THE CHRISTIAN CENTURIES

A New History of the
Catholic Church

THE CHRISTIAN CENTURIES

A New History of the Catholic Church

THE CHRISTIAN CENTURIES

Volume Two

THE
MIDDLE AGES

by

DAVID KNOWLES with DIMITRI OBOLENSKY

DARTON, LONGMAN & TODD
London
PAULIST PRESS
New York/Paramus/Toronto

Published in Great Britain by
Darton, Longman & Todd Ltd
89 Lillie Road, London SW6 1UD

ISBN 0 232 35605 X

Published in the United States of America by
Paulist Press
Editorial Office: 1865 Broadway, N.Y., N.Y. 10023
Business Office: 545 Island Road, Ramsey, N.J. 07446

ISBN 0–8091–0276–5

Library of Congress Catalog Card Number: 63–22123

First edition 1969
Second impression 1972
Third impression 1978
Fourth impression 1979
Fifth impression 1983

Printed in Great Britain by litho at The Anchor Press Ltd
and bound by Wm Brendon & Son Ltd, both of Tiptree, Essex

FOREWORD

A short history of Christendom, embracing both the eastern and western churches, and covering almost nine centuries, cannot hope to contain even an outline of the fortunes of the church in all periods and regions. The aim of the authors has been, therefore, to provide a brief narrative or survey of events for periods and movements of particular significance, while giving wider treatment to institutions and aspects of Christian life and work in the church as a whole in the Middle Ages.

The chapters or sections on the Orthodox Church are by Dimitri Obolensky; they comprise chapters 3 and 7, and sections 3-5 of chapter 25 and section 2 of chapter 26; the remainder of the volume is the work of David Knowles.

A difficulty was caused by the widening breach, at first political and later also ecclesiastical, between Rome and Constantinople. The separation of the churches was due both to political events and to the different ways in which the two parties interpreted points of doctrine and practice. It seemed therefore best, in the ecumenical climate of to-day, that the story of the gradual estrangement should be told by a writer of each of the two allegiances. This entailed some duplication of the narrative without which the motives of the actors and the consequences of their actions would be inexplicable, and after discussion and a careful reading of each other's work the two authors were in complete agreement that this was the only way to present the reader with an historical dialogue, which in this case seemed more valuable than a single account, however impartial. A candid recognition of differences of outlook, as well as of faults and misundertandings on both sides, must be an indispensable basis for mutual sympathy and understanding.

Professor Knowles wishes to thank the following friends, who have kindly read parts of the volume and made many suggestions and corrections: Professor C. N. L. Brooke, Sir Kenneth Clark, Dr Philip Grierson, Professor W. Ullmann.

David Knowles
Dimitri Obolensky

CONTENTS

* By Dimitri Obolensky.

LIST OF MAPS

CHRONOLOGY OF SOME IMPORTANT EVENTS

Political		*Religious*
Persian war with Empire	603-28	
	604	Death of Pope Gregory I
	605	Death of St Augustine of Canterbury
Heraclius emperor	610-41	
Capture of Jerusalem by Persians	614	
	615	Death of St Columbanus
Conquest of Egypt by Persians	611-19	
Mahomet leaves Mecca for Medina. Era of Hegira begins	622	
Siege of Constantinople by Persians and Avars	626	
Heraclius defeats Persians at Nineveh	627	
Death of Mahomet	632	
	635	Arrival of St Aidan in Northumbria (England)
Conquest of Persia by Arabs	637-41	
	638	Heraclius issues Monothelite *Ecthesis*
	649	Synod at Lateran under Pope Martin I condemns Monotheletism
	653	Pope Martin taken captive by Emperor
	654	He dies
	662	Death of St Maximus the Confessor
	663	Synod of Whitby
	669-690	St Theodore archbishop Canterbury
	674-8	Siege of Constantinople by Arabs
	c. 680	Birth of St Boniface
	680-1	Council of Constantinople (6th ecumenical) condemns Monotheletism
	690	Death of St Benet Biscop. St Willibrord archbishop of Utrecht
	692	'Quinisext' Coucil at Constantinople (largely disciplinary; anti-Roman)

Political		Religious
Political		*Religious*
Muslim conquest of Carthage	698	
Muslims invade Spain	711	
	715-31	Pope Gregory II
Siege of Constantinople by Arabs	717-18	
Leo III emperor	717-41	
	723	St Boniface consecrated bishop by pope
	726-30	Edicts of Leo III against images
Revolt of Byzantine Italy	727	
	731-41	Pope Gregory III
Victory of Charles Martel near Tours	732	Calabria, Sicily and Illyricum detached from Roman jurisdiction by the Emperor Leo III
	735	Death of St Bede the Venerable
Fall of the Exarchate of Ravenna	751	
	754	Pepin's donation to papacy
Charlemagne king of the Franks	768-814	
	772-95	Pope Hadrian I
Alcuin joins court of Charlemagne	782	
First landing of Vikings in England	787	Council of Nicea (7th ecumenical) condemns iconoclasm
(Christmas Day) coronation of Charlemagne as emperor in Rome	800	
	804	Death of Alcuin
Lewis the Pious emperor of the West	813-40	
Death of Charlemagne	814	
Division of western empire	817	Monastic meetings at Aachen
	826	St Anskar's first missionary journey to Scandinavia
Treaty of Verdun. Birth of France and Germany	843	Council at Constantinople ends iconoclasm
	845-82	Hincmar archbishop of Rheims
	846	Sack of St Peter's, Rome, by Muslim pirates
	847	Pope Leo IV walls ' Leonine City '
	c. 850	Forged decretals
	858-67	Pope Nicholas I. First period of office of Photius as patriarch
Russian attack on Constantinople	860	
	863	Missionary journey of Constantine (Cyril) and Methodius to Moravia

Political		Religious
		Religious
	865	Bulgarians accept Christianity (Orthodox church)
	867-9	Photian schism
	867-74	Conversion of the Serbs to the Orthodox Church
	869	Death of St Cyril in Rome
	869-70	Council of Constantinople (8th ecumenical; anti-Photian; not recognised in East)
Reign of Alfred the Great	871-99	
	877-86	Second period of office of Photius as patriarch
	879-80	Synod under Photius rejects decisions of recent council
	882	Death of Hincmar
Final collapse of Frankish empire	887	
Magyars occupy Hungary	895	
Western raids of Magyars begin	900	
Russian attacks on Constantinople	907	
	909	Foundation of Cluny
Henry I (the Fowler) king of Germany	919-37	
	927-41	Odo abbot of Cluny
Otto the Great crowned king	936	
	940	Dunstan abbot of Glastonbury
Russian attack on Constantinople	941	
	954-94	Maieul abbot of Cluny
Otto I defeats Magyars at Lechfeld	955	
Otto I crowned emperor of West	962	
Basil II emperor	976-1025	
Conquest of Bulgaria by Basil	986-1018	
	988-89	Conversion of the Russians to the Orthodox Church
	994-1049	Odilo abbot of Cluny
	999-1003	Pope Silvester II
	c. 1000	Conversion of Denmark
St Stephen crowned king of Hungary	1001	
	1007-1029	Fulbert bishop of Chartres
Death of St Vladimir of Russia	1015	
Arrival of Normans in Southern Italy	1016	

Political		Religious
Henry III King of Germany, Italy and Burgundy	1039	
Henry III crowned emperor	1046	Henry III reforms papacy
	1049-54	Pope Leo IX
	1049-1109	Hugh abbot of Cluny
	1049	Synod of Rheims under Leo IX
	1054	Schism of east and west
Reign of Henry IV	1056-1106	
	1059	Papal election decree (cardinals; no mention of emperor)
Norman conquest of Sicily	1061-91	
	1062-74	St Theodosius abbot of the Kiev Monastery of the Caves
Norman conquest of England	1066	
End of Byzantine power in Italy. Defeat of Byzantine emperor at Manzikert	1071	
	1073-85	Gregory VII pope
	1076	Council of Worms 'deposes' Gregory VII. Gregory VII excommunicates Henry IV
	1077	Canossa
	1080	Final excommunication and deposition of Henry IV by Gregory VII
Rise of North Italian communes	1080-1130	
	1084	Sack of Rome by Robert Guiscard. Foundation of Grande Chartreuse by St Bruno
	1088-99	Urban II pope
	1093-1109	Anselm archbishop of Canterbury
	1095	Urban II proclaims crusade at Clermont
First Crusade	1095-9	
	1098	Foundation of Cîteaux
Crusaders take Jerusalem and found kindgom	1099	
Baldwin I king of Jerusalem	1100-18	
Louis VI king of France	1108-37	
	1111	Paschal allows lay investiture to Henry V
	1115-53	St Bernard abbot of Clairvaux

Political		Religious
		Religious
	1119	*Carta caritatis* confirmed by pope
	1120	Foundation of military orders and Premonstratensians
	1121	Abelard condemned at Soissons
	1122	Concordat of Worms
	1123	First Lateran Council (9th ecumenical)
Roger II crowned king of Sicily	1130	
Louis VII king of France	1137-80	
	1139	Second Lateran Council (10th ecumenical)
	1140	Abelard condemned at Sens
Gratian's *Decretum* (*Concordia discordantium canonum*)	*c.* 1141	
Beginning of German *Drang nach Osten*	1141	
	1142	Death of Abelard
Second Crusade	1146-8	
Trial and acquittal of Gilbert de la Porrée	1148	
	1151	Death of Abbot Suger of St Denis
Reign of Frederick Barbarossa	1152-90	
Reign of Henry II king of England	1154-89	
Execution of Arnold of Brescia	1155	
	1156	Death of Peter the Venerable
	c. 1159	*Sentences* of Peter Lombard
	1159-81	Alexander III pope
Conquest of Wends by Henry the Lion	1160-3	
	ante 1164	Death of Peter Lombard
Formation of Lombard League	1167	
Stephen Nemanja, founder of Serbian monarchy	*c.* 1167-96	
	1170	Peter Valdes begins to preach. Murder of Archbishop Thomas Becket
	1170-1221	St Dominic
Reign of Saladin	1174-93	
Defeat of Frederick Barbarossa by Lombards at Legnano	1176	
	1179	Third Lateran Council (11th ecumenical)

Political		Religious
Political		*Religious*
	1181-1226	St Francis of Assisi
Foundation of second Bulgarian empire	1186	
Defeat of Christians at Horns of Hattin and loss of Jerusalem	1187	
Third Crusade	1189-92	
Foundation of Teutonic order	1190	
	1198-1216	Innocent III pope
Charter of Philip Augustus to university of Paris	1220	
Fourth Crusade	1201-4	
	1202	Joachim of Fiore died
Sack of Constantinople; foundation of Latin empire	1204	
First Albigensian crusade	1209	
	1210	Innocent III gives verbal approval to St Francis
Christian victory at Las Navas de Tolosa	1212	
Reign of Frederick II	1212-50	
Philip Augustus wins battle of Bouvines against English and imperialists	1214	
King John of England signs Magna Carta	1215	Fourth Lateran Council (12th ecumenical)
	1216	Honorius III confirms the Order of Preachers (Dominicans)
Fifth Crusade	1219	Consecration of St Sava as autocephalous archbishop of Serbia
	1221	Death of St Dominic
	1226	Death of St Francis
Reign of St Louis IX	1226-70	
Frederick II recovers Jerusalem	1228	
Teutonic order enters Prussia	1228-30	
Bull of Gregory IX to Paris *Parens scientiarum*	1231	
	1233	Gregory IX establishes Inquisition
Mongol invasion of Europe	1237-41	
Final loss of Jerusalem	1244	
	1245	First Council of Lyons (13th ecumenical); deposition of Frederick II
Sixth Crusade (St Louis)	1248-51	

Political		Religious
Political		*Religious*
Death of Frederick II	1250	
Death of Robert Grosseteste	1253	
	1254	Gerard of Borgo San Donnino publishes *Introduction to the Eternal Gospel*
	1255	Bull *Quasi lignum vitae* of Alexander IV confirms position of friars at Paris university
	1257-72	St Bonaventure minister-general
Reign of Michael Palaeologus	1259-82	
Reign of Kublai Khan	1259-84	
Defeat of Mongols by Mamelukes at Ain Jalut	1260	
Recapture of Constantinople by Greeks	1261	
	1266	Franciscan Narbonne constitutions of Bonaventure
	1274	Second Council of Lyons (14th ecumenical). Reunion with Greeks. Papal election conclave provisions. Death of St Thomas Aquinas. Death of St Bonaventure
	1279	Bull *Exiit qui seminat* of Nicholas III approves *usus pauper* of Franciscans
Sicilian Vespers ends French control of Sicily	1282	
End of kingdom of Jerusalem	1291	
	1298	Decretals (Sext) of Boniface VIII
	1300	Bull *Super cathedram* settles relations of friars and bishops
	1302	Bull *Unam sanctam.* Death of Boniface VIII
	1307-12	Destruction of Templars
Death of Duns Scotus	1308	
	1309-78	Papacy settled at Avignon
	1311-12	Council of Vienne (15th ecumenical)
	1312	Bull *Exivi de Paradiso* of Clement V
	1316-34	John XXII pope
Death of Dante	1321	
	1322-23	John XXII issues *Ad conditorem canonum* and *Cum inter nonnullos,* the latter declaring the non-ownership of property by Christ a heretical tenet

Political		Religious
Political		*Religious*
Publication of *Defensor Pacis* by Marsilius of Padua	1324	John XXII declares Lewis IV deprived of empire
Death of Master Eckhart	1327	
Emperor (with Marsilius) enters Rome and sets up antipope	1328	William of Ockham flees from Avignon to join emperor
Stephen Dušan ruler of Serbia	1331-55	
	1334	Origin of Observant Franciscans
	1335-9	Monastic reforming Bulls of Benedict XII
Hundred Years War begins	1337	
Diet of Frankfort by law *Licet juris* declares papal confirmation unnecessary after Electors' choice of emperor	1338	
Charles IV founds university of Prague	1348	
First visitation of Black Death	1348-9	
	1349	Death of William Ockham. Death of Archbishop Bradwardine
	1353-63	Restoration of papal states in Italy by Cardinal Albornoz
	1354-78	St Alexis metropolitan of Moscow
Turks capture Adrianople	1357	Egidian Constitution of papal states
	1361	Death of John Tauler
Philip the Bold duke of Burgundy	1363	
John Gerson	1363-1429	
Death of Petrarch	1374	
Death of Boccaccio	1375	
	1378-1417	Great Schism
	1379	Wyclif begins teaching on Eucharist
Floruit William Langland	1380	
	1384	Death of Wyclif
Austrians defeated by Swiss at Sempach	1386	
Serbs defeated by Turks at battle of Kosovo Polje	1389	
	1392	Death of St Sergius of Radonezh
'Great' Statute of Praemunire in England. End of Bulgarian independence	1393	
Union of Calmar (Scandinavia)	1397	
Death of Chaucer	1400	
English statute *De haeretico comburendo*	1401	

Political		Religious
	1402	John Hus begins to preach
	1409	Council of Pisa. Three popes
Defeat of Teutonic knights by Poles at Tannenberg	1410	
Sigismund, king of Hungary, elected king of the Romans	1410-37	
	1414-18	Council of Constance (16th ecumenical)
Defeat of French by Henry V at Agincourt	1415	Hus burnt at Constance
	1416	Jerome of Prague burnt at Constance
	1417	Martin V elected pope
Philip the Good duke of Burgundy	1419-67	
	1420	The Four Articles of Prague
Hussite wars in Bohemia	1420-41	
St Joan of Arc burnt at Rouen	1431	
	1431-49	Council of Basle (17th ecumenical)
Sigismund crowned emperor at Rome	1443	
	1436	Compacts of Prague between Council and Hussites
Charles VII of France issues Pragmatic Sanction at Bourges	1438	Council moved by Eugenius IV
	1439	Union of Greek and Latin churches
	1448-61	St Jonas, metropolitan of Russia, becomes independent of Patriarch
	1449	Council of Basle dissolves. End of ' conciliar epoch '
Fall of Constantinople. End of Hundred Years War	1453	
First Bible printed at Mainz by Gutenberg. Mahomet II fails to take Belgrade against John Hunyadi	1456	
	1458-64	Pius II pope (Aeneas Sylvius Piccolomini)
	1460	Bull *Execrabilis* against appeals to a council
	1464	Death of Nicholas of Cusa
Printing begins in Italy	1465	
	1467	Separate church instituted in Bohemia
Lorenzo de Medici ruler of Florence	1469-92	
Isabella the Catholic, queen of Castile	1474-1504	
Caxton prints in England	1477	

xxii

Political		Religious
Ferdinand the Catholic, king of Aragon. Ferdinand and Isabella, Catholic Kings of Spain	1479-1516	
Peace of Zurich finally gives independence to Switzerland	1478	
Conquest of Granada by Catholic Kings. Colombus discovers America	1492	
	1492-1503	Alexander VI (Borgia) pope
	1498	Execution of Savonarola

POPES REIGNING BETWEEN 1050 AND 1500

This list is based on the relevant portion of the list in the *Handbook of Dates* edited by Professor C. R. Cheney and published by The Royal Historical Society (1945). I am indebted to the Council of that Society for their kind permission to use the list. In most cases papal status is historically certain, but in cases (e.g. during the Great Schism) where some historical uncertainty exists, the official list of the Roman Church is followed. In one instance, that of the medieval John XXIII (1410-1415) who was usually (as in the Handbook) included as canonical, the official decision was only given as recently as 1958, when the newly elected Angelo Roncalli, by adopting the style of John XXIII, eliminated his namesake from the list, thereby causing some confusion to chronologists. In the lists that follows, the first date is that of *election*; the second that of *death*, unless otherwise noted. Anti-popes are listed in italics.

LEO IX	Dec. 1048	19 Apr. 1054	
VICTOR II	late 1054	28 July 1057	
STEPHEN IX	2 Aug. 1057	29 Mar. 1058	
BENEDICT X	4-5 Apr. 1058	24 Jan. 1059	*deposed*
NICHOLAS II	late Dec. 1058	? 22 July 1061	
ALEXANDER II	29-30 Sep. 1061	21 Apr. 1073	
Honorius II	*28 Oct. 1061*	*late 1072*	
GREGORY VII	22 Apr. 1073	25 May 1085	
Clement III	*25 June 1080*	*Sep. 1100*	
VICTOR III	24 May 1086	16 Sep. 1087	
URBAN II	12 Mar. 1088	29 July 1099	
PASCHAL II	13 Aug. 1099	21 Jan. 1118	
Theodoric	*Sep. 1100*	*late 1100*	*expelled*
Albert	*elected and deposed Feb.-Mar. 1102*		
Silvester IV	*18 Nov. 1105*	*13 Apr. 1111*	*deposed*
GELASIUS II	24 Jan. 1118	29 Jan. 1119	
Gregory VIII	*8 Mar. 1118*	*Apr. 1121*	
CALIXTUS II	20 Feb. 1119	13 Dec. 1124	
HONORIUS II	16 Dec. 1124	13-14 Feb. 1130	
INNOCENT II	14 Feb. 1130	24 Sep. 1143	
Anacletus II	*14 Feb. 1130*	*25 Jan. 1138*	

Victor IV	*15 Mar. 1138*	*29 May 1138*	*resigned*
CELESTINE II	26 Sep. 1143	8 Mar. 1144	
LUCIUS II	12 Mar. 1144	15 Feb. 1145	
EUGENIUS III	15 Feb. 1145	8 July 1153	
ANASTASIUS IV	12 July 1153	3 Dec. 1154	
HADRIAN IV	4 Dec. 1154	1 Sep. 1159	
ALEXANDER III	7 Sep. 1159	30 Aug. 1181	
Victor IV	*7 Sep. 1159*	*20 Apr. 1164*	
Paschal III	*22 Apr. 1164*	*Sep. 1168*	
Calixtus III	*? Sep. 1168*	*29 Aug. 1178*	*resigned*
Innocent III	*? 29 Sep. 1179*	*Jan. 1180*	*deposed*
LUCIUS III	1 Sep. 1181	25 Nov. 1185	
URBAN III	25 Nov. 1185	20 Oct. 1187	
GREGORY VIII	21 Oct. 1187	17 Dec. 1187	
CLEMENT III	19 Dec. 1187	late Mar. 1191	
CELESTINE III	30 Mar. 1191	8 Jan. 1198	
INNOCENT III	8 Jan. 1198	16 July 1216	
HONORIUS III	18 July 1216	18 Mar. 1227	
GREGORY IX	19 Mar. 1227	22 Aug. 1241	
CELESTINE IV	25 Oct. 1241	10 Nov. 1241	
INNOCENT IV	25 June 1243	7 Dec. 1254	
ALEXANDER IV	12 Dec. 1254	25 May 1261	
URBAN IV	29 Aug. 1261	2 Oct. 1264	
CLEMENT IV	5 Feb. 1265	29 Nov. 1268	
GREGORY X	1 Sep. 1271	10 Jan. 1276	
INNOCENT V	21 Jan. 1276	22 June 1276	
HADRIAN V	11 July 1276	18 Aug. 1276	
JOHN XXI	8 Sep. 1276	20 May 1277	
NICHOLAS III	25 Nov. 1277	22 Aug. 1280	
MARTIN IV	22 Feb. 1281	28 Mar. 1285	
HONORIUS IV	2 Apr. 1285	3 Apr. 1287	
NICHOLAS IV	15-22 Feb. 1288	4 Apr. 1292	
CELESTINE V	5 July 1294	13 Dec. 1294	*resigned*
BONIFACE VIII	24 Dec. 1294	12 Oct. 1303	
BENEDICT XI	22 Oct. 1303	7 July 1304	
CLEMENT V	5 June 1305	20 Apr. 1314	
JOHN XXII	7 Aug. 1316	4 Dec. 1334	
Nicholas V	*12 May 1328*	*25 July 1330*	*resigned*
BENEDICT XII	20 Dec. 1334	25 Apr. 1342	
CLEMENT VI	7 May 1342	6 Dec. 1352	
INNOCENT VI	18 Dec. 1352	12 Sep. 1362	
URBAN V	28 Sep. 1362	19 Dec. 1370	
GREGORY XI	30 Dec. 1370	27 Mar. 1378	
URBAN VI	8 Apr. 1378	15 Oct. 1389	
Clement VII	*20 Sep. 1378*	*16 Sep 1394*	
BONIFACE IX	2 Nov. 1389	1 Oct. 1404	

Benedict XIII	28 *Sep.* 1394	5 June 1409	*deposed*
INNOCENT VII	17 Oct. 1404	6 Nov. 1406	
GREGORY XII	30 Nov. 1406	4 July 1415	*resigned*
Alexander V	*26 June 1409*	*3 May 1410*	
John XXIII	*17 May 1410*	*29 May 1415*	*deposed*
MARTIN V	11 Nov. 1417	20 Feb. 1431	
Clement VIII	*10 June 1423*	*26 July 1429*	*resigned*
EUGENIUS IV	3 Mar. 1431	23 Feb. 1447	
Felix V	*5 Nov. 1439*	*7 Apr. 1449*	*resigned*
NICHOLAS V	6 Mar. 1447	24 Mar. 1455	
CALIXTUS III	8 Apr. 1455	6 Aug. 1458	
PIUS II	19 Aug. 1458	14 Aug. 1464	
PAUL II	30 Aug. 1464	26 July 1471	
SIXTUS IV	10 Aug. 1471	12 Aug. 1484	
INNOCENT VIII	29 Aug. 1484	25 July 1492	
ALEXANDER VI	11 Aug. 1492	18 Aug. 1503	

The somewhat complicated successions of the three lines during the Great Schism may be set out as follows:

ROMAN LINE

Urban VI 1378-89 died

Boniface IX 1389-1404 died

Innocent VII 1404-1406 died

Gregory XII 1406-1415 died

(Gregory was deposed by Council of Pisa 5 June 1409 but did not accept the verdict, resigning only 4 July 1415.)

LINE OF PISA

Alexander V 1409-1410 died

John XXIII 1410-1415, died 1419

(John was deposed by Council of Constance 29 May 1415.)

AVIGNON LINE

Clement VII 1378-94 died

Benedict XIII 1394-1422 died

(Benedict was deposed by Council of Pisa 5 June 1409, and again by Council of Constance 20 July 1417, but refused to quit the scene.)

Clement VIII 1423-9 resigned

LINE OF BASLE

Felix V 1439-49

Note

If the Council of Pisa is held to be a pseudo-Council, the deposition of Gregory XII was invalid, and therefore both Alexander V and the medieval John XXIII were ' anti-popes '. In the past, both have obtained a quasi-entrée into the canon, but if John XXIII is ruled out, he takes with him Alexander V.

The way had been cleared for the election of Martin V in 1417 by (1) the resignation in 1415 of the ' Roman ' pope Gregory XII, (2) the deposition by two councils of the ' Avignon ' claimant Benedict XIII, and (3) the flight and deposition by the Council of Constance of the ' Pisan ' claimant, John XXIII. Thus Martin V was undoubtedly canonically elected; on the ' Roman ' calculation the see was vacant by the resignation of Gregory XII, and on the ' Avignon ' reckoning by the twofold deposition of Benedict XIII. The elections of Clement VIII (Avignon line) and Felix V (Basle) were the desperate attempts of faction to prolong the state of uncertainty .

ABBREVIATIONS

MGH	Monumenta Germaniae Historica
PL	Patrologia Latina
PG	Patrologia Graeca
SSS	Settimana di Studi, Spoleto
SSM	Settimana di Studi, Milan (Mendola)
ASS	Assyriological Studies, Chicago
DHG	Dictionnaire d'Histoire et de Géographie ecclésiastiques
DTC	Dictionnaire de Théologie Catholique
RHE	Revue d'Histoire Ecclésiastique

ILLUSTRATION
SECTION

LIST OF ILLUSTRATIONS

A. The Frontiers of the Church

AI. THE CONFLICT OF FAITH IN NORTHERN EUROPE. On the left of the picture, Faith ties up the defeated heathen deity, while on the right the pagan shrine is left unattended – apart, that is, from a sacrificial victim spared by the advent of the Christians. *Bürgerbibliothek, Bern. Codex 264.f 35r. Prudentius*, De Cultu Deorum. *9th c.*

2

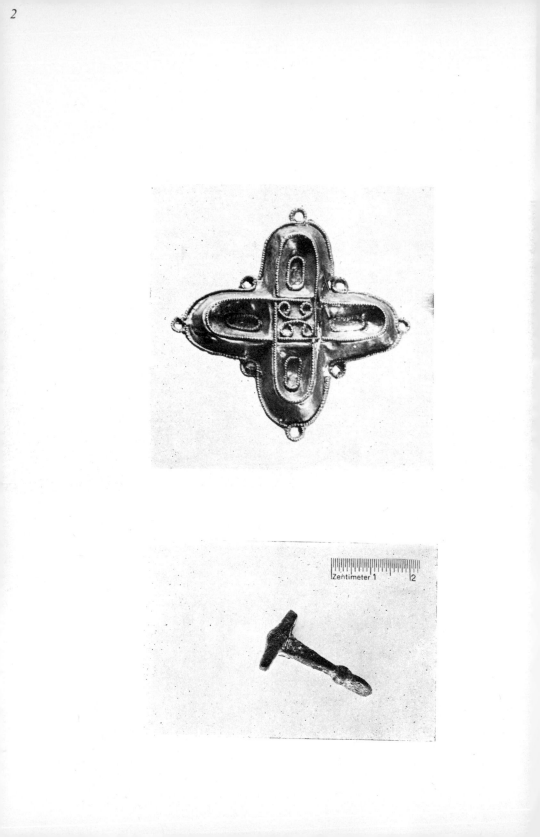

(Above) A4. Left: THE MISSIONARY WORK OF BONIFACE. Right: THE MARTYRDOM OF BONIFACE. Boniface was killed not far from the site on which the hammer (picture A3) was found. This miniature illustrates another, earlier, phase in the conflict in the north of Europe. For the career of Boniface see ch. 2. *Universitätsbibliothek, Göttingen. MS 231.f 87. The Fulda Sacramentary. Late 10th c.*

(Above left) A2. GOLD PENDANT CROSS, WORN AS TOKEN. This small ornamental cross was amongst the possessions of a wealthy lady buried at Canstatt, near Stuttgart. Its interest in this context is that it was worn by its owner as a token of her Christian allegiance. *Late 7th-early 8th c. Length 4.2 cm. Photo: Württemburgisches Landesmuseum.*

(Below left) A3. THOR'S HAMMER, A PAGAN SYMBOL. This tiny hammer was one of several religious ornaments found during excavations at Haithabu-bei-Schleswig. Both Christian and non-Christian religions are represented, and the close juxtaposition of a pagan symbol, such as this, with crucifixes of the same period highlights the conflict of religions in the north of Europe. *Bronze. 9th c. Actual size. Photo: Schleswig Landesmuseum für Vor- und Frühgeschichte.*

(Top) A5. THE SALADIN AND GUIDO REX STRUGGLE FOR THE HOLY CROSS. By the time Guido Rex (Guy de Lusignan, King of Jerusalem from 1185 onwards) and Saladin confronted one another, crusading zeal and morale were rather stronger on the Muslim side than amongst the Christian Crusaders. While Saladin preached the Jihad or holy war, the Christians quarrelled amongst themselves. In 1187 two battles decisively weakened the Christian position and in the second, at Hattin on 4 July, Guy himself was captured. Three months later Jerusalem fell to the Muslims. *Corpus Christi College, Cambridge. MS. 26 f 279. Mid-13th c. By permission of the Master and Fellows.*

(Below) A6. WILLIAM II OF SICILY ATTENDED BY AN ARAB PHYSICIAN AND ASTROLOGER. Relations in Sicily tended to be rather more peaceful than in Palestine. *Bürgerbibliothek, Bern. MS 120.f 97.*

A7. PRESTER JOHN HONOURS THE CROSS. This medieval counterpart of the visitor from Mars hails from beyond the frontiers of the medieval Church with which this book is concerned. In 1122, a stranger is said to have appeared in Rome, claiming to be a Christian king from an unknown land. He described his empire, impressed his listeners, and then disappeared. About fifty years later, a letter, allegedly written by the same ruler, appeared in Europe, addressed to the rulers of Europe. In the letter, Prester John called on the rulers to become his subjects.

The Pope thought the letter sufficiently important to need a reply, and on 27 September 1177 he wrote to Prester John, expounding the Petrine claims and introducing the bearer of the letter, the papal physician Philip, who, the Pope said, would give more detailed explanations. Philip sailed from Venice – and is not mentioned again in medieval literature. *Bibliothèque Nationale, Paris. MS Anciens Fonds Fr. 2810 f. 205.*

A8. ST MICHAEL AND THE THREE MEN IN THE FIERY FURNACE. Faras, on the Nile, at the border of the Sudan and Egypt, was an episcopal see as early as the 7th c. Its bishops belonged to the Monophysite Church and recognised the authority of the Patriarch of Alexandria. Three of the bishops are associated with the wall painting reproduced here, for the peculiar arrangement of the three men, with one to the north of the Archangel and two to the south, corresponds exactly to the positions of the tombs of three 10th c. bishops. Clearly the artist intended his painting to represent them in the role of the three men in the fiery furnace, under the guardianship of St Michael, the protector of the cathedral. St Mich ael, who is portrayed in several places in this cathedral, here assumes the role of one ' whose appearance is like a son of the gods ' (Daniel 3: 25). This wall painting and the tombs of the bishops were excavated between 1961 and 1964 by a team of Polish archaeologists. *Wall painting, Faras Cathedral, last quarter of 10th c. Photo: Professor Michaelowski, University of Warsaw.*

B. The Problem of Authority

(i) CHURCH AND STATE

B1. THE DONATION OF CONSTANTINE. The fresco shows Constantine on the right, kneeling, delivering the tiara to Pope Silvester I. The fresco was painted in about 1246 at one of the high points of papal power in the West (cf. illust. B16). *Fresco in the Chapel of St Silvester in the Church of SS. Quattro Coronati, Rome, c. 1246. Photo: Anderson (Mansell Collection, London)*

(Above) B4. HENRY IV OF GERMANY REQUESTS THE MEDIATION OF MATILDA AND ABBOT HUGH OF CLUNY. The emperor is in the chapel of St Nicholas in the castle of Canossa. *Vatican Library. MS Vat. Lat. 4922.* (Vita Mathildae.)

(Above left) B2. OTTO II INVESTS ADALBERT WITH THE EPISCOPAL STAFF. The date of this incident is 983, and the occasion is Adalbert's elevation to the see of Prague. For the significance of this action and for the later conflict see chs 2 and 14. *Detail from the bronze door on south side of the cathedral of Gniezno, Poland. 12th c. Photo: Bildarchiv, Foto Marburg.*

(Below left) B3. JOHN VI CANTACUZENUS, AS EMPEROR AND AS MONK. John VI was forced to abdicate in 1354. He then became a monk, assuming the name of Joasaph, on the model of the story of Barlaam and Joasaph (the Buddha story) in which the hero, a prince, becomes a monk. He is seen here in both roles. As further evidence for the unity *(symphonia)* of Church and Empire, cf. the letter from the Patriarch Antonius to Vasili I, Grand Prince of Russia, only forty years after the abdication of John VI: ' My son, you are wrong in saying, " We have a Church but no Emperor. " It is not possible for Christians to have a Church and not to have an Empire. Church and Empire have a great unity, and it is impossible for them to be separated from one another.' *Bibliothèque Nationale, Paris. MS Grec. 1242. f. 123 v.*

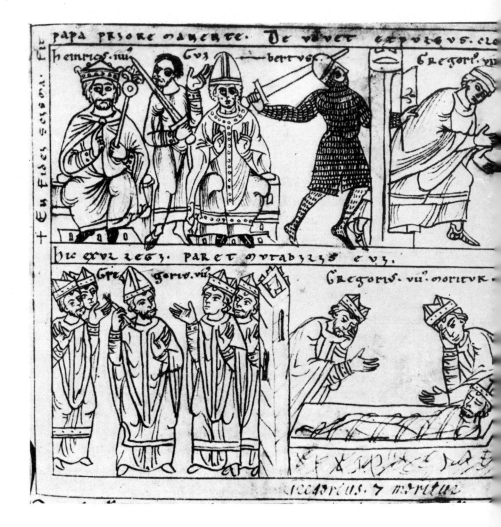

B5. HENRY IV OF GERMANY IN CONFLICT WITH THE POPE. These pictures show Henry IV in a stronger position. Above he is comfortably in control, seated beside his own anti-pope, while Gregory VII is expelled. Below, on the left, Gregory is shown in exile where, on the right, he dies. For details of the conflict, see ch. 14. *Universitätsbibliothek*, *Jena. MS. Bos. G.6.Bl.79. Otto of Freising's* World Chronicle *c. 1170*.

(ii) THE CHRISTIAN RULER

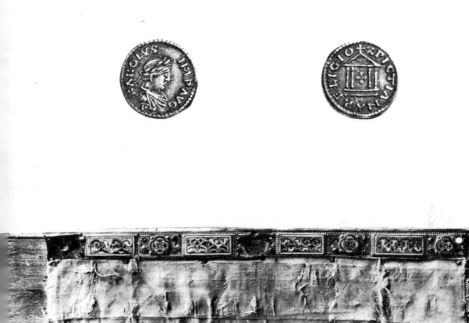

(Top) B6. PORTRAIT COIN OF CHARLEMAGNE. Obverse: KAROLUS IMP AUG Bust and letter F. Reverse: XRISTIANA RELIGIO Temple.

For the propaganda uses of coins see Vol. I, part ii ch. 2. *Silver. After 804. Minted at Frankfurt. By permission of Münzkabinett der Staatlichen Museen, Berlin.*

(Bottom) B7. ARM RELIQUARY. The figures represented on the medallions are (from left to right): Conrad III, Peter, Christ, Paul; and Frederick, the one-eyed Duke of Swabia (1105-47), father of Frederick Barbarossa.

Frederick Barbarossa himself, and his wife, appear on the other side in the company of the Virgin and the archangels. The reliquary was made by order of Frederick Barbarossa in connection with the canonisation of Charlemagne in 1165 and was designed to contain an arm of the new saint. Frederick's understanding of his imperial position knew few limits, and distinguished predecessors from Augustus to Charlemagne and later were summoned from history to bear witness to the glory of the imperial office. *Date c. 1165. Now in Louvre. Photo: Archives Photographiques, Caisse Nationale des Monuments Historiques, Paris.*

(Left) **B8.** THE CROWN OF STEPHEN, FRONT VIEW. (Above) **B9.** BACK VIEW. Date: several studies of the Crown have been carried out, and it now seems clear that it was not all made at the same time. There is no agreement, however, as to whether any part of it can be identified with the crown of Stephen, first King of Hungary, crowned by Pope Silvester II in 1000.

The portraits: the following analysis is based on an essay by Albert Boeckler, ' Die Stephanskrone ', in *Herrschaftszeichen und Staatssymbolik*, Vol. III ed. P. Schramm. p. 731 ff. For further bibliography see this essay.

Front, centre: Christ Pantocrator. Below, on either side of him, are the two Archangels, Michael and Gabriel, while beyond them are the saints George and Demetrius, Cosmas and Damian. All are honouring Christ.

Rear, centre: The Emperor, Michael VIII Dukas (1071-78). Below, on the left of our picture, is his fellow Emperor Constantine Porphyrogenitos (1071-74) while on the right is King Geza I of Hungary (1074-77). The most interesting figure is that of Geza who is to be seen as inferior to and dependent upon the other two monarchs. He lacks certain of the imperial attributes possessed by them; for example, he has no nimbus, and instead of the imperial labarum he has to be content with a patrician staff. Finally, note that his eyes are directed towards the emperors, while they look steadfastly forward.

The most plausible explanation of the purpose of the Crown, in its present form, is that it was sent as a gift by Michael Dukas to Geza in 1074 and was intended to assert Byzantine hegemony over Hungary. It was also intended as a counter-measure against the efforts of Pope Gregory VII who claimed hegemony on the basis of the coronation by the Pope in 1000. *Present location known only to the Pope and the U.S. government. Photo: Bildarchiv, Foto Marburg.*

(Above) B11. THE GERMAN EMPEROR ELECTED BY THE ECCLESIASTICAL AND SECULAR ELECTORS. *Der Sachsenspiegel. Landrecht III, 57. sect. 2. By permission of British Museum.*

(Left) B10. KING EDWARD THE CONFESSOR ANOINTED BY THE CLERGY. *Cambridge University Library. MS Ee 3.59. f. 9: Life of Edward the Confessor. Mid- 13th c.*

B12. CHRIST CROWNS ROGER II OF SICILY. Roger II was of Norman stock, but the ideology of kingship reflected in this mosaic is Byzantine. The king is suitably humble before Christ; but he is still given considerable prominence because the coronation indicates not simply subordination to Christ, but also authority from Christ to rule as his vice-regent on earth. *Mosaic from narthex of church of Martorana, Palermo, Sicily. Mid-12th c. Photo: Anderson (Mansell Collection, London).*

(iii) THE PAPACY

B13. BONIFACE VIII. For the career of Boniface VIII see ch. 27. *Statue in the Lateran, Rome.*
Photo: Archivio Fotograf. Gall. Mus. Vaticani.

bactenus ecterit uuienirūt ⁊ rebellem · regnum
anglie totit sub mtdo̅ conaudent auctoritate ei
aplica denunciantes · qd̅ si per hoc ptinaciā suā
u̅ duxer corrigīdā · ipe manū adbibere curaret
g̅inōes · cū necesse sit eu̅ uince qui p salute ecclie
s̅c̅e diaboliū ⁊ anglos eī debellans · claustra tar
tarea spoliauit · Suffraganeis q̅ cant̄ ecclie
epit · aliis q̅ illius diocesis ptatis in u̅itate obedie̅
tie p sedis aplice lit̄as expssit · ut archiepm ptatu̅
in psem susciperit ⁊ past̄m · eiq̅ caritate debita
obedire curaret · Ut anglia sub gn̅ali tmdo̅
o̅ndouiensis · helyensis atq̅ sit ontlusa ·

prima post festum natiuitatis s̅ Iohis bape   mutante pt̄hea uultuit se si̅ cede
Innoc ix̅ · ([Concilii lugd   Thadeus de suessa p̄curator f̄r̄h̄ca recedit
                                                          [dicit ista dies ne
XIIII

These three sketches in the margin of the Matthew Paris MS illustrate episodes in the exercise of papal authority in the 13th c.

(Top left) B14. THE IDLE BELLROPE. The Interdict of 23 March 1208 involved a suspension of ecclesiastical rites. Hence the idle bellrope in this drawing.

(Bottom left) B15. THE COUNCIL OF LYONS. The Council of Lyons, presided over by Innocent IV, deposed the Emperor Frederick II on 17 July 1245. In this illustration, Taddeo da Suessa, the trusted imperial proctor, is seen leaving the Council.

(Above) B16. THE COUNCIL OF LONDON. The Papal legate Otto addresses the English bishops and clergy at the Council of London, 3 May 1236. At the Council the legate made new proposals for financial contributions to the Pope; these were not greeted with enthusiasm by the members.

Corpus Christi College, Cambridge.
MS 16. Fol. 27b, 107, 186b. Matthew Paris, Chronica Maiora. *Mid-13th c. By permission of the Master and Fellows.*

(Above) B17. THE PAPAL PALACE AT AVIGNON (FLOODLIT). *Photo: French Government Tourist Office.*

(Right) B18. ROME PORTRAYED AS A WIDOW. A comment on the absence of the Pope in Avignon. *By permission of Bibliothèque Nationale, Paris. MS Ital. 81.*

RÓMA

C. The Christian Society

(Above) C2. CLERICAL DIGNITARIES WITH THEIR VASSALS. The relevant section of the *Sachsenspiegel*, an ancient record of law, reads: ' Vassals stand in front of the Bishop, the Abbot and the Abbess, with forefingers extended as is appropriate when one makes a vow. The clerical dignitaries, on the other hand, act as those who give commands, since they lay down the law. ' Der Sachsenspiegel. *Landrecht III. 42. sect. 2. By permission of British Museum.*

(Left) C1. A NOBLEMAN AND A BISHOP DEDICATE A CHURCH. The nobleman is probably Duke Hugh II on whose land the cathedral was built, and his partner may well be the Bishop of Autun, Etienne. *Sculpture, by Giselbertus of Autun, on the capital of N.W. pier of crossing in the cathedral of Autun. Early 12th c. Reproduced from* Giselbertus, Sculptor of Autun, Orion and Trianon Press, Photo: Franceschi.

(Above) C5. A 13TH C. TREATISE ON SURGERY. The miniatures in this handbook follow a regular pattern: scenes from the life of Christ are shown in the top panels, while below there are pictures of more immediate relevance to the medical student. On this folio, the top panels show incidents in the childhood of Jesus, while below a patient is shown who is suffering from a rather gruesome wound on his head. *Photo: British Museum. Sloane MS 1977 f. 39.*

(Top left) C3. A MAN AT PRAYER. This silver belt-end from Mikulcice, Czechoslovakia, shows the man wearing a broad cloak, breeches and boots; his hands are held up in prayer, as was the ancient custom. *9th c. Length 7.2 cm. By permission of Archaeological Institute of the Czech Academy of Sciences, Brno.*

(Bottom left) C4. A WEDDING. *By permission of Bibliothèque Nationale, Paris. MS Lat. 3898 f. 304 v.*

The next twelve pictures (C6 to C17) are intended to illustrate aspects of the ordered and separated life. Pictures C6 and C7 reflect quite different conceptions of the ideal. The first shows a community remote from the rest of society and barely organised. The second, with its key in C8, provides an insight into the basic physical requirements of a highly organised community which, because it is so cultured and ordered, becomes a centre of civilising influences in society as a whole. This model is a modern reconstruction. A letter accompanying the MS and address to 'our dearest son Gorbert', suggests that the plan was originally intended for the 'private study' of Gorbert, Abbot of St Gallen from 816-836. The author of the letter and plan was probably Hitro, Bishop of Basle. and between 803 and 823, Abbot of Reichenau. The Aachen Synods of 816 and 817 published a series of ordinances aimed at standardising the rules governing one monastic life; this plan may be an attempt to express the architectural implications of these regulations. Literature: 'Studien zum St Galler Klosterplan', in *Mitteilungen zur Vaterlandischen Geschichte*. XLII, 1962.

(Above) C6. ROCK CHURCHES IN CAPPADOCIA. *Photo by permission of A. Bryer Esq., Department of History, University of Birmingham.*

(Top right) C7. MODEL OF AN IDEAL MEDIEVAL MONASTERY. *Model by Walter Horn and Ernest Born, based on St. Gallen Stiftsbibliothek MS 1092 c. 820. Photo: Fotowerkstätte Schmölz & Ulrich KG, Cologne.*

(Bottom right) C8. KEY TO THE MODEL. *Key reproduced by permission of Penguin Books Ltd., from* Carolingian and Romanesque Architecture. *Pelican History of Art and Architecture) by K. J. Conant.*

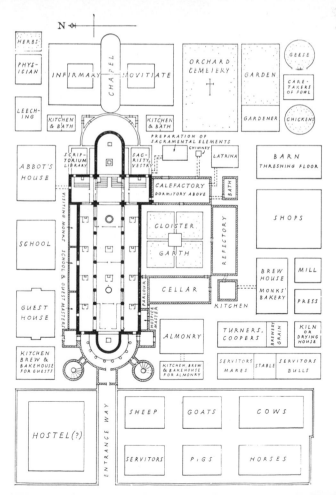

N

HERBS				ORCHARD			GARDEN	GEESE
PHYS-ICIAN	INFIRMARY	CHAPEL	NOVITIATE	CEMETERY				CARE-TAKERS OF FOWL
LEECH-ING	KITCHEN & BATH		KITCHEN & BATH				GARDENER	CHICKENS

PREPARATION OF
SACRAMENTAL ELEMENTS

CHIMNEY

ABBOT'S HOUSE	SCRIP-TORIUM LIBRARY	SAC-RISTY VESTRY	LATRINA	BARN THRESHING FLOOR
		CALEFACTORY DORMITORY ABOVE	BATH	SHOPS
SCHOOL		CLOISTER GARTH	REFECTORY	BREW HOUSE MONKS' BAKERY	MILL
					PRESS
GUEST HOUSE		CELLAR	KITCHEN	TURNERS, COOPERS	BREWERY GRAIN	KILN OR DRYING HOUSE
KITCHEN BREW & BAKEHOUSE FOR GUESTS	PARLOUR	ALMONRY	KITCHEN, BREW & BAKEHOUSE FOR ALMONRY	SERVITORS MARES	STABLE	SERVITORS BULLS

VISITING MONKS SCHOOL & GUEST MASTERS

HOSTEL MASTER

| HOSTEL(?) | | SHEEP | GOATS | COWS |
| | ENTRANCE WAY | SERVITORS | PIGS | HORSES |

(Above) C9. FONTENAY: THE ABBEY CHURCH. *Photo: Archives Photographiques, Caisse Nationale des Monuments Historiques, Paris.*

(Top right) C10. FONTENAY: THE CISTERCIAN MONASTERY, A GENERAL VIEW. Built 1139-47, this is the oldest Cistercian ensemble still in existence. It also happens to be based on the plan most favoured by St Bernard himself. *Photo: French Government Tourist Office.*

(Bottom right) C11. FONTENAY: VIEW FROM THE CLOISTERS. *Photo: French Government Tourist Office (Jacques Boulas, Orléans).*

(Above) C12. MONASTERY OF HOSIOS MELITIOS, HYMETTOS. The arrangement of this monastery – a fortified rectangular outer structure enclosing a courtyard with the church – has its roots in eastern monastic architecture of the 5th c. and domestic architecture of late antiquity. It was built before 1100 for a community which was obviously much smaller than that of Cluny or of the St Gall plan, but it is still large by Byzantine standards of the 9th and subsequent c. Primarily because of fiscal pressures, monastic communities of the east tended to be small, and a community of more than eight persons was regarded as large. For details and discussion, cf. R. Krautheimer, *Early Christian and Byzantine Architecture*, London 1965, p. 247 ff. *Photo: A. Frantz.*

(Right) C13. MONASTIC SKILLS. Several of the illustrations in this section testify to the skills of the monastic scribes. The interesting point about the miniature C13 is that it shows a layman working with a monk. *By permission of Staatsbibliothek, Bremen. b. 21 f. 124v. Date 1039-43.*

(Above) C14. THE MONASTIC CURRICULUM. A list of authors from a 8th-9th c. MS Latin Grammar from Fleury. *By permission of Bürgerbibliothek, Bern. Codex 207. f. 1v.*

(Top right) C15. THE UTRECHT PSALTER, PSALM 43 VERSE 25 (Vulgate). This illustration is one of the finest in the whole Utrecht Psalter. To convey the sense of hopelessness in the first part of the psalm, the artist shows a city besieged and almost overrun. The real problem, however, is not the numerical superiority of the enemy so much as the fact that the Lord, 'above on his holy hill', is sleeping on a couch and is apparently unaware of the fate of his people. The text shown is of psalm 42 (Vulgate). *By permission of the University Library, Utrecht. MS 32, f. 25r. Date c. 820.*

(Bottom right) C16. MONKS IN PROCESSION BEHIND A CRUCIFIX. *By permission of Bibliothèque Nationale, Paris. MS Nouv. Acq. Lat. 1359.*

XLII PSALMUS DAVID
IUDICAMEDSET EMITTELUCEMTUAMETUERI CONFITEBORTIBIINCI
DISCERNECAUSAMMEAM TATEMTUAM IPSAMEDEDU THARADSDSMEUS
DEGENTENONSCA ABHOMI XERUNTETADDUXERIN QUARETRISTISESANI
NEINIQUOETDOLOSOERU MONTEMSCMTUU ETIN MEAETQUARECONTUR
EME TABERNACULATUA BASME
UIATUESDSFORTITUDO ETINTROIBOADALTAREDI SPERAINDOQNMADH
UEA QUAREMEREPPULIS ADDMQUILAETIFICAT CONFITEBORILLI SAL
TETQUARETRISTISINCEDO IUUENTUTEMMEAM TAREUUITUSMEIETDSI
DUMADFLICITMEINIMICUS

A̅ rabit anno p̅dicto q̅ in die
Aſſumptionis uirginis glo̅ꝛi
oſe venerunt a̅ uilla bꝛugen
ſi arater .CC. hominus. quaſi hoꝛa
pꝛandij. Ipſi autem aduuauerīt
ſe in foꝛo et ſtatim ruinoꝛ magnus
fuit per totam ciuitatem. vn̅ de om
nes ueniebant cateruatim ueue

ceperunt compati perſonis et
penitentie condolere et deo gra
tias reddere ſuper tanta pem
tencia̅s quam grauiſſimam re
putabant. Remanſerunt q̅ꝫ
dicti bꝛii genſes in ciuitate co
ta illa die et nocte. Et in die
craſtina que fuit dies dn̅ica in

(Above) C17. Flagellants in procession behind a crucifix *By permission of Bibliothèque Royale, Brussels. MS 13076/7 fol. 16v.*

(Right) C18. St francis of assisi preaches to the birds. *Copy drawing of a 13th c. wall painting in Wiston Church, near Colchester.*

(Above) C20. DANTE. *In Florence Cathedral. Domenico di Michelino. Photo: Alinari (Mansell Collection, London).*

(Left) C19. ST THOMAS AQUINAS. Note the places of honour given to Plato and Aristotle as teachers of Aquinas. The heretic at his feet is Averroës. *From the Church of St Catherine, Pisa. Photo: Mansell Collection, London.*

D. Christian Symbols

(i) THE VIRGIN AND CHILD: Illustrations D1-D10

The first six pictures illustrate the trend towards greater realism and tenderness in the handling of this theme in the period covered by this book. In Pictures D1 to D4 secular 'controls' are present which suggest the distance preserved between the Virgin and other women by the artists. Pictures D5 and D6 show two extreme conclusions of the development – the first vulgar and coquettish, the second warm but dignified. Pictures D9 to D10 indicate two contrasting attitudes towards religious art: the first will have no images, the second makes art in its own image.

(Above) D2, Eve. Hildesheim Cathedral: detail from Bernward's door. *c*, 1015. *Photo: Wehmeyer, Hildesheim.*

(Left) D1. Virgin and child. Hildesheim Cathedral: detail from Bernward's door. *c*. 1015. *Photo: Wehmeyer, Hildesheim.*

fugit ēma re[gina] ɠma in normānniā
cum pueri[s] [f]uiſ ut ibidem a du
[s]te · pa[tre] [s]uo protegatur
[g]etur

[b]us[?] **Ꝍ edwardulus**

(Above) D4. QUEEN EMMA CARRYING THE YOUNG EDWARD THE CONFESSOR. A detail from the life of Edward the Confessor, as a control for D3. *By permission of Cambridge University Library. MS Ee. 3. 59. f. 24. Date probably 1240-50.*

(Left) D3. THE CHICHESTER ROUNDEL *c.* 1230-40. *By permission of Victoria and Albert Museum, London.*

(Above) D6. 14TH C. VIRGIN AND CHILD. *14th c. statuette on the portal of the monastery church, Chartreuse of Champnol. Photo: Archives Photographiques, Caisse Nationale des Monuments Historiques, Paris.*

(Left) D5. 14TH C. VIRGIN AND CHILD. *14 th c. statuette from Villeneuve-les-Avignon. Now in Louvre. Photo: Archives Photographiques, Caisse Nationale des Monuments Historiques, Paris.*

(Above) D8. VIRGIN AND CHILD, DESIGNATED 'SAVIOUR OF SOULS'. This icon was originally intended to be carried on a pole in processions. It is almost certainly the work of a Constantinopolitan artist. *Obverse of two-sided early 14th c. icon from the church of St Clement, Ochrid. Now in Skopje Museum. Photo: Byzantine Exhibition, Edinburgh, 1958.*

(Left) D7. VIRGIN AND CHILD BETWEEN TWO ANGELS. *Ivory convex relief. Syrian or Egyptian, 9th-10th c. By courtesy of the Walters Art Gallery, Baltimore, Md.*

46

(Above) D10. A WOMAN PAINTING A STATUETTE OF THE VIRGIN. *By permission of Bibliothèque Nationale, Paris. MS Fr. 12420 f. 92v. 15th c.*

(Left) D9. AN IMAGE OF CHRIST IS OBLITERATED. This picture in a contemporary psalter illustrates a result of the decrees of the Iconoclast synod of 815. *By permission of the Vatican Library. Barberini Psalter f. 43v.*

(ii) DEATH AND RESURRECTION: illustrations D11-D12

The pictures in this section are concerned with the Christian understanding of death, and above all with the portrayal of the crucified Christ. Note the greater concentration upon the sufferings of Christ as the period progresses.

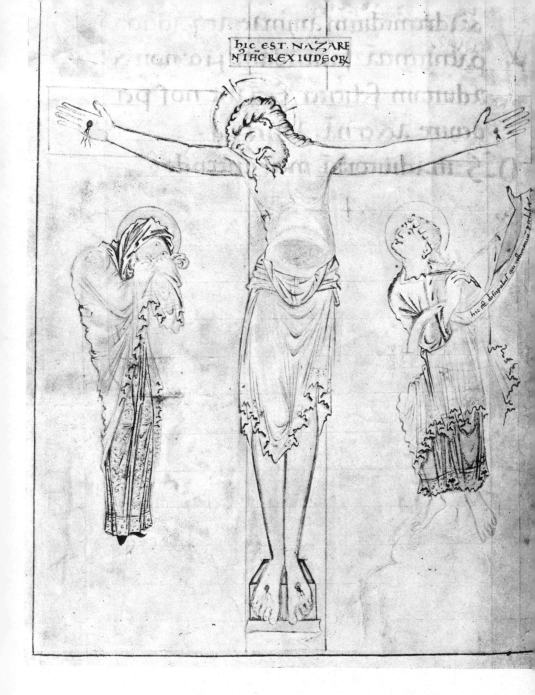

hɪc EST. NAZARE
N IHC REX IUDEOR

(Above) D12. CHRIST CRUCIFIED. *By permission of British Museum. Harley MS 2904. Late 10th c., possibly from Ramsey.*

(Left) D11. CHRIST CRUCIFIED. *9th c. crystal, probably originally from Metz, but now in the Augustiner Museum, Freiburg. Photo: Verlag Karl Alber, Freiburg i.B.*

Christ en croix
France XIIᵉ siècle

(Above) D14. Wooden crucifix. S. *Maria in Capitol, Cologne. 1304. Photo: Bildarchiv, Foto Marburg.*

(Left) D13. French bronze crucifix. *Now in the Louvre. 12th c. Photo: Giraudon.*

(Above) D16. CARVED CRUCIFIX. The figure of Christ is a substitute for a lost carving, but the rest of the cross is original. It is made out of seven pieces of walrus tusk skilfully fitted together. The scenes represented on the plaques are as follows:

Right: The Deposition and the Lamentation.

Left: The women at the tomb and the Resurrection. *Walrus Ivory 22 5/8 × 14 3/4 inches. Mid-12th c. Now in Metropolitan Museum of Art, New York. Photo: British Museum.*

(Left) D15. PAINTED CRUCIFIX. *Early 13th c. In S. Maria degli Angioli, Pisano. Photo: Alinari (Mansell Collection, London).*

D17 and D18. CHRISTIAN GRAVESTONE. The engravings on this gravestone indicate how the group to which this 7th c. Merovingian nobleman belonged, thought of death.

(Left D17) Front: A man with a sword and drinking flask, sorely pressed by snakes. This is the dead man, and the snakes are the snakes of death who are attempting to drag him off to the Underworld. Instead of striking at them, however, he seems to be combing his hair. and this fact shows that he is still defiant and alive. The other side of the grave explains why this is so.

(Right D18) Back: Another man, with a spear in his hand, a nimbus round his head, and a medallion on his chest. The snakes are beneath his feet, in a confused, wriggling heap, and he is surrounded by a strange collection of sharp angular lines. This figure is Christ. He has defeated the snakes of death, and they now lie helpless at his feet. The odd geometrical patterns which branch out from the figure of Christ are probably intended to represent the energy that emanates from the person of the risen Christ. Literature: K. Böhner, ' Der frankische Grabstein vom Niederdollendorf am Rhein ', in *Germania*, 28 (1944-50), p. 63-75. *From Niederdollendorf, near Bonn. 7th c. Photo: Rheinisches Landesmuseum, Bonn.*

24v

S non essent regultrantes
et futuris ministrantes que
viderit et que audiunt .
et illa que crememur in diuersis
temponbus et in suis etatibus p
libios et per sarptinas vbi po
niuit magnas aras. pauca sa
rentur de factis in temponbus

que non viderunt nec saunt
per sariptinas edocemur
si nos bene recordemur. que sii
bona vt amemus. quid ne mal
vt nitenius.   Ergo tu sane co
clude anna sariptinas. et stud
et non amabis vicia In qui
sunt opprobria. Laudandum

D20. THE DANCE OF DEATH. At one time it was thought that the origins of the Dance of Death motif, which appears in several parts of Europe in the later Middle Ages, might lie in Breton folklore; but this now seems unlikely, as this example, the only one in Brittany, is certainly not as old as other examples in Paris and elsewhere. One peculiar feature of this series is that some of the corpses are carrying the heads of animals. This detail was no doubt intended to add to the horrific effect, but it may originate in the use of masks by those acting the devil in medieval mystery plays.

Literature: J. M. Clark, *The Dance of Death*, Glasgow 1950. *Wallpainting in the church at Kermaria, Brittany. Late 14th c. Photo: Archives Photographiques, Caisse Nationale des Monuments Historiques, Paris.*

(iii) THE SAINTS: Illustrations D21-D22

D21. COUNT DIRK II OF HOLLAND AND HIS WIFE AT PRAYER. The picture shows the couple praying to God through the mediation of the patron saint. (Cf. Vol. I, plate 40). *Evangeliarium of the Monastery of Egmond, c. 950. By permission of Koninklijke Bibliotheek, The Hague. 76. F 1, f. 245r.*

(Above) D24. THOMAS BECKET: NORWEGIAN RELIQUARY. This reliquary is almost certainly the work of a Norwegian craftsman. Note several peculiar details. There are five assailants instead of four: the artist included Hugh of Horsea among the murderers. Secondly, part of the sword of one of the assailants breaks off as it strikes the Archbishop's head. Finally, the incident occurs in front of an altar with a chalice on it and a dove above the chalice, thus giving the (false) impression that Mass was being said at the time. Literature: T. Borenius, *Thomas Becket in Art*, London 1930. *From Hedal stave church, Valdres, Norway. Date c. 1250. Photo: Henriksen & Steen, Oslo.*

(Top left) D22. ST SEVERINUS OF COLOGNE. St Severinus was the patron saint of Cologne, and this medallion was worn by a devotee. *Gold Medallion. 11th c. Now in the Erzbischöfliches Diözesan Museum. Photo: Rheinisches Bildarchiv, Cologne.*

(Bottom left) D23. THOMAS BECKET. *British wallpainting. 13th c. Hauxton Church, Cambridgeshire. Photo: Judith Woods.*

(Above) D25. ST JAMES DRESSED AS A PILGRIM. *Late 13th c. wooden statuette from Eggeda i.1 Norway. By permission of Oslo University Archaeological Museum.*

(Top right) D26. PILGRIMS ON THE WAY TO THE HOLY LAND. *By permission of Bibliothèque Municipale, Lyons. 828 (715) f. 15 v. c. 1280.*

(Bottom right) D27. A PILGRIM WHO FOUND THE GOING HARD. The pilgrim appears to have a thorn in his foot, or perhaps he (or she) is simply rather weary. *Carving on a capital in the south transept of Wells Cathedral, England c. 1200-10. Photo: Phillips' City Studio, Wells.*

ça nus elloit li apois aioult en l.ini delincar
nation noftre feignoi: qʒ ꝶ iiij. z vɪ el qn
feine ioʒ del mois. li uaillins Godefroi de
buillon ou·ʒ de loberaine assembla ceus
qui deuoient estre si compugnon de la
uoie. z mut de son pais asigeint au raul

E. Architecture

It is obviously impossible in thirteen plates to give anything approaching a comprehensive coverage of medieval Christian buildings. Those which follow are therefore intended only to highlight some of the more important developments and to illustrate the variety of architectural types in the Christian world.

(Above) EI. CHURCH ON ST MCDARA'S ISLAND, EIRE. This ancient church in County Galway, built c. 700, is one of several surviving early Irish examples which probably replaced earlier wooden structures. Certainly, in their rectangular plan they reflect the influence of simple timber buildings rather than more sophisticated and distant Christian constructions. Several of them have extended side walls, or antae, which were probably intended to carry external timber roof-trusses. In this particular case the antae piers have been continued upwards on to the gable, for a purpose that is not clear. Literature: G. Webb, *Architecture in Britain: The Middle Ages*, London 1965. *Photo: Bord Failte (Irish Tourist Board), Dublin.*

(Right) E2. CHURCH OF HAGIA SOPHIA, SALONIKA. This is one of the best surviving examples of eastern cross-domed churches. The structure of the church, which, in photograph at least, can best be seen from the outside and is here viewed from the north-east, was determined by the demands of the liturgy and in particular by the ritual of the Two Entrances – the Lesser Entrance in which the gospel book is taken to the altar, and the Great Entrance in which the elements of the Eucharist are transferred to the altar. In the period after Justinian, the processions were no longer made along the length of the church from the west, but from either side of the chancel. The domed rooms on either side of the chancel reflect this change. From these rooms, the gospel book (from the south) and the elements (from the north) were carried into the chancel and then, briefly, into the central area of the church where they were shown to the congregation gathered in the aisles and in the galleries. Some 6th c. churches have rooms on either side of the chancel, but it is in the eighth century that fusion with the chancel is perfected. Literature: R. Krautheimer, *Early Christian and Byzantine Architecture*, London 1965, p. 205 ff. *Early 8th c. Photo: Antonello Perissinotto, Padua.*

(Above) E3. BORGUND STAVE CHURCH, NORWAY. This is the best preserved example of the medieval Norwegian stave church. It has been partially restored. The appearance of these churches in the 12th c. coincided with the emergence of the Norwegian Church as a powerful force in Norway under native Norwegian archbishops. Literature: A. Bugge, *Norwegian Stave Churches*, Oslo 1953. c. *1150*. *Photo: Henriksen and Steen, Oslo.*

(Top right) E4. CHURCH AT GERMIGNY-DES-PRES. In contrast to E1 this church, built in 806, does continue an important tradition of early Christian architecture. It follows the Byzantine plan of the inscribed Greek cross, with a central dome. The link with the earlier churches was probably provided by Spanish buildings which Theodulf of Orleans, for whom the church was built, would have known from his early days in Spain. Literature: Nikolaus Pevsner, *An outline of European Architecture*, Jubilee edition. 1960, p. 57 ff. *Photo: French Government Tourist office.*

(Bottom right) E5. CHURCH OF SAINTE FOI, CONQUES. The church of Sainte Foi is one of the great pilgrim churches, built on the pilgrim route to Santiago de Compostela. Its plan, again best seen on photograph from the outside – here from the north-east, illustrates another type of development of the eastern end of the church. In order to ease the passage of pilgrims past a shrine and to provide more chapels for daily mass, an ambulatory or wide passageway was constructed round the apse and radiating chapels were built on to the ambulatory. Literature: K. J. Conant, *Carolingian and Romanesque Architecture, 800-1200*, p. 26, and ch. 8. *Late 11th c. Photo: French Government Tourist office.*

(Above) E6. ABBEY CHURCH, CORVEY, WESTPHALIA: WEST WORKS. This picture illustrates one of the most important innovations of west European architects in the early Middle Ages – i.e. the development of the western end of the church by the introduction of another transept emphasised by towers, and sometimes also by the introduction of another apse (cf. the St Gall plan illus. C8). The innovation has its roots in the Carolingian period but the earliest known example, the Abbey church of St Riquier (790), is no longer standing. *Photo: Verlag Julius Henze, Höxter.*

(Right) E7. ST DENIS, NEAR PARIS: WEST FRONT. The abbey church of St Denis represented a revolution in western architecture, but only the choir and this restored west front remain. For a description of the building of St Denis, see ch. 35. *Mid-12th c. Photo: Archives Photographiques, Caisse Nationale des Monuments Historiques, Paris.*

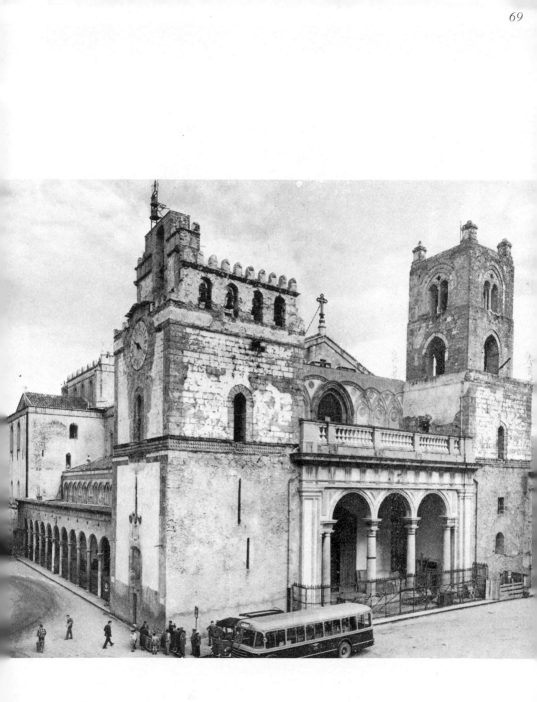

(Above) E9. MONREALE CATHEDRAL: WEST FRONT. The extravagant consequences of a fusion of several traditions are nowhere better illustrated than in the cathedral of Monreale in Sicily. The internal decorations continue the Byzantine tradition (see picture E10), but the architecture manages to combine a variety of traditions, both western and eastern, with questionable success. *12th c. Photo: A. F. Kersting, London.*

(Left) E8. RHEIMS CATHEDRAL: WEST FRONT. The west front of Rheims Cathedral shows how elaborate the basic two-tower type of façade could become. The introduction of more windows and sculpture has transformed the front of the church from a massive fortress into a vast tableau of carved figures set amongst beautifully modelled windows and pinnacles. *Mid-13th c. Photo: Archives Photographiques, Caisse Nationale des Monuments Historiques, Paris.*

(Above) E10. Monreale cathedral: interior looking east. It has been suggested that William II of Sicily, under whose patronage the mosaics were executed, imported teams of Byzantine workmen to do the work. Note the dominant figure of Christ Pantocrator. For further details and literature, cf. D. Talbot Rice, *The Art of the Byzantine Era*, London. *Photo: A. F. Kersting, London.*

(Right) La madelaine, vézelay. (Top) E11. Inner portal. (Bottom) E12. Nave. Note the contrast between the vivid presentation of Christ the Judge on the inner portal and the restrained architecture of the nave. *E11. c. 1130. Photo: A. F. Kersting, London. E12. Early 12th c. Photo: French Government Tourist Office.*

E13. AMIENS CATHEDRAL: NAVE. The added height and the more complicated vaulting and pillars give a greater sense of space and unity than at Vézelay (pictures E11 and E12). There, progress up the nave is through several clearly defined stages; here, the dominant movement is upwards rather than along the church. *Mid-13th c. Photo: French Government Tourist Office.*

PART ONE
604-1048

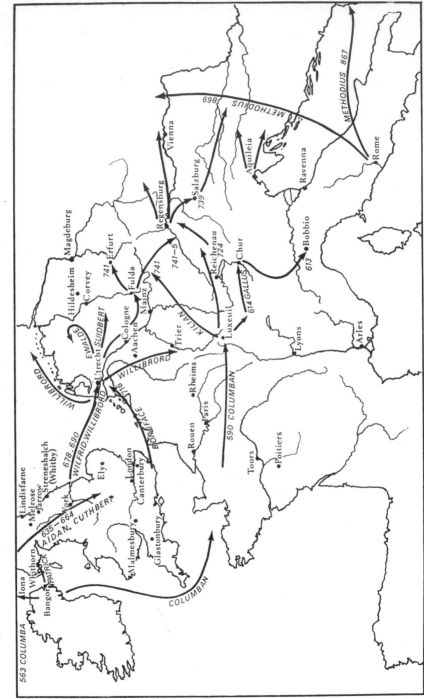

1. The spread of Christianity in northern and eastern Europe 563-740

INTRODUCTORY

THIS volume is designed to carry the history of the Church from the death of Pope Gregory I to the eve of the Protestant Reformation. Long as this period is (604-1500, nine hundred years), it has an undoubted unity, and it corresponds roughly with what most historians for the past hundred years have agreed to call the medieval epoch of European history. A 'period' of history is indeed a purely verbal and arbitrary construction: the stream of history is continuous and deep; revolutions only stir the surface and are themselves the culmination of a long process of change; within any and every period, long or short, there is unceasing movement. Nevertheless, the centuries between the collapse of Roman government in the western half of the empire, accompanied by the decay of ancient, 'classical', civilisation, and the birth of the modern world of nation-states, have certain characteristics and similarities which make them a unity in the same sense that the millennium of the historic Greco-Roman civilisation is, at least to modern minds, a recognisable unity.

During those nine centuries, the peoples of northern and central Europe, who had all moved westwards and southwards towards or into the Roman empire, gradually established a single political and cultural form of society which later began to change slowly into the diversified Europe that we know. Throughout the whole of this period the population of the continent and isles was in the main agrarian, and in the main, also, a society of classes in which that of the landowners great and small dominated and exploited the others under the overhead dominion of a greater lord or king. From the point of view of the church historian, this was the age in which Christianity gradually spread until it covered the whole of Europe from the Ural Mountains to the Atlantic, and from Greenland to the Azores. The peculiar characteristic of the medieval period in western Europe, however, and that which marked it out from what had gone before and what was to come after, was not only that western Christendom was a single religious unit, but that all this great area looked to the apostolic see of Rome as the fountainhead of doctrine, and that with an ever-increasing definition of thought and word the papacy claimed and exercised a doctrinal magisterium and a disciplinary control. Western Europe of the middle ages, therefore, was not only, at least till the end of the fourteenth century, an undifferentiated religious unit, but it was conterminous with a society that looked to the church of Rome and to its bishop as the source of the faith and the seat of authority.

Yet although the ' middle ages ' have a unity and some recognisable broad characteristics, very great changes and developments took place within their framework, and it is not fanciful to see a line of division very near their central decades (A.D. 1000-1050). In the four centuries following the death of Gregory the Great the waters of change ran very slowly in the West. Intellectual and literary life was often static, if not stagnant, and there was little change in political organisation or administrative technique. The innovations that appeared, such as the horse-shoe, the draught collar, the stirrup and the fulling mill, were long in bringing about economic change. In the purely material realm there was no attempt to construct works on the scale of Hadrian's wall or the baths of Caracalla or the Pont du Gard. From about 1000, on the other hand, movement began in every direction. Schools, thought, literature, a reformed and reorganised papacy, a reformed monastic order, architects and builders of genius, with a love for the vast and the sublime – all these new births of the age helped to cover the land with cathedrals and abbeys, while a whole civilisation expanded and proliferated into an infinite variety of achievement. It was at once a renaissance, a re-discovery of the past, and a new creation, the birth of a new world; and whereas in the earlier centuries thought and the mastery by man of the material world and of political life had been fitful and ineffective, in the latter half of the middle ages there was a rapid growth and flowering and finally a transformation into something new.

Within these two divisions, also, we can see dividing lines. From 604 till the central period of Charlemagne's reign (800 is a convenient date to take), it was not clear whither Latin Christianity was going. During much of the seventh century there was a real danger that the central axis of Christendom might be overrun and conquered by the infidel advancing from both east and south-west, while for much of the same epoch the Roman Church was in peril of losing its independence and freedom of action in face of pressure exerted by the eastern emperor. During the same period also, the losses and dilutions experienced by the ancient culture were more marked than the attempts to preserve it or to build upon its foundations, and it was not clear whether, when or where a widespread revival of intellectual and spiritual energy would occur. The reign of Charlemagne saw the establishment of a particular form of literary culture and style in art and architecture that became the norm for two centuries despite the setbacks and irruptions of the forces of heathenism or barbarism that took place here and there throughout the following period. At the same time the Christian empire of the Romans, the western empire, came into being, and from its first beginning as protector of the papacy it came, when transferred to German monarchs, to stand for the secular as opposed to the spiritual power. Yet in politics, as in the things of the mind, contemporary society was as yet incapable of making continuous progress towards a stable and ordered settlement before the middle of the eleventh century.

In somewhat similar fashion the second half of our period divides in the first half of the fourteenth century, and the year of the great pestilence (1349), though in itself too precise and perhaps too late to mark the change of climate, is easily remembered, coinciding as it does with the opening of the long period of French distresses. Until then, all the movements of thought, art, legal lore, institutions and techniques of government had grown steadily in complexity and efficiency, to reach something of a summit in the middle of the thirteenth century during the reign of St Louis in France (1226-1270). At the same time, the struggle between pope and emperor had ended with the victory of the former, and the papacy, already strengthened and exalted, had continued for a century, from Innocent III to Boniface VIII (1198-1303), to dominate western society and politics with ever-increasing claims. Concurrently, artistic achievement, theological and philosophical speculation, and the religious orders had reached, in their different ways, a peak of concentrated and organised excellence. From 1300-1350 onwards the fabric of this culture began to dissolve. A spirit of criticism and individualism broke up the intellectual synthesis, the papal residence at Avignon, followed by the Great Schism, dealt a blow that was all but mortal to the divided papacy, and the recurring pestilences and wars, with their high death-rate and demographic and psychological effects, reduced the numbers and the quality of the higher clergy and the religious orders. At the same time new intellectual interests in literature, art, philosophy and natural science heralded an entirely new mental and spiritual outlook, while regions and countries rapidly developed a spirit of nationality with centralised and jealous governments. Although for almost a century more, under a restored and materially wealthy papacy, some of the forces of change fell into quiescence or at least into latent action, the decadence and disorder of so many years of ecclesiastical life and the new atmosphere created by the humanist worship of the Roman past, added to the geographical discoveries of Portugal and Spain, heralded a revolution which was to break out finally and unexpectedly in Germany, bringing with it the total and permanent fragmentation of western Christendom.

THE EVANGELISATION OF EUROPE

W E may begin our review of the history of these centuries by following the course of the spread of the faith in land hitherto heathen and in those regions, such as Britain and the Rhineland, where the churches established in a province of the Roman empire had been extinguished either wholly or in part by the barbarian invasions. The story is of necessity disjointed and complicated, and its episodes should properly form part of the history of each region and country, but for the purposes of this book a short survey of the expansion of Christianity from the pontificate of Gregory I to the early decades of the eleventh century may be of greater assistance to the reader.

In Italy in 600 there were as yet areas of wild country where the peasant population was still pagan, and in the Lombard territory in central and northern Italy the invaders were nominally Arian. Within a century the whole peninsula was Catholic, though the process of the change cannot be followed at all fully in the records of the times. Meanwhile there had been a steady, if largely unperceived, advance in the unification of faith in other parts of Christian Europe. Arianism, which at one time threatened to engulf the Church, had vanished from Gaul shortly before the date at which our period opens, but in Spain a party of the heresy remained until the Muslim conquest.

In Gaul the great majority of the population was Christian or at least in contact with Christianity in 600, but the Breton peninsula of Celtic immigrants from west Britain displaced by the Saxon invasions remained separate in character and customs from the rest of the Gallic church for more than two centuries, and has retained traces of its origin to the present day. In the north of Gaul the Roman Christianity had been thrust back from what is now Belgium by the tide of pagan invasion to a line running roughly from Amiens to Trier and Cologne, and the reflux had not yet recovered all the lost ground, though Amandus in Flanders and figures that later were seen mistily in heroic proportions, such as Audomar (Omer) and Eligius (Eloi), in what are now Normandy, Picardy and Flanders, won districts here and there back to the faith. In the north and east of Gaul, groups of Irish monks, followers or successors of Columbanus, Gall and Fursa preached and worked in the neighbourhood of their monasteries in the Jura and what is now Switzerland.

In Germany the scattered Christian settlements in what is now the Austrian Tyrol, Switzerland, southern Bavaria and Württemberg had never been wholly obliterated by the invasions. Augsburg and Chur, for example, had remained bishops' sees throughout, and north Switzerland from Constance to Basle had retained the faith. Strasbourg also may have remained in being as a see. Later, in the early decades of the seventh century, Columbanus and his monks had reached Zürich, Bregenz and what became St Gall. Swabia was partially Christian by 700, and the monk Pirmin, whose native land may have been either Ireland, southern France or Spain, had founded Reichenau and its daughters the Bavarian Altaich and the Rhaetian Pfäffers. In Bavaria also Salzburg and Regensburg were founded before 700, though the church in those quarters remained unorganised. Thuringia, where Arian influence had lingered, remained undisciplined and without organisation, though the Irish had colonised Würzburg.

All these tentative and unco-ordinated efforts were later overshadowed by a missionary impulse which had its origins in England.

In the British Isles, when our period opens, the whole of England, save perhaps for Cornwall, and the eastern regions of Scotland were occupied by the pagan invaders, Saxons, Angles, Jutes, Danes and others who had settled there after the withdrawal of the Roman armies and administration. So far as written and archaeological evidence goes, there is no trace of the survival of Christian communities in what is now England, but Cornwall and Wales, still wholly British, had kept the faith and Ireland, not yet threatened with invasion, had recently, as was seen in the first volume of this history, sent out two great missionary apostles, Columbanus to Gaul and Italy, and Columba to Iona in the western isles of Caledonia. From Iona, at the request of the Northumbrian prince Oswald, had come Aidan

(d. 651) to be bishop of Lindisfarne, whence Northumbria and later, under Aidan's successor Finan, Mercia and parts of East Anglia were converted or reconverted.

Meanwhile the Christian faith had come to southern England from another source. One of the most influential of the acts of Gregory I was the mission of Augustine and his companions to England. By this action which, though without parallel in the earlier history of the papacy, was seemingly not designed as the opening of a larger programme, a policy of evangelisation was begun, and begun from Rome, and by an unforeseeable set of consequences a strong nexus between the papacy and a distant church was set up which became far more extensive owing to the evangelisation of north-western and west-central Europe from the British Isles, while at the same time the papacy gained a direct control and a notable prestige among the newly converted peoples which rapidly strengthened its position in face of the eastern empire and in the more remote future gave it powers of resistance in its contest with the German emperors. At first, however, after the initial success in Kent, and the somewhat later mission of Paulinus in Northumbria, there were setbacks in both regions, and it was only by slow degrees, and partly from other sources, that Wessex and East Anglia were converted. Meanwhile, as we have seen, the Christian faith had come to Northumbria from a northern and Celtic source, and had extended to Mercia, a kingdom embracing what are now the north Midlands of England. The differences of customs, above all in the calculation of the date of Easter, of religious sentiment and of discipline between the southern English with their direct links with Rome, and the Celtic church, with its long tradition of isolation, were bound to produce a controversy, if not a collision. Agreement was reached at the synod of Whitby (663), in which a decisive part was taken by a zealous and forceful monk of Ripon, Wilfrid, who had visited Rome and had received the tonsure in Gaul. He stressed the apostolicity and the widespread authority of the see of Peter, and the church in the north accepted the customs and decisions of Rome.

Within a few decades of the settlement of Whitby, some of the energies of the flourishing church in Northumbria were directed overseas, partly by a consciousness of kinship with the Saxons and their neighbours who had remained at home in the age of the great invasions, and partly through contact with the Irish and their vision of exile for Christ's sake and settlement abroad among the heathen. Wilfrid of Ripon, in one of his periods of exile, had preached to the Frisians with some success, and the first notable missionary came from Wilfrid's monastery of Ripon in the person of Willibrord, the so-called apostle of the Netherlands, who crossed to Frisia in 690 and was consecrated bishop by the pope in 695. His success, however, was limited in area (he died in 739) and the decisive moment came with the arrival of Winfrith (672/5-754).

This eminent man, who must rank with such saints as Cyril and Methodius and Francis Xavier among the very greatest of Christian missionaries, was born in Devon, and spent his youth and early manhood in Wessex monasteries near Winchester and what is now the Solent before he felt the call to give the light of faith to the men of his own race living in Europe. Beginning with Frisia in 716, where the inhabitants were long resistant to the gospel, he encountered opposition and retired, only to visit Rome in 718 and to receive a commission from Gregory II to return to Frisia, where he worked with Willibrord with more success (719-22). From the beginning, he had carried on with the Anglo-Saxon tradition of a church bound directly to the see of Peter, and he himself made long visits to Rome in 718 and again in 722, when he was consecrated bishop by the pope and confirmed with his Roman name of Boniface, with a wide commission of preaching and ruling. He then spent many years, till 739, in Hesse and Thuringia, and finally passed to Bavaria, among a population half-pagan with Christian groups and traditions. Here he completely reorganised the church, as he was to do later in Frankland for Pippin, and set up several of the great bishoprics of central Germany.

Boniface had a genius for friendship, and knew how to give as well as to inspire devotion. His letters, of which a considerable collection has come down to us, give a picture of the age, and of his work among the heathen, that is unique in its direct and vivid detail. Thus he writes to Abbess Eadburh of Minster, asking her ' to write for me in gold the epistles of my lord, St Peter the Apostle ', so that the heathen may reverence Holy Scripture, and to Daniel, bishop of Winchester, for a ' book of the six prophets... written with clear and detached letters... since my eyes grow dim I cannot distinguish small and connected letters '; for his part, he sends Daniel as a present from Germany a cloak of mixed ' silk and goats ' wool, and a towel for drying your feet'. Elsewhere we see him in difficulties with the Franks, with whom he has sworn to the pope that he would have no intercourse, and to whose rich and worldly clergy ' our labours and battles with the heathen... seem alien '. [1] He was followed to Germany by friends from England, some of whom he himself had invited; among them were both monks and nuns, and he founded for them abbeys such as Fritzlar and Fulda, and bishoprics such as Würzburg, to serve as bases and fortresses for the missionaries and centres of spiritual life and learning for the infant churches. Among those who came were Willibald,

---

1. M. Tangl, *Die Briefe des heiligen Bonifatius und Lullus* in *MGH Epistolae selectae* I (Berlin 1916) ep. 35, 60; ep. 63, 130-1. In the English translation by E. Emerton (see Bibliography) the pages are 35, 115-16.

an English monk who, on his way back from a pilgrimage to Palestine, had helped to refound Monte Cassino, his brother Winnibald, later bishop of Eichstätt, their sister Walburga, abbess of Heidenheim, and Lull, and he kept up a correspondence with his friends in England that gives a vivid reflection of his personality and of the excellence of the literary education attained in the higher levels of the Anglo-Saxon church. Appointed archbishop ' of Germany ', he settled as bishop of Mainz in 732 and was later commissioned by Pope Zacharias as legate to the Frankish church. Finally, in 754, he and his numerous companions were massacred almost by chance when on a preaching expedition in northern Friesland. Boniface is known with justice as the apostle of Germany, for though much of his life was spent in regions which were at least partially Christian, his was the hand that consolidated the church from Frisia to Thuringia, and who gave to what are now south Germany and central Switzerland their organisation and the earliest of their great monasteries. Above all, he gave to the young church of Germany a framework and traditions of the Roman type. His upbringing in England and his repeated visits to Rome were both responsible for this; he was commissioned by a pope of vision, and regarded himself throughout as an agent and representative of the papacy; the infant and adolescent churches and monasteries of Germany inherited and maintained this tradition. In consequence, when the papacy was in danger of losing its independence to successive imperial claims, and passed through times of humiliation and virtual impotence at Rome, the young churches, from England in a wide arc to Austria, were growing to adolescence with the attitude towards Rome that was to become universal throughout the western church in the course of a few centuries. It may seem at first sight paradoxical that it was in Germany and not in France that the papacy, three centuries later, was to meet its most powerful adversary, but it was unquestionably the ancestral tradition of Boniface that preserved the Roman obedience in many of the dioceses of Germany throughout the struggle between pope and emperor.

The work of Boniface was continued by his disciples, and Charlemagne assisted their efforts in Frisia in the decades before 800. In Saxony, as is well known, he adopted other methods, and the Saxons (or such as remained of them) were driven to the waters of baptism during thirty years of brutal warfare which, unlike so many other attempts at conversion by blood and iron, produced ultimately a permanently Christian people. Thirty years later Anskar (801-65), a monk of Corvey, under the patronage of Lewis the Pious, was consecrated bishop of Hamburg, to which Bremen was later joined, with a general commission to Christianise Scandinavia. Anskar did indeed penetrate to Birka near the modern Stockholm, and later evangelised part of Denmark, but the Viking invasion drove back the frontiers of Christianity, and despite numerous attempts, the conversion of Denmark was not fully accomplished till the early eleventh century, when Knut was king of Denmark and England, and it was from England that Denmark received monasticism and some of its first bishops. England also, though in ways very imperfectly recorded, was chiefly responsible for the conversion of Norway in the late tenth century and Sweden in the early eleventh, though no single missionary attained the eminence of an Anskar or a Willibrord. Monks had a large part in the evangelisation of Scandinavia, and the Danish and Norwegian churches retained permanent marks of the old English connection in their liturgy and religious literature and art. Thus the cathedral at Stavanger is dedicated to St Swithin of Winchester and the modern town displays the patron's name on street names and branded goods. From Denmark the faith was carried to Iceland (996) where a fervent church grew up, and to Greenland (1123) where a medieval church has been excavated recently.

Whereas the evangelisation of Europe west of Germany had been the pacific work of individuals or groups fired with missionary zeal and for the most part working among peoples of their own or kindred race, or at least with no racial hostility towards those who were preaching the gospel, the progress of Christianity on the eastern side of Germany was a slow and irregular penetration, preceding, accompanying or following German arms and often influenced by political considerations and the fortunes of war. Here the people of German stock came up against a Slav population and the fierce and savage tribes on the Baltic coasts. They were moreover hindered in their work of evangelisation by the hatred of conquered peoples, by their own reverses, and above all by a great pagan invasion, that of the Magyars or Hungarians, who drove large wedges into German territory. The first wave of Hungarians were defeated by Henry I in two great battles in 933 in Thuringia and Saxony near the Elbe; the other was halted by Otto I on the Lechfeld near Augsburg in 955.

The Magyars had ravaged Moravia, but Christianity was not wholly destroyed, and German and Moravian priests entered Bohemia, where the ascetic young king Wenceslas (Vaclav) in his short reign (923-9) built churches and endeavoured to spread the faith in the few years allowed him before his murder. Meanwhile under Henry I and still more under Otto the Great the German *Drang nach Osten* began to influence the diffusion of Christianity. The first people to be encountered were the Wends, who put up a stubborn resistance to both the Germans and their new religion, but the see of Brandenburg was founded in 948. Aarhus in Denmark had probably been established in the previous year, and Oldenburg a little later. Otto I had long wished to found a see at Magdeburg on the frontier of east Saxony, and after many difficulties the monk

Adalbert became the first archbishop (968) with a suffragan see at Merseburg.

Shortly before this the progress of the faith in Bohemia had been pressed forward by Boleslav II (ruled 967-999), under whom it is probable that the bishopric of Prague was founded, as a suffragan see of Mainz; here the second bishop was another Adalbert, a monk who, after many vicissitudes and missionary labours, died a martyr's death among the pagan Prussians in 997. Meanwhile the able and ambitious politician Pilgrim, bishop of Passau, was endeavouring to convert the Magyars, whom he hoped to control from a bishopric suffragan to his own see. His efforts failed, and Hungary owed its Christian organisation to the sainted Stephen I (ruled 997-1038), whose arrangements were ratified by Silvester II. He gave the country its hierarchy, with an archbishopric at Gran (Esztergom), and established it as an active part of the western church. A few decades earlier German immigrants had helped to found the Polish see of Poznan (Posen) in 968, but the conversion of the country followed upon that of Mieszko I, the founder of the Polish state, in 967. The church in Poland was organised more completely by Duke (later King) Boleslav I (ruled 992-1025), with an archbishopric at Gniezno (Gnesen), authorised by the Emperor Otto III in 1000, when he visited the tomb of St Adalbert, and canonically erected by Silvester II, who thus gave permanent organisation to the two easternmost churches of the Roman obedience, and at the same time put bounds to the long eastward extension of the archbishopric of Magdeburg.

In these ways, therefore, the greater part of continental Europe was Christian and Roman west of Russia and Bulgaria, and north of the shifting boundary of Islam in Spain, by the middle of the eleventh century. Parts of the three Scandinavian countries with the Baltic coast and its hinterland from Bremen eastwards and northwards, remained pagan, together with pockets of land in central Europe. Eastwards, much of modern Russia-in-Europe and the Balkans had been won for Orthodox Christianity. What remained was to be won for the Church during the twelfth and thirteenth centuries, and the whole held for some three centuries under the control of the two great bodies who claimed to preserve intact the primitive faith of Christendom.

In the far west the conversion had had in it something of mystery, of wonder and of romance. Celtic Christianity, with its lack of unifying discipline and of dogmatic formalism, with its gifts of art and learning, and its abounding energy of expansion which sent its sons to Iceland and to the Danube, has no parallel in the east of Catholic Europe, nor is there any early Christian culture to match that of Northumbria and Wessex, prolonged by its missionaries to Frisia and Germany. In all these countries the waters of salvation spread as if by some inner natural or supernatural force. In the east, on the other hand, the process was tied closely to the expansive force of Germany, and was accomplished by the plantation of monasteries and the foundation of bishoprics. No doubt it was often spiritualised by the presence of saints such as Adalbert and Cyril and Methodius, but the difference remains, and it is for this reason that western missionaries are more distinct figures in the pages of history. Nevertheless, the conquests of Christianity in the German and Slav lands are as impressive in every way in their witness to the innate power of the gospel message to appeal to every race of Europe.

During the period we have been considering Christianity as a whole had suffered losses as great as its gains. These had been caused by the unforeseeable emergence of Islam and the phenomenal speed and extent of its conquests. Mahomet died in 632 and within a century the dominion of his followers extended from Samarkand and the Indus to Cadiz and the Pyrenees, and their armies threatened the walls of Constantinople and Orleans. We are not here concerned with their eastern successes, by which the flourishing Christian communities of Syria, Armenia, Palestine and Egypt were overrun and in great part destroyed. In the west, the Muslims had conquered the Roman provinces of Africa and Mauretania before 700, and in 711 they had crossed into Spain. Two years later almost the whole of the Peninsula was in their hands. Their armies washed like waves past either end of the Pyrenees at almost the same moment that they were pouring across Asia Minor towards Constantinople. Christendom, which had not yet reached its full northward and eastward spread in Europe, was reduced for a time to the Byzantine lands in Thrace and Greece in the east, and in the west to what was little more than a wide corridor of territories from Italy, through Frankland, to England. Never since the first spread of the gospel had its sphere of influence seemed so restricted. Yet at the very moment when the pincers seemed about to close from west and east, relief came. In 674-8 and again in 717-8 the fleets and armies of Islam were beaten back from the walls of Constantinople, and in 732 Charles Martel defeated the invading army of Saracens near Poitiers.

These two victories of Christendom have justly been reckoned as among the decisive contests in world history. That in the west, though at first it might seem to have given no more than temporary relief, was in fact to establish the Pyrenees as the limit of Muslim occupation, while that in the east gave the Byzantine empire another seven centuries of life with renewed power and all that that implied, including the Christianisation of Russia. Of the two, indeed, that in the east was in reality the more momentous, for Constantinople was at once the heart and the head of the Christian empire, and had the city fallen Byzantine civilisation might well have foundered, and the faith might never have spread to the countries between the Danube and the Urals. In France, on the other hand, Muslim activity already stretched out too far to hold what it had grasped, and though the coastal regions of the Mediterranean were to be harassed by the Saracens for another four centuries, there was probably never during that time any danger of a permanent conquest. But perhaps the most significant feature of Charles Martel's victory was the contemporary realisation that it was the victory not of an army, but of Europe, and this realisation was to inspire the myth which later found expression in the *Chanson de Roland.*

THE ORTHODOX CHURCHES
OF EASTERN EUROPE

OST of the Christian communities which arose in the early middle ages in the Slav-speaking areas of the Balkan peninsula, in the lands bordering on the middle and lower Danube, and in Russia, owed their existence, directly or indirectly, to the work of Byzantine missionaries. The conversion of the peoples who dwelt in these countries was, at least as far as the ruling classes were concerned, completed by the end of the tenth century. By the year 1000 there had arisen in eastern Europe a community of nations whose rulers and educated classes were in some measure united by a common profession of eastern Christianity and by the acceptance of a cultural pattern derived from Byzantium. The conversion of these nations of eastern Europe and the growth of their Christian culture were largely the result of a missionary effort by the Byzantine church which, despite several set-backs and interruptions, had been maintained since the sixth century, and whose general pattern is first clearly discernible in the reign of Justinian (527-65).

I. THE PATTERN OF THE EARLY BYZANTINE MISSIONS

By the sixth century the missionary work of the Byzantine church had become closely associated with the aims of the empire's foreign policy.

Both found their motive force and ideological justification in three basic principles: in the conviction, inherited from ancient Rome, that the empire was in theory universal and in practice coextensive with the civilised world, whose nations owed lawful obedience to the emperor in Constantinople; in the view, derived from the Hellenistic thought-world, that the barbarians outside the civilised *Oikoumene* were destined one day to gain admittance to the cultural community of the *Rhomaioi;* and in the belief, rooted in the Judaeo-Christian tradition, that these *Rhomaioi*, dedicated to the service of Christ by the Emperor Constantine, were the new chosen people, whose duty it was to bring the gospel to all the peoples of the earth. The equivalence thus established between the *Pax Romana* and the *Pax Christiana*, between the interests of the empire and the advancement of the Christian faith, explains why most emperors took their duty of converting the barbarians very seriously, and why the history of Byzantine missions was, from the sixth century onwards, determined at every stage by the interplay of religious and political factors. Henceforth the Byzantine missionary appears in a dual role: as an apostolic figure, sent to extend the spiritual frontiers of the Kingdom of God, and as an ambassador of east Roman imperialism, accompanied on his journeys to the barbarians by the pomp and majesty of his secular sovereign. And this association of imperial diplomacy with evangelical work in missionary fields abroad was matched by their close connection on the home front: the receptions accorded in Constantinople to envoys from pagan barbarian rulers combined an elaborate *mise-en-scène*, designed to impress them with the empire's magnificence and power, with an attempt to move their hearts by the spectacle of the liturgy of the Christian church splendidly celebrated beneath the vaults of some of the most celebrated shrines in Christendom, among which the Cathedral of St Sophia held pride of place.

This intimate association of Church and State in the common task of extending the hegemony of the Christian empire was sometimes a source of weakness to both. Some barbarian peoples were too attached to their pagan beliefs to submit willingly to a Byzantine protectorate; others valued their political independence too much to risk jeopardising it by accepting the spiritual jurisdiction of Constantinople. In 528 a certain Grod, king of the Huns who lived near the Crimean city of Bosporus, was baptised in Constantinople. As godson and subject-ally of the Emperor Justinian, he was expected on his return home to guard the political interests of the empire in the Crimean sector. But on this occasion the Byzantine diplomats had played their cards too hastily. Grod's subjects, rather than face forcible conversion to Christianity, rose in revolt and slew their king. A Byzantine military expedition re-established the empire's authority in southern Crimea, but the attempt to Christianise the local Huns failed. [1]

Often, however, the missionary work benefited from imperial support. About 530 an Armenian bishop by the name of Kardutsat, accompanied by priests, went to preach the gospel among another group of Huns, who lived in the steppes to the north of the Caucasus mountains. During the seven years he stayed among them he made many converts and translated some books – doubtless the Scriptures and the liturgy – into the Hun language. The emperor Justinian sent the missionaries a consignment of flour, wine, oil, linen cloths and sacramental vessels. Kardutsat was succeeded as head of the Hunnic Christian community by another Armenian bishop, Maku. This remarkable missionary, we are told by a contemporary Syriac writer, ' built a brick church and planted plants and sowed various kinds of seeds and did signs and baptised many '. [2] Here, condensed into a vivid miniature, are all the essential features of a successful – though, in this case, probably short-lived – Byzantine-sponsored mission to the nations of the steppe: genuine evangelical zeal; the use of vernacular translations of the Scriptures and the liturgy to facilitate the conversion of the pagans; the support – political and economic – given to the mission by the imperial government; the missionaries' attempt to convert the nomads from a pastoral economy to an agricultural way of life, with the aim of providing a more stable framework for the religious and cultural growth of their community; their ability to make their technical skill serve the practical needs of their flock; and the shrewd flexibility of Byzantine diplomacy – for the Armenian clerics who worked to promote the interests of the Orthodox empire among the Huns may well have been Monophysites: this picture is an epitome of many a Byzantine mission to the peoples beyond the empire's northern border.

The same interplay of religious and political motives is visible in the missions sponsored by the emperor Heraclius (610-41). In the Balkans the Croats and the Serbs, who had settled there c. 626 to guard imperial lands against the Avars, were converted by missionaries sent from Rome at the emperor's request. [3] And although their conversion was impermanent – for the Christianisation of Serbia and Croatia had to be carried out afresh in the ninth century – their acceptance of Christianity enhanced

1. John Malalas, *Chronographia*, Bonn 1831, 431-3; Theophanes, *Chronographia*, ed. C. de Boor, I, Leipzig 1883, 175-6.

2. *The Syriac Chronicle known as that of Zachariah of Mitylene*, translated into English by F. J. Hamilton and E. W. Brooks, London 1899, 329-331. The name Maku is doubtful. Cf. E. A. Thompson, *Christian missionaries among the Huns:* Hermathena 67 (1946) 73-9.

3. Constantine Porphyrogenitus, *De administrando imperio,* ed. Gy. Moravcsik, Engl. transl. R. J. H. Jenkins, Budapest 1949, 148-9, 154-5.

for a while their political loyalty and their usefulness to the empire. It was largely in response to the Avar threat – so dramatically demonstrated during the siege of Constantinople in 626 – that Heraclius strove to ensure a favourable balance of power in the steppes of south Russia: here, too, Christian proselytism and diplomacy went together. The alliance concluded by Heraclius with the Turkic Onogurs (or Bulgars) who built up, with Byzantine support, a state extending from the Caucasus to the Don and probably as far as the lower Dnieper, was cemented by the baptism o their ruler in Constantinople in 619 and by the resultant loyalty to the empire of their king Kuvrat (d. 642) who in his youth had become a Christian in the Byzantine capital. [4]

During the two hundred years between 650 and 850 the missionary work of the Byzantine church suffered a set-back. The occupation of almost the entire Balkan peninsula by the pagan Slavs, the desperate struggle against the Arabs, and the Iconoclast controversy, diverted the energies of the empire into a fight for survival, exhausted the spiritual resources of its church, and crippled its foreign policy. Yet even in those dark centuries the Byzantines did not forget that both their religious duty and their political interest lay in preaching the gospel to the barbarians. Attempts were made in the eighth century to convert the Khazars who were now the dominant power in the south Russian steppes. They largely failed, as the rulers of Khazaria preferred the more neutral Jewish faith to the political commitments of Byzantine Christianity. It is noteworthy, however, that the Iconoclast governments of Constantinople were not averse to employing defenders of the images, whom they persecuted at home and exiled to the Crimea, to propagate Christianity among the subjects of the Khazars.[5]

2. CYRIL AND METHODIUS AND THE MORAVIAN MISSION

The revival of the missionary activity of the Byzantine church coincided with a remarkable recovery of the empire's foreign policy towards the middle of the ninth century. Both were closely connected with the political and cultural renaissance which followed the defeat of Iconoclasm in 843; and they had their crowning achievement in the seventh decade of that century, when the influence of Byzantine civilisation, striking out far beyond the empire's northern frontier and thrusting deep into eastern and central Europe, gained the allegiance of a substantial part of the

4. Nicephorus Patriarcha, *Opuscula Historica*, ed. C. de Boor, Leipzig 1880, 12, 24; *The Chronicle of John, Bishop of Nikiu*, transl. R. H. Charles, London 1916, 197.
5. F. Dvornik, *Les légendes de Constantin et de Méthode vues de Byzance*, Prague 1933, 157-68.

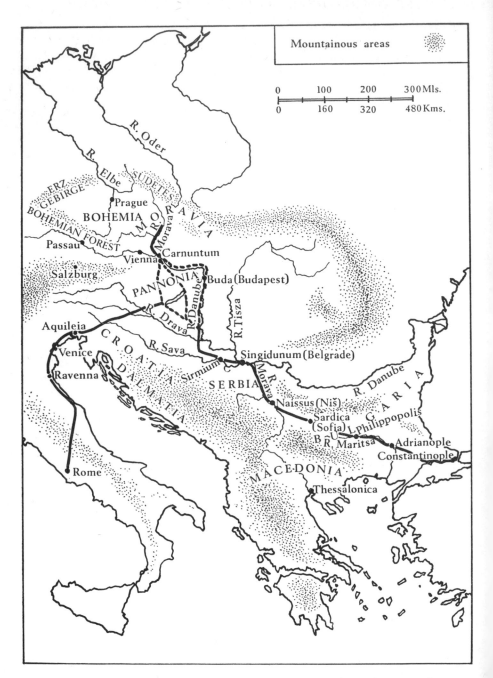

2.   The missions of Cyril and Methodius to Moravia and Pannonia

Slav world. This movement is closely associated with the names of two of the greatest Byzantine missionaries, St Cyril and St Methodius.

Cyril (or Constantine, as he was called before he became a monk in the last few weeks of his life) and Methodius, born in Thessalonica, were the sons of a high-ranking Byzantine official. Methodius, the elder brother, after a brief administrative career as governor of a Slav province–probably in Macedonia–became *c.* 840 a monk in one of the religious houses on Mount Olympus in Bithynia, which was then, next to Constantinople, the foremost monastic centre in the Byzantine empire. Constantine, who showed a great aptitude for scholarship, studied at the University of Constantinople, where he was the pupil and later the successor of the future Patriarch Photius, and was ordained priest. About 851 he took a leading part in a Byzantine embassy to the court of the Arab Khalife, and in 860-1 he headed a religious and diplomatic mission to the Khazars. In 862 there arrived in Constantinople an embassy from the Moravian prince Rastislav, bringing to the emperor Michael III the offer of a political alliance and a request for a Christian missionary acquainted with the Slavonic language of the Moravians. Rastislav, whose realm included Moravia, Slovakia and part of present-day Hungary, saw in these two proposals a means of securing his political independence from Lewis the German, king of the East Franks, and cultural autonomy for his country. The Byzantine government, mindful of the spiritual and temporal advantages to be gained from an extension of its influence to central Europe, concluded an alliance with Rastislav and appointed Constantine and Methodius to head the mission to Moravia. As natives of Thessalonica, which was then a bilingual city, the two brothers had a fluent knowledge of the Slav dialect of neighbouring Macedonia. Before leaving Byzantium, Constantine, basing himself on this dialect, invented an alphabet for the use of his future Moravian flock. It is now fairly generally agreed that this was the Glagolitic alphabet, a highly distinct and original creation, and that the so-called Cyrillic script which bears Constantine's monastic name and on which the modern alphabets of the Bulgarians, the Serbs and the Russians are based, was the result of a later attempt by Methodius's disciples in Bulgaria to adapt Greek uncial writing to the Slavonic tongue. With the help of his new alphabet and with the assistance of a group of linguists in Constantinople, Constantine translated into Slavonic a selection of lessons from the Gospels, starting with the opening words of St John: ' In the beginning was the Word '.

Thus was created a new literary language, Old Church Slavonic, based on the spoken dialect of the Macedonian Slavs, modelled on Greek, largely ecclesiastical in character, and – in view of the close similarity between the different Slavonic languages in this period – intelligible to all the Slav peoples. Throughout the middle ages Old Church Slavonic remained the third international language of Europe and the sacred idiom of those Slavs – the Bulgarians, the Russians and the Serbs – who owed their religion and much of their culture to Byzantium.

The Byzantine embassy arrived in Moravia in the spring of 863. With the support of Rastislav and the help of Slav-speaking clerics whom they had brought from Constantinople, Constantine and Methodius embarked on their missionary work. Moravia had been Christianised in the first half of the ninth century, mainly by Frankish missionaries from Salzburg and Passau, and it is not impossible that Irish monks from Bavaria had also worked in the country in the late eighth century. But the Byzantine missionaries improved on the work of their predecessors by bringing to the Moravians the Scriptures and the liturgy in their vernacular language. It is probable that Constantine translated into Old Church Slavonic the Byzantine liturgical offices, including the Liturgy of St John Chrysostom, as well as a formulary based on the Latin Mass with which the Moravians were already familiar: this formulary, in the opinion of some scholars, was the so-called Liturgy of St Peter, a Greek version of the Roman Mass with some additions from the Byzantine rite. From the Byzantine standpoint the translation of the liturgical offices into a vernacular language seemed natural and legitimate: many nations of eastern Christendom – among them the Armenians, the Georgians and the Copts – used their native languages for Christian worship. But in the western church Latin had, in practice, come to be recognised as the only legitimate liturgical language. The natural suspicion with which the Frankish bishops viewed the liturgical experiments of Constantine and Methodius was aggravated by their resentment at what they regarded as an act of trespass by the Byzantine missionaries on their ecclesiastical field.

The explosive situation brought about in Moravia by this Franko-Byzantine rivalry was mitigated for a while by the authority and far-sightedness of the papacy. Some three and a half years after their arrival in Moravia, Constantine and Methodius set out on a journey southward, in order to have some of their disciples ordained. [6] On their way they secured the enthusiastic support of the Slav prince Kocel, who ruled in Pannonia under Frankish suzerainty; he learned the Slavonic letters and entrusted some fifty of his subjects to the two brothers, as their pupils. During their stay in Venice, Constantine conducted a spirited defence of vernacular languages in a disputation with the local Latin clerics who,

6. It is not clear whether they intended to go to Rome or to Constantinople. On this disputed point, see F. Dvornik, *The Slavs, their early history and civilization*, Boston 1956, 89, n. 2; F. Grivec, *Konstantin und Method, Lehrer der Slaven*, Wiesbaden 1960, 70-3.

according to his contemporary biographer, expounded the 'trilingual heresy', based on the view that Hebrew, Greek and Latin are the only legitimate liturgical languages. It was probably in Venice that Constantine and Methodius received an invitation from Pope Nicholas I. They arrived in Rome during the winter of 867-8.

It seems probable that, in attempting to determine his attitude to the two Byzantine missionaries, the new pope, Hadrian II, found himself in a dilemma. Constantine and Methodius were known to be friends of the patriarch Photius, whom the papacy had refused to recognise, and the news of the *coup d'état* in Constantinople (24 September 867) and of the consequent accession of Ignatius' as patriarch had not yet reached Rome. On the other hand, the reputation of the two brothers stood high; they were bearers of the relics then believed to be those of St Clement of Rome; they were strongly backed by the Slav rulers of central Europe, Rastislav and Kocel; and the papacy, which had recently scored a remarkable success in Bulgaria, [7] could not but welcome the opportunity of detaching Moravia and Pannonia from the jurisdiction of the Frankish clergy and of securing their direct submission to the Holy See. Hadrian II decided to give his full support to Constantine and Methodius: he instructed that their disciples be ordained, that the Mass be celebrated in the Slavonic language in four Roman churches, and that the Slavonic liturgical books be deposited in the Basilica of Santa Maria Maggiore. Soon after this signal triumph of his life-work, Constantine fell seriously ill. In 869, after becoming a monk under the name of Cyril, he died in Rome at the age of 42, and was buried in the Basilica of St Clement.

The future of Slav vernacular Christianity now lay in the hands of Methodius and the pope. In response to a request from Kocel, Hadrian II sent Methodius to Pannonia, bearing a letter to him, to Rastislav and to the latter's nephew Svatopluk, in which he authorised the use of the Slav liturgy in their lands. Before the end of 869 Methodius was back in Rome, where he was consecrated archbishop of Pannonia; he then returned to his missionary diocese, which included Moravia and was based on the see of Sirmium and, in the mind of the pope, was probably intended to counteract the recent defection of neighbouring Bulgaria to the Byzantine church. But the foundations on which Methodius was forced to base his work in central Europe were precarious. The east Frankish clergy, whose earlier prerogatives in Moravia and Pannonia were abrogated by Methodius's new jurisdiction, took advantage of the increased power of Lewis the German in Moravia, and of the deposition of Rastislav in favour of Svatopluk, to secure the arrest of Methodius. Condemned as

7. See p. 304.

a usurper of episcopal rights by a local synod presided over by the archbishop of Salzburg, he was imprisoned for two and a half years in a Bavarian monastery. It was not until 873 that Pope John VIII, having learnt at last of his archbishop's plight, forced the Bavarian king and bishops to release him.

But a new ordeal awaited Methodius. John VIII now forbade the use of the Slavonic liturgy in his diocese. The papacy, it seems, was becoming increasingly unwilling to risk, for the sake of this liturgy, a major conflict with the Frankish church. This papal prohibition was, however, ignored by Methodius. During the remaining twelve years of his life, he continued as archbishop of Pannonia to build his Slav church on vernacular foundations, translating the remaining parts of the Scriptures, the liturgical offices, a Byzantine book of canon law, and various patristic works, and training a Slav-speaking clergy. His work was constantly endangered by the indifference of Svatopluk and the hostility and intrigues of the Frankish clergy. The latter denounced him to the pope for reciting the creed without the *Filioque*. In 880 Methodius travelled once more to Rome. There he successfully vindicated his orthodoxy and persuaded John VIII to recognise once again the legitimacy of the Slavonic liturgy. In the bull *Industriae tuae* (880) the pope stated:

> It is certainly not against faith or doctrine to sing the Mass in the Slavonic language, or to read the Holy Gospel or the divine lessons of the New and Old Testaments well translated and interpreted, or to chant the other offices of the hours, for He who made the three principal languages, Hebrew, Greek and Latin, also created all the others for His own praise and glory. [8]

John VIII's support of Methodius was further strengthened by the sympathetic interest shown in his work by the Byzantine authorities, who were now reconciled with the papacy. About 882 Methodius travelled to Constantinople, at the invitation of the emperor Basil I. He was warmly received both by the emperor and by the patriarch Photius, and returned to Moravia with the approval of his secular sovereign. But the last years of his life were, despite his unflagging literary activity, overshadowed by the spectre of defeat. The papacy, after John VIII's death in 882, was no longer willing to shield Methodius from the German party in Moravia. No sooner had Methodius died in 885, than his principal enemy and rival, Bishop Wiching, hastened to Rome and secured from Pope Stephen V a condemnation of the Slavonic Liturgy. A few months later Methodius's principal disciples, including Gorazd whom he had appointed his successor, were arrested and exiled from Moravia.

The missionary work of St Cyril and St Methodius, undertaken in a

8. PL CXXVI col. 906.

Christendom which, despite the growing tension between East and West, was still conscious of forming a single body, proved to be, at least during their lifetime, a unifying force reconciling three important elements in the civilisation of medieval Europe: the Byzantine, the Roman and the Slavonic.

As citizens of the east Roman empire, Cyril and Methodius loyally performed in central Europe their dual task of missionaries of the Byzantine church and of ambassadors of their emperor. The Byzantine authorities, for their part, continually supported their work. During his last journey to Constantinople, Methodius before returning to Moravia left behind him, at the emperor's request, a priest and a deacon with the Slavonic liturgical books. Soon after his death, some of his disciples, whom the Moravians had sold into slavery, were redeemed in Venice by an envoy of the Byzantine emperor, and were sent to Bulgaria to continue their work. There can be little doubt that in the second half of the ninth century the Byzantine authorities were collecting Slav-speaking priests and stockpiling Slavonic liturgical books for their missionary enterprises in the Balkans and in Russia. The fact that the Frankish clergy did all it could to destroy Slavonic vernacular Christianity in central Europe should not allow us to forget that the Old Rome, too, welcomed and blessed for a while the work of Cyril and Methodius. These two Byzantine missionaries, like most of their compatriots, undoubtedly recognised the primacy of honour in the whole of Christendom vested in the bishop of Rome–the ' Apostolicus ', as he is called in the ninth-century Slavonic biographies of Cyril and Methodius. As for the Slavs, they owe to the two brothers the very foundation of their medieval Christian culture: the Scriptures and the Byzantine liturgy in a translation at once faithful and close to their vernacular; access, through the medium of Old Church Slavonic, to Greek patristic literature and to Byzantine learning; an idiom for the creation of an original native literature, sacred and secular; and a particular outlook, which the Slav writers of the early middle ages inherited from Cyril and Methodius and their immediate disciples, in which each nation, consecrated to the service of God by the liturgical use of its vernacular language, was held to possess its own particular gifts and its own legitimate calling within the family of the universal Church.

Despite the hostility of the Frankish clergy and – after 885 – of Rome, it took more than two centuries to extinguish the remnants of the work of Cyril and Methodius in central Europe. Old Church Slavonic literature and the Slavonic liturgy continued to flourish in Bohemia and Croatia until the late eleventh century, when they were destroyed or submerged by the Roman policy of centralisation and linguistic uniformity. These developments, however, were of marginal importance. The future of Slavonic vernacular Christianity lay elsewhere. Expelled from Moravia after their master's death, Methodius's disciples found refuge in Bulgaria, whose destiny it was to rescue the Slav vernacular culture and to transmit it in a developed and enriched form to the other Slavs who owed allegiance to the eastern church – the Russians and the Serbs.

┌─────────┐
│   4   │
└─────────┘

THE CHURCHES
OF WESTERN EUROPE

I. THE MEROVINGIAN AND FRANKISH CHURCHES 604-888

T HE history of the Frankish church between 600 and the death of Pippin (768) falls into three periods. In the first, when a succession of Merovingian kings were gradually losing control of their kingdom, the old pattern of church life in Roman Gaul was gradually disappearing, while here and there new centres of life such as the abbey of St Denis near Paris came into being. In the second, when the Mayors of the Palace were in power, there was a rapid disintegration of organised church life: bishoprics and abbeys were secularised, synods and councils were no longer held, and one of the last and greatest of the Mayors, Charles Martel, though deserving well of the Church as the saviour of western Christendom, was responsible more than any other for despoiling the abbeys and bishoprics of the country in order to secure and reward those who fought for Christendom and defended it against the invader. In the third, under Carloman and Pippin, a real revival of discipline and a spirit of reform were evident. Pippin, who in fact founded the Frankish kingdom, inaugurated in many ways the aims, ideals and methods of government which his son Charles was to carry to such heights of achievement.

In this, the latter part of the transitional period between the last age

3. Attacks on Christendom

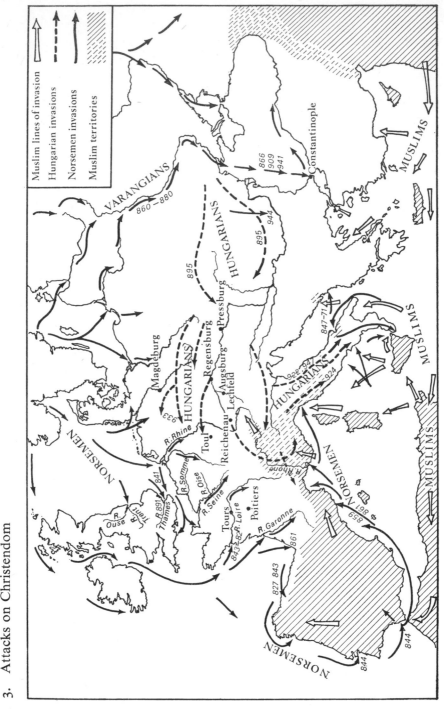

Legend:
- Muslim lines of invasion
- Hungarian invasions
- Norsemen invasions
- Muslim territories

VARANGIANS
860–880

HUNGARIANS
895
944
895
866
909
941
Constantinople

MUSLIMS

Magdeburg
HUNGARIANS
895
Pressburg
Regensburg
Augsburg
Lechfield
933
847–71
922–947
HUNGARIANS
924
NORSEMEN

Reichenau
Toul
R. Rhine
R. Somme
R. Oise
R. Seine
R. Loire
Tours
843–82
Poitiers
R. Garonne
861
827 843
844
844
R. Rhône
NORSEMEN
198
658

R. Ouse
R. Trent
891
841
R. Thames

MUSLIMS

MUSLIMS

of the Roman empire and the emergence of the monarchical Frankish kingdom, the church in Gaul drifted slowly from its position as an extension of Roman Christianity along the roads and rivers of southern Gaul, to that of a regional or territorial church *(Landeskirche)* of which the immediate governor was the king. In the last centuries of organised administration in the West the church had been ruled by bishops residing in the cities or large towns and having complete control over the finances and clergy of their dioceses, and over the considerable estates of their churches. As central government decayed, the bishops stood out as the only source of authority with funds and a firm position, and it was natural that they should fill the void left by the gradual disappearance of the civil authorities and should become the leaders of society. They continued to hold this position under the early Merovingian kings, who could not make use of the normal resources and administrative organisation of civilised society. For a century or so a race of bishops, sprung in many cases from the wealthy and experienced families of the later empire, continued to fill their office with success. They governed the cities, dispensed justice and dealt with public calamities. The church *c.* 700 probably owned at least a quarter of the cultivated area. An able if not spiritually-minded class of men, they were appointed as a matter of course by the king, and lived on easy relations with him and his ministers. No political or social distinction was made between Franks and Romans. In the past, close relations had existed between Rome and the churches of southern Gaul, and Arles had been the seat of a papal vicariate. The standing papal vicar became the occasional legate, and provincial synods under the metropolitan fell into desuetude, but Rome still held its place of esteem as the supreme and final authority on doctrine and morals. At the local level the erection of churches continued as the influence of the church expanded from the lines of the roads and rivers into the rural areas. In the ancient cities there had been originally only one centre of religion, the church of the bishop attached to his dwelling, and in some romance and German languages taking its name *(Dom, duomo)* from its situation. The other places of religious assembly, such as the basilica at the tomb of a saint or chapels at a cemetery, were all under the direct control of the bishop who also had the immediate direction of the priests in neighbouring churches evangelised from his see. Beyond these, what was later to be a parish system was slowly growing up, though on estates and in villages distant from ancient towns the private church was the norm. The priest and the cult were maintained by oblations of bread and wine, by gifts at Easter and other times, and from the mid-eighth century onwards by the tithe. When the proprietary church became almost universal and the lord took many of the sources of income for himself, councils reiterated the obligation of providing a house and a modicum of land for the priest. As for the latter, in all country districts he was usually a man of humble or servile birth appointed by the lord of the land. Gaul was predominantly but not entirely Christian by the end of the seventh century save for large pockets of heath, marsh and woodland. The open spaces of Brittany were occupied by Celtic immigrants with their peculiar customs. Apart from some of the larger city churches and the monasteries, the religious life must have been elementary in its simplicity. The priest, serving a private church for his whole life, needed only a minimum of knowledge: perhaps little more than the two creeds, Apostolic and Nicene, a few prayers, the commandments and rules of fasting, and the marriage law in the matter of relationships. His duties were to say Mass on Sundays and festivals, and to baptise. It was not yet obligatory that marriages should be blessed by a priest, though no doubt this was common practice. The priest's sole connection with higher authority would have been the annual synod at the cathedral in Holy Week, when he obtained the holy oils for the year. A bishop's visitation must have been rare, if not unknown. Sheer paganism doubtless continued to exist for long here and there, and superstitious ceremonies and witch-craft inherited from the Celtic or Roman past still longer and more widely. Apostolic preaching was still a necessary part of a conscientious bishop's life, and though by tradition and canon law he alone had the right and obligation to expound the articles of faith, zealous abbots and priests are often found evangelising the dwellers in remote or wild districts.

Gradually the level of civilised life fell, traditions of Roman surveillance faded, and social inequality developed. A new aristocracy of warriors and landed men arose, with a corresponding debasement of the lower orders into a large servile class; the peaceful life of the late empire, and the gradual adjustments of the invaders, were now replaced by struggles for power between great ones. Among these, bishops were often found as powerful and factious elements; they had in many cases paid for their appointment and appropriated monasteries to support their position. The level of discipline fell; worldly bishops and the secularisation of church property became common, especially under the stress of campaigns against the Saracens and the other wars of Charles Martel, whose period of effective rule (719-41) is often taken as the moment when medieval feudalism as a recognisable species first appears. The need to equip and to endow large numbers of horsed warriors and commanders led both to the marriage of military service with a gift of land and to the insertion of an oath of fealty as part of the transaction, while the necessity of finding lands with which to reward or endow supporters led to the bestowal of church lands and monasteries on lay magnates who enjoyed the revenues and gave, if they gave anything, no more than a subsistence to the monks. Pluralism and the usurpation of abbeys were common practices among the bishops of Gaul in the middle decades of the eighth century. St Boniface could write to the pope in 742 that metropolitans no longer existed and that synods were unknown; the churches were possessed by laymen.

A partial rescue of the church was accomplished by the sons of Charles Martel, largely through the agency of Boniface. Under Carloman's patronage he held a series of national synods in northern Gaul and the Rhineland (742, 744, 745 and 747), in which the office of archbishop (a title which Boniface took from England to replace the traditional name of metropolitan) was restored and yearly diocesan synods were imposed. Boniface himself, as we have seen, was a strong upholder of papal supremacy, but though he might have influence with the clergy, his attitude in this respect could not affect the king. Pippin, to whom recent historians have restored much of the credit for initiating the 'Carolingian' reform, lacked the statesmanship of his greater son but showed himself an energetic and clearsighted ruler in ecclesiastical matters, the friend though not the servant of the papacy. He held important reforming synods such as those of Verneuil and Compiègne (755-7), but they were the synods of a kingdom, not of a province. He curtailed lay proprietorship by leasing lands to churches, established bishops as supreme in their dioceses, and instituted archbishoprics.

All this, however, was piecemeal and partial reform compared with that of Charlemagne. From 768-814 that great monarch devoted a major part of his energies to the establishment and government of a great Christian commonwealth. Leaving to a later page the analysis of his principles and ideas, we may here consider his aims, acts and achievements. From first to last he behaved as the supreme ruler of the Christian realm or, as he himself with a fine disregard for history and geography consistently proclaimed, of the Christian Church. In that task he made extensive use of ecclesiastics as both agents and counsellors and, one had almost said, departmental ministers. When circumstances demanded, he also used the book of canon law of Denis the Short (Dionysius Exiguus) augmented by Hadrian I, the so-called *Dionysio-Hadriana*, presented to the king by the pope in 774, but in the main he treated every matter that arose, practical and theoretical, as something to be decided by himself with such advice as could be obtained, whether privately and personally or in synods and councils. Neither in personnel, nor in the circumstances of decision and action, was any clear distinction made between civil and ecclesiastical affairs. Charlemagne's measures and pronouncements, like those of a private person in his private life, were those of a Christian with his mind fixed upon what he took to be the law of God. While recognising the papacy as the ultimate fountain of doctrine and moral teaching and also, but less distinctly, as the final arbiter of discipline, he assumed and maintained the complete control of ecclesiastical matters within his realm, and this, by the year 800, included almost all western Christendom save for the British Isles. To a degree and an extent never attained with any permanence either before or after in Frankish or German territory, Charlemagne governed the church in theory and in practice, in design and in power. The limitations that human weakness put to the actions of himself and his agents, the very imperfect organisation, the vast distances, the absence of almost all the elements of a civilised bureaucracy and financial machinery, must never be forgotten. There was much that Charlemagne himself could never perceive or desire, much that he could not and did not achieve of what he saw and attempted, but by and large, for a half-century of tireless activity, he defended and directed Christian faith and moral endeavour as he saw them. It is a measure of his success, or at least of the recognition of his good intentions by his subjects, that for half a century laments over the calamities and distresses of ecclesiastics, and the vices and scandals of the times, are muted almost to silence.

Charlemagne appointed his bishops, with rare exceptions, but gave them full powers of every kind within their dioceses. There did not yet exist, and the emperor made no attempt to establish, a complete network of ecclesiastical provinces. The *ex officio* metropolitan of such sees as Rheims, Bourges and Mainz, and the papally appointed archbishop, sometimes existed simultaneously in different localities. Charlemagne used each as an agent in marshalling his bishops rather than as a court of appeal for their benefit. Sure of his men, he used them in assemblies and councils, with or without a lay element, as his advisers and mouthpiece in legislating for the church. This legislation took the form of edicts or ' capitularies ' covering every aspect and detail, moral, disciplinary, liturgical, economic and educational, of the life of a Christian people; it was collected and preserved by contemporaries. No doubt the enforcement of all these laws was imperfect and impermanent. They existed, nevertheless, and at each subsequent centre of reform in the West for more than two centuries they were the norm for all endeavour, and their enactments, and the embryo institutions which they created, were to remain as an influence throughout the middle ages and into modern times. Charlemagne's control of the church extended to its material possessions. While he enforced the duty of giving tithes to the clergy, he also claimed the ultimate right to dispose of church property, and used this to create fiefs out of ecclesiastical possessions, thus assisting the development of the feudal state. Under his rule the wealth of the church increased greatly, in France rather than in Germany, and among the richest proprietors were the Frankish abbeys, though Charlemagne himself was sparing of new foundations.

Charlemagne did not confine his attention to conduct and administration. He regarded himself also as the moderator of doctrine and the defender of the faith against error. In three considerable controversies, those of the worship of Images, of Adoptionism and of the procession of the Holy Ghost, [1] he stood forward as the official defender of the faith and, in council with his bishops and advisers, promulgated what he considered to be Catholic truth. That in two of these questions he and his experts were both ill-informed and theologically ill-instructed, and that in all three the last word lay with the pope, does not alter the fact that Charlemagne, both in council and by writing, behaved as the established judge of orthodoxy. Nevertheless, the independent behaviour of Rome, and the absence on Charlemagne's part of any attempt to engage in a trial of strength or a campaign of suppression with the papacy, serve to warn the historian that the term caesaro-papism or a comparison with totalitarian rulers of other epochs are meaningless unless all the circumstances and ideas of a particular moment are understood and stated before any such labels or comparisons are used. But by whatever name we call it, the control of the church by Charlemagne was to become a precedent and an exemplar throughout the middle ages. Though in many ways no more than a prolongation of the practices already in existence, the person and genius of Charles, the extent of his empire, and the relative thoroughness and success of his achievement, gave to his age an incomparable lustre. It was not only that with him the regional church became the imperial church; that for a short moment an individual ruled over all continental Christendom; beyond this, Charlemagne became a legend and a myth, perhaps the most influential myth in the history of western Europe.

Any successor of such an emperor would inevitably have failed to carry on his work. Even one who rivalled Charlemagne's range of qualities of mind and will, of genius for peace and war, would have been unable to handle the vast and disjointed machine that had grown under the hands of its maker. Nor did there exist any of the framework of government and administration that in a civilised society can often bridge a revolution or a minority rule. Lewis the Pious lacked both character and genius, and the disintegration of the Carolingian empire soon began, but his interests and gifts were in the sphere of religion, not to say of mo-

---

1. See pp. 50-1 (Adoptionism); 87-92 (Iconoclasm); 133-4 (*Filioque*).

nasticism, and here, as will be seen, he left his mark. In other matters his piety had in it a morbid quality, which led to degrading self-abasement; he allowed himself to be chaptered and put to public penance by his clergy in 822 for his brutal (and uncharacteristic) treatment of a rebel nephew, Bernard; and the leadership in ecclesiastical affairs passed to a group of bishops who had been trained in his father's councils. It was they and their successors who dominated the Frankish church for the next fifty years. By comparison with their predecessors of fifty years before and their immediate successors they were learned men, the product of the teaching of Alcuin and his colleagues. They were soon to count among their number not only able controversialists such as Hincmar, but the authors of the forged decretals and capitularies.

The political events of the decades following the humiliation of Lewis the Pious have tended to distract the attention of historians from the intellectual activities of the leading bishops of this generation and from their writings which, it must in fairness be allowed, daunt the reader by their prolixity and often fail to satisfy those familiar with later and more expert theological work. This activity was nevertheless considerable. It is perhaps the strongest evidence of the technical excellence of the schools established by Alcuin, and goes far to invalidate the facile judgments of those who suppose that all constructive thought ceased between the age of Boethius and that of Berengarius. An exception is indeed often made for John Erigena, that strange and learned migrant from Ireland who stands apart from his age with his competence in Greek, his acquaintance with Neoplatonic and Dionysian thought and his parade of dialectic. More characteristic, however, and more significant of the latent power of the West, are the leaders in the two theological controversies of the age, that on the nature of the presence of Christ in the consecrated species, and the essence of the Mass and the Eucharist, which is associated primarily with the names of Paschasius Radbert and Hrabanus Maurus, and that on grace and predestination, originated by that strange, unhappy and unwilling monk, Gottschalk, and carried on by Hincmar, John Erigena, Florus of Lyons and others. [2] In neither of these controversies was the spirit of heterodoxy abroad, and both died down, largely through the lack in all parties of the theological technique capable of analysing and redefining the problems at issue. Both nevertheless have significance both in themselves and as heralds of what was to come. First, they show a wider reading of the Latin Fathers, and a greater ability to seize the essential points than is usually attributed to men of the Carolingian culture. Next, the problems raised, those of the Eucharist and grace, are precisely

2. See pp. 135-7.

those that will time and again prove sources of perplexity and discord in later ages. Thirdly, the disputants may be divided into those who follow Augustine to the end of the road and those who see the difficulties of his opinions and search for a new solution. Here again a twofold stream appears that will be seen again in the schools four hundred years later and again, after another four hundred years have passed, in the convents and schools of France and the Low Countries in the age of the Jansenists.

Throughout the theological, ecclesiastical and political turmoils of the years between the treaty of Verdun (843) and the death of Charles the Fat (888) one name and one alone recurs at every turn. It is that of Hincmar of Rheims, perhaps the most notable bishop in western Europe in the centuries between the great Spaniards of the seventh century and the Germans of the Ottonian empire. A priest of high family, brought up in the abbey of St Denis, the counsellor of Charles the Bald, he was elected by royal favour to the metropolitan see of Rheims in 845 at the age of forty. A theologian of competence and an expert canonist, he was to spend much of his long episcopate of forty years in a series of imbroglios, which overlapped and tangled each other and which set him continually at odds with popes, monarchs, colleagues and theologians. His troubles began with his entry at Rheims, for his predecessor, deposed by royal and papal authority, attempted repeatedly and not without success to rehabilitate himself, while the case of a group of his clerks, the ' clerks of Ebbo ', whose ordination Hincmar declared invalid, was to dog his career for decades. Born to dominate by personality and mental power, Hincmar was a life-long champion of metropolitan rights, and in consequence was compelled at one time or another to fight off both suffragans who disputed his powers and claimed the right of appeal to Rome and popes who were the ultimate beneficiaries of their doctrine. Hincmar was a tireless, if disorderly, writer and his treatises in the predestinarian controversy and his various apologias to Rome show alike his real powers, his sound judgment, his resourcefulness, his resilience, and his diplomatic and political skill no less than his unconcealed self-esteem which gives a touch of the ridiculous to his repeated misfortunes. It was inevitable, we feel, that having at last shaken off the nightmare of the clerks of Ebbo he should both in theory and practice fall foul of a nephew and namesake whom he had chosen as his suffragan at Laon. The Bossuet of the ninth century, capable of more than one blunder and more than one piece of chicanery, he could nevertheless rise on occasion to true dignity and set a tiresome wrangle on the high level where lay its true significance. Alone of his contemporaries he can stand with Nicholas I as undoubtedly great, and there is a dramatic fitness in his death as an old man, fleeing from the Northmen who were threatening his cathedral with destruction, a week after the brutal murder in Rome of Pope John VIII and only a few years before the extinction of the empire of Charlemagne with the death of Charles the Fat (888).

The century that followed the collapse of royal power in Francia was in many ways the most disastrous period of medieval European history. The fragmentation of authority into the hands of feudal dukes and courts and bishops was followed by the substitution of lay magnates for regular abbots in the monasteries, and the consequent impoverishment and often the complete absorption of the monastic property by the seizure by the commendatory lay abbots of the portion of the monastery's property assigned to the support of the monks. When to this was added the ravaging of some of the most fertile regions by the Vikings and the consequent destruction of many of the abbeys, resulting in the death or exile of the monks, a situation developed which might well have seemed to portend the complete ruin of the monastic life and of organised religious discipline.

In the event, a remarkable resilience and power of reaction saved traditional western civilisation in France. The Vikings were fought off, or at least contained in Normandy and other centres and, like the Danes in England, the fiercer Normans rapidly absorbed the religious and political atmosphere of their new fatherland.

2. THE ANGLO-SAXON CHURCH, 663-1066

On an earlier page we glanced at the evangelisation of Britain, culminating in the union of the Roman and Celtic observances at Whitby in 663. The unity there established in principle soon became universal in practice owing in large measure to the work of Theodore of Tarsus and Benedict Biscop, which began within a few years of the synod of Whitby.

In 668 an archbishop-elect of Canterbury, sent for consecration to Rome, had died there. By ecclesiastical custom this left the choice of a substitute to the pope, and Vitalian decided upon Hadrian, a learned African monk then abbot of a Naples monastery. Hadrian demurred, and proposed in his own stead Theodore, a learned Greek monk of Cilicia, then living in the City, possibly as a refugee from Muslim invasion of his native land. He in his turn was unwilling to go without Hadrian; the pope accepted the condition and sent the accomplished Greek scholar and theologian, already sixty-five years old, to organise a church composed of unfamiliar and disparate elements, and in many districts still a missionary province. It was a bold, if also a farsighted, decision; it proved in the event successful and significant beyond expectation. The elderly and alien archbishop reshaped and regularised the church in England, and was a major influence in establishing centres of education and learning which bore fruit in the golden age of the generation that followed.

Theodore was fortunate in a second companion who accompanied him to England. This was a Northumbrian, Benedict Biscop, who had founded a monastery at Wearmouth (county Durham) and who had already visited foreign shrines and monasteries more than once before he made the pilgrimage to Rome. He was there when Pope Vitalian was sending Theodore to Canterbury, and was assigned to the archbishop as interpreter. Theodore rapidly mastered the problems of his task in England, defining and dividing dioceses, holding synods where doctrine and discipline were defined, and reconciling the differences still existing between parties and persons. Among his colleagues were a number of unusually distinguished and saintly men: Cuthbert, the Scottish anchorite of Farne Island, renowned for his austerity and success in preaching the gospel, who was made bishop of Lindisfarne and was to become the patron saint of Northumbria; Wilfrid of Ripon, a tireless, difficult, mercurial bishop and missionary, who died bishop of York, where the see had been vacant since Mellitus; Ceadda, a saintly Celt, bishop of Lichfield; and Erconwald, another saint, for whom Theodore revived the see of London.

Nor was his energy less in giving his church learning. The abbey of St Augustine at Canterbury became under Hadrian a school of letters, Greek as well as Latin, for the south of England. Its culture was carried far and wide in Wessex, from Malmesbury, the home of Aldhelm, in the north to the monasteries of Devon and the neighbourhood of Winchester whence came Winfrith (Boniface) and many of his friends and correspondents. Theodore himself composed scriptural commentaries and a celebrated penitential. The greatest development of learning and art, however, took place in Northumbria, whither Benedict Biscop had returned after more than one tour on the continent, in which he collected books, liturgical texts, relics, objects of art, masons, glaziers and the Roman arch-cantor John. He used all these men and materials to build and furnish his monasteries of Wearmouth and Jarrow, and to establish a semi-Benedictine observance with the Roman chant and liturgy. When he died in 690 he had established in the far north of England a twin community with all the resources needful for learned work.

When Theodore died, also in 690, the church in England was ordered and at peace. He must rank as one of the greatest in the long and distinguished line of the successors of St Augustine.

Among the children dedicated by their parents to God under Benedict Biscop was Bede, who was to spend his life learning, teaching, writing and praying in his monastery. In a small church on the remote shore of Northumbria, and among a people of the second and third generations in the Christian faith, Bede was to become the most learned writer in western Europe, soon famed all over the continent for his work on the calendar and his homilies. Beyond this, he wrote lives of his monastic elders and an ecclesiastical history of his people that for accuracy and human interest is without a parallel in European literature of the age.

The picture he gives is of a church, unorganised indeed in many ways, and lacking almost entirely a hierarchy and the machinery of government, but with a virile and energetic priesthood successful in carrying the gospel throughout the length and breadth of the country, and in supplying the basic needs of the faithful. As for the Christian population, though Bede himself supplies evidence of violence, ignorance and pagan superstition, he also shows a remarkable display of virtue and experience, with many instances of deep spiritual wisdom and sanctity, and a daily practice of religion and a use of the sacraments that would be remarkable at any period of the history of the Church. Insight and holiness of life are revealed in monks and nuns, clerics and laypeople, kings and peasants. He has a whole gallery of memorable portraits from Bishop Cuthbert, Abbot Ceolfrid, Abbess Hilda and royal personages, down to the poet-cowherd Caedmon and simple hermits. Bede's pages are undoubtedly the fullest and most attractive picture we possess of the reception and first unfolding of the integral Christian life, often touching heroic sanctity, on the part of a pagan but sensitive and on the whole frank and simple race of farmers and peasants. That his world is not a visionary creation is shown by the realistic and comminatory tone of his letter to his pupil Egbert, bishop of York, where the darker side of contemporary church life is displayed. That the two pictures are not both the work of an imaginative genius is seen in the independent evidence of high achievement in art and literature and Christian sanctity afforded by his contemporaries and successors in East Anglia and Wessex. As we have seen, the children of the generations portrayed by Bede were to carry their traditions into the field of missionary endeavour and the spread of civilisation abroad.

The golden age of the Anglo-Saxon church endured for a little more than a century, from the coming of Theodore to the first Viking raids upon Northumbria. Besides Bede, his saintly abbots and his scholars, the north of England at the time was the home of great artists. The Lindisfarne Gospels and other contemporary masterpieces of illumination, though inspired by earlier Celtic work, were executed by Anglo-Saxon artists, and the great sculptured crosses of Bewcastle, Dumfries and elsewhere, whose motifs derive from eastern and classical works of art, from Celtic illuminations and from the Old English poetry, were probably the work of contemporaries. In the generation that followed, Bede's pupil Egbert, founder of the school and celebrated library of York, was succeeded in his turn by Alcuin, who left England for the court of Charlemagne, carrying with him much of the learning and the art of his fatherland.

During this century the church in England, now unified under the Roman obedience and the Roman observance, strengthened its hold over the country. The unit of administration was not as yet the parish but the minster *(monasterium)*, a group of monks or priests living together, evangelising and later ministering to the faithful at chapels or mass-crosses within a radius of a dozen miles or so. The process by which the minster was superseded by the parish was slow and has left few traces. In England, as elsewhere, the régime of the proprietary church and, in Bede's day, the proprietary monastery prevailed everywhere, and there, as elsewhere, appeared the common phenomenon of the small monastery sliding down the scale and becoming the seat of a royal official or of a landowner and his family. In England, also, as in north-western Gaul, ' double ' monasteries were common, often taking the form of a large nunnery ruled by an abbess of royal or noble blood with a group of monks attached who, besides acting as chaplains to the nuns, ministered to the surrounding population. All were under the rule of the abbess, and some of these, notably Hilda of Whitby, Etheldreda of Ely, and Milburg of Wenlock, were women of great ability and sanctity, who helped to diffuse learning as well as religion. This flourishing life was halted and in some regions annihilated by the raids and later by the invasions of the Vikings, who first appeared off the coast of Northumberland in 793.

These invasions, and still more the abiding presence in England of predatory Danish hosts in the second half of the ninth century, had the effect of reducing the church in England, where it survived at all, to its very lowest terms of priest and people. King Alfred in a well-known passage deplored the wholesale destruction of all precious things, and the disappearance of all learning and education. [3] The monastic life, it would seem, which was planted most strongly in Northumbria and the Fenland, disappeared entirely, and even south England saw the monasteries reduced to groups of clerks, sometimes with families. Anglo-Saxon England and its church were saved by King Alfred the Great who, besides his abilities as a warrior and a leader, was a man of fervent piety with a deep appreciation of learning and the heritage of the past. Both in his political achievement and in his personal example he stands out as one of the greatest of medieval rulers. Alfred and his able son Edward and grandson Athelstan not only conquered the Danes in battle but forged the unity of England under the kings of Wessex. The Danish king Guthrum became a Christian,

---

3. In the Old English prose preface to Alfred's translations of the *Pastoralis Cura* of Gregory the Great as printed by D. Whitelock in *English Historical Documents*, ed. D. C. Douglas, I (1955) 818.

and the country was for a short time divided between the English in Wessex and Mercia and the Danes to the east in the Danelaw. No doubt small churches and their priests had survived all the shocks, and the conversion of the Danelaw to Christianity was remarkably rapid. Within a century of Alfred's victory the east and north showed little difference as regards the church and its institutions from the south and west.

Religion was, however, reduced to its lowest terms; it rested at what may be called a spiritual ' subsistence level '. Without monks or regular canons, with a married clergy, with scarcely any administrative connection with a Rome that for the time took little interest in transalpine affairs, and with the king as the only sovereign power and unifying element in ecclesiastical as in social life, the English church, seen through the eyes of the seventeenth century, might well seem to resemble the Anglican church of Elizabeth's day. In the conditions of that age only monks could provide a foundation for moral reform and the rebirth of learning. Alfred's attempt on a small scale at Athelney failed, and it was not till the ancient house of Glastonbury was revived by Dunstan in 940 that the seeds of growth were sown. By that time the reforms of Cluny and Brogne were making their influence felt on the continent, and Dunstan with his two eminent fellow-monks and episcopal colleagues, Ethelwold and Oswald the Dane, led a great monastic revival which, under King Edgar (959-75), became a renewing factor for church life in general. Some sixty monasteries and nunneries were founded, including many of the names well known to later English history such as Westminster, St Albans, Abingdon and Peterborough, and the three monastic reformers became bishops: Dunstan at London (later Canterbury), Ethelwold at Winchester and Oswald at York and Worcester. Learning and art began to flourish and for fifty years a majority of the bishops were monks. Churches and monasteries were built on a scale which recent excavations have shown to be larger than was hitherto realised, [4] and the revival, while remaining English, borrowed considerably from the reformed monasticism of the continent, and the reform spread gradually to the ' secular ' clergy. The age of progress was arrested by a new wave of invasion, and England for a time was ruled by a Danish king.

Once more, however, the invader was converted, and there was no lasting disruption of church life. The Old English church, at the beginning of the eleventh century, continued to be in form a survival from the past. In no other country were secular and ecclesiastical affairs so intermingled. While the historian can see clearly the reason for this, to others it might seem paradoxical that the country, that was traditionally more than any

4. Cf. the recent excavations at St Augustine's, Canterbury, Glastonbury (Dunstan's monastery) and above all at Winchester (early English cathedral).

other devoted to the see of Peter, should in practice be so independent that its customs could be reckoned by the Norman kings as the strongest argument in their struggle to maintain independence from the new claims of the papacy. In the first place, although there had never been the vestige of a controversy between king and pope, the absence of any attempt or claim on the part of the papacy to control affairs in England had put upon the king the necessity of acting as the effective ultimate authority. He was assisted in all important affairs by his council of notable men (the Witenagemot) which included all the bishops and many of the abbots. At this council church affairs were dealt with as part of the government of the realm. All elections to bishops' sees took place there and during the last two centuries before the Norman Conquest all matters that would have gone to a provincial or national council came before the Witan. At a lower level, the bishop had a place of honour at the shire court or moot and ecclesiastical causes and pleas were dealt with there by him. In all the royal legislation of the period the laws governing the Christian life in kingdom and parish are decreed without any direct appeal to the bishops, and commands to pay tithes and Peter's pence and to observe Sundays and festivals jostle laws dealing with property and crime. Bishops acted, on the rare occasions when public or controversial action was necessary, in consultation with the king, but in practice this meant very little, for the diocesan and provincial organisation was extremely loose and bishops had very little contact with their clergy. Yet at the same time England had two links with the papacy for which she could claim priority over every other country of northern Europe: the regularity of the journeys or missions of her archbishops to Rome for the pallium, and the regular Peter's pence, collected with legal sanction from the whole country and sent to Rome as a mark of loyal obedience. England was thus, in the early part of Edward the Confessor's reign, something of a survival from an earlier age in a world where king and pope, clerics and laymen, were each defining and enlarging their territorial claims. In England all was as yet undefined. The churches, particularly numerous in London and the towns on the eastern side of the country, were almost all proprietary, and sometimes the property of a consortium. The units of parish and diocese were ill-defined and there was little administrative machinery at the disposal of the bishop. Recent scholarship has shown that discipline and the observance of canonical practice were at a higher level than hitherto had been supposed, but the wind of the Gregorian reform had yet to be felt in England, and in the years immediately before the coming of William the Conqueror no one could have been certain whether England in the future was to form a province of Europe or an outpost of Scandinavia.

National boundaries

German–Slav boundary
  about 800 A.D.

Old German boundary c.700 A.D.

  „   „   „   800–1100A.D.

  „   „   „   1200A.D.

  „   „   „   1250A.D.

  „   „   „   1300A.D.

  „   „   to 1400A.D.

4. Germanic expansion eastwards

3. THE GERMAN CHURCH, 754-1039

A principal instrument of Boniface in organising the German church had been the plantation of monasteries. Fritzlar and Fulda in Hesse, Niederaltaich and Benediktbeurn in Bavaria, and great nunneries such as Lioba's Tauberbischofsheim and the Heidenheim of Walpurga may be taken as examples. The monasteries served a double purpose. Besides giving an example of Christianity in action, and serving as a focus of education and of artistic and craft work of all kinds, the German monastery was often the seat of a missionary monk-bishop, and thus had an institutional as well as a spiritual function in the evangelisation of Germany. Boniface and his companions may have been led to this use of a monastery by the practice of England, where the relationship between monasteries and both diocesan bishops and missionaries had been very close, as at Winchester, Canterbury and Ripon, but the precise form taken by the typical German abbey-sees was peculiar to this region. In the short run it was undoubtedly successful; in the longer run there were troubles when bishops, now royal appointees with little sympathy with the monks, endeavoured to engross the monastery and its revenues, or to use the abbey as an episcopal or an administrative centre, and even to secularise it altogether. Under Charlemagne the process of parochial organisation developed particularly in Bavaria, and was almost complete in Germany in the ninth century. The normal parish there was a community of a different kind from that of the city church of the Roman empire. In the latter the faithful gathered round the bishop and his clergy and formed an integral body the members of which had rights such as a share in the election of the bishop and in the liturgy of the Christian year. In the rural parish of north Frankland and Germany, on the other hand, the parishioners, who were usually the serfs and peasants of a feudal lord, had duties, such as those of tithe-paying and oblations, but no rights. The church was beginning to fall apart into the hard divisions between clergy and laity, and higher and lower clergy, that were to achieve full crystallisation after the Gregorian reform.

Whereas the Frankish church was a development from the Gallic church of the late Roman empire, the German church was largely a new creation. The Roman Empire, after the disastrous attempt to conquer what is now Western Germany, had fixed its frontier — the only land-frontier in continental Europe — along the Rhine and Danube, with an irregular line of fortifications, the celebrated *limes Germanicus*, which crossed the open space between the two great rivers from a little south of Bonn on the Rhine to a few miles west of Regensburg on the Danube. Within that long frontier Christianity was sparsely established, and never wholly eliminated by the invaders. When the Celtic missionaries came, this vestigial tradition helped them on their eastward passage, and doubtless explains, what is at first sight surprising, the presence of Scotti and *Schottenkirchen* throughout the belt of country between the *limes* and the Alps as far eastward as Vienna. We have already glanced at the evangelisation of western and central Germany by a series of Anglo-Saxon missionaries culminating in Boniface and his companions and successors. They won or confirmed for Christianity a wide belt of territory from Frisia, by Hesse and Thuringia to Baden, Württemberg and Bavaria, and left the various regions with an active organisation of bishops' sees and monasteries as centres radiating civilisation and the Christian life.

In the parts of Germany that had never received, or that had lost, the faith the rhythm and direction of the spread of Christianity was different from the gradual diffusion in Gaul. In most districts of Germany the faith had been brought to a pagan population by itinerant missionaries, and their work had been continued by others either from an established centre of church life or from a monastery planted in a heathen land. Moreover, especially in Bavaria and Swabia, the country was mountainous and covered with dense forest. In early days, at least, the bishops came into more direct contact with their flock than did those of Gaul; it was they who planted the faith, and nursed it when planted. In addition, they inherited from Boniface and the other early Anglo-Saxon missionaries the sense of a direct dependence upon Rome, the authority behind their own apostles, and this loyalty was to be an enduring legacy in the German church, remaining as a kind of undertow even during the struggles between popes and emperors. In the second and third generations of Christianity the monasteries, which often grew to be the centres of small administrative towns, counted for much, and for more than three centuries the alternation of conquest and conversion continued on the eastern and northern frontiers in a rhythm to which there was no parallel in the West save in the different conditions of the Spanish march. Nevertheless, the faith gradually sank into the soil and for century after century produced that simple, virile and unhesitating piety that still distinguishes the peasant and the labourer in Bavaria and the Tyrol.

Parochial organisation came relatively early to Germany. A capitulary of Lewis the Pious allotted tithes, house and garden to every church, and in the ninth century the establishment of parishes was carried forward. It has been calculated that there were 2500 parishes in Germany by 850, and they were organised into deaneries.[5] *Chorepiscopi*, or assistant

5. A. Hauck, *Kirchengeschichte Deutschlands*, Leipzig 1933, II, 741.

bishops with a limited field or a roving commission, were not uncommon. Preaching was a duty for the parish priest, who in early times was probably more thoroughly instructed in the faith than his Gallic counterpart, and the hearing of confessions according to the tariff of a penitential was common. Contemporary accounts nevertheless here as in Gaul show the persistence of the old gods and pagan superstition. Though pagan customs and ways of thought were endemic in rural Europe for many centuries after the first conversion, the German forests were nearer to the dark heart of heathenism than were the woods of France and England.

In general there was less differentiation of the classes than in Gaul and Italy. The lower order comprehended all save the nobles, who soon became and remained a caste, and the higher clergy. The German bishops were from the beginning more significant figures than their French contemporaries by reason of the extent of their sees. At one time the territories of Cologne, Mainz and Salzburg covered all Germany east of the Rhine, and later the eastern bishoprics such as Magdeburg had spheres of influence stretching far into the newly conquered lands. This gave them great influence, and in addition potential sources of wealth that became actual as the conquest was stabilised and the land developed. In the later Baltic conquests a large part of the land, as we shall see, was bestowed on the bishops.

The rise of the five great duchies, Lorraine, Franconia, Saxony, Swabia and Bavaria, presented the king with a problem unknown in Francia, and for a short while the power of the dukes became almost royal. A change came with Otto I, who established control over the duchies and assumed the right of appointing to all bishoprics save those of Bavaria, and treated them as fiefs for which the recipients did homage. The principal sees were given comital rank and their holders ranked on a par with the dukes. By this means the bishops were enlisted as supporters and aids of the monarchy, and served to counterbalance the dukes, though with a certain loss of independence consequent on their status as feudal magnates. They also became inevitably political figures of importance, with the administration of their counties, and kings and emperors often elevated their close relatives to major sees. The danger to the church was obvious, for the bishop and his estates were marked down for the royal service, and it was at this point that ' investiture ' appeared, when the bestowal of the staff in token of jurisdiction was transferred from the consecration ceremony to the moment when homage was done. In this way the hierarchy of the empire was tightly woven into the feudal body; the possessions of the see became the possessions of the empire. Bishops were tied still more closely to the land by immunities bestowed by the king in virtue of which they enjoyed the revenues of tolls, courts, markets and the rest. There is truth in the judgment that the German church was on the way to become a national church, as contrasted with the regional church of France, but the German emperors never legislated for the whole church as Charlemagne had done. National in some ways the German church might be, but neither in doctrine nor in liturgy was there ever the least deviation from the other countries of the West, and the bishops, as has been said, retained the traditional attitude to Rome as the source of all authority.

When the last Carolingian king of Germany died in 911 Lorraine and the four tribal duchies, which formed fairly compact unities as regards both population and institutions, had already become the basic framework of the new Germany and although a monarchy, now elective, continued to function the first German king, Conrad I (911-8) failed to gain control of the whole country. His successor Henry, duke of Saxony, opened a new epoch, and his reign (918-36) began that succession of able and eminent monarchs of the Saxon and Franconian dynasties who dominated the continental scene for two centuries and did so much to defend, consolidate and extend the frontiers of their realm and of Christendom.

Henry I, besides subduing the other three duchies and adding Lotharingia to Germany, began the age-long policy of war along the northern and eastern periphery of his kingdom, the *Drang nach Osten*, and the imposition of Christianity upon the vanquished and the allies. He also initiated the policy of alliance with the church by giving to the bishop of Toul the powers of a feudal count. His son, Otto the Great (936-73) continued all these policies. He gained control of the duchies by imposing dukes of his choice and knit the loose fabric, with all its centrifugal tendencies, together by bestowing lands and immunities on the bishops and greater abbots, who were thus drawn out of regional loyalties and bound to the king by fealty and services. They and the lower clergy also were used in every form of government service and in high political councils and missions by reason of the monopoly of education which they enjoyed. They were also often given entire counties to rule on behalf of the king. A corollary of this was an assertion of the royal right of appointment, with the customary additions of feudal homage and investiture with both fief and office–a custom which had become common practice in the West fifty years earlier under Lewis the German. This, though appearing to the historian as a new development, was such an easy, universal and in a sense inevitable evolution from the practice of Charlemagne and his successors throughout Europe that it passed uncontested and almost unnoticed during the eclipse of the papacy.

After his initial successes and his external victories, crowned in due course by the annihilation of the Magyar army at the Lechfeld, Otto turned to his fateful invasion and conquest of north Italy, partly from the German urge to expand and conquer in the rich and brilliant trans-alpine world that has always attracted the northern peoples, partly in order to include the papacy in his sphere of influence and partly with the hope of ultimately reviving the western empire, the bestowal of which was now by a universally acknowledged tradition a prerogative of the pope. When his coronation ultimately took place in 962 the double dealing and inefficiency of the papacy brought about a reversal in the position of the two parties. The emperor was no longer a protector called in by the pope, but a sovereign exercising a protectorate over the Roman church as part of his realm.

After the short and less successful reign of Otto II (973-83) his son Otto III (983-1002) left a far deeper mark. Inheriting much of the wide statesmanship of Otto the Great, he derived from his talented mother, the Byzantine princess Theophano, an intellectual perception absent from the monarchs of Frankish and German blood. He conceived a universal empire of the West, inheriting the ancient Roman empire and even absorbing or eliminating the pseudo-Roman empire of Constantinople. In this empire the pope was the chief priest, or chief bishop, and as in the German kingdom all great churches were royal proprietary churches, so Rome was to be the proprietary church *par excellence* of the Roman (= Christian) empire. Otto therefore chose and removed popes, issued orders to them, and presided over papal synods. But he remained by office and inclination the authentic protector of the church, the friend of saints and the supporter of missionaries, and he was willing to allow both Poland and Hungary to obtain ecclesiastical independence of Germany.

Otto III left no heir and Henry, duke of Bavaria, succeeded with difficulty. Educated for an ecclesiastical career and always a loyal church-man, he none the less held firmly to all royal rights over the church, including that of appointing bishops and dismissing them if need arose, dividing sees and founding them as seemed best to him. An outstanding example of his initiative was the foundation of Bamberg in 1007. But he was also a great benefactor in a material way to the church, giving lands and immunities to reformed monasteries and to bishops whom he could trust. He presided at synods and issued liturgical instructions. He was followed in time by Conrad II (1024-39), a descendant of Otto the Great, a hard, expeditious and just ruler who lacked Henry's devout piety. He appointed to all ecclesiastical offices, often after a considerable sum of money had passed, and treated bishops in a practical, realist fashion as his officials. Approaching a stage nearer to a national church, he allowed

5. Muslim conquests up to 750

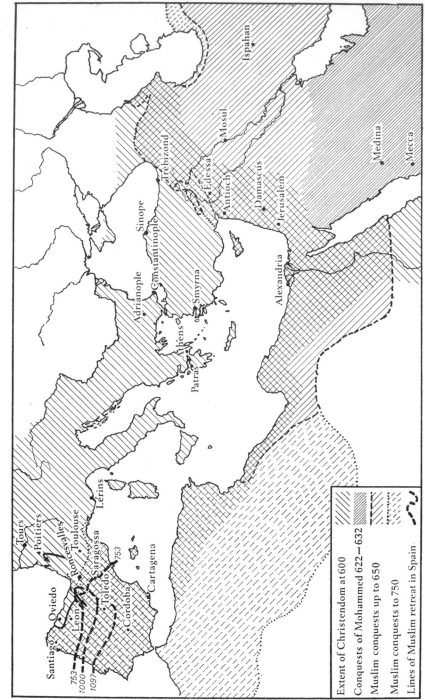

Extent of Christendom at 600
Conquests of Mohammed 622—632
Muslim conquests up to 650
Muslim conquests to 750
Lines of Muslim retreat in Spain.

Ispahan

Medina

Mecca

Mosul

Edessa

Antioch
Damascus
Jerusalem

Trebizond

Alexandria

Sinope

Adrianople
Constantinople
Smyrna

Athens
Patras

Lérins

Tours
Poitiers
Roncesvalles
Toulouse
Saragossa
753

Cartagena

Santiago
Oviedo
León
Toledo
Cordoba

753
1000
1097

no appeals to Rome without his permission, presided at synods, decreed feasts and fasts, moved sees and styled himself the vicar of Christ. When in Italy, he presided with the pope, Benedict IX, at synods. His son, Henry III (1039-56), was less harsh, more intelligent and more religious than his father. He appointed bishops, chiefly from the clerks of his chapel, and abbots, and called and presided at synods. But in north Italy the climate was changing, and it was his fortune to release by his action the avalanche of reform.

The series of able, and even great, rulers in Germany had created a new focus of relatively ordered life in Europe. The endemic stresses and strains within the kingdom or empire, and the ceaseless warfare on the frontier must not obscure for us either the ability of its rulers to conceive wide policies in church and state, and to carry them through, or the new splendour of material and cultural life that developed at the court of Otto the Great and his successors, and at the greater bishoprics and abbeys. Nor should the real energy of the reforming emperors be forgotten. The Germany of this epoch set up a norm of practical and theoretical political action and thought which had a wide influence over the subsequent monarchies of Europe. In part the German church in its higher levels was a derivation and an enlargement from the Carolingian past, but it had new features that were to become–if indeed they were not already– common practice throughout Europe. Such were the appointment of bishops, mainly from the royal chapel, after a large sum of money had passed; the summoning of synods by the monarch; and the forbidding of appeals to Rome.

4. SPAIN, 711-800

When Spain was overrun in the great and rapid invasion of 711-13 many of the inhabitants were killed or enslaved and of the rest many conformed to the religion of the Prophet. A number however of those who submitted remained in possession of their land and retained their faith and the practice of their religion; these were the mozarabs who had a part in the later history of the country. Far in the mountainous region of the north-west, Asturia and Galicia, a focus of resistance held out, and this gradually increased in size and strength until, under Alfonso I ' the Catholic ', 739-57, it comprised the coastline and a strip of mountainous country, the ' kingdom of the Asturias ', some forty to fifty miles wide from the north-west corner to the Pyrenees. It was the first stage of the re-conquest.

A year before the death of Alfonso the independent caliphate of Cordova had been established by refugees from the east, but a few years later the expeditions of Charlemagne had established another small Christian area, the Spanish March. Meanwhile the mozarabic church had reconstituted its organisation as before under the archbishop-primate of Toledo, and remained conservative of the traditions of an earlier age.

At the end of the eighth century the see was held by the elderly Elipandus, whose fortune it was to deal with a certain Migetius, an erratic character who expounded what seemed to be a novel opinion, asserting that Jesus, the son of David, was one of the divine Persons of the Trinity. Whether orthodox in intention and even in expression or not, this offended conservative Spanish opinion, and at a council held at Seville Elipandus sponsored the statement that the human being, the Son of Mary, complete in a nature similar to ours, was at the first moment of his existence, logically before attaining personality, *adopted* by the Son of God, the Word, and Jesus therefore in his human nature was the *adopted* Son of God. This formula which, like the opposing one of Migetius, would seem patient of an orthodox explanation, was attacked by two monks of Asturia of whom one, Beatus, is celebrated for his commentary on the Apocalypse which became an archetypal text for the illustration of the book in the middle ages. He and his colleague Etherius accused Elipandus, violently and unjustly, of Adoptionism, the heresy (wrongly attributed to Nestorius) which held that Jesus was adopted as his Son by God the Father at his baptism, while themselves going far in the direction of the denial to Christ of complete human nature. At the same time, they delated Elipandus to Pope Hadrian I as a heretic.

Hadrian replied by a sober theological exposition, and a condemnation of the ill-sounding phrase ' adopted son '. Elipandus, for his part, referred the phrase for judgment to his learned suffragan Felix of Urgel, a town recently reconquered by the Franks. Felix approved the phrase in the context, and saw himself delated to Charlemagne. Summoned to Ratisbon he recanted but was sent to Rome where he again gave satisfaction. Meanwhile the Spanish bishops had rallied their forces and replied to Beatus and Etherius, reiterating the offending expression ' adopted son ' which they probably understood as equivalent to ' adopted human nature ', and demanded the support of Charlemagne. The latter once more approached the pope, who sent a second and more dogmatic statement, fortified by an anathema, to Spain. Simultaneously Charlemagne, having summoned the bishops of his empire to Frankfurt, together with Alcuin, Benedict of Aniane, and other notabilities, secured a condemnation of the offending phrase ' adopted son ' and provided for the Spaniards two refutations one from Scripture the other, probably the work of Alcuin, a careful and in part a sound and remarkably powerful dialectical analysis of the orthodox dogma. This was not the end of the battle. Felix, at last back in Urgel, reasserted his original thesis and this drew from Alcuin a short patristic exposition and an excellent dogmatic statement, in which he distinguished between the assumption or personal union of the human nature with the divine and the adoption of human beings into divine sonship. This letter crossed (if the expression be allowed) a long treatise of the unrepentant Felix, who was summoned to Aachen and forced to recant, while a Roman council under Leo III (798) reiterated the orthodox doctrine and the anathemas. Felix died many years later in confinement at Lyons. Alcuin, however, had not yet done with the Spaniards. Elipandus, nettled at the treatment accorded to Felix and strong in the mozarabic liturgical traditions, defended once again and with acerbity the phrase ' adopted son ', only to receive a vast reply from Alcuin in which no new argument was used. With that the mists close down upon Spain, not to lift for centuries. For Alcuin and his associates it was the first of a series of theological tournaments in which they learnt to read the Fathers and develop their own powers of thought. Recent examination of this and the other theological controversies of the age has suggested that the counsellors of Charlemagne and Lewis the Pious, and above all Alcuin, were more mentally able and theologically weighty than the last generation of historians allowed. Both as patristic scholars and as careful thinkers they were the first able group that the ultramontane nations had as yet produced.

5. THE REGIME OF THE PROPRIETARY CHURCH

During the centuries between the pontificates of Gregory I and Gregory VII what may be called the domestic or internal economy of the church in western Europe underwent great changes, some of which were among the causes of the controversies of the eleventh century, and some of which have continued to influence ecclesiastical life down to the present day.

Christianity in the fully civilised parts of the Roman empire developed from groups and communities of the faithful in cities, centring upon the bishop, who was surrounded by his clergy of priests, deacons and minor clerics. For many centuries no widespread campaign was launched to convert the peasantry or herdsmen of the rural districts whose name *pagani* (*pagus* = a rural district) or heathen (= men of the heathland) came to be synonymous with *infideles*, those who had no faith. This progress of Christianity from city to city, and later from town to town along the main routes of travel, remained the normal method of extension for the church at least until the end of the fifth century, and the practice gradually grew up of the appointment by the bishop of resident priests in small towns and villages. In this way the basis of a parochial system was formed in Gaul and elsewhere.

Nevertheless the rural areas, particularly in districts such as Africa, the Iberian peninsula and southern Gaul, were Christianised in another way, by the foundation of what we should now call private chapels by men of means upon their country properties. This practice is found everywhere, in Asia Minor as well as in Africa and the West. It was controlled by both civil and canonical legislation. Justinian's *Novellae* acknowledge the right of private ownership of these churches, and the right of the founder and owner to appoint the priest with the approval of the bishop and the safeguarding of the latter's right of surveillance. Gelasius I, on the other hand, legislating for Italian and north African conditions, laid down strict regulations governing the dedication of new churches by private persons. Permission from Rome was necessary, and the founder, while allowed to appoint the priest, was obliged to disclaim all rights over his church, save the bare right of entry and of the presentation of the priest. Originally in the churches of the great cities all property had been considered as belonging to the bishop; when the Church was formally recognised in the empire the ownership passed to the church or community of each place, to be administered by the bishop. Roman law recognised the existence of ' notional persons ' *(personae morales)*, such as communities and colleges, and the church of the city fitted into a familiar legal category. When a multitude of oratories and chapels began to spring up these were regarded by church law also as *personae* with inalienable properties and privileges. The privilege of the presentation of the priest accorded to the founder and his heirs was no more than the legalisation of an existing practice, but it was destined to have far-reaching consequences. Nevertheless, for almost a century after Gelasius I the forces of order were in the ascendant, and in the sixth century what may be called the first extension of the parish-system took place in Italy, Spain and southern Gaul, as it was to take place later in Britain and in northern and eastern Germany. Councils regulated the finances: the revenues from land and its appurtenances were to be administered by the parish clergy; offerings were to be divided into three (or sometimes four) parts, of which one was to go to the bishop and the others to various aspects of the church's activity. There was to be an annual visitation by the bishop and, in the reverse direction, an annual episcopal synod at Paschal time at the end of which the holy oils for the year were to be distributed. Part of the tithe, when later established, was to go to the priest as part of his income.

This steady progress along traditional canonical lines was first halted and then dislocated by the forces of disorder and fragmentation that took possession of western Europe after the great invasions. All central control, all ownership and administration by communities, or by the officials of a centralised government in church and state, gave place to private, personal and local relationships. Historians have long been divided on the immediate and principal cause of this. While French scholars have seen in it an instance of the universal tendency for the individual and the weak party to seek protection by commendation to the nearest wielder of influence and power, the Germans have traced the change to the introduction from Germany of the custom of lords or chiefs possessing private temples with private priests, to which the German principle of law was applied by which all on the land was the property of the lord of the soil *(superficies solo cedit)*, whereas the principle of Roman church law was that the estate of the church was attached to the dedicated altar *(fundus sequitur altare)*. Doubtless both these legal conceptions and social pressures had their influence in various ways and places, as had also, on the higher levels of church life, the German concept of a regional church *(Landeskirche)* under a king, with territorial bishops, as opposed to the Roman concept of city bishops within a universal church. In any case deep-seated currents were moving irresistibly, and a universal shift of authority took place. While among the members of what had been a hierarchy all bonds were relaxed, and both metropolitans and bishops lost the close control of their provinces and dioceses, at the lower level of the individual church and its priest personal relationships and private ownership alone became important. How far the prevalent secularisation of the seventh and eighth centuries may have accelerated and completed the process is doubtful; the fact is certain that the conception of the local church as the private property of an individual and of the priest as the ' man ' of a ' lord ' was current in some districts in 600 and was almost universal a little over a century later. Thus came in the régime of the proprietary church *(Eigenkirchentum)* which was to characterise almost the whole of western Europe for four hundred years. The practice preceded the law, as it did also in the contemporary and kindred institution of ' feudalism '. Gradually the church (and at certain times and in certain measures also the abbey and the bishopric) was regarded as a piece of real property. It could be bought, sold, bequeathed and traded; it could be divided amongst heirs and legatees; and the various sources of its income could be split up and receive individual allocation. Tithes could be given away to a relative or a religious house, as could also the regular oblations. The priest, often a serf of the owner, could be regarded as a feudal dependent, and his office as a gift or a reward *(beneficium)*. The survival of the term ' benefice ' in some European languages solely with reference to a spiritual office is evidence of its universal use in this sense. Churches could be owned by everyone – by private persons, by a consortium, by a monastery, by a bishop, by a king – and a bishop (or a monastery) might own churches far remote from his own diocese or country. With the slow change of outlook in a Europe drifting further and further away from the climate of ideas in the late empire, the adolescent parish system was stunted or dissolved and the parish churches of France, England and elsewhere lost their status of close dependence upon the bishop. The régime of the proprietary church, which appears in Visigothic Spain at the end of the sixth century, and in Gaul before the conversion of Clovis, becomes general in Frankland under Carloman and Pippin and ubiquitous in the age of Charlemagne. In the ninth century it even reached the patrimony of the Roman church, while by a kind of back pressure it was adopted by the apostolic see itself in its relations with monasteries and churches ' commended ' to St Peter.

Meanwhile attempts were being made to give a cover of legality to the existing state of things. In 746 Pippin approached Pope Zacharias with a query as to private churches. The pope replied in traditional terms: they must be consecrated, and the priest appointed, by the local bishop, and they must not have the rights and status of a parish church. This position clearly could not be maintained, and under Charlemagne there were attempts at a concordat. While the right to bequeath, bestow or sell a church was recognised, each church was to have an inalienable dowry and its priest a minimum wage together with a house and land. Payment on the part of a priest on his appointment was forbidden, and all priests of private churches were bound to receive a bishop for his visitation and to attend his synods. Under Lewis the Pious the reform party led by Agobard of Lyons attempted to go further: all priests were to be freemen with no obligation for services of any kind, and the bishop's approval was necessary on appointment. Nevertheless, when the monarchy lost its power of control all attempts to restore at least a part of the old canonical fabric broke down. In 826 Pope Eugenius II gave full recognition to the régime of the private church. A monastery or oratory once properly established could not be taken away from its founder, and he was free to appoint without security of tenure any priest he might choose, subject to the bishop's acceptance. Canonical principles were scarcely saved by the assertion that the lord bestowed the church, and the bishop the cure of souls. Thenceforward would-be reformers were unable to achieve any success as the church was gradually sucked into the feudal system at every level and the bishops consistently lost ground to the seigneurial power. An early Cluniac charter may be cited as typical. In it a church is ' bestowed with its priest's house and all its territory, with tithes, lands, vineyards, meadows, closes, serfs and whatever belongs to the church '. As an historian remarked, the difference between ownership of a church and the ownership of an estate no longer existed. [6]

Gradually the economic, material nature of the transaction became

6. Imbart de la Tour, *Les Paroisses rurales du IVe au XIe siècles*, Paris 1900, 234.

more definitely acknowledged. The gift of a church took the form of a contract, often with a cash payment. Once in possession the owner received a yearly tax, together with presents and legacies. The church was his property and he might even shift it. He also took the greater part of the tithe. The priest was left with a little land and part of the tithe and oblations, but in return for these he paid a tax or did service to his lord. The church in fact became an asset, a piece of real property, which could be treated exactly like any other real property; it could be fragmented vertically and horizontally. A man might own a half-church, or even one-twelfth of a church; on the other hand he might own the nave of the church, or an altar, or the tithes, or a part of the offerings.

Simultaneously, the church and all its appurtenances including its priest were drawn into the feudal net of the region or ' honour ' in which they lay. The church itself was a benefice, in fact a benefice *par excellence*, an *honor ecclesiasticus*. The priest took the oath of fealty and did service to his lord; this was primarily, no doubt, the spiritual service of providing Mass and the sacraments, but also every kind of notarial work and estate management. Subinfeudation by the priest was possible, while in the higher levels the bishop became feudal overlord of his *Eigenkirchen* and exploited them as did lay lords. Churches, like other fiefs, became liable to *spolia* at the demise of an incumbent, and fell into the hands of the overlord during a vacancy. The parish lost altogether its social and ecclesiastical identity, and churches were currently divided into the three classes of bishops' churches, monastic or capitular churches, and the churches of a lay lord.

This process, by which the church, the monastery and even the bishopric became, in different ways and degrees, the ' property ' of an individual, who might be of any rank from burgess or one of a peasant-group, to a duke or a king, has been considered in the foregoing pages in its material aspect, in which the church is a bunch of revenues. It is usually looked at from the other end, that of the supreme owner, the emperor or monarch, with his right of appointment and investiture. Both are aspects of one and the same condition, the ' church in the hands of laymen ', which was the root cause of the reform movement of the eleventh century.

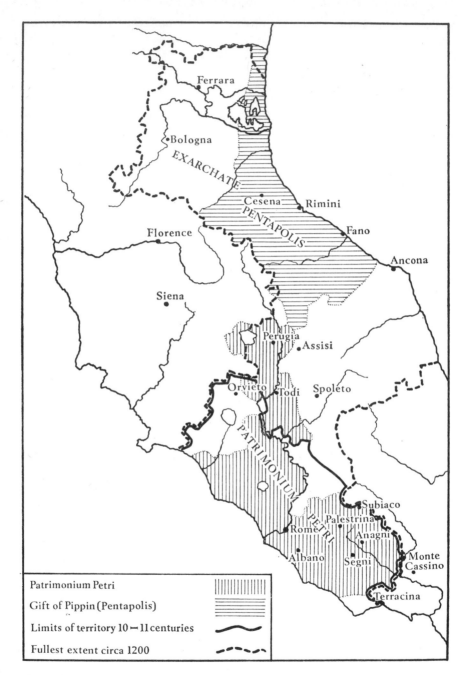

Ferrara

•Bologna

EXARCHATE

Cesena   Rimini

PENTAPOLIS   Fano

Florence

Ancona

Siena

Perugia
•Assisi

Orvieto •Todi   Spoleto

PATRIMONIUM

PETRI

Subiaco
Palestrina
Rome•   •Anagni
Albano   Segni   Monte
Cassino

Terracina

Patrimonium Petri												
Gift of Pippin (Pentapolis)	≡≡≡
Limits of territory 10 – 11 centuries	⌇⌇
Fullest extent circa 1200	- - -

6. The Papal States

THE FORTUNES
OF THE PAPACY 604-1049

T HE history of the papacy in the four centuries that followed the pontificate of Gregory I is more obscure than that of any other period since the third century. Particularly is this so for the history of the popes of the seventh and tenth centuries. During these two periods, as also during the ninth century, popes succeeded each other very rapidly; thus between 604 and 701 there were twenty pontificates; between 816 and 900 also twenty and between 900 and 1003 twenty-three, giving over the three centuries taken together an average reign of less than five years. This of itself would make any narrative based upon successive pontificates meaningless. In addition, there is throughout a dearth of literary record. The scholars of the past hundred years have indeed done much to settle chronology, to date important actions and documents, and to mark the phases of liturgical and artistic activity at Rome, but the quantity of historical, biographical and theological literature originating in or around Rome during these centuries is extremely small. It is not therefore surprising that few popes have left a permanent memorial of their policies and personalities for posterity to assess. Gregory II and III (715-41), both accounted saints, Hadrian I (772-95), Nicholas I and Hadrian II (858-72) and Silvester II (999-1003) stand almost alone in their personal or political eminence.

Regarded in its Roman aspect, the period of four centuries falls into four epochs. The first (604-715) is in many ways a continuation of earlier papal history. The church of Rome, still juridically part of the empire, is closely connected with the theological and other activities of the eastern church. The city itself, partially recovered from the invasions and sieges of the sixth century, is a cosmopolitan gathering, swollen in the middle of the seventh century by Christian exiles and refugees from the Muslim East. The clergy are racially mixed, and from 686 to 752, save for Gregory II, all the popes were either Greek from southern Italy or Syrian. Many of them were estimable men and bear the title of saint. The death of Zacharias in 752 coincided very nearly with both the extinction of the Byzantine exarchate of Ravenna and the rise to power of Pippin in France, and marked an epoch.

In the second of our periods (715-800) a succession of able popes were called upon to deal with a changing situation in Italy and in the West. In Italy the Lombard conquests overran the last foothold of the eastern empire in northern Italy and threatened the adjacent territories administered by the papacy. In Gaul the rise to power of Charles Martel and his successors gave a centre of firm government in the West and the possibility of a strong protector for the popes. For almost a century the process of change continued which issued finally in 800 in the creation of the western empire.

In the third period (800-88) the popes witnessed the maturity and decline of the Carolingian empire; it was a time of activity in the Frankish church, in which liturgical and theological issues were debated and settled, and in which the papacy made its influence felt both as a counsellor of moderation and as a sovereign demanding submission. The end came with the collapse of the Carolingian empire and the emergence of the powerful families of Rome and its neighbourhood as a perpetual source of unrest. Finally in the fourth period the papacy as a world power was in eclipse, while the centre of political activity was transferred to Germany, where the kings (and later the emperors) controlled their bishops and engrossed the papacy. By an irony of history it was by the imperial appointment of a succession of German prelates to the papacy that the power of the Roman families was broken, and a pope with reforming zeal placed in a position that enabled him to take the first steps towards establishing a powerful and independent head of the Church.

By the time of Gregory I the pope was already in effect the civil governor of Rome. The code of Justinian had formally confirmed the position of bishops as judges, financial officers and legal protectors of their cities, and in the case of Rome the pope was given charge of the revenues in grain from Sicily, Sardinia and Corsica, and became the emperor's banker and paymaster. Gregory can be seen at work in these capacities, and two circumstances combined to give the bishop of Rome an exceptionally strong position. In the first place, large gifts of land in Sicily, Sardinia and southern Italy, and Gregory's own inheritance, had made of the pope the richest landed proprietor in the peninsula. In particular, the block of estates from Orvieto in the north to Terracina in the south, with a width of some fifty miles, was known as the patrimony of St Peter from the legend of its origin. Secondly, in 584, by an act of imperial devolution, the exarch of Ravenna was given immediate control of Italy and, when he proved an ineffective guardian, Gregory had of necessity to become the universal provider for his people. From this time the popes were the real masters of Rome, both temporal and spiritual, under the nominal control of the paramount imperial authority, and it was for them to organise the army and defend the interests of the ' republic of St Peter ' against Lombard attacks as well as against imperial exactions.

The exarchate of Ravenna was joined to the patrimony of St Peter by a narrow corridor straddling the Apennines and including Perugia, from which city it continued down the valley of the Tiber to Todi. The territories of the exarchate were overrun by the Lombards, and when in 753 the pope appealed for help to Pippin against their further encroachment, help was forthcoming and finally successful, and as the ultimate result of a gift, of which the terms are uncertain, in 756 the pope acquired, or, as papal sources put it recovered (either as successors to the imperial power, or as owners in virtue of the alleged donation of Constantine), a strip of land along the Adriatic, from the southern edge of Venetian territory, including Ravenna and the Pentapolis of Rimini, Pesaro, Fani, Sinigaglia and Ancona, to which was later added Bologna. The whole complex which, with some later additions and minor losses, remained intact in essentials until the mid-nineteenth century, comprised the papal states of the medieval and modern world. Thus the ' temporal power ' of the pope had consolidated itself through no farsighted planning or ambitious statecraft, but inevitably and by degrees out of the circumstances of the time, and above all through the inability of the eastern emperor to guarantee security and good government to Italy. It became in the eighth century, and was to remain throughout the middle ages and beyond, an apparently ' inseparable accident ' of the papacy, at once a bulwark against attack, a source of power and wealth, and a liability that again and again was to shackle its masters and distract them from their spiritual obligations, and from their duties as unbiased fathers of the whole of western Christendom.

As a necessary accompaniment of the twofold power of the pope as spiritual and temporal ruler of Rome there flourished two classes which had no exact equivalent elsewhere: the clerical and other officials of the Roman church, and the aristocracy of the city, from which popes and their officials were often recruited, and which was in turn and in various different degrees of unanimity the antagonist, the master and the ally of the pope of the day. The group, from which the popes of the first three centuries of our period were normally chosen, was not necessarily composed of Romans by birth and blood. The history of the papacy is ample evidence that they were often men of exceptional ability, but they did not form a large bureaucracy till the eleventh century. Nor, as we shall see elsewhere, did the cardinals emerge as an influential class till the very end of the period we are considering. [1] Nevertheless, there was from early times a numerous body of ecclesiastics, many of them family men, who formed the staffs of the basilical and monastic churches and the financial officers of the papal estates. The Roman aristocracy, who had evolved from the senatorial and official families of the Theodosian empire, and who became in time the quasi-feudal nobility of the City and Campagna, differed from similar groups in other medieval cities both in their jealous maintenance of their title to honour as descendants of the rulers of empire, and in their lack of any effective political power. Throughout the middle ages they gave many of their sons to the Roman church and to the papacy while remaining a potential source of trouble both by their feuds and intrigues within the papal entourage and by their riots and revolts against the papal government. They and their supporters were responsible for many acts of violence at papal elections, in which by tradition they had a part to play, as also during the long periods when the papacy became the pawn of warring clans or powerful individuals.

From the middle of the sixth century until the transference of the papal court to Avignon eight hundred years later, the city of Rome remained a papal city, rendered more illustrious to the men of that age by the tombs of the apostles than by the glories of its past splendour. [2] For a thousand years its public architecture and most of its artistic work were devoted to sacred, or at least to ecclesiastical, purposes. As it was also the only city of western Europe that was a seat of continuous monarchical government and as it remained tolerably wealthy during the early middle ages, Rome became a storehouse and a museum of architectural and other masterpieces of every period and style, and despite warfare, domestic and foreign, and the destruction of old buildings to provide the site and

1. For the origin of the cardinalitial dignity see S. Küttner, 'Cardinalis: the history of a canonical concept' in *Traditio*, III (1945), 129-214, C. G. Fürst, *Cardinalis* (1967) and M. Andrieu in *Miscellanea Giovanni Mercati* (Studi e Testi, 125) V, 113-44.
2. Cf. the hymn of Paulinus of Aquileia (730-802) in honour of SS Peter and Paul: 'O Roma felix quae tantorum principum / Es purpurata pretioso sanguine, / Non laude tua sed ipsorum meritis / Excellis omnem mundi pulchritudinem'.

sometimes also the materials for new, the city became, as it still remains, incomparably rich in examples of artistic genius from every century of the Christian era. Many as were the interludes of destruction or desolation, Rome remained a city of churches and holy places to which pilgrims as well as suitors resorted.

For more than a century after the death of Gregory I central Italy, including the papal territory, remained in theory under the jurisdiction of the emperor, but relations deteriorated and ties loosened as the decades passed. In the early part of the eighth century Italy north of Rome was divided into three political regions, the papal estates, the exarchate of Ravenna to the north of the Apennines, and the Lombard kingdom to the north-west. The maltreatment of successive popes by the emperors of their day, culminating in the attempt upon the life of Gregory III by Leo the Isaurian, and still more the severe taxation imposed on Italy by the emperor, alienated the pope and the population; the king of the Lombards, the erratic if pious Liutprand (712-44), was advancing, and the exarchate of Ravenna was in danger. So also were the papal territories, and Pope Gregory III appealed for help, which was refused, to Charles Martel. Some years later Stephen II, in danger of losing more territory and Rome itself to Liutprand's successor, Aistulf, appealed for protection to Pippin and made a journey, hitherto without precedent, to Ponthion (dep. Marne) in France (754). Pippin agreed to help, and in two campaigns brought Aistulf to terms, giving to the pope the territories recovered from him (756). This was an authentic recognition of the existence of the papal government north of the duchy of Rome, and coinciding as it did with the victory of the Iconoclasts in Constantinople, it marked an epoch. Although relations with the emperor and with the eastern church were restored and endured, with intervals, for three centuries, the decisive step had been taken. The papacy had turned its back on the emperor of New Rome, had shaken off the bonds of allegiance that had hampered its movement, had made for itself a kingdom in Italy, and looked for protection to the king of the Franks. It is not without significance that Stephen II was the first pope (save for Gregory II) of Italian racial descent after a long and almost unbroken run of Greek-speaking popes from 685 to 752. Twenty years later Hadrian I, the heir to many problems and difficulties, turned for help to Charles, newly arrived in power, and was promised the whole of Italy from Mantua to the Byzantine possessions in the south. The promise was never implemented, but in 787 additional territories north of Viterbo and near Farfa were added to the papal states.

The close dependence of the papacy upon the Frankish monarchy was to be big with consequences. More than three centuries previously the popes, faced with the claim of the emperor to rule the church, had elaborated a counterthesis which set the emperor within the church, as its protector under the authority of the pope. This thesis had come to have ever less and less meaning in face of the theory and practice of such emperors as Justinian I, and of the reckless policies of later emperors, together with their virtual neglect of Rome, and their exaltation and exploitation of the patriarchate of Constantinople. After a century and a half of uneasy coexistence with the empire the papacy had now turned its eyes westward, and when Pippin answered his appeal the pope had taken the step of bestowing on the king of the Franks the title of *patricius* of the Romans. *Patricius*, a Byzantine title for a grade of court officials, appears to be a novelty in its new form and application, with the meaning ' lord ' or ' protector ', while the *Romani* concerned are not only the inhabitants of Rome, but all those over whom the Roman church had jurisdiction. By anticipating its conferment by the ceremony, new to Rome, of anointing for the king, the pope gave to the *patricius Romanorum* not only a religious character, but also a close bond with himself. The rank was bestowed by the pope, and was dignified by such a unique consecration. The pope had thus taken the first step towards filling the post and office left vacant by the inability to act on the part of the eastern emperor.

Charlemagne, who had received the title of *patricius* at his anointing in 754, promised Pope Hadrian I in 774 to bestow on the Roman church all the territories taken from it that figured in the donation of Pippin; when Charlemagne had taken the Lombard crown this promise, as no longer desirable, was not implemented. Indeed, the emperor seems to have planned to make of Aachen, his palace-town, a replacement of old Rome in the north, and for a short time it was not only the administrative centre of the West, but the focus also of a great intellectual and monastic revival. The political outlook of western Christendom was, however, permanently changed by an event of which there had been no previous expectation.

Historians are still divided in their opinions, and must confess to a baffling dearth of evidence as to the circumstances, of the imperial coronation of Charlemagne on Christmas Day, 800, which was to prove a moment of such significance for the political and ecclesiastical life of Europe in the future. The pope of the day, Leo III, was a mediocrity of equivocal repute, who had been brought low by domestic enemies at Rome. Charlemagne was in the City for the purpose of investigating the charges against him and of restoring order, and when the pope refused to be judged he was in fact acquitted by his own oath of innocence. [3] Two days later on Christmas Day, when Charlemagne was praying at the tomb of the

3. L. Wallack, 'The Genuine and the Forged Oath of Pope Leo III', in *Traditio* XI (1955), 37-64.

Apostle, the pope placed a crown on his head while the people acclaimed him as Augustus, emperor of the Romans. The pope then ' worshipped ' him. It was a copy of the Byzantine coronation. This, perhaps the most significant moment in medieval political history, remains also an historical mystery. Who had planned the act, and to what end? Leo III gave no other evidence of boldness or statesmanship. Yet the initiative of the coronation would seem to have come from him, and the manner of the act, if not the act itself, would seem to have taken Charlemagne by surprise, though it is unthinkable that he had no notion of what was about to take place. The most likely (but far from certain) explanation of the move is that the pope and his advisers took advantage of a temporary interregnum at Constantinople to complete the long process of shaking loose from the eastern emperor by creating in the West–or by transferring to the West–an empire whose tenant would fulfil the papal conception of a servant and protector of the Roman church. Charlemagne, for his part, may even have planned, by a diplomatic marriage with the bereaved empress Irene, to secure the transference of the empire to the West. In any case, he acquiesced in the accomplished fact, and was in time accepted by the eastern emperor as emperor of the Franks, but he never explicitly recognised the papal definition of his function as minister of the Roman church. One great difference remained to distinguish the eastern from the western empire. The imperial title in the East was not in theory heritable, but succession was ensured by the association as colleague of an heir, as in ancient Rome. Furthermore, in times of crisis it was attainable by a *de facto* ruler. That in the West, as a result of skilful and persevering papal diplomacy and action, came to depend entirely upon the action of the pope in crowning a candidate. This doctrine, once established, was rarely contested in good faith, and never challenged with success until, after more than four centuries, an electoral college with full powers was established, and papal recognition, if not coronation, followed immediately. But by that time the imperial title and office had become something very different in status and political importance. Charlemagne, indeed, took the first and crucial step in shattering the quasi-ecumenical conception of the empire by following the Frankish custom of dividing his dominions between his sons, thus ending the supposed territorial universality, and when his sons continued his policy and quarrelled over their portions the Carolingian empire ceased to be in any sense either universal or hereditary, and in fact declined in power and prestige until the imperial title ceased for a time to have any practical reality in 899. When the Ottonian revival came, the papacy had no difficulty in imposing its doctrine and conditions, however impotent popes may have been in the sequel to maintain them.

The fragmentation of the Carolingian realm and the discords of lesser men gave two powers in the church the opportunity of asserting old claims with a new force and clarity. The activities of the bishops at and about the court of Lewis the Pious and his successors will receive fuller mention on a later page. [4] From them the papacy received at least indirect support, but the immediate advance in its fortunes was due to the appearance of able and active pontiffs.

The first of these, one of the greatest of the popes, Nicholas I (858-67), has been designated as the architect of the medieval papacy and ' the greatest pope since Gregory I '. [5] By his words, and still more by his actions in every sphere, in relation to Constantinople, to Ravenna, to the emperor and to the powerful bishops of France, Nicholas proclaimed the supremacy of Rome and the jurisdiction of the pope over all members of the Church, lay and clerical alike. The direct contact between the papacy and the hierarchy, which had been established long since in Italy, Sicily, Africa and the Rhone valley, had been curtailed by Byzantine conquests, by Lombard encroachments, and above all by the energy of Frankish monarchs since the days of Charles Martel. It had developed in another form at first in England and then in the new territories won for Christendom by Boniface. Now it was applied by Nicholas I as a matter of course in the domains of the descendants of Charlemagne. The long affair of the divorce of Lothair II, one of the earliest of a series of such matrimonial imbroglios to affect the course of European history, and the interminable series of controversies with Hincmar of Rheims, in which the great archbishop was treated summarily *de haut en bas*, were evidence of an attitude towards monarchs and prelates very different from that of the popes of Charlemagne's day.

The successor of Nicholas, Hadrian II, followed his policy, though with less power, but thenceforward the papacy, along with the succession states of Charlemagne's empire, fell into dismal eclipse, of which the death of John VIII in a Roman *émeute* (882) was an early consequence. Five years later the last effective emperor, Charles the Fat, was deposed; he died in 888, and the empire went into sordid liquidation. Three years later Pope Formosus was elected (891-6); he made many enemies and Stephen VII, who succeeded a pope who reigned only a few days, is said to have exhumed the body of Formosus and to have tried the dead pope for various canonical faults, after which the body was thrown into the Tiber. Stephen was followed during the next eight years by eight popes in rapid succession, and the papacy entered into the most distressing

4. See p. p. 136-7, 140.
5. E. Caspar, *Geschichte der Päpste*, II, 514: ' Aber fragt man nach dem grössten christlichen Charakter, so gebührt Gregor unter allen Päpsten die Palme. '

phase of its history, when amid the violence and ambitions of warring nobles in Rome and the duchy the pope repeatedly became a pawn in the hands of a great family.

Nevertheless, the lurid accounts of papal scandals over more than a hundred years, but particularly in the first half of the tenth century, have often been retailed in the past without a critical examination of the sources and with only a narrow field of vision. Not only hostile writers such as Gibbon, but great Catholic historians such as Baronius and Duchesne, have on occasion been too ready to accept questionable evidence. Although at the end of the ninth century the duchy of Rome was harassed and in part overrun by the Saracens and threatened by the Lombard duchies to the north, while the city itself was rent by the faction warfare of great families, neither the continuity of curial administration nor the manifold religious activities of Rome ever wholly ceased. Rome, though largely a city of ruined splendour, mean in comparison not only with its own imperial grandeur, but with the wealth and numbers, the commercial and intellectual life, and the luxurious civilisation of contemporary Constantinople and Cordova, was nevertheless unique in western Christendom. Rich still in churches and shrines with their traditional liturgical observance, and with a twofold administration, papal and governmental, rooted in tradition, the Romans had a high sense of the majesty of their city as the head of the world *(caput mundi)* by reason both of its past glory and of its apostolic authority. Mistress of all, servant of none, Rome, resplendent with the blood of martyrs, was still the goal of pilgrimages from the confines of Christianity. Its walls and its great extent were a marvel. On the right bank of the Tiber, near the Vatican hill and the basilica of St Peter, stood the hospitals or *scholae* of the northern nations, the Saxons, the Frisians, the Franks and the Lombards, together with the palace of the imperial *missi* or commissioners. To the northerners this was the *burh* or *bourg* and the name (Borgo) has prevailed to this day. Further down the river was the new suburb walled by Leo IV (847-55) against the Saracens and bearing his name. Across the river were churches among the ruins and the vineyards, and on the ring of hills from the Quirinal to the Aventine the basilicas, the monasteries and the houses of the papal officials near the Lateran. In all the major churches the monks of the basilical monasteries performed the liturgy, and the pope, the deacons and the suburbican bishops took part in the stational processions and Masses. Other monasteries and nunneries lay in and around the fragments of antique baths and palaces. However little the popes of the age might take the initiative in distant affairs or guide the destinies of the Church, the papacy with its archives remained with its body of traditional law and lore, and its officials, oblivious as they might sometimes be alike of their personal and of their wider responsibilities, never forgot that they were the repositories of doctrine and discipline for the Latin world.

The first period of disorder was ended by the rise to power as senator of Theophylact, a noble who was put in charge of the papal treasure and army by Sergius III (904-11). For fifty years he and his descendants and relatives were in fact rulers of Rome, though an occasional pope, such as John X, might assert his rights. Theophylact shared power with his able wife Theodora, and his daughter Marozia, for some time mistress of Sergius III, married first Alberic, marquess of Spoleto, secondly Guido of Tuscany, and thirdly Hugh of Provence, king of the Regnum Italicum. From 928 Marozia was for a number of years the actual ruler of Rome, and as such able to appoint her son by Sergius III pope as John XI. Her domination was ended by the revolt of another son Alberic, who seized power in 932 and compelled his mother to enter a convent, thus ending the span of years called by some modern writers, echoing Baronius, the Pornocracy, a title misleading in itself and resting partly at least on a series of scandalous happenings for which the unreliable chronicler Liutprand is a principal authority. Alberic ruled Rome for twenty-two years as Senator and Prince of the Romans, at the head of a military aristocracy, and during this period the popes exercised no temporal power; they were appointed and dominated by the Senator. Nevertheless they were in general competent and acceptable men, and during Alberic's rule certain reforms were made in the church both in Rome and in the duchy. Above all, Alberic was a patron of monasticism. Of the many monasteries in the city a number had become secularised and none followed the Rule of St Benedict. Alberic summoned Odo of Cluny to Rome in 936 and the great abbot reformed a number of houses, giving them the Rule, though his efforts and those of Alberic failed to rehabilitate the decayed abbey of Farfa. Many new houses of monks and nuns came into being in Rome and the environs, and the ancient abbey of Subiaco recovered its position.

Alberic died in 954, leaving his son Octavian to succeed him, but the young man, only eighteen years old, was almost immediately elected pope as John XII. His pontificate marked an epoch, though not by reason of the character or actions of the pope. Otto the Great, the first effective monarch of the whole of Germany (ruled 936-73), had previously crossed the Alps in 952 to settle Italian affairs, and had asked in vain for imperial coronation. In 960 the youthful pope John XII, able but wordly and immoral, appealed for help in his territories to Otto as overlord in circumstances not wholly clear. The emperor reached the city early in 962, and on 2 February was crowned as emperor of the Romans. Local independence was guaranteed to the pope, and so far as words went he was confirmed not only in the traditional Patrimony, but also in the wider territories promised in 774. He and the Roman leaders took the traditional oath of fidelity, and Otto retained supreme dominion over papal territory, with two commissioners, one imperial the other papal, to reside in Rome. Thus both in its occasion and in its circumstances the coronation of Otto the Great resembled that of Charlemagne, which was indeed its model. Yet the significance of the event was different. In the first place, great though Otto may have been, he was no Charlemagne, though Germany was to hold together, as the Carolingian empire had failed to do, and a succession of monarchs were to receive imperial coronation. Secondly, political ideas had changed. Charles had looked upon himself as the David of the Christian Israel, with the pope as his priest. Otto and his successors gave their attention first and foremost to the secular government of their kingdom, in which the bishops were feudatories and the papacy a kind of attached *Eigenkirche*. Thirdly, while Italy was to Charles's empire a distant and semi-independent annexe, to the monarchs of Germany it was to become a part, albeit a restive and defective part, of their realm, the ' axis ' of European diplomacy.

Eighteen months after his coronation the emperor returned to Rome in answer to the appeals of the pope's enemies. John XII was brought to trial on a variety of charges, public and private, reasonable and implausible. He eluded judgment, but was deposed and Leo VIII, a curial official, was appointed by the emperor; it was an uncanonical and dangerous precedent which offended both Roman and papal tradition. The diploma issued by the emperor on the occasion included a clause imposing upon the elect an oath of allegiance to the emperor, and the Roman leaders took an oath of a similar kind, which implied an obligation to consult the emperor before a papal election. Both of these undertakings were unprecedented, and earlier documents, the diploma issued by Otto in 962 and the oath of fealty to the emperor takèn by the Roman people in 824, were duly interpolated to serve as precedents. [6] John XII fought his way back into Rome but died shortly afterwards; his successor, Benedict V, was elected without reference to the emperor who thereupon returned to besiege Rome and restore the exiled Leo VIII. Otto's next pope, John XIII, was a respectable choice, but when the great emperor died imperial and Roman popes struggled for power and there was more than one outbreak of savagery. In the years that followed the best of the imperial popes, Benedict VII (974-83), ruled the city firmly, and in conjunction with the emperor passed a decree against simony. He also continued the earlier monastic reform with the assistance of Abbot

6. W. Ullmann, ' The Origins of the Ottonianum ', in *Cambridge Historical Journal* 11 (1953), 114-28.

Maieul of Cluny, who is said to have refused the tiara in 974 and who reformed St Paul-without-the-Walls. The pope also founded St Alexius on the Aventine as a mixed community of Greek and Latin monks following the rules of Basil and Benedict. The house became fervent and learned, and included among its inmates St Bruno of Querfurt and St Adalbert, archbishop of Prague. It was long since Rome had taken the lead in spiritual matters and St Alexius marks the beginning of the great age of monastic rejuvenation in central Italy. For the papacy, however, the real dawn had not yet appeared and for another half-century Rome, though nominally within the control of the kings and emperors of Germany, was in fact dominated by the Roman houses of the Crescentii and of Tusculum. For several years at the end of the century John, son of a Crescentius, governed Rome as Patrician while the pope, John XV, was confined to the ecclesiastical sphere. Here he was active in replacing many of the lay and hereditary officials of the papal chancery by cardinals, bishops and abbots who had no hereditary rights. He was thus responsible for the gradual transference of curial power from the Roman aristocracy in its lay representatives to clerics depending more closely on the pope, a *conditio sine qua non* for the reform of the papacy itself and for the supply of agents dedicated to its service. At the end of the century the papacy emerged from the war of factions first during the enlightened rule of Rome under the regency of the empress-mother Theophano (989-91) and for a few years of true revival with the rule of the learned and farseeing Silvester II (999-1003), the direct choice of Otto III, his old pupil, whose pontificate in its various aspects and its mingling of new life with old habits, is as it were a false dawn of the true revival that was to come. The pope and his patron left the scene at almost the same moment, and the Crescentii resumed their control of the papacy until in 1012 their rivals, the house of Tusculum, succeeded in introducing their candidate as Benedict VIII. This pope, who acted as a successful warrior baron and defeated the Saracens at sea, also crowned Henry II as emperor, and held with him a council at Pavia in 1022. The last and perhaps the worst of the Tusculan popes was Benedict IX (1032-44), youthful, immoral and cruel, who obtained office by simony. He resigned the papacy in favour of the pious Gratian, Gregory VI, on the promise of a pension. This earned for Gregory deposition at the hands of Henry III, who appointed the bishop of Bamberg pope as Clement II. Together pope and emperor promulgated a decree against simony, but Clement died within a year, and his successor, Poppo, bishop of Brixen, reigned less than a month. For his third appointment Henry chose Bruno of Toul, who succeeded as Leo IX (1048), and for the first time for almost two centuries a pope of ability, energy and spirituality was in office.

6

THE SOURCE OF AUTHORITY

I N the era when the whole of that portion of the world which came within the purview of monarchs and popes was conterminous with Christendom, and when, at least in the West, the culture was predominantly religious and clerical, the debate upon the relationship of priest to king was at times the dominant intellectual exercise of the best minds of the Carolingian epoch, and it was to throw the whole of Europe into turmoil in the following age.

Ever since the conversion of Constantine the supreme authority of the Church, whether regarded as the collective episcopate of the eastern portion of the empire, or as the Roman papacy in the West, had been called upon to solve a problem new to its experience, that of the proper relationship of a Christian autocrat to ecclesiastical authority. This problem was from the beginning intractable because the first ruler to present it was at once a convert who postponed to the last moment his entry into full church membership, a conqueror to whom the Church owed in totality its new position of freedom and privilege, and a man of dynamic genius who had absorbed, before his conversion, much of the prevailing conception of a godsent, charismatic, orientalised monarch.

Until the conversion of Constantine the Church had been a minority group within the vast Roman empire. Christians, following the teaching

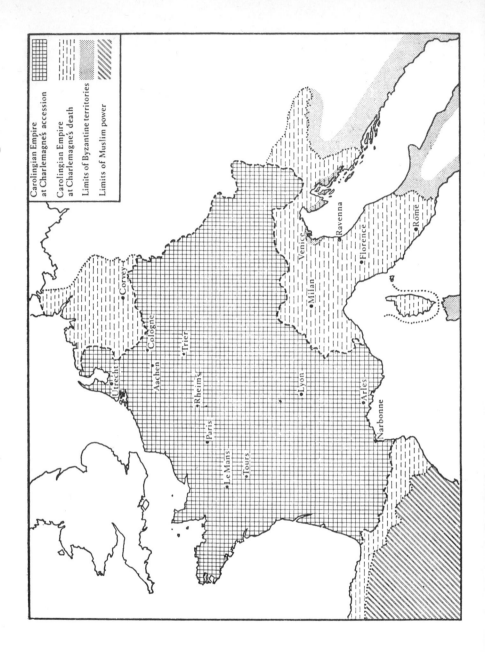

Corvey

Cologne

Trier

Utrecht

Aachen

Rheims

Paris

Le Mans

Tours

Lyon

Arles

Narbonne

Milan

Venice

Ravenna

Florence

Rome

7. The Carolingian Empire in 814

of St Paul and St Peter, [1] gave obedience in all things lawful to the regularly constituted secular power while remaining themselves entirely autarchic. When the emperor declared his adhesion to the Christian faith, the Church could no longer regard him as an external power, a magistrate representing divine authority only in worldly matters, and this only in so far as he ruled justly and lawfully. Still less could the Church accept in its entirety the concept of a numinous, semi-divine ruler. A tension was gradually set up which has never since been fully relaxed, the familiar tension between ' Church ' and ' State '; indeed, it might be argued that the distant consequences of the conversion of Constantine were to prove as harmful to the Church as the immediate results were beneficial. From the beginning the Christian emperor conceived it as a principal part of his task to assist the Church to attain her purpose in the world, and the step between assistance and dictation was a short one. For long the emperor's word alone could convoke the universal Church to council; he alone had a vantage point from which he could advise or command its leaders; and it was inevitable that even a well-intentioned emperor might allow a statesman's or an autocrat's desire for peace and unity to outweigh a pastor's or a theologian's zeal for truth and firm discipline. In the fifth century a change began which culminated in the reign of Justinian I. The rôle of protector was taken up into that of governor. The modern term caesaro-papism has become unfashionable, and it is true that even Justinian allowed in theory a magisterial and spiritual supremacy to the bishop of Rome, but in practice he behaved as the divinely chosen, sole and absolute governor and legislator of the church throughout his empire. Later emperors, no doubt, lacked the combination of genius, character, power and opportunity that Justinian enjoyed; moreover they often acted in a despotic, even brutal fashion that was incompatible with any reasoned theory of their position. Nevertheless, the emperors at Constantinople continued to regard themselves as divinely appointed representatives of God charged with the moral and spiritual responsibility for an empire that was conterminous with Christendom.

If the converted emperor and his successors by their active leadership probably delayed the emergence of a single authority in the liberated Church, the claims made by them of a divine authority over all Christians stimulated the popes of Rome, who as the centuries passed had become more explicit in their assertion of their inheritance of the promise and commission given to Peter, to assert a rival claim to religious sovereignty. By Gelasius I and Justinian I the opposing views were openly declared. The pope presented the priesthood as the paramount authority in a society which was ordered in temporal matters by the emperor; the

1. Romans 13: 1-7; I Peter 2: 13-17.

emperor thirty years later conceived himself as ruler of a Christendom
to which the priesthood gave spiritual care and nourishment. Thus while
the pope set the emperor firmly within the Church of which he, the pope,
was pastor, the emperor, in practice if not in theory, acted as a king-priest
with traditions drawn from both ancient oriental monarchies and the Old
Testament.

The issue remained still unresolved in the pontificate of Gregory I,
who showed great deference to the emperor while using to the full the
papal centralisation of authority in the West, and under his rule the
' divided mind ' is still apparent, for he addresses the emperor with deference as his lord, while kings of the western world, however supreme, are
regarded as his ' sons '. For more than a century after the days of Gregory
the popes continued to admit the temporal sovereignty of the emperor
over themselves and the territory which in practice they administered for
him; they announced their election to him and received his approval, they
dated their documents by his regnal year, and professed their loyalty to
their sovereign at Constantinople.

Concurrently with the first appearance of opposition between pope and
emperor tension had developed between the patriarch of Constantinople
and the pope at Rome. The patriarchate of the imperial city, a latecomer
among the patriarchal sees, owed its dignity to its seat at the centre of
government and the explicit resolution of the council of Constantinople
(381) which gave it precedence second only to Rome. The prestige of the
see grew, and emperors were ready to exalt the position of the patriarch
vis-à-vis the pope as a direct consequence of their success in subordinating
him in their own scheme of the order of things. This very subordination
in its turn stimulated the patriarch to assert his equality with, and even at
moments his superiority to, Rome. The popes, therefore, at least from the
sixth century onwards, had always two opponents to their claims, the
emperor and the patriarch, and the disappearance from any kind of
ecclesiastical power-politics of the other patriarchs after the Muslim
conquest had the effect of weakening the Roman position in practice, even
if it might seem to strengthen it in the realm of theory.

Meanwhile in the West popes had become accustomed to treat the whole
of the Italian peninsula south of the see of Milan, together with Africa
and on occasion Spain and southern Gaul, as an ecclesiastical province
over which they had direct or indirect oversight, and regarded the rest of
the western world as a sphere within which they could take any action
which might seem to them good. Thus while the whole of western Europe
could in a sense be regarded (and was so regarded by the Byzantines)
as a vast western patriarchate, it was in fact divided into two zones: the
province of Rome, in which the bishops were directly and wholly under the

papal jurisdiction, and received from the pope a pallium symbolising this; and the wider extent of Christendom north of the Alps, in which the metropolitans of a city or region ruled over autonomous provinces, consecrated their bishops and held their synods. The jurisdiction of the metropolitans was inherent in their churches, and Rome intervened only on appeal or when matters of grave concern arose between metropolitans. On the other hand, the papal missionary churches, first that of Britain and later those of Germany, were treated almost as if part of the papal suburbican province. Augustine, Willibrord and Boniface received the pallium and took the oath of obedience to the pope. Boniface attempted, without lasting success, to make this arrangement in the Frankish church; Charlemagne, with other motives, was more successful in obtaining for his metropolitans the pallium as a sign of honour, and thus unintentionally introducing them into the Roman orbit, in which papal action was required to bestow rights of jurisdiction.

This relationship, which seems a natural one to those familiar only with the Catholic church of modern times, was not one that could prevail in the political climate of the early middle ages; it continued for long in England, where no strong monarchic influence opposed it in a divided land, but it could not survive on the continent, where Frankish and German conceptions of kingship were predominant and where popes were content to allow the initiative to pass from their hands. In the land of the Franks, when a strong monarchy came into being with Pippin and his Carolingian descendants, the necessities of government and the native conception of kingship combined to place in the king's hands the control of the church. In a simple society, nominally Christian but almost entirely illiterate, in which the only educated group and the only literature were clerical, it was inevitable that a principal task of an energetic monarch should be the care and direction of the Christian life in all its aspects, and the long reign of Charlemagne was to become the type and exemplar in this respect for the French monarchy until the Revolution.

Charlemagne surrounded himself with a group of clerical advisers, of whom Alcuin was the chief, who not only supported him in his policy but went on to provide a basis of ideas with which to justify and canonise it. The outcome of their thought was what has been called ' political Augustinianism ', by which is meant a political theory based not precisely on Augustine's *City of God* as it was intended by the author to be understood, but upon political ideas which reflected, in the realm of temporal and spiritual activities, the interpenetration of natural and supernatural, divine and human powers, that occurs, or seems to occur, in so much of Augustine's thought. Charlemagne himself is known to have admired and hearkened to the writings of Augustine, and he regarded himself as divinely appointed to rule the City of God. The task of the clergy was to pray for, and administer the sacraments to, the people of God. The task of the emperor was well expressed in the celebrated programmatic statement which, though doubtless written by Alcuin and reflecting the views of the court clerics, is an accurate expression of Charlemagne's thoughts:

> Mine it is to defend on all sides the holy church of Christ from pagan incursion and infidel devastation abroad, and .within to add strength to the Catholic faith by a clear statement and an acceptance of it. Yours it is, raising your hands to God like Moses, to aid our arms in order that by your intercession... the Christian people may everywhere be always victorious over their enemies. [2]

Any account of the actions and policies of Charlemagne must assume in the reader a recognition of the almost complete lack in the West of the regular, bureaucratic administration which the eastern emperor commanded, and without which laws and programmes are of little avail. In the Byzantine state, as in modern France, a stable and competent bureaucracy ensured the continuance of the machinery of government even when the titular head of the administration was incompetent or ephemeral. The reader should also be aware of the failure of the emperor and of many of his agents to exhibit in their own lives examples of Christian moral excellence and contempt of worldly things. But when all these reservations have been made, Charlemagne still appears as a ruler distinguished by his care for the well-being of the Church. The great body of legislation throughout his reign covers every aspect of church life; he convoked reforming synods, and sent inspectors from among the clergy to tour his empire. Of the two plenipotentiaries *(missi)* who went together through all the districts of his realm one was a cleric and both might on occasion be bishops; the rights of the bishops and of church lands, the education of the clergy, the requirements of the liturgy, the safeguarding of small churches and their incumbents and their funds, the sanctity of marriage and the avoidance of scandalous conduct–all these received legislative treatment during his reign. His capitularies, based on current canon law where that was applicable, remained as a desirable norm and as a model of reform for two centuries and more in Gaul. Beyond this was the emperor's care for the faith, seen not only in the articles of belief which he proposed for all his subjects, but on the three important occasions to be considered later when, doubtless moved by his advisers, he took the initiative in opposing what he and they considered false doctrine.

Charlemagne, in much of this, carried on the autocratic traditions of his father and, as a supremely able and practical ruler, gathered more and

2. *Epistola ad Leonem papam* in MGH *Epistolae* IV, 137.

more executive power into his hands. Illiterate in the technical sense he may have been, but he was an exceedingly intelligent man, and it is impossible to be certain how far his clerical advisers constructed for themselves the basis of ideas on which his government was alleged, in the manifestoes of the time, to rest. It is certain, however, that the part that they, and in particular Alcuin, played was very considerable.

Charlemagne himself, in the latter part of his reign, undoubtedly wished to revive the image of the Roman empire in the West. His buildings at Aachen, with their names of *palatium* and *Lateranum* and the reference to ' new Rome ', make this clear. As a corollary, he asserted for himself over the church of the West the same powers of governance as were claimed by the eastern emperor. Four years before the coronation of 800 he claimed to be ' lord and father, king and priest, the governor of all Christians ', and others claimed for him the vicariate or vicegerency of Christ; he was the ' ruler *(rector)* of the people of Christ '. For this position Alcuin, Theodulf and others provided a basis in the kingship of Saul and his successors in the kingdom of Israel. Charlemagne was the new Moses, the new David, priest as well as king; not as possessing the powers of sacramental conse-cration conferred by the possession of holy orders, but as having in virtue of his kingly position, and later of his anointing, the jurisdictional rights of the priest, by which he could appoint to ecclesiastical office, convoke councils, and give legal binding force to decrees on faith and morality. The imperial status given to Charlemagne by the pope in 800 was thus interpreted in a very different sense by the two parties to the act. For the pope, Charles had been appointed the official protector and champion of the apostolic see; for Charles, the coronation had sealed what was already a fact, that he occupied the place in the West that had in the past been held by the Roman emperor, and his rule extended in theory, if not in fact, over all Christians of the West. Henceforth, there were *de facto* two empe-rors. In theory a sheer diarchy, as opposed to a collegiate rule, was incompatible with the claims of both the emperor of new Rome and the pope of old Rome; in practice, the theoretical impossibility was either ignored or transcended.

In any case, the claim of Charlemagne's theologians could not be formally accepted by the pope or papal theorists. It was as unacceptable as the claim of Justinian, but like his, it could be silently tolerated or ignored until a time of reckoning arrived. For the papacy, quite apart from its traditional, basic, dogmatic claim to hold the supreme commission promised to Peter, was by this time committed to another claim to sove-reignty.

We have seen how, by the accident of events, the popes came to exercise the functions of temporal sovereigns over central Italy. For this authority the papacy now claimed to have august title-deeds. In the last decade of the fifth century, and outside the papal chancery, a group of forgeries, called the Symmachan as dating from the pontificate of Pope Symmachus (498-514), had been produced in Rome, one of which was the celebrated *Legenda sancti Silvestri*. This purported to be a life of Silvester I, and described his healing of Constantine I and the emperor's baptism, at which he gave the pope the primatial position over the Church, together with possession of Rome, from which the emperor withdrew to found a new capital. This story was the basis of a far more tendentious fabrication known as the *Donation of Constantine*. According to this Constantine handed over to Pope Silvester all the imperial garments and insignia, as also his palace, the city of Rome, all the provinces of Italy and the cities of the West, islands expressly included. By this act the pope became a pendent to the emperor, with equal powers over the West. Not only this, but it seems clear that the author of the *Donation* intended to suggest that Constantine had relinquished Rome so as to leave the sovereign power of the pope in possession: in other words, that Constantine had become emperor at Constantinople by papal permission; this permission could equally well be withdrawn.

The date of the spurious *Donation* is uncertain, but it is certainly not later than the early years of the ninth century. Recent criticism has gone far to show that it was fabricated to assist the appeal of Stephen II to Pippin (754) by establishing that the papacy had been robbed by the Lombards of territories given by Constantine, thus obscuring the historical fact that some of them had recently belonged to the eastern empire. This document, unlike the *Legenda*, was most probably composed in the papal chancery, though not necessarily with the connivance of the pope. Whatever influence it may have had at the time, it soon became venerable with age and one of the most·effective weapons in the papal armoury, though it must be emphasised that neither the *Legenda* nor the *Donation* were in any way responsible for the much older and traditional doctrine of the papal power as descending from Peter. By the time of Gregory the Great the papacy had long since acted, at least in certain matters and theatres, as having an authority which was not only unique in character and extent, but was also in a real, if not as yet a fully defined way, paramount above all other authorities. Popes had presented general councils with formulas of faith; their assent had been recognised as necessary before the canons of a council were universally binding; their representatives had taken precedence and intervened with decision in the debates. Popes had pronounced upon every kind of doctrinal and disciplinary issue and had judged cases of all kinds that had been referred to them; their right of appellate jurisdiction in matters of importance had been admitted, if grudgingly, by the eastern church. [3] They had appointed legates in Gaul and elsewhere. They had a permanent representative at Constantinople. They had acted as exercising full power in establishing the Church in England. Nevertheless, during the two centuries following the age of Gregory I, they were often overshadowed or neglected by secular rulers; their action was impeded and on occasion questioned or opposed, while at other times almost all papal activity ceased owing to a lack of will or wit in the holders of the papal office. Yet if, under the strong rule of Pippin and Charlemagne, the papacy largely renounced its initiative within the Frankish territories, outside, as in Britain, and on the periphery, as in Frisia, Saxony and Bavaria, popes acted with complete freedom in authorising the actions, establishing the powers and confirming or altering the decisions of Boniface, his companions and their successors.

In the long course of papal history it has happened time and again that a pontiff has arisen who has drawn swiftly and deeply upon the potentialities of his office and has spoken and acted with unexpected and unfamiliar strength not through any abuse of power, but through a keener vision of the nature of the authority he holds. Such a one was Nicholas I (858-67), who, reigning at the moment when the bishops of northern Francia were establishing their independence of the imperial power, himself acted both within and without the Carolingian realm as one holding immediate and complete authority over individual bishops and their metropolitans, reversing elections and settlements, hearing appeals and calling cases to the papal court. In the matter of Lothair's divorce he stood as the final judge of legal and moral questions even in the case of a monarch, and even with the sanction of excommunication. This last point is crucial. Both in East and West popes showed themselves ready to excommunicate – that is, to sever from communion with the Roman church conceived as the universal Church – those of whatever rank or station who had acted disobediently. Not all popes, however, acted thus, and in the space of more than four hundred years there were several intervals and two periods of considerable length when the papacy withdrew into impotence either through a personal lack of fibre or as having been caught up in the intrigues and brawls of Roman faction.

It was the fortune of Nicholas to encounter the affair of Photius, which will be treated elsewhere, and from its beginning he took a high line, condemning the patriarch as an intruder; his own legates were cashiered in consequence of the pope's mistaken trust in an enemy of Photius, and in a letter to the emperor claims were made to powers hitherto never exercised in the East, such as the right of Rome to summon parties to Rome for the

3. Cf. the decrees of the Council of Sardica in 343-4 in Denziger-Schönmetzer, *Enchiridion Symbolorum* no. 136 [57e].

examination of their case even though no appeal had been lodged by them. Nicholas uses language about the papacy which was not exceeded in strength even by Gregory VII. Set up as princes over the whole earth the popes are an epitome of the whole Church; all Christians are subjected to the papal rule; without the Church of Rome there is no Christianity; the pope is master of the bishops; the monarch who treats a bishopric as his personal property is exceeding his powers. The pope is mediator between Christ and man, and it is through him that the powers of both emperors and bishops flow. How much of the language and thought of Nicholas's utterances came from his *alter ego*, Anastasius the Librarian, an equivocal character who had been by turns an ambitious aspirant to the papacy, an excommunicate, and a laicised priest, and whose violence of language and action needlessly embittered negotiations both at Constantinople and with Hincmar at Rheims, must be a matter of opinion, [4] as must also be the extent of the influence of the False Decretals upon Anastasius and his master. Probably they were a convenient corroboration rather than a formative influence. In any case, the language of the pope's letters is at times drastic, almost brutal, in its remorseless logic. It is the first taste of that ruthlessness of expression that reappears in Gregory VII and Boniface VIII. It could be used with effect only by a strong man, and after the reigns of Nicholas's successors Hadrian II and John VIII it is not heard again for almost two centuries, but the correspondence and acts of these forceful popes remained in the chests of the curia, like the bow of Odysseus, ready to be drawn again when the needful strength of arm was once more present.

When the empire had been restored under Otto the Great, much of the doctrine of the imperial authority was adopted by the German monarchs, but with the difference that it was, so to say, externalised. All executive power lay with the secular arm, but no German king, with the possible exception of Henry II, regarded himself as the father and ruler of the church in the West. There was a subtle, but real, change of outlook. Whereas Charlemagne, as a divinely appointed ruler, guided his people who, seen from another point of view, composed the Church – for both eastern and western emperors regarded their empires as ecumenical – the German monarchs ruled only the German realm, of which a part was the territory held by the pope bound by an oath of fealty; they claimed the practical right of government over bishops, who were the leading feudal magnates, and over the papacy, the church in special dependence on the emperor. On occasion emperors, such as Conrad II in particular, are styled vicars of God or of Christ, but this was a time-honoured style which

---

4. W. Ullmann is partial to Anastasius; for another view see A. Lapôtre, *De Anastasio bibliothecario Sedis apostolicae*, Paris, 1885.

attached itself to actions of the monarch rather than to his person. The German emperor was not divinely appointed to take the place of Christ as head and guide of the church; rather, he performed certain acts in virtue of his kingship and so doing represented Christ. Thus so far as a theory or programme could be deduced from actions, the Carolingian empire is seen to have absorbed the spiritual territory of the church more completely than did the German line, but it was in fact far less of a menace to spiritual independence. Charlemagne was working by means of churchmen for what he held to be the best interests of the church; the German emperors, even at their most devout, were preoccupied with the secular interests of their realm, of which the papal territory was only one part, important though it might be.

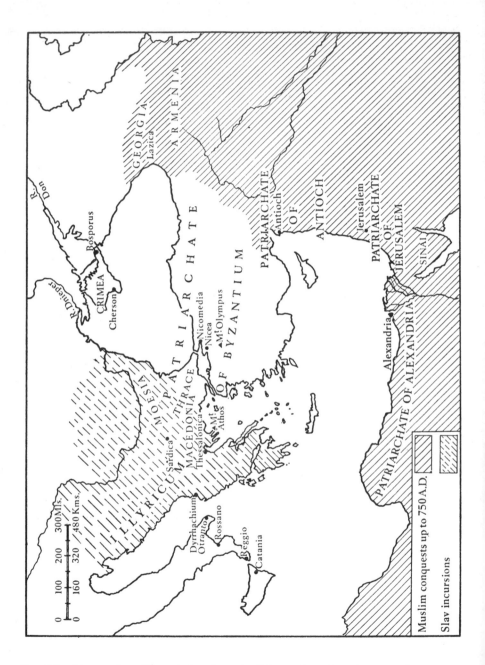

8. The Byzantine Church in the 7th, 8th and early 9th centuries

THE BYZANTINE CHURCH

I. EASTERN CHRISTENDOM IN THE SEVENTH CENTURY

THE seventh century, which marked a decisive turning-point in the history of the east Roman empire, was a time of far-reaching changes in the life of the eastern church. The political and military events within the Byzantine empire and beyond its eastern and south-eastern borders transformed the ecclesiastical map of eastern Christendom, and endowed the Byzantine church with new cultural features which it was to retain throughout the middle ages. The victories of the Persians in Syria, Armenia, Palestine and Asia Minor, their conquest of Egypt (611-19), and the simultaneous invasions of the empire's Balkan provinces by Avars and Slavs, seemed to herald the last days of the Roman empire in the East. The capture and sack of Jerusalem (614) and the consequent removal of the relic of the Holy Cross to Persia, deeply shocked the Byzantines; and the ensuing struggle against the Persian empire assumed in their eyes the features of a holy war. The subsequent recovery of Byzantium, due mainly to the administrative and military reforms of the emperor Heraclius (610-41), and in which the Church played its part by contributing handsomely to the financial burden of the war and by stirring up patriotic fervour – a notable example was the inspiring rôle played by the patriarch Sergius during the unsuccessful attack on Constantinople by Persians, Avars and Slavs in 626 – led to the reconquest of the empire's provinces in Asia and Africa (622-8) and to the triumphal return of the Holy Cross to Jerusalem. But this recovery proved ephemeral. Within fourteen years of the Byzantine victory over Persia, the Arab armies had conquered the imperial provinces of Syria, Mesopotamia, Armenia and Egypt; and although in the two supreme trials of strength between Byzantium and the Umayyad caliphate, in 678 and 718, the Arabs were repulsed before the walls of Constantinople, most of the empire's eastern provinces, including the sees of Alexandria, Jerusalem and Antioch, were by the mid-seventh century lost to Islam. Antioch was later temporarily recovered (from 969 to 1085); but the patriarchates of Alexandria and Jerusalem were never again under Byzantine control.

The Arab conquests were certainly facilitated, especially in Egypt, by the religious disaffection of the local Monophysite population toward the central government in Constantinople, which for the past two centuries had striven to enforce conformity with the doctrines of Chalcedon. Later Monophysite writers claimed that the Christians welcomed the Arabs as liberators: Abu'l Faraj (Barhebraeus), writing in the thirteenth century, passed this verdict on the conquest of Syria: ' The God of vengeance delivered us out of the hands of the Romans by means of the Arabs... It profited us not a little to be saved from the cruelty of the Romans and their bitter hatred against us '. [1] And a tenth-century writer ascribes these words to the Coptic patriarch Benjamin (623-62): ' I was in my city of Alexandria, and found a time of peace and safety after the troubles and persecutions caused by the heretics '. [2] In the vindictive harshness of these judgments there is no doubt some partisan exaggeration. Yet it cannot be denied that the religious and political hostility of the Copts and the Syrians towards the ' Melkites ' of Constantinople made it easier for them to accept the rule of their Islamic conquerors.

The Arab conquest of the empire's eastern provinces sealed the failure of the attempts which the Byzantine emperors had made for the past two centuries to win back the Monophysite communities and to enforce acceptance of the Council of Chalcedon, sometimes by persecution, sometimes by doctrinal compromises. After his victory over Persia, Heraclius made a determined effort to gain the loyalty of the Monophysites in Armenia, Syria and Egypt, who had enjoyed a favoured status under their Persian masters. He began to propagate the doctrine of Monoenergism, which seems to have been invented in the early years of his reign by

1. Cited in A. J. Butler, *The Arab conquest of Egypt and the last thirty years of the Roman dominion*, Oxford 1902, 158.
2. *Ibid.* 445.

Sergius, patriarch of Constantinople; by affirming that Christ had two natures but a single active force (ἐνέργεια) this teaching seemed to open the door to a compromise between the Orthodox and the Monophysites. Heraclius's attempts were at first successful – even Pope Honorius I was persuaded to support them – and by 633 it seemed that the whole empire was united in the nominal acceptance of Chalcedonian orthodoxy. However, a union based on theological equivocation and political expediency could not long survive. Sergius's teaching was strongly attacked by the monk Sophronius (who later became patriarch of Jerusalem) and by St Maximus the Confessor; but Heraclius was more convinced than ever that, in the face of the Arab invasions which threatened to engulf all of his eastern provinces, only religious unity could save the empire. Shifting his theological ground, he abandoned – again, it seems, under the inspiration of the patriarch Sergius – the increasingly discredited Monoenergism for a new doctrine which asserted that although Christ had two natures, he had only one will (θέλημα). The emperor attempted, by an edict known as the *Ekthesis* (638) to impose Monothelitism on the whole Church. Its results were wholly disastrous: the Monophysites rejected it as too Chalcedonian; the Arabs continued their triumphal advance through the Near East; it led, after Heraclius's death in 641, to the brutal persecution of the Chalcedonians; and it resulted in a conflict between the sees of Rome and Constantinople. The papacy – with the exception of Pope Honorius – consistently opposed Monothelitism; in vain did the emperor Constans II, to avoid a complete break with Rome, issue a *Typos* in 648, forbidding any further discussion of ' active forces ' and ' wills ' in Christ. The Lateran council, convened by Pope Martin I in 649, solemnly condemned the Monothelite doctrine. The emperor's revenge was a display of brutal power. In 653 the pope was arrested, taken to Constantinople and tried before the Senate on charges of high treason. After suffering humiliations and gross ill-treatment, Martin was exiled to Cherson in the Crimea, where he died soon after. A similar fate overtook the monk Maximus, the leader of the Greek anti-Monothelite party and the greatest theologian of his age. He, too, was arrested in Rome and brought for trial to Constantinople. All attempts to induce him to accept the *Typos* failed. Imprisonment, deportation and physical torture failed to break his resistance. The confessor died in exile in Lazica in 662.

But Constans II's cruelties were causing a revulsion of public opinion in Byzantium. Moreover, the Byzantine authorities were beginning to tire of the continued religious disunity in the empire. The Monothelite compromise, now that the eastern provinces were firmly in the hands of the Arabs, had largely lost its political *raison d'être*. The breach with Rome was causing growing uneasiness among the orthodox followers of Maximus. However, the final solution of the Monothelite crisis was delayed by the exigencies of war. Between 674 and 678 Byzantium was faced with a desperate struggle against the Arabs. This fight for the survival of eastern Christendom was decided in 678, when the Arabs were forced to raise the siege of Constantinople. This victory over Islam, achieved by the Emperor Constantine IV, proved to be as far-reaching in its effects upon the history of Christendom as the repulse of the Arabs from the walls of Constantinople by Leo III in 718, and the victory of Charles Martel at Poitiers in 732.

The way was now open to religious reconciliation. The Sixth Ecumenical Council (680-1), convened in Constantinople by Constantine IV in agreement with the pope, condemned Monothelitism and amplified the Chalcedonian definition by the doctrine of two wills in Christ:

> We... declare that there are two natural wills and two natural energies, which are indivisible, immutable, inseparable and without confusion, in Christ, according to the teaching of the holy Fathers. And the two natural wills are not opposed to each other... but His human will followed, and it does not resist and oppose, but rather is subject to the divine and almighty will. [3]

The council anathematised the principal clerical propagators of Monothelitism, including Pope Honorius and the patriarch Sergius, but passed over in silence the two imperial ringleaders of the heresy – Heraclius and Constans II: imperial patronage still weighed heavily on the Church.

The Sixth Ecumenical Council took place in a world that was very different from the Byzantine empire of A.D. 600. In the East, Byzantium had lost Syria, Palestine and Egypt; and at the end of the hardest struggle for survival it had yet known, the empire was able, only with the greatest difficulty, to repel the Arab onslaught on Constantinople. The situation in the Balkan provinces of the Byzantine empire had also, during the seventh century, altered beyond recognition. The invasions of the Avars and the Slavs, which had started in the sixth century, resulted in the occupation of the greater part of the Balkan peninsula by the Slavs. In this pagan barbarian flood the Christian communities and bishoprics of the peninsula which, except for Thrace, were then within the jurisdiction of the Roman church, were, with few exceptions, submerged or destroyed. For some two centuries – the seventh and the eighth – most of the Balkan peninsula, including much of Macedonia, Greece and the Peloponnese, lay outside the effective political control of Byzantium and was lost to Christendom.

The Arab and the Slav invasions had two far-reaching effects upon the future development of the Byzantine church. The loss of the eastern

3. C. J. Hefele, *A History of the Councils of the Church*, transl. W. R. Clark, V, Edinburgh 1896, 174-5; C. J. Hefele and H. Leclercq, *Histoire des Conciles*, III. Paris 1909, 509.

provinces greatly increased the power of the patriarch of Contantinople. Freed from the competition of his former rivals of Alexandria and Antioch, resting his claims on the status, second only to that of the bishop of Rome, accorded to his see by the Second Ecumenical Council, styling himself (since the late sixth century) ecumenical patriarch, the bishop of the Byzantine capital became henceforth the unquestioned leader of eastern Christendom. The Slav invasions, on the other hand, interposed for several centuries a wall of pagan barbarism between the eastern and the western parts of Christendom; and both the destruction of Christianity in Illyricum and the physical barrier thus created to the relations by land between Constantinople and Rome contributed, at least as much as the Arab domination over the Mediterranean, to the growing estrangement between the eastern and the western churches. In the history of this estrangement the seventh century represents a significant turning-point. Latin, the official language of imperial administration, was during that period replaced by Greek, and rapidly forgotten in Byzantium; and knowledge of and interest in the West declined rapidly even in the educated circles of Constantinople. The legal and administrative traditions of the Roman empire and its political claims to universality continued to mould the eastern empire of the *Rhomaioi;* but in language, culture and religion Byzantium became in the seventh century largely a Greek empire.

What of the day-to-day life of the eastern church in the seventh century? If from the theological controversies and the ecclesiastical policies of the emperors we descend to less exalted spheres, what do we know of the life of the lower ranks of the clergy, the development of monasticism, the morals of the educated laity in the capital, and the faith of the humble folk of the provinces? Our evidence on these matters, scanty though it is, comes mainly from hagiographical works and from the canons of the Trullan, or Quinisext, Council. This synod, convened in Constantinople by Justinian II in 692, was accepted by the eastern church as an extension and an integral part of the Sixth Ecumenical Council, but was rejected by Rome because of its condemnation of certain customs of the western church and its re-affirmation of the twenty-eighth canon of the Council of Chalcedon.

The Acts of the council paint a picture of Byzantine society, clerical and lay, that is scarcely edifying. A decline in Christian morality, a ritualism often indistinguishable from superstition, and an attachment to pagan practices are among the vices which the council castigates most severely. But this sombre picture, suggesting a serious breakdown in ecclesiastical discipline in a still semi-Christianised society, should be balanced against the achievements of the Church's ministry in the often harrowing circumstances of the seventh century; we should note the development of the Byzantine liturgy, then beginning to acquire, from a synthesis of different traditions, its medieval form; the liturgical expression increasingly given to the veneration of the Mother of God; the further development of Greek hymnography, in which the theological experience of the past was transmuted into religious poetry of a high order, and which was exemplified in the penitential canon of St Andrew of Crete (*c.* 660-740); and the shining examples of spiritual perfection, illustrated in the lives of the saints which continued to be avidly read, studied and admired by all sections of Byzantine society. The *Pratum Spirituale* of John Moschus, with its stories of the monks and hermits of Palestine, Egypt and other places, glorifying the virtues of asceticism, charity and attachment to Orthodoxy, addressed primarily to the humble folk and reflecting conditions of the late sixth or early seventh centuries, continued to enjoy an immense popularity. [4] And another popular work of hagiography, the Life of St John the Almsgiver, patriarch of Alexandria in the early seventh century, famed for his love of the poor and championship of the oppressed, shows how highly the virtues of charity and compassion were prized by the people of Byzantium. [5]

2. THE ICONOCLAST CRISIS

The Iconoclast dispute, which for over a hundred years (726-843) divided the Byzantine church into two bitterly irreconcilable factions, provoked a great deal of violence and persecution, generated much political and social unrest in Byzantine society, and generally speaking proved to be one of the turning-points in the history of the eastern church, was a complex phenomenon some of whose essential features continue to elude the historian. Its origins are not entirely clear; the degree to which non-religious factors affected its course and outcome remains controversial; and our understanding of the doctrinal background of the dispute is impaired by the fact that on two separate occasions, which followed the temporary restoration of the veneration of images in 787 and its definitive re-establishment in 843, the writings of the Iconoclasts suffered wholesale destruction, and can hence be reconstructed only from the evidence of their enemies. Yet modern scholarship has succeeded to a large extent in overcoming these difficulties. It is now possible to draw a reasonably full and objective picture of this remarkable controversy.

4. PG 87, col. 2851-3116; French transl. M. J. Rouët de Journel, *Jean Moschus, Le pré spirituel*, Paris 1946; cf. N. H. Baynes, ' The pratum spirituale ': *Orientalia Christiana Periodica* 13 (1947), 404-14.
5. *Leontios' von Neapolis Leben des Heiligen Johannes des Barmherzigen Erzbischofs von Alexandrien*, ed. H. Gelzer, Freiburg and Leipzig 1893; H. Delehaye, ' Une Vie inédite de Saint Jean l'Aumonier ': *Analecta Bollandiana* 45 (1927), 5-74; *Three Byzantine Saints: contemporary biographies translated from the Greek*, by E. Dawes and N. H. Baynes, Oxford 1948, 193-270.

Yet it is not easy, nor always possible, to disentangle its many inter-woven strands. Certainly it had a social and economic aspect, which appears particularly clearly during the second phase of Iconoclasm (815-42), but can also be detected in the eighth century. The Iconoclast faction derived its strength from the circus parties of the capital, from small craftsmen, and especially from the army, inspired by fervent loyalty to the leadership and later to the memory of its great military commander, the Iconoclast emperor Constantine V; the city proletariat seems in the main to have remained faithful to the veneration of icons. Iconoclasm has also been described as a predominantly anti-monastic movement; but this statement requires qualification. It is true that during the first phase of Iconoclasm the monks were firmly loyal to the icons, and that in the latter part of Constantine V's reign many of them became martyrs and confes-sors; moreover, after the revival of Iconoclasm in 815 the Iconodule party was led and inspired by the abbot Theodore and his monks of the monastery of Studios in Constantinople. Yet no evidence exists of anti-monastic measures by the Iconoclasts before the sixties of the eighth century; and after 815 an appreciable number of monasteries sided with the Iconoclasts. We may further detect, in the attempts of the Iconoclast emperors to enforce their theological views upon their subjects, a resur-gence of that Byzantine political philosophy which sought to subject the Church to the imperial power, and which was later decisively checked by the final defeat of Iconoclasm. It was this mentality that prompted Leo III to state in a letter to Pope Gregory II: ' I am emperor and priest,' [6] and Leo V to declare to his bishops in 814: ' I too am a son of the Church, and as a mediator I shall listen to both parties and after a comparison of the two I shall determine the truth. ' [7]

And yet, however important these problems were in the context of the Iconoclast controversy, its central issues must be sought in the realm of doctrine. The dispute, essentially, was about the objects of Christian belief and the nature of Christian worship, individual and corporate. Iconoclasm derived its original and basic element from the hostility towards all forms of religious art which a section of the early Church had inherited from the Synagogue and drawn from Old Testament prohibitions of images (e.g., Exodus 20: 4). In the eighth century this hostility was widespread in Asia Minor, where it was probably fanned by the prevailing Muslim aversion to the representation of the human form, and there is no doubt that Leo III was influenced by the views of the bishops of that region.

6. Βασιλεὺς καὶ ἱερεύς εἰμι : Mansi 12, col. 975; cf. *Zeitschrift für Kirchengeschichte* 52 (1933), 85.
7. Theosterictus, *Vita S. Nicetae Confessoris*, ASS Aprilis I, xxix; cf. P. J. Alexander, *The Patriarch Nicephorus of Constantinople*, Oxford 1958, 131.

However, the tradition of hostility to religious art went back a good deal further in time. The cult of holy images representing in the main Christ or the saints, first attested in the fifth century and widespread by the late sixth, became in the seventh century a general feature of Byzantine popular devotion. The popular nature of this cult often caused its votaries to ignore in practice the distinction between the image and the imagined, and thus to cross the slender boundary between genuine veneration and superstitious idolatry. The understandable distrust felt by many Byzantine churchmen – often the more educated – for this seemingly uncontrollable devotion found some support in the patristic tradition, notably in the letter of Eusebius of Caesarea to the Empress Constantia Augusta, in which the author, in accordance with Origenist ideas, denied the theological validity of any pictorial image of Christ. The Iconoclast position, which at first owed much to a fear of pagan idolatry, was later reinforced by Christological arguments put forward by Constantine V. He held that the true image is consubstantial with its prototype, and that icons of Christ are heretical, for they either separate or else confuse his two natures. Both these propositions the Iconodules strongly denied. They maintained that the image differs from the prototype according to its essence (κατ' οὐσίαν), and that its veneration is no more idolatry than the honour paid to imperial effigies is a form of emperor-worship. It is interesting to observe that in defending the symbolic nature of religious representations the Iconodules used arguments put forward by pagan writers of the second and third centuries who distinguished between the statues set up to honour the gods and the gods themselves to whom alone worship was offered. But the key argument of the Iconodules was based on the doctrine of the incarnation, as defined by the Council of Chalcedon. Already implicit in the eighty-second canon of the Trullan Council, it was first propounded clearly and consistently in the first half of the eighth century by St John of Damascus, the leading theologian of his time. For him the icons are not only ' silent sermons ', ' books of the illiterate ', ' memorials of the mysteries of God ', but visible signs of the sanctification of matter made possible by the incarnation. Because the Invisible and Indescribable became visible and describable in the flesh, images of Christ in his visible and human aspect are truly representations of God. The essential link established by the Damascene between the meaning of icons and the theology of the incarnation, and the equally essential distinction he drew between ' worship ' or ' adoration ' which are due to God alone, and the relative ' veneration ' due to images of Christ and the saints, underlie the dogmatic definitions of the Seventh Ecumenical Council, and remain the foundation of the Orthodox church's teaching on religious art.

Iconoclasm gained the support of the public authorities of Byzantium in 726, when the emperor Leo III openly declared his opposition to the veneration of religious images. The destruction, on the emperor's orders, of a highly venerated icon of Christ provoked a riot in the capital, while Leo's iconoclast intentions led to an insurrection in Greece. The crisis was further aggravated in 730, when Leo III issued an edict forbidding the cult of icons and ordering the destruction of all sacred images. His iconoclast programme thus acquired the force of law. The government took immediate measures to coerce the opposition: the icons were forcibly removed from the churches, mural paintings depicting religious subjects were defaced, liturgical objects and vestments on which these subjects were portrayed were confiscated, saints' relics were desecrated and burned; though precise details on the persecution of Iconodules in the reign of Leo III (d. 741) are lacking, there is evidence that many of them were put to death, mutilated or exiled; and the patriarch Germanos, who refused to subscribe to the edict of 730, was forced to resign. Iconoclasm reached its peak in the reign of Leo's son Constantine V (741-75). A gifted statesman like his father, he proceeded at first with great caution and only launched his iconoclast policy after assuring his position by skilful propaganda and judicious episcopal appointments; but, in contrast to his father, he held extreme and highly articulate theological views. In 754 the emperor convened a church council in Constantinople, attended by 338 bishops, which unanimously condemned the veneration of icons as a form of idolatry, decreed their destruction and excommunicated the leaders of the Iconodule party, notably its greatest theologian, St John of Damascus. This ' headless synod ', as it was called by the Orthodox because no patriarch was present (neither the pope nor the eastern patriarchs had sent representatives, and the see of Constantinople was then vacant), bolstered up the iconoclast programme with theological arguments. Constantine V's government, secure in the doctrinal support of virtually the entire Byzantine episcopate, proceeded to implement the council's decrees. Destruction of religious art and an increasingly brutal persecution of Iconodules were now accompanied by a régime of terror instigated by the state authorities against the monks who, in this period, were the staunchest supporters of the veneration of images. Many of them were forced to flee to outlying regions of the empire where orthodoxy was still maintained, particularly to the Crimea and to south Italy.

The reign of Constantine V was later regarded by the Orthodox as marking the climax of persecution and heresy. The government was not content to proscribe the images and their defenders; prayers to the saints were forbidden, their relics destroyed, and even the cult of the Mother of God was attacked. Most of these excesses, however, ceased after the emperor's death. His successor, Leo IV (775-80), though an Iconoclast by conviction, pursued a moderate policy, partly under the influence of his wife Irene, who was a fervent Iconodule. Persecutions against the monks ceased. And when after Leo's death Irene became Regent on behalf of her young son Constantine VI, the Iconodule party was able to oust its opponents from power. Its victory was not achieved without a show of force. In 786 a church council convened by Irene in Constantinople to restore the cult of images was broken up by soldiers of the imperial guard, faithful to the memory of their idol, Constantine V. Only when these rebellious regiments were replaced by loyal troops transferred to the capital from Thrace was Irene able to secure the triumph of orthodoxy. In 787 a council, consisting of some 350 bishops and presided over by the Byzantine Patriarch Tarasius, assembled in Nicea. It annulled the decisions of the council of 754, declared Iconoclasm to be a heresy, and solemnly restored the cult of images. The crucial definition of this assembly – known henceforth in the east Christian world as the Seventh Ecumenical Council – on the veneration of icons reads as follows:

> We define with all accuracy and care that the venerable and holy icons be set up like the form of the venerable and life-giving Cross, inasmuch as matter consisting of colours and of small stones and of other material is appropriate in the holy church of God, on sacred vessels and on vestments, on walls, on panels, in houses and on roads, as well as the image of our Lord and God and Saviour Jesus Christ, that of our undefiled Lady the Holy Mother of God, those of the angels worthy of honour, and those of all holy and pious men. For the more frequently they are seen by means of painted representation the more those who behold them are aroused to remember and to desire the prototypes and to give them salutation, honour and veneration (ἀσπασμὸν καὶ τιμητικὴν προσκύνησιν), but not the true worship (τὴν ἀληθινὴν λατρείαν) of our faith which befits only the Divine Nature; and to offer them both incense and candles in the same way as to the form of the venerable and life-giving cross and to the holy books of the gospel and to other sacred objects, as was the custom even of the ancients. [8]

Irene's restoration of the veneration of icons did not break the strength of the Iconoclast party. The accession of Leo V in 813 inaugurated a period of thirty years during which Iconoclasm was once again the official doctrine of the empire. In some respects this period marked a return to the religious policy of Leo III and Constantine V: a council held in St Sophia repudiated the Seventh Ecumenical Council, and decreed the destruction of icons (815); in the same year the patriarch Nicephorus, a leading theologian of the Iconodule party, was deposed; and the reigns of Leo V (813-20) and especially of Theophilus (829-42) were marked by perse-

8. C. J. Hefele, *A History of the Councils of the Church*, transl. W. R. Clark, V, 374-5; C. J. Hefele and H. Leclercq, *Histoire des Conciles*, III, 772-3; cf. G. Mathew, *Byzantine Aesthetics*, London 1963, 103-4.

cutions whose principal victims were the Studite monks. Yet this second wave of Iconoclasm seems to have lacked the vigour and assurance which characterised the movement in the previous century. The persecutions were on the whole milder and more intermittent; the council of 815, despite its unconditional condemnation of the images, declined to equate icons with idols; and the intellectual armoury marshalled in this period on both sides of the controversy appears, by comparison with the theological disputes of the eighth century, largely imitative. By the time Michael III ascended the throne (842) the force of Iconoclasm was largely spent; and the final restoration of the veneration of images proclaimed in March 843 by a synod in Constantinople, convened on the initiative of the empress Theodora, began a movement of pacification of which the Byzantine church and society, crippled by the violence and intolerance generated by the Iconoclast controversy, were so sorely in need. This event, still commemorated as ' The Festival of Orthodoxy ' in the Orthodox churches on the first Sunday of Lent, is for the eastern church both an epilogue to the epoch of the Ecumenical Councils and the prelude to the history of the medieval Byzantine church.

3. RESULTS OF THE ICONOCLAST CONTROVERSY

The Iconoclast controversy affected the subsequent history of the eastern church in a variety of ways. Its results were particularly far-reaching in the fields of art, monasticism and church-state relations; and in addition it proved to be a significant landmark in the history of the relations between the churches of Byzantium and Rome.

(a) *Painting, relics and hymnography*

The intimate relationship between images and Christological doctrine, established by the Seventh Ecumenical Council and sanctioned by the Festival of Orthodoxy, led to the adoption of a new pattern of church decoration, characteristic of Byzantine religious art during the next three centuries. The mosaics and wall-paintings with which the interior of the churches were now profusely adorned were executed according to strict theological principles and in close connection with the liturgical function and the architectural framework of the buildings. The biblical symbolism, the eucharistic connotations and the hierarchical arrangement of these decorations combined to produce a symbolic image of the cosmos. From the cupolas and apses, representing heaven and portraying Christ the All-Ruler, his Mother or the Angels, to the lower level of the niches and lunettes on which were painted scenes of Christ's life on earth, and down to the third and lowest plane depicting the figures of saints, the descending hierarchy of heaven and earth bore witness to the central doctrines of the

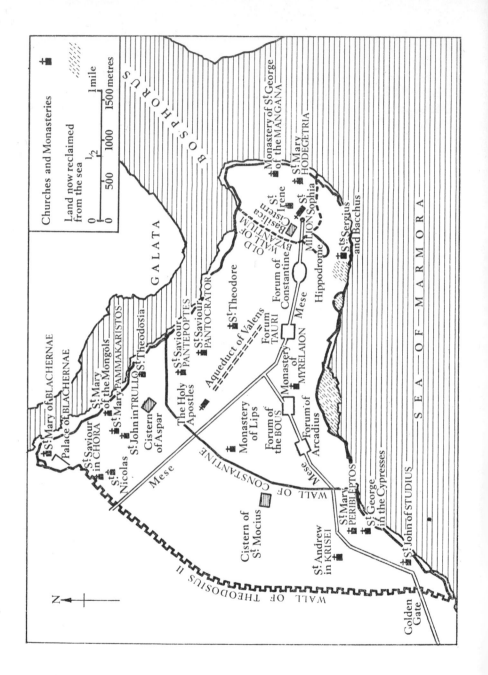

9.   Plan of Constantinople

Christian faith and illustrated the main events of the liturgical year. The medieval Byzantine church had itself become an icon.

The increased popularity of religious art in Byzantium after 843 was not confined to mosaics and frescoes. The veneration of panel paintings and the closely related cult of sacred relics now reached unprecedented heights. The supernatural grace and help which the faithful sought in them were considered to extend, in the case of nationally venerated relics, to the entire body politic. Constantinople especially possessed world-famous relics which, in the belief of the Byzantine folk, ensured supernatural protection to their city and to their empire, such as the body of St Stephen the first martyr, the head of St John the Baptist, and the celebrated image of Christ ' not made by human hands ' (ἀχειροποίητος) supposed to have been given to King Abgar of Edessa, and brought to the city in 944. Above all did Constantinople glory in and, in moments of national danger, rely on the personal patronage of its heavenly protectors, the Divine Wisdom, whose temple was St Sophia, and especially the Mother of God, whose robe, preserved in the church of Blachernae by the city walls, was regarded as the city's Palladium. This aura of sanctity which continued, until the fall of the Byzantine empire, to surround Constantinople, was in the eyes of eastern Christians rivalled only by the glory of Jerusalem. For them Constantinople, ' the eye of the faith of the Christians ', ' the city of the world's desire ', was indeed the New Jerusalem. [9]

The ninth century was also a decisive period in the development of the Byzantine liturgy. The Byzantine rite, which had been evolving since the fifth century, acquired by then all the essential features which it still possesses. A great number of hymns were composed during the Iconoclast period – notably by John of Damascus and Theodore of Studios – which form the basic material of several liturgical books of the Orthodox church: of these the *Triodion* and the *Pentekostarion*, and a new version of the *Oktoechos*, were compiled in the Studios Monastery during the ninth century (the *Oktoechos* after 843). After the defeat of Iconoclasm the monks, the leaders of this liturgical revival, adopted fresh elements from the Jerusalem ritual, and the resultant synthesis between the Palestinian and the Byzantine rites became henceforth the official rite of Constantinople and the empire. The liturgical tradition of Byzantium displays in this period the same tendency towards systematisation and uniformity which we observe in post-Iconoclastic Byzantine church decoration. It was then that east Christian hymnography was fixed and incorpo-

9. Τῆς Χριστιανῶν ὀφθαλμὸν ὑπάρχουσαν πίστεως : L. Sternbach, *Analecta Avarica:* Rozprawy of the Academy of Cracow 15 (1900), 304; Ἡ κοσμοπαμπόθητος αὕτη πόλις: Constantine the Rhodian ' in *Revue des Études Grecques* 9 (1896), 38.

rated in a rich and elaborate liturgical corpus which remains one of the crowning achievements of the medieval Byzantine church.

(b) *Byzantine monasticism*

The defeat of Iconoclasm also led to a powerful revival of monasticism in the Byzantine empire. If in the fourth century the ascetic took the place of the martyr as the supreme embodiment of the ideal of Christian perfection, the two types achieved a temporary fusion during the Iconoclast persecutions, when the monks suffered much in the cause of orthodoxy. It was only natural that after the restoration of the images the prestige and popular appeal of monasticism should increase still further in Byzantine society. Coenobitic monasticism had been reformed, strengthened and minutely regulated by St Theodore (759-826), abbot of the monastery of Studios in Constantinople, which became in this period the leading monastic foundation in the east Christian world. Theodore's regulations, based on the Rules of St Basil, inspired numerous monastic constitutions *(typica)* in the Byzantine empire and in the Orthodox Slav countries. Monasticism was often a mixed blessing for the empire which from 843 onwards accorded it honour and protection: the tendency of so many monasteries to acquire large landed estates – which several emperors tried vainly to check – proved to be an incessant drain on the imperial treasury; the decline of monastic discipline, particularly in the eleventh and twelfth centuries, was the chronic despair of ecclesiastical reformers; and an influential and well organised party consisting largely of monks, first clearly detectable in the Iconoclast period and traceable to the end of Byzantine history, tended to support an ultra-conservative position in the interpretation of canon law, were hostile to secular learning, and opposed all concessions to expediency, even when these involved no compromise in matters of doctrine. By no means all monks belonged to this extremist, ' zealot ' party; but its influence remained powerful in ecclesiastical affairs. Yet viewed as a whole, monasticism played a vital and creative rôle in the Orthodox church of the middle ages: in every generation the monks provided bishops from their midst; contributed to the art, the literature, the hymnography and the liturgical tradition of the Church; gave spiritual advice and moral comfort to laymen of all stations in life, from the emperor downwards; were a living witness to the moral discipline of the Christian life and to the sacramental reality of the Church; and acted as the bearers of a continuous tradition of contemplative prayer which, cherished in the hermitages and monastic communities of the Byzantine world, acquired a fresh theological foundation and a powerful influence on the religious life of eastern Europe in the late middle ages. Nowhere was the vitality of Byzantine monasticism more apparent than on Mount Athos; there, on the southern tip of a secondary peninsula that juts out from the northern seaboard of Greece into the Aegean, and on which hermits had begun to settle as early as the ninth century, the Greek monk Athanasius founded in 963 the monastery of the Great Lavra. St Athanasius's coenobitic foundation, established under the personal patronage of the emperor Nicephorus Phocas, was the first of many monasteries founded on Mount Athos during the middle ages by different nations – Greeks, Georgians, Bulgarians, Russians, Serbs and even Amalfitans. They embodied the three main types of east Christian monastic life, the coenobitic, the eremitical and the intermediate form represented by the *lavra* (a collection of hermit cells grouped round a common teacher), in addition to which the ' idiorrhythmic ' type, which allows the monks much individual freedom, appeared in the late fourteenth century. Throughout the middle ages and down to modern times ' the Holy Mountain ' has been a supra-national centre of the Orthodox world and an incomparable repository and teacher of the spiritual life.

(c) *The Church and the Imperial power*

The fact that the triumphal vindication of monasticism in 843 coincided with the defeat of Iconoclasm has a further significance. The monks, whose calling testifies to their belief that the Kingdom of God is not of this world, were throughout the Iconoclast crisis struggling to assert the autonomy of the spiritual order. They, and no one more than their leader, St Theodore the Studite, strongly opposed the claims of the Iconoclast emperors to possess the right of defining the doctrines of the Church. Neither these claims, nor the opposition to them, were new in Byzantium; both were but exacerbated by the bitterness of the Iconoclast controversy and by the violence it engendered. Even Leo III's claim to be ' emperor and priest ' was not without precedent in Byzantium; and it is noteworthy that the emperor's right to the ' praesidium Ecclesiae ' was recognised by Pope Leo the Great. [10] Although these assertions should not be taken too literally – since no Christian emperor ever claimed the right to administer the sacraments, and imperial definitions of doctrine were conditional upon its prior proclamation by the episcopate – there is no doubt that the east Roman emperors, from Constantine onwards, regarded themselves as vicegerents of God and mouthpieces of the revealed truth. But attempts of the emperors to coerce the episcopate and to arrogate to themselves the right of initiative in defining dogma were, in general, regarded by the Byzantine church as an intolerable abuse. In protesting against the efforts

10. ' Debes incunctanter advertere, regiam potestatem tibi non ad solum mundi regimen, sed maxime ad Ecclesiae praesidium esse collatam ': Mansi 6, col. 325.

of the Iconoclast emperors to impose their will and their beliefs on the church, St Theodore the Studite was but restating the views earlier expressed by St John of Damascus, St Maximus the Confessor and St John Chrysostom.

The doctrinal autonomy of the Byzantine church and the power claimed by its authorities to impose the moral law on the emperor increased considerably after the defeat of Iconoclasm. The relationship between imperial power and ecclesiastical authority in medieval Byzantium is not easy to define with precision, and no brief summary can do justice to its complexity. It would be true to say that after 843 the emperor continued to hold a supreme and sacrosanct position in Byzantine society; that the canons and rules of the church required his sanction before they became effective; that in the last resort he could usually depose a recalcitrant bishop or patriarch; and that the freedom of the Church frequently suffered from the emperor's heavy-handed patronage. But it is no less true that the emperor was explicitly bound to preserve the Orthodox faith by a solemn promise which he made at his coronation; that the canons of the church were drawn up and issued by the ecclesiastical councils; and that later imperial attempts to intervene in doctrinal matters, which were due not to the emperors' desire to enslave the Church but to their wish to enforce compromise solutions with a view to preserving peace and unity within the State or securing military aid from the West, were always in the end defeated by the church's refusal to tamper with the purity of the Orthodox faith. Recent studies of Byzantine society have shown how misleading is the term ' caesaro-papism ', by which earlier scholars sought to describe the alleged enslavement of the Church by the emperors. Its inadequacy can be judged in the light of three essential facts: firstly, despite the interpenetration of the spiritual and temporal spheres in Byzantium, there existed in the mind of the church an unbridgeable gulf between the political prerogatives of the state and the sanctifying and saving function of the church; secondly, the emperor's sovereignty was limited both intrinsically, by its subordination to divine law, orthodox doctrine and the duties of ' philanthropy ' imposed upon him by the nature of his office, and extrinsically, by the spiritual authority of the bishop and the moral authority of the ascetic holy man; and thirdly, although the Hellenistic notion of the emperor as ' the living law ' and of his sovereignty as the earthly image, the icon, of God's monarchy in heaven was always accepted in Byzantium, in practice the relations between church and state underwent a significant development, from the weighty intervention of the early emperors in ecclesiastical affairs, through the bitter struggles of the Iconoclast period, to the ninth century settlement that followed the restoration of the cult of images in 843. This settlement is epitomised in the statement of the *Epanagoge*, the law-book compiled about 880 in the reign of the emperor Basil I:

As the Commonwealth (πολιτεία) consists of parts and members, by analogy with an individual man, the greatest and most necessary parts are the emperor and the patriarch. Wherefore agreement in all things and harmony (συμφωνία) between the Imperium and the Sacerdotium bring peace and prosperity to the souls and the bodies of the subjects. [11]

This doctrine of the ' symphonic ' relationship between Church and state was no revolutionary innovation: indeed this passage of the *Epanagoge* has a close parallel in the introduction to the Sixth Novel of the emperor Justinian, published more than three centuries earlier. But, as an expression of the Byzantine mind, this formula approximates more closely to the facts of the post-Iconoclast age than to the reality of the sixth century. This shift of emphasis in the relationship between the spiritual and the temporal spheres which resulted from the defeat of Iconoclasm is reflected in the imperial art of Byzantium: the imperial portraits, which before the ninth century illustrated above all the triumphal and victorious aspects of the emperor's sovereignty, after 843 show him mainly paying homage to or being invested by Christ. In emphasising the emperor's piety, rather than his secular triumphs, the art of medieval Byzantium faithfully mirrored the ascendancy acquired by the church over the different facets of Byzantine culture.

(d) *Byzantium and Rome in the eighth century*

Finally, the Iconoclastic controversy contributed to the further estrangement between the churches of Byzantium and Rome. The papacy, during this controversy, consistently supported the veneration of icons and denounced the heretical views of the Byzantine emperors, who were still nominally their sovereigns. The Iconodule party and especially the Studite monks looked to Rome as the guardian of orthodoxy. It was only to be expected that the Iconoclast emperors would pursue a policy hostile to the Roman see. About 732 Leo III detached from the pope's jurisdiction the provinces of Calabria, Sicily and Illyricum (the latter comprising virtually the entire Balkan peninsula, with the exception of Thrace) and subordinated them to the patriarchate of Constantinople. The animosity against Byzantium which this action provoked in Rome, and especially the weakness of the Byzantine military position in Italy, so strikingly demonstrated when the exarchate of Ravenna fell to the Lombards (751), threw the papacy into the arms of the Franks. The resultant alliance

11. *Epanagoge*, tit. iii, cap. 8, ed. Zachariae von Lingenthal, *Collectio librorum juris graeco-romani ineditorum*, Leipzig 1852, 68.

between Pope Stephen II and King Pippin in 754, which foreshadowed
the coronation of Charlemagne as emperor (800), meant that the papacy
had turned its back on the Byzantine empire.

And yet, despite the rivalries of jurisdiction, the political animosity and
the bitter memories of Iconoclasm, the Byzantine and the Roman churches
still remained, in many respects, closely interwoven parts of a single
organism, and no one yet doubted, in the East or in the West, that Christendom was one body. The complexity of the relations between the two
churches–antagonistic in one sense, but marked by an intimate mutual
involvement on the other–are strikingly evident in the disputes which,
between 858 and 880, were associated with the name of the patriarch
Photius.

4. THE PHOTIAN DISPUTE

The Iconoclast controversy left an aftermath of bitterness in the Byzantine
church which, despite the settlement of 843, was not healed for at least a
generation. The ' intransigent ' and the ' moderate ' parties, whose
opposing views have been noted above, clashed over the attitude to be
adopted towards the former Iconoclast clergy who sought reconciliation
with the church: the former urged that they be treated with uncompromising harshness, the latter, in accordance with the principle of ' economy ', argued that both charity and common sense demanded that their
former lapse be overlooked. The patriarch Ignatius, appointed by the
empress Theodora in 847, was in sympathy with the ' intransigents '. But
following the *coup d'état* of 856, which deprived Theodora of power,
Ignatius was forced to resign, and in 858 Photius was elected patriarch of
Constantinople. At the time of his election he was a layman, a professor
in the University of Constantinople, and the president of the Imperial
Chancellery; he was hurried through the necessary stages of ordination
within a week. A ' moderate ' by conviction, Photius was a distinguished
scholar and, in terms of personal ability, probably the most outstanding
of all Byzantine patriarchs. Shortly after his appointment, he sent a letter
to the pope announcing his accession; simultaneously, the pope was
invited by the emperor Michael III to send legates to Constantinople to
take part in a council, convened to reiterate the condemnation of Iconoclasm, which was still at that time a living danger to the Byzantine church.
On the legates' insistence, however, the council of 861 agreed to discuss
first and foremost the issue between Ignatius and Photius. The council,
with the legates concurring, recognised Photius as the legitimate patriarch.
But Pope Nicholas I, influenced by the tendentious reports of supporters
of Ignatius who had come to Rome, refused to endorse the action of his
legates. A synod of the Roman church declared Photius's election to be

uncanonical, and reinstated Ignatius (863). These decisions were ignored by the Byzantine authorities; considerable resentment was felt in Constantinople at what was regarded as an unjustified interference of the pope in the internal affairs of the Byzantine church; and an open schism thus broke out between the churches of Rome and Constantinople.

Their relations were soon further envenomed by events in Bulgaria. In 865 the Bulgarian ruler Boris was baptised by Byzantine missionaries, who began at once to convert his subjects to Christianity. The next year, however, Boris, hoping for better terms from the western church, asked the pope for an ecclesiastical hierarchy. Part of Bulgaria had belonged to the ecclesiastical province of Illyricum, to whose loss the papacy had never reconciled itself, and Nicholas could not but welcome the opportunity of extending his jurisdiction over Boris's realm. Roman missionaries were promptly dispatched to Bulgaria. The Byzantine response was equally understandable. The southern regions of Bulgaria – northern Thrace – had never belonged to the Roman jurisdiction; the threat of Frankish political influence spreading, in the wake of the western missionaries, almost to the gates of Constantinople seriously alarmed the Byzantine government; and the authorities of the Byzantine church learnt to their dismay that the Roman clergy in Bulgaria was insisting on the addition of the word *Filioque* to the Nicene Creed.

In 867, in an encyclical letter addressed to the eastern patriarchs, Photius denounced the *Filioque* as an heretical doctrine.[12] In the same year a council held in Constantinople and presided over by the emperor excommunicated and deposed Pope Nicholas I. At this moment of extreme crisis another palace revolution in Constantinople suddenly transformed the situation. Michael III was assassinated, and his successor and murderer, Basil I, compelled Photius to resign and reinstated Ignatius as patriarch (867). Communion with Rome was restored. In 869-70 a council, held in Constantinople, excommunicated Photius. But the legates of Pope Hadrian II, who attended this council, faced with the growing strength of the Photian party, were powerless to prevent the return of Bulgaria into the fold of the Byzantine church, a new *volte-face* skilfully engineered by Boris. The final act of this long-drawn out drama ended in general reconciliation. In 877 Ignatius died, and Photius reascended the patriarchal throne. Both sides now showed a spirit of moderation. Pope John VIII, who considered that the primacy of the Roman see had been vindicated, was willing to recognise Photius; and the latter, while refusing to apologise for what were regarded in Rome as his past misdeeds, showed due defer-

12. PG CII, col. 721-41.

ence to the Holy See, and a willingness not to press Byzantine ecclesiastical claims on Bulgaria. In 879-80 a new council, attended by papal legates, was held in Constantinople. It recognised Photius as the legitimate patriarch, annulled the former condemnatiòns issued against him, abrogated the decisions of the council of 869-70, and with pointed though not intemperate reference to the *Filioque*, condemned any addition to the Nicene Creed. These decisions were accepted in Rome; Photius remained during his second tenure of office (877-86) in full communion with the papacy; and peace was restored to Christendom. Photius, dismissed once again from office by the emperor Leo VI, retired into obscurity, though still an active polemical theologian, and died at an unknown date.

The reciprocal ignorance, the outbursts of mutual intolerance, and the conflict of jurisdictions that marked much of the Photian dispute were bound up with two issues of crucial importance which henceforth came to dominate the discussions between the Roman and the Byzantine churches: the papal primacy and the *Filioque*. These must now be briefly examined.

5. BYZANTIUM AND THE ROMAN PRIMACY

The historical importance of the Photian dispute lies mainly in the fact that it marked the first open clash between the Roman conception of the primacy of the see of Peter, as defined by Leo the Great and Gelasius, and now pressed with new vigour by Nicholas I, and the view held by the eastern church of the nature of ecclesiastical authority and government. The eastern church recognised that the Roman see had primacy over all other churches, and that the pope was the first bishop in Christendom. This primacy of Rome was from the fourth century onwards explicitly acknowledged by most Byzantine churchmen. The nature of this primacy – which the Byzantines ascribed less to the apostolic origin of the Roman see than to its location in the former capital of the Roman empire and to its virtually unblemished record of doctrinal orthodoxy – was never defined by them very precisely. It was rather more than a mere primacy of honour and at least on some occasions implied their recognition of the right of any cleric, condemned by his own ecclesiastical authorities, to appeal to Rome in accordance with Canons 3, 4 and 5 of the Council of Sardica (c. 343). But the Byzantines never accepted – nor did the Council of Sardica sanction – the privilege, claimed by Nicholas I, of summoning any cleric to his court or re-trying in Rome cases affecting the vital interests of their own church. They rejected, both then and later, the Roman view of primacy which gave the pope supreme power throughout the Christian Church. And they bitterly resented the attempts of Nicholas I to lay down the law in the dispute between Photius and Ignatius, which they regarded as an uncanonical interference of the head of one patriarchate in the internal affairs of another. This has always been the traditional attitude of the Orthodox church towards the bishop of Rome: it was given eloquent expression in 1136 in these words of Nicetas, archbishop of Nicomedia, addressed to a bishop of the western church:

> My dearest brother,... we do not deny to the Roman church the primacy amongst the sister [patriarchates]; and we recognise her right to the most honourable seat at an Ecumenical Council. But she has separated herself from us through her pride when she usurped a monarchy which does not belong to her office.... How shall we accept from her decrees that have been issued without consulting us and even without our knowledge? If the Roman pontiff, seated on the lofty throne of his glory, wishes to thunder at us, and, so to speak, hurl his mandates at us from on high, and if he wishes to judge us and even to rule us and our churches, not by taking counsel with us but at his own arbitrary pleasure, what kind of brotherhood, or even what kind of parenthood can this be?... We should be the slaves, not the sons, of such a church, and the Roman see would be not the pious mother of sons but a hard and imperious mistress of slaves... I ask your pardon when I say this about the Roman church, for I venerate her along with you. But I cannot follow her along with you through everything; nor do I think that she should necessarily be followed through everything. [13]

This attitude was characteristic of the articulate and fair-minded section of the Byzantine church at a time when the divisions between East and West had not yet hardened into a definitive schism: recognition of the papal primacy was combined with the conviction that a monarchical government of the universal Church was contrary both to the canons and to tradition; respect for the Roman see and its occupant was combined with the belief that the doctrinal infallibility of the Church was expressed not through the mouth of a single bishop, no matter how exalted his office, but by the entire Church, represented by its bishops gathered in an Ecumenical Council. The belief in the fundamental equality of all bishops rested on the doctrine, so clearly expressed by Ignatius of Antioch, that the Church is fully manifest wherever the bishop, who represents the eternal priesthood of Christ, celebrates the Eucharist in the presence of the faithful.

And yet, though the Byzantines were convinced that both canon law and the patristic tradition justified their rejection of the claims of the bishops of Rome to exercise direct jurisdiction over the eastern churches, they were on less firm ground when they attempted to define the nature of the papal primacy and the relationship of the eastern churches to the Roman see. The Byzantine response to the Roman claims was often hesitant, sometimes inconsistent, and – in contrast to the clarity and

13. *Anselmi Havelbergensis episcopi dialogi*, lib. iii, cap. 8, PL CLXXXVIII, col. 1219-20; cited in S. Runciman, *The Eastern Schism*, Oxford 1955, 116.

consistency of the Roman doctrine – lacked the basis of a fully developed ecclesiology. This lack of clarity shown by Byzantine churchmen in defending their position against papal claims may be due partly to their emphasis on the sacramental reality rather than on the juridical structure of the Church, and partly to the close interrelation which existed in Byzantium between the concept of spiritual authority and the idea of empire, in the light of which the papal claims appeared to many Byzantines to be more a political than an ecclesiological problem. It seems, indeed, that the true nature of the papal claims was not, at least until the thirteenth century, fully understood by the Byzantines, who tended to ascribe them to the popes' desire to extend their personal power. They attempted to counter the Roman claims to ecclesiastical supremacy by the theory of the Pentarchy, already existent in the sixth century, developed in the ninth and fully formulated in the eleventh, according to which the government of the Church is jointly vested in the five patriarchs – those of Rome, Constantinople, Alexandria, Antioch and Jerusalem. But this theory was tinged with the same confusion of primacy with power which the Byzantine theologians imputed to Rome, and proved difficult to reconcile with the emergence of the Slavonic autocephalous churches in the late middle ages.

6. THE FILIOQUE

If the Byzantine response to the ecclesiological implications of the papal claims was neither fully clear nor wholly consistent, the reaction of the eastern church to the second basic doctrinal issue of the Photian dispute – the *Filioque* – was unequivocal and theologically coherent. The addition of the word *Filioque* to the Nicene Creed, an addition which expresses the doctrine that the Holy Spirit proceeds not from the Father alone, but from the Father and the Son, seems to have first been made by the Spanish church in the sixth century, as a safeguard against the Arianism of the Visigoths. From Spain the addition spread to France and Germany, and was eagerly adopted by Charlemagne, who used it as a weapon against the Greeks whom he accused of heresy. In Rome, however, the *Filioque* was not accepted until the early eleventh century, the popes holding that, although the addition was theologically justified, it was not desirable to tamper with the version of the creed that had been accepted by the whole of Christendom. But the use of the disputed term by the Roman missionaries in Bulgaria touched off a controversy which became the basic theological issue between Greek and Latin Christendom throughout the middle ages, and which still divides the Orthodox and the Roman Catholic churches.

The Byzantine church objected to the *Filioque* on two grounds. In the first place, any alteration to the creed had been expressly forbidden by the

Ecumenical Councils; and nothing short of another such council was competent to rescind this prohibition. Secondly, the *Filioque* was, in its view, theologically untrue. In his *Mystagogy of the Holy Spirit*, Photius argued that this doctrine upsets the delicate and mysterious balance between unity and diversity within the Trinity.[14] This complex and technical controversy cannot be adequately summarised here. But it may be suggested that in attempting to express the Trinitarian mystery in theological terms, the Latins and the Greeks often started from different points of view: the Latins emphasised above all the single essence (οὐσία, *substantia*) as the principle of unity within the Trinity, in the light of which they regarded the relations between the Three Persons; while the Greeks preferred to start from the distinction between the Three Persons *(hypostases)*, and to proceed from there to consider their unity of essence. Both points of view, in the opinion of eastern theologians, are legitimate, provided that the mysterious equivalence between the common essence and the distinct *hypostases* is not overlooked by an attempt to overemphasise the one at the expense of the other. In the Greek view the doctrine of the *Filioque*, by stating that the Holy Spirit proceeds from the Son as well as from the Father, was an unjustified inference from the dogma of the consubstantiality of the Father and the Son, weakened the monarchy of the Father, tended to sacrifice the distinction between the *hypostases* to the divine simplicity of the common essence, and implied a theology in which the mystical reality of the Triune God is to some extent obscured by a philosophy of essence.

7. THE BREACH OF 1054

The problem of the *Filioque* figured, though less prominently than in the ninth century, in the dispute between the Roman and the Byzantine churches which led to the dramatic breach of 1054. The causes of this breach, which has been inappropriately dignified with the name of ' the Great Schism ', were many and complex; and the historian of today, whatever his personal views on the doctrinal issues involved in the controversy, cannot but subscribe to the judgment of Pope John XXIII that responsibility for the breach in Christendom was divided. Among the immediate causes of the mid-eleventh century crisis were in the first place the attempts of the papacy to enforce uniformity of liturgical usage in the Greek churches of south Italy which the Normans were gradually wresting from the Byzantine empire, and the contemporary measures of the Byzantine patriarchate to impose conformity to Greek usages on Latin churches in Constantinople; and secondly the mounting antagonism

14. PG CII, col. 280-392.

between the universalist claims of the reformed papacy and the equally strong desire of the Byzantine church, more conscious than ever of its prestige as the partner of the most powerful and civilised state in Christendom, to preserve its traditional autonomy. The document composed by Leo of Ohrid, head of the Bulgarian church, doubtless at the instigation of Michael Cerularius, patriarch of Constantinople, and full of intemperate abuse against Latin practices – notably against the use of *azymes*, or unleavened bread, in the Eucharist – was followed by the dispatch of an embassy from Pope Leo IX to Constantinople, headed by Cardinal Humbert (1054). The latter's histrionic postures, abusive language and truculent behaviour were almost matched by the intransigence and self-righteous arrogance of the patriarch of Byzantium. The scene that took place in Constantinople on 16 July 1054, when Humbert and his fellow legates laid a bull of excommunication against Cerularius and his chief supporters upon the altar of the church of St Sophia, has acquired a melancholy and perhaps excessive notoriety; it was followed by the burning of the bull by order of the emperor Constantine IX, and the solemn excommunication of Humbert and his associates by a synod in Constantinople.

8

ROME AND CONSTANTINOPLE (I)

I n the first volume of this History the most significant theme after the conversion of Constantine was the gradual unfolding of Christian doctrine under the pressure of attack from heterodox teachers, an Arius, a Sabellius, a Nestorius, and a Pelagius who, whatever their intentions, did in fact hold views, or use expressions, which were not according to the apostolic tradition of the faith. In the first part of the present volume this theme shifts to one of church government and Christian unity: the development of papal government and the rift between the eastern and western churches. These themes, so pregnant in their consequences for both East and West, which were to give to each of these great divisions of Christendom characteristics and attitudes of mind which might never have been theirs had events fallen out differently. In part connected with the theological theme of earlier centuries, they were also a direct outcome of new political and social tensions and growths.

In the early years of the seventh century the able and energetic emperor Heraclius (610-41) devoted much of his care towards restoring the unity of the East, long broken by the Monophysite schism which had created the Jacobite church and had captured Egypt, Syria and Mesopotamia, flourishing in particular under the brief Persian occupation. He was assisted by the patriarch of Constantinople Sergius, himself by origin Syrian and

Jacobite, who had adopted a formula which seemed capable of uniting the Jacobites with the other churches. This was the assertion that the person of Christ had only a single principle of activity (the so-called doctrine of ' mono-energy ') despite the existence of two natures, the divine and human, as defined by the council of Chalcedon (451). Heraclius accepted this formula, and used it as a means of conciliating the Monophysites both before and after his victory over the Persians, and a union was in fact effected between Constantinople and Armenia, Egypt and other regional bodies previously separated. Nevertheless, the formula was strongly opposed by Sophronius, patriarch of Jerusalem, and the theologian Maximus, later known as the Confessor, on the grounds that it did in fact impair the doctrine of the two complete and separate natures in Christ. Heraclius therefore solicited the approval of Pope Honorius for the statement that the Word made man had only a single principle of activity. The reply of Honorius provided matter for controversy both then and thereafter, but there is now a measure of agreement that he failed to recognise the theological significance of the proposal of Sergius. Thinking to eliminate over-subtle terminology, and anxious to avoid any appearance of disunity within the personality of Christ, he endorsed the position of Sergius, which he did not fully comprehend, and stated that there was no conflict of will in Christ. Meanwhile Sophronius had clearly enunciated the doctrine of two wills in Christ, the human and the divine; Sergius had protested, and (638) changed his term ' single energy ' to ' single will ', holding this to be the correct interpretation of the Council of Chalcedon, whereupon the emperor Heraclius, in a decree which became known as the Ecthesis (or exposition) imposed it upon the church. Honorius died, and two years later Pope John IV, at a synod held in Rome, condemned the doctrine of the single will in Christ, now known as the Monothelite heresy. Shortly after, the Arab conquest of Egypt and Armenia weakened the Monophysite party and shifted the centre of gravity of Christendom westwards and northwards.

Controversy nevertheless continued between successive popes and emperors and ultimately the patriarch Paul of Constantinople was excommunicated by Pope Theodore (647), while the emperor Constans II in a proclamation known as the Typos (or rule) of 648 abolished the Ecthesis but reiterated an earlier prohibition of all discussion on the unity of wills or energies in Christ. Ignoring this, Pope Martin I in 649 summoned a synod at the Lateran at which the two wills of Christ were asserted and proclaimed in an augmented version of the creed of Chalcedon, while the Ecthesis and the Typos were condemned, and Sergius and his successors anathematised. This decision was accepted throughout the West, and in those parts of the East that were no longer controlled by the emperor. The latter retorted by seizing the person of the pope and bringing him to trial at Constantinople. The charge was one of treason, for failure to obtain ratification of his election from the emperor and for alleged conspiracy against the emperor in Rome, but in reality the crime was that of opposing the emperor's will. Martin was treated with extreme brutality, and died in exile in the Crimea. Maximus the Confessor, arrested in Rome at the same time, was exiled, tortured and mutilated.

The pressing danger of Arab aggression and the general disgust at the treatment of Maximus and others brought about a reconciliation between Rome under Pope Vitalian and Constantinople, and the advance of the Arabs and the siege of Constantinople (674-8) postponed further action till 680, when the emperor Constantine IV convoked a council attended by papal legates. At this, the Sixth Ecumenical Council, the creeds of the previous councils were reaffirmed and the doctrine of two wills in Christ proclaimed, with the anathematisation of the erring patriarchs of Constantinople, Alexandria and Antioch, with whom the name of Pope Honorius was associated. Pope Leo II accepted the acts of this council and transmitted them to the West.

The peace thus re-established did not, however, last for long. The young and unbalanced emperor Justinian II, desiring to emulate his great namesake, called a council in 692 to promulgate disciplinary and legal reforms; known as the Quinisext (the ' Fifth-Sixth ') it was intended to supplement the two previous councils. While admirable in its measures of reform at home the council, under the guidance of the emperor, showed a studied lack of deference to Rome. Papal decrees were ignored or criticised and disciplinary and liturgical legislation, adapted to the customs of the Byzantine church (e.g. in the marriage of clerics), was decreed for the whole of Christendom. Finally, an article proclaimed absolute parity between the sees of Rome and Constantinople. When Pope Sergius refused to sign the decrees an attempt was made to arrest him, but he was defended by the troops of Ravenna against the emissaries of the emperor. Nevertheless, peace was once more restored, and in 710 Pope Constantine II journeyed to Constantinople where he was received with honour and agreement was reached between East and West at a conference with the emperor, Justinian II.

Thus during the century that had passed since the death of Gregory the Great no great external change, no irreparable cleavage, had occurred in the relations between Rome and Constantinople. In part this was no doubt due to the short pontificates and mediocre personalities of many of the popes, as also to the Greek and Syrian nationality of several of their number and of their counsellors; in part also to the misfortunes of the empire during this century, which made a breach with Rome politically and diplomatically undesirable for Constantinople. Nevertheless relations had been stretched to breaking-point and memories had become embittered. While on the one hand the disasters that had overtaken the East and the permanent loss of Egypt, Syria and Armenia had reversed the balance of numbers and power as between the eastern and western churches, and had greatly reduced the extent of the authority of the Byzantine emperor, the new state of things had accentuated national pride in Constantinople and had made it more easy for an emperor, however unbalanced or insecure, to control the patriarch and the church with its rites and beliefs. At Rome on the other hand, relations with the emperor had become permanently embittered by memories of the shocking treatment meted out to Martin I and the attempt to kidnap Sergius I. Though the influx of Greek and Syrian refugees from the Balkans occupied by the Slavs and from the regions conquered by the Arabs had kept Rome in close touch with eastern sentiment, the political situation of Italy and the loose attachment of Ravenna to the empire were tending to a separation of interests and loyalties. The Monothelite controversy, into which the popes had been drawn unwillingly and in which they had shown to little advantage at first, while later standing firmly for the traditional faith, only to suffer indignities and punishments and danger to life and limb, had created a deep feeling of distrust and repulsion in curial circles. Nevertheless, traditional loyalty towards the emperor and memories of past association had been strong enough to restore, at least to all appearances, the old relations between Rome and Constantinople.

The amity thus painfully restored had endured for less than twenty years when it was again ruptured by a religious issue of eastern origin. This was the disastrous controversy over the devotional use of images, known as the régime of the image-breakers (Iconoclasts).

The issue was raised of set purpose by the emperor Leo III the Isaurian, who had recently deserved well of the whole of Christendom by resolutely fighting off the determined attacks of the Arab besiegers of Constantinople (717-18), thus saving ' the sum of things ' for the church and western civilisation and preserving the great centre of Byzantine government and culture for another seven centuries of life. Eight years later, after long and skilful propaganda, and after having forced the resignation of the patriarch and brushed aside the strong resistance of Pope Gregory II, the emperor forbade the cult of images throughout his dominions and commanded their wholesale destruction. Pope Gregory III, speaking for all Italy as well as for the church of Rome, protested vehemently, whereupon the emperor increased the rates of taxation in south Italy, confiscated the papal estates in Calabria and Sicily, and (c. 732) cut off from Rome and attached to Constantinople the whole of Greece and the Balkan peninsula

(Epirus, Illyria and Macedonia) together with Sicily and south Italy.

Leo's son and successor Constantine V, who for a time was too occupied with domestic revolts to devote his energies to controversy, restored friendly diplomatic relations with the papacy, but in 754 he summoned and held near Chalcedon a council, consisting solely of bishops of imperial territories. Completely orthodox save in one important respect, it condemned the manufacture, possession and veneration of images whether in public or private, fixing severe spiritual sanctions, while at the same time forbidding (as the event showed, in vain) all violent or unauthorised destruction. The emperor followed this up by an edict decreeing the punishment as heretics of any offenders, and the next twenty years saw fierce, if spasmodic and intermittent, persecution, particularly of monks, throughout the eastern empire until the death of Constantine in 775. Under his son and successor Leo IV, and still more under the latter's widow, Irene, there was a move towards pacification and after consultation with Pope Hadrian I and some difficult manoeuvres, a council, the Seventh Ecumenical, was held at Nicea in 787 where with considerable expedition the traditional teaching was proclaimed as to the reverence due to images, and the distinction between the worship (τιμητικὴ προσκύνησις) due to them and the adoration (λατρεία) given to God alone. Satisfactory as this was for Roman theologians, any overt acceptance of the council was hindered by a curious episode at the court of Charlemagne.

Thither the acts of Nicea had been despatched in an extremely faulty and misleading translation which on some important points gave a sense directly contrary to that intended by the Greek. Charlemagne, in consequence, convinced that the council of 787 had swung far back across the line of orthodoxy in reaction to the canons of 754, proceeded with the aid of his theological advisers, and in particular of Alcuin and Theodulf, to traverse the whole field of supposed eastern error in a great capitulary concerning images, better known as the *Libri Carolini*. It was the very moment when diplomatic relations between the eastern and western courts had been compromised by the failure of negotiations for a marriage alliance between the young emperor Constantine VI and a daughter of Charlemagne, and the latter's move against the Greeks was undoubtedly intended as a manifesto of western authority and orthodoxy. The despatch of the *Libri Carolini* was followed up by a council at Frankfurt in 794 at which the recent council of Nicea was reprobated. Pope Hadrian I refused to ratify this decision, but nevertheless hesitated to welcome and accept the Nicean decision, and the eastern church was soon thrown back into confusion by a new turn of power.

Meanwhile another cloud had appeared on the horizon that was ultimately to prove far more pregnant with fatality: this was the first serious development of the *Filioque* controversy. An account of this has been given elsewhere;[1] it is enough to remark here that the moderation and good sense of Popes Hadrian I and Leo III prevented a breach for the time. So the matter rested for sixty years.

The peace in the matter of images imposed by the empress Irene and the Council of Nicea in 787 did not long endure. The emperor Leo V, who seized power after the catastrophe to Byzantine arms in battle with the Bulgarians at Adrianople (813), lost no time in reopening the campaign of Iconoclasm, and the persecutions were now directed partly against the monks, who drew inspiration from the celebrated Theodore the Studite. A return to peace and orthodoxy did not take place till 843, an occasion which has been given permanent commemoration as the festival of orthodoxy, the triumph of the true faith of the seven councils, now recognised as whole and entire. On that date a new epoch opened in the eastern church, an epoch of stability and of apostolic expansion on a scale hitherto undreamed of at Constantinople, which was to give Byzantine Christianity a solidity and a self-confidence that had been lacking ever since the emergence of the Muslim armies. For the present, however, the conversion of the Slavs lay in the womb of time, and the attention of both Greeks and Latins was again diverted by a sour and vexatious controversy, occasioned by the appointment of Photius as patriarch of Constantinople in 858.

The complicated series of events that ensued has been related in outline elsewhere.[2] This is a field in which recent scholarship, and in particular that of F. Dvornik, has thrown much light and in particular has made of Photius, whom the Orthodox church has always regarded as a saint and a principal theologian, a less sinister figure than before in western eyes. Nevertheless, the thirty years in which he and his cause dominated the course of events in Constantinople were a true watershed in the history of relations between East and West. Within that span of time both at Rome and at Constantinople men of genius, working upon earlier tradition, gave to it, if not a new formulation, at least a new sharpness of outline and a new actuality, and this novel presentation was in due course stereotyped on both sides for the ages to come. While Photius was led by the demands of his position to study and to rebut the claims of Rome to a primacy of jurisdiction and to a unique magisterium of doctrine, and sought out and expounded all that the tradition of the eastern church and its ancient saints and doctors knew of a theology of the Holy Trinity that excluded the Procession of the Holy Spirit from both Father and Son, Nicholas I, led on by political events, encouraged by eastern divisions

1. See pp. 99-100; 133-4.
2. See pp. 98-100.

misinformed by an enemy of Photius, and supported, perhaps even overborne, by his singularly able 'secretary of state', the Librarian Anastasius, proposed and applied in the fullest manner possible the papal claims to supremacy of jurisdiction, and presented the Roman church as the epitome and mother of all Christendom. In this clear doctrinal confrontation the political and theological acumen of Photius and the success of his Bulgarian aims on the one hand, and the drastic, overbearing attitude of Nicholas I on the other, added a rivalry and a bitterness to the relations between the churches at the only level on which they had contact with each other. If in Constantinople the intrigues and deeds of violence in the palace are shocking, at Rome the dubious, if not sinister, repute of Anastasius the Librarian and his relatives is far from reassuring when he is seen to be associated with the policy, if not dictating the words, of the pope. The acts and writings of both parties in those fateful years erected a barrier between the churches which still remains an obstacle in the way of mutual understanding.

The patriarchate of Photius, his personality and his writings left a permanent mark upon the political and theological thought of the church of Constantinople. There was, however, no break in the relations between East and West, though in the decades that followed the brief pontificates and, later, the moral eclipse of the papacy made intercourse between the parties, as well as our information as to its extent, extremely scanty. An incident of trifling importance occurred at the end of the century (899-923) which led both to a renewal of intercourse and to a fresh embitterment. This was the fourth marriage of the emperor Leo VI. According to Byzantine canon law second and (later) third marriages were undesirable but valid, whereas a fourth was not legally recognised. Leo VI presented his patriarch, the distinguished Nicholas Mysticus, with a *fait accompli*, which he proposed to confirm by an appeal to the four other patriarchs, of whom one was the pope. Sergius III in reply to the appeal put forward the traditional western teaching which set no limit to the number of successive marriages that could be reckoned as valid, and Nicholas was promptly dismissed. Returning to office under the next emperor he broke for a time with Rome, but relations were at last resumed. Nevertheless, the episode had helped both to underline the differences between East and West and to confirm the patriarchs in their desire for independence of action and decision. During the century that followed little is known of the relations between Rome and Constantinople. In both places there was a succession of brief and undistinguished, not to mention also irregular and violent, pontificates. There was a later tradition in the East that relations were again broken off *c.* 1000, but this cannot be supported by clear documentary evidence.

Meanwhile a great change had been taking place in the fortunes both of the eastern empire and of the papacy. At Constantinople a series of distinguished military emperors had reconquered Asia Minor, part of Syria, Bulgaria and part of south Italy. Something of a national or imperial sentiment and pride sprang up. The patriarch of Constantinople could now see himself as the head of a church including Bulgaria and Russia, and the Italian conquests brought about a new political rivalry with the West. Meanwhile the papacy, at first under German tutelage, but later with independence regained, was defining ever more fiercely its traditional claim to supremacy. While the East, confident in its revived power and in the cultural and largely lay element in its revival, regarded the West as rude and barbarous, the papacy, now possessed of self-confidence and a supply of energetic supporters and publicists, regarded the East as decadent and heretical. It is only by realising the great change in the mentality of both parties, and the strong ideological influences at work on both sides to stimulate the newly acquired strength of each, that we can understand the sudden and fatal *dénouement* of the mid-eleventh century. The patriarch Michael Cerularius (1043-58) was an ambitious and forceful character, eager to assert the autonomy of his see and the inferiority of the Latins. Despite the political developments caused by the Norman conquests in south Italy, which drew pope and emperor together and favoured an alliance, Cerularius showed indulgence to violent and sacrilegious attacks on the Latin churches and ' reservations ' in Constantinople and caused a manifesto to be published denouncing the ritual of the Latins as rendering reunion impossible. Unfortunately, the task of answering these charges was entrusted to the extreme, impulsive, injudicious Cardinal Humbert of Moyenmoutier, who fulfilled his commission by rehearsing the Roman claims in their fullest extent.

Nevertheless, political considerations brought about a *détente*, for each party hoped for the other's help against the Normans, and Humbert in an evil hour was chosen to lead a papal delegation to arrange a union between the churches. When he arrived at the capital the skilful diplomacy of the hostile patriarch, who had no wish for an understanding, and the unperceptive rigidity of the cardinal brought about the end that Cerularius desired. While the two parties sparred with words, and Humbert wrote a vehement polemic, the death of the pope deprived the legate of his moral, if not also of his canonical powers as negotiator, and Humbert, realising that a breakdown in the negotiations was imminent, hastened to excommunicate the patriarch in St Sophia before sweeping out of the city. The emperor tried in vain to recall the parties to a conference; Cerularius summoned a synod which condemned the conduct of the papal legates and followed this up with a long manifesto traversing the whole history of the differences between the churches and presenting himself as the head of the Byzantine church in its totality. Cerularius indeed was disgraced and died shortly after, but both the city populace and the governing classes (though by no means all bishops and monks) were in full sympathy with his aims. On the Latin side the reformers, now sweeping forward with their ideological programme, gave little thought or care to what had happened. The break of 1054 was not indeed absolutely and technically final. The relations between Latins and Greeks remained neighbourly in many places. Nevertheless, the events of 1054 can be seen in retrospect as a point of no return, and if, in the long and melancholy history of the breach between the churches, the deeds of individuals were of significance, a heavy weight of responsibility must lie upon Cerularius and Humbert. In the story of western Christianity 1054 is a date comparable to 1517, even if the principal actors were unaware of the significance of the events, and were more concerned with church discipline or contemporary diplomacy than with the unity of Christendom.

The historian, looking backwards over the four and a half centuries since the death of Gregory the Great, may be allowed a moment's reflection on the whole issue. In the first place, the great differences in institutions, in outlook, in habits of mind, and in political fortune between Greek and Latin Christianity were from early days very real, and have been duly emphasised in an earlier volume of this History. It should not be regarded as axiomatic that these differences of themselves would have led inevitably to a schism. Other regional differences, as for example, those between Celtic Christianity and continental Europe, or those between long-existing uniate Greeks and other rites and the Roman church, have in fact either disappeared or endured without breaking unity. Certainly Christians themselves should be slow to admit the inevitability of centrifugal forces within the mystical body of Christ. Wherein, then, shall we find the seeds of division in this case? Primarily, it may be, in the intrusion from the days of Constantine the Great of the imperial power, regarded as having a divine commission of tutelage, as an influence and an authority within the life of the church, accompanied as it was by the shift of the centre of gravity in government and administration from Rome to the East and by the subsequent decline of the economic and cultural significance of the West. For a long and critical period in the development of the corporate life of the church her destinies were in consequence linked with, and in a sense controlled by, an emperor to whom all owed loyalty, to whom many looked for advancement, and with whom lay the initiative in all matters affecting the external action of the church as a whole in such matters as councils and legislation. There was in consequence no possibility for the scattered churches, or for the patriarchs when they came to be recognised as leaders, or for the common sentiment of Christians, or even for papal Rome, to make any practical move towards establishing an independent common centre of unity or method of government. At the same time it was all but inevitable that the bishop of the capital of the empire should come to occupy a position of great importance, and that the emperor should find it in his interest both to exploit and to control the office and its holder. When in the course of time western loyalty to the empire waned and disappeared, and a new link was forged with a new empire which in time threatened to engross the papacy, if not the western church, almost as thoroughly, though not so permanently, as the old empire of the east, the external tensions making for schism were so strong as to be humanly speaking irresistible. The Greeks could not but feel that Rome had chosen to be alien. These forces of division were aided by the conquests of Islam, which eliminated the balancing weight of the other eastern patriarchs, and by the subsequent conquests of the Macedonian emperors which made the church of the capital fully metropolitan, and opened a new vista of missionary enterprise. It is true that, regarding things solely on the level of history, the tradition of Christian unity was strong, and the tradition of the primacy of some kind of the apostolic see of Peter was primitive and widespread. Events, however, were to show that human weakness and unwisdom were too strong for higher considerations of the common good to prevail. In the closed world of the ninth or eleventh century – closed to the minds of the age, whatever might be the movements of Muslim, Hungarian or Northman – when all thought was Christian and when intercourse between East and West was rare and very slow, legal distinctions, ritual differences, and alleged heretical opinions seemed far more dangerous and abominable than the bitterness and hostility aroused by acts of violence, mutual excommunications and extravagant manifestoes. No doubt the errors and faults of individuals and groups were many and grave. The irresponsible and brutal acts of power on the part of emperors, with regard both to Rome and their own hierarchy, the accidental but serious shock of the Iconoclast campaign, the weakness and debasement of the papacy, the factions of Rome and Italy, the intolerant, unspiritual jousting of Anastasius the Librarian or Humbert of Moyenmoutier, the almost complete lack of wide and charitable vision on the part of both popes and patriarchs of Constantinople after the pontificate of Gregory I – all these had their share in making the calamity fatal. It was perhaps inevitable, but it was none the less regrettable, that the whole long controversy (save for a few moments of violence) was conducted at a high diplomatic, not to say political level, and often by correspondence that was outdated by events long before it was received, and that the union of Christendom should so often have been imperilled by transient, personal accidents and considerations. Certainly the historian may feel that the schism was not rendered inevitable by any deep separation in a matter of faith or morality. The beliefs and practices and devotions of those of deep spirituality on either side were in essence the same, and the questions of authority and ecclesiastical jurisdiction, which in the nine centuries that have passed since 1054 have become so central to the controversy, and so apparently frustrating, had not explicitly come to the fore until the days of Nicholas I and Photius. With wisdom and a sense of responsibility on both sides the Petrine claims of the Roman church to govern and to define as well as to preside and to pronounce might have been presented less starkly and less roughly, and might have developed gradually by common agreement as the needs of the Church showed the way. Historically, no doubt, the decline in prestige of the papacy, and the identification of its fortunes with those of the western empire, alienated the East irrevocably, and shattered whatever solidarity of feeling still remained. Simultaneously, the expansion of the Orthodox church, which in the event went far to compensate for the loss of the provinces of western Asia, kept alive the spirit of missionary enterprise and gave the eastern church a forward-looking enthusiasm which had been lacking for centuries. She could now continue in a new way her defence of Christendom in the East, and oppose to the Roman church an almost equal stretch of territory and mass of faithful peoples. In the era between the reign of Charlemagne and the pontificate of Gregory VII the clashes of the great ones on either side could divide; in later centuries it needed more than agreement between an emperor and a pope to restore unity.

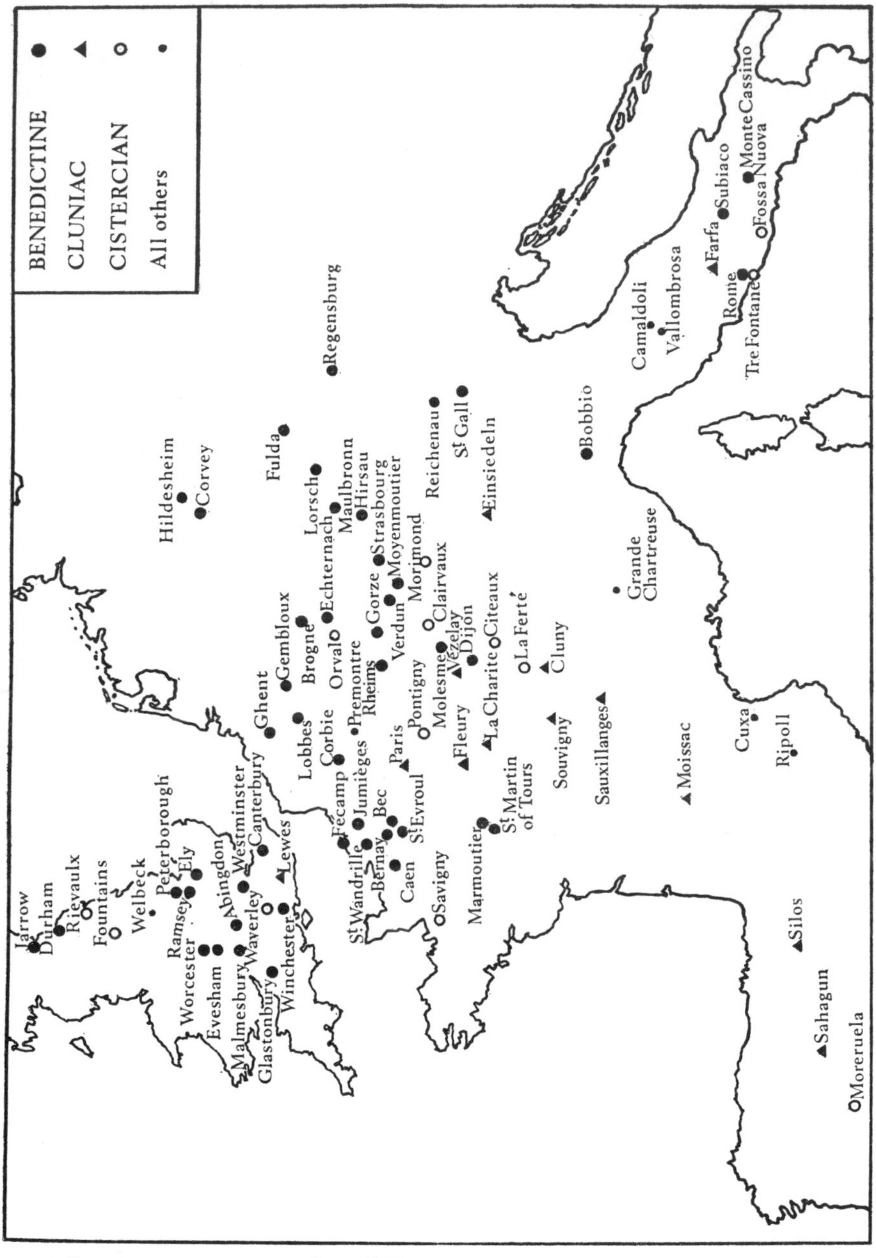
BENEDICTINE
CLUNIAC
CISTERCIAN
All others
Jarrow
Durham
Rievaulx
Fountains
Welbeck
Peterborough
Ely
Ramsey
Worcester
Evesham
Abingdon
Westminster
Canterbury
Waverley
Malmesbury
Glastonbury
Winchester
Lewes
Hildesheim
Corvey
Regensburg
Fulda
Lorsch
Maulbronn
Hirsau
Strasbourg
Moyenmoutier
Reichenau
St Gall
Einsiedeln
Ghent
Gembloux
Brogne
Echternach
Orval
Lobbes
Corbie
Premontre
Rheims
Gorze
Verdun
Morimond
Clairvaux
St Wandrille
Fécamp
Jumièges
Bec
Bernay
Caen
St Evroul
Paris
Pontigny
Molesme
Vézelay
Dijon
Citeaux
La Ferté
Cluny
La Charité
Fleury
Savigny
Marmoutier
St Martin of Tours
Souvigny
Sauxillanges
Grande Chartreuse
Moissac
Cuxa
Ripoll
Silos
Sahagun
Moreruela
Bobbio
Camaldoli
Vallombrosa
Farfa
Subiaco
Rome
Tre Fontane
Fossa Nuova
Monte Cassino

10. Important monasteries of Europe

9

THE MONASTIC CENTURIES (I)

THE period of European history between the death of St Benedict (*c.* 548) and that of St Bernard (1153) has become known as 'the monastic age' or 'the Benedictine centuries', and St Benedict of Nursia has been called 'the Father of Europe'. However extravagant such phrases may seem, they are permissible as an arresting way of expressing an historical truth. During the five centuries in question, as distinguished from the preceding and subsequent ages, monks of all kinds, whether regarded as individuals or in community, were an integral feature of continental and insular society, which they affected on every level, spiritual, intellectual, liturgical, artistic, administrative and economic, moulding its character and shaping its development. Before that epoch, European monasticism was a purely religious phenomemon, regional in its impact; after it, the influence of the monastic life declined until the Reformation. By contrast, during the period we are describing, monasticism was no longer merely a vocation for the few who lived apart from the world; it became an important way of life appealing to a large and influential section of society which, owing to the virtual monopoly of learning and spiritual doctrine enjoyed by the monks, became in many ways more significant than the body of secular clergy in the life of the Church, and ultimately impressed many of its practices and ways of thinking upon the whole of western Christendom, moulding the thoughts and ideals of ecclesiastics and laymen alike, while touching also the peasant and the serf. As for almost the whole period the Rule of St Benedict was the guiding code for the majority of monks, the legislator himself, in an age when patrons, earthly and celestial, were much in demand, was rightly regarded as the patriarch and patron of all monks.

The Benedictine centuries, however, do not form an undifferentiated whole. Four main divisions of the period can be distinguished. In the first, the pre-Carolingian centuries, monasticism spread slowly from Italy and the southern and south-western parts of Gaul to the remainder of what are now France and western Switzerland, while England received monastic immigrants from Gaul, Rome and the Celtic regions, and in its turn planted missionary abbeys in the Rhineland and Bavaria. A feature of this period was the gradual building up of the wealthy landed monastic community.

The second period was one of attempted centralisation, followed by widespread secularisation and decline reacting one upon the other. The project of Charlemagne to unite all the monasteries of his empire in the observance of the Rule was perfected by his son, Lewis the Pious, who gave to the monks of the empire a code of daily life and liturgy that remained a norm for three hundred years. Further than this he could not go, and the monastic order shared in the decadence and secularisation of the late ninth century.

The third period saw a series of revivals which merged at last with the still wider and more intense European reform. Cluny, a mustard seed that became a mighty tree, was followed by the movement in Lorraine and others in England, Normandy, south Germany and Italy. It was in this era that the traditional Benedictine monachism attained to its full stature as a liturgical life with a strong literary and artistic culture.

The fourth period saw the appearance of a new monachism, both in eremitical and coenobitic forms, in Italy and in France. This will form the subject of a later chapter.

At the end of the sixth century monastic life had been established in the West for more than two hundred years, since the foundation by St Martin of Ligugé (near Poitiers) and Marmoutier (near Tours) in 360 and 372. Lérins (410) and Marseilles (415) had become celebrated, the former as a nursery of bishops, the latter as the home of John Cassian. In the sixth century St Cesarius of Arles (c. 500), the anonymous and enigmatic Master (c. 520), and St Benedict, abbot of Monte Cassino (c. 535) had written their rules, and monasteries were to be found along the littoral of the Mediterranean from Catalonia to Calabria, while in Rome and a few other great cities basilical communities existed. In Gaul, Fleury

(6th century) and St Benignus at Dijon (550) and St Remi of Rheims (*c*. 550), had come into being, with a number of monasteries at centres of pilgrimage, such as Poitiers, Tours and Paris, and a few royal foundations. These for the most part made use of no comprehensive rule; the abbot applied the liturgical and other customs common to all monks in the region or diocese. In the Celtic lands, on the other hand – Ireland, Galloway and Wales – monasticism had rapidly come to be the ruling element in the Christian life of the region affected, as well as being the focus of all learning and piety. Already Celtic missionaries or emigrants were beginning to export their spirituality and their learning to continental Europe. By 600 Armorica (Brittany) was occupied by refugees from Britain and thence evangelists passed eastward, while towards the end of the sixth century St Columba (521-597) had founded the celebrated monastery of Iona (563), which was to be the centre of radiation for missionaries to the western and northern isles, and later for the Lowlands of Scotland and Northumbria.

At almost the same date St Columbanus (540-615), after a long preparation at Bangor, crossed the sea to Armorica and thence proceeded to the Vosges, where in 590 he converted the ruins of a Roman spa (Luxovium) into the abbey of Luxeuil, one of a group of three houses under his rule. After many adventures and many missionary journeys in Switzerland, he crossed the Alps to found Bobbio (613) in the Apennines north-east of Genoa, where he died in 615. Austere, and a prodigy of energy and zeal, Columbanus imparted some of his own faith and intense piety both to his monks and to the kings and nobles whom he met. In the fifty years after his death two generations of his disciples, the abbots of his monasteries and the children of his patrons, helped to spread the traditions of Luxeuil at Jumièges (654), Fontenelle (St Wandrille, 649) and St Ouen (645) among monasteries, and Faremoutiers (*c*. 625), Jouarre (630) and Chelles (653) among nunneries. Among other celebrated houses founded at this time were Corbie (in Picardy; 657), St Trond (660), Stavelot and Malmédy (649), Lobbes (in Hainault; 660), St Pierre and St Bavon at Ghent (660-70). The dynamic force of many of these flowed from St Columbanus and his posthumous fame, and the abbeys concerned used his rule, but gradually from *c*. 630 onwards the Rule of St Benedict came to dominate the scene, at first side by side with Columbanus's rule and then victoriously alone. The conquest was complete before the end of the eighth century, and Charlemagne could expect a negative answer when he asked whether any other rule existed.

The victory of the Rule was due entirely to its excellence in combining the qualities of a practical code and a spiritual directory. It was never imposed by authority before 800, and there is no clear evidence of the manner of its introduction into the Gallic scene. The hoary legend that it was introduced by Benedict's disciple St Maurus at Fleury may possibly conceal an historical fact that the translation of the relics of the saint in 673 made of Fleury a foyer of influence in France.[1] The Columban spirit, even when diluted by a generation's residence in Gaul, was quite different from the Benedictine. More austere, more demanding and more individualistic, it made of the monastic life a struggle on the part of the monk to attain complete self-renouncement in the hands of his abbot; the Benedictine Rule with its emphasis on humility, on the father-and-family relationship, and on the authority of the Rule, put the emphasis on social charity, mutual understanding, and spiritual advancement by daily work and prayer. This outlook, which at once encouraged and was supported by the new view of the monastic life as a way for the many, when added to the clear and adequate administrative framework contained in the Rule, are sufficient to account for its immediate and lasting success.

While the monastic life spread and found its code, the normal monastery became something other than the simple microcosm of the Rule which we can glimpse also in other documents of the sixth century. From a small and predominantly lay community, engaged in domestic, craft and agricultural work, it had become a largely clerical body; from a life of prayer and work in which the liturgical section was simple and relatively short, there had developed a horarium in which the solemn Mass took pride of place, and in which numerous prayers and offices drew out the hours spent in choir. Serfs tilled the lands, servants and dependents plied the crafts and performed much of the service of a large establishment. The copying and illumination of manuscripts, and original composition, together with teaching, became normal claustral employments. Elaborate rituals and customs glossed and embroidered the simple directions of the Rule. Finally, from being the vocation of the individual retreating from the world in the company of a few like-minded associates, monasticism was on the way to become a profession, a social factor with a function in and for the world of its day.

Contrary to the common opinion of Benedictine tradition followed by older historians, neither the Rule nor ' Benedictine ' monasticism spread rapidly northwards from central Italy. Monte Cassino fell to the Lombards in 581, and there is no evidence that either its monks or their Rule made any impact upon Rome.[2] In the city itself the basilical monasteries

1. The controversy over the relics of St Benedict still continues. Cf. P. Meyvaert, ' Peter the Deacon and the tomb of St Benedict ', in *Revue Bénédictine*, 1955, 3-70.

2. G. Ferrari, *Early Roman Monasteries* (Vatican City, 1957) 406, remarks: ' There is no evidence of a monastery in Rome which employed exclusively the Rule of St Benedict much before the tenth century '. B. F. Hamilton, *The Holy See, the Roman Nobility and the Ottonian Emperors* (London University thesis, 1960), 233, adds: ' It is difficult to

flourished for a century or more and then declined; they were reinforced from 650 onwards by refugees and immigrants from the south and east who founded or occupied a number of monasteries in or near Rome, besides covering Apulia and Calabria with monasteries of the Greek type. Not till the eighth century were there new foundations in Italy of ' Benedictine ' character, and it is noteworthy that when Monte Cassino was restored c. 720 the tone was set by the Anglo-Saxon Willibald. In this the north was repaying its debt to Rome, for while the influence of Columbanus and of the stream of Celtic monachism was merging into the older and more traditional waters of European religious life a new and powerful invasion was beginning from Anglo-Saxon England.

The band of missionaries sent to the island by Gregory the Great, and the earliest reinforcements to their ranks, were Roman monks, though there is neither evidence nor likelihood that they observed or took with them the Rule of St Benedict. It is certain that they founded the monastery of SS Peter and Paul (later St Augustine's) at Canterbury; it is probable, also, that for some time at least they staffed the cathedral of Christ Church. A little later, the gradual spread of monastic life, for both men and women, in Essex, Kent, Sussex, Wessex and the Thames basin is unquestionable, though its provenance is uncertain. For nuns, at least, and in the particular form taken by the monasteries of which Streaneshalch (Whitby) is the most celebrated example, where Abbess Hilda ruled over monks as well as nuns, the model was Gallic. Very soon a wholly independent stream of Celtic monasticism reached Northumbria, ultimately from Iona, immediately from Melrose, and a number of monasteries came into being, such as Lindisfarne and Ripon, under the impulse of the great monk-missionaries and bishops Aidan and Cuthbert. The first certain introduction of the Rule was due to Wilfrid, himself a monk of Ripon and later in exile as bishop of York, but the true founder of English ' Benedictine ' life was Wilfrid's contemporary Benedict Biscop, founder of the monasteries of Wearmouth and Jarrow, soon to be the home of Bede the Venerable. Biscop, from his stay at Lérins and his many pilgrimages to Rome, had brought back the customs of many monasteries, but there is no doubt that the Rule had a privileged position among them. Both Wilfrid and Biscop were contemporaries of Archbishop Theodore, who was accompanied to England in 669 by the Neapolitan abbot Hadrian. Hadrian succeeded Biscop as abbot of St Augustine's, Canterbury, and henceforward for almost a century, in the golden age of the Anglo-Saxon church, the two fields of monasticism developed until they covered most of the populated districts of England. Both met and merged with a Celtic

---

justify the qualification " much " '. In his opinion, the introduction of the Rule dates from the first visit of St Odo in 936.

stream, but whereas in the north the traditions of Cuthbert and Lindisfarne affected both ascetic and artistic activity, in the south the Irish at Glastonbury and Malmesbury influenced only the Latinity and perhaps the calendar of Aldhelm and his associates. It was an age of small houses, but of intense literary and artistic work. It was of European significance, on account of its missionary activity in which both Northumbria and Wessex took part. From the north and from Ripon came Willibrord, the apostle of Frisia, the bishop of Utrecht and the founder of Echternach, together with Suitbert and others (690-739). From Wessex went Winfrith (Boniface) and his relatives and disciples Wigbert and Lull, monks of Nursling, Glastonbury and Malmesbury, followed by a group of devout women. These and others, as we have seen, carried the Benedictine Rule along with the Christian faith and culture to the provinces on the northern and eastern fringes of the Frankish dominions.

The first period of the expansion of monasticism, largely from southern and eastern Gaul, was halted by the invasion of the Rhône and Loire valleys by the Arabs from 719 onwards, and by the widespread secularisation and appropriation of abbeys under Charles Martel, by means of which Charles himself, or the founder of the house and his descendants, assumed possession of the revenues, save for a pension to the community, together with the right of appointing the abbot. In effect, this often led to control by a lay or episcopal ' abbot ', and the impoverishment, or even the disappearance, of the monastery proper. This process continued under Charlemagne, who was not a notable founder or benefactor of the monasteries. He did, however, include monks within the scope of his legislation; they were to observe the Rule of St Benedict and all that it implied, and to undertake the task of teaching in schools for externs attached to the monastery. This legislation, which remained in part inoperative, was carried into practical execution by Charlemagne's son, Lewis the Pious, who called to his assistance Benedict of Aniane.

This abbot had founded an austere monastery near the Mediterranean west of Marseilles which had become the mother of several houses, while Benedict had received Charlemagne's approval as an agent of reform and had been used by Lewis when ruler of Aquitaine. On his accession to the empire Lewis summoned him to court and founded for him the abbey of Inde or Cornelimünster near Aachen (815), to serve as a model and nursery for reformers. Shortly after, a great synod of the abbots of the empire was held at Aachen (July 817) at which a code of constitutions (capitulare monasticum) was approved, and a year later (818-19) Lewis approved of the division of the revenues of proprietary monasteries into portions assigned to the abbot and to the community, thus safeguarding the latter from the depredations of lay and episcopal abbots. This division gradually became almost universal. Finally, Benedict of Aniane produced a collection of rules *(codex regularum)* and a commentary on the Rule emphasising its excellence. It was Lewis' intention that with Inde as a seedbed, and a staff of inspectors, a standard should be set up and maintained for the monasteries of the empire, following a single code of constitutions based on the Rule.

This great design, like other grandiose schemes of the Carolingian empire, failed to achieve its end. Benedict himself died prematurely (821) and the fragmentation of the empire and political dissensions destroyed all possibility of a central control. The time had not yet come when reformers or monarchs could create the machinery necessary for maintaining in being a great organisation. The reform of Benedict of Aniane is nevertheless an important milestone in monastic history. It established a precedent, and men of the middle ages found reproduction more congenial than creation. For two centuries monastic reformers looked back to the meeting of 817 and to the *Ordo qualiter* (a directory summarising its liturgical results) for guidance and support. More important still was the solidarity that had been created among the monks of the empire, rooted in the observance of a single rule. Henceforward, on the forensic level, all reforms would attempt some kind of union within a group. On the level of ideas and sentiment the influence of Benedict was still more pervasive. Now for the first time all the monks of western Europe looked to St Benedict as to a patron or patriarch, and upon themselves as the *familia S. Benedicti*. So deeply did this conception penetrate monastic writers of the three following centuries that they, and modern historians following them, have attributed to the seventh and eighth centuries the attitudes of the ninth, and created the myth of an unbroken chain of ' Benedictine ' tradition from the abbot of Monte Cassino to the age of Charlemagne.

In France the first partition of the empire (843) began a new era of secularisation, soon to be followed by the wide-ranging ravages of the Northmen. The former profoundly modified the right of free election and imposed heavy exactions and feudal services and dues in cases where the estates were not altogether dismembered. Everywhere in the western parts of the empire monasteries disappeared or fell into poverty. In Germany and what is now Switzerland conditions were less deplorable. The abbeys were more recent foundations and were often either the sees of bishops or outposts of civilisation, and in the latter part of the ninth century they took up the torch from France and were, for a time, worthy heirs of the Carolingian renaissance. Fulda in Franconia, Corvey in Saxony, St Gall in Swabia and Reichenau on the lake of Constance were pre-eminent, and for a time these houses were cradles of learning and literature without a rival north of Italy. Here Smaragdus wrote his commentary on the Rule, and the monasteries, unlike their French contemporaries, were also assistants at the birth of vernacular poetry. Here, more than anywhere else, the great abbey, situated at the centre of wide estates peopled with serfs and peasants, formed a great complex of buildings containing, besides church and claustral buildings, the elements of all the social services – schools, hospitals, courts and accommodation for travellers, pilgrims and almsfolk. Here, the decline, foreshadowed in Bavaria by the Hungarian invasion and hastened by the growth of *Eigenkloster*, seigneurial and episcopal, was not critical till the beginning of the tenth century.

The turn of the tide in monastic history in France is marked by an event which attracted little contemporary attention. This was the foundation of Cluny in southern Burgundy by Duke William of Aquitaine *c*. 909, under Berno, a reforming abbot of the day. Cluny resembled in almost every respect other earlier and later attempts at reform. The peculiarity, which was to make possible the later success of the venture, was its freedom from all local encroachment, whether of lord or bishops, in consequence of its commendation to the apostolic church of St Peter in Rome. This ensured at first the merely negative benefit of the preservation of independence for Cluny; when the papacy became once more a dynamic force more than a century later it gave the abbey a distinguished position of privilege. Meanwhile, Cluny grew slowly under a succession of saintly, able and long-lived abbots. The first of these, Odo (927-42), began the great task of spreading reform in both Burgundy and Italy, particularly in the Rome of Alberic. He also began the long association of the abbots of Cluny with the kings and emperors of Germany. Maieul (948-94) continued the work of reform in Burgundy and Italy, and summoned William of Volpiano to make of St Benigne at Dijon another focus of fervour. Hitherto, no special bond of dependence united Cluny to the houses that had adopted her reform. The creator of the ' order ' of Cluny was Odilo (994-1049). Not only did the number of dependencies double in his time, but he laid down the main principles of their organisation. First among these was the policy of strict subordination to Cluny, and to himself as abbot, on the part of all those who wished to follow the customs and share the privileges of Cluny. The machinery was simple. All dependencies, save for a very small privileged class, were, if abbeys, reduced to the rank of priory; they were then received into the Cluniac system on condition that they adopted in totality the Cluniac customs, and that their monks made profession to the abbot of Cluny, who appointed their prior. They paid a small annual tax to Cluny, similar to the *census* paid by Cluny herself to Rome. Dependence passed in a vertical line, thus La Charité depended upon Cluny, Lewes (England) depended upon La Charité, Castle Acre (Norfolk) upon Lewes, and Bromholm (cell of Acre) upon

Castle Acre. There was no horizontal spread of equal constituent houses as in later monastic orders. Statutes for the whole body were framed by the abbot and community of Cluny; there was no general legislative assembly and no devolution of powers or use of lieutenants on the part of the abbot of Cluny, who consequently spent much of his time away from the mother abbey, visiting its daughters and dependents, reforming and instructing newcomers to the family, in addition to his occupation in the business of the Roman church or of the emperor. The Cluniac organisation had therefore something of a feudal character, with the abbot of Cluny in place of the king or emperor, and monastic profession to the abbot corresponding to feudal homage.

All the procedure adopted by Odilo was taken over and accelerated by Hugh the Great (1049-1109), who carried every aspect of the Cluniac system – elaborate monastic observance, splendid architecture, large numbers and control of the dependencies – from a moderate to an immense scale. The order grew from some seventy houses to at least 1200, the community of Cluny from fifty to 300, the church, entirely rebuilt, from a large to a spectacular fabric, the largest church in Christendom. For almost the whole of the eleventh century she was the spiritual centre of western Christendom, at a time when few popes were able, or were allowed by their opponents, to treat Rome as their permanent home. In consequence, she was able to impress her spirit upon the age. Her ' message ' was the liturgical service of God, the unceasing round of choral duties, the *opus Dei* of St Benedict now swollen out of all recognition with the solemn Masses, the elaborate chant and the additional offices and litanies, carried out by a huge community in a great church amid the splendours of gold, silver and jewels, of vestments of silk and golden thread, illuminated by countless tapers and lamps. Manual labour had long since been crowded out of the monastic day, and at Cluny there was comparatively little literary or theological work. In the arts, on the other hand, Cluny produced numerous executants, especially in the illuminating of manuscripts, and Cluniac houses were the patrons of an architecture and school of sculpture and decoration that spread outwards from the larger Cluniac houses to the neighbouring churches, and along the lines of travel or pilgrimage. Since Cluny was in existence as a focus of reform more than a century before the papacy reasserted its leadership, historians have sought to assess the share of the great abbey in the struggle against lay ownership and imperial domination. In general it may be said that Cluny took no part in campaigning for either cause, but that her own exemption and that of her dependents from the jurisdiction of bishops and lay lords, and her status as a centre of monastic reform, made of her at least a benevolent ally of the reforming papacy. In the great contest between pope and emperor Hugh was respected and consulted by both parties; later, Cluny was used by the papacy as a recruiting-ground for its agents.

Although pre-eminent, Cluny did not stand alone as a centre of reform. Her influence was largely confined to lands of the romance languages. In Lorraine and the modern Belgium a series of reforms had begun with that of Gerard of Brogne, near Namur (923). Among houses reformed by him were the two great monasteries at Ghent, St Peter and St Bavon, and several Norman refoundations such as St Wandrille and Mont St Michel. More important was the reform of John of Gorze, near Metz (933), which spread to a large number of Lotharingian houses. Like Cluny, Gorze was noted for its lengthy liturgical duties, but it had a note of austerity foreign to the later period at Cluny. Unlike Cluny in its treatment of the monasteries reformed by its discipline, Gorze allowed them to retain their self-government while following a common observance. The movement spread and ultimately embraced some 150 houses in Germany and Lorraine, and in fact, though probably not in intention, the success of Gorze helped to restrict the spread of Cluny's influence in the empire. Gorze was patronised by both Otto the Great and Otto II, and the houses of the Lorraine reform, unlike those of Cluny, remained radically the property of their secular founders; they were not commended to Rome and in consequence remained under the jurisdiction of the diocesan bishop. As a result, their influence on the secular clergy was greater than that of Cluny and many of the monks became bishops; they thus had a considerable, if not a direct, influence upon the general movement of reform in Lorraine which anticipated and later powerfully assisted the Roman reform, and gave to the Roman church, among others, Bruno of Toul, later Pope Leo IX, and Cardinal Humbert of Moyenmoutier. Indeed, it is probable that Hildebrand himself became a monk at or near Toul when he had crossed the Alps with the deposed Gregory VI. Finally, a word must be said of the Greek or Basilian monasteries of southern Italy which in the tenth century, largely through the influence of the Calabrian St Nilus (d. 1005) moved again northwards, establishing an outpost within sight of Rome at Grottaferrata and the abbeys of St Paul and St Saba to join the existing houses in the City itself.

It is characteristic of the Benedictine centuries, and indeed of traditional monachism of every age, that centres of fervour and reform appear here and there unexpectedly, like a summer fire in grassland, sometimes with transient effect, sometimes with permanent results. Mention has been made of one such focus in Anglo-Saxon England, which saw the foundation of abbeys of monks and nuns – Westminster, Glastonbury, St Albans Abingdon and the rest – that continued in being, as venerable institutions, until the final dissolution more than five centuries later. Another such was the Norman monasticism of the tenth and eleventh centuries. The northern invaders, who had settled in the basin of the Seine and in the neighbouring maritime regions, assumed with remarkable rapidity the religious practices of western Europe and the earliest monastery was founded at Jumièges *c.* 940; this was followed by foundations from Lorraine, as mentioned above, in 961-3, and from 1001 onwards by the activities of the Cluniac William of Dijon at and around Fécamp. This great man, who as William of Fécamp was the first of the series of eminent spiritual writers of the age, gave a new life to the Norman abbeys, and the barons of the duchy vied with one another in founding houses, so that when Duke William invaded England there were already some twenty-seven houses of men in existence. Besides giving lustre to Normandy, these abbeys rejuvenated monastic life in England, making new foundations, giving notable abbots and new blood to the old houses, and above all fostering a spirit of artistic and literary activity and a taste for large-scale building. As the Norman abbeys lay outside the Cluniac network they maintained the existing independence of English monasticism. In consequence, the ' black monk ', later known as Benedictine, houses in the British Isles remained independent, self-governing units, and the relatively few Cluniac houses that were founded after the Conquest were for the most part small and uninfluential. The eleventh century revival in Normandy and England, together with the contemporary revival of Monte Cassino, provide examples of a new type of monastic family, that devoted to intellectual, literary and artistic work. In Normandy Bec with Lanfranc and Anselm, and in Italy Monte Cassino with Desiderius, were houses of unusual distinction.

One of the last centres of monastic reform of the traditional kind in the eleventh century was Hirsau in the diocese of Speyer. Founded by William, its abbot from 1069 to 1091, Hirsau followed the Cluniac observance; indeed, the well known and most eleborate account of Cluniac liturgical and daily observance, the customary of Ulrich, was composed for Abbot William's guidance and sent to him as from Hugh the Great of Cluny, with permission to make such alterations as he deemed necessary for the different conditions of Hirsau. That abbey and its associates never became members of the Cluniac body, but Hirsau was chosen by Gregory VII, along with Cluny and St Victor of Marseilles, as a focal point of reforming activities and the anti-king Rudolph of Swabia was there shortly after his election, though William was subsequently forced to leave Hirsau by an unfriendly imperial bishop, taking refuge in the sister abbey of Schaffhausen.

Hirsau is of significance in monastic history on another count also. Its repute attracted numerous laymen of the smaller nobility, who took the monastic habit there in middle life as *conversi* or ' lay monks '. They were not ' lay brothers ' of the kind so soon to be established by the Cistercians, but ' lay ' or ' bearded ' monks of the kind found at Canterbury in Lanfranc's day, unable as ' illiterate ' to take orders, and occupying themselves in various tasks in church and cloister. They are evidence of a widespread demand for an extension of the monastic life, and deserve a place in the pre-history of the lay-brotherhood.

The history of the traditional black monk way of life has now been taken down to the end of the eleventh century. Until shortly before that date it had a monopoly in western Europe as the single available form of the monastic life, and can be seen in every kind of fortune and misfortune, now fervent, now relaxed, here flourishing, there decaying, with new centres of life appearing and vanishing. In the last century of its undisputed sway, indeed, groups were being formed, of which Cluny was by far the largest and most highly organised, which spread and maintained particular forms of observance, but the machinery of Cluny was already creaking and bending under the weight of numbers, while in other groups the links that bound the members were too light to stand a serious strain. All were about to be challenged by radical and powerful reformers, and were never again to stand as the only representatives of the monastic life. Yet the traditional monachism remained, and their descendants remain today, as self-governing communities following the Rule of St Benedict interpreted benignly, and it is they, and not the reformers, who assumed and still bear the name of Benedictine.

THEOLOGY 604-1050

T HE period between the pontificate of Gregory I and the theological renaissance of the late eleventh century has often been regarded as intellectually and theologically sterile. It is true that no theologian of the first magnitude appeared between Gregory the Great and St Anselm; true also that no systematic teaching of theology existed before the rise of the school of Chartres soon after the millennial year. There were however several theological controversies which left a permanent mark on western dogma, and more than one theological development of great importance for the Christian life. Above all, it was in these four centuries that the practice of sacramental confession as we know it came into being and spread over the whole western church, while the allied practice of indulgences began to develop towards the end of this period.

As is well known, the history of penance is a difficult topic. No sacrament has changed its external form so radically. The penitential discipline of the early Church, formalised in the church of Rome, was public, solemn, for heinous sin, and not repeatable; it was a second and final reintegration of a public sinner into the full life of the Church. This procedure gradually fell into desuetude and was ultimately replaced by the private and frequent confession of and absolution from sins small and great, which came to be one of the principal pastoral concerns of the parish priest. This evolution –

or revolution – took almost five hundred years (500-1000) to accomplish and its history is one of the strangest episodes in the evolution of Catholic piety.

So far as any clear evidence goes, the only form of penance in the early western church (for here as in other matters the practice of the East developed more rapidly but less completely) was the yearly public penance of confessed sinners in Lent. They were guilty of faults accounted grave such as murder and adultery, for which they received penances of varying severity in addition to the fasts and humiliations of public penance. It was clearly a discipline which could only endure as a reality in small communities of earnest Christians, such as were the churches of Italy and Africa before Constantine. Like other practices, it lingered on under altered conditions, when the profession of Christianity was normal and city churches embraced large sections of the populace of every degree of fervour. Clearly under such conditions many would commit sins of a gravity formerly expiable only by public penance, but it is also clear that such penance was not universal, and there must have been a great and growing number of sinners who never took part in it. At its best it had two grave inconveniences: it was unrepeatable, and a second fall was only remissible on the deathbed; and it was not available to clerics. It has often been argued that private absolution and penance must have existed side by side with the public; if so, it has left no trace whatsoever in the records and it is perhaps an anachronism to attribute to the fourth or fifth centuries attitudes of the guilty conscience which have become ingrained in Catholics for centuries by the practice of auricular confession.

The great change was due ultimately to Egyptian monasticism, which gave birth almost at once to ascetical theology. The confession of faults to an abbot or senior was recognised as meritorious in itself and as giving actuality to spiritual direction. The practice followed monasticism over the West, but it seems certain that it was in Ireland that a further great development began. In the Celtic church there, where monks were the powerful factor and diocesan bishops almost unknown, public penance on the Roman model did not exist. Within the monasteries a scale of penalties for faults, both sinful and merely disciplinary, existed, and monks acting as spiritual advisers to lay-folk began to compose similar tariffs of penance (the ' penitentials '). These Celtic practices were accepted in the Anglo-Saxon church and the system was perfected there by A.D. 700; it was acceptable to a society already familiar with the complicated tariffs of compensation for thefts, homicides, bodily injuries and the rest. Confession even for laymen became common and was administered with the help of ' penitentials '. The practice was authorised in England by the great archbishop Theodore who, though coming directly from Rome, was as a Greek monk familiar with a somewhat similar system in Asia Minor. Bede, Egbert and Alcuin were all advocates of private confession, the last-named in particular was a zealous apostle of the practice among the Carolingian reformers. It had already reached the continent and spread widely through the agency of the Columban and other Irish monks. The Carolingian reformers were, however, also liturgical archaists and desired to re-establish the public penance of the Roman church. The public penancing of Lewis the Pious is an extreme instance of this feeling. They stressed the lack of authority, the great variety and the tendency to laxity in the penitential literature, and for a time the doctrine was current that for public faults public penance, and for private faults private confession should be the norm, while papal letters and regional councils endeavoured to establish a *modus vivendi* on these terms. Clearly, however, public, unrepeatable penance over the length and breadth of Europe, where the whole population was nominally Christian, was quite impracticable, and when attempts at reform ceased in the ninth century private penance remained in the field. As the conception of public penance faded, there came in gradually the single régime of confession either private to a priest or semi-public to a bishop or pope, with penances graded according to the heinousness of the sin. Already in the tenth century it was a common practice throughout north-western Europe to demand of the faithful a Lenten confession in preparation for paschal communion, while in monasteries frequent private confession was made obligatory and accusations in chapter were confined to disciplinary or scandalous faults. It remained only to discuss the essential constituents of penance and its necessity when the theology of the sacraments was perfected in the late twelfth and early thirteenth centuries. The celebrated decree of the Fourth Lateran Council *(Utriusque sexus)* in 1215, imposing annual sacramental confession of grave sins before the obligatory paschal communion, did no more than give legal sanction to a long existing state of practice; its importance was primarily theological and pastoral, in giving a stimulus to moral theologians.

The two last centuries of the development of frequent auricular confession saw another familiar practice become common, that of indulgences. Though theologically distinct, its evolution was influenced by penitential practice. The theological foundation of an indulgence is the doctrine of the power of the keys, by which Peter and his successors and representatives can apply the treasures of merit (or love) accumulated by Christ, his mother and the saints to the remission of punishment incurred by others for sins committed, even after the guilt has been forgiven by repentance and confession. This had long been recognised in principle, and was implied in the practice which grew up in post-Carolingian Europe of the commutation of the penance laid down in a penitential tariff for another satisfactory act, different or less, such as hearing Masses, almsgiving or prayers. In the tenth century it became common for the bishops of southern France or northern Spain to assign a remissive value to pilgrimages to Compostela and elsewhere quite apart from their knowledge of specific sins on the part of the individual. The slip-over from the commutation of a penance to its remission was accomplished when the reward of remission was offered to all complying with certain conditions, and when it was stated that a particular act or prayer was the equivalent of so many days of regular penance. An important extension came when an ' indulgence ' was held out as enticement to fight for the faith either in Spain or in the East, and the unparalleled offer of a plenary (i.e., total) remission of temporal punishment for crusaders by Urban II was a landmark. It was natural that the papacy should strive, if the metaphor be allowed, to arrest the fall of the currency by forbidding bishops to bestow more than a relatively small remission, but from the twelfth century to the present day indulgences have continued to be one of the commonest features of devotional life and at the same time a source of some perplexity (all questions of abuse apart), for it is with indulgences as with sacramental grace: the task performed with due dispositions is never vain, but who can say what fervour is needed to obtain a full remission? Moreover, though popes and theologians have always, when solicited, maintained that indulgences are concerned with the punishment incurred by the sinful act, and not with the removal of the guilt of sin, the language even of authority has at times left much to be desired, while the uninstructed faithful from the eleventh century onwards have been confused in mind and have often regarded indulgences as a talisman or a passport to heaven.

Another theological issue of importance was debated throughout our period: that of the need for reordination of heretical, schismatic or irregular clergy before admission or readmission to the exercise of their orders. As is well known, the clear recognition of seven, and only seven, sacraments, and of the nature and effect of the various sacraments, was not attained in the West before the twelfth century. In particular, the classical doctrine of the ' character ' bestowed on the soul by the sacraments of baptism, confirmation and order had not been explicitly formulated. In the early Church a long and bitter controversy had been waged as to the necessity of re-baptising (and later reordaining) heretics and schismatics, St Cyprian being the protagonist of the rebaptisers. While the baptism controversy was finally settled against the African Father, that on reordination smouldered long in both East and West. While St Augustine would seem to have held what has become the orthodox doctrine others, offended at the thought of the most sacred powers surviving the worst of betrayals or the sentence of excommunication, demanded reordination on repentance. Nor did Roman practice show entire consistency, and a dictum of Innocent I that no one could give what he did not possess (i.e., an excommunicate bishop could not confer sacerdotal powers) was cited for centuries by the reordainers. The question cropped up again and again in an acute form largely owing to the very wide definition of heresy then current. Thus in England after the Council of Whitby there was a question of the orders of clergy who held to Celtic practices, and Theodore, again with memories of current practice in Rome and in the East, introduced reordination. It was maintained by Egbert and figures in insular penitentials. During the same period feuds, scandals and irregular elections at Rome led to the nullification of orders and reordination of opponents by victorious partisans (e.g., after the anti-pope Constantine II, 767-9, and the pope Formosus, 891-6) and the issue of one of Hincmar's many stern tussles hung upon the status of clerks ordained by Ebbo, after his irregular resumption of office as bishop. The reform movement of the twelfth century brought the question to the forefront of the stage. Simony and incontinence were 'heresies' in a priest or bishop, to be fought with every canonical weapon. Were those guilty of these faults, and as such excommunicate, any longer priests or bishops? If so, one granted the transmission of orders and all means of sanctification to heretics. In this *mêlée* of ideas the leading theologians were divided and popes acted inconsistently. Peter Damian, the great doctor in the matter, and Cardinal Deusdedit the canonist were against reordination, Cardinal Humbert and the canonist, later pope as Alexander II, Anselm of Lucca, were for it. Leo IX, Gregory VII and Urban II were inconsistent in practice. As the controversy continued and theology developed various refinements were proposed. One school wished to oblige reconciled heretics to submit to a new laying-on of hands, omitting the anointing and other ceremonies. Another school took the view that ordinations 'within the church' were valid, i.e., a heretic so ordained still had episcopal powers, and could ordain. But ordinations 'without the Church' were invalid i.e., a priest or bishop thus ordained by a heretic could not himself ordain or consecrate. The matter had not been theologically settled when Gratian and Peter Lombard complied their manuals in the mid-twelfth century, but in practice reordination was becoming rare.

Perhaps the most fateful of the issues raised in this period was the matter of the *Filioque*. The so-called Nicene creed first promulgated by the Council of Constantinople in 381 contained the words '(I believe) also in the Holy Spirit, Lord and Giver of Life, who proceeds from the Father, etc.' In this form the creed was in use at both Rome and Constantinople for more than four centuries. In Spain, however, from at least the middle of the sixth century (the profession of faith at the council of Toledo in 589 is the first known occurrence) the words *Filioque* ('and from the Son') were added. In Spain, as in the East, and in contrast to Italy and the West, the creed was recited during Mass; the addition therefore must soon have become familiar and along with many other Spanish customs spread to Gaul. When and where the insertion was first made is not known, and there is no reason to suppose a controversial intent. In fact theologians of the early and middle patristic age in both East and West had seen in the Son as well as in the Father the source of the personal being of the Holy Ghost, but while the East had preferred the expression 'from the Father through the Son', the west had chosen 'from the Father and Son'. In other words, theologians of both the eastern and western churches before the epoch of controversy would have considered the words *Filioque* taken by themselves to represent one of several expressions of the mystery of the Trinity, and not an heretical deviation. Nevertheless, the eastern church had always regarded the credal formula of 381 as intangible, and any addition to it was bound to cause trouble. It must be allowed in all fairness that the Spaniards, however unintentionally, had provoked criticism. At Rome, however, where the creed was not recited at Mass, no change had been made, and the fatal clash might never have occurred had Charlemagne, at odds with the empress Irene, not set his theologians the task of putting the Greeks in the wrong wherever possible. Accustomed now by long usage to the *Filioque*, Alcuin and his collaborators pointed to its absence in Greek professions of faith at the second council of Nicea, not yet approved by Rome, but Pope Hadrian I replied by showing the orthodoxy and ancient tradition behind such an omission. Nothing daunted, when further breaches occurred between Byzantium and Aachen, the Frankish theologians pursued their point and at the Council of Cividale in 796, pronounced against the Greeks on the procession of the Holy Ghost and the *Filioque*. Some years later, in 809, Charlemagne once more demanded of his theologians, of whom the chief was now Theodulf of Orleans, treatises in justification of the *Filioque* clause, which had long been recited in the creed in the imperial chapel at Aachen. Theodulf replied with a long and learned collection of texts from the Fathers, both Latin and Greek, and at a council held at Aachen it was resolved to send representatives to Rome begging the pope to order the recitation of the clause in the Roman creed, so as to deprive the Greeks of the useful argument they drew from its omission. Leo III replied that he agreed fully with the imperial theologians in the matter of doctrine, but was not prepared to exacerbate feeling by changing the Roman practice. As a counter-proposal, he suggested that all churches of the West should discontinue the chanting of the creed at Mass. This proposal was unacceptable to the emperor, but the pope stood firm, and for the moment a collision between the churches of East and West was avoided.

In contrast to the theological writings of Charlemagne's lifetime, in which Alcuin, Theodulf and others acted as official spokesmen of the emperor in attacking supposed errors occurring outside Frankland, the debates of the following generation took place between individuals or groups of the clergy of France and Germany, and ended without any final or official doctrinal pronouncement.

The first concerned the Eucharist and more especially the manner of Christ's presence in the consecrated host; it is of interest as posing for the first time some of the problems that were to exercise theologians for many centuries at a later date. It was opened almost unwittingly by Paschasius Radbert, later abbot of Corbie, who composed a long treatise on the Eucharist for the monks of Corvey, the German daughter-house of the French abbey. Throughout this he insisted on the reality of the presence of Christ behind the veil of appearances. It is the body of Christ, born of the Virgin and sacrificed on the cross, that is now offered again as victim. So far, Radbert was only expressing more clearly than any of his predecessors the traditional doctrine that had developed in the West, but he went on to describe the body of Christ as if spatially existent on a reduced scale in the host, and present by a miraculous transformation or creation. He was attacked almost at once by a group of contemporaries including Hrabanus Maurus, who, professedly reproducing the doctrine of Augustine, regarded the presence of Christ as something realised by the faith of the recipient when united with the Lord in the sacrament. So far as words went he might seem to neglect the objective reality of the presence and of the sacrifice though this was probably not his intention. Ratramnus, a monk of Corbie, was equally opposed to the realism of Radbert, but asserted strongly the presence of a divine, if spiritual, reality in the consecrated host. This was a nearer approach to one aspect of Augustine's teaching than Hrabanus had made. Radbert replied by disclaiming any intention of supposing a mensurable or material presence of Christ, but continued to hold firmly to its absolute reality and to the identity of the Christ present in the host and the Christ born of the Virgin.

The controversy, as we shall see, was revived from another point of view two centuries later, and a theological opinion similar in many respects to that of Radbert prevailed. Ratramnus, for his part, as a faithful Augustinian, was felt as an influence by Aelfric in England, and was to be excavated five centuries later still, when some of the Reformers appealed to him as a medieval forerunner.

A second controversy, which was at once the more hotly debated and the more obstinately prolonged, concerned predestination and was provoked by Gottschalk. This unfortunate man, originally an oblate at Fulda, where he was befriended by Walafrid Strabo and Servatus Lupus, claimed and won his freedom from the monastic state, but spent the remainder of his life, some forty years, in wanderings and controversies in and out of monasteries and prison. Early in his travels he was accused of proposing dangerous views on predestination, a subject untouched since the Council of Vienne had summed up the results of the Pelagian controversy. Gottschalk's views were in fact rigidly Augustinian: he maintained a double predestination, to glory or to reprobation, admitted the consequences of the loss by original sin of man's freedom to do good, denied God's will to save all men, and restricted the sacrifice on the Cross to those predestined to glory. He was answered by Hrabanus Maurus, who took no notice of Augustine's premises or arguments; for him the matter was simply one of God's prevision, not his predestination, of good actions and bad. Condemned by a gathering at Mainz in 848, Gottschalk was prosecuted by Hincmar of Rheims, who secured his condemnation and punishment at a royal council at Quierzy in 849. Not content with this, Hincmar proceeded to write a short treatise on predestination in which, without following Hrabanus all the way, he insisted that Christ had died for all men. He also invited the opinions of others, thus eliciting from Prudentius of Troyes and Servatus Lupus pronouncements not greatly differing from those of Gottschalk. Prudentius accepted the reprobate race of mankind (the *massa damnata* of Augustine) and the double predestination of Augustine's extreme declarations, as did also Ratramnus. John the Scot, called in likewise by Hincmar, took a Neoplatonic view of evil and offered to settle the question by dialectic. John was taken to task by Prudentius, who abounded in the sense of Augustine, and by the church of Lyons, which showed itself equally Augustinian. Hincmar, now in the midst of his troubles with the clerks of Ebbo, accepted the proposal of Charles the Bald to hold a synod at Quierzy in 853, at which four propositions were passed by the fathers: (1) predestination to glory was accepted; the reprobate, by the fact of their omission from those chosen, have no hope of salvation, and their final end is seen by God as the inevitable result of their (free) sin; (2) the freedom to do good, ruined by sin, is restored by grace; (3) God has a universal will to save all; (4) Christ suffered for all men. These produced numerous protests, and two years later the emperor Lothair gathered a council at Valence which decreed (1) that there was a twofold predestination; that of the elect preceded God's knowledge of their good works, that of the reprobate followed upon God's knowledge of their evil deeds; (2) Christ died for all the baptised, whether elect or no. There were attempts on both sides in France both to reject and to repeat these decrees, and Hincmar wrote an immense treatise against them, but the attempts failed, and Hincmar wrote a third treatise, in which he put forward the Greek tradition as less severe than that of Augustine. Meanwhile Gottschalk, the mover of all the trouble, died unannealed outside the Church *c*. 866-70.

These controversies did not exhaust the energies of the writers of the time. Paschasius Radbert summed up the opinion of his time on the assumption of the Virgin in a long letter written in the person of St Jerome which, though recognised at the time as by a contemporary, lived this exposure down in the tenth century and was used liturgically as an authentic piece of Jerome's, and later by apologists of the cult of Mary. John the Scot, known also as Erigena, i.e. Irish, who had, alone of his age in the west, mastered the Greek language, provided a translation of works of Dionysius the Areopagite and later produced an account of the universe in Neoplatonic terms which, with all its technical, linguistic and perhaps also dogmatic infelicities was the only attempt between Augustine and Nicholas of Cusa to use a philosophic system, or rather a scheme of things, derived principally from Plotinus, to express the whole of Christian theology. Modern scholarship is in general agreement that Erigena was orthodox in intention, though his expressions were not always accurate or happy, and it was not until he was misunderstood and misused by deviationists in a world becoming more and more sympathetic to Aristotle that he was condemned as unorthodox.

Nothing has been said in this chapter about three other controversies which took place in this period. Two, the matter of the twofold will of Christ and that of the worship due to images, primarily concerned the eastern church and are mentioned elsewhere in this volume. [1] The third, that of Adoptionism, a deviation peculiar to Spain, received mention in a chapter concerned with that country.

1. See pp. 30-1; 81-92; 105-7.

CANON LAW FROM DIONYSIUS EXIGUUS TO IVO OF CHARTRES

WHEN the Christian Church under Constantine I became a single, visible, organised body, the need for a framework of law to define its authorities and activities became gradually apparent. In the eastern provinces this need was met almost as soon as it was felt, in part by the disciplinary enactments of the general and provincial councils, which had now become a recognised feature of church life, and in part, particularly from the sixth century onwards, by the imperial codes and decrees which accepted the visible church as an essential element in society and legislated for it as a body with a privileged status. Thenceforward in the East ecclesiastical legislation, in so far as it dealt with the organisation and activities of the church, was for long a section of state legislation, promulgated either by the emperor himself or by a council approved by him.

In the West a different state of things prevailed. There, too, the decrees of general and regional councils interpreted and developed ancient traditions, but from the fourth century onwards the popes asserted their authority both by actions and by letters issuing commands or resolving doubts (the later ' decretal ' letters, of which the earliest surviving example is from the pontificate of Siricius, 384-98), and these decisions were recognised as valid for subsequent generations unless superseded by further directives. Moreover, popes in their letters asserted their primacy in matters of discipline and morals, and their right to receive appeals from any other church.

For long, all the various sources for the ordering of the church were scattered, but in the reign of Theodoric, which in so many ways witnessed an Indian summer of Roman creative power in philosophy, in liturgy and in discipline, a renaissance of canonical study issued in several collections of conciliar decisions and decretals by the Scythian monk Denis the Short (Dionysius Exiguus) which, known as the *Dionysiana*, were to be the basis of all subsequent canon law in the West. In the decades that followed the eastern and western church law began to take different paths. In the East, all was absorbed and rationalised by Justinian, who covered both civil and ecclesiastical fields in his legislation. In the West the Roman collections began to penetrate Italy and Gaul, but their advance was halted by the gradual decadence of Roman legislation. The pontificate of Gregory I, though providing directives and precedents for action in many directions, did little towards the promulgation or standardisation of church law as such. At the opening of our period, therefore, the Roman collections of Denis and others, together with other collections made in Gaul, offered a confused mass of directions. Only Spain, in its newly found unity and orthodoxy, continued to hold frequent councils and to produce collections such as the various versions of the *Hispana* (*c.* 633), some of which, by following a strictly chronological order within the sections arranged according to their sources, pointed towards a rationally devised synthesis of law. The Spanish collection had also the distinction of being by far the richest collection of the early middle ages, containing councils and other sources not tapped by Denis the Short.

Simultaneously, in the Celtic church, where bishops had little jurisdiction and monasticism was the norm of Christian perfection, the literature of the penitentials began to appear. These had in essence nothing to do with authoritative legislation; they were in origin aids to the priest in administering the sacrament of penance, particularly in apportioning the kind and degree of punishment or sanction to be applied. Nevertheless, in default of other and official guidance, the penitential literature came to cover all kinds of moral and disciplinary matters, as for example all the problems of relationship and impediment connected with marriage and illicit unions, or those relating to the reception of the sacraments. Meeting as they did a real need in a church which practised both moral austerity and frequent confession, they were introduced widely on the continent by insular immigrants who diffused the Celtic monasticism, but since they were in essence no more than the decisions of private individuals, they often differed widely from one another on important points, and occasionally, as in the matter of the lawfulness of divorce and remarriage of the innocent party, ran counter to the doctrine and practice of continental Christendom. Thus towards the end of the Merovingian epoch great confusion of precept and practice prevailed in Europe north and west of the Alps. While in Rome, Milan and some other ancient cities the traditional canonical discipline was retained, in Gaul fragments of debased canon law circulated by the side of *Hispana* and the penitentials, while the cessation of conciliar and synodal meetings, and the disintegration of episcopal rule, increased the confusion. The inconveniences that followed drew the attention of Charlemagne to this, as to other, causes of confusion in his empire, and he applied to Hadrian I for guidance. The pope despatched an enlarged copy of the Dionysian collection in 774, and this was ultimately promulgated for the empire at Aachen in 802. The gift of the *Dionysiana* marked an epoch; henceforward the Carolingian empire had for its canonical basis a short and manageable code setting out the old Roman discipline. Alongside of the *Dionysio-Hadriana*, and often coalescing with it, was the seventh-century *Hispana* with later additions, known in its fullest form as *Dacheriana* from its seventeenth-century editor, Luc d'Achery. These two sources together made up a corpus of authentic western and Roman legislation.

Scarcely had this law become familiar to the Carolingian empire when it was augmented and contaminated by the remarkable series of fabrications often, if incorrectly, known from their most important element as the False Decretals or the ' pseudo-Isidore '. Whatever be thought of the motives of their composition, they remain the most influential manifestation of the mental ability of the second generation of Carolingian scholarship. These texts, which have gradually emerged after successive epochs of scholarly labour from the layers of misunderstanding–conservative, controversial and historical–that had encrusted them, can only be understood when the circumstances of a precise moment of history have been displayed. Charlemagne's conception of an empire which was the City of God upon earth, directed by himself and served by the priesthood, had been taken over, under the weaker rule of Lewis the Pious, by the leaders of an educated and selfconscious hierarchy, but with the significant difference that the emperor was now the minister of the bishops, and more particularly of the archbishops, who were the true rulers of the City of God. In fact, however, the immediate and principal problem for the leaders of the clergy was how best to defend themselves and the possessions of the church from the attacks of lay potentates in that troubled age, while at the same time the bishops had a vivid realisation of the dangers that might easily come from overmighty metropolitans. An answer was found in the production of a body of civil and canonical legislation, supplementing and interpreting the existing body of law, by a small but extremely active and able body of the clergy. Their compositions consist of four principal collections: an augmented and in part fabricated version of the Spanish code, known from the provenance of a celebrated manuscript as the *Hispana of Autun;* the *Capitula of Angilramnus;* the *False Capitularies* and the *False Decretals*. The second of these is a short treatise on criminal procedure in the case of ecclesiastics, and was put out as the work of Pope Hadrian I. The third, ostensibly the work of Benedict of Mainz, makes numerous additions to the legislation of Charlemagne and Lewis the Pious in the interests of ecclesiastical authority and liberty, thus supplementing, in the direction desired by the writer, the authentic short collection of capitularies made by Ansegis. The fourth, which is by far the largest and most influential, purports to be the work of Isidore Mercator (a fictitious person), and it also is concerned with the liberties of the church, but is in fact principally interested in the powers of the diocesan bishop and thus in those of the pope, to whom belongs complete jurisdiction, direct and final, general and personal, over the whole Church. This power is displayed by two groups of letters, all of them unauthentic and fabricated for the occasion, purporting to be the work of the early popes from Clement I to Miltiades, and from Silvester I to John III. All four contain, in various proportions, straightforward, authentic matter; genuine writings excerpted, rearranged and conflated; and sheer fabrications. As no contemporary discusses these documents, or makes any mention of the authors, their motives and their dates, a wide field is left for the ingenuity of critics. The date can be deduced without difficulty from the contents of the works and a knowledge of the circumstances of the time, and there is general agreement that all were written by a small group of clerics who were concerned to free the Church from the assaults and encroachments of the secular magnates, and to assert traditional canonical discipline as against Celtic tendencies and irregularities. More specifically, they claimed the right of clerics to a trial before an ecclesiastical court, and that of bishops to appeal from their metropolitan to the apostolic see. One of the most striking characteristics of the group is their exaltation of the powers, prerogatives and supremacy of the pope of Rome. Nevertheless, it is certain that the Roman church had no share in, or knowledge of, the composition of these collections; the papacy was exalted and its prerogatives enhanced simply in order to safeguard the freedom of all ranks of the clergy from secular and metropolitan domination such as is known to have been gaining ground at the time.

Explicit internal evidence as to the provenance of these works is wholly lacking, and when Rome by general agreement had been eliminated as the source, modern scholars put forward in turn three possible localities as homes of the group: Rheims, Le Mans, and the court at Aachen. At Rheims the great archbishop Hincmar was passing through a series of controversies in which some of the False Decretals might have proved useful; Le Mans was a diocese threatened by the aggressive Breton duke Nominoë; the court harboured a group of learned clerks who might have witnessed a recent advance of secularisation. A majority of recent scholars favours Rheims, but the court cannot be ruled out as the focus of the enterprise. Whoever they were, the group, probably a small one, worked swiftly and with a remarkable range of material both scriptural and canonical, both authentic and apocryphal, and showed great discrimination in both choice and composition. While the capitularies are mainly composed of existing material rearranged and re-dated, many of the decretals are entirely new fabrications, and the author takes care to lend verisimilitude to his work by gratuitous fabrication of texts on theological and other matters unconnected with his main practical purpose. The date of the whole corpus can be fixed by internal evidence to within a few years on either side of 850.

When the conditions of the age are borne in mind the forgeries [1] must be pronounced a very successful piece of work; they imposed themselves on posterity for some seven centuries. As happened with other forgeries of the epoch, some contemporaries showed themselves suspicious, but once the documents had achieved wide and distant circulation they were immune from any criticism that the age was capable of providing. There is no evidence that they had any effect in their primary purpose of buttressing the clergy in the general decadence of the empire. Nor did the Roman church make much immediate use of the present offered to it. Indeed there is evidence that both Hincmar and Nicholas I were chary of using Isidore's work. Nevertheless, the collections spread gradually; the Decretals in particular were copied· again and again, but it is certain that, so far from having originated the forgeries, the Roman church was slow to use them. It was not till two centuries later, when the papal party of reform were searching for support in their struggle, that their publicists, and popes themselves, found in the pseudo-Isidore an arsenal of texts. By that time the forgery could not be exposed, and was in fact not suspected, and the cogent passages, genuine and unauthentic alike, were copied everywhere and passed into all the collections before being finally canonised by Gratian.

---

1. Most medieval ' forgeries ' were not what we should call criminal counterfeits. They were reconstructions of what the writer supposed had once existed, or at least what he thought should have existed, though sheer dishonesty became more common when official documents multiplied. How far the disinterested man of that age considered such actions reprehensible, at least before *c.* 1100, is very hard to determine.

This collection of forged documents, possibly the most comprehensive and successful of all medieval counterfeits, was, as has been said, not originally executed to forward the papal claims. The pseudo-Isidore asserted no right that had not already formed part of the papal programme as set out by a succession of great popes from Leo I to Nicholas I, and although the dossier was at Rome by 854, and was used by Anastasius the Librarian in controversy with the Greeks, it did not influence the growth of ideas or the course of events. As has been well said, the forgers were concerned to forward and to exploit for their own purposes the traditional and accepted doctrine of papal supremacy. They did not invent an ideology; ' what they did forge was the decree that was to " prove " this ideology '. [2] Both before and after the date of the False Decretals the Roman church put forward its case firmly and independently. Nevertheless, on several points of judicial procedure, such as the right of all to appeal to Rome, the extension of the clerical *privilegium fori* which entitled clerics to trial before an ecclesiastical court, the protection of those accused against force and despoliation before trial, the False Decretals helped to form, and not only to confirm, canonical tradition.

In the two centuries between the Isidorian forgeries and the Gregorian reform a number of important collections appeared, all of them prolix, disorderly, and containing materials from all available sources. Among them may be noted the so-called *Collectio Anselmo dedicata* (*c.* 885-90), a strongly papal compilation made at or near Milan and using the forgeries; the collection of Abbo of Fleury (*c.* 990), also strongly papal, and above all, the *Decretum* of Burchard, bishop of Worms (composed 1008-12). This vast and influential collection, culled from all sources, including the False Decretals, and arranged with numerous manipulations and falsifications by Burchard himself, was the work of a reformer anxious for a free church but the friend of Otto III and Henry II, at once proclaiming the papal supremacy in doctrine and jurisdiction and making of the pope a modest nonentity in practice. For Burchard, the diocesan bishop is the prop of society both spiritual and temporal; he admits lay ownership of churches *(Eigenkirchen)* while denouncing secularisation; he is in fact a sincere reformer operating within the existing framework of society. Burchard's work was in some respects tendentious. He omitted all but a few of the texts supporting the paramountcy of Rome, and he did not hesitate to omit, alter and extend passages that did not suit with his opinions. Nevertheless, his personality and position in the empire, together with the sheer bulk of his work, won for his writings a currency that endured for a century.

2. W. Ullmann, *The Growth of papal government*, 178.

The generation that followed Burchard's saw a great change. The reformers in the party that ultimately won for itself the name of the Gregorian Reform sought formulas and authority for their programme in the ancient discipline of the Roman church, and instituted a search throughout the archives of Italy for collections of papal and conciliar pronouncements. In this search a vast quantity of material was uncovered, which made possible the critical and academic study of civil as well as of canon law, for the *Authentica, Novellae* and *Pandects* of Justinian probably formed part of the mass that was excavated. The first aim of the reformers, however, was to assemble collections of texts bearing immediately upon the topics at issue, such as papal supremacy, the freedom of the church, and clerical celibacy. Inspired by Cardinal Hildebrand both before his elevation as Gregory VII and after, his colleagues produced a series of compilations. One of the first was the so-called *Collection in 74 Titles* (*c.* 1050), a short gathering made in the papal interest and containing selections from the writings of Gregory the Great and the False Decretals; this was embodied in several later collections. Among subsequent more elaborate works were those of Anselm of Lucca (*c* .1083), Cardinal Deusdedit (*c.* 1087), and Bonizo, bishop of Sutri and (later) Piacenza (*c.* 1085). The two first were strongly, and Bonizo fanatically, Gregorian. The achievement of Anselm was to eliminate Celtic, Frankish and Germanic elements from the canon law, and to reintroduce Roman pronouncements hitherto unused. He paraded a strong battery of papal pronouncements against simony, the marriage of priests and lay ownership of church property. Cardinal Deusdedit concentrated on the primacy, powers and property of the Roman see. The programmatic *Dictatus papae* of Gregory VII belongs to, and may be based upon, the work of these men.

Influential as these collections were, they did not eliminate all opposition. Others continued to copy Burchard and his predecessors, or to select texts more favourable to the imperialist position, and the activity of canonists developed throughout north Italy, France and western Germany. Collections were copied and extended by papalist, imperialist and neutral writers without any advance in critical or methodical presentation. Lanfranc, for example, who taught at Bec and was a reformer, but neither a Gregorian nor an imperialist, compiled a working selection of canon law from Hadrio-Dionysian and Isidorian material for use in the reform of the English church.

A change came at the end of the century with Ivo of Chartres (bishop 1091-1116). Ivo, whom we shall consider more fully elsewhere, made his collections in the early years of his episcopate, *c.* 1093-4. In his *Decretum*, an unwieldy compilation from Burchard, Carolingian legislation and elsewhere, he had a store whence he himself extracted a short, methodical and extremely popular encyclopedia of canon law known as the *Panormia* (*c.* 1095). Ivo's significance is twofold: he was by temperament and choice a moderate, and on principle he worked as a practical statesman in the world as it was. He preached the necessity of mutual respect and assistance between throne and altar, which implied compromise on inessentials. His contemporary, Urban II, was reaching the same conclusions by his use of the dispensing power and his distinction between immutable and reformable legislation. At the same time the theological movement in France, which had now come to a discussion of the sacraments, was widening the field of canon law, while the dialectical and critical methods of the schools were beginning to draw out the principles and seeming contradictions of the canons. It is certain that Ivo used the *sic et non* method a decade or two before Abelard's celebrated preface. Meanwhile, the civil law had leapt forward as the first intellectual discipline to become organised with technical methods of teaching. The tendencies of the age, the needs of the reformed papacy and of bishops throughout Europe, the rivalry of the civilians and the disarray and intrinsic contradictions of the material all called for some kind of rationalisation. The answer to these exigencies was found by the Bolognese monk and teacher Gratian.

PUBLIC WORSHIP AND
THE DEVOTIONAL LIFE

THE spiritual life of the middle ages, as seen in the external observances of public and private worship and prayers, changed its character steadily throughout our period while remaining faithful to a permanent tradition of doctrine and liturgical practice. Speaking very generally
we may say that between the age of Gregory the Great and that of
Innocent III the devotional life manifested itself primarily in the liturgical
services, of which the principal members were the Mass and its satellite
functions such as the ceremonies of Holy Week and other festivals and fasts,
and the Divine Office of psalmody and prayers. These were publicly performed in large churches, and in private by monastic communities, and
though the monastic rite in the Divine Office differed considerably from that
of the Roman church and other local rites, all were nearly allied species of a
single genus, and practices and customs spread easily from one to another.
This liturgical life was seen in its fullest development only in cathedrals,
basilical churches and monasteries, and when the Gregorian reform came
to influence circles other than the clerical and monastic, the devotional
practices of layfolk were derived from the liturgy and monastic customs
and took the form of a selection from, or a shortened form of, the offices
of monks and canons, such as the offices of the Blessed Virgin and of the
dead, together with litanies and selections from the psalter such as the

penitential or gradual psalms. After the age of Innocent III, as we shall see, and guided chiefly by the friars, devotional practice was adapted more and more to the needs of the laity and to the conditions of town life.

The Mass or eucharistic sacrifice had always formed the core and centre of Christian service and devotion, and by the beginning of our period a eucharistic liturgy of a simple type, embodying all the principal elements of the medieval and modern western Mass, was common to all regions. At Rome itself, in the golden age of liturgical and musical composition and ceremonial, an elaborate but austere rite was developed from the year's liturgy in the papal churches, and by means of the so-called Roman directories *(ordines)* the solemn Mass was defined which gradually became the norm elsewhere, and existed till recent changes in the rubrics for solemn Mass in the Roman missal. In this, the lessons and gospels and the whole of the canon from sanctus to postcommunion, together with the collects and secret prayers, have remained almost unchanged throughout the centuries for the cycle of the liturgical seasons from Advent to Pentecost and for the Sundays following that festival. The so-called Leonine, Gelasian and Gregorian sacramentaries represent a gradual development of the rite and an augmentation of prayers and prefaces from the fifth to the eighth centuries at Rome, and the lectionary of epistles and gospels attained its final form *c.* 750. In the centuries that followed cognate or similar liturgies developed in many of the cities of Italy. At Rome, the full choral liturgy was carried out at a number of basilical churches, in many cases by a community of monks established for that purpose, and similar practices were found in some churches north of the Alps. In this western liturgy the Mass, conducted in full view of the congregation, who took part in the offertory and processions, was expressed in the brief, dogmatic, unemotional but deeply impressive formulae of prayers and prefaces characteristic of Rome, with a selection of verses from the psalms and passages from the Scriptures that often display an exquisite if mysterious relevance to the doctrines of the faith or to the mystery commemorated by the day's festival. In its ambit were comprehended all the religious exercises that in later ages came to form separate parts of the worship. In addition to the basic scheme of prayers, offering and sacramental reception of the sacred elements, there was a sermon, which took place after the reading of the gospel, and the elaborate chant which accompanied the Mass and the litanies, processions and prayers that often preceded it.

The core of the eucharistic liturgy, the indispensable canon whose origin is lost in the mist of apostolic times, had received various small modifications in different cities and regions, while at Rome itself the *Kyrie eleison*, the fraction of the host, and the *Agnus Dei* had been inserted in the service from eastern models by Sergius I (687-701). ' Low ' Mass without deacon

and subdeacon had become common by 600, and in the following century
the practice of using round white hosts made of unleavened bread, with
small hosts received orally by the faithful, became the norm and supplanted
the use at the sacrifice of the loaves and wine provided at the offertory.
In 751 Pippin decreed the adoption of the Roman liturgy in his kingdom,
and the Roman chants, carried to the north first by Chrodegang of Metz,
entered Frankland at least in some places, of which Rouen was one.
Charlemagne, some decades later, applied to Pope Hadrian I for a sacramentary of the Roman church. The pope, not without difficulty, secured
a copy of the Gregorian sacramentary with the rite of the papal chapel.
This, with some Frankish additions, formed the basis of the liturgy in the
royal chapel of Aachen. Thence it spread throughout the Carolingian
empire and eventually, c. 1000, travelled back to Rome to form the missal
that was to radiate thence over the whole Catholic world. Thus it may be
said that whereas from the fifth to the end of the seventh century Rome
was a centre of creative liturgical composition, the initiative thereafter
was taken by the Gallic church, and the resulting amalgam was in large
part adopted by the Roman curia and then once more transmitted to the
western church.

    The tendency of the Gallic liturgists was to lengthen and dramatise the
liturgy. Censings were multiplied, solemnity was given to the reading of
the gospel, sequences and extra prayers were added in the form both of
collects and of prayers within the framework of the liturgy, giving expression to thoughts and intentions previously left unspoken. Thus the prayers
Deus qui humanae substantiae at the preparation of the chalice, the *Suscipe
sancta Trinitas* before the Preface, the two prayers, *Domine Jesu Christe*
and *Perceptio corporis tui* immediately before the priest's communion,
and the *Placeat* before the final blessing, came into the missal. Long
prayers before and after Mass were gradually accumulated, some of which
are preserved in the preparation and thanksgiving still printed in the
Roman missal. Celtic penitential influence added some prayers of which
the *Confiteor* is the sole survival, and a number of psalms were introduced,
of which the introductory *Judica* (now lost), *Lavabo* at the washing of
hands and *Dirigatur* at the censing of the altar are fragmentary traces. For
a long time there was great diversity between various churches in small
matters, and to the present day the rite of Milan differs considerably, and
that of Lyons slightly, from the Roman rite, while among religious orders
the Carthusians and Dominicans have preserved the form they originally
adopted from local custom. Still later additions were the elevation of the
consecrated host which was not standardised at Paris till 1210, the final
ablutions, and the gospel of St John at the end, while crossings, kissing of
the altar and genuflexions were multiplied. As will have been noticed, the

recent changes and omissions in the Roman missal have removed many of the additions mentioned above.

Until the end of the eleventh century the texts necessary for the celebration of Mass were distributed in three books, the sacramentary containing the canon and part of the ordinary; the lectionary, with lessons, epistles and gospels; and the antiphoner, containing the words of the introit and other chanted portions of the ceremony. Gradually these three books were combined, owing to the increase and multiplication of private Masses, and the missal, a conflation of all three, began to appear. As for vestments, the original garments and clothes of daily life gradually attained conventional shapes and coloured vestments became common; the so-called five ' liturgical colours ' were standardised in the age of Innocent III, though additional varieties persisted long afterwards.

The days from Psalm Sunday to Easter Sunday, known later as Holy Week, the liturgical week *par excellence* of the whole year, underwent an amplification of a kind similar to that of the normal Mass. The familiar rite of Palm Sunday is drawn from several different sources. The procession of palms was early borrowed from Jerusalem, the source of so many Christian rites and practices, but the blessing of the foliage with its rite and prayers only arose later in Spain and Frankland, to appear at Bobbio in the eighth and Bavaria in the ninth century. The Frankish version was made up of prayers alone, while the German contained the outline of a Mass, and a shortened and conflated form of this rite, the basis of the present service, reached Rome only in the eleventh century. The knocking at the door (which has disappeared from the reformed rite) came from Gaul later still, along with the hymn *Gloria, laus et honor* of Theodulf of Orleans. The singing of the Passion appears *c.* 1000, but it was four centuries before the *turba* or crowd was added to the three soloists; hence the absence of any indication of its share in the chant in the older missals.

The Triduum of Thursday to Saturday contains a core of very ancient practice, crystallising in the Roman rite. Good Friday in particular, especially as newly restored in the recent reform, preserves a very old, non-liturgical (i.e. non-eucharistic) service of lessons and litany. The adoration of the cross, probably borrowed from Jerusalem, was introduced early in the seventh century, and to it was appended the Greek rite of the pre-sanctified some fifty years later. The complete modern rite was elaborated in Gaul and Spain *c.* 900, and the sepulture of the cross and consecrated host, recovered on Easter morning, came a little later. In the greater part of the West this was replaced (and partially absorbed) by the solemn removal and adoration of the host after Mass on Maundy Thursday, but the earlier rite survived till recently in parts of Germany and Austria. The core of what was for a millennium the rite of Holy Saturday, but is now once more the vigil liturgy of Easter day, is very ancient. It is a survival, more complete than that of Christmas, of the liturgy of the vigil-service originally held on all Saturday-Sunday nights. The ' prophecies ' are ancient, and may well be survivals of the pre-historical ' office ' of the day, followed by the Eucharist and pre-dating the dawn office of Lauds which is omitted, as a full ' hour ', on that occasion alone in the year's cycle. This ancient liturgy is now preceded by the blessing of the new fire and the paschal candle, a late eighth-century importation from Gaul to Rome.

The Divine Office evolved long after the eucharistic liturgy was complete, though psalmody and readings from the Scriptures had always formed part of the official order of Christian prayer. The original nucleus at Rome consisted of vespers, the vigil office and mattins (the modern Lauds). A parallel, but more rapid development had meanwhile taken place in monastic circles, with the three ' day ' or ' little ' hours added, to be augmented by prime in the fifth-sixth century and rounded off by compline.

By the end of the eighth century there were some fifty monasteries in Rome, of which nineteen were basilical, and the monastic office subsequently ' contaminated ' the Roman rite, from which in its turn it borrowed several features, including the total office of the Triduum of Holy Week, but each form retained its individuality in its arrangement of psalmody and lessons. In each, also, the ferial office preceded the festal. Until the opening century of our period the liturgical calendar was very simple. Christmas with its ' double ' the Epiphany, an early borrowing from the eastern church, Easter and Pentecost were the only special feasts. The late seventh century, marked by the pontificate of the first Greek pope Sergius I (687-701), saw the introduction of a group of eastern feasts of the Blessed Virgin including the Nativity (8 September), the first day of January, originally regarded simply as a feast of Mary, the Purification (2 February), the Annunciation (25 March), and the Assumption (15 August). The eighth century saw a notable development of the Roman calendar. The feasts of martyred saints had long been held in the church of the cemetery in which the relics lay. In the middle of the eighth century both the bodies of the martyrs and the titles of their churches were transferred into the city, and the celebration of the feast followed, soon to be shared by the papal court when the ' stations ' were established at the various churches as meeting-places for the papal procession. These commemorations of the Roman martyrs still remain as the foundation of the Roman calendar. At about the same time a number of other martyrs, long familiar by reason of the apocryphal ' acts ' of their passion, received liturgical commemoration, among them the apostle Andrew and SS Laurence, Cecilia, Sebastian, Agnes and the Roman martyrs John and Paul.

Whereas the fifth and sixth centuries had witnessed the compilation of the Roman sacramentaries and lectionaries, and had produced the masterpieces of collects and prayers that still evoke our admiration with their dogmatic clarity and their economy of words, the seventh century was the age when the masters of the Roman curia composed the anthems and responds of the 'temporal' offices which remain as monuments of unsurpassable excellence in the liturgical art. Those of Advent, of Christmastide, of Lent, of Passiontide, and of the weeks of paschal time, with their felicity of selection of scriptural texts in which the Latin seems to catch the harmonies of Hebrew poetry, and with the deep but restrained emotion of their allusion to the Christian mysteries, must always remain the despair of modern imitators. They are unsurpassed also in the dramatic force they give to a word or a question, and in their skill, resembling that of an Aeschylus or a Shakespeare, in ' loading ' a passage or an office with significant key words. Equally at ease in times of penance and in times of joy, they give to every season its peculiar colour and tone. Working in succession for almost a century, these nameless masters, to whom the Roman office of the dead may also be attributed, deserve recognition as the creators of the cycle of liturgical offices which is one of the most precious jewels of the Christian tradition.

The basilical monasteries of Rome and a few other large ' cities ' in the West were an influential, but relatively short-lived species. Founded in Rome solely to supply liturgical service, and without any parochial rights or duties, they were independent of the priest of the church, who had no authority over them. Their abbot was appointed by the pope, and was often a secular cleric who administered their funds, and the monks, who often passed out into the papal service, were in effect little different from regular canons. Chief among these monasteries in the seventh century were the three attached to the Vatican basilica of St Peter, and it was from this church, the ' head of the world ' and the lodestar of pilgrims, that the divine office of the Roman model spread out over Europe. Benedict Biscop at Wearmouth (c. 680), and Chrodegang at Metz (754) are only two of the leaders of religion whose love of the Roman fashion of worship led them to transplant it in entirety to their own distant churches, and Chrodegang, Remedius of Rouen and Pippin between them diffused it over the whole Gallican church. The Roman liturgy varied slightly from basilica to basilica and from time to time, but it was standardised by Amalarius the great Carolingian liturgist.

When the feasts of the martyrs were received along with their relics into the churches of Rome, they took their ' office ' with them, and at first the saint's office (or part of it) was celebrated in addition to the office of the day. Then the ferial office dropped out on all save a few of the greatest feasts, such as that of SS Peter and Paul, and by the thirteenth century it had vanished even from these. The centuries between 650 and 1050 saw the Roman liturgy attain, in the words of its eminent historian, to ' a pitch of perfection which was destined not to be surpassed, or indeed maintained. ' [1]

The arrangement of psalmody and lessons as outlined above persisted throughout the middle ages. The only notable changes, in both secular and monastic rites, were concerned with the abbreviation of the lessons. But there was for long a difference between the two which has yet to be mentioned. The Roman office remained for centuries innocent of hymns. These, first introduced into Christian devotional practice by St Ambrose of Milan, remained for a long time extra-liturgical. Ambrose himself composed a number of austere and beautiful hymns in an iambic quantitative metre that followed the classical rules of scansion. These, and others in the same metre, appeared for the first time in liturgical setting in the Rule of St Benedict, and they still remain unchanged in the ferial offices throughout the week, and at the ' little ' hours on feasts and ferias throughout the year. To these were added, by monks and some secular churches, poems or groups of stanzas of the Christian poets of the late empire. The earliest instance of a metre other than the simple iambic was perhaps the *Pange lingua* of Venantius Fortunatus, but at the time of the Carolingian renaissance the door was flung open, and hymns in several of the classical lyric metres entered, among them the magnificent *Ut queant laxis* for St John the Baptist by Paul the Deacon in the Sapphic metre, and others such as the Sunday *Nocte surgentes* and *Ecce jam noctis*, and the familiar *Iste confessor*, as also the admirable trochaic *Urbs beata Jerusalem* and the iambic trimeter *O Roma felix*. Many of these may have come in first in secular churches, but by 1000 they were almost universal, though the great basilicas held out on principle and the Roman office contained no hymns till the end of the thirteenth century.

We may end this section with a few scattered notes. The so-called Athanasian creed, composed in Spain probably *c.* 580, appears at Sunday prime under Hayto, bishop of Basle, in 836; at Cluny it was recited daily in Ulrich's time (1070). The daily (so-called ' little ') office of the Blessed Virgin appears early in the eleventh century, and its diffusion was partly the work of St Peter Damian; here again Rome was resistant to innovation. The office of the dead, on the other hand, which had no direct connection of origin with the much older Mass and funeral service, was a pure Roman creation of the eighth century, originating as a funeral ' vigil ' and spreadling rapidly and widely as a separable office. The commemoration of all

1. P. Batiffol, *Histoire du bréviaire romain* (Paris, 1893), 140. ' L'office romain... était arrivé à un état de perfection qui ne devait être ni dépassé ni maintenu. '

peace-parted Christians (All Souls) had its origin, as is well known, at Cluny on the initiative of St Odilo (d. 1049). Meanwhile in the monastic office the additional psalms and prayers were accumulating: the gradual psalms before the night office, the penitential psalms before prime, the psalms, called the *familiares*, for relatives and benefactors, and the extra short offices of All Saints, the Holy Cross, and others.

Thus by a gradual process, extending over at least six centuries, the liturgy of the year, the ceremonies of a few particular days and occasions and the devotional or optional offices and litanies, had reached their fullest richness of development, at first in Roman, later in Gallican and monastic circles, by about the beginning of the eleventh century. They were to influence lay piety for almost two centuries more, and to remain almost unaltered until the liturgical reforms of Sixtus V and the recent more radical changes of the past fifty years, culminating in those connected with the introduction of the vernacular and the revival of concelebration authorised by the Second Vatican Council.

It is not easy to compose a picture of eucharistic piety in the medieval centuries from the scattered and often discordant evidence of fact, precept and counsel. Throughout, we may distinguish three classes of the faithful: monks and nuns; clerics other than those officially bound to celebrate Mass; and layfolk.

As for monks in central Italy in the mid-sixth century, it seems that in the monastery of the Master's Rule Mass was celebrated by a visiting priest on Sundays, and that he consecrated bread or wafers to suffice for a daily distribution of Holy Communion by the abbot, who was not a priest, and there are clear indications in the Rule of St Benedict that frequent, perhaps daily, communion was the custom, though there is no suggestion of daily Mass. [2] In Carolingian days daily communion is recommended by Theodulf of Orleans, and in the tenth century the practice is commended for English monks and nuns in the *Regularis Concordia* (*c.* 970). A century later Lanfranc's statutes for the Canterbury monks make no mention of communion, and fifty years later the Cistercian customs do no more than exhort monks who are not priests to communicate weekly, preferably on Sunday. During the whole of this period it was becoming slowly more common for all choir monks to proceed to major orders, and monastic customaries make allowance for daily private Masses. In the eleventh century, indeed, there is evidence that Mass was offered on occasion more than once daily out of devotion by priests, while in the mid-thirteenth century the practice of daily private celebration is noted among the virtues of St Thomas Aquinas. Parish priests were bound

---

2. For this see A. de Vogüé, *La Règle du Maître*, 3 vols. Paris 1964-5, I, 63-4 with references to the text. Cf. *Regula S. Benedicti*, ch. XXXVIII.

to celebration on Sundays and feasts, and clerics were exhorted to frequent reception of the Eucharist, but it is impossible to know what in fact was the practice.

For layfolk we have the evidence of Bede (*c.* 730) that the Roman laity received daily communion, and he recommended the practice to his disciple Egbert at York. In the Carolingian epoch, however, the reiterated prescription of councils varied in detail. At Tours in 813 communion three times a year (Christmas, Easter and Pentecost) was decreed, while at Aachen (836) weekly communion on Sundays was recommended. In the eleventh and twelfth centuries thrice a year was the common prescription, with Maundy Thursday sometimes as a fourth occasion, and the fourth Lateran council, so far from making an innovation, represented something of a regression, though the single occasion of the paschal communion was given new and solemn sanction. If counsel rather than the decree of councils is regarded, we find Peter Damian advising daily communion for the devout, and Gregory VII, in one of his rare letters of personal direction, recommending frequent, perhaps daily, reception to his penitent the countess Matilda. Both Gregory and others appeal to St John Chrysostom and other Fathers, and cite the familar dictum of St Augustine that he neither praised nor blamed a daily communicant. Peter Lombard recommends daily communion, and St Thomas, in agreement with Albert and Bonaventure, laid down the teaching, which became stereotyped, that daily communion was lawful and desirable for the earnest Christian acting on the advice of a spiritual guide. While Aquinas and others use the argument that the Holy Eucharist, to which they saw a direct reference in the Lord's Prayer, is a daily bread (and thus, *per contra*, not to be received twice a day), the argument that reception by all who assist at Mass is a liturgical normality, where grave sin is absent, is not found. The thirteenth century, as is familiar, saw a great increase in devotion to the Blessed Sacrament in its visible species, but it is not clear that this was accompanied by a more frequent reception. Indeed, there are indications that this became more rare rather than more frequent in the fourteenth and fifteenth centuries. The author of the *Imitation*, while devoting to the Sacrament a treatise that has become a spiritual classic, nevertheless supposes a frequent rather than a daily reception, and in the early sixteenth century we know that Thomas More's custom was to receive communion at moments of serious concern in his life.

CHRISTIAN CULTURE IN THE WEST

THE centuries between Gregory the Great and Gregory VII stand apart from earlier and later epochs in the history of European learning and letters. They witnessed the final extinction of the direct stream of thought and education that had risen first in Greece a thousand years before, and the first flickering revivals that were to grow into the medieval European civilisation of the middle ages. As the ancient world receded from sight it began to assume the character of a golden age. Hitherto Christian writers had either stood altogether apart from pagan literature, or had been parties in different ways and degrees to the love-hate relationship towards classical culture which had inspired in different ways such men as Jerome, Augustine, and Gregory the Great. It was perhaps natural to feel hostility towards a literature which was the principal attraction of a way of life that could still pose as a rival to Christianity, and which was permeated by the spirit of wordly splendour and moral laxity, and to decry its merits while one could still enjoy as a parasite all the amenities with which that culture had adorned human life. But when Christianity was left alone to fight the battle of civilisation in the West under the gloom of a leaden sky in a savage land, it was natural to look with other eyes upon the civilisation of the past, and from A.D. 600 to 1050 the cultural history of western Europe is a series of attempts, far separated in time and space, to recreate the glories of the past by amassing and imitating its learning and literature. Nothing in literary history is more strange than these attempts – now in Ireland, now in Northumbria, now in Wessex, now in Touraine, now in Bavaria – to copy exactly the expressions and metres and vocabulary of ancient Rome under conditions so widely different from the days of ' Virgil or Juvenal. The literary monuments of these attempts are as exotic flowers or fruit appearing on the grafted branches of woodland trees which, in Virgil's phrase, marvel at their strange foliage and alien fruit. [1] The leaders of these revivals adopted a very different attitude to ancient literature from that of Jerome or Augustine. To them the ancients are a marvel; all knowledge comes from them; they are the only models; to imitate and reproduce them is the one hope of the age. Alcuin, indeed, was to go a stage further. The liberal arts are not the work of man, but of God, who has created them as a part of nature for man to find and to develop. The ancients did their part, how much more eagerly and successfully should Christians emulate them; and Alcuin in a well known passage enunciates the functions of Christian humanism. In the morning of his life he had sown in Britain; in the evening of that life he ceased not to sow in France. His one desire was to build a new Athens in France, or, rather, an Athens better than the old, for the old had only the science of the seven arts, but the new has in addition the seven gifts of the Holy Ghost. [2] This attitude of reverence towards letters and learning is a characteristic of writers of this age, in which education and literary activity – one had almost said literacy itself – was the province of churchmen, whether monks or clerics. In their own phrase, they spoiled the Egyptians; they used the techniques and forms of Virgil or Cicero to clothe the expression of their beliefs and devotions. The history of literature in this age is therefore part of the history of the Church. Whereas in previous centuries Christian writings had formed only a part of the literary activity of the declining empire, now it was the turn of the Church to take over from the ancients and to inspire and control every form of writing.

It might have been expected that the focus of the new life would continue to be found in Italy and southern Gaul. This was not so. Instead, literary activity, like a fire in grass, blazed out now in the extreme west, in Spain, and thence described a wide arc at the periphery of the Christian world, in Ireland, in Northumbria, in Wessex and in Germany, until the flames from the circumference met in a greater fire at the centre of Charlemagne's empire.

The brief and brilliant age of Visigothic Spain opened with the conversion of King Recared I in 589 and closed with the invasion of 711. One of

1. Virgil, *Georgics* II 82: ' Miraturque novas frondes et non sua poma '.
2. Alcuin, ep. 43 in PL CLX col. 209. Cf. *Epistolae* ed. E. Dümmler, 277.

the earliest figures and certainly the most significant of all historically was Isidore (565-636) bishop of Seville from 599 till his death. Isidore is without question one of the ' founders of the middle ages '. Almost all his works are in a sense satellites of the immense encyclopedia known as the *Etymologies* which in fact embraces history, medicine, law, theology, architecture, agriculture, seafaring, and even the domestic sciences. In all these Isidore, with an impersonal simplicity controlled by a sense of moral and religious values, digests and deploys the garnered wealth of the past. Himself the last of the long line of encyclopedists deriving from Alexandria on the one hand and Varro on the other, Isidore was to become a mine and treasure-house to be pondered and plundered and plagiarised by countless writers for eight centuries, while his theological and biblical learning won for him a place on the fringe of the doctors of the Church and alongside Bede and Richard of St Victor in Dante's Paradise. His brother Leander, also of Seville, theologian and correspondent of Pope Gregory, is a less familiar figure, but Julian of Toledo produced another medieval classic in his *Prognosticon* which remained for centuries the *locus classicus* on the fortune of the soul after death. Eugenius and Ildefonsus of Toledo, Beatus, commentator on the Apocalypse, and Valerius, to whom we owe the preservation of the *Peregrinatio Aetheriae*, were of the next generation. The wholly unforeseeable catastrophe of 711 put an abrupt end to what might have been a principal agent in European development. As it was, Spain, which with the expulsion or forcible conversion of the Jews under King Sisebut, and with its reception of eastern influences from Greece and Syria, foreshadowed so much of its later destiny, had a powerful influence upon the literature and learning of Ireland, and thus the mozarabic liturgy and (possibly) the *Hisperica famina* made the voyage from Finisterre to Bantry Bay. [3]

In Ireland the great age of the saints and earliest artists was giving way to that of the emigrants. The death of St Columba at Iona in 597 and of St Columbanus at Bobbio in 615 places those two leaders outside our scope and marks the end of the first wave of expansion. Ireland made her contribution to Latin medieval literature with the writings of Adamnan and the poems of Sedulius, but her chief claim as a nurse of learning lies in the part played by Irish monks in educating visiting scholars from Britain and above all in diffusing manuscripts and a love of learning far and wide from the Hebrides to Regensburg and Bobbio. If the depth and extent of their classical scholarship has sometimes been exaggerated—there would seem to be no clear evidence of any insular knowledge of Greek beyond vocabularies and proverbs – their appreciation of Latin poetry and

3. P. Grosjean, ' Confusa Caligo. Remarques sur les *Hisperica Famina* ', in *Celtica* III (Dublin, 1956), 35-85.

their influence on the production and circulation of Latin classical texts was profound. Nevertheless, while north Britain and some south-western monasteries may have received instruction from the Irish, the rise of a literary class among the Anglo-Saxons was primarily due to continental influence. The Northumbrian Benedict Biscop, the importer of books and customs from Rome and Gaul, and the Cilician archbishop Theodore, who brought standards of Greek education to Canterbury, laid the foundations of the schools of Northumbria and Wessex. In the former the monks of Jarrow-Wearmouth, in close association with the Celtic clerics of Lindisfarne, established traditions of literary and artistic excellence; in the latter Aldhelm of Malmesbury was foremost among the masters who diffused a love of letters and a sound literary training throughout southern England. The finest flower of this age was the monk of Jarrow, Bede the Venerable. Typical of his age, if also eminent among his contemporaries in his writings on chronology, notable for his preference for a literal rather than an allegorical interpretation in his biblical commentaries, Bede in the last years of his life rose far above all around him in his *Ecclesiastical History*. In his use of documents, in his criticism of sources, as a narrator of genius and as a writer of pure, idiomatic, unrhetorical Latin he stands alone. [4] His is the most valuable historical writing in the west between the Latin silver age and the Italian Renaissance. Though written on the margin of the world by a monk who never travelled far from his monastery, Bede's writings spread rapidly. He had disciples, among them Egbert, later archbishop of York and founder of the school there, and within his immediate circle we can see much of the purity of language and historical sense of the master. It is indeed characteristic of Anglo-Saxon Latin writing of this period (if we except Aldhelm) that it is never artificial or pretentious. In the generation following Bede the letters of the Devonian Boniface and his companions and correspondents have the same combination of direct speech and sincere thought.

Theirs, however, was not the strain of learning that was to lead to the Carolingian renaissance. Among the pupils of Egbert at York was Alcuin (735-804) who himself in 778 became master of the schools there and of the library which he has described with enthusiastic detail. Alcuin, returning from Rome in 781, met Charlemagne at Parma and consented to become head of the palatine school at Aachen. Charlemagne, though his own education had been scanty, had ideas of great magnificence and a firm resolve to bring about a rebirth of learning. Alcuin was for eight years at

4. E. Lehmann towards the end of a long scholar's life (in 1959) could declare: ' Mir ist sein Latein immer ein Rätsel... wo und von wem Beda diese vorzügliche Latein gelernt hat '. *Settimana di Studi, Spoleto* IV, 581 (see Bibliography). Gregory the Great may have been an early model, but if so, Bede surpasses his master in lucidity and felicity of language.

the head of the movement, ' the first minister of public instruction ', as he has been called or, with greater propriety, ' prime minister in things of the mind '. [5] When, after a short sojourn in England, he returned finally to Gaul as titular abbot of Tours, he was the real, if not the official, soul of the Carolingian revival, always countenanced by, and in close correspondence with, the ' great barbarian ' himself.

Alcuin's designation as ' intellectual premier ' is apt, because his action and influence extended far beyond the sphere of education, and were far more direct and specific than those of a theoretician or literary dictator. Thus he was entrusted with standardising correct spelling, and as controller of the imperial and monastic *scriptoria* he was able to extend the use of the beautiful and clear script known as the Carolingian minuscule. In another field, Charlemagne laid upon him the task of publishing a reformed and standard edition of the vulgate Bible and of the essential liturgical books, a commission which of necessity included a reform of the chant with the aid of the early Roman gradual and antiphoner, as also the introduction into the Roman rite of a number of Gallican elements. As head of the palatine school and later as abbot of Tours he was able to train and send out eminent pupils to carry with them his scheme and technique of education. Finally, it was to Alcuin that the emperor turned when he felt called upon to assert a point of orthodox doctrine, and when the Adoptionists of Spain or the Iconodules of the East or the opponents of the *Filioque* at Constantinople incurred Charlemagne's displeasure, it was on Alcuin's advice and often with Alcuin's pen that they were corrected. We may be allowed to think that on the two latter points Alcuin was misguided and perverse, and that on the first he showed intolerance, but he has perhaps received less than his due as a theologian. His writings show a truly wide range of reading among the Fathers and councils, and a good selection of texts supporting his opinions. Alcuin was not like Bede, a great historian, nor was he a thinker of power, but as a tireless and enthusiastic diffuser of letters and art, both sacred and secular, at a moment, and under circumstances, peculiarly fateful and propitious, he must always take a very high place among the benefactors of European civilisation. Seldom if ever has a single man so gathered up all the threads of a culture and transferred them from one loom to another. He, more than any other man, is the father of French medieval letters and learning, and of all that has derived from them.

Charlemagne's principal aim had been to create an education for the clerics on whom the administration of his empire was to rest. In capitularies and councils two kinds of school were repeatedly mentioned; the

---

5. Guizot, *Histoire de la civilisation en France* II (Paris, 1853), 167, calls Alcuin ' le premier ministre intellectuel de Charlemagne '.

school of the bishop in every cathedral town, and the cloister school of all monasteries, to be open to external students. Beneath these lay the instruction of the parish priests, to be given freely to the children entrusted to them by parents. As for the matter of education, Alcuin in his treatise on education summarised, but did not depart from, the tradition of the schools or scholarship of the late Roman empire. His treatise is a landmark, but not an innovation. In the Roman empire secondary and even higher education had been almost exclusively literary and rhetorical, and the effect of a rhetorical training on Latin literature and then later on all medieval Latin writing before the scholastic age can scarcely be exaggerated. From the days of Persius and Juvenal, who were to be the models of ethical declamation, down to Bernard and Hildebert, something of rhetoric tinges almost all works of literature, whether in prose or verse. Nevertheless, since the conception of education as a training for public life and forensic speaking had long since disappeared, the end now proposed was to use the learning of the past as a means of understanding Scripture and commenting upon it and the writings of the Fathers. The curriculum was inherited from Rome: the seven (originally nine) liberal arts of grammar, logic, rhetoric, geometry, arithmetic, astronomy and music, of which the three first formed the *trivium* and the four last the *quadrivium*; but all but the first three had fallen out of the educational programme many centuries earlier, and in Alcuin's system grammar and rhetoric alone were developed; the other subjects, when included at all, being treated in a literary way or purely as an exercise of memory.

The aim and achievement of Charlemagne and Alcuin was therefore to produce a literate and well-read clergy, and the thirty years after the emperor's death were to show how well the foundations had been laid. In the history of European culture, the greatest achievement of this first stage was the production of a technique of calligraphy and reproductive accuracy, and if the Carolingian renaissance had done no more than exploit this skill, it would mark an epoch. In fact, it did more; it gave birth to a generation of ecclesiastics who had read widely in all the literary remains of the western church, and it gave a literary education to a group of laymen.

The name of Alcuin is an indication that Charlemagne accepted or invited men of talent wherever he found them. The two members of the Aachen ' academy ' next to him in importance also came from outside the empire. Paul the Deacon, a Lombard who became a monk of Monte Cassino and wrote a celebrated commentary on the Rule of St Benedict, was a versatile scholar who wrote a history of the Lombards, and a life of Gregory the Great, besides putting together a collection of extracts from the sermons of the Fathers that went down the middle ages. In addition he composed one of the greatest of Latin hymns, the *Ut queant laxis*, in honour of John the Baptist. The other, Theodulf of Orleans, was a Visigoth banished from Spain, and a man of wide interests and cultivated taste in literature and art. Favoured by Charlemagne, who gave him the bishopric from which he took his name, he was used on diplomatic missions and in theological controversies, sharing with Alcuin the authorship of the *Libri Carolini*. He also wrote a hymn which is still in honour, the *Gloria, laus et honor*, soon embedded in the liturgy of Palm Sunday.

The generation that followed were all, mediately or immediately, the pupils of Alcuin and his friends. At the German abbey of Fulda Hrabanus Maurus, a direct disciple, earned the title of ' schoolmaster of Germany ', and himself taught letters to Servatus Lupus, monk of Ferrieres. Reichenau, on Lake Constance (Germany), was the monastic home of the poet and letter-writer Walafrid Strabo. Hrabanus, encyclopedist and theologian; Lupus, the indefatigable borrower of books and copier of manuscripts and humanist writer of letters; Walafrid, who describes in detail the plants in his monastery garden; these are, with Einhard, the biographer of Charlemagne, the greatest figures of the second generation. All are in their way literary humanists, lovers of ancient poetry for its own sake. Of another family, but also bearing the impress of Carolingian learning, are such men as Hincmar, indefatigable controversialist, and the unknown group who produced the forged decretals and capitularies.

Much has been written in recent years to challenge or to confirm the reputation of the Carolingian renaissance. What, precisely, was reborn? How far was any part of it either admirable or durable? It has been said that there was nothing original in the work of the Carolingian scholars, that it was no more than a technically improved version of what had gone before, that it was restricted to a few literary genres without any philosophical or theological depth, and that it vanished leaving Europe as dark as, if not darker than, before. It may be admitted that no great works of literature and no original thought resulted from it, and that the reign of Charlemagne did not inaugurate a new era in western intellectual life. Its achievements were at a lower level, that of grammar and Latin composition, the method, the system and the framework of education. But at this level, and within its own sphere, its work was durable. The method, the framework and the system of education had been set on the lines that were to be followed for more than three centuries.

The Carolingian renaissance owed more to its titular patron than did the Periclean or the Medicean age. Without the monarch's direct and purposeful agency there would have been no revival. Though himself technically uneducated, Charlemagne admired learning and was alive to its necessity in a church which must necessarily supply the counsel and the laws, and much of the administration, of his empire. Hence his celebrated capitularies establishing, at least in theory, a system of education at the levels of parish, monastery and cathedral. Hence also his establishment of a palace school and his creation of a group of distinguished scholars drawn at first from beyond the Alps, the Channel and the Pyrenees, such as Alcuin, Paul the Deacon and Theodulf. These men, and others invited or attracted by the emperor, formed a company that was at once an academy and a cabinet of the American model to advise their master on all matters of theological or educational policy.

All these achievements made the Carolingian revival different both in degree and in importance from any other revival of learning before the eleventh century. In the first place, and largely owing to the ideas and propaganda of Alcuin, literary achievement, based on a study and an imitation of the ancients, was now regarded as desirable and praiseworthy. Christian culture was to equal all that had gone before and to surpass it aided by divine illumination. The pen was a nobler tool than the spade in the monk's hand. [6] This view, that the writings and thought of the Greco-Roman world had attained to a human excellence to which Christians could add greater perfection, was a new and influential one. Secondly, the organiɔation of *scriptoria* throughout the monasteries of the empire, in which copies of the classical and patristic authors were systematically multiplied in the ' Carolingian minuscule ', gradually provided the libraries of Europe with large collections of masterpieces to read and to imitate. For many of the Latin classics a manuscript of the early ninth century is the oldest complete text. This was a revolution, smaller indeed and more limited, but still comparable to the impulse given to learning and letters by the invention of printing. Thirdly, the capitularies of Charlemagne and the manuscripts written in the monasteries remained to serve as an inspiration and material for future revivals. The best witness to the work of Alcuin and his colleagues is the theological and controversial activity of the age of Hincmar. The Carolingian revival waned, like all others in the early middle ages, because it lacked the background of administrative machinery and organisation that in fully developed civilisations can sustain institutions even when genius is wanting.

PART TWO
1049-1198

THE GREGORIAN REFORM

THE great movement of reform in the western church which extended over the space of a hundred years has often been misrepresented by historians and misunderstood by their readers through a lack of adequate breadth of treatment. In the past attention was often directed almost exclusively to the contest between empire and papacy, and, within that contest itself, to the controversy over the particular point of lay investiture. It is only within the last fifty years that this great dispute, the contest *(lis) par excellence* for German historians, has been seen more correctly as one aspect of a vast movement of moral, disciplinary and administrative reform affecting the whole of society and not only the papacy and the clergy. Seen still more fully, even the wide province of ecclesiastical and religious reform is only one aspect of the emergence of western Europe from its intellectual tutelage into an adolescence of mental and practical capability; it forms, in fact, a part of the new life which in other manifestations has been called the renaissance of the eleventh and twelfth centuries. The centralisation of the papacy, the monastic revival, the rebirth of canon and civil law, are all features of the same movement of the spirit which inspired the new dialectic, the growth of the schools, Romanesque art, and Domesday book. Yet even so we are not surveying a landscape sufficiently wide. The eleventh century looks back as well as forward. Just as the matter of investiture is only a facet of the laicisation of the Church and the universal *Eigenkirchentum*, so the advance of the papacy is only comprehensible if the long tradition of the Roman see is borne in mind. Indeed, the contest of empire and papacy cannot rightly be understood unless the earlier relations of the papacy with Charlemagne, and with the emperors of eastern Rome from the time of Constantine downwards, have been examined and remembered. So it is, that the short space of thirty of forty years, which witnessed the full development of the reform known to posterity by the name of Hildebrand or Gregory, and which reached a climax in the pontificate of Gregory VII, can only be understood if it is considered as the direct outcome of more than seven hundred years of opposing theories and actions. By the same token, those years form a watershed in European history beside which, as a short epoch of significant and permanent change, only the similar periods of the Reformation in the sixteenth century and of the French Revolution in the eighteenth can be considered as comparable. The monastic revival and the rebirth of speculative activity will be considered elsewhere; here we are concerned only with what may be called the political history of the reform.

The moral and spiritual rebirth throughout the period, if considered in all its aspects, is seen to have been largely the work of monks, and it is usual, and appropriate, to see its first beginning in the foundation of the abbey of Cluny *c.* 910. Up to that date, ever since the early years of Lewis the Pious a century earlier, there had been a general decline of religious life, and all revivals had been short-lived. With the foundation of Cluny we see the birth of an institute that was to endure throughout the creative period of the middle ages, to last indeed until it was swept away, along with other remains of feudal Europe, by the French Revolution. But Cluny did not stand alone. The foundation of Brogne in northern Lorraine a few years later (914), and that of Gorze near Metz twenty years after Brogne (933) show that a true spirit of reform was stirring, while in south Italy, at the very same moment, there appeared the first of a new family of eremitical and monastic saints. The monastic reformers, however, had no direct influence on the head and members of the hierarchy of the Church. They are notable in a wider context than that of their own order only as providing fixed points of regular life, and nurseries from which the individual reformers were to come a century later. These, as monks, left a monastic impress on all their work; they looked upon their world as from a monastery, and the remedies they proposed were monastic in character.

We have seen that Silvester II, whose career and historical significance are strangely similar to those of Hadrian VI in a later age, was energetic during the short space of four years in defending the claims of his see and was responsible also for founding the hierarchies of Hungary and Poland.

The death of the emperor in 1002, followed by that of the pope a year later, ended this foretaste of spring, and although the new king, Henry of Bavaria, originally destined for the Church, was a devout and conscientious ruler who ultimately achieved canonisation, he had no intention of abandoning the traditional royal control of the German and Lombardic church and its bishops. The reign of Henry II, indeed, saw a period of achievement when the monarch of a united Germany presided over a reforming papacy with something of the spirit of a Charlemagne. At Rome, the baronial house of Tusculum came into power and provided a series of popes of whom the most notable, Benedict VIII, combined the part of a successful warrior baron who regained territories lost to the papacy and defeated the Saracens with a fleet from Genoa and Pisa, with that of an active pope who worked with and accepted the control of the emperor. In 1022, in a council at Pavia, the two sovereigns of Christendom promulgated, among other measures, a canon reaffirming the celibacy of the clergy, and even extending the canon against incontinence to all clerks. Probably, however, this decree was inspired by feudal and economic motives, to prevent the alienation and release from feudal hands of property attached to private churches. In any case, pope and king once again died prematurely and almost simultaneously (1024), and under the unspiritual Conrad II a young and probably dissolute pope renewed some of the scandals of the past. After an interval of confusion, in which at one moment three claimants disputed the papal office, the decisive turn came when Henry III at the synod of Sutri deposed the worthy but technically simoniac Gregory VI, patron of the rising Hildebrand, and appointed first Suitger bishop of Bamberg (1046) as Clement II and then (1047) Poppo, bishop of Brixen, as Damasus II. While this showed clearly enough where the real power lay, it was nevertheless a break with the claims and feuds of Rome, and when Damasus died after a few months Henry appointed his relative, Bruno, a reforming bishop of Toul. With his entry upon the scene a new epoch began.

To what extent, and in what ways, did the Church of the mid-eleventh century need reform? And who were the first reformers? Genuine spiritual reform may come from two sources: from individuals unusually gifted with virtue, energy and spiritual wisdom, and from a zealous and enlightened authority. The latter agency was almost entirely absent at the Roman centre before 1049, and the imperial government was unable to take the place of the pope as Justinian I and Charlemagne had taken it. Not only were genius and prestige lacking, but the German monarchs had never in practice claimed, with Charlemagne, to govern the whole Church as the divinely appointed ruler of all Christendom; theirs it was to rule their difficult kingdom, in which bishops and abbots were great feudatories holding of the king, but the spiritual life of Christendom was, in theory at least, under papal jurisdiction. Moreover, the empire was no longer by any stretch of words or ideas coextensive with Christendom. Not only the British Isles and much of Italy, but the whole of France and a growing number of peripheral national churches, such as those of Poland, Bohemia, Hungary and reconquered Spain, looked directly to the pope without any mediation through the emperor. A few imperial publicists, followed by some modern historians, might write as if the Staufen emperors, like Charlemagne, controlled the whole of western Christendom, but this was not the case, and the contest between empire and papacy was not in 1070, still less fifty years later, a struggle between two contestants for a single territorial unit. Reform on a large scale, therefore, could not come from even the best of emperors.

That the papacy needed reform was clear enough. Though Roman scandals have undoubtedly been exaggerated, both by contemporaries and by historians down to the day of Duchesne, the unworthiness of very many of the popes for two hundred years, their entanglement in Roman feuds, and their administrative inability to deal with the affairs of the whole Church, need no demonstration. Widespread reform could only come from the centre, and from a centre that was itself pure and powerful.

Whether, or in what sense, the great body of Christians needed reform at that moment more than at any other can scarcely be decided. In the eleventh century the vast majority of western Christians were illiterate peasants bound in one way or another to the land they worked. By this time almost all were within reach of a church and a priest and could attend Mass and receive the sacraments. What use they made of the rudimentary Christian teaching and the skeleton of Christian life and worship in which they had a share we cannot say. But as yet, save perhaps in a few cities and towns of Italy, the programme of reform did not include, as it included in the later middle ages, a revolution or reorganisation at the parochial level. At the other end of the scale, monastic reform, within certain conventional limits, had preceded any movement for general reform, and though fervent individuals were engaged throughout the century in initiating and spreading strict observance the monastic order in general was not one of the objects of concern in high places. Indeed, it was because many of the early reformers, monks themselves, had their own order relatively in hand that they could turn their attention to other classes. As will be seen, their panacea was to monachise the church by a general summons to the regular life and by giving a monastic rule of life, so far as was possible, to the secular clergy and the laity. There remained the clergy from the pope downwards: bishops, priests and the lower orders. Here the basic evil, only now becoming clear, was the submersion of the priests of the church in lay society. The papacy, when not labouring in the mire of Roman faction, was in harness to the German kings; the bishops, almost without exception, were chosen by lay magnates, enriched by royal and other benefices, caught up in feudal engagements, and largely occupied in administrative services for their temporal lords. At the worst, they had bought their office for a price. The lower clergy, with very few exceptions, were either directly attached to the service of a lord, great or small, or served for a subsistence income a church that was regarded as a piece of real property, of which the major part of the income went away to one or more proprietors. It is true that this submergence of the clergy was not due to any explicit policy of lay rulers, and that in all the polemical writings of the age before the revival the paramountcy of the spiritual over the temporal was asserted or assumed. Nevertheless, in the world as it then was, the clergy high and low had all but ceased to have a corporate or a disciplined or even a distinct life of their own. With the pope a Roman baron and petty sovereign, and at times also chaplain and servant of the emperor, with bishops, often very wealthy, as leaders among the feudal baronage, and with priests as small peasants, married and often mere links in an hereditary chain, there was no organised body of clergy and no possibility of its serving as a leaven or as a light for the rest of the world.

The reformers themselves concentrated their attention and their propaganda upon two universal evils and one great remedy. The evils were, in the language of the time, ' simony ' and ' nicolaism '; the remedy was disciplinary action on the part of a free and powerful papacy. Neither evils nor remedy were novel; what was novel in an age when problems of every kind were being isolated and defined, was the widespread desire to deal with a state of things rather than with isolated instances, and to find or create a law and a machinery for accomplishing this. In the course of this campaign there emerged in the West, for the first time, an organised class, the clergy or great body of clerks, tightly bound together under bishops who themselves were tied tightly to the bishop of Rome, with a law and interests that separated them from the laity, who were to occupy a lower place.

Simony, a sin as old as Christianity, was originally the perverse belief that supernatural gifts or charismatic powers could be purchased for money. It had subsequently been used of the purchase or sale of spiritual or sacramental actions or offices, and was extended to cover all services or fees given or demanded on appointment or ordination to the priesthood or episcopate. As the original sin was a confusion of grace with magic, and a wholly false conception of the working of the Holy Spirit in the Church, it was labelled as a heresy. Sacramental theology was still in its infancy, and the bestowal of holy orders had not yet been treated on the analogy of baptism; it was therefore easy for the opinion to become common among the reformers that a simoniacal transaction prevented the transmission of spiritual powers and that orders and sacraments bestowed simoniacally were null; the distinction between licitness and validity in the exercise of a power had not as yet been fully employed. How frequent fully simoniacal transactions at the level of episcopal appointments had become cannot be said. Precise instances of the payment of large sums for bishoprics are lacking before the tenth century, and the worst cases and greatest frequency would seem to have occurred when the campaign of the reformers was already under way. Simony of a less obviously reprehensible kind, such as the payment by a bishop of the equivalent of a feudal ' relief ' on the acceptance of a fief, or by a priest on the lower level of an ' entrance fee ' to a church, were more widespread, though the former became common only when the feudal machinery had become elaborate and standardised. Nevertheless, the reformers undoubtedly had a strong case, even if they exaggerated or mistook some of the instances they quoted. What they were at bottom resisting was lay proprietorship of church property and offices, with the consequent enslavery or robbery, as well as the moral degradation, of the Church.

Nicolaism, the second evil, is a name of uncertain origin which came to stand for clerical incontinence. Chastity or celibacy was part of the ancient canonical discipline of the western church, but breaches of this discipline, and indeed a total neglect of the precept, had become more and more common in western Europe after the collapse of Roman civilisation. Here again statistics are necessarily wanting. Reformers often exaggerate, but there is a large and constant body of evidence to show–as might be expected in a vast and undisciplined body–that marriage, or concubinage, was widespread and common. The term ' marriage ' is not incorrect: at this time Holy Orders were not a canonical impediment invalidating an attempted marriage, nor was the presence and blessing of a priest a necessary condition. Many priests in all countries had undertaken a permanent union carrying with it all its legal consequences and rights. Nicolaism therefore had results beyond its intrinsic personal effect. It led naturally both to the inheriting of churches (as benefices) and to the dissipation by gift or will of church property. It led also to social and economic difficulties peculiar to the age. Though the priest was often of servile or villein status, his office raised him among his fellows and his consort was often of free birth. Sons ' followed the mother ', and the lord was thus deprived of the offspring of his serf as well as of some of the church's wealth which came to him by gift or inheritance. Thus the economic motive sometimes allied the lay lord with the reformer. But generally speaking, when all churches were in the hands of a proprietor, lay or clerical, and when the diocese was a geographical region or a congeries of churches rather than an integrated unit of pastoral administration, when the priests, socially the equals of their fellow-villagers and often illiterate, were married or at least shared their house with a woman and children, the priesthood could do little towards reforming society. To this must be added, on the evidence of Peter Damian and others, the prevalence of every kind of sexual vice and irregularity in the population of the towns of north Italy and Provence. The party of reform were justified in thinking that all these irregularities could be attacked only by recreating a pure and disciplined priesthood, governed by bishops who were under no relationship of dependence in regard to their secular lord, but who were freely elected and consecrated according to canon law, and directed by a pope resolved and able to affirm and to sanction the traditional canonical discipline of the Roman church.

While the activities and writings of reformers such as Bishop Wazo of Liège and Peter Damian had been notable during the first half of the eleventh century, the crucial moment when individual attempts were replaced by action from the centre may be placed in 1049, when Leo IX arrived in Rome accompanied by the young Hildebrand and was soon joined by a cohort of like-minded Lorrainers, such as Hugh Candidus, Udo of Toul, Frederick of Lorraine and Humbert of Moyenmoutier, all of whom were shortly to become cardinals. This internationalisation of the cardinalate was in itself the striking assertion of a programme though it did not yet become a permanent practice. The new pope, chosen long before as a young deacon to lead troops for his bishop, and retaining to the end some of the qualities, such as speed of movement and rapid decision, of a great commander, started his work at once with a paschal synod in Rome at which earlier decrees against simony were reaffirmed. Leo, indeed, supported by Humbert, seems to have held that ordinations by simoniacs were invalid, and wished to impose reordination, but the synod would not proceed thus far. After the meeting the pope left immediately for the first of his long journeys to Cologne, Aachen, Trier and Toul. At Rheims in the autumn he held a synod to extirpate simony, followed by another at Mainz. The following year he toured central and south Italy, condemned Berengarius at Rome, visited north Italy and crossed the Alps for Toul and Augsburg (February 1051). In central Italy again in the autumn and following spring (1052) he went north for a third time and joined Henry III at Pressburg. Thence with some encouragement from Henry he led an armed force across the Alps against the Norman invaders of south Italy, who were threatening papal territory at Benevento. His army was defeated, he himself was captured, and died (1054) shortly after coming to terms with the Normans and despatching to Constantinople the embassy that was to serve the cause of unity so ill.

Leo stands at the doorway of a new world: a devout and spiritual man, by his synods, his journeys and his policy of ' visiting ' the churches beyond the Alps, he was the first to display the papacy as an immediate and drastic agency of reform throughout the Church. The friend of a truly devout emperor, he did not solve, and perhaps did not realise, the problem of lay control of episcopal and papal elections, and he seemed to many unwise in drawing the sword against the Normans as he has seemed also unwise in sending Humbert to Constantinople. Though himself spiritual, he did not consistently stand above events as the father in God of all Christendom.

He was succeeded by a young relative of the emperor, Victor II (1054-7), who was content to accept his patron as co-president at a council and who spent much of his pontificate in Germany. He in his turn was followed by Frederick, brother of the duke of Lorraine, a reformer who had recently become a monk to avoid any action the emperor might take for his share in the embassy of 1054 to Constantinople. Placed as abbot over the un-willing monks of Monte Cassino and then created cardinal he was soon to be elected canonically by the clergy at Rome as Stephen IX during the minority of Henry IV. His short reign (1057-8) was marked by the appear-ance of Humbert's treatise *Adversus simoniacos*, which is distinguished from all previous writings against simony by its clear advocacy of two remedies. The first, a corollary of Humbert's steadfast assertion that sim-ony was a heresy, and that in consequence simoniacal ordinations were invalid, was the proposed annulment of all orders or sacraments conferred or administered simoniacally. The second was the complete restoration of canonical election with a consequent elimination of lay control. Humbert's treatise, it has been generally recognised, was the direct cause of the papal election decree of 1059. On the death of Stephen IX the Roman nobility elected the bishop of Velletri, who took the name of Benedict X; Hilde-brand, on embassy at the imperial court, returned to put forward as candi-date a reformer, Gerard, bishop of Florence, who became Nicholas II, and on 13 April, 1059, the celebrated decree was promulgated giving the right and duty of papal election to the cardinal bishops supported by the other cardinals and approved by the clergy and people of Rome, with no more than a salute to the king of Germany. Not unnaturally the German bishops riposted by condemning the pope and quashing his decrees: it was the first exchange of salvos in the great strife.

The pope had already strengthened his position by negotiating an alli-ance with Robert Guiscard and reiterating the election decree at a synod in 1060, omitting the allusions to the people of Rome and the king of Germa-ny, and adding sanctions. In addition, he renewed the decree on simony and the celibacy of the clergy of Leo IX, decreed the establishment of houses of canons with a recall to ' the apostolic life ', and forbade the faithful to hear the Mass of a concubinary priest. We can see here the hand of Peter Damian, whose theologically moderate opinion the pope followed in the matter of reordination. Finally, clerics were forbidden to receive churches at the hands of laymen, though it is not clear how far this was intended as an absolute and immediate measure. Taken together, the pontificates of Leo IX and Nicholas II had gone far in the direction of what we know as the Gregorian reform, and the premature death of the latter (1061) was a misfortune for the Church. After an interval of three months Anselm of Lucca was canonically elected as Alexander II, whereupon a German council at Basle elected Cadalus, bishop of Parma and sometime Nicolaite as Honorius II. Humbert the extremist was now dead, and Peter Damian worked for an understanding with the German court. This was effected by the action of Alexander II, but at the expense of sacrificing a principle by referring the issue between Cadalus and himself to a commission of Godfrey of Lorraine and the court of Germany. It was on this occasion that Damian composed a treatise advocating a close understanding between pope and monarch, and he went on to write to Anno, archbishop of Cologne, suggesting a general council to clear matters up. This drew from Hildebrand a sharp rebuke, which itself gave occasion for Damian's allusion to Hildebrand as his ' holy Satan ', but the council duly took place at Mantua in 1064; Alexander II was confirmed in office; so also was the king of Germany as arbiter of the papacy. For the rest, Alexander II was an assertive, reforming pope. He proceeded against unchaste priests and simoniacs and forbade assistance at their Mass. Meanwhile in Germany during the regency of the empress Agnes for her son Henry IV simony had reappeared in strength. Bishoprics and abbeys were sold at the royal palace, all appointments in Germany were made in the name of the king, and Alexander II was uncertain in his opposition. Nevertheless, for all his occasional weaknesses and inconsistencies, the pope developed centralisation by sending legates about Italy and France, England and Spain, and even German affairs came back to him in the last resort. He directed the Spanish crusades and set his face against the attempted divorce of Henry IV; he also claimed suzerainty over south Italy, Sicily and Spain. His was a notable pontificate.

Alexander II died on 21 April 1073. On the following day the Roman populace acclaimed Cardinal Hildebrand and the cardinals proceeded to elect him in canonical fashion. Born between 1015 and 1020 of plebeian stock in Tuscany, he was brought up in a Roman monastery where he may have become a monk, though more probably Lorraine was the region of his profession, and he then assisted Gregory VI, whom in 1046 he followed, unwillingly, into the exile imposed upon the deposed pope by Henry III. Returning after a short period with Leo IX he acted as legate for him in France. Appointed archdeacon of the Roman church by Nicholas II, he became the trusted counsellor of the pope. In his own register as pope, which can be augmented by letters and documents from other sources, we can discover his ways of acting, his principles, his motives and his ideals more fully than those of any pope since Gregory I. We can see an inflexible and logically argued insistence on the paramount powers and God-given authority of the Roman see which, when regarded in isolation, may appear repellent in its stark claim to universal reverence and unlimited obedience, infallibility and unaccountability, but a careful reading shows also the necessary counterpoise of a spirit of genuine religious feeling, of wide charity and of personal humility. The pope's authority is to be used only to forward the cause of justice, understood as the will of God known in his commandments, and justice and peace are key-words throughout all Gregory's pronouncements.

We cannot doubt that Gregory VII began his pontificate with a desire for peace and understanding with all. He recognised as valid lay appointments where no money had passed and absolved all offenders from the excommunication incurred over the matter of the Milan election (see p. 176). In his first Lenten synod of 1074 he reiterated without change his predecessors' decrees against simony and unchastity, and repeated the prohibition against assisting at the Mass of an unchaste priest. Meeting with resistance and convinced of the need for more drastic measures the pope, at the Lenten synod of 1075, after renewing the decrees of 1074, renewed also that of 1059 prohibiting the reception of an abbey or bishopric at the hands of a layman, but neither now nor on its first issue was this decree promulgated as for universal observance. [1] Indeed, Gregory made it clear from his actions that, provided the appointment was free from simony, he was prepared to let it stand. In a sense the decree was not novel; it was a return to Roman canon law of six centuries earlier. It was however in fact a novelty in two ways: first, it ran counter to a practice at least three centuries old, by which emperors, monarchs and feudal lords had freely bestowed bishoprics and abbeys without let or hindrance. Even allowing for the medieval regard for the distant past as a golden age to be recaptured when possible, a sudden break with the immediate past and with actual practice in a matter such as this was politically a revolution. Secondly, the papal decrees abolished, by ignoring, the subsequent assent of the monarch to a canonical election. This had been allowed explicitly, and had even been enjoined by popes, since the time of Charlemagne. To withdraw this time-honoured custom was a very serious step, which assumed the validity of Gregory's interpretation of the papal prerogative.

1. The decree of 1075 is not extant; that of 1059 is in MGH *Legum* sect. III Constitutiones et acta publica imperatorum et regum, I, 547 (Jaffé-Wattenbach 4405).

It was in fact at this very moment that the celebrated *Dictatus Papae* was drawn up (1074-5). While the old view of this as a manifesto or published programme is probably incorrect, it certainly presents papal powers as Gregory saw them and intended to use them. [2] It is a logical translation into practice of the unlimited commission of Christ to Peter, but although almost every phrase can be found in earlier decrees (including the False Decretals which, however, did little more than state crisply what was commonly acknowledged), the *Dictatus* nevertheless outlines a doctrinal programme, terse and comprehensive, which if put into execution would show a command of power and a degree of centralisation never exercised or contemplated hitherto.

In fact, it is the consistent implementation of the *Dictatus* that gives supreme importance to the rule of Gregory VII. The centralisation of power, based on the conviction of possessing at once universal authority and universal responsibility, took many forms. In regard to the hierarchy, Gregory VII minimised the importance of the primatial status and reduced the powers of the archbishop to the consecration of his suffragans and presiding at synods, while the diocesan bishops were supervised directly from Rome. The pope continued and developed the use of plenipotentiary legates, either temporary for a particular commission or permanent for a region. An outstanding example is that of Hugh of Die, the energetic, zealous and intransigent archbishop (after 1082) of Lyons, more Gregorian than the pope. Elsewhere may be seen Altmann of Passau (Germany, 1080), Anselm of Lucca (Lombardy, 1081) and Amatus of Oleron (south-west France, 1075). The activities of these men were considerable; whether the protests aroused by their drastic methods were justified remains uncertain, but in some cases, at least, the pope revised their sentences of deposition and excommunication, and his letter to Hugh of Die recalling to his notice the tolerance and discretion of the Roman church should be noted in any assessment of Gregory's character. Yet another instrument of reform was found in a new activity characteristic of the period, that of the polemists and pamphleteers. Nevertheless, legates were not always able to deal satisfactorily with slippery customers such as Hermann of Bamberg and Manasses of Rheims.

Yet if the original aim of Gregory was to maintain good relations with Henry IV, full agreement was impossible. The outlook of the two leaders and the uncompromising programme of the pope in face of the unreliable

---

2. The suggestion of G. B. Borino, that the *Dictatus Papae* is an index or reference-list to passages from canonical collections, in ' Un ipotesi sul " Dictatus Papae " di Gregorio VII ', in *Archivio della R. Deputazione Romana di storia patria* 67 (1944), 237-52, is accepted by K. Hofmann in *Studi Gregoriani* I, 533-40, and has been characterised by S. Küttner, *ibid.* II, 401, as ' one of those happy historical insights which have only to be formulated to be at once recognised as truth '.

yet politically able king rendered a concordat impossible. The breach was to come over the bishopric of Milan. After riots the populace in 1075 demanded another bishop in place of the canonically elected Atto, and Henry nominated Tedald. On the crest of the wave after suppressing the revolt against his rule in Saxony, the king ignored the pope's protests, and summoned an assembly at Worms (January 1076) at which his excommunicated counsellors and bishops, who had refused to attend Gregory's synods and execute his decrees, consented to depose ' the false monk Hildebrand '. Henry, for his part, wrote to the pope developing his claim to divine appointment as the temporal vicegerent of Christ wielding one of the two swords of the gospel. Gregory replied by suspending Henry from kingship (Lent 1076), freeing his subjects from their oath of fealty and, finally, excommunicating him. The last act was a move on the part of the papacy that had no precedent. The German princes, in part reverencing the papal excommunication and in part glad of an excuse for rebellion, met at Tribur (16 October) and decided that the king must come to Augsburg on 2 February 1077 and plead his cause in the presence of the pope. Gregory agreed to this and in the middle of an exceptionally severe winter set out for Germany. The promised escort was not forthcoming, and rumours were about that Henry was moving south. The pope therefore took refuge in an impregnable castle of the countess Matilda, who throughout a long life showed herself the staunch champion of the papacy. The castle of Canossa stood (and still stands) on a spur of the Apennines, and Henry, accompanied by a handful of men, appeared before its gates at the end of January professing repentance and begging for absolution. Gregory delayed for three days, then, whether overborne by the pleadings of Matilda and Abbot Hugh of Cluny, the one cousin, the other godfather of the young king, or, as is more probable, unable in his capacity of supreme father in God to resist the prayers of a penitent who gave every outward sign of sincerity, he yielded and lifted the ban. Henry's supporters (as representing in this the king himself) gave security on oath for his future conduct; it is disputed whether he was restored to the exercise of his kingly powers, but Gregory declared he did not take this step.

Gregory had acted well in the spiritual sphere, in that of politics he had forfeited a great advantage. His allies among the German nobles regarded his action as a betrayal, and proceeded to ignore Henry and elect Rudolph of Swabia in his place despite the efforts of papal legates to obtain a delay. A period of three years of confusion followed in which the pope lost the initiative and many of his supporters in Germany. Finally Gregory, perhaps fearing further loss of support, proceeded to a second excommunication (7 March 1080) to which were added a deposition, a prophecy of disaster, and the recognition of Rudolph as king. This alienated almost the whole German episcopate who, joined by discontented colleagues from Lombardy, met at Brixen (25 June) and deposed Gregory, electing as anti-pope Guibert, archbishop of Ravenna (Clement III). This last step was clearly uncanonical, and many German bishops wavered, but the death of King Rudolph in battle (15 September 1080) not only removed Henry's only rival possessed of a colourable title, but seemed to many a judgment of heaven in the opposite sense to that which the pope had so confidently predicted. Henry was now free to move south, while a war of pamphlets set forth his claims to rule by both heredity and divine right in opposition to the reassertion of the uncompromising claims of the papacy in Gregory's second and programmatic letter to Hermann of Metz. The pope was forced to take refuge in the fortress of Sant' Angelo while the emperor and his bishops once more deposed him and enthroned Clement III (24 March 1084) who immediately placed the imperial crown on Henry's head (31 March). Two months later Gregory's ally, Robert Guiscard, retook the city, but the consequent sack turned the citizens against Gregory and he abandoned Rome to his rival, who re-entered at once. The pope eventually took refuge in Salerno, where he died (25 May 1085), unbroken in spirit and freeing from censure all his opponents save the emperor and anti-pope, giving judgment on his own life with the well-known words: ' I have loved justice, and hated iniquity, therefore do I die in exile. ' [3]

Gregory and Henry, like Thomas and another Henry in England a century later, were antagonists in a quarrel that will always divide the sympathies of those who consider it. In both cases almost all admit at once the fortitude, the logical integrity and the spiritual superiority of the churchman, and the energy and political ability of the king and the strength of custom in favour of his cause. In both cases, also, the king weakens our sympathies by his violent behaviour and moral instability, while the pope and archbishop alienate us by their rigid and extreme utterances and claims. Gregory VII, however, is a greater figure than Thomas Becket. He was not an innovator, inasmuch as all his claims either could be substantiated from some ancient canon law or papal utterance, or were a legitimate deduction from his claim to inherit the office and the promises given to Peter, but no one before had ever claimed the right to remove a king or to absolve his subjects from their allegiance, and no one before had acted so consistently and so implacably in implementing his claims. Again, though nothing in the *Dictatus Papae* is formally new, its shattering declarations cause dismay at a first glance and, like other stark pronouncements of authority, seem unbearably rigid and egocentric to the general reader, but lose some of their harshness after the application of careful technical exegesis[4]. Gregory himself undoubtedly gains in stature when closely examined; there is a spiritual concern and motive in almost all his words and acts. If the papacy was to be rescued from tutelage, and the Church as a whole from lay control and moral weakness, severity and drastic action were inevitable, but we may wonder if Gregory VII is not, in some of his utterances, and in his prodigality of threats of excommunication, taking the first step on the path that leads to the extravagance and unreality of the claims of Boniface VIII. However that may be, he carried the papacy irrevocably forward towards that freedom from control which was its need and its right. We should not be justified in thinking of the struggle as one between Church and State. No contemporary would have attributed to the State a natural right to exist and to settle its own destinies as against those of the Church. Both emperor and pope were within the Church, and it was the ultimate weakness of the anti-papal party that they could never imagine or demand a state of affairs in which the pope and clergy did not dispense and judge the gifts of God and spiritual causes. The most they could do, once they had abandoned appeal to custom, was to claim for the king a divine right to govern Christendom and control the activities of Christians in all matters that did not imply the possession of strictly priestly powers. The pope could claim the right to institute emperors or deprive them of their power; he could even claim that a pope instituted the very office of emperor; and kings and emperors had always to admit that even those prelates whom they elected needed a consecration, and acted on a commission, with which they had nothing to say. Gregory VII did not end the struggle between *sacerdotium* and *imperium*, but he freed the spiritual power from tutelage and ensured that it should stand on its own feet not only throughout the later middle ages, but in centuries to come under circumstances very different from any that the eleventh century had known.

The later years of the pontificate of Gregory VII, as seen by contemporaries, must have seemed disastrous for the papacy and the cause of reform. The pope had been driven from Rome and had died in exile, the emperor, crowned by his anti-pope, was free to act as he pleased, the pamphleteers on both sides were active with their theories and proposals; one imperialist, Benzo of Alba, was even suggesting that the emperor should reside at Rome with a papal appointee and revive the ancient empire. Nevertheless the cause of reform was not lost. The reigns of

4. E.g., by S. Küttner, ' Liber Canonicus, a note on " Dictatus Papae " ', in *Studi Gregoriani* II, 387-401, and W. Ullmann, ' Romanus Pontifex indubitanter efficitur sanctus: Dictatus Papae 23 in retrospect and prospect ', *ibid.*, VI, 229-64.

Leo IX, Nicholas II and Gregory VII had encouraged the growth of a reforming spirit throughout Europe, and many of the bishops and cardinals were convinced Gregorians. It was this public opinion in high places which saved the Gregorian programme in the coming years.

For the moment there was uncertainty. Didier of Monte Cassino was canonically elected a year after Gregory's death, but he did not formally accept office as Victor III for ten months. A cultured but weak man, he died six months later, whereupon the cardinals chose Eudes of Chatillon, bishop of Ostia, henceforward Urban II. The new pope was of noble birth, sometime scholar at Rheims under St Bruno and then archdeacon, who had left his career to become a monk at Cluny (1073-7), whence he had been called to the curia. Devout and with sound political sense, he aimed at maintaining the full Gregorian programme, but with tact and latitude. Meanwhile, the schism of Henry IV was prospering both in Germany and around Rome, where the anti-pope was in possession. Urban, less autocratic in temper than Gregory, formally renewed condemnations of simony, nicolaism and lay investiture, but made no attempt to enforce the last and was ambivalent in the matter of the reordination of simoniacs. Nevertheless, he showed energy in governing the church beyond Italy, encouraging especially the exemption of monasteries and the foundation of houses of regular canons. Rome was a prize to be fought for. Urban recaptured the city in 1089, only to escape when Henry invaded Italy in 1090-2 to replace Clement III, who retired in his turn when Henry went north in 1092. Meanwhile canonists and pamphleteers continued to support reform and Urban II became more active and more rigorous. At a great council at Piacenza (March 1095) the orders of those ordained by the anti-pope were declared invalid, as were those of excommunicates; simony and nicolaism were once more condemned. In July 1095 Urban began a journey to France in the cause of reform that was to have vast and unforeseen consequences. The pope had recently received an appeal for help from the eastern emperor Alexis; he had also witnessed the success of the crusade in Spain. He passed by Le Puy, where he met its bishop Adhemar, and Saint Gilles, where he took counsel with Raymond IV, count of Toulouse, and called a reforming council at Clermont for 18 November. There once more reforming decrees were passed, it was also forbidden that those appointed to bishoprics or abbeys should take the feudal oath, and Philip of France, long persistent in adultery, was excommunicated. Then, on 27 November, Urban preached his celebrated sermon launching a crusade, no longer to assist Alexis, but to capture Jerusalem. Neither the numbers present, nor their enthusiasm, were as great as is generally related, but the project originally proposed to Frenchmen only was accepted, and with Philip I unavailable as leader, the position was given to Adhemar as papal legate. Enthusiasm grew, and became at first warm and then almost hysterical. The single army originally envisaged became four – from south France, from the royal domain, from the imperial territories and from Norman south Italy, not to speak of popular bands scarcely armed. Meanwhile crowds in Rhineland cities opened the crusade with massacres of Jews.

The opening of the epoch of crusades in the East, almost by accident, still remains a momentous episode. It seems clear that the pope's original scheme was a very modest one; he had no intention of creating a diversion from the controversy between Henry and the papacy, or of removing possible trouble-makers. Nevertheless, it was a serious, and in the event an inauspicious precedent, that the pope should encourage and reward a great and unprovoked war, which lasted for two centuries in its various phases, and served to inspire other military adventures that led to blood-shed and cruelty. At the time, however, the launching of the crusade undoubtedly enhanced the prestige of the papacy; the pope, unlike the emperor, could influence the whole of Europe.

Meanwhile Urban continued his active work throughout the West. He renewed the use of legates, created a number of primates and practised centralisation and direct papal action, while at the same time renewing decrees against investiture and homage to lay lords. He stiffened disci-pline in other ways by claiming jurisdiction over monasteries and endeav-ouring to abolish the lay advocate or *Vogt*, and in October 1098 held a council at Bari where the procession of the Holy Ghost from the Father and from the Son was defined. He died on 29 July 1099, after a pontificate which, beginning without great promise, developed into one of the most important in medieval history, in which for the first time a pope stood forward as the personal leader of Christendom.

He was succeeded by Cardinal Rainier, an Italian monk, who took the name of Paschal II (1099-1118). He opened his pontificate by condemning lay investiture, thus channelling the controversy with the monarchs of Europe into a single stream. Before taking the narrative further, it may be well to review the past history of this great issue. In the earlier phases of the strife between pope and king, the essential points had been the claim of the monarch to appoint his bishops and, as a further demand often accompanying but not necessarily connected with this, to exact or at least to receive a payment of some kind. The latter practice, on any showing an abuse, was simony; the former was merely the most important manifestation of the lay control of the Church and, in the supreme case of the papacy had disappeared in practice with the election decree of Nicholas II in 1059. There still remained, even if an election was free and canonical, the question of investiture. Bishops and abbots were feudal landowners; hence, when they entered into possession of their fief, they did homage with an oath of fealty, and by an age-old custom, received at once their office and their lands from the lord by ' investiture ' with ring and staff. In the first phase of the contest, the emphasis of the reformers centred on the iniquity of lay appointment to a spiritual *office*. This was an understandable position, which could be opposed indeed by a thorough-going imperialist, but which was not directed of itself against the whole of feudal practice. Investiture, however, and homage seemed to be of the essence of any entry into possession of lands, and so long as this practice was regarded as combining the gift both of *office and estates*, it remained a stumbling-block to all efforts for peace. During all this time, canonists and controversialists had been issuing their pamphlets on either side. The majority were clearly committed to partisan and often extreme views, but as the dispute wore on it became clear to many that the feudal framework of society was something that had to be accepted as a condition of life, and as an institution that had not existed when the canon law was first composed. Some kind of compromise must therefore be devised. The first writer known to have proposed some kind of theory, as distinct from toleration in practice, was Guy of Ferrara *c.* 1086, and Ivo, bishop of Chartres from 1090, helped to diffuse the notion of a compromise such as was eventually attained, and of which the agreement between Anselm and Henry I of England was a foreshadowing. This rested on the assumption that investiture with property and the oath of fealty were not of themselves uncanonical for clerics; the essential matter was the distinction between the spiritual office and the temporal fief. For the moment, however, Urban II had disavowed this opinion and even stiffened his own methods.[5]

Paschal II, as has been said, began his pontificate by condemning lay investiture outright, and thus opened a new and bitter phase of the quarrel. Meanwhile Henry IV and his son and namesake were fighting a civil war against one another, and when the former died in 1106 the latter continued to act entirely uncanonically in the appointment of bishops. The pope reiterated his condemnation of investiture at the Council of Troyes (1107), though almost at the very moment the English version of the controversy and the French were settled by compromises on the lines of Ivo's teaching. Suddenly the great quarrel rose to a crisis. Henry V, anxious to obtain imperial coronation, proposed to visit Rome; the pope, while still maintaining his ground, agreed. When the king was not far from the city, reiterating his claims, Paschal II produced an entirely novel solution: the Church would renounce its right to properties held of the king, and the king would renounce his right to investiture. It was a solution which, had it been possible of adoption, would have revolutionised the religious and

5. Cf. A. Fliche in Fliche & Martin VIII, 333-4.

social fabric of Europe, with incalculable consequences in the history of the papacy and the Church. It would have accomplished what reformers of all the medieval centuries wished to achieve: it would have lifted the Church (for other feudal tenants would have followed the lead) out of the control of the lay power and, with still greater effect, out of the clutches of mammon. It was, however, a proposal impossible of execution for exactly the same reasons as is the equally unreal proposal in the modern world that some countries or all countries should disarm themselves. Had Paschal II previously shown himself a St Francis his proposal would at least have been the challenge of a saint. His previous and subsequent actions suggest rather that it was a quixotic, almost irresponsible suggestion. Henry, with quick political intuition, seized his chance. He accepted, on condition that the pope should obtain the consent of the bishops. Paschal agreed, and the compact was made under this condition; it was to be ratified at the beginning of the coronation ceremony. Henry duly renounced investiture, but when the pope renounced *regalia* on behalf of the Church a storm broke in St Peter's, that quickly became a riot. Neither the bishops nor the lay lords would allow the compact. Henry seized the person of the pope, and after a captivity of two months Paschal yielded; investiture was permitted and the pope consented to crown Henry as emperor, whereupon Henry departed in triumph for Germany, leaving the pope outwitted and humbled. Europe and the Church, however, were not what they had been a century earlier. There were very many bishops, not only in France and Italy, who were now convinced and staunch Gregorians, and letters of advice and of abuse showered upon the pope. He must repudiate his promises, which had been extracted under duress. Meanwhile the emperor, as an emperor of the French eight hundred years later was also to do, had forfeited much of his goodwill by his use of violence towards Paschal. Ivo of Chartres assisted matters by his sober mediation, and at the Lenten synod of 1112 the pope retracted his concession of investiture, and in March of the same year a council at the Lateran quashed the '*privilegium*' of 1111 to Henry. [6] The emperor, who was kept away by troubles with his turbulent subjects, did not invade Italy again till 1116, when the pope retreated before him. Henry retired with little effected, and Paschal II returned to Rome, where he died in 1118.

His successor, Gelasius II, died after a bare year of office, and was followed by the imperious Gregorian Calixtus II, previously archbishop of Vienne. By this time the contest had become one of words and theories rather than of practical issues, and both sides wished for peace with the least possible loss of principle or face. Agreement was very near at Mouzon

6. Otto of Freising records the play on words, '*privilegium*' (*pravus* = evil) for privilegium, which became familiar.

in north-eastern France in 1119, but distrust of Henry led to an over-brusque withdrawal on the pope's side. The final concord was attained on 23 September 1122, when the agreement or Concordat of Worms was signed. Free election (for Germany, in the king's presence) was to be followed by investiture by the king's sceptre and homage on the part of the elect. With this compromise, which was never accepted by the papacy as any-thing more than a provisional act of mercy *(misericordia)* tempering just claims, the great controversy that had convulsed the upper reaches of the Church for some sixty years came to an end. It was a compromise of practice. The great theoretical dispute of the primacy of power was left undecided, to be renewed again in thirty years and continued in one form or another down the ages. Superficially seen, it might seem a drawn battle. Kings continued to work their will with episcopal appointments and to ignore papal commands as before. But on a long view, for the medieval centuries at least, the pope had won a notable victory. He had succeeded in fighting off the royal and imperial claims to paramountcy, and had established the spiritual order in command of the Church, with its claim intact to command also the whole of society. In later struggles the Church could be resisted and attacked, but she could not be ignored.

THE MONASTIC CENTURIES (II)

A DISADVANTAGE of the division of European history into periods is that many writers and readers fail to remember that the river of human activity is continuous and that even when, as in 1517 and in 1789, it appears to plunge over the cliffs of a Niagara, the waters below the falls are of the same stream as those above. The metaphor must not be pressed, for again and again in the course of ages the elements that determine physical and intellectual superiority are blended in harmonious combination to produce genius in this region or in that and new spiritual power wells up from unseen depths; but the historian must always distrust the picture of a new age emerging as if by magic from formless chaos.

The great stirring of life in every field of mental activity that began to be visible in the eleventh century made its first appearance in north Italy and central France. In Italy in its early stages the revival was primarily moral and institutional; in France the educational and intellectual factors were more in evidence. This distinction soon vanished, but it is natural for a church historian to look first towards Italy, the fatherland of the great saints and reformers of the eleventh century. These men, almost without exception, were monks, and the space of time between the pontificate of Silvester II (998-1002) and the death of St Bernard (1153) is an epoch of reform and expansion in the monastic world, just as it is one of reform and expansion in the history of papal government.

The remarkable and original developments of monastic life did not take place in a void, nor were they without harbingers. Monte Cassino had risen once again to prosperity early in the tenth century, and almost at the same time Subiaco became rich and influential as a result of the benefactions of Alberic II, duke of Rome. Reformers from Cluny and elsewhere, in the days of Odilo and William of Dijon, had worked at Farfa, at Cava, in Rome and in north Italy, and though the fervour of a revival might soon cool, it would be wrong to regard Italian monasticism as wholly decadent even when the raids of the Saracens had ruined many houses. Nevertheless, what monasteries there were, in Rome and elsewhere in Italy at the end of the tenth century, conformed to the traditional type of liturgical community life, and the Rule of St Benedict, interpreted in a conservative sense, was now spreading its influence in Italy.

Yet at the same time an entirely new spirit was beginning to make itself felt. Those whom it inspired aimed at a more austere and often at an eremitic type of life, and they found their directing principles either in the teaching of the fathers of the desert or in a literal, severe interpretation of the Rule of St Benedict. The forerunners of this movement may well have been the Greek monks of south Italy, refugees from the Saracen invasions, or those driven out of Asia Minor, but the leaders and their programmes were Italian, and among them are eminent the names of Romuald, John Gualbert, and Peter Damian. Romuald of Ravenna (c. 950-1027), originally a Cluniac monk, aimed at restoring the monasticism of the desert with its solitude and severity. He left as his legacy the hermit-groups of Fonte Avellana and Camaldoli in Tuscany and the Apennines. John Gualbert of Florence (c. 990-1073), likewise a Cluniac of San Miniato, passed to Camaldoli but went on to found a community at Vallombrosa following the Rule with strict enclosure and perpetual silence. Peter Damian of Ravenna (1000-72) spent many years at Fonte Avellana as a hermit before being caught up into the counsels and activities of the curial reformers, but his principal influence upon the monastic life was through his writings, which are a searing indictment of the depraved society of north Italy. In these three men and their followers we can see the characteristics which in them were new, but which soon became typical of the age. For individuals, the monastic life in its severest, semi-eremitical form was held up as the most perfect, indeed as the only true way of following Christ; on the institutional level they favoured an eremitical rather than a coenobitical monasticism, and a strict interpretation of the Rule inspired by the counsels of the saints of the Egyptian desert. Apart altogether from the intentions of their founders, Camaldoli and Vallombrosa were to be of great significance in monastic history. Camaldoli, a family of hermits meeting together only at certain times in church or chapter, was the first of a group of institutes, of which the Carthusians are the most celebrated, in which the members combined the monastic and eremitic life and practised considerable austerity. Vallombrosa was the prototype of another group: in this the community lived in strict seclusion, while all administration was performed by lay brothers *(conversi)*. Whatever the ultimate origin of this category of religious, it was to be remarkably fruitful from Romuald's day to our own.

In another respect also these two ventures were original. Both were made up of two establishments. At Camaldoli the hermits dwelt high up on the mountain-side; below, an austere community provided recruits for the solitary life. At Vallombrosa the monks lived in comparative seclusion on the mountain; below was the convent of the lay brothers and a hospice for guests. The austerity of these two institutes forbade a wide diffusion, and though both still exist after nine centuries they have always remained primarily Italian, and it is impossible to prove, though it is most likely, that they influenced the new ventures north of the Alps.

There, as in Italy, monastic decay was far from universal. William of Volpiano, a Cluniac monk, had made of St Benigne at Dijon a house of fervour and the centre of a considerable congregation; he had also helped Duke Richard II to establish a flourishing monastic life in Normandy. Several other ' orders ' of traditional observance came into being, at Bec, La Chaise Dieu, Molesmes, and St Victor de Marseille, and continued to flourish for two or three centuries. Side by side with these were the new ventures. At Muret St Stephen of Grandmont established in 1076 an order of extreme, not to say savage, austerity and poverty. At Fontevrault Robert of Arbrissel, by turns preacher and hermit, set up a large double monastery following the Rule of St Benedict severely interpreted; the men acted as chaplains and directors to the numerous nuns, many of them from royal or noble families.

Muret and Fontevrault were new creations, but they did not aim at meeting the need that was so widely felt for a rejuvenation of the traditional monastic life that would answer the aspirations of the age. In the decades around 1100 several attempts were made in this direction. At Savigny, in a wild valley on the borders of Brittany and Normandy, Vitalis, another itinerant preacher of fame, founded a monastery (1088) following the Rule of St Benedict with austerity. This soon became the head of a congregation with houses in France and England. At Tiron, a few years later, Bernard, a whilom Cluniac abbot, founded a monastery with an emphasis on work in the fields. After an initial success, with a few foundations in Wales and

Scotland as well as France, the Tironian order gradually reverted to type as a traditional Benedictine group. At La Chartreuse in the mountains near Grenoble Bruno of Cologne, late master of the schools of Rheims, settled with some companions in a ' desert ' similar to Camaldoli, which Bruno may have known. The founder was soon called to Rome and later created another hermitage in Calabria, where he died, but the Chartreuse continued to exist and acquired by stages detailed constitutions and the status of an order. The life resembled that of Camaldoli, with certain offices and duties in common, but unlike Camaldoli, it was a desert ' domesticated ', with small houses built round a cloister and a quasi-monastic complex of buildings. By a rigid observance of their rule of life and a resolute policy of accepting only those spiritually, psychologically and physically adopted for the régime, the Carthusians were the only medieval order to escape laxity. They remained, and have remained to the present day, a small *élite* among the religious orders of the Church.

This could not be said of the institute that found the exact answer to the needs of the age. The first fathers of the Cistercian order, like so many others, began as a group of hermits, and it was only after founding a house at Molesmes and seeing it lose its sense of vocation, that they devised a programme for their third attempt at Cîteaux (1098) which was to stand the test of time.

Hitherto reformers dissatisfied with the liturgical, cloistered, complicated life of the great black monk abbey, where even the fervent were caught up in the administrative duties of a great land- and property-owning corporation, with guests and pilgrims to receive, rents to collect, and a solemn round of long and elaborate ceremonial to perform, and whose abbot was a feudal lord and royal councillor, had either adopted a hermit's life, or had as it were begun again at the beginning with a small and indigent establishment that lacked the extravagances and conventions of an ancient and wealthy community. In both cases there resulted either complete failure or a gradual reversion to type. Now, the fathers of Cîteaux resolved to be thorough and ruthless. They refused to receive lands, churches, manors, courts, rents, feudal dues and serfs. They took as the programmatical motto for their life ' the Rule to the last dot ' *(ad apicem litterae)*, cutting off all food, clothing and objects not specified in the Rule. They cut off also almost all liturgical or devotional exercises not mentioned in the Rule, thus abolishing at a stroke the numerous minor offices, litanies, prayers, processions and the rest, which centuries of piety had added to the *Opus Dei* of the Rule. Almost all went, but they were children of their age and could not bring themselves to abandon the daily Mass and the office of the dead. Thus without further ado they restored the balance of the horarium and the division of the working hours between public prayer, meditative reading, and physical work. They had become what Monte Cassino had been, a self-contained family with a simple round of prayer and work. Now, they went a step further. They had asked for, and had received, nothing but land, and waste land at that. They had to fend for themselves. And so, perhaps more through necessity than by design, they made of hard, manual labour a part of their daily duty. In this, they went beyond the practice, though perhaps not away from the spirit, of St Benedict, but they soon made a more original move. A community of monks working only for a few hours a day, and not at all on festal days, could not develop or work the fields, or breed and care for the beasts, necessary to support a large community; they had no serfs and no money to hire labour. They adopted, perhaps from Vallombrosa or Hirsau, lay brothers *(conversi)*, but made of them something altogether new, allowing them to follow a semi-monastic régime and become fully members of the family, save for chapter-rights and service of the choir and altar. The vocation met exactly a spiritual and social need in an age of expanding rural economy and population, and recruits flocked to the Cistercian abbeys, far outnumbering the choir monks. The lay brothers were epoch-making also as a labour force. Working on wide estates which were entirely free of the customs and hampering methods of manorial strip-field economy, and deployed during the week by turns at ' granges ' often at a distance from the abbey, the *conversi* were a mobile and elastic instrument of exploitation, and soon raised the arable and pastoral economy of the white monks to a high level of excellence.

Meanwhile, the first fathers of Cîteaux, and in particular the second abbot, the Englishman Stephen Harding, showed themselves able also to deal with the problems of an expanding order. The watchword was uniformity: service books, customs, buildings, horarium, discipline; all were to be identical everywhere. To maintain this two expedients were adopted, known indeed in ancient times, but long fallen into desuetude: the annual general chapter, with legislative and judicial powers, meeting at Cîteaux, and the annual disciplinary visitation of each abbey by the abbot of the founding ' mother '-abbey. This constitutional framework was evolved, step by step, and summarised in the short document known as the *Carta Caritatis*, the ' Charter of Love ', which must rank, along with the Rule of St Benedict, as one of the very few cardinal documents of monastic constitutional history. Composed in several stages for a relatively small group of monks it proved adequate to contain an immense order, and many of its provisions soon became common form for all subsequent institutes.

Equipped with this constitutional and economic machinery, and strengthened by the sanctity of the founding fathers and of Bernard, the portentous abbot of Clairvaux, the Cistercians expanded rapidly and enjoyed a vogue throughout Latin Christendom that had no parallel in earlier times and that endured for more than a century. At the death of St Bernard in 1153 the order already counted 343 abbeys of which sixty-six had been founded by the saint himself. In 1300 the number had risen to 694. The Cistercians of the golden age chose sites in remote and wild country, which they developed with skill and pertinacity, and the ruins of their abbeys are still a feature of the landscape, and the haunt of the archaeologist, and often also of the sightseer, in every country of western Europe. Within thirty years of the foundation of Cîteaux, they had become the cynosure of Christendom; they had antiquated the Cluniacs and had made of themselves the first formal and articulated religious order. While avoiding the Cluniac ' tyranny ' by ensuring the domestic autonomy of each house, and denying any special powers to the abbot of Cîteaux, they nevertheless succeeded, by their uniformity, their mutual interdependence and their common seat of authority in the general chapter, in standing out as a closely knit, well-disciplined body with a spirit and interests of its own.

The aptness to the age of the Cistercian vocation, and the excellence of their institutions, inevitably provoked imitation. Foremost among these was the order known from their first house as the canons of Prémontré or Premonstratensians, and from their white habits as the White Canons. These, founded near Laon in 1119 by St Norbert (c. 1080-1134) of the Rhineland, were originally destined for preaching and missionary work, but the pull of the Cistercians and friendship with St Bernard led their founder to accept the monastic element in their life, and they adopted many of the constitutional arrangements of the white monks. From early times there was a tension of ideals both within each house and between the Germanic and Latin countries; in the former the apostolic vocation predominated, in the latter the monastic and contemplative character, but the differences never issued in division. In central Europe and in the northern Netherlands their expansion was even more rapid and spectacular than that of the Cistercians, and they achieved wonders in reclaiming marshes and clearing forests. East of the Rhine, also, they provided bishops to many German sees. In France and the British Isles, on the other hand, they were for long almost indistinguishable from the Cistercians both in the manner of their life and in their agricultural and pastoral activities.

Besides these two great families, the age gave birth to several other new institutes. One, that was confined to England, was that of the Gilbertines, primarily an order of religious women, directed by regular canons who lived sometimes apart, but more often in a monastery forming a pendent to a larger nunnery that lay on the opposite side of a church in which each community had its separate choir. Lay brothers and lay sisters were added to form a complex governed by elaborate constitutional and disciplinary machinery, under a Master, Gilbert of Sempringham. This order was all but confined to the large counties of Lincoln and York and its founder offered in 1147 to merge with the Cistercians, but the white monks, engaged in absorbing the large group of Savignac houses, declined the offer.

Still more characteristic of the age were the two original so-called 'military' orders: the Order of the Temple (Knights Templars) founded to escort and protect pilgrims to the Holy Places and soon to become the *corps d'élite* of the crusading armies, and the Order of the Hospital of St John (Knights Hospitallers) who devoted themselves to the care of travellers, sound or sick, bound to or from the East. In both the military and clerical members lived by a monastic rule, thus blending, in a manner conceivable only in that age, the two callings, monastic and military, that appealed so strongly to contemporary sentiment. In the East they lived as armed religious in masterpieces of military architecture of which the Krac des Chevaliers is the most celebrated example. In Europe, and particularly in western Europe, they rapidly constructed a network of residences known as commanderies or preceptories to serve as recruiting centres, posts of administration and the collection of revenues, and hospitals for the sick and aged brethren. The orders were governed by a Master and Grand Commander respectively with a general chapter and smaller council, and were organised in regional groups. Both orders lost their original function with the evacuation of Palestine, and the Templars, as we shall see, came under attack and succumbed, but the conception of a military order continued throughout the middle ages to inspire crusaders in other parts of Europe, particularly in Spain and in the eastern marches where Germans and Poles waged war against the heathen.

2. THE AUSTIN CANONS

While the growth and diffusion of the monastic and quasi-monastic orders, old and new, are a favourite topic of medieval historians, less attention has been given to the development and spread of another numerous and important class, that of the traditional canons, 'regular' and 'secular'.

The phrase 'canonical life' was originally used of the clergy who were the assistants of the city-bishop, and who were distinguished from the private chaplains and lesser clergy of various kinds, but in the early middle ages it began to take another meaning. From the days of St Augustine of Hippo, there had been isolated attempts to gather the clergy of the bishop's household into a common life based on that of the first Christians, which implied celibacy, a common store of food and clothing, and a quasi-monastic way of life. In times of decadence this type disappeared, to return with each serious reform, and a kind of rule for 'canons' was compiled by St Chrodegang of Metz (715-66) from the Rule of St Benedict and other sources; when Charlemagne attempted to reform and unify all groups of the clergy this rule was an important element of the *Institutio Canonicorum*, and was promulgated in 816-17 by the council of Aachen. This, like other Carolingian reforms, foundered in the political storms and invasions of the tenth century, but the document and the conception behind it remained. In the empire, and particularly in the towns, numerous large houses of canons sprang up and endured, and in France and England also there were revivals in the tenth and early eleventh centuries. Economic and social conditions, however, had combined to destroy both the common life and the close connection with the bishop in cathedral colleges. A prebend was assigned to each canon, and the common dorter and refectory usually disappeared. The revival of the collegiate life was one of the first aims of the reformers in north Italy and south France, and several important houses, such as St Ruf near Avignon, and St Martin des Champs at Paris, were founded before the pontificate of Leo IX. The matter received official attention when, on the motion of Hildebrand, the discipline of the canonical life was discussed at the Lateran council of 1059, and a moderately worded decree urged a return to ' the apostolic life, that is the common life '. Thenceforward the growth was rapid, particularly in Italy and France; in Europe to the west and north the importation of the new model was less urgent, and was hindered by the barriers imposed by the contest of empire and papacy.

Before the end of the eleventh century the majority of the canons' houses were in towns, where they were occupied with pastoral work. There was no kind of uniformity, no common rule or constitutions beyond those of Aachen; in other words, the ' canons ' were still primarily groups of clergy imitating the common apostolic life of the early Church. The great change began some years before the pontificate of Urban II (1088-99), with the adoption of the so-called Rule of St Augustine as a code by isolated houses, and mention of this rule is frequent in papal privileges and confirmations henceforward, though it was not till the twelfth century that it was regarded as the sole ruling code. This ' Rule ' had been ignored for more than six centuries, and its origins and form have been the object of critical discussion in recent years. In the form which became popular in the early twelfth century, and which is still used by Augustinian canons and other religious orders, it is probably an adaptation for men, made by Augustine or an early writer, of the saint's letter (no. 211) to his sister, the head of a community of nuns (the ' first ' Rule). It is in no sense a complete rule, and was prefaced in manuscripts previous to the twelfth century by a very short and austere outline of a regular life (the ' second ' Rule). This was soon abandoned as impracticable and subsequently the masculine version of the Rule (the ' third ' Rule) was augmented by collections of constitutions peculiar to the house or order. Gradually the adoption of this Rule, the need for a distinguished and ancient founder, and the example of the new orders all around, made of the majority of the canons' colleges (for a minority remained permanently ' secular ') a religious order claiming to derive from the days of St Augustine. In the beginning of this movement there were several species of canons' houses: the chapter of a cathedral or the staff of a basilica, the urban foundation (or *Stift*) common in Lorraine and Germany, the small so-called ' castral ' group adjacent to the founder's castle, a common type in Francia and England, and the small rural group placed by a landowner in what had been a well-to-do proprietary church. In addition there were the stricter and more fully organised groups, such as the Victorines and the Arrou-aisians. In general, the climate of the age and the example of other orders tended to ' monachise ' the canons, who now became known as the Augustinian or ' black ' canons as distinct from the 'white' Norbertines, and many of the larger houses became almost indistinguishable from houses of the black monks, but the Austin canons in general remained the least austere, the least secluded and the most loosely organised of the regular orders, as it were the extreme left wing of the great phalanx in which the Carthusians and Camaldolese were on the extreme right. Nevertheless, they gave birth to many saints and bishops in the twelfth century and probably, by reason of their numbers and place in the world, were more present to the consciousness of men of their time than they are to that of the modern historian. In all parts of Germany they were more numerous than Cistercians and Premonstratensians combined; over fifty foundations were made in the province of Salzburg between 1071 and 1166, and in Gerhoh of Reichersberg (1093-1169) they found an agent and an advocate of the first importance.

3. CLUNY

While these developments and innovations were proceeding, the older forms of monasticism were continuing, and in some cases expanding, their way of life. By nothing more significant than a coincidence, the epochal year 1049 marked a period at Cluny, for in that year the young aristocrat, Hugh de Sémur, became abbot, who for sixty years was to rule the great abbey, to carry it to its highest point of fame, and to feel in his last years the first chill of winter. The rapid growth was due primarily no doubt to the great and ever increasing celebrity of Cluny. To belong to her was at once a distinction, a safeguard and a guarantee. This celebrity was itself partly due to the personality of Hugh, soon called the Great, and his repute for wisdom, sanctity and influence. Nor can we doubt that Hugh showed himself more ready than his predecessors to accept invitations to reform or to control others. Nevertheless, it must in fairness be said that the spread of the monastic spirit, reform in the widest sense, not empire-building, was Hugh's foremost aim. He seems in all ways to have planned magnificently. Under him the community of Cluny herself increased three-fold to almost three hundred, while the buildings expanded to meet the new need and Hugh built the third basilica of the abbey on a scale that was only to be surpassed of set purpose, by a few feet, in the sixteenth century basilica of St Peter at Rome. Under his rule the prestige and fame of Cluny rose to its highest point.

Even so, the seeds of a decline were sown in his time. Cluny had been and still remained purely monarchical. The keystone of the great fabric was the profession made by all to the abbot of Cluny, and in theory all were monks of the mother house. There was no constitutional machinery apart from the normal conventual chapter of monks at Cluny. No attempt was ever made to establish representation or devolution. The vast machine worked of its own momentum supervised by the abbot of Cluny whose years were spent in almost continuous travel. Cluny, designed as an escape from the clutches of the feudal system, was itself a semi-feudal family, held together by a sentiment of loyalty and a need for protection, cemented by the solemn promise of obedience by every monk. Initiative was stifled and fervour damped. In addition Hugh himself was responsible for two sources of weakness, the reception of an ever-increasing stream of recruits and their admission after what was often no more than a token period of probation lasting for a few days only. Life at Cluny, and doubtless at other houses also, was clogged by numbers, and of these many had no true vocation to the life. The insecurity behind the splendour was seen when Hugh died and his brilliant but unstable successor Pons caused discord and even violence within the cloister. The ship righted herself under another young aristocrat, the able and zealous abbot (1132-56) later to be known as Peter the Venerable, but the shock, and the successful competition of the new orders, ended Cluny's domination of the scene. Meanwhile her way of life, and its external show, had been attacked by a new and power-ful rival who had taken the place of Hugh as lord of the ascendant. St Bernard's polemic against the Cluniacs and the apologetic of Peter form one of the classical debates on matters of spiritual principle within the western church and opinion is still divided in support of the two cham-pions. Did evangelical zeal oppose laxity, or did puritanism condemn hu-mane Christianity? Did zeal cloak the Pharisee, or did the sheep's clothing of charity conceal indulgence and luxury? The historian must at least record that Peter the Venerable became a considerable reformer, while the Cister-cians within fifty years had themselves lost much of their first fervour.

Before the twelfth century was out the flowing tide of monasticism had reached its high-water mark, and though new foundations were made here and there, especially at the periphery of Latin Christendom, the point of saturation had been reached. In the two centuries between Silvester II and Innocent III the monastic order and its congeners had appeared in a new social, religious and institutional form. Speaking very generally, we may say that a class had become a vocation. The monk, from being primarily an intercessor for society and a discharger of liturgical service, had become an individual seeking the fulness of evangelical perfection. Camaldolese, Carthusians, Cistercians and Premonstratensians were not in their age of fervour a part of feudal society but an escape to the desert. In the spiritual sphere the communion with God, the mystical life, was once more the distant goal of the monk. Institutionally the articulated, united, supra-national religious order had been born, and certain of its features, such as the general chapter and visitation, with all their machinery, were to become common property. This great surge into the monastic life cannot be measured by statistics but some idea of its extent may be gathered from the experience of England, where information is available more plentifully than in any other country. There, in the century and a half from 1066 to 1216 the number of religious houses rose from about sixty to over 700, while the population of monks, nuns and canons rose from about 1000 to about 15,000.

This great wave of enthusiasm was born of the conviction that the monastic life, with its renunciations and its devotions, was the Christian life *par excellence*. The evangelical and apostolic ideal of Christian perfection, preached to all and capable of realisation by all, had in a sense become obscured in a long age of violence, ignorance, and insecurity with its consequent sense of sin and punishment for sin, and its need of a refuge and a discipline. These the monastic life had supplied and its waters of salvation had now even overflowed and returned back into the world. The monastic practices and devotions had become the food of devout men and women not consecrated by orders or distinguished by vow. Not only lay brothers and sisters, but laymen and women felt the pull. In a very real sense the western church had become monachised. And at the same time the monastic orders, growing large and rich, were themselves beginning to take their colour from the world around them. For a brief space, between the day of Innocent III and the Great Pestilence, they stood at the height of their outward magnificence, still inspired by something of their early ideals. But they were no longer moulding the religious feeling, or representing the highest religious ideal, of their world.

The principal motive behind all these new institutes of monks and canons was a religious one, and the principal reasons for their rapid expansion were also religious, both in the founders of monasteries and in the recruits that came. Nevertheless social and economic causes can be seen at work in the unprecedented rush to the cloister. A more peaceful and cultured society needed and appreciated the opportunities for learning and artistic achievement, and the increase of population provided more recruits for this as for every other calling. Finally, the economic cause is clearly visible in the large numbers of Cistercian lay brothers, drawn mainly from the thriving peasant class (as in the English Danelaw) and from non-servile families exploiting marginal lands.

4. BERNARD OF CLAIRVAUX AND PETER THE VENERABLE

The first half of the twelfth century was the last and most spectacular phase of the period known as the ' monastic centuries ', and it is fitting that it should have been dominated by one whose life was an example and whose words were an exposition of the monastic ideal. Bernard, monk of Cîteaux and first abbot of Clairvaux, held for some thirty years a position of influence in the western church such as has been occupied by no other person unsupported by the papal rank, and by few even of the greatest popes. The time and the man were an exact match. A century earlier it would have been impossible for a religious genius, however great, to bring his influence to bear upon a disjointed, undeveloped Europe. A century later even a Bernard would have been trammelled and frustrated by the rigidly drawn network of the centralised church. Bernard's mature life was passed in a society centred upon Cîteaux and Clairvaux, which was for a brief space the spiritual powerhouse of western Christendom. There was a brief period when, in absolute spiritual freedom as a simple monk, he operated in a society which recognised, even if it did not observe, his own principles. None of his many adversaries or rivals disposed of the political or official or material force that could have silenced or thwarted him. In himself he had in rich measure the qualities that fitted him for mastery –the social ease of noble birth, great moral and spiritual courage, literary and rhetorical gifts of the first order; absence of worldly ambition and material desires; an ardent self-assurance and an iron determination; a transparent sincerity which was not incompatible with great tactical dexterity; and a real and practical love of his fellows which did not lead to any indulgence or even to any moderation when he attacked what he believed to be evil.

The young Bernard, appointed founding abbot of Clairvaux in 1115, emerged after a few years of difficulties and trials to a position of spiritual leadership that he held till his death in 1153. During the greater part of that time he occupied a position as reformer, as counsellor, as agitator, as preacher, as director and as theologian to which it would be hard to find a parallel in the history of the Church. While remaining throughout abbot of a great monastic family that was the cynosure of Europe and the mother in thirty years of over sixty daughters from Rome to Northumberland, he was also constantly summoned out of his monastic enclosure. It was he whose prestige confirmed Innocent II as rightful pope, he who brought about the condemnation of Abelard and Arnold of Brescia and the submission of Gilbert de la Porrée. He challenged the great family of Cluny, and defeated with his fire and his love Peter the Venerable himself. He preached to heretics, settled disputed elections; he deposed unworthy bishops, he converted multitudes by his preaching, as the students of Paris; by his letters, as the great Suger; and by the fame of his sanctity. Single-handed he sent France and Germany forth on crusade. He saw his monks become abbots, bishops and cardinals and finally he was able to counsel and chide a spiritual son on the Apostolic throne. He guided other saints in other institutes, such as St Norbert and St Gilbert, he gave a rule to the Templars and inspired that of the Premonstratensians. Studies have been made of his influence upon bishops, upon other orders of monks and canons, upon nuns, upon men and women in the world – indeed upon almost every group in the society of his time. The last of the Fathers with his treatises on the love of God, on the incarnation and on free will, he is also an eminent founder of modern piety with his devotion to the human life and suffering of Jesus and his Mother, to the mysteries of the Annunciation and the Nativity, to the Holy Angels and to the Holy Souls. He is both the greatest master of the teaching of the Rule of St Benedict and the first great autobiographical mystic in western Europe. He was justly acclaimed by John of Salisbury as the greatest preacher since St Gregory the Great, and has been hailed as the most eloquent writer of Latin between St Leo the Great and Petrarch. In an age of accomplished letter-writers he stands supreme, and almost alone among medieval writers he can intoxicate the reader of today. A matchless leader of men, he could attack with fury and pursue with remorseless energy, only to end a long controversy in peace and amity. He could use the arts of persuasion with a mastery of timing and methods which seemed to many to be harsh and even sharp practice, yet he could also win hearers by what he himself called a ' coruscation ' of signs and wonders unequalled in attested hagiography. He was a fire, a portent, and yet a man of courtesy and gentle affection. He was hated and feared by many in his lifetime, just as he was passionately defended and admired. Historians have found, and still find, matter for blame and judgment in his actions, but none has denied his genius. He was indeed a nonpareil, and set beside him, all other spiritual leaders of the medieval world, even a Gregory or a Francis, seem less massive figures. Since his death, as during his life, he has always been the object of a diversity' of judgments, but his place as a writer, as a man of action, and as a saint is secure among the greatest names of the European past.

Below St Bernard in prestige, in eloquence and in theological depth, but nevertheless one of the most influential men of Europe for a full generation, was Pierre de Montboissier, Peter the Venerable, almost exactly the contemporary of his great rival, and abbot of Cluny from 1122 to 1156. Called as a young monk of thirty-two to the helm of a great vessel in distress, and fighting forever a desperate battle against the laws of moral gravity, he came more than once into collision with St Bernard, most notably in the long exchange of letters in which each argued the case of his monastic allegiance, Bernard the reformer and the idealist, Peter the man of peace called not to destroy and to tear up, but to nurse the smoking flax and the bruised reed, who could yet recognise the justice of Bernard's strokes of the lash and apply to Cluny the medicine of Clairvaux. In his fine courtesy, and in his sympathy with Héloise and Abelard, he anticipates the best qualities of a Fénelon. Always on the road to visit his far-scattered family, or to discharge missions of diplomacy secular and ecclesiastical, he ranged in his travels from Rome to England, from Burgundy to Spain. He was the friend and correspondent of almost all the monarchs and of all the popes of his day. In the realm of letters his correspondence, though less rich in matter and style than the dossiers of Bernard or John of Salisbury, is indispensable for the political and monastic history of his times. During thirty years the vast network of Cluny, still an imposing colossus bestriding Christendom, and the luxuriant tree of Cîteaux, whose branches covered the earth, were ordered and controlled by two men of eminent distinction of mind and a holiness of life unmarred by any taint of worldliness or ambition. Such a phenomenon had never before been seen in western Christendom, and it has not been seen again.

THE CHURCH
IN THE TWELFTH CENTURY

I. ENGLAND 1066-1216

OF all the foes who battered at the walls of Christendom in the early middle ages, the most destructive and in the long run the most influential were the Scandinavians, or, as they were called by their early victims, the Vikings. It is still impossible to account historically for the numbers and, above all, for the outstanding practical and political abilities of the Norsemen. Nothing in what is known of their previous history, or of the subsequent fortunes of the countries from which they came, helps to account for their share in the making of Europe. Yet great as were their conquests, they might well, but for the opposing ambitions of Norsemen and Danes, have created a Scandinavian state covering the whole of the British Isles and much of the French and German coastline. We have already seen how the Danish invaders of Great Britain were rapidly absorbed, and received from those whom they conquered a civilisation superior to their own. Within a century of its occupation by invaders the Danelaw, as it was called, had become a peaceful Christian region distinguishable but not essentially different from its Anglo-Saxon neighbours.

Of all the Scandinavians the regional group known as the Normans were the most dynamic. It is difficult to think of any group in recorded history of the same size that can have impressed the stamp of their character so widely and so deeply. From the small territory north and south of the lower Seine which came to be called Normandy a succession of knights went out to hold most of the fertile land of England, lowland Scotland, south Wales and east Ireland; others conquered and held Sicily and the lower half of Italy; others again went further to dominate Greece, Cyprus, Antioch and Palestine. In all these countries they instituted forms of government and administration that were superior in efficiency to anything similar in the West. Such people – one cannot write such a people – were necessarily an influence upon Christian Europe, and indeed neither the crusades nor the cathedrals of this period would have been the same without the Normans.

The Northmen in the only district that bears their name soon became Christian and from the beginning of the eleventh century onwards Normandy steadily advanced to ecclesiastical and to political maturity. Monasteries were founded and flourished under William of Dijon, and recruits came from mighty and baronial families; many of the bishops were taken from the abbeys. Great churches were built that set the style and the scale. The bishops and abbots were drawn into the net of feudal dependence on the duke, and under William, later known as the Conqueror, a remarkable degree of organisation and reform was effected. When the duke prepared to invade England, ostensibly to claim his inheritance and avenge the perjury of Harold who had succeeded Edward the Confessor, he obtained a banner and a blessing from Pope Alexander II, possibly by favour of Hildebrand. When victorious he proceeded to reform what Norman monks considered a decadent church. Norman bishops and abbots were appointed, Lanfranc abbot of the Conqueror's abbey of Caen and the most celebrated theologian of the West was called to Canterbury. Synods were held, canon law was applied, Courts Christian instituted, churches were built, and a stream of monks crossed the Channel to establish new monasteries, to become abbots, and to take possession of estates newly granted. The church in England lost its anachronistic character of a Carolingian state-church, and accepted a reform of the kind that Humbert or Damian would have praised, but it was a reform without the pope. Both Lanfranc and William had come to know the reform of the mid-century but neither was a Gregorian in the current sense. Lanfranc, confident in his own powers as archbishop, aimed at a reformed church strictly governed by the duke, with himself as a kind of northern patriarch controlling also the churches of Wales, Scotland and Ireland. The pope was to be honoured but held at a distance. Lanfranc wished for no legates and William I wished neither for legates nor to see his own bishops receiving orders from Rome or visiting the curia.

So matters remained while the king and archbishop lived. Lanfranc's design of a kind of patriarchate for the British Isles vanished as unpracticable and undesirable, but his reorganisation and rejuvenation of the church in England remained as his monument. Unjustified as may have been some of the Norman charges against bishops and monks, there is no doubt that the English church benefited greatly from the Norman conquest. Above all, it gave England solidarity with the continent and for three centuries men and ideas passed freely back and forth. Had William's mission failed, England might well have formed part of the Danish kingdom.

Lanfranc's successor, the great Anselm, caught between an unprincipled king and the demands of the papacy, had a less happy term of office punctuated by two periods of exile, and under Henry I was faced with an ' investiture ' contest of his own. A compromise was finally arranged in 1107, anticipating the agreement at Worms of 1122. Anselm found his true vocation in his spiritual correspondence; in that and in the memory of his sanctity and intellectual eminence he added lustre to the annals of his see.

Henry I had proclaimed, though in practice he limited, the freedom of the church, and under the disturbed rule of the weaker Stephen this promised liberty was taken to imply complete freedom for papal centralisation. Legates visited England and held councils, the canon law was studied and put into practice and even some episcopal elections were free. A change came with Henry II, a ruler of great energy and ability, if unspiritual, lax of morals and violent in temper. His lifelong aim was to concentrate all administration, both feudal and ecclesiastical, in his own hands and with this end in view to reassert many of the royal rights which his ancestors had claimed but which had been eroded by the infiltration of Gregorian principles. Among these rights were the control of episcopal and papal excommunications and appeals to Rome, the appointment of the bishops and the jurisdiction over ' criminous clerks ', i.e. the royal right of punnishing clerks found guilty of serious crime by the Courts Christian. Archbishop Thomas Becket, the king's whilom friend and chancellor, newly (1162) appointed at the king's desire to Canterbury, pleaded the canons in his resistance to the royal demands and claimed complete and final jurisdiction over all clerks. [1] This and other controversies, and temperamental difficulties on both sides, led to the archbishop's refusal to accept the so-called Constitutions of Clarendon (1164) and to his exile for six years, in which he received hospitality from the king of France and qualified support from Alexander III, who could not afford a complete breach with the king. Ultimately an agreement was patched up and the

1. The archbishop's interpretation of the canons has recently been defended by C. Duggan, ' The Becket dispute and the Criminous Clerks ', in *Bulletin of the Institute of Historical Research* (London) XXXV 91, 1-28.

archbishop returned to England in triumph, to be murdered a few weeks later in his cathedral by four knights acting on an impulsive utterance of the king. Miracles were reported at his tomb; canonisation followed in 1173, and his shrine became a major goal of pilgrims from all over Europe. Sympathy has always been divided over the cause and the conduct of the king and his archbishop; Henry was intractable and unreliable, Thomas flamboyant and combative; each had a case and each made mistakes. There can be no doubt, however, that Henry's aim was to control his bishops in ways incompatible with canon law and the principle of a free church, and that Thomas in the last analysis died a martyr for the freedom of the spiritual power.

The canonisation of St Thomas brought immediate victory for his cause in the matter of the right of clerks to trial and sentence in the Courts Christian, though later a compromise was effected here as in so many other matters. For the next forty years or so the church in England was externally at peace, though internally disturbed by quarrels and lawsuits between bishops and monasteries. Another conflict broke out in the reign of King John who from the beginning ignored canonical procedure in appointing his bishops. In 1207, after a disputed election at Canterbury and appeals to Rome, Innocent III appointed Cardinal Stephen Langton to the metropolitan see. John refused to accept him and after many attempts to reach an understanding England was placed under an interdict (24 March 1208) which lasted for five years, and the king was only brought to submission by his formal deposition by the pope in favour of Louis, son of the French king Philip Augustus. In his submission (1 June 1213) John offered his kingdom in vassalage to Innocent III, recognising his suzerainty and promising a tribute. The pope for his part undertook to protect the king against those who opposed his rights with the assistance of his legate Pandulf. Almost immediately a kaleidoscopic change took place. Barons and clergy, oppressed by the king during and after the interdict, banded together under the archbishop to impose terms upon him in the celebrated Magna Carta of 1215. Innocent III, underestimating the king's violence and unreliability, and ignorant of the customs and traditions of English law and feudality, suspended the archbishop, excommunicated the ' rebels ', and declared the Charter invalid. The subsequent period of anarchy and confusion ended only with the death of John (19 October 1216), but the papal legates Guala and Pandulf played a large and beneficent part in the re-establishment of good government under the young king Henry III.

The church in England had suffered under King John. The bishops, torn between loyalty to the king and obedience to the pope, had lost much of their income and some estates, had been forced into exile and had, in many cases, died leaving their sees vacant for years. The religious orders had been mulcted of large sums only a few years after their subscriptions to the ransom from imprisonment of Richard I, the crusading king; some houses of the Cistercians, particularly hard hit, had disbanded, while the monks of Canterbury were for years in exile for their opposition; finally all classes had suffered morally and spiritually in the interdict, almost without a precedent both from the length of its duration and width of its impact. No doubt some of the damage done was permanent, but to all appearances the recovery was swift and for the church in general the subsequent age was one of growth, of improved organisation and administration, and of a new spirit of religion which made the thirteenth century perhaps the most solidly remarkable in England of all the medieval centuries.

2. FRANCE 900-1150

Whereas in Germany the history of the church after the division of the Carolingian empire must always be considered with reference to the king or emperor of the day, in France the power of the monarch rapidly declined, and his sphere of influence was reduced. To make headway against the universal collapse of authority and the barbarian invasions in north, east and south a remedy was found in the devolution of power to the local lord which resulted ultimately in a network of feudal dependencies.

This absence of central secular authority gave to the bishops as a class a position of considerable influence. Already under Charlemagne, and still more under his immediate successors, they had controlled the church individually and collectively more effectively than any other regional hierarchy, and the councils and controversies of Hincmar of Rheims and his contemporaries have for us a distinct, if distant, family resemblance to those of later centuries. Internally, also, the French church of the early ninth century with its archdeacons, deans, and embryo parishes, with its episcopal synods and councils, was more fully organised and articulated than any other. This relative homogeneity was shaken by the gradual lessening of central authority, by the growth of feudalism and lay proprietorship, and by the stress of invasion, and the first half of the tenth century was one of disorganisation and distress for France in which the régime of feudalism and the proprietary church (abbey and even bishopric) became universal. The light of a new day came first in the monastic world with Cluny emerging in Burgundy and the influence of Gerard of Brogne radiating from Lorraine; then came the rebirth of the church in Normandy at the end of the tenth century, with the resurgence of the bishoprics and the foundation of abbeys. With the royal power in eclipse, the bishops as a body became active again in councils and in preaching the ' truce of God ', the abstinence from feudal warfare for part of the year, while at Chartres and elsewhere the episcopal schools began to flourish. From about 1030 the royal power reaffirmed itself and a new age began, in which the feudal baronage, under the influence of the climate of reform, began to found monasteries and colleges, secular and later regular, and to bestow their proprietary churches on religious houses. It was an age, less than a century in duration, in which the monastic life was the spiritual remedy for all ills; abbeys and priories were founded as centres of intercession and small groups of monks (followed later by the canons) were used to occupy proprietary churches, and to provide a liturgical service of prayer for castles and villages. The more careful payment of tithe helped on the process of delimiting the parish which became increasingly important as an administrative unit when the process of subinfeudation fragmented a large village into several manors. On the highest level the church began to take the shape it was to wear for the remaining medieval centuries. The king reasserted the Carolingian custom of supervision and approval of episcopal elections and added to these the *regalia* and feudal rights of investiture and of the enjoyment of the revenues of a see or abbey during vacancies. The king, and dukes and counts also, summoned councils at which they presided, and encouraged the visits of bishops to their court. The monarchy however was still relatively weak, whereas the papacy was extending its influence from decade to decade, and there was in the eleventh or twelfth century no general reassertion of the rights of the episcopate in face of papal claims such as had been seen in the days of Hincmar, which has been called by a modern historian ' the Gallicanism of the ninth and tenth centuries '.

Meanwhile the waves of the Gregorian reform had flooded in. From the middle of the eleventh century legates with ever greater frequency toured the country holding councils and settling disputes. Under Gregory VII this activity was intensified, and permanent legates with initiative and full powers exercised a quasi-papal supervision. Later, and particularly during the pontificate of Urban II, a less drastic exercise of legislative and administrative power was usual, though the influence of the papacy was felt decisively by the repeated presence of popes upon the soil of France over a space of fifty years, holding councils, preaching crusades and receiving or despatching legates and emissaries to and from the emperor and other monarchs. The church, firmly stamped with Gregorian principles by the legate Hugh of Lyons and others, became a principal source of support to the papacy, and with the last decades of the eleventh century the golden age of French ascendancy had begun in Europe. On her soil were born almost all the new religious orders that transformed the face of Europe;

in her cities developed the cathedral schools and the school of schools at Paris, mother of knowledge; and it was France that gave to the Church the galaxy of saints and of bishops, preachers and writers whose names will recur in these pages. A steady increase in the population gave recruits to the monastic life and in particular to the lay-brotherhood and to the nunneries. A succession of rulers of varying ability with a steady policy of unification and firm government achieved a consolidation of power and a growth of the territory under royal control. For a crucial period (1130-1151) Abbot Suger of St Denis advised and in part controlled the government, the earliest of the class of clerical first ministers who were to fill such a place in French history, the class to which Georges d'Amboise, Richelieu, Mazarin and Fleury were to belong.

The French church at this time escaped the sharp tensions that were felt in England, in Italy and in the empire. Louis VII was pious and deferential. It was only towards the end of the century that Philip Augustus began to assert and defend what he conceived to be his rights. Gradually, with Paris becoming a unique centre of intellectual life, France was advancing towards the commanding position she was to attain in the political, cultural and ecclesiastical life of Europe in the thirteenth century.

3. GERMANY AND THE PAPACY 1125-1190

In Germany during the twelfth century the pattern formed that was to remain in its shifting outlines throughout the middle ages. At the economic and social level were the towns, rapidly becoming richer and more populous, and as time went on many became independent tesserae in the mosaic of the empire. On the political level the duchies and counties grew ever more numerous through accidents of inheritance. Among them the greater, under warlike and ambitious rulers, engaged in a perpetual struggle for self-aggrandisement, one aspect of which was the possession of the imperial title. At the head of all was the emperor for the time being, concerned both to reduce overpowerful vassals, to bring some kind of order among the many members of the empire and to control the church which in large part depended on his authority for episcopal elections and assisted him to rule. In addition some emperors, and among them the two greatest, aimed at re-establishing their sovereignty in Italy and their control of the papacy, attracted by the wealth and lustre of Italy and in particular of Sicily. In this last aim they were opposed with greater or less success by the popes. As a consequence the diplomatic and military history of the twelfth and thirteenth centuries is largely concerned with the clashes in policy between pope and emperor. The former, often harassed by rebellion in the city of Rome, had always to negotiate alliances to find a makeweight to the emperor's power. The latter was always ready to take advantage of a divided papal election, and to foster and perpetuate a schism.

Henry V died three years after the Concordat of Worms, and with him ended the Salian dynasty. His nephew was passed over by the electors and Lothair of Saxony was chosen. In secular affairs able and vigorous, but dogged by mischance, he was a devout monarch willing to accept the consequences of Worms and the Gregorian reform. Under his rule (1125-37) Germany experienced and accepted the tide of papal activity that had flowed a little earlier over France and England. Elections were canonical, free from both simony and external control, privileges and protection were solicited and granted, and the Holy See was recognised as the ordinary court of great affairs and the court to which all litigation could be carried on appeal. Legates went about the country on their missions, settling disputes, holding or assisting at synods and councils. On Lothair's death the electors again transferred the monarchy, electing Conrad of Hohenstaufen (1137-52), who followed the same course as Lothair. By the time of his death more than a quarter of a century had passed in which Germany had received the same influences and churchmen had formed the same associations as in the rest of western Europe. The roots of difficulty, however, still remained. The lack of basic political unity deprived the German bishops of a centre of loyalty and a spirit of solidarity such as both the English and the French bishops possessed in different ways, while on the other hand management of the hierarchy was almost a necessity for any monarch who desired to control his restless subjects. Moreover the myth of the empire, Carolingian and Ottonian, remained as a most powerful incentive to ambition, almost indeed as an obligation upon a king of Germany to assert his rights.

Conrad's successor, his young nephew Frederick I, Barbarossa (1152-90), was perhaps the most clear-sighted statesman and the most energetic and able warrior of all the German kings. He was in addition a man who inspired both affection and devotion, and a politician who knew how to retreat when disaster threatened without abandoning his aims. As a king he was committed, if he would survive, to a long and laborious struggle to control his subordinates and govern Germany. As a leader he had before his eyes the image of Charlemagne and Otto, but the empire he tried to re-establish was that of the Saxon dynasty, not that of Charles the Great. In other words, he thought in terms of a secular ruler, not in those of a theocratic emperor. Both emperor and pope were divinely appointed with different spheres of authority; Frederick did not claim to summon councils to declare doctrine or to impose forms of worship. But in all the external acts of government within his domain the monarch was to be supreme. From the beginning of his reign he disregarded the spirit and often the letter of the Concordat of Worms. He appointed and deprived bishops, dealt with disputed elections and other controversies and forbade appeals to Rome. He claimed the rights of *regalia* and *spolia* that had lapsed.

Before the advent of Barbarossa the currents of church life had been disturbed by a schism. On the death of Honorius II divisions in the curia produced a double election (1130) which was rendered possible by the absence of any rule as to the majority vote. In all probability both parties proceeded with irregularity, but the superior moral qualities of Innocent II, confirmed by St Bernard who was called in to pronounce by Louis VI, assured him the support of France and England, and later of Spain and the emperor Lothair III. Rome and Italy resisted for a time and two campaigns by Lothair and one by St Bernard were needed to change the alliance of Rome and Milan. The death of Anacletus II ended the schism (1138).

Innocent II was followed by short-lived pontiffs. The next pope of note was Eugenius III (1145-53) a Cistercian and a former novice of St Bernard at Clairvaux. The holiest and most unworldly pope of the century, he showed himself also a skilful steersman in troubled waters. He is remembered principally as the recipient of Bernard's ' Reflections for a pope ' *(de Consideratione)* which became at once a *locus classicus* both for theologians of the papacy and for reformers of all ages. He is remembered also as the pope who launched in 1147 the disastrous second crusade. Eugenius was followed after the brief pontificate of Anastasius IV by Hadrian IV, the only Englishman to become pope. Born on the estates of St Albans, he failed to secure entrance to the abbey, and became a canon regular at St Ruf near Avignon. As abbot of the house at loggerheads with his canons he was cited to Rome where Eugenius III recognised his talents and retained him as cardinal. In this office he acted as legate in Scandinavia where he reorganised the hierarchy of Norway but was unable to effect the union between Northmen and Goths in Sweden which was attained shortly after. His qualities of energy and statesmanship ensured his election to the papal throne in 1154. Faced by an opponent of genius he showed himself a match for Frederick Barbarossa; he crowned him Emperor but he reiterated and strengthened the papal claims of Gregory VII and sought to exclude Frederick from any right in Rome. Before the inevitable conflict developed the pope died (1159) leaving unfulfilled the promise of a memorable reign, notable among other acts for the extension of the English Peter's Pence to Scandinavia and for the bull *Laudabiliter*, bestowing suzerainty of Ireland upon Henry II. His friendship with John of Salisbury is commemorated in that scholar's letters.

His death was followed by another disputed election. Roland Bandinelli, a celebrated Bologna canonist and chief counsellor of Hadrian IV in his struggle with the emperor, had a large majority and became Alexander III, but Octavian, a Roman noble of the emperor's party, found support and the electoral decree of Nicholas II, which presupposed unanimity among the electors, gave no help. There is little doubt that Alexander III's election was valid, but tumult and a double coronation followed, and the supporters of both claimants appealed to the emperor's arbitration. Frederick called a synod at Pavia, which Alexander refused to recognise. Thinly attended, it was dominated by the emperor and pronounced for the antipope Victor IV. The schism which ensued divided Europe. Alexander excommunicated both emperor and anti-pope and by vigorous action in France won all western Europe apart from the empire to his allegiance, though Henry II of England, when at odds some years later with Thomas Becket, threatened withdrawal. Victor IV died shortly (1164), and a group of imperial bishops, whipped in by the resolute imperial chancellor Rainald of Dassel, uncanonically elected a successor, and at a meeting at Würzburg (23 May 1165) Frederick extracted an oath from all prominent lay and clerical subjects to repudiate Alexander III. The anti-pope, Paschal III, though clearly illegitimate, dutifully canonised Charlemagne, who remained in the German calendar thereafter. The struggle between the pope and emperor continued for more than ten years, with its active theatre in Lombardy; it was ended by the decisive defeat of Frederick by the Lombard league at Legnano in May 1176, which was followed by a reconciliation with the pope at Venice in July 1177.

Alexander III, handicapped at first by the difficulties of his succession and the long struggle against the emperor, was blessed by a long pontificate of twenty-two years which allowed his gifts of mind and character scope and made his reign the most distinguished of the century. The pupil of Abelard and Gratian, with equal competence in theology and canon law, he was the first of a series of great lawyer-popes that continued for a hundred years, and by his numerous decretal letters of which more than seven hundred are extant, he helped to form the discipline of the Church and of Christian life, and in so doing to foster and to give distinction to the science of canon law. He extended the competence of the ecclesiastical courts by claiming for them jurisdiction over church property as bound up with a spiritual entity *(jus spirituali adnexum)*, and comprehended in the claim marriage, dowries, tithes, wills, contracts under oath, advowsons and the like. As a disciple of Abelard he distinguished in his moral teaching between ignorance and negligence, and between culpable and invincible ignorance. His actions and his competence helped to increase the number of appeals to Rome, but he did not of set purpose draw all business into the papal net. He left his mark on every legal topic he touched. It was he who finally established the sole right of the pope to canonise saints, and established the procedure which remained in force for five centuries. He accelerated and clarified the process by which monasteries paying an annual tax *(census)* to Rome and those exempt from episcopal control as royal proprietary churches *(Eigenkirchen)* became canonically exempt, and he isolated the formula *(nullo mediante*, i.e., ' with no intermediate authority ' between themselves and Rome) which established exemption. In the long history of the struggle against lay proprietorship of churches he expressed in terms of papal law the decision of his master Gratian, which in its turn reflected the practice of the reformed church. He recognised the patron's right of presentation *(advocatio*, advowson) to a living, while denying to him the right of ownership of the ' church '. This right, and the practice of impropriation by a religious house, have been called by a great historian the elder and younger daughter of the régime of the proprietary church *(Eigenkirchentum)* [2].

Alexander III, upright and of blameless life, though without the fire and simplicity of a saint, must rank high among the popes of the middle ages. His personality is hidden from us, save in so far as it survives in his decretals, but his statesmanship and his mental power are evident [3]. After his death the papal policy during a series of short pontificates varied between hostility and accommodation, but no disaster occurred before Frederick's death on crusade in 1190.

The reign of Frederick I and the pontificate of Alexander III witnessed political events of the greatest significance for Germany, and equally important changes in the climate of opinion. The fragmentation of the duchies during Frederick's struggle for the mastery, culminating in the despoliation of Henry the Lion, was decisive in setting the pattern of the map of Germany for the next seven centuries. Similarly the victory of the Communes of northern Italy over the emperor at Legnano determined the map of north Italy and decreed that Lombardy should never for long be an integral part of the empire. In Europe at large, the struggle between Alexander and Frederick had made it clear that the empire could no longer pretend to represent western Christendom. France, Spain, Burgundy and the Angevin empire were now of equal if not greater importance as a block and would go their own way. Henceforward, whatever ancient battle-cries might be raised, the emperor could not claim to speak for Christendom.

---

2. U. Stutz, ' Gratian und die Eigenkirchen ', in *Zeitschrift der Savigny-Stiftung für Rechtswissenschaft* 45 (Weimar 1911) Kanonistische Abteilung I, 12. ' So enstand als zweite Tochter des Eigenkirchenrechtes und als jüngere Schwester des Patronates die Inkorporation ', Cf. *ibid*. 27. ' Gratian spricht... der Eigenkirchenrecht... das Todes-urteil '.
3. The veil is lifted for a moment in the letter of the pope to the English hermit Godric of Finchale, asking his prayers. Cf. W. Holtzmann, *Papsturkunden in England* III, (Göttingen, 1952), 163.

Moreover, the unprecedented diffusion of the centralised religious orders, and the devotion to the papacy of great leaders such as Bernard and Norbert, had given to Europe a new cohesion and solidarity. At the same time the acceptance of Gregorian dichotomy between clerical and lay sections of society was becoming universal and, for the time, irresistible, and the clergy would look to Rome as their centre. Nevertheless the struggle of the reformers against the possession of the church by lay magnates had been only half successful. Neither emperors nor individual monarchs such as Henry II of England would ever agree to abandon entirely their claims to select the personnel and enjoy some of the fruits of the wealthy church.

4. SPAIN IN THE MIDDLE AGES

In the two centuries that followed the Adoptionist controversy very little is known of the fortunes of the mozarabic church. On the whole, freedom of worship and social intercourse were general, and although proselytism or propaganda was punishable the martyrs and confessors whose legends have survived seem to have been mostly those who for whatever reason themselves provoked or invited repression. Gradually, however, small kingdoms formed along the northern coast reaching down towards central Spain – Leon, Castile, Navarre – and in the ninth century (829) the cult of St James established itself and was located at Compostela (866) where a large basilica was consecrated in 899. Thenceforward the Christians in the north were continually tilting at the Muslim frontier and though the Moors also had their periods of advance, particularly under the great warrior known as Almanzor (Mahomet ibn Abi-'Amir, active 976-1002), and during the internecine wars of the Christians, by the mid-eleventh century the three kingdoms of Castile, Aragon and Navarre were in being, contacts were established across the Pyrenees and the pilgrimage to Compostela was becoming fashionable; it was both the result and the occasion of a string of monastic foundations on or near the route, and of the two-way traffic of architectural and sculptural practitioners and their art-forms. Round the Mediterranean coast, also, a chain of monasteries, of which Cuxa was one, were closely linked by visits and pilgrimages with each other and with Italy. Later, from 1008 onwards, came the penetration of the Cluniac monks, who gradually established their control over almost all the Spanish houses.

It may have been Cluniac influence that brought about the entry of the papacy, under Alexander II (1061-73), into Spanish affairs. The original purpose was the general reform of the church, and the agent was the legate Hugo Candidus, who in his second visit directed his energies to the replacement of the mozarabic rite by the Roman.

No doubt the curia had records of the Adoptionist ' heresy ' and of the support it had derived from liturgical phrases, but the pope's motive was also a desire for uniformity. Whatever regret be felt at the all but complete disappearance of an ancient form of Christian euchology, the subsequent history of Spain might seem to justify Alexander's policy. Spain, in the course of a few years, became and was to remain completely one in doctrine and usage with the Roman church. This achievement was rapidly followed up by the papacy. There had been discords and disruptions in the Muslim principalities and the Christian princes to the north were preparing an invasion (1064). This was organised, supported and blessed by Alexander II and may be considered the first papal ' crusade '; the territory recaptured was to be held under the suzerainty of the Holy See. Gregory VII took up and extended this claim, regarding it as the reassertion of an ancient proprietorship, possibly in consequence of the Donation of Constantine. He met with opposition from Alfonso VII of Castile, but imposed his will upon Aragon, Navarre and Catalonia. Later he was successful also in Castile, which accepted the Roman rite and in 1085, a few days before the death of the pope, King Alfonso recaptured Toledo.

Urban II continued the policy of his predecessor and pressed forward the reform, aided by his confrères the Cluniac monks who had remained distrustful of Gregory VII, but his hopes were dashed by domestic disturbances in Spain, the defeat of Alfonso VII by a new Muslim invasion, and the rivalry of the archbishops of Toledo and Compostela. Nevertheless, a new ' crusade ', assisted by allies from Provence and Genoa, achieved the reconquest of the Balearic islands and of Saragossa; Lisbon and most of Portugal was liberated from 1147 onwards. Little progress was made in Spain until the beginning of the thirteenth century when a ' crusade ' organised by Innocent III and supported by French arms won a decisive victory at Las Navas de Tolosa (1212), the first step in the drive towards the final liberation of the peninsula. Cordova fell in 1236, and Seville in 1248, bringing with it Cadiz and other cities; Murcia had become subject to Castile in 1241 and was finally secured in 1266. Valencia had been taken in 1238. Thus before the end of the thirteenth century the reconquest of Spain was virtually completed, save for the newly organised Muslim kingdom of Granada.

Ecclesiastical reorganisation went hand in hand with reconquest, and Spain gradually took its place in the medieval church. Cluniac and other monks had been numerous in the northern kingdoms since the early eleventh century; the Cistercians filled what spaces were available in the twelfth and at the beginning of the thirteenth the Spaniard Dominic of Old Castile gave a powerful new order to the church. Great cathedrals were built at Avila, Salamanca, Zamora, Coimbra and elsewhere. Already with the recapture of Toledo Spain had become for a short time, like Sicily, a Mecca for ecclesiastical careerists from the north, several of whom were, or were accompanied by, scholars in search of the ancient treasures of thought and science now embedded in Arabic. From *c.* 1140, for almost a century, Spain was a hunting-ground from which the translators despatched or carried their booty northwards to Paris, Montpelier, Oxford and other northern universities. It was not until western scholars had absorbed and exploited the mass of this new learning that Spain herself founded her own academies. Salamanca dates from 1255, but this university and others did not attain international celebrity before the Golden Century.

The mention of Spain raises the problem, difficult for our minds to comprehend and resolve, of papal suzerainty over various countries. Suzerainty (overlordship), a feudal concept, stands uneasily for a position of authority lower than modern sovereignty and higher than patronage. Gregory VII certainly conceived himself as having, as pope, the right and duty of controlling the faith and morals of the public as well as the private life of Christendom; all monarchs were therefore accountable to him in their public as well as their private capacity, in so far as morality and justice, as distinct from administration and ownership, were involved. Suzerainty implied a solemn recognition of this, with the corresponding feudal obligations of loyalty and protection. But there were various grades of sovereignty. The pope was immediate and sole sovereign of most of Italy; in the Empire he asserted paramount spiritual power; he was the protector and guide of monarchs in countries not fully christianised, as Spain, Denmark, Hungary, Bohemia and others. In these suzerainty implied freedom to impose a hierarchy and canon law. In a few countries, as France and England under William the Conqueror, he did not succeed in imposing suzerainty.

The reconquest of Spain, which added to the area and lustre of Christendom, brought new problems and revived old tensions. The traditional term ' reconquest ' has been used, but recent historians have stressed, what earlier racial prepossessions ignored, that Spain in the first twelve centuries of the Christian era had always been a country of mixed racial ancestry, and that during the Muslim ascendancy Christianity had never been extinct. By the same token, those who fought in the wars of ' reconquest ' were a cross-section of the population, and after the achievement of national sovereignty the mixture of races continued. The Christian population of the north was swollen by mozarabic colonies who did not at once change their rites and outlook, while free Muslims remained to form a religiously alien element and Jews, either refugees from districts of oppression or old inhabitants of Muslim cities, flooded over the country and were received at first without hostility. Thus once again the old tensions of the seventh century were building up which were to have such grave consequences in the future. Some of the greatest figures in the episcopate, such as Paul of Santa Maria, bishop successively of Cartagena and Burgos, and his son the still more distinguished Alfonso of Cartagena, were Jews or of Jewish descent; so also, it may be, was Cardinal John de Torquemada. Yet in Spain, even more decisively than in France and England, there was a strenuous vindication of royal authority, backed by a parliament, the Cortes, which, even earlier than in England, denied legal validity to papal juridical advances. The regalian rights of the kings were wide, as were also, on the other hand, the privileges of the clergy. When the Great Schism occurred, Spain nevertheless remained as a whole aloof from the conciliar party; her bishops and theologians were traditional papalists, and she supported for long the Spanish Pedro de Luna, pope at Avignon under the name of Benedict XIII (1394-1423).

5. SCANDINAVIA

While the first attempts of missionaries from Francia and Germany to evangelise Denmark and Sweden had been repulsed or had met with merely temporary success, the efforts of Anglo-Saxon evangelists, many of them monks, had succeeded in the tenth and eleventh centuries in planting the faith and founding monasteries in Denmark and along the south-western fjords of Norway. Evesham Abbey sent a colony to Odensee, and Stavanger retains to the present day many traces of its devotion to St Swithin of Winchester. Missionaries to Sweden reached the Malar lake, and Sigtuna, where Anskar had founded his church, and later Uppsala, a centre of primitive religion, became Christian settlements. Of the three countries Denmark, whose kings then ruled over the south-western part of Scania, was the earliest to resemble the other Christian kingdoms, with a hierarchy centred upon Lund, and a parish organisation. Neither feudalism nor the proprietary church nor the right of presentation (advowson) existed in Scandinavia in the eleventh century; in Norway the king exercised rights, but elsewhere the priests were appointed either by the bishop or (especially in Sweden) by the community of the parish. The early twelfth century saw the arrival of the Gregorian reform, partly under Cistercian influence. Lund in Scania had inherited from the dissolved archbishopric of Hamburg-Bremen metropolitan rights over all Scandinavia, and Eskil, the friend of St Bernard, introduced the white monks at Alvastra and Nydala before retiring to die at Clairvaux (1181). Eskil was succeeded by another great archbishop, Absalom (1178-1201), the founder of Copenhagen, who diffused the canonical reforms.

Norway, with its scattered population, had a more rudimentary organisation, with many customs and bishops from England, whence came also the earliest Cistercian foundations at Lyse, near Bergen, and Hovedö, near Oslo. The whole establishment was reformed and given its permanent shape in a memorable legatine visitation (1152) by the English cardinal Nicholas Brakespeare, who set up Trondheim as the metropolis, and added to its four Norwegian suffragans the sees of Iceland, the Faroes, Orkney, and Sodor and Man. He also established canonical election of bishops, the right of these to appoint parish priests, and the payment of Peter's Pence. These reforms were maintained by the able Eysten (Augustine), archbishop of Nidaros (Trondheim, 1161-86), but there followed a generation of strife between the hierarchy and the kings who endeavoured to reassert their old rights, the bishops were exiled, and Norway had experience of a struggle not unlike that between Thomas Becket and Henry II in England.

Sweden, the most backward of the three countries, was for long Christian only in the wide central belt around the great lakes between the modern Göteborg and Stockholm. Sigtuna lost its early primacy when Uppsala was given metropolitan dignity by Alexander III shortly after the martyrdom in Finland c. 1157 of its bishop Eric. The first bishop of the see had been the Englishman Stephen, a monk of Alvastra. Thenceforward the Swedish church developed slowly along normal lines, though Lund long retained primatial position. During the remaining medieval centuries Scandinavia and the littoral of Finland became wholly Christian, though pagan practices continued in forests and mountains, and in distant Faroe and Iceland. The gradual introduction of a feudal monarchy entailed recurrent trials of strength between church and king, but on the whole, and especially in Denmark, the church retained more freedom than in western Europe, while in Sweden the monasteries and bishoprics, with their vast estates, were of admininstrative value to the king as against the military and peasant classes. The island of Gotland, which became an appendage of Denmark, was wealthy and populous as an entrepôt of Baltic and European trade, and renowned for the number of its churches and houses of friars.

6. THE CRUSADES 1098-1274

The crusade in the East, an unprecedented and unforeseeable movement of religious enthusiasm, originating in an impulse to meet a particular crisis, became for almost two centuries a recurrent episode, comparable to a volcanic eruption, in medieval society, and remains perhaps the most striking of those movements of feeling, translated into action, that have appeared to the modern mind as characteristically and exclusively medieval. The word unprecedented has been used, and with justice, of the international voluntary mass expedition to Palestine to conquer or defend the region of Christ's life on earth. Taken in the wider sense of a military venture undertaken for a professedly religious purpose, the first crusade had forerunners in the military expeditions, supported and encouraged by the papacy, to reconquer the north of Spain from the Muslims and in the Norman Conquest of England, specifically blessed by the papacy. At the other end of our period the idea, the name and the religious and military techniques of the crusade were for more than four centuries applied to military expeditions organised, with greater or less show of justice, to conquer or to repel foes of the Church, whether heretics as the Albigenses, or pagans as in Prussia and the Baltic lands, or invaders such as the Turks between 1453 and the late seventeenth century. Nevertheless the seven crusades, all of which entailed the transfer overland or oversea of a large and mixed force representing Christendom and blessed by the pope, stand together as a medieval phenomenon, apart from all other holy wars, and as such remain on the fringe of church history.

The origins of the first crusade and the motives of its promoter still remain in dispute. Warriors from Normandy and France, encouraged by a papal indulgence, had assisted in the reconquest of Spain, and Toledo was theirs in 1085. In the same year Antioch had been captured by the Turks who had previously (1071) occupied Jerusalem. In the latter year also the decisive battle of Manzikert had stirred Gregory VII to rouse western Christendom to the aid of the East and of the Holy Places. More recently (1085) the emperor Alexius I had appealed for help to Urban II. This was probably the immediate occasion, though not the real cause, of the plan for a crusade mooted at Piacenza and proclaimed at Clermont in 1095, but the pope no doubt saw also the advantage of turning against the enemies of the Church the swords of Normans and others who were disturbing Europe. As a statesman, he must also have seen the chance offered to the papacy of taking the lead of western Christendom. He appealed to his hearers to rescue the Holy City from the infidel. His invitation was accepted instantaneously and with a far wider enthusiasm than the pope could have foreseen, and the subsequent planning had to deal with an accomplished fact. The overall supervision of the volunteer army was given to Adhemar, bishop of Puy, as legate; the possessions of absent crusaders were put under papal protection, and the crusaders were promised, if they fell on crusade, remission of the punishment due to their sins. As for the warriors, every kind of motive was no doubt to be found in their ranks, but in the first crusade many must have entered through sincere desire to fight the battles of the Lord and to smite his enemies. The course of the crusade need not be followed here. The death of the able, wise and spiritual Adhemar removed the only man who, standing above party, could have maintained the crusading ideals and settled the religious

polity of the Latin kingdom of Jerusalem. This became a purely feudal
state, in which the existing patriarch of Jerusalem was deposed in favour
of a Latin patriarch, while the needs of the crusaders gave birth to the
hybrid creation of military and religious zeal, the military order, which in
its twofold form, of the Temple and of the Hospital, was the mainstay of
the defence of the Latin kingdom of Jerusalem.

The second crusade was occasioned by the Turkish advance and the
capture of Edessa on 25 December 1144. Appeal was made to Eugenius III
who invited Louis VII to organise a crusade. Both king and pope turned
to St Bernard, who accepted the task – unwillingly as he subsequently maintained – and, acting in the pope's name, proclaimed a crusade at Vézelay
on 31 March 1146. The scenes of fifty years earlier at Clermont were
repeated and Bernard followed up his success by a tour of France from
Languedoc to Flanders. Pope and king had thought in terms of a French
crusade; the Germans had taken little part in the first, but Bernard, summoned to the Rhineland to quell a private crusade against the Jews started
by a Cistercian, went on to preach the eastern crusade in Germany and to
persuade Conrad III to lead his people. The account of his tour, corus-
cating (his own word) with signs and wonders, forms the vivid and extraordinary narrative of the book of miracles *(Liber Miraculorum)* included
as a part of his *Life*. The crusade was a disastrous failure; Bernard, never
one to yield to hard facts, agreed to organise a second wave of crusaders,
but the enterprise was not undertaken. St Bernard and his many followers
were hard put to it to explain the failure of an enterprise to which the great
leader had devoted such enthusiasm and which had seemingly been blessed
by signs from heaven. Bernard put the blame fairly and squarely on the
shoulders of the crusaders and recalled the parallel of Moses and the
Israelites. A modern historian can do no more than note the zeal with
which a great religious leader could use his immense moral power to send
armies of men to death by disease or in battle.

The disaster which seemed imminent in 1146 did not in fact develop
and the Latin kingdoms held out for another thirty years. Not till Saladin's
appearance (1179) did danger again threaten. This time there was no
respite. Defeated in 1187 at Nazareth and the Horns of Hittim, where the
flower of the military orders fell or were captured, the Christians lost
Jerusalem in 1187 and were driven back to their single stronghold of Tyre.
This shocked the whole of Europe. The pope changed the colour of his
seal and Samson, the great abbot of Bury St Edmund's, took to wearing
a hair shirt and abstained from meat. A spontaneous wave of enthusiasm
sent the three great monarchs – Conrad, Philip and Richard – to the East.
Once more the pope, by means of two legates, summoned a crusade and
was prodigal of plenary indulgences both to those slain and to survivors,

and demanded from bishops a contribution towards its expenses, which was augmented in France and England by the so-called Saladin tithe imposed by the monarchs with support from the bishops. This time the direction was not papal, but imperial, and after Frederick's death, no overall direction existed. Despite its fame in history and legend, the success of this crusade was meagre, but the Christians obtained a long if narrow strip of territory along the sea.

The fourth crusade was not directly caused by any disaster in the East; it was the work of Innocent III alone, who devoted much of his energy in the first years of his pontificate to repeated attempts to stir up the monarchs of Europe and the emperor of the Greeks to a concerted attempt to regain the Holy Land for Christendom. When all failed, he pressed on by a direct call to the bishops and the faithful and succeeded in setting recruitment in motion. A large army began to form, which was to embark, in the Pope's plan, from Sicily. Instead, the leaders made arrangements with Venice for transportation. Venice was hostile to Byzantium and the German leaders of the crusade had been approached by a pretender to the eastern throne. The emperor Alexius III begged the pope for reassurance, which Innocent gave, that no attack would be made upon his dominions, but in 1203 the crusading fleet at Corfu decided to sail upon Constantinople. The pope protested in vain; on 17 July the city was taken and the pretender Alexius installed as emperor (Alexius IV). Eight months later Alexius IV was murdered in a revolt; the city was again taken by the crusaders and pitilessly sacked, after which the leader Baldwin of Flanders was elected Latin emperor. Thrace, Greece and the islands were parcelled out to Venice and various barons. The crusade had ceased to exist, after committing a crime which poisoned the relations between Rome and the Greek church for centuries, and which still haunts like a spectre the imaginations of many Christians in the East.

Innocent III did not abandon his hope. From 1213 onwards he took all the traditional steps in calling a crusade (the fifth), with all its indulgences, remissions and protection. Departure was fixed for 1 June 1217. Innocent did not live to see the day but the crusade duly departed, failed to take advantage of its victories and broke itself in capturing Damietta. The emperor Frederick II, who failed to join the party, had a crusade of his own as excommunicate in 1228 which was a purely secular enterprise that won for him the title king of Jerusalem.

That city was lost to the Christians in 1244 after their defeat at Gaza; for some years previously Gregory IX had been endeavouring to rouse the sovereigns of Europe, but some small expeditions had done little. In December 1244 Louis IX (St Louis) took the cross when seriously ill but it was not till 1248 that his crusade (the sixth) started with the support, moral and financial, of Innocent IV. The king was absent from France for about six years in alternating victory and defeat, with a short period of captivity as prisoner of war. Twenty years later the Mameluke Baibars, victor of Gaza and now Sultan of Egypt, took Caesarea (1265) and Jaffa and Antioch (1268). This brought about the last of the crusades (the seventh), under King Louis and the Lord Edward, heir of Henry III of England. St Louis died before Tunis and Edward after some successes arranged for a ten years' truce in Palestine. Fighting broke out a dozen years later and the two great cities of Tripolis (1289) and Acre (1291) fell. It was the end of Frankish occupation in the Levant and the end of the movement and of the enthusiasm that had given birth to the name and the ideal of a crusade.

The crusades in Palestine and its neighbourhood were at once characteristic of and peculiar to the mental and religious climate of the twelfth and thirteenth centuries. Save perhaps in the narrow realm of military tactics and architecture they were signally devoid of lasting consequences. No system, no institutional, theological, political or diplomatic principles, nor indeed any growth or change of method can be discerned in their history. By preaching the first crusade and thus displaying the papacy as a unifying force and a dynamic agency that could excite or direct the enthusiasm of the whole of Europe, Urban II gave to the Gregorian reform a new aspect, which was to remain powerful for centuries, even if in after years the legacy of responsibility was to lie heavy on the papacy, and lead to endless and fruitless toil, and to cruel wars of spoliation and conquest dignified by the name of crusade. Among the crusaders almost every type of motive was to be found, from exalted self-sacrifice to a love of fighting for its own sake or for the prestige and material success it might bring. In the past much has been said of the religious or romantic ideals of the crusaders; today the spectacle of popes and preachers inciting multitudes to enterprises which from our vantage-point we can see as inevitably doomed to sordid and bloody failure has in it something repugnant. Though the attempt to reconquer Palestine was seemingly feasible, the success of a motley array led by jealous captains without a rational and detailed plan of campaign was bound to end, as analogous attempts at large-scale international co-operation in our own age have ended, in disunion and disaster. An unprovoked and offensive warfare can with difficulty preserve a religious character. We can only record that earnest pontiffs of the stature of Urban II and Innocent III, and men of the moral and spiritual quality of St Bernard and St Louis, gave untiring and unqualified support, and life itself, in the cause of the crusade.

7. THE FOUR COUNCILS AT THE LATERAN

The twelfth century saw the reappearance, on western soil, of a series of councils which in course of time became recognised as ecumenical in the western church. As we have seen, both emperors and popes had from time to time convoked assemblies to debate and pronounce upon matters of doctrine and discipline, and in the eleventh century the reforming popes had made use of synods, and particularly of regular Roman synods, to promulgate their programmes and to fix sanctions. None of these, however, had aimed at universality, and it is a sign of the times that in the twelfth century popes were able to summon to council, with considerable success, all the bishops and other prelates of western Europe. The earliest of these meetings were concerned primarily with the announcement and registration of important political agreements in which the papacy was concerned and in the enunciation of points of discipline rather than of doctrine.

The first was summoned to the Lateran by Calixtus II for the Lent of 1123, at a moment when the Concordat of Worms (1123) was imminent, but not yet achieved. It was attended by more than 300 bishops. In effect it reiterated and gave precision to the measures of reform during the past seventy years. Simony, nicolaism, lay control of clerical persons and property were condemned, and decrees in favour of pilgrims and crusaders were passed, while others forbade monks to administer sacraments or offer public Masses for the lay people.

This council was followed up by a group of regional synods, at London (1125, 1127), Rouen (1128), Toledo (1129), Clermont (1130), Rheims (1131), and Pisa (1135), applying the Roman programme to the various churches.

A second great assembly was convoked at the Lateran by Innocent II for 1139. Though attended by more than 500 bishops it did little more than reiterate the reform legislation of the councils of the previous decades. Indeed there is little difference either in solemnity or matter between this council and that held by Eugenius III at Rheims in 1148, which ended with a global confirmation of all decrees passed since the time of Gregory VII.

The third Lateran council was convoked for 1179 by Alexander III, when his contests with rivals and with the emperor had yielded to peace. The assembly contained at least some representatives from almost every country to the number of more than 300, among whom was the bishop of Chartres, John of Salisbury. Many of its decrees were mere repetitions of past legislation. One decree however, perhaps the work of Alexander III himself, decided that in future papal elections, when unanimity was lacking, the candidate who secured two-thirds of the votes of all cardinals should be deemed elected. This provision, which has ever since remained in force, removed a principal obstacle to clear and unassailable papal elections, and in the event no anti-pope appeared until a totally different cause led to the schism of 1378. In addition the council laid down the conditions, including requisite age (thirty for a bishop, twenty-five for a cure of souls) for valid elections to ecclesiastical offices, with appropriate sanctions; simony, nicolaism and dissipation of church property were once more stigmatised. A new and important decree apportioned a benefice in each cathedral to a master; he was to teach without fee, and the licence to teach was to be freely given to all qualified candidates. Finally, a series of decrees, some new others old, regulated Christian society; the Jews, Muslims and heretics were considered and in the case of the last a series of new and important measures were taken which will be glanced at later.

Innocent III throughout his pontificate had in the forefront of his programme a new crusade and the reform of the Church. The crusade organised by him had failed disastrously in 1204, but after an interval of years he returned to his plan, and the fourth Lateran council, convoked in 1213 and held at the Lateran in November 1215, contained in its agenda the crusade and a wide programme of reform covering every department of the life of the Church. Nothing is known of the machinery of the council, save that its decrees were accepted at a session on 30 November and that in some respects they departed from what is known to have been the policy of the pope, but a contemporary account [4] suggests that the decrees, framed by the curia, were presented to the fathers, who had little opportunity for debate. With the single exception of Trent it was and has remained till our own time the widest in scope of all the ecumenical councils, but in contrast to Trent its dogmatic chapters were few and relatively unimportant; the most celebrated passage is that in which the word ' transubstantiation ' is applied to the Eucharist for the first time in an official pronouncement. The word occurs in the brief statement of faith which heads the decrees and which is shortly followed by the well-known section on yearly confession and Easter communion. These, and other miscellaneous decrees, besides their influence on sacramental practice and theology, are of significance as being the first attempt by a council inspired by the papacy to legislate for the Christian life as lived by layfolk. The dogmatic canons were followed by a restatement of measures against heretics. As for the clergy, their lives were controlled by a whole series of decrees. Episcopal election was to be canonical and free. The education and selection of the clergy, and the rules as to benefices, were overhauled. Preaching was enjoined, and the careful administration of the sacraments, and the lives and activities of the clergy, especially parish priests, were regulated. As for the

4. S. Küttner and A. García y García, 'A new eyewitness account of the Fourth Lateran Council', in *Traditio* 20 (1964) 115-78.

regular clergy, all were to adopt the Cistercian system of general chapters and bishops were to exercise their ancient right of visitation. No religious order was to be founded with a new rule. The laws of marriage were at once strengthened and rationalised and ecclesiastical judicial procedure was reformed. Taken as a whole the Lateran decrees are a remarkably thorough review of the life of the Church, both spiritual and external, and the contrast is striking between their wide and practical legislation and the bankruptcy of dynamic and realistic proposals in the later conciliar epoch. Like all medieval legislation they were imperfectly implemented, and applied in some regions more thoroughly than in others. Where, as in England, they were put into practice with tolerable thoroughness, they helped to make the century that followed an epoch of distinguished achievement. It was not the fault of the pope or the council that the centralising and autocratic tendencies of the papacy and the canonists tended to harden and to narrow the flexibility and breadth of the canons of the Fourth Lateran council.

THE SHAPE
OF THE MEDIEVAL CHURCH

I N the two centuries between the pontificates of Silvester II and
Innocent III the external form and activities and framework of the
Church developed greatly in every direction. Alike in the appearance
of corporate uniformity and in the grasp of control by the papacy this
was a time of crucial importance. To some contemporaries and to many
subsequent observers the changes appeared revolutionary; to others at the
time and to the upholders of the central tradition of the Roman church
the eleventh century appeared as a renaissance, a taking up of the threads
of a loom that had been inactive since the sixth century, and the twelfth
century seemed an extension of this process to the cisalpine countries. Both
views have an element of truth in them. The principles and many parts of
the machinery, intellectual, theological and administrative, used by the
great churchmen of the eleventh century were both ancient and hallowed
by long acceptance, but the men who used and developed them were of a
different race, of a different culture and with new problems and capabilities. Hence the profound truth which is also a paradox, that in many
ways the middle ages, the centuries between two civilisations in Europe,
ceased early in the eleventh century, and the clock which had run down
in the sixth century began again to keep time; while in another context
the eleventh and twelfth centuries were an age of flower and fruit after a

hard winter, the harvest of seed sown by Charlemagne and his agents.

The life of the Church may be considered in two aspects in this as in every age. On the one hand there is the life of the great body of faithful scattered over Europe, each generation, or rather the unceasing stream of generations, living the same round from birth to death with the same creed, the same ministers and the same rites and sacraments, untouched in essentials by the changes and movements among the office-holders and men of letters. On the other hand there is the small group of leaders who work chiefly in and upon a framework of dogma, law and administrative procedure – the Church and churchmen in a narrow sense.

In the widely scattered church of western Christendom, which in the year 1000 was still almost entirely rural, one decade, one century, grew slowly out of another, each a child of its age. In default of all statistics, it is hard to answer even such elementary questions as, when was this or that region fully and confessedly Christian? Or, when was this territory or that fully covered by what we should now call the parochial system? Both questions, and in particular the first, are complicated by the invasions, German, Scandinavian, Hungarian and the rest, which sometimes obliterated a Christian landscape and made a new evangelisation necessary. A recent historian has remarked, as if it were a certainty, that during the eleventh century, and not before, Europe became wholly Christian [1]. Such a generalisation is too broad to be of value. Parts of France, such as the Rhône valley and an area from Paris eastwards and southwards, and much of the Celtic parts of the British Isles, were fully Christian in the seventh century or earlier; on the other hand, pockets of wild land remained pagan after 1100, and the beliefs and practices, with their roots in a psychology derived from millennia of non-Christian life, often remained to entwine themselves with Catholic rites and doctrines or to exist side by side with them or to retreat beneath the conscious level to reappear in fears and magical practices, race hatreds and heresies.

As for the organised system of a pastoral clergy, we are on ground that can be accurately mapped only if the necessary facts are known. In detail, this is not yet the case, but there is good reason to think that the habitable districts of France, Germany and England were parochialised, or perhaps it would be better to say, were adequately supplied with priests and churches: France before 800, Germany as a whole as early as the mid-ninth century, and England during the ninth century, though later the country was partially disorganised by the Danish invasions as parts of France also were by the Northmen. As we have seen, a majority, and probably a large majority, of the churches were ' proprietary ', but this did

1. R. W. Southern, *The Making of the Middle Ages*.

not imply in rural areas that the priest was a ' private chaplain '. He might owe specific duties to his lord, but he was in principle at least available for the spiritual needs of the people of the village. What this meant in practice we can only guess. The priest was ordered by synods and capitularies to teach his flock the creed, elementary prayers, and the Christian virtues, together with the principal commandments of the Church. He was also enjoined to preach upon the gospels of the Mass, and to gather the promising boys of the district for elementary instruction in letters. What his personal relations would have been with the adult members of his flock we cannot tell. Ordinarily, he would have been by birth a man of their class, with very scanty learning. He would mingle with them in cultivating his glebe and other strips of land, at the market and probably also at the ale-bench. In the ninth and tenth centuries a large proportion of the clergy in every land would have been joined, often by formal marriage, otherwise by an informal but not degrading relationship, to a life-long consort. When marriage was valid without the assistance of a priest, when communion was rare and confession spreading but slowly, it is difficult to picture the village priest's pastoral life. The historian, however, must not forget that he is writing of baptised and believing Christians, and that the basic problems of the human mind and of human conduct and passion are present in all societies, and that the help of a good man and his advice are always prized.

At this level a change in the eleventh and twelfth centuries is perceptible, in so far as the spread of education and the reforming decrees of councils and synods filtered down to the parish, or were acted upon by devout landlords. The practice of celibacy spread, however slowly, and the inheritance of churches by the sons of their priests became rarer. The rural population gradually became aware of the new monasteries, founded by orders old and new, that were springing up on every side. They were, as we know from the narratives of contemporary conversions, ' sermons in stones ', and the increase in literacy from the new schools, and the growth of the rural population with its consequent pressure on land, were among the disposing causes of the enthusiasm that greeted the Cistercians and the new monastic vocation of the lay brotherhood. That, and the corresponding increase in the number and variety of the orders of nuns, were major influences in the development of religious sentiment in the century 1050-1150. The monastic life was now open to all of sound bodily habit, and the Cistercians and Premonstratensians must have creamed off, for more than a century, many of the potentially devout over the whole population, while their sisters found a home, as professed nuns or lay *conversae*, in the new nunneries of Fontevrault and Sempringham. Much has been written of the motives of the founders and inmates of these new monasteries that covered the land. Certainly we may accept that motives other than the purely religious had a part. Fashion, fame, the hope of valid intercessory prayer in life and forever after death no doubt entered into the calculations of donors, while the security of shelter and a quasi-superstitious trust in the round of monastic service, or sheer fear of the consequences of sin, may have led many to the novitiate. But the monastic buildings of the twelfth and other centuries, standing as we can imagine them in their multitude and in their solemn beauty, or as we see them now in fragments or ruins, remain as evidence that numberless men and women of that age were willing to spend much thought and money, and to follow hard ways, for an end which brought them no comparable return in terms of material or social gain, or physical or merely human satisfaction.

The twelfth century, particularly in its later decades, saw also a steady growth of urban population. Hitherto Italy had been the only region of western Christendom where towns in any number existed, and where urban life was the lot of a notable section of society. In the old Italian cities and towns, which themselves had decayed between A.D. 500 and 1000, as also in the rarer towns of southern France, the church organisation had resembled that of Rome. There was a cathedral of some size, with a baptistery, and a ring of suburban. churches, often sited in cemeteries. In the tenth and eleventh centuries the cities of north Italy increased in size, as did also the towns of the Rhône valley and the Midi, and both these districts were soon to be rivalled by the manufacturing and merchant towns of the Low Countries and the Rhineland. In these places, where closely knit groups existed within a relatively small commune, and where the monastic life was less in evidence, there began to spring up for the first time a spontaneous lay piety, neither monastic nor clerical in origin, and indeed often strongly anti-clerical in feeling. It is the first appearance in western Europe of the temper that was later to lead to the congregational groups, orthodox and heretical, that included the Lollards and Beguines, the sects of the Reformation and the nonconformist churches of the Anglo-Saxon world. Already in Milan and Lyons the Humiliati and the Waldenses were beginning to show the characteristics of their class: desire for associations of prayer and good works outside the liturgical framework; love of preaching and Bible-reading in the vernacular; dislike of sacerdotal and sacramental aspects of religion; disputes about the Eucharist; praise of poverty; impatience of hierarchical control. In Italy and France, apart from the ferment of Catharism, these groups were in origin neither rebellious nor heterodox. They wished only to fill a spiritual void in their lives, and could find little help from either the lower or the higher levels of the city clergy. In some places, particularly in Germany and eastern France, houses of regular canons were beginning to meet some of the needs of the townsfolk, and the hope (which the event was to belie) that similar benefits would come to the rural parishes was to lead to widespread foundations of canons throughout the twelfth century. In other regions, particularly in northern towns of Scandinavian settlement, a multitude of small private churches sprang up, owned by a consortium of burghers before they were ultimately absorbed into the parochial system.

Meanwhile, a newly developed ability to plan and execute schemes of government and administration, together with the self-confidence that was a mark of the age, were on their way to change the whole aspect of the medieval Church, or rather to make of a casual series of individual actions the regular working of an articulated machine. The contests of emperors and popes, and their effect upon the status and prestige of the papacy, were outward signs of a far more general movement, to which this contest gave momentum. The papacy, which for four centuries had been content, save at a few moments of crisis, to remain as a distant, venerated source of power and unity, asserting itself only on appeal or in bestowing routine favours, now began to extend its initiative and its actions over the whole Church, and to grasp every link and lever of government. Free from domestic and imperial tutelage, the popes, now freely elected by and from the curial clergy, set themselves to organise their own governmental machine. Throughout the centuries, at least since the age of Constantine, the Roman church had maintained at least a rudimentary archive and secretariat, which must have attained considerable proportions under the able and active popes of the fifth century, and again in the pontificate of Gregory I, of whose methods and agents of administration we are reasonably well informed. In the centuries that passed after Gregory's death the secular government of the papal territories had sometimes passed out of the immediate control of the pope, but regular government of the duchy of Rome had been recovered after the collapse of the exarchate of Ravenna in 751, and in the Carolingian age the papal administration had been supervised by two imperial agents *(missi)*. Later, the effective power passed to the Roman nobility, and in the tenth century it was vested in Alberic as prince. On his death the popes resumed control, which they retained with a greater or less degree of efficiency thenceforward, though the continuity was interrupted by exile, war, the occasional rise to power of a Roman noble, and the success of anti-popes. Throughout, the chancery and treasury dealt with both civil and ecclesiastical affairs. They were staffed by clerics and laymen, and popes were frequently drawn from among the higher officials, of whom the most influential was often the librarian *(bibliothecarius)*, who acted as the pope's secretary. Others were the head of the chancery *(primicerius)*, the treasurer *(vestararius)* and the collector of revenues *(arcarius)*. There were also numbers of officials running the papal household originally under the *vicedominus,* but in the eleventh century under the cardinal archdeacon. This fairly elaborate hierarchy of officials had continued to exist, so far as names went, during the various troubles of the papacy, but in the realm of financial administration it had ceased to work for the benefit of the popes, and had been in the hands of the Roman barons who used it largely for private gain. It was among the achievements of the reformed papacy to take in hand the recovery of the sources of papal revenue and their efficient exploitation. Leo IX was here as elsewhere a pioneer, and he was fortunate in having in Hildebrand an agent of energy and great competence. It seems clear that first as arch-deacon and later as pope, Gregory VII was the architect of a reformed financial establishment and was responsible for beginning the process of recovery of revenue. The primary source of income was the patrimony and the territories subsequently added by emperors and kings to the papal possessions. In addition, there were the traditional contributions made by certain churches, of which the English ' Peter's Pence ' was an important example, and the payment made by various vassals of the Roman church. To these was added, in growing number but without great financial importance, the tax levied upon exempt monasteries. Besides these, there were all the great but ' invisible ' incomes of individual members of the curia derived from fees, charges for bulls and privileges, and the still greater sums given as douceurs to various influential members. From this date down to the final extinction of the papal states in the nineteenth century, popes were burdened and distracted by a constant struggle to realise their assets, and to secure from their territories, without excessive loss by inefficiency and peculation, a reasonable proportion of the income which would, if secured, go far to make the papal administration viable. In the decades after the death of Gregory VII, economic reform continued, and a new age began with the appointment by Urban II of a monk of Cluny as head of the papal finances; he was to apply to the papal treasury the methods elaborated by the great abbey in realising her income from scattered estates.

The reforming papacy, and in particular Gregory VII, had made use of every traditional instrument that came to hand in the work of extending its control and of bringing to bear upon the whole Church the influence of reforming measures. Pre-eminent among these measures were, in the realm of principles, the rejuvenated canon law, and on the level of practice, the machinery of supervision, visitation and judicial decision.

As we have seen, Gregory VII and his lieutenants used the ancient canon law as an incontrovertible authority both in framing and in executing their programme. In the eleventh century law, like theology, was still treated in a patristic, literary fashion. An energetic bishop like Burchard of Worms, or a propagandist like Anselm of Lucca, collected and compiled from the remains of the past as best he could, and from the days of the pseudo-Isidore to those of Ivo of Chartres there was little formal or methodical advance. Thenceforward canon law rapidly became a science, a discipline, a career, and a factor of paramount importance in the life of the Church.

Unlike Roman or civil law, which enjoyed a similar phase of rejuvenation and formalisation at the very same moment, canon law had no classical texts corresponding to the Justinian corpus. It was, and has always remained, a heap rather than a building. Precepts of the Old and New Testaments, decrees of popes and of general and provincial councils, elements borrowed from the legislation of Justinian, passages extracted in good faith from the successful forgeries of earlier ages, and in particular from the forged decretals, all were collected together in an enormous pile. In this collection there were many contradictory regulations and many of doubtful authenticity. Meanwhile civil law, with a clear text and the glosses of Irnerius and others, was rapidly becoming a mental and professional discipline, with its centre at the nascent university of Bologna. A similar discipline and technique were needed by the canonists, and we have noted the attempts of eminent bishops to create them. What greater men had failed to accomplish was achieved by the Camaldolese monk Gratian, c. 1140, working probably in the monastery of San Felice at Bologna. His work, *A harmony of discordant laws (Concordia discordantium canonum)* has been described as ' one of those great textbooks which, appearing just at the right time and in the right place, take the world by storm ' [2]. True within limits, this judgment does less than justice to Gratian. It is not only that he had in a high degree the juristic qualities that enabled him to select the vital and essential passages and topics; not only that his collection was vaster and more complete than any that had preceded him. Added to this, Gratian was the first to choose a logical arrangement and to cover jurisprudence; moreover his was not merely a legal collection, but a scholastic one also. It was a collection made not only for memorising or for reference, but for discussion and decision. In all this Gratian's work, the *Decretum* as it came to be called, resembled its younger sister the *Book of the Sentences* of Peter Lombard. In one way, indeed, it became in the long run even more celebrated, for the *Decretum*, a purely private venture, became, as the *Sentences* never became, synonymous with canon law itself, and continued, with the inevitable subsequent additions, to be current far longer than the Lombard's work—current, indeed, till within living memory (1918). Gratian influenced the history of canon law in two ways. He provided not only a textbook but a text, which could be used as a basis

2. H. Rashdall, *The Universities of Medieval Europe*, I, 127.

for commentary and discussion by a succession of masters, known as the Decretists, for almost a century. Secondly, he gave the stamp of currency, once and for all, to a number of spurious pieces. Once accepted and acted upon by decretists, a spurious text was in fact legitimised.

Yet on canon law the last word could be said by no one, not even by Gratian. Unlike the texts of Justinian, which were regarded as a sacred legacy from the past, canon law could be augmented and even altered, either by the addition of pertinent texts unknown to Gratian or dismissed by him, or by the decrees of reigning popes. In the centuries between the two great Gregorys popes had seldom pronounced on matters of morality and discipline, but in consequence of the recent wide range of papal initiative such pronouncements were to become more and more common. Decretal letters, as they were called, addressed to individuals as distinct from the more public despatch of the more solemn bulls, were doubtless preserved in duplicate in the papal archive, but there was no promulgation or publication. Yet a decretal decision, when known, was authoritative in any court and did not admit of appeal. The practice therefore grew up among enlightened bishops of collecting and indexing decretals addressed to themselves or their neighbours. These private collections, several of which were made in northern France and especially in England, became in time the nuclei of larger ones, till ultimately the work of collection and comment rose to academic level and was accomplished by celebrated masters of Bologna such as Bernard of Pavia (1191). Finally, they were officially edited and issued by the curia as decrees known in academic circles as *extra Decretum vagantes*. The century from 1130 to 1230 has been characterised as a period – and it is perhaps the only historical period – in which the study of law, civil, canon and regional, was the principal intellectual occupation of a majority of those engaged in teaching and research. The rediscovery of the history of canon law, with the careers and doctrines of its principal exponents, has been one of the major achievements of the past century of medieval studies.

The papacy had from time out of mind maintained the right of all catholic Christians to appeal to the apostolic see, with the consequent acknowledgement of the right of the pope to judge all causes with a final verdict, but these rights were rarely exercised in the early middle ages save by pontiffs of exceptional strength of purpose, such as Nicholas I, and in cases of unusual or controversial importance. From the age of Gregory VII onwards, however, appeals became more and more common and were encouraged by the popes, who also made good their claim to summon up to Rome any case which had been, or seemed likely to be, mishandled in a lower court. As the volume of appeals grew, and disputes of every kind on property rights and elections were carried to Rome, cases often bore upon details of time and place and person entirely outside the ken of the curia. To deal with these another old practice was revived and became common. This was the appointment of local judges-delegate either to collect evidence or to conduct the whole case and pronounce a judgment from which no appeal was allowed. Between 1130 and 1230 a great number of commissions of this sort were issued to bishops, abbots and other dignitaries, some of whom must have devoted much of their time and energy to this kind of work. Even so, the *causes célèbres* of the period, such as that of the rights of the monastic chapter of Canterbury *vis-à-vis* its archbishop, came sooner or later into the curia. Arrived in Rome, the cases not susceptible of a routine decision came before the pope either at an informal audience, or assisted by his unofficial small council or by the cardinals in consistory. The popes before and including Innocent III treated such an occasion as a plain, free-spoken meeting, at which the advocates pleaded and the pope at length gave a personal judgment, often explicitly based on canonical principles. Skill in canon law naturally assisted a curial career, and from the middle of the twelfth century many of the cardinals, as well as the advocates, were taken from among the doctors of Bologna. With the elevation to the papal throne of Roland Bandinelli as Alexander III the great era of papal legalism began, in which canon law became both an instrument of high policy and a basis for the construction of theories of government.

Concurrently with the extension of its judicial activity the papacy was engaged in controlling episcopal elections. As we have seen, simoniacal elections and royal appointments to episcopal sees were among the principal objects of attack by the reformers, and the ideal consistently held up was the ancient procedure of election by the clergy of the church assisted by neighbouring dignitaries. The part of the people, originally decisive, was tacitly obscured. This ideal was realised only very intermittently. The leading monarchs in the twelfth century succeeded after the compromise of Worms and similar arrangements in transferring the election to their presence where, even if freedom was proclaimed, the danger of opposing the royal will or inclination was great enough to stifle independence. Nevertheless, the popes by insisting on at least the canonical form in elections made it possible for disputed elections to be carried to Rome on appeal, with the corollary of direct papal appointment under certain conditions, and by the beginning of the thirteenth century the ideal of a free local election was retreating before the opposing encroachments of pope and king.

In order to make its power effective at a distance the reformed papacy made frequent use of legates, temporary or quasi-permanent. This practice dated from the second century of the Christian empire, but it had fallen into desuetude between the sixth and the eleventh centuries. It was revived by

Leo IX and thenceforward popes, and particularly Gregory VII, made frequent and effective use of it. Active reforming agents such as Peter Damian and Humbert, cardinals, abbots and even lesser clerics were constantly employed on both routine and controversial business. Often, like Carolingian *missi*, they travelled in pairs, visiting monarchs and holding synods. Characteristic of Gregory VII was his employment of a legate, a trusted supporter, who was a resident bishop of an important see. Subsequent popes tended to use legates only for a particular purpose, *legati a latere*, though these also on occasion might remain for a year or more in the region to which their commission was directed. Gradually the legacy *a latere* (i.e., ' from the side of the pope ', a direct and particular representative) was standardised and usually entrusted to a single prelate, though his task might vary from a particular diplomatic exchange (and this was frequently executed by two legates) to the general oversight or reform of a region or country, where the legate would hold synods, visit monasteries, depose or appoint abbots and settle episcopal elections. Occasionally, with a wider sweep, he might order the establishment of the church and the erection of sees over a whole region, as did Cardinal Brakespeare in Scandinavia. A legate, acting within his commission, might exercise all the administrative and judicial functions of the pope, often with no possibility of appeal *(remota appellatione)*. Legacies of this kind throughout the twelfth and thirteenth centuries were a normal means of bringing local law and discipline into line with the latest papal decrees.

The pope, like other bishops of large cities, had always been surrounded and advised by a body of clergy. The principal members of these groups, priests and deacons, had come to bear the qualification of *cardinalis*. This word had as its chief applied meaning that of ' principal ' or ' essential ', but it has been shown that its original sense in the clerical context was from a rare use of the word in architecture or joinery to mean ' firmly inserted ', whence it came to be applied to clerics who formed part of (or were ' incardinated ' in) the regular staff of a particular church. In Rome, in the time of Gregory I, the name was given to the priests of the oldest churches or ' titles ' and to the deacons serving the various Roman districts. To them were later added the bishops of the suburbican churches, whose function for several centuries was to deputise for the pope at the various ' stational ' processions and liturgies. In early times the popes had no official or recognised inner circle of advisers. Important matters were debated at a Roman synod or council composed of the bishops in papal territory and others happening to be in the city. These synods were held at irregular intervals and ceased altogether when the papacy was in eclipse. The reforming popes made frequent use of them, with a wider intake of bishops, and they became a sounding-board for papal declarations of policy. Later, in the twelfth century, they were used by popes, now able to summon gatherings from the whole of Europe, to register important diplomatic agreements and to issue reforming decrees. The series was crowned by the great council (Lateran IV) of 1215, after which popes tended to govern the Church directly by means of the curia.

During the same period the popes had used a small council of close advisers, the meetings of which became known as a consistory, and the name was applied to the advisory body itself in the pontificate of Alexander III. By the end of the pontificate of Innocent III this gathering had come to consist principally of prelates bearing the title of cardinal; the original use of the word cardinal had been forgotten, and it was now understood in its other signification of ' chief ' or ' most important '. This group had advanced gradually to a position of influence, principally by reason of their place in papal elections. In early times the bishops of Rome had been appointed solely by the Roman clergy and people, and from among their number. Among the clergy the cardinals of every degree formed an important, but not necessarily a controlling group, containing as it did the archpriest and the archdeacon of the Roman church, and usually also the librarian or secretary of the late pope. At least as early as the tenth century it became customary for the pope to be chosen from the cardinal priests or the Roman deacons – the translation of a bishop for the purpose being regarded as irregular if not invalid – and of the three classes the deacons, being normally *en disponibilité*, were often chosen for administrative posts or diplomatic missions. The cardinals came fully into prominence when the cardinal bishops were given the dominant voice in papal elections by the decree of 1059, in which the assent of the Roman people was reduced to a confirmatory acclamation and the rôle of the emperor to a shadowy assent which was later abolished entirely. Hitherto the cardinals, with very rare exceptions, had all been Romans or sub-urbican clergy, but the reforming popes appointed distinguished abbots and monks, such as Humbert of Moyenmoutier, Peter Damian and Abbot Desiderius of Monte Cassino, to suburbican titles, and used them as legates and emissaries of reform. Henceforward the cardinals appear as a group influencing and executing papal policies, and as such to be canvassed by interested parties. As residence in the curia and occupation with papal business was the purpose of the office, there was as yet no move towards recruiting the college from the resident episcopate outside the Roman region. This phase of the history of the cardinalate reached its climax in the period between Alexander III and Innocent III, when the body of cardinals surrounding the pope shared with him the overall government of the Church in weekly or bi-weekly consistories.

In the twelfth century the reorganisation of the external fabric of the

Church, which had begun from and with the papacy, began to spread to the whole body. Hitherto both diocesan and parish boundaries had often been vague; the former through lack of administrative activity and through the fragmentation caused by proprietary churches and immune or exempt jurisdictions, the latter from lack of episcopal supervision and through private encroachment or enterprise. Gradually the boundaries of dioceses were firmly drawn and the division of the whole territory into parishes was completed, though wide areas of forest, marsh, moor and mountain still remained extra-parochial. The towns lagged behind the country; sometimes the original parish had become unworkably large, sometimes the whole urban area was studded with small churches.

Along with organisation went administration. Hitherto the cathedrals had been staffed in various ways. In some places ' canons ' of the Carolingian type had lost all their organisation, and outside the ambit of ninth-century reform there would often be merely a group of married priests living in houses round the cathedral. In the eleventh century there had been a widespread endeavour to restore a communal, celibate life, and this had been followed by the establishment of ' regular ' canons who later became Augustinians. At the end of the century energetic bishops began to introduce an administrative chapter with the so-called ' quadrilateral ' of officials; dean, chancellor, treasurer and precentor, with fixed prebends. In the diocese archdeacons and rural deans were gradually introduced. Meanwhile, as the bishops became more concerned with establishing their rights, several points of friction developed. First, there were clashes between the bishops themselves. In the past more than one kind of hierarchical grouping had been practised. In the eastern church a small number of patriarchs had exercised a loose control over the bishops of a large region, with traditional powers of supervising elections and holding synods. In the West a few sees such as Lyons and Toledo had acquired something of the status of a primacy, with real if ill-defined jurisdiction. Later there was a grouping of sees under a metropolitan such as Rheims or Canterbury or Salzburg. Canterbury, indeed, from its foundation by Gregory I, bore the unfamiliar title of archbishopric, and from England this title was carried by Boniface to Germany, whence it spread in time to the rest of Europe owing to its adoption by the Roman curia. In the period immediately after Charlemagne there was an attempt by some metropolitans, of whom Hincmar of Rheims was an outstanding example, to exalt the office of metropolitan to a position of importance which would have made its holder in practice the supreme ruler of a region. As late as the end of the eleventh century Lanfranc of Canterbury aimed at making his church the effective metropolitan of the British Isles. In Scotland and Ireland his success was personal and temporary only, but in Wales it was permanent, where the framework remained till the disestablishment of the Church of Wales in 1922, and he succeeded in establishing his claim as archbishop to receive from all the bishops of his province and of Wales the profession of canonical obedience. It was while pursuing this policy that he claimed primatial rights over York, thus initiating a vexatious series of disputes that echoed down the centuries. Similar litigation arose elsewhere, as for example at Hamburg. In general, archbishops everywhere in the course of the twelfth century established a judicial and supervisory position over their province, with the right of convoking and presiding over synods.

Jurisdiction over monasteries provided another source of friction. From the time of Gregory I the papal practice of ' exempting ' an abbey from episcopal control and interference had made its appearance, as a corollary to the use made by the popes of monks as missionaries or as bastions of orthodoxy or agents of reform. Sometimes this exemption took the form of creating an enclave in a diocese, within which the abbot enjoyed juris-dictional powers and could invite any bishop to perform for him the functions for which episcopal orders were needed. More rarely, a small district was included in this exemption, as at Monte Cassino in Italy. Concurrently, especially in northern countries, kings bestowed on monas-teries an ' immunity ' from all impositions and interferences which included those from a bishop. There were solid reasons for this action, for bishops in many countries endeavoured, sometimes with success, to obtain posses-sion of a monastery for use as their headquarters and cathedral. Some of these monasteries, in an epoch of uncertain rights, took out a counter-insurance by commending themselves to the church of St Peter and becoming censual abbeys. Cluny had done this on its foundation; other houses, such as the royal *Eigenkloster* of Battle in England, slipped across from royal immunity to papal exemption. In the twelfth century there were a number of acrid disputes between monasteries and the local bishops who wished to engross them. As a result, there was a gradual regularisation of status, by which monasteries, immune either by papal or royal grant, came to apply for, and to receive, canonical exemption. Here, as in many other respects, the long pontificate of Alexander III saw the crystallisation of the canonical formula and the definition of status. Though in general the monks were encouraged by the papacy to exploit any title, however dubious, they might have for exemption, these efforts naturally encoun-tered heavy opposition, and litigation continued in many instances well into the thirteenth century or even longer.

When Rome was thus encouraging recourse to her protection, there was a natural disposition to make use of her interested benevolence, and during the twelfth century a stream of requests from religious houses, chapters and private individuals flowed to Rome, soliciting a confirmation of possessions, privileges and constitutions. The papal chancery, like the papal consistory, enjoyed a vast increase of custom, with the resultant multiplication of functionaries and complication of methods of writing and witnessing, and the inevitable multiplication of forged charters. The golden age of medieval forgery was perhaps the century between 1070 and 1170, when law was in a state of precipitation and formulas were still fluid, and all parties were fighting desperately for what they considered their rights.

The course of events in the twelfth century, taken as a whole, may be said to justify the title ' Victory of the Papacy ' by which the period is sometimes characterised. If Gregory VII died in exile, while an imperial anti-pope lorded it in Rome, Innocent III came nearer than any pope to be the effective general manager of both church and state in Europe, launching a crusade, appointing an emperor-elect, issuing commands for the governance of England, and dictating decrees for ratification by the Lateran council. Yet to regard the century as merely an extension of its predecessor would be misleading. In the realm of politics, the claim of the papacy to be, not only one of the two powers of the world, but the supreme sovereign of all, had never been willingly conceded by lay rulers, though under Innocent III it came near to being admitted in practice. In the realm of ecclesiastical government the triumph had been almost complete. The church that emerged from the fourth Lateran council was a comprehensive, orderly, rationalised machine, driven by the papacy. But in the realm of spiritual achievement the advance was neither continuous nor wholly successful. The Gregorian reform was part of a wider spirit of renewal which embraced the foundation and direction of new orders, together with bishops and kings not wholly imbued with Gregorian ideas, and a multitude of devout landowners and others. It was a century of great men and of saints: perhaps no century between the fourth and the sixteenth could be reckoned its equal in this respect, but the movement of reform had ceased by the middle of the century. The spiritual reform from the centre had indeed ended long before that. The twelfth century was not one of great popes; perhaps Alexander III alone deserves that title, and if so, it is by reason of his legal and administrative genius rather than of his sanctity or statesmanship. Nor did any pope impress his contemporaries by reason of holiness of life save in a measure Eugenius III. Ecclesiastical diplomacy took the place of apostolic zeal, and papal policy rather than spiritual purity was in the forefront of curial activity. The Gregorians had found a means to attain their end; the end now was no longer seen clearly; it was becoming obscured by the means.

THEOLOGY   1050-1216

I N the eleventh century several important theological issues had been raised and had called forth a considerable body of writing. The eucharistic controversy, the question of reordination of those ordained by heretics or schismatics, the discussions of Anselm–all these had inspired theological writings of varied importance, culminating in the monographs of Anselm which must always take rank among the supreme achievements of medieval genius. Yet despite this activity, theological study at the cathedral schools had changed little during the eleventh century, still consisting chiefly of a study of the Bible and of a small number of patristic and later writings. Dialectic, in spite of Berengarius and Anselm, had as yet scarcely influenced the official masters of the schools, and this no doubt made it easy for Abelard, in his own eyes and those of his enthusiastic students, to score victories over the conservative teachers when he passed over from dialectic to theology. Nevertheless, by 1100 a new era was beginning. From lecturing on the Bible with its Gloss, masters were compiling *Sentences*. These, in the technical sense of the word then current, were *flores* or anthologies culled from the Scriptures and Fathers to illustrate the various doctrines, and under the hand of Ansellus (or Anselmus) of Laon and contemporary masters they were developing into an ordered presentation of texts. Gradually these *Sentences* came to contain a number of opinions or judgments on the theological issues, the word *sententia* gradually shifting its meaning from ' selection ' to ' opinion ', ' pronounce- ment '. Collections of *Sentences* multiplied, and attempts were made to consolidate or harmonise their conclusions; such works were called *sum- mae sententiarium*. Abelard turned theologian was asked repeatedly by his students to present a picture of the whole field of theology, to explain its difficult parts and to provide rational arguments for the doctrines. This he did in his *Introduction to Theology*, thereby giving to the discipline a name *(theologia)* novel in this sense, and an exhaustive treatment equally novel. Meanwhile two other thinkers of distinction were at work. At the newly-founded abbey of St Victor at Paris Hugh was accomplishing in a discursive way and in the manner of St Augustine a summary of the whole economy of creation, redemption and sanctification, while Gilbert de la Porrée, like Abelard a dialectician, but a Platonist and a patristic scholar to boot, was translating Catholic doctrine into his own vocabulary and idiom, an attempt that won for him the hostility of St Bernard. As many students passed, like John of Salisbury, through many schools, the streams of Abelardian criticism and Victorine ' contemplation ' were beginning to merge in the later *Summae Sententiarum*.

Gratian's achievement in canon law and its immediate success may well have been the final impulse that drove the stream of theological teaching into a parallel channel. Peter the Lombard, a compatriot of Gratian and a former pupil of Abelard, now a master at Paris, produced (*c.* 1150) what came to be known as the *Four Books of the Sentences*, in which the whole of the Christian faith and economy, from the Creation to the Last Judgment, was set out with the relevant scriptural texts, and the conciliar, patristic and magisterial decisions and opinions, on which the Lombard made his own observations and pronounced judgment. Both Gratian and the Lombard took their framework with its confrontation of contradictory texts, and their method of resolving disputed questions, straight from the *Sic et non* of Abelard who in his turn had perfected a technique already introduced by the lawyers of Ivo's day. The Lombard's work followed Gratian's with an interval of less than ten years and each revolutionised the teaching tradition of his own discipline. Gratian's *Decretum*, as it was called, and the Lombard's *Sentences*, became the sole and universal text- books for their subjects. Each invited comment, and within a few years each had become the peg on which the great masters of Bologna and Paris hung their criticisms, explanations and additions. For the next five cen- turies indeed a regular duty of the young bachelor in theology was to read the *Sentences*, and an infinite number of commentaries was produced. Bonaventure, Thomas Aquinas, Duns Scotus and William of Ockham are only the most celebrated of those whose reputations were made by a commentary on the *Sentences*. The Lombard was only displaced when Aquinas, Bonaventure, and Scotus took his place in the schools of the Counter-Reformation, and he was being studied by Anglican theological students at Oxford when Newton was writing his *Principia* at Cambridge.

The historians of theology and canon law have not always appreciated the very considerable influence of the canonists in the development of doctrinal expansion. The sacraments, for example, and in particular the discipline of penance and Holy Orders, had been constantly topics for legislation and papal decision, and the tradition thus established had been expressed or modified by canonists in their ordinary task of presenting and explaining the canon law. Similarly the primacy and prerogatives of the Roman see had been debated in the dialectic of rival schools and the principal claims of the papacy, as expressed in the *Dictatus papae*, itself possibly not so much a programme as an index of significant canonical topics, had been formulated by canonists long before theologians had conceived of a treatise ' on the Church '. In this field indeed, for better or for worse, it was the canonists who made the running, if the phrase be allowed, over the whole period from Gregory VII to Martin V. On the other hand, the canonists who led the theologians in the development of critical methods in the early twelfth century were themselves borrowers thenceforward from the *Sic et non* of Abelard and its further exploitation by theologians.

We have already glanced at the controversy concerning the reordination of bishops and priests previously ordained by bishops in heresy or schism. Uncertainty in practice continued till the early years of the twelfth century, and division among theologians later still, until the distinction had been made clear between jurisdiction and the sacramental character. The first purely theological controversy of the new age was eucharistic, and is connected with the name of Berengarius (d. 1088), archdeacon of Tours and a pupil of Fulbert of Chartres, whose teaching on the sacrament was in the Augustinian tradition and perhaps based upon that of Ratramnus. He challenged Lanfranc, then teaching at Bec and known as a supporter of the views of Paschasius, to defend his opinions, but before he did so Berengarius had been excommunicated by a Roman synod in 1050 and after imprisonment in Italy solemnly professed the current orthodox doctrine of the real presence, set out in somewhat materialistic language at Tours in 1054, and again at Rome in 1059. He continued, however, to propound his old opinions, which provoked Lanfranc's *De corpore et sanguine Domini* which asserted as orthodox and defined in precise terms the change of substance from bread and wine to the ' essence ' of the Lord's body, while the appearance *(species)* remained unchanged. Berengarius answered in his *De Coena Domini* that the change which occurred was purely spiritual and refused to admit that the material bread and wine were replaced by the body and blood of Christ. This took him once more to Rome, where he made anew a profession of orthodoxy in 1079, though he probably never admitted the full implication of the current definition of the doctrine. Despite his chequered career, Berengarius was, and to the end of his life remained, a prosperous and respected teacher of the new dialectic. This indeed, rather than theology, was his true *métier*, and modern critics have suggested that his difficulties were in essence grammatical rather than theological, and that he was forced by his doctrine of the intimate connection between a word and the thing of which it was an expression to deny the possibility that the bread in the priest's hands *(hoc)* could be at the same moment *(est)* the body of Christ *(corpus meum)*. However this may be, Lanfranc maintained what was certainly the common opinion in the western church, that the bread was *changed into* the body of Christ, and with the new dialectic he expressed this in set terms for the first time. His was accepted as the orthodox explanation, and the term transubstantiation, though not employed by him (it was probably a coinage of Peter Damian) came into common use and was ultimately canonised by the fourth Lateran council. It was indeed a clear statement in philosophical language of what the ordinary reflecting Christian believed. Its disadvantage, in addition to that of expressing a mystery in terms of Aristotelian metaphysics, was that it gave a handle to a crude and materialistic conception of the host as merely veiling a physical body and to a devotion expressed in the phrase ' seeing God ' at the elevation of the host in the Mass. It helped also, by emphasising the presence of the incarnate Son, Jesus, son also of Mary, upon the altar, to strengthen the tendency to regard the Mass primarily as an act of the priest for and on behalf of the laity, and thus to obscure other aspects of the Eucharist as the principal means of joining the faithful in and into Christ's mystical body. It certainly encouraged devotion to the reserved Sacrament as providing God's presence in a church and to processions and blessings in which the host was revered as Christ. Similarly, the conception of the Eucharist as a sacrifice offered *by* a priest *for* individuals gradually superseded a widely held patristic conception of it as the offering of the mystical body of sanctified humanity to the Father as God by Christ as the head of the Church, but it may be thought that the later development was in fact theologically the more unambiguous. In any case, the private Mass, the multiplicity of Masses, and the devotion to the Mass as a paramount means of liberating souls from the punishment incurred by sin, were direct consequences of the growth of the belief expressed in the term ' transubstantiation '. How far this shift in attitude and practice was due to characteristics of western thought, and how far to the change from urban communities to illiterate peasant and serf congregations must remain a matter of opinion.

Anselm in the realm of speculative theology is chiefly remembered for the cause he assigned to the incarnation, the answer to the question he had asked: 'Cur Deus homo?' The Latin Fathers and in particular St Augustine and St Leo had stressed the mediatory nature of the redemption. Man had sinned and was now under the dominion of sin; no mere man could give due satisfaction to God. Nor could God *qua* God; but a divine Person who had assumed a human nature could do so. Concurrently with this another stream of tradition regarded man as the slave of the devil, unredeemable save by adequate ransom. This conception, which Augustine also accepted, gained ground and one of these two explanations was given by all writers of the early medieval age. Anselm's presentation was a fuller version of the familiar argument of St Leo the Great, that only a sinless man who was also God could satisfy for man's sin, which had in it an infinite quality as the offence against an infinite Being. Anselm thus firmly rejected the ransom theory and the rights of the devil.

Abelard reacted against the legal or forensical implications of both the 'ransom' and 'satisfaction' explanations. His views were not constant, but for a considerable time, at least, he regarded the Passion of Christ as the consummation of the 'exemplary' purpose of the incarnation, which was to instruct and stimulate mankind in the perfect love of God. This view, which as an exclusive explanation was condemned by implication at Sens in 1140, had the blessing of the Lombard, though he was equally kind to the 'ransom' opinion.

Another aberration of Abelard touched the central point of Christology. Concerned to safeguard the transcendence of the Divinity, Abelard taught that the human nature was as 'nothing' *(nihil)* to the Divine Person, thereby reviving in a different form the heresy of Adoptionism or, as it was called in its new form, nihilism. This opinion was taken up by Roland Bandinelli (later Alexander III), by Peter Lombard and, with a difference, by Gilbert de la Porrée, and spread widely in France and later in Germany. Alexander III as pope twice forbade vain discussions of this and similar topics; finally in 1177 he formally condemned the Abelardian doctrine.

The revived dialectic found in the doctrine of the Trinity, with its attribution of nature and person and its apparent relevanc to the problem of universal terms, an irresistible attraction and pitfall. Roscelin, who allowed only a verbal reality to universal terms, applied this to the divinity and came, so far as words went, to proclaim the existence of three distinct divine beings. Abelard, attacking Roscelin, went to the other extreme of regarding the Names as little more than attributes or 'appropriations' – Power, Wisdom and Love – of a single God. Gilbert de la Porrée likewise,

under the influence of his own logical definitions and his realistic metaphysics, regarded the deity, the divine essence, as consisting of the form
common to all Three Persons but not itself God, thus calling forth
St Bernard's celebrated declaration of the absolute simplicity of God.
The Lombard was impeccably orthodox, but his teaching provoked an
attack from Joachim of Flora, who saw in it a divine quaternity of Father,
Son, Spirit and divinity. This opinion was condemned by the Fathers of
the Fourth Lateran council, who accepted a resounding declaration of trust
in Peter, and it was left to the scholastics and in particular Aquinas to
reform the doctrine in terms of subsistent relationships (i.e., the Persons)
in one undivided Godhead.

Abelard reacted also against the current Augustinian conception of
original sin as carrying a physical weakness, almost a moral disease of
mind and will, and regarded it simply as a penalty, consisting of the loss
of a title to eternal beatitude, while grace in consequence became an
assistance rather than a physical enablement for meritorious action. In this
also he was opposed by St Bernard who reiterated the traditional view in
his treatise on grace, but no real progress in elucidating the nature of the
assistance or enablement was made before Aquinas.

It was in the realm of sacramental theology that the twelfth century saw
undoubted progress. Hitherto in the West, as in the East to the present day,
baptism and the Eucharist had stood pre-eminent as rites conveying particular gifts of grace. The anointings and laying on of hands at confirmation,
holy orders and the rite of the visitation of the sick were also generally
regarded as ' sacraments ' of divine institution, but the double ambiguity
of the word sacrament, both verbal (either ' mystery ' or ' bestowal of
sanctification ') and in its loose application to any established practice
of devotion, long hindered an attempt at rigid classification. This was
achieved at length by the discussions of Hugh of St Victor and the
Lombard, as was also the distinction between the words by which the grace
is bestowed and the material which the minister uses. The exclusive number
seven, however, was not defined as a matter of faith until the appearance
of the creed or confession approved for the Greeks in 1439. The two
sacraments not mentioned above, penance and matrimony, were long in
entering the final list partly because of their intractability in complying
with definitions and analysis, but chiefly because of the long development
of penance and the existence of matrimony in other legal systems and social
customs before and since the foundation of the Church. As we have seen,
the practice and virtual obligation of auricular confession were well established in the West before 1100, but the theology was still fluid. Was confession to a priest merely a dispensation from the régime of public penance
and readmission to communion by the bishop? Were the powers of the

priest merely delegated or did the bishop simply give permission for the priest to use powers bestowed on him at ordination? Did the priest absolve from sin, or merely declare the sin to have been remitted, or simply pray for its remission? What disposition was needed in the penitent? If he were fully contrite what more could absolution give? If not, how could it give anything? Can forgiveness be obtained without confession, and, if not, what obligation of confession exists? Some of these questions were settled by practice and law before the theologians had answered them satisfactorily, but the Lombard was able to set out formally the three constituent elements of contrition, confession and satisfaction. The nature of the contrition required and the direct effect of absolution were topics to be discussed for many centuries to come. In practice the decree *Omnis utriusque sexus*, making an annual confession to the parish priest the condition of full membership of the Church, was the final and universal establishment of a primary duty for those with the care of souls. One of its results was to multiply manuals intended to help the physician of souls; another was to make the new orders of friars coadjutors and rivals of the secular clergy in their most intimate spiritual relationships with their flock.

Matrimony, though more simple in its theology and performance, was to remain the most complicated in administration. Custom and scriptural authority, old and new, had erected a forest of obstacles based on relationship, natural and spiritual, and on status, social custom and personal engagement, while the Church had never, in the first millenium of her existence, imposed an absolute obligation of sacerdotal presence for lawfulness. As the medieval centuries passed, the impediments of relationship were rationalised and the obligation of receiving the blessing of the Church strengthened.

Great as were these developments, perhaps a still more influential change was the gradual clarification of the distinction between natural and supernatural, reason and revelation, nature and grace. Clear as was the evangelical and early patristic teaching of the existence of two separate realms, the world and the kingdom of heaven, several historical circumstances, over and above the intrinsically mysterious nature of the topic, delayed any attempt at a philosophical or theological analysis. One was that in each individual Christian soul the two lives, the two principles of action, and the two ends were in fact and in experience inextricably mingled. A second was that any analysis needed philosophical terms for its expression, but these were for long unavailable, since all patristic writers with a background of philosophic thought had Platonic and Neoplatonist affinities. To Plotinus all being was spiritual and in a sense divine. A transcendental Creator bestowing a new life upon some, but not all, of his creatures could have no place within this system. It is true that the

latest and greatest of the Fathers, Augustine, at issue with Pelagius, separated nature and grace with a metallic force of definition, but it is equally
true that the Pelagian polemics are almost a watertight bulkhead in the
vast works of Augustine, and that in his speculative and spiritual medita-
tions on the Christian life, and even in the *City of God*, his deeply Platonic
associations prevent him from defining or even from considering the limits
of human intelligence and volition. The problem indeed lay quiescent and
undefined for more than six hundred years, but when logic and dialectic
were reborn in the eleventh century it became urgent. How far could reason
go in understanding or proving the doctrines of the faith? How far, in
actual fact, had human reason, in the person of a Plato or a Cicero, gone
in anticipating truths of the faith and of morality? We have seen something
of the strife between the masters. They might be sceptics, rationalists, or
spiritual men, but without the aid of the lost Aristotelian system they were
fighting in the dark. An Anselm or a Hugh could claim to prove or at least
to explain a doctrine, an Abelard or a Gilbert could hope to confine a
dogma within the framework of a verbal or logical definition. It was only
with the recovery of Aristotle's metaphysics and psychology that human
nature with all its powers and potentialities could be seen in a ' pure '
state, and defined as such, with no thought of the human race as it is,
wounded by original and actual sin, and elevated by revelation and grace.
That definition with all its consequences was set out for the first time in
all its fulness by Aquinas.

   Finally considerable development took place in the definition of the
privileges of Mary. Her physical virginity before, during and after the birth
of her son, the justice of her title as Mother of God, a fulness of grace
implying absolute sinlessness throughout life, were elements of the heritage
of faith received from the patristic age. Her bodily assumption into
' heaven ', though not to be defined for centuries, was commonly held in
the West, largely through eastern tradition, and was never seriously questioned. The matter of her sinless conception, the question, that is, of the
preservation of her soul from the first moment of its existence from the
stain of original sin, had not been debated before the eleventh century.
It had been implicitly taught in the eastern church as a consequence of
Mary's absolute fulness of grace and position as a second Eve. Meanwhile the feast of the Conception of Mary had become common in the
eastern church and its outposts in south Italy. This, instituted on the analogy of the miraculous conception and sanctification of John the Baptist,
celebrated a similar but legendary account of the conception of Mary – that
is, the feast celebrated the reputedly miraculous conception by her mother
and the simultaneous sanctification of Mary's soul; it did not rest upon or
itself express a precise doctrinal basis. This feast was introduced into some

English monasteries before the Norman Conquest, probably from Greek sources in Italy. Suppressed along with other English devotional peculiarities at the Conquest, it was reintroduced by Anselm, the nephew and namesake of archbishop Anselm, who had been abbot of St Sabas in Rome before coming in 1121 to be abbot of Bury St Edmunds. Before that time emphasis had been laid on Mary's absolute purity by Anselm, and his confidant and biographer, the monk of Canterbury Eadmer, c. 1125 wrote a treatise in defence of the re-introduced feast; in this he provided the first theological statement to appear in the West of the Immaculate Conception, based upon Greek materials, and what is called the argument of suitability. Though frequently quoted in the sequel, it had no wide effect at the time, for attention was diverted by the well-known attack of St Bernard upon the liturgical celebration instituted by the canons of Lyons. This began a theological controversy that lasted for more than two centuries. St Bernard, whose intense devotion to the Mother of God was well known, took exception to the (to him) novel doctrine partly as infringing the universal law of original sin in the children of Adam, but more through the ruling Augustinian opinion that original sin was transmitted by an act induced by concupiscence, an act therefore in a sense sinful and certainly not fit to be the object of a cult. Thenceforward the issue was controversial. There were two problems to solve. All human beings need the redemptive merit of Christ. But if Mary had no guilt, not even of original sin, how could she need or receive redemption? Further, if, as it came to be generally agreed, the active physical conception on the part of the mother did not enter into consideration, at which point did the act of God take place? If the soul were sanctified before infusion into the material from which the body grew, then only the soul of Mary not her humanity would be immaculate. If on the other hand sanctification took place after the soul's creation, then the conception would not be immaculate. In the thirteenth century Aquinas cleared the issue by his teaching that original sin consisted in the absence of grace and not in a quasi-physical transmission of a sinful quality, but it was left to Scotus to solve the difficulty caused by the need of redemption, by teaching that Mary was preserved from original sin by the foreseen merits of her Son. During the later middle ages Dominicans and Franciscans were bitterly divided on the issue and the Franciscan Sixtus IV in two constitutions of 1477 and 1483 found it necessary to declare the lawfulness of the feast and of the teaching behind it.

The century that followed the death of St Bernard and the appearance of the Lombard's great work, and closed with the almost simultaneous deaths of St Thomas and St Bonaventure, embracing in that short space the rise of the universities, the reception of Aristotle, and the golden age of scholastic theology, was singularly free from theological controversy of what may be called the classical type, in which a new opinion is pronounced by one party, denounced by another, hotly debated, and finally settled by an eminent doctor or by a conciliar or papal pronouncement. One reason for this was no doubt the preoccupation of all theologians with the routine debates of the schools, which often ranged the leading masters on opposite sides of a question. Another, perhaps, was the absorption of all parties in the task of subjecting the whole body of traditional doctrine and opinion to the discipline of logical analysis and deduction. Indeed, the greatest achievement of the schools between Abelard and Duns Scotus was the gradual extraction of the whole rich body of Christian teaching from the writings and decrees of past ages – this was largely accomplished by the masters of the schools in the twelfth century – and the formation from this mass of a systematic, coherent body of theology expressed in technical language and in logical order – this was the work of the great masters of Paris in the thirteenth century. The peculiar achievement of the men of genius in the latter epoch, such as Alexander of Hales, St Bonaventure, St Albert and St Thomas, was that they bound together the body of their theology with a few great leading speculative principles, those of a Neoplatonism, mingled with other elements, as in the ' Augustinian ' complex of Alexander and Bonaventure, or those of Aristotle as expressed by Albert and Thomas. The traditional material was common to all. The strength of the two great Dominicans lay in the resources of Aristotelian thought, which covered all, from the logical and dialectic foundation to the furthest metaphysical conclusions, and supplied a language and technical terms in which every doctrine could be expressed, such as the ' subsistent relationships ' of the Holy Trinity and the ' substances ' and ' accidents ' of the Eucharist, whereas others used an amalgam of Aristotelian logic and Neoplatonic psychology or (as Duns Scotus and his successors) devised a new philosophical framework of their own.

It is only recently that the work of specialists such as Dom Lottin, Mgr Landgraf and others has laid bare the collection of the theological and positive material as opposed to the philosophical and speculative construction, and much work has yet to be done before assessment can be made of the total theological contribution made by the great scholastics to the mass of traditional material sifted out by the Summists. The main lines of the picture are however clear: that the doctrinal basis often, even in the details of its expression, came down from the first five centuries. The achievement of the twelfth and thirteenth centuries was to collect, to penetrate, to prolong, to correlate and to classify the whole by means of a philosophical discipline that was itself in large part a legacy from ancient Greece, but had been extended and rendered elastic and capacious by medieval genius.

When we survey the development of theology in the twelfth century, our gaze is necessarily directed to the birth of new disciplines and techniques, and to the shift of enterprise from the monasteries and the cathedral schools to the universities, to the victory of logic over letters as the basic pursuit of young students. We must not, however, forget that what has been called ' monastic theology ', the literature of the ' monastic middle age ' continued side by side with academic theology well into the thirteenth century. Meditative, reflective, scriptural and patristic in character, it prolonged the Augustinian conception of the Christian theologian, rising from thought to prayer and contemplation. The victorious entry of the friars into the schools and their zeal for philosophy and dialectic has obscured for many observers the monastic tradition to which they clung. The familiar and classical teaching of St Thomas on the active and contemplative lives has in it much of the monastic tradition, as well as elements from Aristotle and Denis, while for the Franciscan school of St Bonaventure theology is far less a discipline of the intellect than it is a guide of the soul to spiritual vision and ecstatic union.

MEDIEVAL THOUGHT 1000-1200

I T is a characteristic of western medieval civilisation that all the higher mental activities, save those of an empirical or practical nature such as medicine or civil law, or those with a purely scientific end such as mathematics or optics, were controlled by religious principles and directed towards religious ends. In consequence, philosophy, art and literature form part of ecclesiastical history, whereas in earlier and later epochs their contacts with religion are casual and comparatively rare. A corollary of this general statement is that the disciplines and institutions connected with these activities are found to be controlled, if not monopolised, by religious authority.

In the dark ages there had been two organs of education, the cathedral school and the monastic school. For parts of Italy we must add the urban grammar and law schools, but these stand outside the main picture of the times. Cathedral and monastery dispensed a single form of education, the ghost of the rhetorical education of the late Roman empire, which was itself a stunted version of the full Hellenistic education, and consisted solely of the grammar, rhetoric and dialectic of the ancient *trivium*. What had been the more advanced *quadrivium* of geometry, arithmetic, astronomy and (theoretical) music was in this epoch either entirely omitted or treated as a merely bookish discipline. Within the *trivium* the order had been changed, with dialectic now second; this was an index of its minor importance. It was no longer an instrument for discovering ultimate reality or truth, but a subject to be read up and subsequently ignored. The education was focused upon literary achievement and led on to a study of the Scriptures and patristic writings; in other words, to what the age knew as theology. Speaking generally, from the days of Hincmar of Rheims (c. 850) to those of Lanfranc of Canterbury (? 1010-89) the monasteries were the most active centres of culture.

A change began slowly a little before the year 1000, showing itself first in the cathedral schools of Lorraine, and northern and central France, where Chartres was from the first pre-eminent; it was a shift of emphasis and interest to dialectic, which returned to its place as the final stage of education, and could thus be prolonged and expanded indefinitely. A sign or sympton of the revival is the rise of Gerbert of Aurillac, an alumnus of Chartres and sometime master of the school of Rheims, to be tutor in the imperial family and finally pope. Gerbert (Silvester II) was a lone swallow, but henceforward half-a-dozen cathedral schools were becoming attractive to eager groups of students. Dialectic, now used as an instrument of knowledge, was their principal pursuit, and a class of masters was springing up that passed from school to school or even (somewhat later) taught outside a school, attracting and retaining their pupils even in their peregrinations and receiving payment for their services. All students and masters save in medicine and civil law were clerks, and therefore under ecclesiastical jurisdiction.

The revived dialectic did not owe its origin to new or rediscovered writings. It rested simply on elementary Aristotelian logic, with the time-honoured *Introduction* of Porphyry, mediated to Latin schools five centuries earlier by Boethius, but these short treatises had nuclear power within them, long unsuspected, and the mind of Europe was now fit to release it. From a dead formula logic became a technique and a method that could be applied to all knowledge, and the masters of the eleventh century were able to handle an instrument which had failed to do its work in the hands of a Paschasius Radbert or even of an Erigena. Dialectic, however, now as long before in Greece, threatened to introduce rationalism and to become a peril to faith and authority, and theologians and bishops were faced with the beginnings of a problem that has never since wholly ceased to exercise them.

An outward consequence was the first major theological controversy in the western church, the denial by Berengarius, in the name of dialectical reasoning, of the real presence of Christ in the consecrated elements. Berengarius is significant chiefly as having caused theological authority to harden its expression, not indeed contrary to tradition and common belief, but in a way that for long banished the more spiritual approach of the Augustinian school such as may be seen a century earlier in the English Aelfric, and that might seem to countenance a coarser and more mechanical piety even if, in the long run, it provided eucharistic doctrine with a bulwark against erosion.

Lanfranc, a thinker of no great power or originality, was acclaimed as the brightest luminary of his day. His pupil, who succeeded him both at Bec and at Canterbury, was known as teacher and writer only to a few, but Anselm of Aosta, known to his contemporaries as a saintly abbot and an unfortunate archbishop, stands out to posterity as a thinker and theologian equalled by two or three only in the golden age of scholasticism. Anselm, while making no parade of novelty and thinking to stand in direct descent from Augustine, was in fact profoundly original in using a piercing intellect and a limpidity of thought and style to express in a series of reasoned disquisitions, usually couched in dialogue form, all that the mind can grasp of the supreme mysteries of the Christian faith: the existence of God, the divinity of Christ, human free will and divine predestination. Without expressly intending it, Anselm gave an exhibition of the true function of dialectic in theology. In his own field he was never surpassed, and his celebrated proof of the existence of God has been misunderstood, controverted, accepted and redrawn from his day to our own. St Thomas was to use the techniques of dialectic and the definitions of philosophy more elaborately and with a wider range; St Bonaventure was to implement more completely the Augustinian programme of theology as the mistress of a Christian's journey to God; but no one again combined the trustful use of human reasoning with the spiritual intuition and warmth of feeling that are the marks of Anselm's genius.

Anselm spoke and wrote for a few pupils, at Bec and at Canterbury. He lived apart from the schools of his day and had little immediate influence upon them. While he was uniting dialectic with theology, the dialecticians such as Roscelin the nominalist were breaking altogether with the traditional conception of theology which regarded it as the study of Scripture in order to draw out, with the aid of the Latin Fathers and councils, opinions and conclusions *(sententiae)*. One way of merging the two streams of authority and reason was to be found, or at least indicated, by the second great thinker of the early scholastic movement, a mind as subtle as Anselm's and as original, though its workings were hindered and clouded by a character that contrasted with Anselm's at almost every point – self-centred, impetuous, ' compact of jars ' – and a temperament that led him through a series of swerves and disasters.

Abelard, like Berengarius, has been hailed as a harbinger, as the first martyr in the struggle for freedom of thought. Criticism has here again replaced him in his age as having a sincerely religious mind, but the mind of a dialectician and a prince of debaters rather than that of a theologian or a spiritual master. His predicament was that of Berengarius, though felt at a deeper level and expressed in an idiom more comprehensible to the modern world. After a series of clashes with those who taught him dialectic, such as Roscelin and William of Champeaux, he remained, in his own eyes at least, master of the field and turned to the realm of theology for further victories. Victories indeed he had. He saw and met the need of a multitude of students, nurtured on dialectic, for an ordered and rational explanation of Christian doctrine that might replace, or at least prolong, the existing disjointed collections of scriptural and patristic authorities, and his *Introduction to Theology*, of which he produced several editions, was the first step towards the great *Summae* of the thirteenth century. He won also the undying love and devotion of Héloise. That Abelard with all his brilliant talents did not himself become a great theologian is an index of his limitations. He lacked the necessary profundity and spiritual wisdom; he did not aim, as did Anselm, at the sympathetic penetration and consequent understanding of the mysteries of the faith; he did not even acquaint himself with the material amassed by the wisdom of the past; he preferred to use the statement of a dogma as a basis for elaborate dialectical superstructure. He lacked also the judgment, the balance and the selflessness of a great thinker. He repeatedly put himself in positions from which he could not retreat without ignominy, as in his celebrated collision with St Bernard. Modern scholarship has acquitted Abelard of intentional error, and has gone far towards justifying some of his positions, which approached nearer and nearer to orthodoxy in successive editions of his writings. St Bernard was, as always, vehement, overbearing, and a master of manoeuvure, and he failed entirely to appreciate the scientific purpose behind Abelard's opinions. On the other hand Abelard's methods and aims, especially in the hands of lesser men, would have twisted theological studies away from their true field of dogma with something of the same result that Nominalism was to have two hundred years later, and he was undoubtedly theologically inaccurate in many details and unnecessarily provocative in his novel use of technical terms and unfamiliar opinions. Nevertheless, his lucid and finely tempered intelligence made of logic a mental discipline and a science fit to exercise able minds; he did not shrink from demolishing mechanical explanations or obscurantist positions; and in ethical theory in particular his emphasis on the deliberate choice of the individual as opposed to the unthinking adherence to the letter of the (perhaps imperfectly known) law was to become classical in the great age of scholasticism. Add to this that on the level of technique the process of methodical doubt as expressed in the method of *Sic et non*, though not an original discovery, owed much of its universal acceptance to Abelard's advocacy.

Abelard, more than any other individual teacher, made of Paris the home *par excellence* of the arts student. His defeated opponent, William of Champeaux, shared in giving the city theological lustre by his creation of a school in the abbey of St Victor. There, a succession of masters, eminent among whom were Hugh and Richard, combined patristic learning and a traditional Augustinian outlook with a liberal use of dialectic. The work of Hugh of St Victor, indeed, is the crowning achievement of the first phase of scholastic theology in which scholars, not yet academical professors with a syllabus and an horarium, could meditate on traditional teaching and illuminate it with dialectic.

The direct legacy of ancient thought to the new Europe of the eleventh century consisted, so far as texts went, of no more than the fundamental parts of Aristotle's logic as mediated and explained by Porphyry and Boethius. The remaining parts of Aristotle's system were entirely unknown. Of Plato and Neoplatonism, on the other hand, no texts were available but a fair amount was known. Thus the methods and trial of Socrates, some features of Plato's political and educational theory, and above all his theory of Forms were tolerably familiar, and in due course the myth of creation in the *Timaeus* was available in Latin. Less was known directly of the formal doctrines of Neoplatonism, but the works of St Augustine, who beyond all others was the Doctor of western Europe, were so permeated by Platonic and Plotinian thought as to influence the outlook of almost all the thinkers and theologians of the twelfth and thirteen centuries, while the writings of Denis the Areopagite coloured all mystical teaching and influenced the theology of the angels and the sacraments. Augustine, indeed, influenced either directly or through his followers and imitators all early medieval literature, all religious sentiment and forms of meditation, all introspective psychology, and the very style and vocabulary of almost all writers. In theology and philosophy it was not only his teaching that was of paramount influence; his whole outlook on the world of men and things, above all his characteristic blending of the natural and the supernatural, or rather his acceptance of human life as it is in fact lived by the Christian, a human creature and yet a child of God, impressed itself upon the whole fabric of medieval religious thought so as to seem not merely one interpretation, but the only possible outlook. This rested, as a philosophy, upon a basis of Platonic thought as rethought by Plotinus, and Augustine's ' unitary ' view of Christian life was in many respects his version of the teaching of Plotinus, a monism of spirit. In consequence, it was easy for a medieval thinker, such as the masters of Chartres in the early twelfth century, to adopt a Platonic outlook.

In the middle of the twelfth century the awakened spirit of research and criticism, which already had to its credit the rediscovery of two great systems of law, turned its attention to the Arab civilisation of Spain, which was now in process of coming under Christian rule, and from the middle of the century onwards western scholars in Spain, and to a lesser extent also in Sicily, began to search out and to translate the philosophical works of Persian, Arabian and Jewish thinkers such as Avicenna, Avincebrol, Averroës and Maimonides. Still greater was their eagerness to translate from the Arabic the hitherto unfamiliar works of Aristotle which, after a long and circuitous journey through Syria, Persia and Egypt, and after passing through several languages, were to re-enter the stream of European thought by way of Toledo and other Spanish cities newly regained for Christendom. There, northern scholars were at work, both the newly appointed ecclesiastics and the wandering men of letters and science such as Adelard of Bath and Gerard of Cremona, and the works of Aristotle and the Arabians arrived one by one at Paris and Oxford.

THE SPIRITUAL LIFE (I)

EVERY generation of Christians has in essence the same spiritual life. All have faith in the divine redeemer whose life and commandments they know from the Scriptures and the teaching authority of the Church. All live as Christians by virtue of the supernatural gifts of faith and sanctifying grace, which are nourished by the sacraments, and in particular by the eucharistic sacrifice and sacrament. Yet during the passage of the Christian centuries the forms of devotion and the rhythm of sacramental life have both developed and changed from century to century, and country to country. Above all they changed during the long period in which the focus of western Christendom passed from the ancient Mediterranean world and its culture into the new European family of nations.

These changes and developments may be observed on many levels, but for our purpose three may be selected. There is the level of the lay life of the people. What, we ask, was the manner of Christian life among the countryfolk and townspeople of Europe in a particular century? Next, there is the higher level of those who stand out visibly as having specially devoted their lives in some formal way to the service of God: the clergy considered as devotees: the various forms of regular and religious life. Finally there is the literary expression of ascetical and devotional literature, which both reflects and influences the devotional climate of a particular epoch.

As for divisions within the nine hundred years of our survey there is, first, the long run of four centuries known as the ' monastic ' centuries in which the monks, and in an ever-growing majority the monks following the Rule of St Benedict, were the sole and almost ubiquitous representatives of a dedicated life. The hermits and anchorites were an extreme, not a rival, variety of this class. Then, during the twelfth and thirteenth centuries, the single monastic tradition split into a number of allied schools, such as the Cistercian, the Victorine, the Carthusian and eremitical, and later the Franciscan and Dominican. Finally, from around 1300, conditions began to resemble that of the modern world. Books and individual masters, whose doctrines and methods were available to all literate men and women, took the place of rules and institutes, and the faithful formed their devotional and spiritual life by choosing one or selecting from many.

The common Christian life in the households of villagers and scattered peasants of early medieval Europe can only rarely be seen at all distinctly. We are fortunate enough to have, however, in the writings of Bede the Venerable (d. 735) numerous glimpses of daily life in England of his day. One of the most striking impressions that we receive both from him and from all sources is the speed with which the original conversion of Europe was effected once the missionaries established themselves in a region. Documentary and architectural evidence shows that the land was soon covered with a multitude of churches, wooden and stone, and that they were adorned with precious vessels and vestments. While the church was primarily built to house the altar for Mass and the font for baptism it was also the place of prayer to which all had recourse at times of distress. How closely life and literature were bound to the fabric of the church is seen in the fragments of the poem *The Dream of the Rood* which occur on the shaft of the cross at Ruthwell (Dumfries, Scotland) and elsewhere. In sparsely inhabited districts crosses were often erected at gathering places where priests or bishops on preaching tours could preach and baptise and confirm. Though many pagan practices and superstitions remained, the simple elements of the Christian faith, above all the crucifixion of the Redeemer and the Last Judgment with its harrowing details, sank deep into the popular consciousness. Bede's long letter to his pupil Egbert archbishop of York (November 734) is a *locus classicus* of a bishop's duties and of the state of religion in that age. Bede has plenty to criticise in his contemporaries but can add:

> ...how salutary for every class of Christian is the daily partaking of the body and blood of Our Lord; ...there are innumerable people, blameless people, boys and girls, young men and maidens, old men and women who could without a grain of doubt participate in the celestial mysteries every

Sunday, and also on the nativities of the holy apostles or martyrs, in the way you have yourself seen it done in the holy Roman and Apostolic Church. [1]

In the same letter Bede insists upon the virtues of confirmation and notes as common the practices of almsgiving and the offering of Masses for the dead. This was the basic piety taken from England by the missionaries to Frisia and Germany, and which we recognise in the accounts of Willibrord and Boniface.

Naturally, however, Bede gives far more space to instances of sanctity and devotion among monks and hermits. Here again we are impressed by the numbers of monks, nuns and hermits drawn from the first generation or two of a converted country. Many of these display a maturity and simplicity of experience remarkable in any age of the Church. What is more remarkable is their number. In England, as in Ireland and throughout the West from the sixth century onwards, the monastic life was regarded as the only recognised form of the fervent Christian life. It was a ' conversion ' for all save those who had grown up from infancy within the walls of the monastery. The sixth and early seventh century had seen its diffusion over Italy, southern Gaul, Ireland and the western isles, England, Wales and Brittany, and in the age of Gregory the Great the Irish were repaying their debt to the continent. In the centuries of change and of missionary activity the monastic life was still a flight from the prevailing evil of the world. Its aim in the Rule of St Benedict, which itself absorbed and continued a climate of thought, was to learn obedience, and so to return to God; to enrol in the service of Christ. There was no question of comparing the spiritual ideal of monasticism with that of clerics or fervent Christians; the monastic life was the fervent Christian life. Its appeal to the English and the Germans was almost as great as it had been to the Irish and to the French.

Gradually, however, the nature of the vocation changed. The retreat-monasteries, typified by Lérins and the austere Columbanian abbeys, gave place to the larger ' mixed-rule ' houses embedded in the social life of the region, and in the large and wealthy Merovingian houses the monks became a class, the professional intercessors, for the rest of men, the executants of a long and elaborate ceremonial of praise. The liturgical service came to absorb and take over from personal sanctification as the *raison d'être* of the monk. Nevertheless the reading of Scripture and other edifying literature was a part of the life, and one which greatly influenced thought. Besides Scripture, and above all the Psalms and biblical canticles, the monks had the Fathers, and in particular the homilies on the gospels of the four doctors of the Latin church. Two of these above all others sank

---

1. Bede's letter to Archbishop Egbert of York (754), in D. Whitelock, *English Historical Documents*, ed. D. C. Douglas, I, 743.

deep into the monastic consciousness: St Augustine, who here as elsewhere marked the age, and from whom it adopted his distinction between the active and contemplative lives; and St Gregory the Great. In the past Gregory has often been represented as the characteristic Benedictine doctor, drawing out the implicit teaching of the Rule. Such a view is no longer tenable. Gregory stands clear of ' Benedictine ' influence and his achievement is to have presented the teaching of the Greek Fathers, in particular Clement of Alexandria and St Gregory of Nyssa, complemented by that of Augustine, in a simple form that his monks could absorb. Nevertheless, Gregory, considered by posterity as a ' Benedictine ', became in fact the teacher *par excellence* of the black monks and was thus a principal agent in the diffusing of the ambiguous conception of the contemplative life that was to confuse spiritual treatises for many centuries.

In any survey the hidden and silent sanctity must elude us. In its external manifestations the monastic *ascèse* became more and more the discipline of a life of liturgical prayer. Intercessory prayers were multiplied and in public and private devotion more and more time was given to prayers to the saints, especially the Blessed Virgin, the apostles and the Holy Angels. As the primitive church and even the missionary church receded into the distance, relics of the apostles and martyrs, or failing them, relics of the patronal saint, became more and more precious. In Gaul and Germany and England the patron was regarded as the true owner and lord of the church, ever present to save in times of peace or catastrophe. It was an instance of that tendency that became common in the political and ecclesiastical insecurity of medieval Europe, for numinous protectors who had once lived on earth to seem more real, or at least more pliable, than the Deity or the Judge of the living and the dead. The monastic ideal, particularly at Cluny, was less that of the Rule, in which the monk advanced in love, humility and obedience by means of all the duties of community life, and more that of the dedicated servitor who by means of an almost perpetual stream of vocal prayer and praise helped to form the earthly counterpart of the heavenly choir.

In these centuries we can see certain devotions developing. That to the Blessed Virgin, fertilised in the seventh century by the influx of eastern monks and clerics, now blossomed in the new festivals such as the Assumption and the Purification, in the dedication of Saturday to her special commemoration and in the ' little Office ' of Our Lady recited daily. That to the Holy Cross likewise grew by the institution of festivals and the multiplication of relics, while the custom of praying for the dead, present throughout the Church from early times, crystallised in the daily office of the dead. Spiritual instruction in writing during this age was largely repetitive, a distillation of each generation's experience of *lectio divina*. Perhaps the great difference is the emphasis on meditation and devotion as compared with the practical teaching on virtue in the Rule of St Benedict. Traditional monastic doctrine reached its summit with the writings of St Anselm preceded by John of Fécamp and followed by Hugh of St Victor. All three, but Anselm most of all, represent the blend of Benedictine practical humanity with the Augustinian conception of contemplation as a divine light enabling the mind to penetrate the truths of faith and the Scriptures. In this spirituality there is no schematic rigidity, neither is there dogmatic clarity. Anselm never proposes stages of the spiritual life or an analysis of the natural and supernatural powers of man. Growth in holiness comes from a life of liturgical prayer, meditation and fraternal charity. In his dialogues it is impossible to fix the moment when reason gives way to supernatural intuition.

A change began in the eleventh century, when Italy gave the lead to Europe. The two great apostles of the eremitical life, St Romuald and St Peter Damian, appeal to the individual and call to the abandonment of all things for the kingdom of heaven. Their doctrine, put into practice at Camaldoli, is of a life silent, solitary and austere, and Damian is the first professed enemy of learning in western Europe. The new orders, such as the Vallombrosans, the Grandimontines and the Carthusians, all have this note of austerity and seclusion. It is the age of monachisation for the Church. The world is positively evil, and the way of salvation is the monastic life, the ark of refuge, a second baptism. It must be made possible for everyone to share in it: clerics must become ' regular ', laymen can become monastic converses, knights and hospitallers can keep the monastic Rule; all can use as a prayer shorter versions of the Office. Concurrently a new devotion to the Mass was making itself widely felt. The custom of ordaining all monks had now become almost universal; this carried with it a multiplication of private Masses and a custom for the devout of celebrating more than once a day. In monasteries the daily Mass, unknown to St Benedict, had been duplicated with the Chapter Mass and was later triplicated with a Lady Mass. An almost invariable feature in saints' lives is the recitation of numerous extra vocal prayers and psalmody, or frequent visits to shrines and chapels for prayer. At the turn of the century the new movement crossed the Alps, and for the first time rival tendencies of spiritual teaching appeared.

The Cistercians aimed primarily at recreating primitive conditions, those of the desert and of the Rule. This implied austerity, but it was also a call to freedom of spirit. The horarium became open, with more time for reading, which could be used also for prayer, and the noviciate, from being a short period of assimilation and acclimatisation to a round of liturgy, became a year of training and instruction. The combination of an open horarium with simplicity and austerity brought with it a new flowering of mystical prayer. Bernard of Clairvaux and William of St Thierry opened a new and splendid chapter. Though both are wholly traditional, even if representing different streams of tradition, both have a directness of appeal and a personal warmth that give their writings permanent actuality. Bernard throughout his works asserts once more the practical counsels and commands that develop the Christian and monastic virtues. His teaching on obedience and humility illuminates the Rule for all centuries. In his wide acceptance of ' devotions ' – to the passion and cross of Christ, to the Blessed Virgin in her virginity and motherhood, to the Holy Angels, and in particular the Guardian Angels, and to saints, St Joseph, St Peter and St Benedict – he gives utterance to the aspirations of his time which set the norm for centuries to come. But above this there is the direct invitation to something higher, to a personal union of love with the Son, the Word of God, to the mystical experience in its plenitude. The term ' contemplation ' recurs throughout the monastic centuries and continues down the middle ages in the pages of spiritual writers; it is an ambiguous word and its precise sense often eludes us, but Bernard breaks through all schematic barriers; he is concerned with facts and experience, and tells his monks what he himself has known. In this he is the first great medieval master to open the series of mystics who illustrate their doctrine from their own lives; some of his pages anticipate a Ruysbroeck or a Teresa. Here too, in his frankness and his appeal, Bernard is of today.

Equally personal though with a different emphasis is his friend and biographer, William of St Thierry. Writing to the monks of the Grande Chartreuse, and showing an acquaintance with the tradition of pseudo-Denis, he perceives and defines supernatural, infused contemplation in phrases that recall the deepest utterances of the desert Fathers. He is the first writer of the western world to distinguish clearly, in his ' golden letter ', between mystical, supernatural knowledge and love and the ' contemplation ' of the schools.

Yet another Cistercian, this one from the north of England, has been raised to celebrity in our own time. Ailred of Rievaulx, though a man of considerable mental power, is no rival to William in originality of thought. In charm of personality, however, and as combining a gift for self-revelation and self-surrender with a real power of speculation, Ailred of Rievaulx, father and guide of one of the largest communities of Europe, and of a widely separated family of daughter-houses, counsellor of the great all over England, is revealed to us in the *Life* by Walter Daniel and in his own treatise on spiritual friendship. Had the large collection of his letters survived he might well have taken a place among the greatest in this field.

Compared with these three, the luminaries of the Victorine school appear at first reading frigid and scholastic, and some readers will remain always in doubt whether they are describing contemplation from within or from without, as theologians or as seers. Both Hugh and Richard of St Victor know from experience that the soul in grace can penetrate divine truth, and Richard, by his subtle transference of the soul's activity from knowing to loving, helped to make the Areopagite's teaching acceptable to those nurtured on the experience of the Christian centuries. When taken still further by a later Victorine, Thomas of Vercelli (Thomas Gallus d. 1246), as a practical doctrine of the spiritual life, the teaching of Richard of St Victor helped to form the great Rhineland school of the fourteenth century.

Hitherto the experiences of women mystics had played little part in the spiritual literature of the age, but in the twelfth century, when for the first time founders and abbots began to make provision for the spiritual direction of nuns, women mystics and writers begin the long line that leads through so many saints to the mystics of our own day. The first appear in the convents following the Rule of St Benedict in Germany. Hildegarde of Bingen (d. 1179) is an ancestress of the long line of visionaries. In hundreds of letters to correspondents great and small she answers spiritual and theological queries from what she has herself seen or heard in the spirit. Extraordinary as were the circumstances of her life, the counsels of Hildegarde are traditional and sober. Elizabeth of Schonau, an ecstatic with many of the characteristics of a stigmatic, speaks as a prophetess rather than as a spiritual guide, and in her life and her messages to all classes she stands between St Hildegarde and Mechtild.

The elder Mechtild (1207-82/97), originally a Beguine at Magdeburg and later a nun at Helfta, wrote an autobiographical treatise on the spiritual marriage for her Dominican confessor. She was the eldest of a succession of mystics at Helfta: St Mechtild of Hackeborn (1241-99) and her sister Gertrude of Hackeborn, and above all St Gertrude the Great (1255-1301/2). Gertrude is the fully expanded flower of medieval Benedictine mysticism. She writes in the tradition of 'nuptial' mysticism but finds in the liturgy the nourishment and expression of her spiritual life, which is centred above all in the humanity of Christ, where she has been seen as one of the originators of the devotion to the Sacred Heart. The group at Helfta is unique among the convents of the Benedictine way of life. There were no doubt many saintly nuns; we hear of them among the Gilbertines in England in the twelfth century; but they remain nameless for us. The group at Helfta is at once the most celebrated among the traditional Benedictines and the last to have a significant place in the main stream of European spirituality.

THE RELIGION OF THE LAITY

THE western church during the first five centuries of its history had been predominantly a great family of urban churches each of which was a lesser family of the faithful grouped under the bishop and his assistant clergy. In this society the individual church, clergy and people together, was the essential unit, and its religious life was expressed in terms of communal worship and action in the liturgy and quasi-liturgical services. Though the clergy by virtue both of their orders and of their jurisdiction were the guardians of doctrine, the dispensers of the ' sacraments ' and the ministers and celebrants of the Eucharist, they did not as yet link with their brethren of other cities to form a class by themselves with privileges, interests and devotions different from those of the laity. The clergy were small groups, partly chosen directly or indirectly by their own people, and supported by them.

From the fifth century onwards a double change is visible. On the one hand, the gradual growth of a regional, as opposed to an urban episcopate, and the administrative use made of the higher clergy by emperors and other rulers, tended to separate at least the higher clergy from the folk of the individual church, and thus to accentuate the development of a class sentiment among them. On the other hand, the introduction and phenomenal appeal of the monastic life provided another sharp division between those who had ' left the world ' for a life of greater spiritual fervour, and those who, whether clerics or laymen, continued to live ' in the world '. The movement of general reform, when it came, rose largely among or from the monastic communities, but in its administrative aspect it exalted the powers and increased the segregation of the clergy in general and of the hierarchy in particular. Speaking loosely it may be said that it was the Gregorian reform that finally separated the clergy from the laity as two divisions within the church. This separation was emphasised more and more, and in a short time ' the church ' and ' churchman ' came to stand for the clergy as opposed to the laity. By the time of the Fourth Lateran Council this process was complete. There were now three great classes in the church: the clergy, the ' religious ' (monks, canons and friars) and the laity, and the last-named were beginning to lose the tradition that the monastic ascesis was the only way to salvation. Wolfram von Eschenbach (c. 1210) is sometimes indicated as the first writer to put forward the thoughts and ideals of a devout but forward-looking and original layman.

Long before this there appeared movements of religious sentiment among the lower orders of the population. They are seen first as a movement to return to the apostolic life of the primitive Church, with emphasis upon the elements of preaching, common life and poverty, and a corresponding denunciation of clerical wealth. The Pataria of Milan, the success in the next generation of preachers such as Vitalis of Savigny and Robert of Arbrissel, the influx of lay brothers at Vallombrosa, Grandmont and Cîteaux are all symptoms of the new spirit. Towards the end of the twelfth century companies and sects are beginning to appear among the artisans and small bourgeoisie in the growing industrial towns of Lombardy and south France. Before the end of the century there are already in existence the elements that were later to form the basic outlook of so many groups of medieval men and women, orthodox and heretical. A common trait of all these movements was the exaltation of physical, material poverty. It was an ideal that was to have a peculiar and in some cases a disastrous fascination for the two following centuries. Present both in heretical groups and in the orthodox Humiliati and Poor Catholics, it was consecrated and raised to its highest power by St Francis.

Concurrently, the Gregorian reform was beginning to affect the landowners great and small. The monastic reform movement and the Gregorian decrees against lay ownership of churches had influence here. The foundation of abbeys by monarchs and great feudal lords had been a necessary factor in the expansion of the old orders, nowhere more than in Normandy and in the territories acquired by the Normans. Soon the lesser barons also established small groups of monks or canons in or hard by their chief castles. When the reformers attacked lay ownership of churches and tithes many landowners salved their consciences either by giving of their property to a monastery, or by founding a priory of monks or canons in one or more of their larger churches. This practice helped especially to multiply the small houses of Austin canons, which were later to prove a liability rather than an asset to religion.

The crusades, however we analyse their causes and the motives of those who took part in them, were in part at least an evidence of the power of religious ideas over the minds of all men of this age. A little later, the attraction of great numbers to the lay brotherhood of the Cistercians and other orders shows how deeply the monastic and penitential ideal had sunk into the consciousness of all classes. The twelfth century was indeed a time when the economy and population of Europe were expanding, and many of the recruits to the Cistercian abbeys were of the free peasant class; the fact that numbers brought with them to the monastery their small holding of land shows that the lay brother's vocation was not always, perhaps not often, the last resource of a landless man.

The Fourth Lateran Council took cognisance for the first time of the laity and legislated for them. With the greater frequentation of the sacraments and means of education the demand for high qualities in the preacher and the confessor was met by the enlightened parish priest, and still more by the orders of friars. In the thirteenth century the framework of the religious life of the parish, such as we know it in its survivals in the modern world, was beginning to take shape. There was the parish Mass, with morning and evening psalmody, the regular if not frequent confession, the occasional discourse from the rector or vicar, and the more eagerly awaited sermon from the friar at the churchyard cross. For the first time in western Europe large urban groups were making their needs and tastes known, and devotions and practices grew up, sponsored by the friars, which had no roots in the cloister. Examples may be found in the stations of the cross and the Christmas crib, the former an importation from Palestine and the latter powerfully encouraged by St Francis, and both closely associated with the Friars Minor; the rosary, the fittest survivor of many similar devotional practices, was sponsored particularly by the Preachers at a later date. Devotion to the Sorrows of Mary and her place in the mystery of the redemption became common and was indeed a motive in the foundation (1233) of the Servite order.

The growth, or at least the wider manifestation, of devotion to the human nature of Christ and to the mysteries of his life commemorated in the liturgy has always been noted as a feature of the twelfth century. The age was peculiarly conscious of sin and judgment, and the crucifix and the Last Judgment were the favourite motifs in churches small and great. St Bernard was both an instance and a cause of the growth of a more loving approach to the Saviour and of a new emphasis on his human sympathies and his condescension to his creatures, especially in the mysteries of his incarnation and childhood. This was accompanied by a more tender devotion to his Mother, seen not only as the Mother of God in hieratic majesty, but as the maiden of the annunciation, the young mother in the stable and the faithful companion by the cross; as the advocate at Cana and the Mother of all the children of God redeemed by her son. The assumption had long since been adopted from the Greek Church; it became during the middle ages the principal feast of Our Lady apart from the gospel mysteries. A little later, the question of her immaculate conception, though long remaining a technical controversy, drew, even from those who opposed its theological presentation, expressions of unbounded devotion to the actual sinlessness and uniquely favoured position of Mary.

Another development is visible in the devotion to the consecrated host. In certain regions, of which England was one, the custom of reserving the host in a hanging pyx before the high altar was widespread; the sight of the sacred vessel gave a focus to the devotion of all who entered the church. In the twelfth century the elevation of the host for adoration at the consecration became common and was soon regarded as the distinguishing moment of the Mass. The public adoration of the host followed naturally. The liturgical reservation on Maundy Thursday gave rise to two separate devotions, the ' sepulchre ' in which the host was placed on Thursday to be saluted and restored to the pyx on Easter morning, and the solemn procession bringing the reserved host to the Mass of the Presanctified on Good Friday. In some regions also the host was carried in the procession of Palm Sunday as a representation of the Lord and adored at the churchyard cross. There were therefore precedents for the solemn procession of Corpus Christi when the feast was introduced in the mid-thirteenth century. The many expressions of devotion to the Blessed Sacrament in the life of St Francis showed the tendency of the age, which was enshrined in the liturgy by St Thomas Aquinas.

Piety towards the faithful departed, familiar in the Church from early times, received a position in the liturgical year through the devotion of St Odilo of Cluny which gradually spread in monastic circles, but it was not till a later century of the medieval period that the establishment and performance of chantries, offices and Masses for the dead became a distinguishing mark of the age. In the twelfth century private piety found satisfaction chiefly in the recitation of psalms or fixed numbers of *Paters* and *Aves*. The reception of the Eucharist by the laity seems to have been less frequent than in some former ages. Whereas frequent communion was common in Bede's Northumbria, and the *Regularis Concordia* of the tenth century exhorts monks to daily communion, the original Cistercian constitutions prescribe a weekly (Sunday) communion for monks who are not priests, while reception is permitted only seven times a year for the lay brethren.

The growth of towns helped to bring about many popular and social developments. The ideals of the age, with its love of poverty and preaching and the imitation of the human life of Christ, were polarised in the new orders of friars. Whereas the monks and canons found benefactors among the landowners, the friars, who chose the towns, were helped principally by the leading burgesses and smaller men. Spiritually the friars were the principal formers of the lay piety of Europe in the later middle ages. They gave what the Church had hitherto lacked, systematic preaching and administration of the sacraments of penance and the Eucharist, and this essential basis of the devout life was followed up by the institution of the ' third order ' for laypeople, which gave the elements of the devout life – regular prayers, simple exercices of penance, and the restraints of certain indulgences or amusements – to men and women leading a family life and conducting the business of a town. With this background it was natural that pious associations should spring up, and the religious activities of the guilds, including the ' mysteries ' and ' moralities ', the founding and maintenance of hospitals and almshouses, and the proliferation of confraternities followed naturally. The coming of the friars and the decrees of the Lateran council opened a new epoch in the pastoral life of the Church. The Lateran council gave to the clergy a programme and to the laity certain directions, which bishops and parish priests translated into a practical code, while the friars, who were soon also trained priests, – indeed, the only priests trained to exercise their office – provided doctrinal and moral instruction from the pulpit, and moral and spiritual direction from the confessional. We are of course speaking of the friars considered as a body and in their golden age, and as such they were a new and beneficent power both in the parish and on the mission field.

With their coming, the spiritual centre of gravity shifts from the monasteries to the friaries and parishes. The two first orders were followed by the Carmelites, by the Austin hermits and by the Servites, and from about 1250 to 1350 medieval piety was at its apogee. In cities such as Florence or Siena, Amiens or Lyons, York or Bristol, Cologne or Regensburg social, artistic and intellectual life was saturated with religious associations and motifs. The first age of a specifically lay piety preceded the ' birth of the lay spirit ', and the century when the clergy, secular and regular, went out to meet and to teach the people ended with the bitter words of Boniface VIII in *Clericis laicos*: that the enmity of laypeople towards the clergy was a familiar observation. The century that followed was in many ways disastrous for Europe and for the Church. Yet in the realm of spirituality it was at certain times and places, especially in Italy, the Rhineland and England, remarkable for its blossom of mysticism, though this of its very nature remained the preserve of a few individuals. It was also a century of lay saints and lay writers, but if the greatest poet north of the Alps, William Langland, wrote, like Dante, a religious poem, it was one that examined the microcosm of man, not the universe of God, and saw love indeed as the answer, but a love hidden and disguised both on the cross and in the world of men.

No account of the social aspects of medieval religion would be complete without some mention of pilgrimages. Pilgrimage, the journeying to distant parts from a religious motive, is not peculiar to Christianity, and has been a familar fact of Christian life from the earliest times to the present day. Devotional journeying to the Holy Places in Jerusalem and to the tombs of the Apostles in Rome has never ceased in the western church. Nevertheless, medieval pilgrimages differ from those in earlier and later times partly in their ubiquity, partly in their recognition by popes, bishops and private spiritual discipline as a meritorious and ' satisfactory ' means of obtaining remission of the punishment due to sin, and partly in the peculiar esteem in which they were held by all classes. Apart from the natural attraction of travel and the equally natural desire to visit the home or the tomb of a venerated leader or saint, three religious motives at least combined to impel pilgrims from the eleventh century onwards: the sense of attaining closer contact with Christ, his Mother and his saints in certain places; the hope of benefiting from a physically healing power; and the prospect of earning an indulgence or the remission of an unusually severe penance.

The oldest of all pilgrimages was that to the Holy Places in Palestine. It was that which drew Şt Jerome and his devout *clientèle* from Rome, and Egeria from Spain. Second only to this was the visit to Rome, at first to the tomb of the Apostles and martyrs, and later to the presence of the vicar of Christ. Gradually others appeared: the ninth-century pilgrimage to the reputed shrine of St James at Compostela, that to Cologne, the reputed tomb of the Magi, and that to the scene of the martyrdom of Archbishop Thomas at Canterbury. Gradually the face of Europe was covered by pilgrimage churches great and small, with international, regional or merely local attraction, some containing authentic relics, others reputed relics of the Passion or the life of the Blessed Virgin or some heavenly visitation such as the imprint of the archangel Michael at Monte Gargano near Ancona, others again wonder-working images such as the crucifix of Lucca or the Virgin of Chartres. In England, besides Canterbury, the image of Our Lady at Walsingham and the Holy Blood of Hales Abbey drew multitudes from afar.

The modern reader must feel amazement at the dangers and difficulties encountered, and still more at the time and money consumed on these long journeys, of which many first-hand accounts survive in all languages. He must wonder, also, at the appeal they made to all classes, from kings, cardinals, bishops and nobles, to monks, friars, burgesses and at the lowest level penniless and mendicant individuals. Both charity and commerce aided the pilgrim; hospices sprang up at or near the great pilgrim routes and the danger-points of mountain passes and river-crossings, while guides, shipmasters, mountebanks and innkeepers throve on the traffic. As has been recognised abundantly in recent years, pilgrimages surpassed all other agencies in diffusing liturgical and devotional practices and architectural, sculptural and decorative forms and motifs. This was particularly the case on the long route to Compostela from the feeding-roads of Tours and Toulouse, through Poitiers and Moissac, down which spread the plan of the great Romanesque church and (more than a century later) the art of northern France, while the northward flow took the earliest Romanesque sculpture from Moissac to Paris.

The *locus classicus* of the later medieval pilgrimage is the Prologue to the *Canterbury Tales* of Chaucer (1387), who records the springtime urge felt by all classes to take the road to distant shrines, and who includes in his company of twenty-nine a cross-section of society lay and clerical, reputable and disreputable. Of these – assembled, it must be remembered, by a satirist, not by a statistician – perhaps one-third show signs of genuinely religious feeling. Among the rest the Wife of Bath, ' who hadde passed many a straunge streem ', had found time amid her cloth-making and five husbands to pay three visits to Jerusalem, in addition to pilgrimages to Rome, Cologne and Compostela. By a happy chance we are able to check fiction by fact in the almost contemporary career of the mayor's daughter of King's Lynn, Margery Kempe, whose autobiography shows her journeying to the Holy Land and Rome (1412-15) and Compostela (1417-18). Her pages bring before us the physical discomforts and mischances, the quarrels and hazards of accident and illness, while at the same time showing the comradeship, the real charity and the fundamentally religious aim of many of the pilgrims.

LITERATURE IN THE ELEVENTH AND TWELFTH CENTURIES

SINCE education and opportunity for study and writing were enjoyed only by churchmen, and particularly by monks and regular canons, the writings of churchmen, mainly on religious subjects, make up the bulk of the literature of the age. Educated in Latin, and members of a supra-racial culture which delighted to call itself *Latinitas* where we should speak of 'western Europe' or 'western Christendom', they wrote in a Latin which approximated at a greater or less distance to the language of Augustine or (in the twelfth century) of Sallust or Suetonius. The masterpieces of Anglo-Saxon poetry and the poems of the elder Edda retreated for a time before the flood; the *Chanson de Roland* and its companions, 'the earliest pipe of half-awakened birds', lie outside our purview. But although literature, in the form of poetry, history, biography and letter-writing, had a long start over dialectic in medieval Europe, since it had come down in an unbroken tradition from the later empire, yet the genuine revival was slow in coming, and the age of maturity was less than a century in length.

In the early decades of the eleventh century the results of the German renaissance under Otto the Great were still apparent, and the south German monasteries were the focus of the greatest literary activity. An example may be seen in the work of Othlon of St Emmeran and Fulda

(1010-1070), one of the most sensitive of those to be inspired by the model of Augustine in his *Confessions;* his memoirs, indeed, must rank high in the small class of medieval autobiographies. Though all his writings abound in personal touches of psychology and literary reminiscence which place him among the humanists, Othlon was professedly an anti-dialectician and a somewhat unconvincing opponent of an education based on pagan poetry.

More interesting is the monk of Reichenau, Hermannus Contractus, 'the Cripple' (1013-54). Paralysed from infancy, unable to move and barely able to speak, Hermannus in his brief life made himself the most renowned mathematician and astronomer of his age. His works on arithmetic, on measuring time, and on the astrolabe were classical text-books for centuries and attracted the attention of the emperor Henry III and Pope Leo IX, while his universal chronicle is for the years 1040-54 an original, accurate, valuable and clearly written source. He was also a poet of note, though the attribution to him of the anthems *Alma Redemptoris* and *Salve Regina* cannot be upheld.

No other region, in the first half of the eleventh century, can vie with south Germany, but it may be noted that Adam of Bremen, Ralph Glaber of Dijon and Peter Damian were for part of their lives contemporaries of the two German monks. Adam, who continued his account of the doings of the archbishops of Hamburg down to 1075, was a moderately accurate and critical historian. Ralph Glaber ('the Bald'; 985-*c.* 1050) is an example of a type of religious recurring in all the medieval centuries, of which Rathier of Verona is an earlier, and Fra Salimbene a later example. Talented, restless, credulous and garrulous, his History of France and Burgundy is valuable as a source, but still more valuable for the living picture he presents of monastic superstition and insubordination. It is from him and others of his family that historians have somewhat too easily received the impression that the medieval monk lived in a world of portents and devils. Peter Damian (1007-72) is a figure of far greater historical significance. A schoolmaster in his youth, with his wide know-ledge of classical literature, his metrical skill and his rhetorical eloquence, he is an impressive witness to the excellence of the literary education of the lay schools of northern Italy at a time when north of the Alps clerics, and for all practical purposes monks, had a monopoly of learning. As a young man he joined the strict Camaldolese of Fonte Avellana and was soon distinguished as an ascetic and reformer of the most thorough and ardent type, who would gladly have applied monastic discipline to all clerics, and emptied rich monasteries into the hermitages of the Abruzzi. In his *Liber Gomorrhanus* he cauterised simoniacs and nicolaites with a pen dipped in acid and sulphur as burning as those of Juvenal or Swift. His writings abound in the bitterest outbursts against pagan and secular learning, poetry, dialectic and the rest. Like Jerome long before and Bernard soon after, Damian uses all his art to destroy art. By choice a solitary, yet called to travel and to negotiate; vowed to silence, yet embroiled in all the controversies of the day; the enemy of culture, and a born writer; an ascetic and apocalyptic seer, yet with a vein of true and metrically subtle poetry, as the well known *Ad perennis fontem vitae* and other hymns show, he is unquestionably one of the most influential and representative men of his age.

The growing literary resources of the Church soon found an outlet in controversies which they had done much to render possible. Although the eucharistic controversy started by Berengarius had been decided by Lanfranc's treatise and ecclesiastical authority, a dropping fire of treatises, many of them by monks, was kept up for fifty years. More widespread and lasting was the output of literature in the investiture contest. Quite apart from collections of canon law and personal letters, at least 130 such treatises and pamphlets have been printed by modern scholars. Of these some fifty came from Italy, fifty from Germany, twenty from France; a few from England and Spain. Clearly the reserves of literary talent and energy available to the contestants were considerable. Very often the treatises show persuasive and polemical skill and, more rarely, gifts of invective and irony. As a whole the pamphlets on the investiture contest, the *Libelli de Lite*, make it abundantly clear that there was now in Europe a copious supply of men of letters at all the great administrative centres and monasteries, able to enter upon a full-dress controversy implying broad legal and intellectual principles, with a mature and sophisticated technique.

Towards the end of the century, indeed, luxuriant vegetation was everywhere springing up. Many of the participants in the investiture controversy distinguished themselves in other fields. Thus Bruno of Asti, bishop of Segni (1045-1123), wrote in every kind of genre and was perhaps the most remarkable of contemporary commentators on the Scriptures, with Rupert of Deutz as his only rival. Reinold of St Blaise (1054-1100) who contributed no less than fifteen pamphlets, ranking among the wisest and most moderate of the whole collection *de Lite*, was also a chronicler of merit. Contemporary with the pamphleteers was a notable group of writers of pure literature. They, like almost all the other writers of the time, were clerics, often abbots or bishops, but their personal characteristics resemble in many respects those of literary men of every age. One of the most remarkable is Baudry (1046-1130) abbot of St Pierre-de-Bourgueil in 1089 and archbishop of Dol in 1107. An indefatigable traveller through France and England, tireless, ambitious and vain, and a man of a hundred friends, Baudry became as abbot the poet most in request throughout France for epitaphs, inscriptions, memorial verses and such-like occasional pieces, writing chiefly in hexameters and elegiacs. Author also of several long poems, and well read in most of the Latin classics, he composed two series of imaginary letters, purporting to have been exchanged between Paris and Helen, and Ovid and Florus. He would have found a kindred spirit in Marbord of Tours (1035-1123), bishop of Rennes from 1096, whose reputation must rest chiefly upon his epigrams, epitaphs, satires and pious poetry. Though not unlike Baudry in life and character, Marbord had greater literary and moral powers, and his poems soon came to form a literary textbook.

A third name is that of a true genius. Alone perhaps of all writers of verse of his age Hildebert of Lavardin (1056-1133), bishop of Le Mans (1096) and archbishop of Tours (1125) was a poet of genuine inspiration who was also a strong and active prelate. Besides biblical poems and lives of the saints there are two brief pieces on which the reputation of the author must principally rest, panegyrics of pagan and Christian Rome, *Par tibi Roma* and *Dum simulachra mihi*. Penetrated with a sense of the grandeur of ancient Rome, and a master of the technique of Ovid, Juvenal and Martial, he regards the ruins of the capital of the empire very much as one of the last of the Romans might have regarded them, yet he is equally aware of the beauty and dignity of the Rome of the martyrs and popes. The friend of Anselm, Bernard, Anselm of Laon, Berengarius, William of Champeaux and Ivo of Chartres, Hildebert, with Ivo and St Anselm, goes to make up a trio of lettered and edifying bishops of which any age of the Church might be proud.

Indeed, the first half of the twelfth century saw the high summer of medieval Latin literature. The fields and tastes of the writers reflected the models of the schools. Above the undergrowth of monastic annalists and chroniclers rose some who deserve the title of historian. Orderic Vitalis, monk of St Evroul, and William, monk of Malmesbury, the former certainly, the latter probably, of mingled English and Norman blood, bring to life for us the courts and abbeys of the Anglo-Norman kingdom. Of the two, William is at once the more prejudiced and yet the more perceptive, with a style and vocabulary based on Sallust and Lucan and an exemplar in Bede the Venerable. Guibert, abbot of Nogent, brings us near to the emotions of the crusaders with his *Gesta Dei per Francos*, while a little later Otto the Cistercian, abbot of Morimond and bishop of Freising, gives a critical and in some ways a reflective picture of the Europe of his nephew, the emperor Frederick Barbarossa.

Akin to historical narrative, and often the work of an historical writer, biography forms a brilliant chapter of the twelfth century renaissance. Here an ancient and twofold tradition existed: that of the secular biography, descending from Plutarch and Suetonius by way of Einhard's life of Charlemagne, and that of hagiography, originating with the life of St Anthony by Athanasius and descending a long family tree by way of Gregory the Great and Sulpicius Severus. The eleventh and twelfth centuries were a golden age of the genre. We have only to compare the posthumous treatment of Anselm, Bernard, Thomas Becket and many others with that of Grosseteste, Albert the Great and Thomas Aquinas to perceive the change between the twelfth and thirteenth centuries. Biography certainly benefited by the expansion in historical writing, but a far more powerful influence was the interest now taken in a leader or a saint in both his human and his spiritual capacities. Many of the lives thus written reach a very high standard. Examples may be seen in Eadmer's *Anselm*, William of St Thierry's *Bernard*, Walter Daniel's *Ailred*, and William FitzStephen's *Thomas of Canterbury*, but almost all the great saints and leaders found a biographer, with the style varying from the simple episodic narrative of William of Malmesbury's version of Hemming's life of Wulfstan of Worcester, and the outline sketch of Suger of St Denis, to the minute domestic portrait of Samson of St Edmundsbury. Biography outlasted almost all the literary forms of the twelfth century, but the near-contemporary yet very different *Magna Vita* of St Hugh of Lincoln and *Vita Prima* (by Thomas of Celano) of St Francis appear as the end of a long-lived family. Numerous as were these lives, their appearance was restricted to certain regions such as north Italy, France north of the Loire, the Low Countries and England. Southern France, Spain and (at first) Germany produced very few.

Autobiography is rarer than biography; among its practitioners Guibert de Nogent stands out as an ' Augustinian ' with a hand of greeting to Othlon his senior and Ailred his junior. A masterpiece more powerful and moving, if less disarmingly simple, is Abelard's *History of my misfortunes*.

Most characteristic of all the literary productions of the age is the personal letter. Till recently historians were content with accepting and using their riches in this respect, but in the past few decades the method of compilation and manner of assembly of these collections have been studied. More than at any other epoch the private letter, nowadays exploited by the recipient, was then reserved in draft or copy by the sender for further use. There is explicit evidence that not only ' literary men ' such as Baudry, but saintly personages such as Anselm, Bernard and Peter the Venerable collected or countenanced the collection of their letters with a view to circulation (we should say publication) during their lifetime, and these collections embrace not only formal letters and those of spiritual or theological instruction, but the most personal, emotional and even violent items of their correspondence. Many of St Bernard's letters and those of others, published during the lifetime of the recipient, would give more than sufficient grounds for instituting a process for libel in the modern English courts. These collections of letters are a major source for the history of medieval culture and for a knowledge of the great men concerned. Hildebert's letters, written in a pure classical Latin, reflect excellently the mental power, moral force and exquisite sensibilities of their author. Those of John of Salisbury have all the characteristics of that keen judge of men. The exchange between Abelard and Héloise, whatever opinion we may hold of its composition or contents, must always stand among the most impressive monuments of passionate love and tragic dilemma. Anselm of Canterbury stands pre-eminent, not as a humanist but as a humane and sensitive friend and master; as a writer of letters and meditative prayers he takes as high a rank as he does in theology. Master of a peculiarly melodious style, Augustinian in many of its cadences but more uniformly harmonious than Augustine's, Anselm is here, as in his thought also, a man far in advance of his time. Reading his letters of direction to monks or noble ladies, his letters of friendship to nuns and bishops, we forget that we are in the age of Domesday Book and the first crusade, and think rather of François de Sales. Above all is that master of language, the abbot of Clairvaux. In his letters the whole range of sentiment is disclosed, from savage denunciation to delicate affection and deep spiritual emotion. His correspondance presents critical problems which may never be resolved. The abbot of Clairvaux, like lesser men, allowed his secretaries wide liberties and some of his letters were written by them and ' signed in his absence '; in the case of others there is evidence that the text now printed is a version revised by the original writer. None the less enough remains of the pure vintage to place Bernard among the greatest letter-writers of the past. No one, it may safely be said, has ever used Scripture with such daring and such paradoxical felicity, no one has called men to the hard ways with such siren tones.

Contemporaries of these great letter-writers would probably have pointed to their sermons rather than to their correspondence. It was indeed a great age of homilists, but those who have compared Ivo and Hildebert to Bossuet and Bourdaloue as summits of eloquence in France must not forget that many of the *sermones* and *homiliae* printed in Migne were written to be read, and if a few were delivered it was to small audiences in a monastic or cathedral chapter-house or the hall of a synod. The preachers who, like Orpheus, drew crowds through the forests, are not on record; we cannot recall the tones of Robert of Arbrissel. Here again Bernard is supreme. His sermons still kindle fire, but they are those delivered to his monks, not those that drove men to the crusades.

No pages on the renaissance of the twelfth century would be complete without mention of the man after whom the whole age has been named, John of Salisbury, who died bishop of Chartres. John is the greatest humanist of all, neither a spiritual guide, nor a philosopher, nor a theologian, nor a homilist, though he was a connoisseur in all these fields. To him the study of letters was both a preparation for and a part of the full life of a Christian, and we may think that throughout his own life this great humanist preferred the part of a spectator to that of an actor. Pupil of Abelard and Gilbert, friend of the English pope Adrian IV, secretary to Archbishop Theobald and Thomas of Canterbury, client and critic of St Bernard, John of Salisbury knew and observed many of the chief actors in an age rich in great men. Consistent in his exposition of the principles of law and justice, he was neither a revolutionary nor an enthusiast, and his judgments on his contemporaries are as cool and delicately shaded as those of a Saint-Simon or a Sainte-Beuve. He has a wider knowledge of Latin literature, and a keener appreciation of its fine points, than any other medieval writer. If Bernard of Clairvaux is a saint and an ascetic who nevertheless knows all the arts of rhetoric and of manipulating men, John is a scholar and stylist who is also a convinced churchman and Christian humanist. Taken together they show to perfection the richness and the variety of their age.

ART AND MUSIC 600-1150

I. THE VISUAL ARTS

ART in its widest significance is an activity of man in all ages and circumstances and of itself does not come within the field of church history. Yet it is also true that man has always used art to illustrate and express his highest aspirations, and to honour the objects of his worship, and that therefore what is called religious art, the use of the various arts in public and private worship, is an important aspect of the history of religion in any epoch. When religion, and specifically the Christian religion, concerns only a section of a culture or a nation, as in the ancient civilisations and the modern world, religious art forms only a small section of art history and the main currents of inspiration and execution derive from the secular or non-religious society of the age. But during the middle ages, from say 500 to 1400, in both eastern and western Christendom, the fine arts were preponderantly and in some periods exclusively the expression of religious sentiment or intuition, or concerned with the construction or beautifying of places of religious worship. No history of the medieval church, therefore, can exclude a survey of art from its purview.

In the present chapter we shall be concerned with the western church only. There it would be true to say that on the continent of Europe, at least, all work of the major arts – painting, architecture, sculpture, music – and most work of the minor arts – manuscript illustration, metalwork, carving – was directed towards a religious end and inspired by religious themes and practices, at least from the time when our period opens till the expansion of civic life and the dawn of Italian humanism in the early fourteenth century. During the whole of this period the most ubiquitous, imposing and characteristic art was undoubtedly architecture. No one, if asked to name the most beautiful and typical monument of medieval civilisation, would hesitate to instance a great cathedral. Architecture, indeed, and that alone, has left us memorials of every medieval epoch in every country, almost all containing some element of beauty and many standing out among the highest achievements of the human mind and hand. For a thousand years churches were being built and rebuilt all over Europe, while sculpture, music and painting were more local but nevertheless widespread activities.

Western architecture follows a rhythm and shows changes analogous to and often roughly contemporary with the phases of thought and literature, though the changes in fashion of building are carried through more slowly, and local influences of every sort are far clearer and more powerful in buildings than in books. Thus the great change from the traditional, imitative, Mediterranean Romanesque style to the original, northern, multi-formed Gothic took place slowly and at different moments, beginning in France and England early in the twelfth century, and was still in progress in Germany in the middle of the thirteenth. Within the Romanesque age there are at least three distinct periods. From 600-800 all building, save perhaps at Rome and a few cities of Italy, is small in scale and a dwindling memory of the past; from 800-c. 975 is a time of local developments and origins, some of them considerable and permanent in effect; from c. 975-1100 there is an immense and universal explosion of construction leading to a peak of achievement in which vast buildings express a perfection of design and form. In the Gothic age many subdivisions by time and region can be made, but in general three periods of transition, of maturity, and of exaggerated emphasis of motif or decoration can be seen almost everywhere.

In the two centuries between Gregory I and Charlemagne little remains to show change or advance in building. In cities and towns that had been centres in imperial days the churches were more than able to suffice for the shrinking population, and Gaul, still partly a missionary land, was content with small churches of simple construction, as was also Anglo-Saxon England, though even in that distant and sparsely populated land a minster at Brixworth (Northants, now dated c. 680) might be an imposing work. A change came in the lifetime of Charlemagne. A great age is always reflected in its buildings, and the patronage and cosmopolitan talent at the court of Charlemagne set in motion a period of construction of which monuments still survive. The palatine chapel of Aachen, inspired by St Vitale at Ravenna but an original and influential work, Theodulf's church at Germigny-les-Prés directly Spanish, indirectly Armenian in inspiration, the large monastic churches of St Riquier (799), Corbie, Rheims and elsewhere, the elegant gateway at Lorsch and other buildings, either stand yet or can be largely reconstructed from descriptions, representations and excavations. Most of them were in the northern half of Charlemagne's dominions, Neustria, Austrasia (Lorraine) and Alemania (south-west Germany) and were distinguished externally by numerous turrets and large box-like masses, though in the districts evangelised earlier by Boniface the old basilica of St Peter's at Rome was still the model. A feature of this region was the so-called 'westwork', a lofty transept repeating almost exactly the eastern end of the building and used now as a porch, now as a burial place, now as a second sanctuary and choir or for an exhibition of relics. Henceforward architecture developed steadily and the new wave of Romanesque influence spread from Lombardy. One of its first important manifestations was along the Mediterranean coast and its hinterland north and south of the eastern Pyrenees. Spain from 800 onwards erected simple but stylised churches as far west as Oviedo and Namanco, and Cuxa in the French Pyrenees shows a large church of the typical Romanesque plan c. 950. In England Brixworth had a basilical plan and Earls Barton an impressive if immature tower. The age of Otto the Great in Germany (936-73) saw the evolution of the typical German church, with eastern and western transepts, towers at the crossing and others at the transept ends, high cliff-like walls and small windows. These buildings were often very large, surpassing in length and height anything built since Roman days. Hildesheim (c. 1000), Gernrode (961) and the cathedral of Speier (1030-60) remain to impress even those who have seen the triumphs of Gothic art.

From c. 1000 onwards a veritable fury of building seized upon Europe through France to Spain and central Germany. Excluding a few notable but uninfluential buildings such as St Mark's at Venice (1066), the normal plan was Romanesque with a basilical nave and eastern apse; the larger churches had an eastern transept with apsidal chapels, and the church was crowned or flanked by the familiar belfry with rounded or arcaded windows at the summit which can still be seen throughout Lombardy, southern France and northern Spain. Architectural progress was rapid and by the middle of the century magnificent and majestic churches were springing up in every quarter. In the forty years between 1040 and 1080 there were constructed such widely differing churches as the second church at Cluny (1043), San Miniato at Florence (1062), Pomposa (1063), Jaca cathedral, Spain (1063), Pisa (1063 onwards) and Silos, to say nothing of the great Norman churches at Caen (1062, 1068), Jumièges (1037-66) and elsewhere, and the original Romanesque abbey at Westminster. The large group of Norman abbeys, indeed, built between 1000 and 1070 and the prolongation of the Norman design in England during the fifty years following the establishment of the Normans (1075-1125) standardised a plan and established a scale of grandeur that in some respects was never surpassed. The long aisled nave, the transepts with eastern apses to each wing, the short presbytery and great eastern apse, the whole covered by a wooden ceiling and a low tower over the crossing, became common form. The nave often 180 feet in length, and considerably longer at Winchester and St Albans, was presumably intended for the processional walk of a large community, or to accommodate crowds at a church of pilgrimage. It imposed at once a proportionately great height. Fifty years later than the abbeys of Normandy a still more splendid and beautiful plan was evoked, seen in various forms in the great churches of the pilgrimage road from northern and central France to Compostela. Tours, Limoges, Toulouse and Santiago di Compostela itself are typical examples. They have transepts larger and broader than the Norman churches, with four eastern-facing apses, and the apse of the presbytery is surrounded by a wide ambulatory with a chevet of five apsidal chapels. This was to be the final and classical layout for a great abbey or cathedral, and was adopted by the Gothic architects, whose only major changes of plan were an elongation of the presbytery and a widening and doubling of the aisles of the nave so as practically to eliminate the transept as a feature of the ground-plan. In England the square end and retrochoir replaced the apse. The highest point attained by the Romanesque plan was the third church at Cluny (1086-1121) where a long narthex led to a long and wide nave with double aisles, two transepts each with four absidal chapels and an ambulatory with a chevet of five apses. In contrast to Gothic buildings, most Romanesque churches were completed as planned and Cluny with its seven towers and seventeen apses, its long nave and gables at every height, and an overall length greater than any church until St Peter's five hundred years later of set purpose surpassed it by a few feet, must have been – and indeed those who saw it acclaimed it as being – the most sublimely beautiful church in western Europe.

It is not often that we are able to discern what we should now call the attitude of medieval men towards the fine arts, but we have at least one striking confrontation in the early twelfth century. At the beginning of that century art and architecture of all kinds were rising to a pitch of magnificence such as had not hitherto been seen in Europe north of the Alps. The monks of Cluny, and indeed their contemporary world, would have been proud to apply to themselves the words of the Psalmist: ' Lord, I have loved the beauty of thy house, and the place where thy glory dwelleth '. No better example of the feeling could be found than the passage with which Theophilus, probably the monk Roger of Helmars-hausen in north-west Germany, begins his treatise (*c.* 1125) on the practical execution of every kind of metal and glasswork, and of jewelry. This passage is one of several that occur in the work, and there is no reason to doubt its sincerity:

> Be eager and anxious to look at this little work on the various arts... If you will diligently examine it, you will find in it whatever kinds and blends of various colours Greece [sc. Byzantium] possesses; whatever Russian knows of workmanship in amber or different kinds of niello: whatever Arabia adorns with repoussé or cast work, or engravings in relief; whatever embellishments of gold Italy applies to all kinds of vessels or to the settings of gems and carved ivories; whatever France esteems most in her richly multicoloured windows; whatever the skilled craftsmen of Germany make for our admira-tion in intricate work in gold, silver, copper, iron, wood and stone... Every time you make good use of my work pray to Almighty God to have mercy on me. He knows that I have written these summary instructions out of no love of human approbation nor desire of temporal gain... but it is to increase the honour and glory of his name that I have ministered to the necessities of the many and have had regard to their advantage. [1]

The great abbot Peter the Venerable would have applauded these words and would have rejoiced to show their author his own great church. Not so St Bernard. He too had seen Cluny, and had not been impressed:

> I will not dwell, he wrote, upon the vast height of their churches, their unconscionable length, their wholly unnecessary breadth, their richly polished panelling, their elaborate paintings, all of which distract the eyes of the wor-shipper and hinder his devotion... but I pass over all this; we are told all this honours God. But I, a monk, would put to my fellow-monks the question that a pagan put to pagans: ' Tell me ', said he, ' you priests, what is gold doing in the holy place? '

Bernard knows what it does:

> You throw money into your decorations to make it breed. You spend for profit. Your bejewelled wheels (you call them crowns) set with lamps, and as bright as flames, your candlesticks as tall as trees, great masses of bronze of exquisite workmanship, and as dazzling with their precious stones as the light that surmounts them, what, think you, is the purpose of all this... will it melt a sinner's heart and not rather keep him gazing in wonder? O vanity of vanities —no, insanity rather than vanity.

Perhaps (Bernard continues) you may answer me with the verse ' Lord I have loved the beauty of thy dwelling ':

1. Theophilus, *De diversis artibus*, book I preface (ed. and trans. C. R. Dodwell, Edin-burgh, 1961), 4 (slightly altered).

Very well; let us have such things in a public church; harmful as they are to some, they may help others. But what on earth can be said for what you put in your cloisters where the brethren sit to read? Those ludicrous monsters, hideous ugliness masquerading as beauty! Those lascivious apes! Those wild men of the woods! Those centaurs! Those half-human animals! Those tigresses with their spots and stripes! The monks will not want books when they have statues to look at; they will have no desire to meditate on the law of God, when they can spend the whole day gaping at all these marvels. Merciful heaven! If you are not ashamed of your sickening folly, at least give a thought to what it costs. [2]

We may think that Bernard's magnificent rhetoric obscures his deeper conviction, that God is adored only in spirit and in truth. Suger, in those early days, had himself known what it was to get a letter from Bernard. He had admitted the justice of the abbot's moral strictures, and they became friends, but on the point of beauty and symbolic design he never gave way. He surely remembered Bernard when he wrote his eloquent apologia:

Thus from my delight in the beauty of the house of God, the variegated brilliance of the jewels has called me away from external cares, and devout meditation has led me to dwell upon the spiritual virtues, bearing me away from material things to those that are immaterial. Then I seem to myself to be resting on the outer edge of the world, which is neither wholly in earth's mire nor wholly in heaven's purity, and by God's grace I am rapt from low to high in spiritual ascent... To me, I confess, it has always been a conviction that all that is most precious, and more precious still than that, should serve primarily for the administration of the Holy Eucharist... If by a new creation our human substance were replaced by that of the Cherubim and Seraphim, it would still give insufficient and unworthy service for a Victim so great and so ineffable... There are those who tell us that a holy mind, a pure heart and a right intent suffices for this ministration, and I would grant that these are the principal, proper and peculiar qualifications. But I maintain that we should do homage also to the rite of the Holy Sacrifice, as to nothing else in the world, with the outward splendour of the holy vessels, with all inward purity and all outward magnificence. [3]

Two ideals, two points of view, were indeed in stark opposition. For the Cluniacs no expense was too great, no ornament too elaborate, for the house of God. Created beauty led the mind up to the Creator. For the Cistercian all that pleased the eye or gratified the feelings was the pride of life, the love of the world. The invisible God lost the worship due to himself alone, and the mind was distracted from its true object.

Meanwhile the uniformity demanded by the Cistercian *Carta Caritatis* was strictly observed, and in almost all the multitudinous abbeys of the white monks the plan is in all its main features identical. Moreover the

2. Bernard, *Apologia ad Gulielmum* c. XII 28, 29 (Migne, PL CLXXXII col. 914-16).
3. Suger, *De rebus in sua administratione gestis* (ed. and trans. E. Panofsky, Princeton, 1946), 63-5 (altered in places).

architectural style was exported with the plan. Cîteaux and Clairvaux and several early foundations were in the architectural region of Burgundy, and Fontenay a daughter of Clairvaux was taken as the model for design and plan. Consequently, in the first fifty years of expansion the transitional Burgundian style was reproduced from Scotland to the Pyrenees, from Scandinavia to Spain. While primitive or small abbeys had an aisleless and sometimes even a barn-like church, the normal practice was a large aisled building with four eastern chapels in the transept and a short presbytery. With their beautiful simplicity and often perfect homogeneity the Cistercian churches, intact or ruined, in their isolation by hillside and forest, or reflected in the untainted streams that so often wash their foundations, are precious treasures in the European landscape, but it may be that we see them at their best. In their days of activity the walls of the church were whitewashed and every vista was broken by a plain wainscot screen; the ornaments were of latten and the crosses of wood.

Architecture, alone among the arts of public display, continued to be practised at least on a minor scale and in some part of Europe throughout our period. It would be natural to treat next of sculpture and painting, regarded as major fine arts, but in fact they were almost entirely in abeyance for more than three hundred years save in isolated centres in Italy. Elsewhere in the Europe of the ' dark ages ' art was reduced to the small-scale techniques that could be practised by an individual in isolation. The basic art of the early middle ages was the writing and illumination of books. Here it was that art-forms were received from a variety of sources, such as designs on fabrics and small precious objects imported from Persia or Byzantium, and hence it was that these motifs were transferred to metalwork, miniature sculpture and carving, and finally to large-scale sculpture, painting and stained glass. It was for this reason that monks, whether Greek, Spanish, Celtic, French or German, played such a part in the creation and transmission of art forms and iconography. The study of the traffic in forms and designs is still in its early stages, but already it has shown us a Europe covered with a web of relationships. Mozarabic Spain was open to the influence of Islam and of Persia; Italy received not only Byzantine forms but those of Asia Minor and Transcaucasia. The spread of monachism westwards took with it some of the motifs of Egypt. The Celtic idiom, so distinctive and apparently original, has been shown to be impregnated with oriental designs, while the free, abstract, non-illustrative Celtic art is interrupted from time to time by a figure of an evangelist taken from an Italian or Greek model which itself goes back to an ancient archetype. In its turn the ' insular ' style, which embraced both Celtic work and the mingling of this with Scandinavian figures, passed by travel with the pilgrim Irish, or by gifts from Britain to the

Carolingian monasteries, to give its character to continental art. For several centuries, then, as we have seen, three currents converged upon France and Germany; the Celtic-insular from Britain, the Byzantine-classical creeping up from Italy or across from the court of the emperor, and the oriental-mozarabic entering from Spain at the two ends of the Pyrenees.

Almost all this corpus of book-production and decoration was monastic. It is astonishing that the Celtic monachism, architecturally and economically so ill-housed and ill-protected against the harshness of nature, and without the background of a developed intellectual or political life, should have been physically able to give birth to such a multitude of masterpieces of design and colour of which the survivals can be only a very small percentage. The Book of Kells and the Lindisfarne Gospels, whatever their precise provenance, [4] are among the supreme works of art of the West. The Celtic styles continued to develop and multiply in Ireland and Britain until the Danish and Viking invasion; they passed to Europe with the pilgrims and missionaries and finally, in the age of Charlemagne, by deliberate gifts and fertilisations on the part of Alcuin and his colleagues. The insular style as such avoided figures and, save when it directly copied or embodied human representations, such as those of the evangelists or Christ, it had little religious content. Its religious significance lies in its use almost exclusively in service books such as gospels, sacramentaries, psalters and the rest. If we are to reconstruct in our imagination a Celtic monastery or important church, we must picture to ourselves books and ornaments such as chalices, censers and candlesticks of great beauty, but architecture of a primitive, almost formless kind. The Celtic genius has never shown itself in great buildings. The early Carolingian artists were influenced by Celtic styles, but the northern flow of gospel and service books from Italy led to imitations of the antique particularly in the Rhineland. The school of Alcuin at Tours was more influential and lasting. There, besides the insular script known as the Carolingian minuscule, a new style of illumination was evolved based on ancient models, largely Greek, and therefore more pictorial. At this time also, and probably in or near the Rheims of Ebbo and Hincmar, the masterpiece known as the Utrecht Psalter was produced, a graphic commentary on the psalms based on Byzantine work, but original not only in its ' existentialist ' interpretation of the psalms but in its excited, realistic movement. The book was to find a home in England for more than 600 years and to influence a succession of English draughtsmen between 1000-1150.

---

4. The Lindisfarne Gospels were doubtless illuminated as well as written there, but the closely related Books of Durrow and Kells, traditionally Irish in origin, may have been executed at Iona or elsewhere in Celtic North Britain. So L. Bieler, F. Masai and others.

For almost two centuries after the decline of the Carolingian empire there was a decline also in artistic activity. Revival came in Germany and the reign of Otto II (973-83), whose wife was the Greek princess Theophano, saw the rise of a new pictorial style based on Greek models and centring upon the monasteries of Reichenau[5] and Echternach. Henceforward there was artistic activity everywhere: in Italy at Monte Cassino and Lucca; in England in the designs and delicately blended colours of the so-called ' Winchester ' (more correctly south English) school, a regional offspring of the Carolingian manuscripts imported by reformers from Alfred the Great onwards. At the same time the changes of style can be seen in the successive illustrations of the Apocalypse of the Spanish abbot Beatus, where the strident lines and colours gradually soften in France under English and Ottonian influence. In England a peak of achievement was reached shortly before 1000, and though there was a slow decline the school was still probably superior to any rival in France in 1066, and in particular to the Norman style, an offshoot of the English, which ultimately drove the traditional native art underground in the 1120s and 1130s. In the period that followed in England a fusion took place, and another brilliant epoch began, distinguished by the great Bibles and Psalters of Winchester, St Albans, Bury and Canterbury. Here once again cross-fertilisation occurred and illustrations of the Ottonian school inspired the master who executed the so-called ' Albani ' or Hildesheim Psalter at St Albans in the middle of the twelfth century.

After all the hazards of time, painted manuscripts remain in sufficient numbers to represent their age, and many of them have preserved almost unchanged their original brilliance and sharpness. It is not so with painting, which in the Romanesque period was almost always done in distemper on stone or plaster surfaces of the interior of buildings. Churches great and small were painted from crypt to ceiling. Of all this wealth little remains after the frequent architectural remodelling, the assaults of the elements and the lapse of time. Moreover the materials were imperfect and the technique in many cases unsure. Nevertheless, we must realise that almost all the churches, save those of some religious orders, were a feast of colour and, as they have been called, ' painted Bibles ' for the people. The Last Judgment over the chancel arch, the Christ or Virgin in the apse, the saints and biblical scenes from Old and New Testament along the walls were there throughout the years to sink deeply into the consciousness of the worshipper, all the more so if they were bold and simple designs that presented the person and told the story without complication and dis-

---

5. The claims of Reichenau have been disputed, particularly by Dr C. R. Dodwell, cf. ' Reichenau reconsidered ', by C. R. Dodwell and D. H. Turner, in *Warburg Institute Surveys II* (London 1965).

traction. This large-scale painting took its motifs from manuscripts such as the illustrations of the Apocalypse of Beatus, and later there was mutual interchange with sculpture.

Alongside the illuminated books lay another technique, that of carving in bone, i.e. ivory or walrus tusk. In an age when the cloister or monastic workroom was the only secure *atelier* this small-scale art attracted genius that in another age might have turned to sculpture. Ivory had long been a favourite medium for Byzantine artists, and the Carolingian monks copied antique models. Later, the carvers took their motifs from contemporary manuscript paintings. In England particularly a school of the highest technical ability and artistic genius developed. The carvers delighted in handling seemingly intractable problems and some of the relatively scarce survivals are masterpieces of composition that would stand out in any age, such as the groups of figures in and around a crozier or covering every centimetre of the surface of a crucifix. Metalwork combined with enamel and jewelry was another skill of the cloister. In this the artists of the Ottonian age in Germany were supreme. At Hildesheim a school of bronze casting flourished for two centuries and lecterns, fonts, candlesticks and altar frontals remain to attest the magnificence of its art. The large-scale casting was doubtless the work of craftsmen in the cities, but the early twelfth-century manual of Theophilus, in all probability the work of a monk of north-west Germany, [6] shows that metalwork in objects of relatively small size was an occupation of gifted monks, and that they still accomplished the work with a sense of its manifestation of the beauty of God's creatures dedicated to the service and adornment of his churches. In England for two centuries from the time of Dunstan (950-1150) we find numerous instances of monks, some of them gifted administrators, who were skilled artists in metalwork and carving. The great monastic church, indeed, from the mid-twelfth century onwards, if not long before, was full of candlesticks, lamps and other ornaments and vessels of every kind, and of every precious metal, many of which had been made in that or another monastic house. Thenceforward craftwork of all kinds, as well as illumination, gradually became laicised and commercialised, at least to the extent that it was executed by individual lay artists, who lived by the sale of works of their hands.

Yet another genre of art was developed in the eleventh century to beautify the church. Stained glass is alluded to in the late tenth century, but no examples survive before the twelfth, when the techniques of firing the glass and later of obtaining further effects from paint were perfected.

6. Cf. C. R. Dodwell in the introduction to his excellent edition of *De diversis artibus* of Theophilus (Edinburgh 1961). He suggests that the book was written early in the twelfth century by a monk of Helmarshausen.

Here again Abbot Suger at St Denis begins an epoch, with his use of a sequence of windows to convey the teaching of the Areopagite or illustrate the theology of the redemption. The early glass, which reaches its perfection at Le Mans and Chartres, makes its effect principally by its mosaic of small pieces of rich colour held in position by a lacework of lead. The figures resemble those of contemporary manuscript illustrations, small groups or symbolic figures, and the iconography both of windows and statuary follows that of the miniature artist until well on in the thirteenth century.

Sculpture has been left to the last because it was the last of the arts to appear in full maturity in its Romanesque shape. In Spain and perhaps in Lombardy (which can be neglected for the moment as being in another stream of influence) it had survived the dissolution of the empire and the Moorish occupation, and continued in a rough but not unattractive form particularly in northern Spain till it was taken up by more advanced practitioners.

These appeared almost simultaneously in Burgundy, in Languedoc and in northern Spain, and the matter of priority is still in debate, turning principally upon the date of the sculpture round the sanctuary at Cluny. In any case work of genius was being produced in Spain at Leon, at Silos and at Compostela in the last third of the eleventh century, while the great tympana of Moissac and Vézelay, the portals of Aulnay and the carvings of Toulouse and Poitiers fall in the first quarter of the twelfth. Thenceforward till the middle of the twelfth century in France and for thirty years more in England as at Rochester and Malmesbury, monumental tympana and exquisitely rich portals and cloisters, still fully Romanesque in style, were constructed with a multitude of small figures forming a pattern to frame the judgment, or the descent of the Holy Ghost. Even in small churches, such as Kilpeck (Hereford) or Barfreston (Kent) the carving and ornamentation is very rich. The great figures and beasts gradually move from barbaric force to human majesty, taking their attitudes and the lines of their draperies from the manuscripts of a few decades earlier. Almost all this work is anonymous, but a master of genius has recently been found in Gislebertus of Autun.

In central Italy, Lombardy and Provence sculpture was flowering contemporaneously but in a more restrained and classical style, producing monuments of more mature power but without the peculiar grace and dawn-fresh beauty of the best French or Spanish work. Here the influence of classical models is felt and the low Romanesque carving of Lombardy is soon overtaken by the magnificent work at Pisa and Parma, while in Provence, at St Trophime of Arles and St Gilles du Gard, the capitals and even some of the figures might be relics of imperial antiquity. We do well to remember that the Italy of Hildebrand and the Lombardy of Henry IV were alive with great new building works, and with architects and artists of the highest genius. While the struggle of empire and papacy was at its height, the two most beautiful groups of buildings in medieval Italy, in the Piazza of St Mark of Venice and the cathedral enceinte at Pisa, were unfolding their new splendours.

2. MUSIC

In the art of music even more than in those of architecture, sculpture and painting, the place taken by monks and ecclesiastics in composition and execution was predominant if not exclusive. The medieval term *(musica)* music, it must be remembered, denoted the vestigial remains of one of the members of the ancient quadrivium, which was concerned solely with the quasi-mathematical science of harmony in all its ramifications. Of the fine art the only branch of any historical significance, between the decay of ancient music and the eleventh century at earliest, was the chant of the church known later as Gregorian or plainchant. This, familiar to modern ears from its revival and critical reconstruction in the past seventy years, has its origin still hidden in mist and darkness. The earliest manuscripts hitherto discovered with musical notation (' neums ') date from the end of the ninth century while at the same time contemporary authority for the musical expertise or activity of Gregory the Great is lacking. On the other hand recent critics who suggest an eighth-century and northern origin for the melodies of the Roman gradual fail to give weight to some certain facts of musical history, viz. the aural tradition of all chant before *c.* 850 and the care taken in numerous cases to ensure that the Roman text and the Roman chant were propagated by missionary and reforming circles. In particular the sources of early English history including Bede and his pupil Egbert between 593 and *c.* 750 show repeated receptions in England of service books and choir masters from Rome, and the same process is seen in the attempts of Pippin and Charlemagne to secure unity and purity in liturgy and chant. In an age when the transmission of a text without a living practitioner was useless the argument for the diffusion of a single, ancient and Roman chant of the gradual in Britain and the lands evangelised by English missionaries, and of the mission of the same chant to Metz under Chrodegang and Corbie in the days of Amalar, would seem an assumption which is not invalidated by any evidence hitherto produced. That the Gallican elements of both liturgy and chant existed and were amalgamated with the Roman core by Carolingian scholars and practitioners is certain, and these were in turn carried back to Rome to become the common heritage of Europe. Meanwhile, and in this case demonstrably later than the age of Gregory I, the chant of the office and in particular of the festal antiphons and of the Sanctorale was taking shape, chiefly in northern Francia. At the same time the chanted portions of the Ordinary, which soon by convention came to form a musical unity – *Kyrie, Gloria, Sanctus* and *Agnus Dei* – were receiving numerous and magnificent settings of which only the *Kyrie Rex Splendens* is attributed to a definite individual, St Dunstan of Canterbury (*c.* 960-70). So far as can be seen, if the seventh and eighth centuries were the golden age of Roman music, the ninth and tenth saw the finest compositions of the monastic precentors. There resulted a corpus of church music which has never been surpassed in gravity, variety and flexibility for the voices of boys and men. With their variety of solo, antiphon and chorus they gave perhaps the highest aesthetic satisfaction enjoyed by any in that age. It was noted that the stone barrel-vault was particularly resonant for the voices of a large choir. Henceforth for two centuries the monks led the way with compositions and innovations, and with technical discoveries. The most important of these, the musical staff, was introduced line by line in the decades around 1000. The monk Guy of Arezzo (*c.* 990-1050) was not its inventor but he popularised the method and it was probably he who applied to the notes of the octave the *ut, re, mi, fa, sol* syllables of the hymn *Ut queant laxis* of St John the Baptist. The creative period of the monastic office, both in words and plainchant, ended in the twelfth century; thereafter new Masses and offices were created either by a cento of old phrases or by new compositions which had lost the spirit and the art of the creative age. It is probable that in monastic houses the chant for the proper of the Mass, at least, and for the Office remained traditional and with little deformation until the beginning of the thirteenth century, save among the white monks where the attempts at simplification on the part of Stephen Harding and St Bernard had unfortunate results. Later, a steady if slow corruption of plainchant and its replacement by the more modern forms of choral singing continued until the fifteenth century.

Meanwhile, from the ninth century onwards in the West, the practice of elaborate modulation (the *melisma*) upon the last vowel of the text, which had begun many centuries earlier at Rome with regard to the *Alleluia* after the gradual, spread to other places in the Mass such as the *Kyrie*. This *melisma* known as a ' trope ' grew to enormous length and received the support first of a few words and then of a whole poetic composition which became known as a Prose or Sequence. These last were finally detached from their dependence on the *Alleluia* and became an independent art-form set to simple melody. Concurrently almost every part of the Mass and some elements of the Office were ' troped ' with a luxuriance suited to the rank of the feast celebrated. At the height of the fashion, in the eleventh and twelfth centuries, the execution of the many tropes added very greatly to the length of the liturgy, and formed one of the counts in the Cistercian case against the black monks. As for the numerous sequences, they remained in the missal until the reform of Sixtus V, which retained only five in the Roman rite.

Side by side with tropes and sequences, which were musically only a development of plainchant, a new form was coming into being. This was the *organum*, originally a treble voice singing an octave above the choir, then a voice accompanying the melody either a fifth or a fourth below, then a combination of these two practices, and finally a voice or voices moving in harmony with the melody. In this way polyphony was born, and its resources were soon exploited in monastic and cathedral choirs, with the voices of children matched with those of monks or clergy. Up to this point the musical development had moved principally within the monasteries, but further progress was barred partly by reformers and partly by the dwindling of the class of child oblates. The future developments of descant or measured music were probably made to an increasing extent by lay musicians, though the new forms continued to filter back into the monastic choirs to become a target for visitors and purists. In music, as in all other artistic and intellectual pursuits, the monasteries lost the initiative before the days of Innocent III. It was left to the friars, and later to lay piety, to put into currency the *laudi*, the hymns and the carols that form part of the legacy of the medieval world.

PART THREE
1199-1303

$$\boxed{24}$$

THE THIRTEENTH CENTURY

WHEN Celestine III died in 1198, the cardinals rapidly and unanimously elected the youngest member of their college, the thirty-
seven-year old deacon Lothario dei Segni, who took the name
of Innocent III. One of the youngest popes thus succeeded a nonagenarian
who had been born before Bernard entered Cîteaux and who had probably
been taught by Abelard years before his condemnation. [1] Lothario had
studied theology in Paris and canon law at Bologna under Uguccio before
his elevation to the cardinalate at twenty-six under his uncle Clement III.
Under Celestine III he had retired from an active share in curial government, but his colleagues must have recognised not only his exceptional
qualities, but also his realisation of the crisis that was upon the Church and
his consciousness of ability to surmount it. In any case, Innocent, once
elected, entered as directly upon the execution of his programme as if he
had been for years in power. In one respect, indeed, he was fortunate. The
absence of an active emperor of the calibre of Frederick I or Henry VI
allowed him to deal with Christendom as a single field without having on

1. The cry of Wilhelm von der Vogelweide is well known: ' Owe der babest ist ze junc!
Hilf, herre, diner kristenheit '.

his hands a feud with the monarch of half of it. German affairs, though vexatious and dangerous, were only one department of his activity.

Innocent, throughout his relatively short pontificate, had three ends always before him: the organisation of a crusade; the extension of direct papal control over the whole of the Church, including the lay populations and their temperamental sovereigns; and the reform of Christendom, both lay and clerical. Before his elevation he had never experienced the cure of souls or even the care of the priesthood; he had studied theology, but his greatest interest and competence had been displayed at Bologna, where Uguccio had moulded his outlook, and Innocent's genius was not that of a profound thinker or zealous pastor, but of a lawyer expressing principles and judgments, and subordinating means and measures to an end clearly seen. What surprises the student of his pontificate is the multitudinous variety of his activities, his tenacity of purpose never shaken by failure or marred by rigidity, and his rapidity and clarity of judgment. Though never an opportunist or an improviser, Innocent had a politician's sense of the possible and of the actual, and a remarkable resilience which served more than once to prevent the consequences of a mischance or miscalculation from overtaking him. His pontificate is the brief summer of papal world-government. Before him the greatest of his predecessors were fighting to attain a position of control; after him, successors used the weapons of power with an increasing lack of spiritual wisdom and political insight. Innocent alone was able to make himself obeyed when acting in the interests of those whom he commanded. We may think, with the hindsight of centuries, that the conception of the papacy which he inherited and developed was fatal, in that it aimed at what was both unattainable and undesirable, the subordination of secular policy to the control of a spiritual power, but this conception was as acceptable and desirable to his age as has been to our own the conception of an harmonious and peaceful direction of the world by a league or union of nations.

Innocent, in the judgment of posterity, made a number of serious mistakes. He misjudged the ability of Venice to use his crusade for her own ends, he allowed his age-old prejudice of a European and a curialist to condone in part the criminal destruction of Constantinople and to underestimate the powers of recovery of the eastern empire. He misjudged, it seems probable, the characters and aims of Raymond of Toulouse and Simon de Montfort, and summoned from the deep spirits whom he could not exorcise. Here again, perhaps, he was too much a man of the thirteenth century to exalt natural justice and Christian charity above zeal for the extirpation of heresy. He misjudged, or at least it seems so to Englishmen, the forces at work in the island kingdom, and took the part of an obedient vassal who was also an untrustworthy and tyrannical king.

In the tangled web of Germany he put policy above faithfulness, and in the end left an inheritance of trouble for his successors. Yet in all these affairs he remained master, where others would have been overwhelmed.

Against these errors, if such they were, Innocent could show his wise and masterly administration of the whole of Christendom by his letters and judgments, his recapitulation of the whole of Christian life in the decrees of the Lateran council, his application to all religious of the salutary constitutions of the Cistercians, and above all, his farsighted and truly apostolic wisdom in accepting and encouraging the new ideals and aims of St Dominic and St Francis. It has been well said of Innocent that he was ' dynamic rather than magnetic, a man to be admired more than to be loved ', [2] but the few direct glimpses of him that we have from the *Lives* of Francis, from Gerald of Wales, or from Thomas of Marlborough, show a man who could meet very different types of character and suit his words and judgments to their capabilities. While it is true that his writings and his words as presented in writing do not move us as do some of the personal utterances even of Gregory VII, it is impossible to dismiss the whole of Innocent's government of the Church as an exhibition of power politics or the exercise of an ambitious and egoistical man or even as an achievement of mere clearsighted efficiency. He appears rather as one who was indeed concerned to use and extend all the powers of his office to forward the welfare of something greater, the Church of Christ throughout Europe, and the eternal welfare of her children. He has been called the greatest of the popes. Such titles are perhaps foolish, but Innocent III must certainly rank as one of the very ablest, and we can only conjecture how great his achievement might have been had he lived another twenty years. Yet ' the greatest pope ' would surely need the cachet of sanctity, such as was possessed by Leo I, by Gregory I and even also by Gregory VII. Innocent III, though eminent for piety, lacks the Christ-like touch of sanctity. Nevertheless, the judgment which sees in him no more than a mitred statesman, a papal Richelieu, a loveless hierocrat, does not square with the evidence. The man who, in the midst of business, could recognise and bless the unknown and apparently resourceless, radical Francis was not only farsighted but spiritually clearsighted. He died when the world still needed him, when he might have saved the papacy, as he saved the Church, from imminent disaster. He died at Perugia; his court left him, and his robes and goods and very body were pillaged by his servants. Yet he did not die alone, for it is all but certain that Francis had been present at his side.

2. E. F. Jacob in *Cambridge Medieval History* VII, 2.

2. FOUR LUMINARIES OF THE GOLDEN AGE

If the eleventh and twelfth centuries are germinal and dynamic, giving birth to the ideas and the institutions that were to form the framework of the new medieval civilisation and culture of Europe, and if they manifested the energy and the travail of birth of new ways in men of determination and a single aim, such as a Hildebrand, a Bernard, and a Becket, the thirteenth century is generally acknowledged as one of the rare periods in European history in which a culture matures and brings forth fruit in plenty with a perfection of form and a harmony of qualities that mark a summit of human achievement, a momentary union of the elements that make up, as it were, the mind and personality of an age. The Periclean age in Athens, the Augustan age in Rome, the Medicean age in Florence, the Elizabethan age in England are similar epochs of varying importance in the history of Europe. The thirteenth century was in some ways a wider and more comprehensive focus than any of these, for it included a culture that covered the whole of western Europe on either side of an axis running from Sicily to Scotland, a culture that had no single master-point of diffusion within its central area, and one which attained eminence in almost all forms of higher human activity save the purely scientific. A history of the Church has, of itself, no direct connection with changes of civilisations, or with the waxing and waning of genius, but the thirteenth century is unique among such periods of maturity as being the fruit and flower of a profoundly religious society, whose higher activities, with only a few exceptions, were either religious or closely connected with religion. It was an epoch rich in great men and men of genius, and most of these were men whose names must appear in any church history of the times. It will therefore not be alien to our theme if we look briefly at four figures whose names would appear in any list of the eminent representatives of their age: St Francis of Assisi, St Louis of France, St Thomas Aquinas and Dante Alighieri. Three of them are saints, canonised in general acclaim before the official pronouncement, and the fourth, if not a saint, has been often claimed as a mystic and was certainly in a broad sense a theologian, besides being the only one of the small group of supreme world-poets who is first and foremost a poet of religion. All four are quintessentially medieval, but three out of the four have in at least some important respects a timeless and therefore a modern quality in their genius, and each was the first within his sphere to show this quality.

St Francis, all would agree, is one of the best known and best loved of the saints. In the modern world, indeed, he has probably the widest appeal of all, though perhaps not always precisely in virtue of his sanctity, and he of all the saints seems, as he seemed to his contemporaries, most Christ-like. His achievement was to create the friars both as a new genus of religious and as an ' image ' in men's minds, and thereby to be justly regarded as one of those primarily responsible, however unwittingly, for meeting a vehement and widespread demand in the religious world of his day, and for domesticating within the Church a great movement of sentiment that was on the brink of heterodoxy and rebellion. Yet it is not this great achievement of founding a family, which ever since has been among the most numerous of all the religious families, that is the secret of his immense popularity. This is due to the exquisite delicacy and loving-kindness of his personality, as also to his awareness of beauty in all natural creation and, we may add, his new-seeming attitude to Jesus Christ, to his Passion and to the life of religious perfection. Together with St Bernard he stands at the very source of modern as of late medieval devotional life, while remaining, in his life as in his ideal of poverty, a child of his age and of Umbria, inviolable, seraphical, a man of sorrows, a visionary presence, *il poverello*.

St Louis is at once the most comprehensible and the least modern of the four. Modern research has set him four-square as a column of the French monarchy, and a founder of its strong judicial and financial administration. His contemporaries admired and respected him, indeed, but could recognise him as one of themselves, acting as they wished to do, but with inimitable strength and justice. He is, for all time, the model of a Christian king and knight, tempering justice with mercy, firm in the assertion of his traditional rights against a domineering papacy and an encroaching vassal, severe to evildoers and traitors, faithful and benign in all his human relationships. Yet where he is most medieval he is hardest to comprehend. His crusading ardour, his knightly prowess, his zeal for the crusade which to the modern eye appears as a betrayal of his duty to his country and his kingly office, all these suit well with a romantic conception of the middle ages but accord not so well with our conception, or the Greek conception, of a ruler and a statesman. While with St Francis it is the romantic vision that tends to attract us away from the real man with his mental and physical agonies, in the case of St Louis we beat against the bars of his crusading chivalry to discover a familiar face behind the visor. Each in his different way shows, as all saints show, a facet of the eternal Christ; each is a devout, orthodox, obedient Christian – yet how alien to our experience!

With St Thomas Aquinas we reach one who uses clear words to speak directly to our mind. Paradoxical as it may seem, he is in some ways the most ordinary, the most comprehensible of our four. Once granted the life and ideals of a friar, we might find more than one Aquinas today, less the unique genius and the radiant sanctity, at Fribourg or Le Saulchoir. His achievement was to rethink the whole corpus of Greek speculation in the light of the law and the gospel, and to use the simplest and most comprehensible of all philosophical techniques to serve as the steel frame for the fabric of Christian theology. It was his achievement also to restore to human activity, thought, art and politics, an authority and a worth that the course of history, aided by Neoplatonism and the consciousness of sin, had taken from them in the eyes of Christian divines. With him, it is the outward showing that is unfamiliar: the steady progress with question and article, major, minor and conclusion, objection and response, through matters great and small, sublime and ridiculous. We miss the interest in men and things, in literature and life, that other great thinkers and theologians, an Augustine as well as a Plato, have displayed; but the thought itself, to those who accept his principles, is timeless.

With the fourth, Dante, we are upon the edge of two worlds. A child of his age in his interests and passions as in his fortunes, he is as ' medieval ' as St Francis or St Louis. Yet suddenly from out a world of politics and problems so different from ours, the world of Boniface VIII and the Franciscan extremist, Angelo of Clareno, a voice of poetry touches a new chord of intense, personal, passionate and yet sublimated love, and seizes with precision of language the beauty of nature that Francis might see but could not express, and the gamut of emotions that no poet had touched since Lucretius, Virgil and Catullus. All medieval Italy comes before us in his pages, but his greatest achievement is to make poetry of theology and to rise above merely human things to the truths of faith, the theological virtues, the beatitudes, mystical love, the Mother of God and heaven itself. It was he who created for Italy and for all men of wide culture the portraits of St Bernard, St Francis and St Dominic, St Bonaventure and St Thomas, that have passed into the general consciousness of Europe. More than this, he made poetry of Christian dogma and theology, and so poured into the bloodstream of western poetry conceptions and ideals that have rarely been adopted by transalpine poets but which remain current in the minds of lovers of great literature and which have done much to recommend Thomism and the contemplative life outside the bounds of the Catholic church. Dante might well stand, if not as the patron saint of laymen, then as the patron of the lay apostolate. Though anything but a yes-man, and often appearing as the hammer of popes, who could write his *Monarchia* as though *Unam sanctam* had never been, he is fundamentally loyal to the papacy for he has in all ways the ' mind of the church '. Though not, as has sometimes been believed, a Thomist *pur sang*, he is as far away as the Master from Nominalism or Pelagianism. Though in some ways an intellectual anti-clerical, he has been the sole poet for popes and cardinals and bishops without number.

He remains the supreme poet of the Catholic culture of the middle ages, medieval in his loyalties and hatreds, and in his hopes and ideals for his own Italy and for a harmonious world order, a Catholic to the marrow of his bones in his faith, in his theology and in his mystical vision of Paradise, and a poet of all time in his expression of the deepest human emotions, of ideal love, of the beauty of nature and art, and of the Christian faith and the Christian's eternal destiny.

$$\boxed{25}$$

PAPAL SUPREMACY
THE SPREAD OF THE FAITH

I. THE PAPACY AND GERMANY 1190-1253

IN the reign of Henry VI a political event occurred which opened a new phase, the fourth and last, in the contest between empire and papacy. In November 1189 King William of Sicily died. Sicily was a papal fief, but the kingdom would pass, by right and general consent, to Henry VI, the husband of the dead king's heiress, Constance. The Neapolitan nobility, fearful of German rule, elected Count Tancred of Lecce in his stead, and Clement III, consulting the political interests of the papacy, accepted their choice. Henry VI proceeded to subdue Sicily and to decline his oath of fealty to the pope.

The Sicilian question was to dominate curial policy for more than fifty years. North of the papal states the empire had always claimed the allegiance of Lombardy and had recently occupied the lands of Tuscany which had been bequeathed to the pope by the countess Matilda (d. 1115). If Sicily were now added to the empire the papacy would be isolated and surrounded by imperial territorial sovereignty. The long feud that followed could hardly be avoided, but it was to have disastrous and permanent results for both papacy and empire.

Henry VI died when the stage was set for the contest (September 1197), and within a few months his opponent made way for Innocent III (January 1198). Both the kingdom of Germany and the future of Sicily were now open to a new order of things. There were two rivals for the German crown, Otto, son of Henry the Lion, duke of Saxony, and Philip, younger son of Frederick Barbarossa and so brother of the late king. Innocent claimed the right of decision, and after long hesitation came down for Otto; his legates crowned the elect after extracting an oath renouncing his claim to Sicily and most of northern Italy, but the German princes refused to acknowledge the papal right of election, and elected and crowned Philip in opposition. It was a disastrous situation. Innocent refused to recognise Philip, who successfully imposed himself on the greater part of Germany, till 1208. Then, almost immediately after papal recognition, Philip was murdered, and Innocent had perforce to turn once more to the candidate he had abandoned; Otto, for his part, once more accepted the papal conditions. The pope went on to make further claims in a Germany too divided to raise opposition. Elections were to be free and conducted by the cathedral (or monastic) chapter alone, and the full canonical system of papal reservations and devolutions was to be accepted. Otto on his side, to win the support of the German prelates, allowed appeals to Rome, and the possession of all spiritual rights immediately upon election; moreover he abandoned claims to *regalia* and *spolia*. It was an important stage in the evolution of the territorial bishoprics with secular authority. Once more, however, Innocent's plan went wrong. Otto drew back from his undertaking to renounce Sicily almost immediately, and conquered the island and mainland kingdom for himself, thus earning excommunication and deposition at the hands of the pope. He died in 1218.

Meanwhile the empress Constance, the widow of Henry VI and by rights regent of Sicily for her son Frederick, had died, leaving him as ward to Innocent III. Now in Germany the princes, without papal leave, elected the boy to succeed the excommunicated Otto as Frederick II. Innocent accepted the fact, but the price of his approval was an oath of vassalage for Sicily, with a guarantee of its independence of the empire, and a promise on behalf of the new emperor to confirm Otto's regulations of freedom for the bishops of Germany. At an assembly at Eger (12 July 1213) Frederick accomplished the latter part of the bargain by his oath which made the undertaking a law of the empire. It was followed by the equally revolutionary *privilegium* of 1220 granted in return for the election of his son as king, and giving the clergy complete exemption from secular jurisdiction and from royal and imperial interference of every kind. His abdication of jurisdiction may have been unavoidable, but it marked an epoch in the history of the empire. Henceforward the church in Germany stood to the papacy and canon law on the same footing as in other European countries. In the contests that followed the bishops were often divided among themselves, but there was never a possibility that they would unite as a body with the emperor against the pope.

Innocent III died before his protégé was able to cause serious anxiety. Honorius III, though a pope of peace, continued the process of papal centralisation in Germany as elsewhere. Yearly visits of bishops to Rome, reports on their dioceses and requests for advice became normal. The provision of Roman officials to German prebends and the taxation of clerical bodies for crusades were introduced. The observance of canonical rules for election, the reception of legates and the holding of synods were common practice. Frederick, in fact, whatever his personal attitude to religion may have been, remained throughout his reign, save for individual actions at moments of extreme tension, fully observant of the oath at Eger. His quarrel with the papacy had almost nothing in it of the old *Eigenkirchentum* save a few theoretical utterances.

The quarrel between pope and emperor broke out ostensibly and in the first place from Frederick's delay in implementing his promise to go on crusade, made in 1215 and not honoured for twelve years, but the radical and permanent matter at issue was the king's refusal to relinquish the control of Sicily. He had crowned his son Henry in 1212 and promised Innocent that he would resign Sicily in his favour. Not only did he fail to do this, but by crowning his son king of the Romans at Aachen in 1222 he made it clear that he had established for him the succession of the empire, including Sicily. Frederick, brilliant, magnetic, changeable and fundamentally unreliable, was throughout consistent in his basic policy, which in fact contained two irreconcilable elements, control of Sicily and peace with the church and papacy. The two chief requisites for carrying out the policy were likewise mutually irreconcilable and unattainable, concord of all parties in Germany and the assistance of the German bishops. With such a policy, a contest with Rome was inevitable. The papacy, committed under Innocent III even more completely than before to a leading rôle in the politics of Europe and therefore to a rivalry in the political field with the empire, could not tolerate the imperial domination of Italy, north and south. It would indeed be almost true to say that the papal claim to universal suzerainty eliminated the empire as an unnecessary and even as an intolerable political entity. When shortly after Frederick's death the Rhine league of towns was formed (1254), to be followed by others culminating in the great Hanseatic league, all the elements of disunion were in existence in Germany which were to prove so influential in the sixteenth century and which endured until submerged in modern times by the events of the past hundred years. As for Frederick's desire for a Germany free from disturbances, the collaboration of the church, an essential part of the programme, could never be certain with a church now almost entirely independent, while the independence of the princes had been established almost as completely by the constitution in their favour of 1231 which gave them independence and legislative power.

The contest between Frederick and the papacy which reached its first crisis with his excommunication and deposition in 1227, continued until the virtual defeat of the emperor in 1245, soon followed by his death in 1250. Restored to the communion of the church after his crusade in 1230, he fell under the ban again in 1239 and was subsequently harassed by the proclamation of a crusade against him in 1240 and the solemn declaration of deposition at Lyons in 1245. Thenceforward the pope, Innocent IV, deployed all the forces at his disposal against the emperor: a legate was appointed to rouse Germany; an anti-king was set up; every kind of ban was placed on clergy supporting the emperor, with corresponding privileges for the papal party, while money was used lavishly to induce or to reward changes of front. Frederick answered by manifestoes claiming autonomy for the ruler of a state. Whereas Honorius III had been slow to act, Gregory IX was drastic in the pursuit of his policy, while Innocent IV threw every ounce into the attack. The final outcome was the complete and final disappearance of the empire not only as a source of religious leadership for Europe but also as a political factor of European importance able to combat the papacy with material forces. The descent from Henry III to Henry IV, to Conrad III, to Barbarossa and to Frederick II is the descent from a sovereign dedicated to the service of the Church to an emperor without any motive of a religious nature. Frederick's character, his beliefs, his aims and his achievements will always give rise to the most diverse judgments. Had the course of events and his own versatile energy allowed him a period of peace, he might have re-established the imperial rights in Germany and given cohesion to the empire. It was not to be. Brilliant as was his genius, and enduring as were many of his acts and laws, particularly in Italy, he had unwillingly perhaps, but deliberately, and as an act of policy, cut away the foundations on which the empire rested and made it certain that Germany for centuries – indeed until 1870 or 1918–would be a nation in fragments. As for the four popes Innocent III, Honorius, Gregory and Innocent IV, they had, largely through the folly of their opponents, destroyed the enemy that for almost two centuries had struggled to contain the papacy, and had brought Germany back under the direct control of Rome which had been largely lost three centuries earlier, but they had achieved this as politicians rather than as pontiffs, with a lavish and ruthless use of spiritual sanctions.

The contest between empire and papacy, which derived ultimately and perhaps inevitably from the union in the person of Charlemagne of the theocratic kingship and the imperial tradition, occupied the minds and energies of emperors and popes and countless lesser men for two centuries. It has bulked large in modern historiography, partly no doubt because the creators of modern historical technique were themselves Germans whose prime interests were medieval. Those of other nations have felt some impatience at this. But when the influence of this mighty contest upon the story of Europe is carefully weighed it may be thought that in both the religious and the political spheres no strife has been more influential. Had it never been, who can say what external form would have clothed the dogmatic fact of the Petrine commission in western Europe? And who can say whether the revolt of the sixteenth century would have taken place? Certain it is that only in our own day have the political shape of Europe and the concept of the destiny and character of the papal office begun to take forms uninfluenced by the memories of the age of Hildebrand.

Be this as it may, the fifty years that followed the death of Frederick II mark a divide. The papacy was to be attacked again, sooner and more bitterly than could have been thought possible by Innocent III or even by Innocent IV, but the enemies now were national sentiment and secular government, the creators of the modern state.

2. THE BALTIC CONVERSIONS

In the early twelfth century the Elbe was still approximately the boundary of organised Christendom and of Germany, with a Slav population in greater or less density to the east and Poland as a bastion beyond them separating the Hungarians from the Baltic tribes. These, reckoning from west to north-east along the coastline, were the Pomeranians between the Oder and the Vistula, the Prussians from the Vistula to the Niemen, the Lithuanians from the Niemen to the Drina, the Letts and the Estonians from the Drina to the gulf of Finland. Evangelisation proceeded first from the two bishoprics on the Elbe, Bamberg and Magdeburg. Otto of Bamberg (d. 1139) by means of force, and St Norbert (d. 1134) more peacefully pressed eastwards, and the latter encouraged his Premonstratensians and the Cistercians to follow or even to precede the evangelists. In the event the ' sphere of influence ' of Magdeburg extended for several hundred miles east of the Elbe and beyond the Oder. In 1147 the German landowners, alerted by the preaching of St Bernard, found crusading among the Slavs more attractive than distant expeditions in the Levant, but the use of force was not justified by results and the conversions proceeded slowly and by peaceful means. Later in the century the advancing Germans gradually closed the gap between Germany and Poland and the whole territory was divided between the two peoples by papal decree.

Meanwhile the Swedes were evangelising what is now Finland, and the Danes Finnish Estonia, while Meinhard of Holstein pushed the gospel along the coast of the Baltic to Lithuania (1184). The process was continued by Albert (d. 1229) a man of energy and wide views who founded Riga (1201) and became its first bishop. In 1204 he founded a crusading order, the Brothers of the Sword, to whom he gave the rule of the Templars. Albert was encouraged and assisted by Innocent III, who also encouraged Cistercian missionaries in Prussia. Here the progress of evangelisation was hastened by the arrival of the Teutonic Order of Hospitallers. This Order, founded during the third crusade on the lines of the other military orders to assist and defend German pilgrims, had, like its fellows, flourished in wealth and numbers. Its attention was directed to the Baltic lands where conditions were more familiar and the prospects of religious and material success more favourable than in the East, and the long connection between the Order and German history began. At first progress was peaceful, but after the death of Innocent III a revolt of the pagan population of Prussia threatened to undo much of the work achieved. At the same time Christendom in eastern Europe was receiving another heavy blow from the Mongol invasion which reached in places almost as far as the earlier Hungarian horde.

The Prussian revolt provoked a war of twenty years waged by the Teutonic Order and its allies. It was ruthless, and many of the pagan natives were massacred, while in their stead Germans from the west were introduced. After the Prussian war came the advance of the Order in Lithuania where conditions of warfare continued for a century (1283-1383) with massacres on both sides and changing fortune. During this time the Teutonic Order, to which in 1237 Albert's Brothers of the Sword had been united, moved its headquarters, which after leaving Acre in 1291 had been fixed at Venice, to Marienburg on the Vistula a short distance inland from Danzig. By so doing the Order became a great territorial power with its wealth and activities centred upon the regions between Russia and Poland and the Baltic, and between 1343 and 1404, in its golden age of power and ability, it conquered and converted the whole coastal series of peoples from Estonia to East Pomerania. In the settlement of Latvia the bishops had received two-thirds of the land and the Brothers of the Sword one-third; in the settlement of Pomerania and Prussia the proportions were reversed. As the bishops and their chapters were independent of the Order, which depended nominally upon the pope, the Baltic countries had the same patchwork appearance of feudalism as the main regions of Germany, though the administration of the whole country was regulated by the Order and considerable liberty was given to both bishops and towns. The predominance of the Teutonic Order was finally impaired by a long war with Poland in the fifteenth century, as a result of which the Poles obtained control of Prussia and parts of Pomerania and Lithuania, thus planting the seeds of tragedy for later centuries. In the fifteenth century the religious and moral fibre of the Teutonic Order declined greatly.

The Teutonic Order has been the object of much admiration and of much modern denigration. Its early crusading days, when a spiritual and Christian motive was uppermost, were followed by a long period of warfare with every kind of foe, pagan and Christian, and many acts and policies can be justly criticised as inhumane, while the martial and administrative successes of the Order cannot but win admiration. On the whole the harshest criticisms, which in our century have often unjustifiably identified the Order with the allegedly fierce and warlike spirit of Prussia, need to be revised. A modern historian, not himself a German and writing after some experience of Prussian domination of Europe, has pronounced the work of the Order as ' one of the most glorious achievements of the middle ages ' and ' the greatest triumph of medieval German civilisation '. [1]

3. THE BULGARIAN CHURCH

The medieval Bulgarian state, founded in 681 by Kuvrat's son Asparuch, who led his Turkic Bulgars across the Danube and established them in the north-eastern corner of the Balkan peninsula, on former Byzantine territory now occupied by the Slavs, was until 864 officially and aggressively pagan. Christianity had, however, been spreading from Byzantium among the Bulgars' Slav subjects during the first half of the ninth century. The immediate cause of the conversion of Bulgaria was a political event – an alliance concluded by the Bulgarian ruler Boris with Lewis the German. This alliance, with the consequent danger of Frankish influence spreading to Thrace and Macedonia, was a threat to Byzantium's vital interests in this area. The emperor Michael III moved an army to the Bulgarian frontier (864). Boris capitulated at once; he undertook to renounce the Frankish alliance and to receive Christianity from Constantinople. In 865 Boris was baptised and was given the name Michael, in honour of his imperial godfather. A revolt of the Bulgar nobility against his decision to enforce baptism on all his subjects was ruthlessly suppressed, and the triumph of Byzantine Christianity in Bulgaria seemed assured. The patriarch Photius wrote a long letter to Boris, explaining the doctrines of the Church and the duties of a Christian ruler. [2] There are reasons to think that the Bulgarian prince was not altogether satisfied by this learned disquisition. His was the awkward problem that faced, in one form or

1. A. B. Boswell in *Cambridge Medieval History* VII, 268.
2. PG CII, col. 628-96.

11. The non-Greek Orthodox Churches of the Balkans

another, every ruler of a nation newly converted to Byzantine Christianity: how was he to reconcile his recognition of Byzantine supremacy with his natural desire to remain master in his own country? A separate ecclesiastical hierarchy, under a Bulgarian patriarch, might have gone some way towards solving his dilemma; but on this matter Photius was ominously silent. And so, disappointed with the Greeks, Boris turned to his former ally, Lewis the German, and in 866 requested him to send a bishop and priests to Bulgaria. At the same time he sent an embassy to Rome asking the pope for a patriarch. For Pope Nicholas I, who was thus presented with the opportunity of regaining ecclesiastical control over part of Illyricum, this was good news indeed. Determined to subject the young Bulgarian church to the Holy See, he sent at once two bishops to Bulgaria and composed a reply to a list of 106 questions which Boris had sent him. This papal letter, known to the medieval canonists as ' Responsa Nicolai ad consulta Bulgarorum ',[3] a shrewd and sagacious document, shows that Boris, though his knowledge of Christianity was rudimentary in the extreme, was quite capable of exploiting the rivalry between the Byzantine and the Roman sees to gain as much independence and prestige as possible for his own Bulgarian church. But the pope, while reassuring Boris as to the propriety of wearing trousers and having one's bath on Wednesdays and Fridays, proved to be less than satisfactory on the matter which was the nearest to the Bulgarian ruler's heart: Boris's request for a patriarch he adroitly side-stepped: for the time being, Boris was told, he would have to content himself with an archbishop. However, since Byzantium had, it appears, grudged him even a bishop, Boris considered that he had got the better deal out of Rome and swore to remain a faithful servant of St Peter.

By 870, however, Boris and his people were back in the Byzantine fold. To a large extent, no doubt, this *volte-face* was the result of Byzantine diplomacy: the papal librarian Anastasius referred pointedly and with unconcealed chagrin to the ' gifts ' (' munera ') and the blandishments (' sophistica argumenta ') showered by the Greeks upon the Bulgarians during these four years in order to detach them from Rome. [4] The Byzantines were careful in 870 to avoid repeating the mistake that had, four years earlier, thrown Boris into the arms of the pope. The Bulgarian church was now to be headed by an archbishop who, though canonically subject to the patriarch of Constantinople, enjoyed a considerable measure of autonomy. Thus did the rivalry between the sees of Rome and Constantinople, the shrewd finesse of Boris of Bulgaria and the flexible diplomacy of the

---

3. PL CXIX, col. 978-1016.
4. *Praefatio in synodum octavam*, PL CXXIX, col. 20.

Byzantine empire contribute to the foundation of the first Slavonic national church.

Some fifteen years later the young Bulgarian church reached a further stage on the road to cultural autonomy. Boris must have realised that only by acquiring a native clergy and the Slavonic liturgy and letters could his people continue to assimilate Byzantine civilisation without prejudice to their cultural and political independence. And so when the disciples of Methodius, after their expulsion from Moravia, travelled down the Danube and arrived in Bulgaria, they were cordially received by Boris. Clement, one of their leaders, was sent to Macedonia, where he worked among Boris's Slav subjects for thirty years, preaching the gospel in Slavonic, celebrating the Slavonic liturgy according to the Byzantine rite, and training a native clergy. Thanks to St Clement (who was appointed bishop in 893) and to his companion, St Naum, Macedonia became a renowned centre of Slavo-Byzantine culture, and Ohrid, its chief city, the cradle of Slavonic Christianity in the Balkans. Meanwhile, in the Bulgarian capital of Preslav, another school of Slavonic literature was developing under the patronage of Symeon, Boris's son and successor (893-927). It was here, probably in the closing years of the ninth century, that the Glagolitic script was replaced by the simpler Cyrillic alphabet, more directly based on Greek. During the next hundred years the schools of Ohrid and Preslav produced a sizeable library of religious and secular books, most of them translations or adaptations from the Greek, but including some original works, such as the first grammar of Old Church Slavonic, and an apologia for the Slavonic letters. This literary movement proved to be of even greater importance than the vernacular culture of Anglo-Saxon Northumbria, with which it has been compared: for, by making Byzantine sacred and secular literature accessible to the Slavs, it fostered for many centuries the cultural life of the peoples of eastern Europe.

There is no doubt that the Cyrillo-Methodian vernacular tradition was a prime factor in the rapid progress of Christianity in Bulgaria. A sign of this progress was a remarkably vigorous growth of monasticism. The reign of the Tsar Peter (927-69) witnessed a veritable proliferation of Bulgarian monasteries, particularly in Macedonia. The thirst for sanctity and the ascetic life was expressed by such men as St John of Rila (d. 946), who lived for many years as a hermit in a hollow oak and then in a cave in the Rila mountains, and who became the patron saint of Bulgaria. Yet the rapidity of this growth of monasticism was a source of its weakness. By the middle of the tenth century, if not before, the impermanent nature of many of these monasteries, the frequently ephemeral nature of monastic vows, and the fairly widespread decline of religious discipline, were causing many monks either to relapse into worldliness, or to become homeless vagabonds and a prey to heterodox teachings. Moreover, the Cyrillo-Methodian heritage, with its characteristic blend of Byzantine and Slav traditions, was being obscured and distorted. Symeon's lengthy wars against the Byzantine empire, which brought Bulgaria close to economic exhaustion and left an aftermath of bitter anti-Byzantine feeling in the country, were followed by a wholesale introduction of Byzantine customs and institutions which accentuated the social and economic rift between the ruling classes and an increasingly impoverished and restless peasantry. These two factors – the critical condition of monasticism and the disaffection of a large section of the peasantry – contributed to the rise of Bogomilism, the most important heretical movement in the medieval history of the Balkans.

The Bogomil sect was founded by a Bulgarian priest of that name, some time between 927 and 969. Its teachings combined a neo-Manichaean form of dualism imported into the Balkans from the Near East (mainly by the Paulicians of Armenia and Asia Minor) with an ' evangelical ', anti-hierarchical and anti-sacramental form of Christianity, and with an attitude of revolt against the authorities of church and state. The central doctrine of the Bogomils was that the visible, material world was created by the devil. This led them to deny the incarnation and the entire Christian conception of matter as a vehicle for grace, to reject baptism and the eucharist, and to spurn the order of priesthood and the visible organisation of the church. Their moral teaching, which was as consistently dualistic as that of the primitive Manichaeans, drew some of its inspiration from heretical tendencies latent in tenth-century Bulgarian monasticism: they condemned those functions of man which bring him into close contact with matter, especially marriage, the eating of meat and the drinking of wine. Though it is doubtful whether the same degree of continence was enforced on all members of the sect, the moral austerity of the Bogomils was, until the fourteenth century, recognised by their fiercest opponents; and it is with some justification that they have been described as the greatest puritans of the middle ages. The Bulgarian priest Cosmas, writing c. 972, accuses them also of practising civil disobedience: ' they teach their own people not to obey their masters, they revile the wealthy, hate the elders, ridicule those in authority, reproach the nobles, regard as vile in the sight of God those who serve the monarch, and forbid every serf to work for his lord '. [5] No doubt this and other features of Bogomilism underwent some change when the movement, in the course of the next few centuries, spread over the entire Balkan peninsula, penetrated into the

5. H.-C. Puech and A. Vaillant, *Le traité contre les Bogomiles de Cosmas le prêtre*, Paris 1945, 86.

Byzantine empire, and contributed to the rise of the Cathar or Albigensian heresy in Italy and southern France. At least in its early phases Bogomilism was primarily a peasant movement, directing into heterodox channels the religious and social aspirations of a large and dissatisfied section of the community. Its recorded history in the Balkans did not survive the Turkish conquest.

The independence of the Bulgarian church, whose head had been accorded patriarchal status by the Byzantine authorities in 927, was ended by the Byzantine conquest of Bulgaria in the late tenth and early eleventh century. From 1018 to 1187 Bulgaria was a Byzantine province. During this period the primates of Bulgaria, the archbishops of Ohrid, though autonomous in theory were controlled fairly closely by the authorities of Constantinople. Some historians have argued that a determined attempt was made by the Byzantine masters of the country to eradicate the Cyrillo-Methodian tradition and to impose the Greek language in the liturgy of the Bulgarian church. No clear evidence on this point is provided by the sources. If this policy was ever attempted, it certainly failed. Yet, to judge from the contempt with which the Greek archbishop of Ohrid, Theophylact, who held office between 1090 and about 1108, referred to his flock in his letters to Constantinople, [6] the Byzantine clergy who in this period controlled the affairs of the Bulgarian church cannot have felt much sympathy for its cultural traditions.

In 1187, after a successful revolt against Byzantium, Bulgaria regained its national independence and in the thirteenth century became once more, as it had been in the ninth and early tenth centuries, one of the great powers of Europe. Its ruler Kalojan (1197-1207), seeking legal recognition for his realm, turned for support to Rome. This prompted Innocent III to send a letter to Kalojan (1199) which inaugurated a correspondence between the pope and the Bulgarian sovereign which continued for five years. Kalojan, shrewdly observing the parlous state of the Byzantine empire, whose capital was invested (1203) and then sacked (1204) by the forces of the fourth crusade, expressed his willingness to subject his country to papal jurisdiction if Innocent III would agree to recognise the imperial title he had assumed and to promote the self-appointed archbishop of Trnovo (Bulgaria's new capital) to patriarchal rank. The pope, who saw clearly that Kalojan was pursuing the policy, inaugurated in the ninth century by his predecessor Boris, of playing off Byzantium against Rome for the greater advantage of Bulgaria, was determined to establish his authority over the country while making as few concessions as possible to the ambitions of its ruler and to his desire for ecclesiastical autonomy. The final results of these diplomatic exchanges in which, to judge from the

6. PG CXXVI, col. 308-557: see in particular col. 308, 309, 444.

extant correspondence [7] between the two parties, not a single point of doctrine or ritual was raised, were the coronation of Kalojan as king (though not as emperor) by a papal legate and the recognition by the pope of the Bulgarian archbishop as primate (though not as patriarch) of Bulgaria (November 1204). In exchange the Bulgarian ruler acknowledged the papal supremacy.

A union based on political expediency and doctrinal equivocation had little chance of survival. Bulgarian culture remained basically Byzantine; Kalojan, with cool disregard for constitutional niceties, continued to style himself emperor (tsar) and to call his primate Patriarch; and, to the despair of the pope, he turned against the new Latin masters of Constantinople and inflicted a heavy defeat on them in 1205. Henceforth relations between Bulgaria and Rome went from bad to worse. John Asen II (1218-41), the most outstanding of the rulers of the ' second Bulgarian empire ', put an end to his country's subordination to the Roman church. In 1235 the Byzantine authorities in Nicea recognised the autocephalous status of the Bulgarian patriarchate of Trnovo, subject only to its nominal recognition of the primacy of the Byzantine patriarch.

In the middle of the fourteenth century a notable revival of religious writing and art on the one hand, and of contemplative monasticism on the other, took place in Bulgaria under a renewed and powerful influence of Byzantine culture. Both movements reached their peak in the reign of the Bulgarian tsar John Alexander (1331-71), and continued until 1393 under the guidance of the Bulgarian patriarch Euthymius. In Trnovo, the capital, a school of literature developed under royal patronage, whose output included the translation into Church Slavonic of Byzantine historical, hagiographical and liturgical works. Bulgarian monasticism flourished anew, under the impulse of the hesychast movement which in the fourteenth century spread throughout eastern Europe. [8] Alongside the famed Bulgarian monasteries founded in the tenth and eleventh centuries – Rila in the mountains south of Sofia, Bachkovo in the Rhodopes and Zographov on Mount Athos – new monastic foundations became influential centres of hesychast spirituality. Chief of these were the hermitage of Paroria in the Strandja Mountains to the north of Adrianople, and Kilifarevo near Trnovo. The former was founded by the great hesychast master, St Gregory of Sinai, and extended its influence to Constantinople, Serbia and the lands north of the Danube. The latter, founded c. 1350 by Gregory's disciple, St Theodosius of Trnovo, also acquired an interna-

---

7. The correspondence between Innocent III on the one hand, and Kalojan and the Archbishop of Bulgaria on the other, is printed in PL CCXIV, col. 825, 1112-18, and PL CCXV col. 155-8, 277-96, 551-4, 705-6, 1162.
8. See pp. 357-8.

tional importance. This last flowering of medieval Bulgarian literature and monasticism came to an end in 1393, when Trnovo fell to the Turks, and the country became a province of the Ottoman empire. The patriarchate was suppressed, and the Bulgarian church was directly subordinated to the see of Constantinople.

Relations were fairly close in the fourteenth century between the Bulgarian monasteries and the Rumanian principalities north of the Danube. The origins of Christianity among the Rumanians are obscure; there is no doubt, however, that Byzantine Christianity and the Slavonic liturgy and letters spread from Bulgaria to the lands between the lower Danube and the Carpathians in the early middle ages. The foundation in the fourteenth century of the independent principalities of Wallachia and Moldavia led to the establishment, under Byzantine jurisdiction, of the metropolitanates of ' Ungro-Wallachia ' at Argeș (1359) and of ' Moldo-Wallachia ' at Suceava (1401). Church Slavonic was to remain the language of the Rumanian church until the seventeenth century.

4. THE SERBIAN CHURCH

Although the national Orthodox church of Serbia was only founded in the early thirteenth century, the Serbs were no late-comers to Christianity. Indeed the opposite is true, for we know that they were converted – albeit impermanently – by missionaries sent from Rome at the request of the emperor Heraclius. [9] More definite evidence comes from the ninth century, when the Serbs were drawn into the Byzantine orbit by the active Balkan policy of the emperor Basil I and, between 867 and 874, accepted Greek Christianity. Bishoprics were then established in Belgrade and Ras (near present-day Novi Pazar). On the Dalmatian coast, Byzantine influence successfully competed against Frankish hegemony until 879, when the Croat church finally acknowledged papal authority. For the next two centuries the Serbs were powerfully attracted to Rome, whose prestige spread through the Latin cities on the Adriatic coast. A Serbian ruler of the maritime province of Zeta (present-day Montenegro) acknowledged the ecclesiastical sovereignty of Pope Gregory VII. Both he and his successor received royal titles from Rome. By the twelfth century, however, the influence of Byzantine Christianity in Serbia began to revive. In the inland district of Raška, the future nucleus of the medieval Serbian kingdom, it had always been strong, and the proximity of Ohrid and other cultural centres of Macedonia had, since the late ninth century, brought into this area the Slavonic liturgy fostered by the disciples of Cyril and Methodius.

It was in the late twelfth and the early thirteenth century that the

9. See p. 18.

religious and cultural destiny of the Serbian nation which, like Bulgaria in the ninth century and Russia in the tenth, had stood at the crossroads between East and West, between Byzantium and Rome, was decided for all time. This, essentially, was the work of three men who between them laid the foundations of their country's medieval greatness: Stephen Nemanja, the founder of the medieval Serbian state, and his two sons Stephen and Sava. Nemanja, though he was baptised by a Latin priest, was a convinced and active member of the eastern church. In 1196 he abdicated in favour of his son Stephen, and retired as a monk first to the monastery of Studenica, his own foundation, and later to Mount Athos. There, on the Holy Mountain, his younger son Sava had founded the Serbian monastery of Khilandar, which was soon to become one of the foremost centres of Serbian monastic culture. At Khilandar father and son planned the future of Serbian Christianity within the framework of the eastern church. Meanwhile the new Serbian ruler, Nemanja's other son Stephen, pursued the traditional policy of a delicately poised balance between Byzantium and Rome. The establishment in 1204 of the Latin empire of Constantinople as a result of the fourth crusade radically altered the balance of power in south-eastern Europe and strengthened for a while the pro-Roman party in Serbia. Stephen accordingly exchanged his first wife, a Byzantine princess, for the grand-daughter of the all-powerful Doge of Venice, promised spiritual fidelity to Innocent III, and in 1217 was crowned king by a papal legate.

But the gravitation of Serbia to the Greek church was too powerful to be long delayed by these tactful manoeuvres. Two years after Stephen's coronation, Sava travelled from Mount Athos to Nicea, where the exiled Byzantine authorities had started to rebuild the shattered structure of the Greek empire. There, in 1219, after reaching agreement with the emperor Theodore Lascaris, he was consecrated autocephalous archbishop of Serbia by the patriarch of Nicea. It is probable that Sava's journey had the approval of his brother, the Serbian king. Sava then returned home to organise his new national church. The Serbian church became thenceforth autocephalous, being granted the right to elect and consecrate its own archbishop; at the same time a nominal control was retained by the Byzantine authorities, the Serbian church having the obligation to commemorate liturgically the Byzantine patriarch in the first place, before the Serbian archbishop. Thus does the foundation of the national church of Serbia provide another example of a compromise between Byzantine hegemony and Slav independence, achieved to the mutual advantage of both.

By rooting his church in eastern Christendom, in the monastic tradition of Mount Athos, and in the national life of his native land, St Sava imprinted on medieval Serbian Christianity some of its most characteristic and abiding features. The close association between the Serbian church and the descendants of Nemanja, who ruled over their country until 1371, found visible expression in the many monasteries founded and endowed by the Serbian kings. The architecture and wall-paintings of their churches – Studenica, Žiča, Mileševa, Sopoćani, Gračanica and Dečani are world-famous examples – rank high among the products of east Christian art. The archiepiscopal see, first established in Žiča in the valley of the Ibar, was c. 1233 transferred to Peć. More than one Serbian ruler of the thirteenth and fourteenth centuries showed leanings to, or at least sympathy for, the Roman church. Yet anti-Roman feeling seems to have increased in Serbia after the Council of Lyons (1274), at which the pope, in agreement with the emperor Michael VIII, proved only too ready to suppress the autonomy of the Serbian and Bulgarian churches. And in an official document of the Serbian realm, issued in 1354 – the legal code of Stephen Dušan – Roman Catholicism was described as the ' Latin heresy '.

In the reign of Stephen Dušan (1331-55) Serbia became the most powerful state in the Balkans: Macedonia, Albania, Epirus were wrested from the Byzantine empire, and Dušan, in pursuance of his dream of establishing a new Serbo-Greek empire on the ruins of Byzantium, assumed the imperial title (1345), styling himself emperor of the Serbs and Greeks. To confer validity on this title he needed a legitimate coronation; according to current Byzantine notions no one but a patriarch could crown an emperor; the patriarch of Constantinople could not but regard his assumption of imperial rank as an act of gross usurpation: so Dušan on his own authority promoted his primate, the archbishop of Peć, to the rank of patriarch. A few days later, at Skopje, the Serbian patriarch crowned him emperor (1346). The Byzantine authorities reacted vigorously to what was, from their point of view, an ecclesiastical and political revolt. In 1350 Callistus, patriarch of Constantinople, excommunicated Dušan and the whole Serbian church. The ensuing schism between the Byzantine and the Serbian churches was only terminated in 1375, when Prince Lazar, ruler of the northern part of the now disintegrating Serbian realm, faced with the threatening advance of the Turks in the Balkans, persuaded the ecumenical patriarch to revoke the anathemas laid upon the Serbian church and nation, and to recognise the Serbian patriarchate.

However, this attempt to restore in the face of the Turkish menace a measure of unity to the Christian peoples of the Balkans came too late. In 1389 the Serbian armies were defeated by the Turks at the battle of Kosovo, whose story, soon distilled into legend and poetry, was to nurture so powerfully the Christian and the heroic traditions of the Serbian people.

For a further seventy years a diminished principality survived in the northern part of the country. There medieval Serbian art and literature flourished for the last time. The ' despots ' of northern Serbia were as zealous in building and endowing monasteries as their royal predecessors had been. The wall-paintings in the churches of Ravanica (1381) and Manasija (1406-18) illustrate the attempt by the Christian artists of Serbia, on the eve of the final Turkish conquest (which came in 1459), to transmute the contrasts of a troubled existence into a vision of spiritual beauty.

5. THE RUSSIAN CHURCH

The conversion of Russia was initiated in that same remarkable decade in the history of Byzantine missions – the sixties of the ninth century – which witnessed the embassy of Cyril and Methodius to Moravia and the baptism of Boris of Bulgaria. Like the latter event, it was precipitated by an incident that spelled danger to the security of the Byzantine empire. In 860 Constantinople was attacked by a fleet of Viking ships: the assault, which was repelled with considerable difficulty, was launched by the Swedish overlords of the eastern Slavs who, under the name of *Rhos*, were emerging as the dominant power along the water road linking the Baltic with the Black Sea. The Byzantine authorities were quick to realise how much the empire's security depended on these Russian barbarians being brought as quickly as possible under the civilising influence of east Rome. They lost no time in trying to convert the Russians to Christianity. And in 867 the patriarch Photius was able to announce that the Russians, a nation formerly notorious for its bloodthirsty savagery, had now accepted Christianity and were living under the spiritual authority of a Byzantine bishop, as ' subjects and friends ' of the empire. Here again, as in the case of Bulgaria's conversion, it is worth noting that in the eyes of the east Romans the acceptance of Byzantine Christianity by a barbarian nation subordinated this nation to the emperor's political sovereignty. A few years later the Russians accepted an archbishop from the patriarch Ignatius.

This is practically all we can glean from the scanty remarks of the Byzantine sources about what historians have called ' the first conversion of the Russians '. We do not know the fate of this first Byzantine diocese in Russia; it was doubtless centred in Kiev, the capital of the realm. Most probably it was engulfed by the pagan reaction which swept over Russia in the last decades of the ninth century. Yet an almost continuous chain of evidence points to the existence of a Christian community in Kiev from the early years of the tenth century to Russia's final conversion in the reign of Vladimir. In 957 Princess Olga, regent of the realm, went on a mission of peace to Constantinople; there, amid splendid court receptions, she was

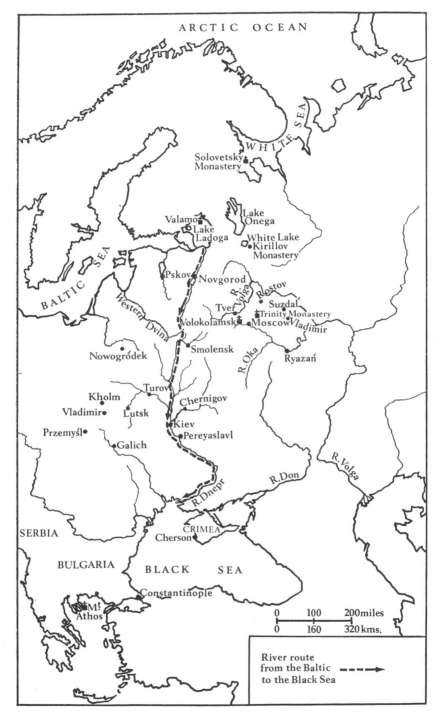

ARCTIC OCEAN

WHITE SEA

Solovetsky
Monastery

Lake
Onega

Valamo
Lake
Ladoga

White Lake
Kirillov
Monastery

BALTIC SEA

Pskov
Novgorod

R. Volga

Rostov

Western Dvina

Tver
Suzdal
Trinity Monastery
Volokolamsk
Moscow
Vladimir

Smolensk

Nowogródek

R. Oka

Ryazań

Turov

Kholm

Chernigov

Vladimir
Lutsk

Kiev
Pereyaslavl

Przemyśl

Galich

R. Dnepr

R. Don

R. Volga

SERBIA

CRIMEA
Cherson

BULGARIA

BLACK SEA

Constantinople

Mᵗ
Athos

| 0 | 100 | 200 miles |
| 0 | 160 | 320 kms. |

River route
from the Baltic
to the Black Sea

12.   The Russian Church

baptised by the Byzantine patriarch. And though Olga was unwilling or unable to impose her religion on her subjects at large, and two years later made an abortive attempt to obtain a German bishop from Otto I, her relations with the empire paved the way for the triumph of Byzantine Christianity in the reign of her grandson Vladimir.

The circumstances of Vladimir's conversion are still in several respects obscure. This is due partly to the fact that contemporary Byzantine sources are totally silent on the matter, and partly to the wide discrepancies between our two principal authorities, *The Russian Primary Chronicle* and the Arab historian Yahya of Antioch. The former emphasises, and no doubt rightly, the religious motives of the conversion, but probably embroiders on reality in making the Russian ruler opt for Byzantine Christianity mainly because of what his envoys told him of the transcendent beauty of the liturgy in the church of St Sophia in Constantinople. [10] The Arab account relates Vladimir's baptism to the political negotiations between Byzantium and Russia in 988 – the Russian ruler agreeing to help the emperor Basil II against the latter's rival, the rebellious general Bardas Phocas, and to accept Christianity in exchange for the hand of the emperor's sister. [11] These negotiations are well attested, and there seems no valid reason to deny that Vladimir's baptism in 988 or 989, followed shortly by that of the ruling classes of his realm, was, like the conversion of Boris of Bulgaria, an act both of faith and of statesmanship.

The obscurity surrounding several aspects of Vladimir's conversion continues to hang over the first fifty years in the history of the church he established. Under whose authority was it then placed? In the absence of direct and contemporary evidence, controversy has raged, and some scholars have argued that the Russian church was between 988 and 1039 dependent on the Bulgarian church, subject to Rome, or autocephalous. In the opinion of the present writer, however, circumstantial evidence strongly suggests that the Russian church was from the beginning directly subordinated to the Byzantine patriarchate. This evidence includes the statement of Yahya of Antioch that the emperor Basil II sent Vladimir ' metropolitans and bishops ' who baptised him and his people; the rôle played by the Greek clergy of the Crimea in the Christianisation of Russia; the building of Vladimir's first stone church in Kiev by Byzantine architects; his marriage with the emperor's sister; and his spiritual adoption by the emperor, symbolised by his assumption at baptism of the name Basil.

10. *The Russian Primary Chronicle*, transl. S. H. Cross and O. P. Sherbowitz-Wetzor, Cambridge, Mass. 1953, 96-116.
11. *Histoire de Yahya-Ibn-Sa'ïd d'Antioche*, ed. and trans. I. Kratchkovsky and A. Vasiliev, Patrologia Orientalis 23, 3 (1932), 423.

From 1039 until 1448 the Russian church, headed by the metropolitans of Kiev (who after 1328 resided in Moscow), was a metropolitan province of the Byzantine patriarchate. Among the main tasks that faced the Russian clergy in the eleventh and twelfth centuries were the establishment of dioceses in the principal cities of the land and the struggle against old Slavonic paganism which, though outlawed by Vladimir, still possessed powers of resistance and popular appeal. In Russia as in the Balkan Slavonic lands, Christianity was imposed from above and remained, for at least a century, primarily the religion of the ruling classes. It was not perhaps until the fifteenth century that the conversion of the countryside was virtually complete, and Christianity succeeded to any marked extent in remoulding the peasant culture. Among the educated classes the church proved a powerful and constantly renewed channel for the spread of Byzantine civilisation. Through the Slavonic translation of the Greek *Nomocanon* – a digest of canon law and of imperial ordinances – the Russians were, like the Bulgarians and the Serbs, introduced to the two basic principles of Byzantine political philosophy: the theory of the ' symphonia ' relationship between Church and State, and the doctrine of the universal Christian empire, whose centre was Constantinople.[12] The former gave an ideological foundation to the close collaboration between the medieval Russian church and the princes of the land; the latter, though it was temporarily and uncharacteristically rejected by one Russian ruler in the late fourteenth century, endowed the Byzantine emperor in the eyes of the Russians with the authority of a natural and divinely appointed master of the Christian commonwealth, the supreme lawgiver of Christendom, whose dominion was believed to extend, at least in a spiritual and ' metapolitical ' sense, over all Christian rulers and peoples. The art of Byzantium, which bore remarkable fruits on Russian soil, both in the early, Kievan, period and again during the ' Palaeologian renaissance ' of the fourteenth and fifteenth centuries, and which as early as the eleventh century began to be modified by local schools of architecture and painting, served to propagate in Russia the theological and liturgical tradition of the eastern church. The impact of the Byzantine artistic tradition on medieval Russia can still be clearly perceived in the decoration of the church of St Sophia in Kiev, whose foundation stone was laid in 1037: its mosaics with their Greek inscriptions, arranged according to a strict hierarchical pattern and dominated by the figures of Christ Pantokrator in the dome and of the Mother of God in the apse, are among the more notable examples of mid-Byzantine art; while the curious frescoes on the tower stairs, which represent the intricate pageant of the Byzantine court, its

12. See F. Dvornik, *Byzantine Political Ideas in Kievan Russia:* Dumbarton Oaks Papers 9-10 (1956), 73-121.

feasts, chariot races and acrobats, are striking evidence of the spell cast upon the Russians by the distant splendours of Constantinople, ' the city of world's desire '. Literature as well as law and art was powerfully influenced by Byzantine Christianity. Like the Bulgarians and the Serbs, the Russians were able to draw at the dawn of their Christian history on the resources of the Cyrillo-Methodian vernacular tradition. The Slavonic translations of Cyril and Methodius and of their disciples were first brought to Russia in the tenth century, mainly, it seems, from Bulgaria. A substantial library of works, both religious and secular, translated from the Greek was collected in Kiev, to which Russian scholars began, espe- cially in the reign of Vladimir's son Yaroslav (1019-54) to add their own translations. In the same eleventh century the Russian educated *élite* began to produce in Old Church Slavonic (which gradually blended with the local vernacular speech) original works of literature, some of which– notably the *Primary Chronicle*, the *Sermon on Law and Grace* by Hilarion, metropolitan of Kiev, and the *Lives* of the early Russian saints (Boris, Gleb, and Theodosius) – rank high in the history of their medieval culture. This Christian culture of early medieval Russia was far from narrow or exclusive. It grew up under the aegis of Byzantium and in close contact with central and western Europe, with which before the Mongol conquest of the thirteenth century Russia was linked by trade and diplomacy and also by a consciousness of belonging to one world of Christendom.

The cosmopolitan character of early Russian culture was undermined during the centuries of Mongol rule (1237-1480). Relations with Byzan- tium continued, it is true, and even revived in the fourteenth century. But the struggle for national survival, of which the rising principality of Moscow was the spearhead, circumscribed the religious and cultural horizon of the Russians. The Russian church received favoured treatment under Mongol domination, and even obtained immunity from taxation in 1270. Its leaders, and notably the native metropolitans St Peter (1308-26) and St Alexius (1354-78), consistently supported the Muscovite princes in their bid for power and in their growing resistance to the Mongols. The Russian attitude to the Roman church, which in the Kievan period had, on the whole, been not unfriendly, now hardened into open hostility. A turning point in Russia's relations with western Christendom was reached in the 1240s, when the Prince of Novgorod, St Alexander Nevsky, repulsed the attacks of the Swedes and of the Livonian and Teutonic Knights against the Russian Baltic borderlands.

It was in the field of monasticism that the medieval Russian church made its most lasting and characteristic contribution to the history of eastern Christianity. At the dawn of its history, in the late tenth and the early eleventh century, Russian monasticism was able through its close contacts with Mount Athos and Constantinople and through the Slavonic translations of classic ascetical writings – notably the *Historia Monachorum*, the *Lausiac History* of Palladius, the *Pratum Spirituale* of John Moschus, and the *Vitae* of Cyril of Scythopolis – to draw the principles of its organisation from three separate streams of Byzantine asceticism: the solitary, the semi-eremitical, and the coenobitic types of life. Each of them made its individual contribution to the history of Russian monasticism. The choice offered by these alternatives was seldom an easy one: indeed the latent tension between them was never resolved in medieval Russia, any more than it was in eastern monasticism as a whole.

Of the seventy or so monasteries attested in Russia before the thirteenth century, some two-thirds were princely houses, patterned on the numerous Byzantine monasteries created by emperors and wealthy individuals in the hope of ensuring for themselves a place of burial and perpetual prayer for the repose of their souls. But the greatest of all monasteries in early medieval Russia, the Kiev Monastery of the Caves, had no secular founder, no original patron, and no initial endowments. It arose in the first half of the eleventh century when a Russian by the name of Anthony, who had been professed a monk on Mount Athos, returned home to establish a hermitage on a hill outside Kiev. Mount Athos, from which the Monastery of the Caves derived its original form and inspiration, was to remain during the whole of the middle ages a school of Russian spirituality and a meeting-place for Slavonic and Byzantine culture. The next stage in the history of the monastery is associated with another Russian, Theodosius, who was its abbot from *c.* 1062 to 1074. He imported the Studite Rule from Constantinople and established the coenobitic way of life. Thus did the organised pattern of a monastic community, living, praying, and working together under the supervision of an abbot, supplant in the monastery, at least for a time, the eremitical and more individualistic ideal of St Anthony. The personality of St Theodosius, marked by a deep and unassuming humility and by the virtues of moderation and ' discretion ' so valued by many masters of the spiritual life, had a powerful impact on the subsequent development of Russian monasticism.

After the crippling blow of the Mongol invasion, monasticism began to revive in Russia in the fourteenth century. But the new monasteries of the fourteenth and the fifteenth centuries were, for the most part, very different from the eleventh-and twelfth-century houses. These were nearly always situated in towns, or in their immediate vicinity; most of the Russian monasteries founded in the late middle ages were, by contrast, built far from human habitation. Their founders, seeking solitude and silence, were drawn to the vast forests that stretched north of Moscow towards the White Sea and the Arctic Ocean. The flight ' into the desert ' began on a large scale in the second quarter of the fourteenth century. The leading figure in this movement, St Sergius of Radonezh, founded in the middle of the century in the forests north of Moscow the celebrated coenobitic monastery of the Holy Trinity. Sergius, whose spiritual features bear a fairly close resemblance to those of Theodosius, was to become the most widely revered of all Russian saints. From him and from his monastery stem the two main types of late medieval Russian monasticism: the highly organised and disciplined communities, with an emphasis on liturgical observance and social service; and the contemplative hermitages of the type known in the Greek world as the *lavra* and in Russia as the *skit*, whose mystical and ascetic ideals were influenced by the tradition of Byzantine hesychasm. In the second half of the fifteenth century the leading representatives of these two currents of Russian monasticism were, respectively, St Joseph of Volokolamsk and St Nil of Sora.

The last decades in the history of the medieval Russian church were dominated by the problem of ecclesiastical self-determination. Muscovy's rejection of the Council of Florence immediately followed the return from Italy in 1441 of Isidore, the Greek Metropolitan of All Russia, who had signed the Decree of Union and had as a result been appointed cardinal and papal legate. Isidore was, by order of the grand Prince Basil II, deposed and imprisoned. In the same year he escaped abroad. After a period of embarrassed hesitation, during which the Muscovites' unwillingness to remain under the spiritual jurisdiction of a unionist patriarch conflicted with their reluctance to sever the age-long canonical dependence of the Russian church on the see of Constantinople, a council of Russian bishops, convoked by Basil II in Moscow, elected Bishop Ioan of Ryazan' as Metropolitan of All Russia (1448) without Byzantine permission. Even then, however, the Muscovite authorities professed obedience to the mother church of Constantinople, ' except for the present recently-appeared disagreements '. This ambiguous situation was brought to an end by the fall of Constantinople to the Turks (29 May 1453) and by the consequent collapse of the Union of Florence. Seeing that the Greek church was now in the power of a Moslem ruler who conferred investiture upon its patriarch, the Russian church retained the autonomous status it had acquired *de facto* in 1448, a status which, by common consent of the other Orthodox churches, was in 1589 converted to that of an auto-cephalous patriarchate.

$$\boxed{26}$$

ROME AND CONSTANTINOPLE (II)

I. THE WESTERN VIEW, 1204-1439

THE crusaders had deviated to Constantinople against the express directions of Innocent III and he was alarmed to hear of their first capture of the city (1203). The nominal purpose of this was the enthronement of the exiled pretender Alexius IV, Angelus, which duly took place, but before the pope or the European monarchs could adjust themselves to this situation, which Alexius had promised would issue in a union between East and West, the new emperor had been murdered in a revolt and one of the conspirators had been enthroned in his place. This provoked another assault upon the city (1204), this time followed by pillage, sacrilege, destruction and crime of every kind, and the victors placed Baldwin of Flanders upon the imperial throne, thus inaugurating a Latin empire. Nevertheless a Greek emperor existed, Theodore Lascaris, son-in-law of Alexius III, and Nicea, his capital, held out against the invaders, as did also Trebizond and Epirus. The crusaders had scattered to seize the available fragments of the eastern empire, and Macedonia, Thessaly, Greece and the isles were soon occupied by adventurers engaged in consolidating their gains.

Baldwin was quick to report his accession and his loyalty to the pope, and Innocent, who had heard nothing of the sack of the city, received the news with enthusiasm, expecting a speedy return of the Greek church to the Roman obedience. Shocked as he was when he heard of the barbarous and disgraceful behaviour of his crusaders he was by nature resilient, as he was also in outlook a man of his age, and the prospect of a Latin eastern empire seemed to him a divinely ordained and successful outcome of his plans. That his crusade had got out of hand and, after attacking and destroying a great and highly civilised Christian community and its dynasty, had petered out in the occupation by western chieftains of regions lately held by the Byzantine emperor, was a sinister portent of which he seems not to have seen the significance. The Latin empire, after its first shocks, fared better than its original banditry deserved, and the Latin patriarch and the Balkan countries in general were an addition to the papal sphere of influence. Innocent III was fully occupied in protecting the church and its property from further looting and confiscations. The Orthodox church was not, however, extinct, and the patriarch at Nicea with the emperor had more real power and significance than had the Latins in Constantinople. Innocent might have been well advised to treat for some kind of understanding with the real church of the East; instead he tried to bind the Latin patriarchate and the lesser bishops firmly to Rome, though he showed his statesmanlike qualities by the moderation of his liturgical and doctrinal demands. He was, however, in common with almost all his contemporaries, unwilling to accept any treaty with the Greeks unless it was preceded by unconditional surrender on the controversial points of doctrine and discipline, and unless the Greeks accepted the Latin empire as a *fait accompli*. These conditions were wholly unacceptable to the mass of educated Greek Christians, and no further advance towards union could be made.

Honorius III and Gregory IX continued the policy of Innocent III in giving their support to the Latin empire as an essential factor in any future crusade, and in a hostile attitude towards the Greek emperor at Nicea. The Greeks for their part looked forward to the expulsion of the Latins and held fast to their own traditions. Nevertheless political considerations turned the Greeks toward negotiation with Rome, while Innocent IV, a wiser statesman than his two predecessors, saw that there was no future for the Latin empire. Negotiations were opened for reunion and Innocent was willing to go further than any medieval pope before or after in his concessions; the two churches were to have equal rights in Constantinople and a general council was to be held in the East. When all seemed to be in train for a settlement Innocent IV died. A few years later Michael Palaeologus, the first of a great new dynasty, seized power in Nicea (1259) and recaptured Constantinople (1261). The new emperor, anxious to strengthen his position, made persistent attempts to reopen negotiations with Rome which were ultimately reciprocated by Urban IV; but these, and indeed all subsequent exchanges between East and West, were political rather than religious in motive and concluded between the parties without reference to the body of opinion of the Orthodox church, which remained steadfastly opposed to Latin domination and formal or ritual concessions.

The atmosphere of political calculation was changed on the Latin side by the advent of Gregory X (1271-6), the most spiritually-minded pope of the thirteenth century (if Celestine V is left out of the reckoning), whose pontificate has some resemblances to that of the late Pope John XXIII. Gregory desired reform, reunion and the restoration of Christian control in Palestine, and the second of these aims seemed likely to assist the attainment of the third. With this programme in mind he convoked the second Council of Lyons for 1274. His hopes for union were shared by Michael VIII Palaeologus, though with political considerations in the forefront of his designs. To him papal protection appeared the only insurance against the ambitious designs of Charles of Anjou, king of Naples. In the months that followed the latter worked against the papal plans, while the emperor had to use force to silence his own clergy. In the event, he was represented at Lyons only by the ex-patriarch of Constantinople and one other prelate who duly promised obedience to the pope in their own and the emperor's name and who joined in the chant of *Filioque* in the creed. It was an empty show. The emperor had fended off Charles of Anjou, but when Gregory X died two years later his spiritual approach was not continued. The king of Naples regained his influence over papal policy, and the forces of Orthodoxy reasserted their protests in Constantinople. Recriminations on both sides occurred and after seven years the union ended with a repudiation by Andronicus II and with the excommunication of the emperor by Martin IV. The various attempts of eastern emperors, hard pressed by political fortunes, to renew relations with Rome during the fourteenth century, belong to Byzantine rather than to papal history. They became more urgent in the fifteenth century and were entertained seriously by the Council of Basle and still more eagerly by Eugenius IV who used the demands of the Greeks for a convenient rendezvous in Italy as an excuse for transferring the council to Ferrara and later to Florence with the hope, which was in fact justified, of winning new prestige to the restored papacy by achieving the union of the churches, which was desired more earnestly in the West than ever before. The emperor John VIII himself journeyed to Florence, and a sizeable body of Byzantine bishops and theologians took part in a series of set debates on the theological, ritualistic and disciplinary points at issue. They sat as Fathers of the council on an equality with the Latins, and the principal topic of discussion was the *Filioque* clause. With the new learning to help them the western scholars and divines made a good showing in patristic and scholastic controversy and the Byzantines were overpowered both by political pressure and by the expertise of the westerners in the scholastic disciplines with which they were familiar. A few even, including Bessarion, later cardinal, were sincerely convinced of the justice of Catholic claims. Ultimately on 6 July 1439 the bull of union was signed by all the Byzantine delegates present with the exception of Marcus Eugenicus. For the Greeks this was not a matter of submission to Rome, but an agreement that the western opinion was not heresy. The union was denounced at once by the monks and most of the population of Constantinople and its environs and many of the signatories recanted. Though the emperor remained firm the tragic events of the next fifteen years rendered the union void. An agreement with the Armenian church a few months later was equally ineffective, but fairly large numbers of eastern Christians in the Ukraine, Transylvania and elsewhere remained in union with Rome and from them descend several of the Uniate churches still in existence.

2. THE EASTERN VIEW. SCHISM BETWEEN EASTERN AND WESTERN CHRISTENDOM

The precise significance of the events of 1054 has been variously assessed by historians. Perhaps their importance lies primarily in the interpretation placed on them by post-twelfth-century writers who believed that the clash between Cerularius and the papacy marked the definitive break between the eastern and the western churches. It is difficult today to subscribe to this view. By applying a purely formal criterion, it could be argued that the schism between the Byzantine and the Roman churches began when the names of the popes ceased to be included in the diptychs of the church of Constantinople; this occurred in 1009. Yet in 1089 a synod of the church of Constantinople declared that this omission was due to a careless mistake. More significant is the fact that in Antioch, which the crusaders conquered in 1098, two rival ecclesiastical hierarchies, the one Greek, the other Latin, existed side by side from 1100 onwards. Yet if on this reckoning there was henceforth schism in the patriarchate of Antioch, there was none in Jerusalem until *c.* 1188, when the local Orthodox ceased to recognise the Latin patriarch. On neither side did public opinion consider that the events of 1054 marked a definitive schism. It is true that the excommunications of that year were not lifted [1] – though it should be remembered that they were personal, and did not implicate the Byzantine and the

---

[1]. They were lifted on 7 December 1965, by joint decision of Pope Paul VI and the ecumenical patriarch Athenagoras I.

Roman churches as such. It is also true that, largely as a result of the Norman aggression in the Balkans, the commercial imperialism of the Italian maritime cities, and especially the crusades, mutual hostility hardened during the twelfth century. Yet the majority of Christians in East and West, and the more enlightened churchmen on both sides, still believed in the existence of an undivided Christendom. In the closing years of the eleventh century, Theophylact, archbishop of Bulgaria, one of the most distinguished Byzantine scholars of his time, severely criticised his compatriots for slandering the customs of the Latin church. ' I do not think', he wrote, 'that the errors [of the Latins] are numerous, or that any of them can cause a schism '. Even the *Filioque*, the one western tenet of which he strongly disapproved, was, he believed, due ' less to wickedness than to ignorance', [2] resulting from the fact that the Latin language is not rich enough to convey the required subtleties of thought. Equally eirenic voices could still be heard in Latin Christendom. In the early twelfth century St Bruno of Segni, abbot of Monte Cassino, wrote to the Benedictine community of Constantinople: ' We truly hold, and steadfastly believe, that although the customs of the churches are distinct, nevertheless there is one faith, indissolubly united to the head, that is Christ, and he himself is one and remains the same in his body '. [3]

To ascribe an exact beginning to the schism between eastern and western Christendom is, no doubt, impossible. Too many contingent factors – political, economic, cultural – affected their mutual relations at different points in time and space to enable the historian to decide with any confidence when he may begin to treat the history of each of the two halves of Christendom as a self-contained whole. On the level of popular feeling, the crusades, with their legacy of disappointed hopes, misunderstandings and mutual ill-treatment, certainly marked a decisive turning-point. The fourth crusade, which led to the brutal sack of Constantinople and resulted, for more than half a century (1204-61), in the forced latinisation of the Byzantine church and in the partition of the European territories of the empire among the Franks and the Venetians, left an aftermath of bitterness in the Greek church that has still not been exorcised. And yet, however much the folk of Byzantium, disgusted at the desecration of their shrines, their churches and their hallowed city by men who called themselves Christians, may henceforth have hardened their hearts to the West, it may be doubted whether even the treachery and brutality of the Latins in 1204 quite erased from the minds of both the victims and the aggressors the sense of a still united Christendom. The later history of the

2. PG CXXVI, col. 224, 228-29.
3. PL CLXV, col. 1085.

Byzantine church contains many examples of peaceful and mutually beneficial contacts between the eastern and the western traditions.

It may, indeed, be doubted whether these factors – psychological, political, cultural – which contributed so much to the sense of estrangement, and eventually of hostility, between the two halves of Christendom would have led to a breach between them, if they had not been exacerbated and reinforced by doctrinal differences. In the last resort the two churches confronted each other, clashed and separated on two basic issues, the one concerned with Trinitarian theology, the other with ecclesiastical government. The *Filioque* and the claims of the popes to be the ultimate judges of dogmatic truth and to exercise direct and universal jurisdiction throughout the Christian Church remained unacceptable to the Orthodox church of the East. The fact that at the Councils of Lyons and Ferrara-Florence these two Latin doctrines were accepted by the emperor and a handful of Byzantine ecclesiastics only emphasises the truth of this statement and places it in more vivid relief.

3. ATTEMPTS AT REUNION: THE COUNCIL OF LYONS (1274)

The Union of Lyons was, from the Byzantine point of view, due solely to the fact that the emperor Michael VIII wished, through the good offices of the pope, to exert pressure upon Charles of Anjou, king of Sicily and Naples, to persuade him to call off his projected campaign against Byzantium which threatened to restore the defunct Latin empire of Constantinople. It is very likely that by signing the Act of Union the emperor saved his country from this deadly menace. He made no attempt to conceal from his subjects that in so doing he was moved solely by considerations of political expediency. The price he paid at home for his diplomatic triumph was a heavy one: the refusal of the Byzantine church to subscribe to the *Filioque* and to the doctrine of papal supremacy led to violent social unrest, aggravated by state persecution, particularly against the monks. The shortlived Union of Lyons – whose results show how little the emperors of the later middle ages were able to enforce doctrinal solutions upon the Byzantine church – was finally wrecked by the decision of Pope Martin IV to support Charles of Anjou against Michael VIII (1281) and by the Sicilian Vespers, a successful assault upon the French which removed the danger of an Angevin attack on Byzantium (1282). Michael VIII died in the latter year, excommunicated both by the Roman and by the Byzantine churches.

Further attempts to heal the schism were made during the fourteenth century. A relatively small group of Byzantine intellectuals were genuinely attracted to the idea of reunion with Rome, among them the theologian Demetrios Kydones (c. 1324-c. 1397) who translated Aquinas' *Summa*

Theologiae into Greek. But the vast majority of the Byzantine clergy and people remained strongly opposed to a union which would involve recognition of the papal claims and acceptance of the *Filioque;* and the attempts of successive emperors to re-negotiate ecclesiastical union as a price for military assistance from the West came to nothing, despite the growing danger from the Ottoman Turks, who in the mid-fourteenth century began their conquest of the Balkans. The sincerest of these attempts was made by the emperor John V during a journey to Rome in 1369: but his personal conversion to the Latin faith in no way involved his subjects and brought no political advantage to his empire.

4. THE COUNCIL OF FLORENCE (1439)

The last and most thorough effort to resolve the differences between the Roman and the Byzantine churches was made at the Council of Florence. This council, which assembled in Ferrara in January 1438, was transferred to Florence early in 1439, and ended with the proclamation of union on 6 July 1439, was attended by a large Greek delegation, led by the emperor John VIII Palaeologus and the patriarch of Constantinople. The Greeks negotiated from a position of weakness, due in large measure to their desperate need to obtain military aid from the west against the growing threat of the Turks to Constantinople, and to the inadequate funds they possessed to maintain their delegation. Pope Eugenius IV and his theological advisers, led by the able Cardinal Cesarini, insisted on an unqualified acceptance of the Roman position on all controversial questions. Despite these facts, the doctrinal discussions – especially on the *Filioque*, the principal issue – were prolonged and thorough; and, with the notable exception of Mark Eugenicus, metropolitan of Ephesus, the leading theologians of the Byzantine party – above all, Bessarion, metropolitan of Nicea, and Isidore, metropolitan of Kiev and All Russia – showed themselves genuinely anxious to restore unity to the Christian Church. In the end all the Greeks present at the council – except Mark Eugenicus, whose defence of the Byzantine doctrinal positions had been more vigorous than constructive – signed the Act of Union. Thereby they formally accepted, on behalf of the eastern church, the Roman teaching on the *Filioque*, on the pope's supremacy (though the formula defining his power in the Church was, in deference to Greek susceptibilities, phrased with some ambiguity), and on Purgatory; the Greeks, however, were allowed to continue to use leavened bread for the Eucharist.

The Union of Florence proved to be, for the cause of Christian reunion, as defective and impermanent as the Union of Lyons. In the non-Byzantine Orthodox churches – in the patriarchates of Alexandria, Antioch and Jerusalem, in Russia, in Rumania and in Serbia – it was almost immediately rejected. In Byzantium, where the hope of effective military aid from the western powers was slow to die, a minority among the clergy, the intellectuals and the common folk, as well as the two last emperors, John VIII and Constantine XI, continued to support it. But once again imperial authority proved incapable of forcing its will on the church. Most Byzantines considered that their authorities had bartered the purity of the Orthodox faith for doubtful political advantages. Several prelates who signed the decree of union at Florence repudiated their signatures on their return home. It was not until 12 December 1452 that the Union was formally proclaimed in the Church of St Sophia. A little more than five months later Constantinople fell to the armies of Mahomet II, and the Union of Florence died with the Byzantine empire.

5. GROUPS AND PARTIES IN THE LATE BYZANTINE CHURCH

For the ecclesiastical historian the importance of the Council of Florence lies not only in the fact that its discussions and decisions embodied the most determined effort ever made to heal the breach between the eastern and the western churches; by accentuating and polarising the different views that existed in Byzantine society on the question of reunion with Rome, the council was also a significant landmark in the internal history of eastern Christendom. During the last two centuries of Byzantine history four distinct attitudes to this problem are detectable in the Greek Orthodox world. At the two opposite extremes were the doctrinal relativists who held that the problem of reunion was essentially a political one and that the salvation of the empire, if military aid could be obtained from the West, was worth a few theological concessions; and the unenlightened traditionalists, content with repetitious denunciations of the ' Latin Heresy '. The two other groups which comprised most of the leading intellectuals approached the problem in a less emotional and more creative manner. The first of them, known to their compatriots as *Latinofronoi*, may broadly be termed the ' Unionist ' party. Their approach to doctrinal problems was influenced by the ultra-conservative tradition which characterised Byzantine theology after the defeat of Iconoclasm and until the first half of the fourteenth century, in which the fear of fresh doctrinal formulations was combined with a somewhat mechanical use of patristic texts and of stereotyped theological arguments. They were further convinced that union with Rome was essential for the salvation of the Byzantine empire, whose supreme mission, in their view, lay in the preservation of the Greek classical tradition. This tradition, it may be noted, had been sedulously cultivated in Byzantium, particularly since the ninth century, despite the church's periodic condemnation of those who displayed inordinate enthusiasm for the ancient Greek philosophers.

The use of ' official ' theology, and the tendency to identify the sacred cause of Hellenism with the historical destiny of the Byzantine empire, characterised the leaders of the Greek ' Unionist ' party at Florence, above all Bessarion of Nicea. Their formalistic theology enabled them to accept with complete sincerity the formal concordance between the Latin and the Greek doctrines expressed in the Act of Union, while their cult of Hellenism, whose cause they did so much to foster in Italy, raised their desire for union above the level of a nationalistic and political opportunism.

6. ST GREGORY PALAMAS AND THE HESYCHAST TRADITION

The last group comprised theologians, scholars, churchmen and masters of the spiritual life who sought both to achieve a genuine identity of thought and experience with the Fathers of the Church, and to reinterpret their teaching creatively. The problem of reunion with Rome was not their central concern; yet by their authentic rediscovery and actualisation of the patristic tradition they seemed to open up, after centuries of sterile controversy, the way to a dialogue in depth between Greek and Latin theology. Their common background was the tradition of hesychasm.

The theory and practice of contemplative prayer, whose aim is a state of quietude (ἡσυχία) and inner silence which follow man's victory over his passions, are rooted in the earliest traditions of eastern Christian monasticism. In the course of time ' the prayer of the heart ' became associated with the frequent repetition of ' the Jesus Prayer ' (' Lord Jesus Christ, Son of God, have mercy on me '); and by the twelfth century at the latest the recitation of this prayer came to be linked with certain bodily techniques (such as the regulation of breathing), as a means of achieving spiritual concentration. The hesychast method of prayer became widely diffused in the Byzantine world in the fourteenth century, which witnessed a notable revival of eremitical and coenobitic monasticism throughout eastern Europe; it found an influential master in St Gregory of Sinai (d. 1346) who united the spiritual teaching of St John Climacus (d. c. 649) with the contemplative traditions of Mount Athos; and it was given a dogmatic justification and a permanent place in the theology of the Orthodox church by St Gregory Palamas (1296-1359), archbishop of Thessalonica, whose teaching was confirmed by two councils held in Constantinople in 1341 and 1351. The sacramental basis of his spirituality was indebted to earlier writings, notably to those of St Symeon the New Theologian (949-1022), the great Byzantine mystic. His theology, with its emphasis on the incarnation and on the biblical doctrine of man capable of ' deification ' by grace, was likewise based on the patristic tradition; and he derived from St Basil and St Maximus the Confessor the elements of that distinction, to which he was the first to give dogmatic precision and a theologically developed form, between the essence and the 'energies' of God. According to this distinction, which arises from the necessity of reconciling the belief that God is by nature wholly un-knowable with the doctrine that, through divine grace, men can be 'partakers of the divine nature' (2 Peter 1: 4), God in his essence is totally inaccessible, yet reveals and communicates himself through his 'energies' or 'operations'; these 'energies' have no existence apart from God; they are God himself in his action and manifestation in the created world. The mysterious relationship between the essence and the 'energies' of God – a relationship which is at once identity and distinction – safeguards the total transcendence of God while ensuring the reality of man's mystical experience of and union with God in his ' energies '.

The distinction between God's essence and his 'energies' has an important bearing on the Orthodox doctrine of the Trinity. For if, according to the essence of God, the Holy Spirit proceeds from the Father alone, the Spirit viewed as divine 'energy' proceeds, wrote Palamas, 'from the Father, through the Son – and, if one wishes, from the Son' (διὰ τοῦ Υἱοῦ, εἰ βούλει, καὶ ἐκ τοῦ Υἱοῦ) [4]. Thus did Palamas's doctrine on the uncreated 'energies' of God open the possibility – already foreseen by Gregory of Cyprus, patriarch of Constantinople (1283-89) – of a fruitful *rapprochement*, if not of complete agreement, between the Latin doctrine of the *Filioque* and the eastern theology of the Trinity. It is perhaps unfortunate that the teaching of Gregory Palamas was not more thoroughly discussed at the Council of Florence. But the historian may still record the fact that in the last century of Byzantine history, against the background of a politically moribund empire, the Byzantine church was able to develop a theology, both traditional and creatively adapted to the needs of the time, which might have narrowed the gulf between the two halves of Christendom; in the dark centuries that lay ahead for Greek Christians, this theology brought them and their fellow-Orthodox in eastern Europe the doctrine of God's energies and uncreated light, capable of making man a partaker in the divine nature and of transfiguring the world.

---

4. Cited in J. Meyendorff, *Introduction à l'étude de Grégoire Palamas*, Paris 1959, 315.

THESIS AND ANTITHESIS
IN CHURCH AND KINGDOM

FOR some sixty years, from the election of Innocent III to the death of Innocent IV (1198-1254) a succession of able popes of marked individuality ruled the Church. All were men of personal probity, high ideals and great intelligence, and all devoted themselves to maintaining and extending the supremacy of the apostolic see. All moreover were trained in the discipline of the canon law as taught at Bologna and practised in the curia. We have seen already that one of the greatest of their predecessors, Alexander III, had a similar formation, and the most eminent of their successors in the next fifty years, Boniface VIII, recalled to his opponents on a celebrated occasion that he had spent forty years in the study of the *Decretum* of Gratian and the decretals. [1] This circumstance was of the greatest significance for the development of papal policy, for there can be little doubt that the wide application of the ancient and basic doctrine of papal supremacy, which was deduced by Gregory VII and his successors from the traditional canons of the Church, owed its later extension primarily to the canonists, though the final elaboration

---

1. ' Quadraginta anni sunt quod nos sumus experti in jure. ' Cited by J. Rivière, *Le problème de l'Eglise et l'Etat*, 77.

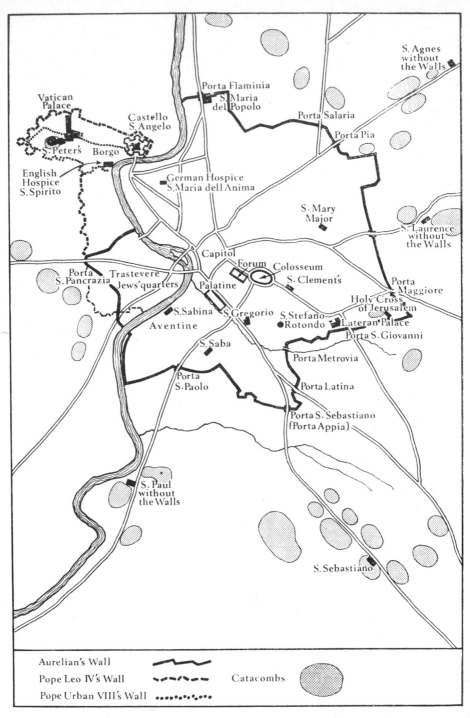

S. Agnes
without
the Walls

Porta Flaminia
S. Maria
del Popolo

Porta Salaria

Porta Pia

Vatican
Palace

Castello
S. Angelo

S. Peter's   Borgo

English
Hospice
S. Spirito

German Hospice
S. Maria dell'Anima

S. Mary
Major

S. Laurence
without
the Walls

Capitol

Forum   Colosseum

Porta
Maggiore

Porta
S. Pancrazia

Trastevere
Jews'quarters

Palatine

S. Clements

Holy Cross
of Jerusalem

S. Sabina

S. Gregorio

S. Stefano
Rotondo

Lateran Palace

Aventine

Porta S. Giovanni

S. Saba

Porta Metrovia

Porta
S. Paolo

Porta Latina

Porta S. Sebastiano
(Porta Appia)

S. Paul
without
the Walls

S. Sebastiano

Aurelian's Wall

Pope Leo IV's Wall

Catacombs

Pope Urban VIII's Wall

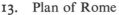

13.   Plan of Rome

was the work of publicists trained in the schools of Paris. [2] It is true, as recent scholarship has clearly shown, that canonical thought was not monolithic, and we shall see on a later page that a conciliar or corporate theory of the Church's constitution had been long defended by a series of canonists, but in the century between the pontificate of Alexander III and the early manhood of Benedetto Gaetani (Boniface VIII) the main stream of canonist thought ran steadily in the direction of universal papal dominion, and in the case of three of the four popes concerned (Honorius III being the exception) what had been learnt at Bologna was practised in Rome; opinions were translated into actions, which in turn supplied a foundation for further opinions. Innocent IV, indeed, elected pope after a brilliant career in the schools, not only practised what he had preached, but preached again as pope on what he had practised. This mutual and close interaction between theory and practice in what may almost be called the ' two bodies ' of the popes of this time must be noted in any discussion of medieval papal claims. When all reserves have been made the training of a canonist can still be seen as a hot-house warmth or a forced draught, bringing fruit to precocious maturity or coals to an excessive heat.

The searching examination of recent years has brought many modifications to the outlines of past histories, but it is still broadly permissible to regard the Gregorian reform as directed towards the separation of the provinces of the spirituality and the temporality, with the proviso that the pope was spiritual father of all, and with special reference to the emperor, who held his power as a ministerial agency for the good of the Church, and could be rebuked, excommunicated and even deposed if he were unprofitable to the common good. The notable popes of the twelfth century, and in particular Hadrian IV and Alexander III, held to this doctrine principally in their struggle with the emperor Frederick I Barbarossa.

Innocent III, inheriting advanced canonistic opinions from Uguccio of Pisa, his master at Bologna, entered upon his pontificate with the doctrine that spiritual and temporal power were both of divine ordaining, but that the spiritual was the greater both in dignity and in extent. His own temperament and genius, and the European circumstances during his pontificate, led him to enter and to dominate the field of politics throughout Europe, primarily as the spiritual father standing above the warring interests, and specifically as the judge and doomsman in all

2. Before Gratian, and for some decades after his work, canon law was a common heritage to which many churches and individuals had contributed and to which popes, as well as lawyers, had recourse as to an authority in their search for a legal ruling. From Gratian onwards it became increasingly a papal code, the object of academic study and comment.

matters, including high public policy, in which sinful human action might produce harmful effect. Much of this activity was personal and practical, the action of a very clearsighted observer who was able to view the European scene from above and to use his position and his personality for good and in the cause of peace, but Innocent had always an intellectual framework for his actions, and revealed it on a celebrated occasion when called upon by King John of England to judge between himself and the alleged unjust action of King Philip of France. He did not, he said, judge between feudal lord and vassal about a fief, but about a matter between men where sinful action entered in *(ratione peccati).* [3] Wide as was the door thus opened, the autonomy of the secular power was nominally preserved. Nevertheless there are statements scattered through the letters of Innocent III that widen and deepen the scope of his claims. The pope is the vicar of Christ, the vicar of God, set over peoples and kingdoms to pluck up and destroy, to build and to plant, with a fullness of power that is divine rather than human. The papal authority is to the regal as the sun is to the moon; the latter is not only a lesser, but a borrowed light. Despite these and other similar assertions, it would seem that Innocent regarded the secular ruler as having a power subordinate, indeed, but a real and not merely a derivative authority. His own political actions, which in number and breadth in fact exceeded those of any other pontiff before or since, were primarily those of a spiritual father with great prestige and wide interests and responsibilities rather than those of an authoritarian autocrat; and that was doubtless the reason why they were often successful and rarely resisted or resented. It is clear, and it must not be forgotten, that at this epoch the whole of western Europe was filled with the conviction that it was a society coextensive with the Church of Christ and that the pope was the divinely commissioned head of that Church. The conviction that natural, social and political rights existed, themselves established by the Creator inside the very structure of rational being, had long been obscured and survived only in fragments of ancient lore or as outcrops of hard practical necessity that were treated empirically as they might appear. The field was thus open for a logician or a lawyer – to say nothing of a realist politician in the papal chair – to press to the limit the apparently necessary consequences of such an argument as ' Christ, who is God, is the supreme head and king of all men. He has given all power to Peter and his successors: therefore.... '

The two immediate successors of Innocent III continued his policy without greatly developing his doctrine, but as both lacked the genius

3. Innocent III *Epistolae* vii 42 (PL CCXV col. 326). ' Non enim intendimus judicare de feudo... sed decernere de peccato cujus ad nos pertinet sine dubitatione censura quam in quemlibet exercere possumus et debemus. ' Cf. also ep. V, 128.

of Innocent and inherited the consequences of his mistakes or misfortunes they, and especially Gregory IX, give an impression of a more ruthless and less paternal use and proclamation of power. With Innocent IV there is a notable difference. As a celebrated master in the schools he was distinguished by his extension of the papal dominion beyond the assertions of Innocent III, and as a man he displayed both his strength of purpose and the lack of his great predecessor's spiritual outlook and political wisdom. In his view Christ had inaugurated, and Peter and his successors continued, a new authority to govern the world from the summit of authority. All lesser rulers, at least in the West, including the emperor, are beneath the pope; it is for him to approve the election of an emperor and depose him if unfit, for the emperor holds his office of him. The significance of the opinions and rule of Innocent IV, however, do not lie primarily in his expositions of theory, but in the manner of his use of his plenary powers. It was by the great expansion of the financial claims of the papacy, by the use of the right of providing Roman and other clerks to benefices all over Europe, and by his ruthless use of the spiritual weapons of excommunication and interdict in contests that were in the last resort political rather than spiritual, that Innocent IV brought about a subtle change in the function of his office. So at least it appeared to many of those directly affected in purse or person. It seemed to them that while Innocent III claimed and used supreme authority for the better ordering, in his judgment, of those over whom he ruled, Innocent IV used a still more powerful grasp of power for the benefit of the papacy itself, its policies, its schemes and its dependents. The popes of every age save the very first epoch of Christianity have had to deal with so many diverse parts and interests, both temporal and spiritual, of the universal Church, that it is always possible to find some errors in the wisest and some things well done in the worldliest. Innocent IV was in many ways a great man, and he was by no means a wholly worldly man. Many of his decisions were wise and many of his actions beneficial. The man whom Grosseteste rebuked visited St Clare on her deathbed, and it has recently been customary, as it is certainly fitting, to defend him against a kind of blanket charge of being the cause of all the calamities that were to befall the papacy. Nevertheless his reign is a turning-point in the history of that office. From Leo IX to Gregory IX it may be said that the papacy, regarded simply as a European institution, was of great benefit to Europe and worked almost solely for the benefit of those who acknowledged its authority. At no time was it to cease being of some benefit, apart from all consideration of its position as the rock of Peter and keystone of authority, but from the pontificate of Innocent IV onwards its critics multiplied, not wholly without reason.

The popes between Innocent IV and Boniface VIII were for the most part neither canonists by training nor statesmen of genius, moreover in default of a recognised emperor they were not concerned to carry on the great controversy. The canonists, however, eminent among whom was the great Hostiensis, continued to develop their theories. Hostiensis, whose influence was deep and lasting, followed Innocent IV in holding the superiority of the spiritual power, to which the secular power acted in a ministerial capacity and in the case of the emperor derived its power directly from the spiritual. He allowed to the secular power an ordinary and proper sphere of action, but this was derivative and could be re-assumed by the spiritual power in cases of sin or any other defect.

Meanwhile what is now called political thought was drawn into their field of study by the theologians, partly by the controversy between popes and Frederick II, partly by the reception, as one of the last remaining portions of the Aristotelian corpus, of Aristotle's *Politics*, in which for the first time the schoolmen met with a theory and a society based on the concept of man as a social animal, with rights and duties in which religion, in the Christian sense of the word, had no part. There was, in the mid-thirteenth century, little mutual goodwill between the canonists and the theologians; this antipathy is indeed one of the very few evidences of personal opinion on the part of St Thomas Aquinas. [4] It is therefore not surprising to find few echoes of the extreme positions of Innocent IV or Hostiensis in the Parisian masters. St Thomas himself would seem in his mature work, possibly influenced by the newly arrived *Politics* of Aristotle, with its emphasis on political activity as natural and essential to mankind, to have held a version of the Gelasian doctrine of the two powers. The tendency of the times, however, was towards extreme positions, and his disciple Ptolemy of Lucca, who had curial interests, in continuing St Thomas's *De regimine principum*, used the Aristotelian axiom of the single supreme cause to support his view that all authority can be reduced to a single source, viz., the spiritual power, which is of its nature superior to the temporal power as the head to the members and the soul to the body. Ptolemy supported his reasoning by the alleged historical action of Constantine, who surrendered the empire of the West to Pope Silvester.

This ambitious fabric of ideas raised by popes and canonists was to be shaken to its foundations when it came into collision with the fact and power of the opposing ideas of nationhood and the secular state.

The death of Nicholas IV in 1292 had been followed by a conclave two years long in which the parties of Orsini and Colonna produced an unbreakable deadlock. To end it the desperate step was taken of electing an old and saintly hermit in the Abruzzi who had founded a new, austere

4. Cf. *Summa Theologiae* IIa IIae Q88 art. 11.

and quasi-eremitical body following the Rule of St Benedict. Celestine V, as he became, proved wholly incompetent to govern the Church or the curia and in five months he resigned. The many enemies of his successor challenged both the legality and the freedom of Celestine's withdrawal which had, they alleged, been obtained by force and fraud by Cardinal Benedetto Gaetani. The latter, as Boniface VIII (1294-1303), was to carry the papal claims to temporal dominion to their extreme point, and thus to bring about a *débâcle* from which the repute of the papacy did not fully recover for more than two centuries. A trained canonist who himself had among his other qualities an unusual clarity of thought and expression, he had in his entourage theologians such as Ptolemy to supply their part in his pronouncements. Violent, egoistical and authoritarian by temperament, convinced of the truth of the doctrine of the spiritual power as enunciated by Innocent IV and Hostiensis, and supported by a group of theological thinkers who had arrived at a similar conclusion by a different route, he had the misfortune to encounter an opponent whose aims and opinions reflected a new outlook, and whose methods and agents were less reputable than those of Frederick II.

St Louis IX, though devout and wholly without personal ambition, had never failed to assert against the papacy what he conceived to be the traditional rights of the monarch with respect to the church in France, and which were in reality the remains of the régime of the private church translated into feudal and royal practice. He had been followed by his son Philip III, who had continued his tradition while remaining on good terms with the papacy. His grandson Philip IV was stronger, more energetic, and more able, but at the same time unscrupulous, avaricious and realistic, not to say materialistic, in all his actions. Philip IV, indeed, his character, and the great significance of his reign for the development of French constitutional and administrative history, offer more than one point of comparison with the English king Henry II. Two important circumstances made the character of his controversy with the pope different from previous clashes between the spiritual and temporal powers. The one was his status as king, not emperor; the other was the new spirit, whether it be called secularism or *realpolitik*, that characterised his policy. Both worked in his favour, for each deprived the pope of a hold, so to say, that his predecessors had grasped. With the king of France none of the arguments or obligations existed that had made it impossible for the emperor to break loose from the papacy, while an avowedly secularist policy equally deprived the pope of any moral or spiritual grip of his opponent.

Trouble began with the attempt of Boniface, in the provocative bull *Clericis laicos* of 24 February 1296 ('Laymen have always been hostile to the clergy'), to put an end to the taxation of churchmen without papal permission. Philip IV replied by forbidding the export of any coin from France, which the pope in turn answered by the comminatory bull *Ineffabilis* (20 September 1296) in which he claimed the right of supervision over all the acts of the king. A truce of four years followed during which Philip continued his taxation, appropriated the revenues of vacant benefices and imprisoned a bishop whom he proposed to judge. His independent and ultimately truculent attitude towards the pope, as also his ruthless domestic policy, was abetted, if indeed it was not suggested, by a group of able, but rootless, insecure and unscrupulous ministers, Pierre Flote, the chancellor, Guillaume de Nogaret, Pierre Dubois and Guillaume de Plaisians.

Boniface met their resistance with the bull *Ausculta fili* (5 December 1301) in which he treated the king as an erring son who might soon exhaust his father's indulgence and who would soon feel his wrath if unrepentant. When this had no effect upon Philip the pope summoned a council of French bishops to Rome to give counsel how the king might be brought to a better frame of mind and might reform his own conduct and that of his ministers. Meanwhile Philip's counsellors had put into circulation a parody of *Ausculta fili* with an insulting reply, and from both sides a stream of treatises issued that in extent and ideological interest surpassed those of any controversy since the days of Gregory VII. From the royal camp came among others the well known *Disputation between a clerk and a knight* and the more dignified but no less drastic *Rex pacificus*. On the papal side a series of able theologians pressed papal supremacy to the extreme point, among them Henry of Cremona, and the Augustinians Giles of Rome and James of Viterbo. All these tracts may well have been written in the early part of 1302. Then on 18 November Boniface fulminated *Unam sanctam*, a masterpiece of firm and lucid language, resting largely upon the writings of Giles of Rome, which proclaimed that the ultimate rule of the world must be in the hands of a single power, and asserting the claims of the papacy to be the only source of God-given authority, whom kings must consult and obey and to which royal power was only ministerial. The bull ended with a sharp definition that submission to the Roman pontiff was necessary for salvation for every creature.

The bull *Unam sanctam* has been regarded as the culminating point, the *ne plus ultra* of the claims of the medieval papacy, and there can be little doubt that Boniface himself meant it to be an assertion of the paramountcy, if not the monopoly, of power enjoyed in the temporal and spiritual spheres by the pope. In terms of strict theological criticism, however, his definition does no more than reassert the claim based on the Petrine text of Matthew 16: that is, the spiritual authority of the pope over the whole Church of Christ, to which all men are called as to the ark of salvation.

Unam sanctam, indeed, made no direct reference to Philip, and negotiations were resumed which might have led to an agreement. Boniface, however, refused anything less than a complete submission, and threatened excommunication. Philip for his part issued a comprehensive list of charges, which included heresy, against the pope, and circularised cardinals and monarchs with charges against him. In September Boniface prepared the bull *Super Petri solio* releasing Philip's subjects from their allegiance; a few days later Nogaret, who had been sent to Italy, and who had sharked up a band of bravoes and partisans, broke into Anagni on 7 September and captured the pope. He was speedily recaptured, but died from shock a month later.

A successor was quickly elected, a man of milder temper who did little in his nine months of rule; then after two years of intrigue, the archbishop of Bordeaux took his place, a subject of King Edward I. He surrounded himself with French cardinals and settled at Avignon, a papal enclave, which was to remain the seat of papal government for more than sixty years (1309-78).

These events, which both shocked and profoundly influenced European sentiment, marked a turning-point in papal fortunes. It is true that publicists and theologians of the papal party continued to expound views on the papal supremacy which improved even upon those of the author of *Unam sanctam*. Ptolemy of Lucca, Agostino Trionfo and others exalted the papal prerogatives with all the resources of hyperbolical expression, and no pope made the least motion towards disowning the claims of *Unam sanctam*. At the same time the situation of the papacy and the events of the time prevented any practical consequences and political conclusions from being drawn and the papacy was to be harassed by every kind of attack and misfortune for more than a century.

The ' Babylonian captivity ', the new trends in philosophy and theology culminating in Nominalism, the rise of a secularist outlook on political life seen in the writings of Marsilius of Padua and William of Ockham, combined to make the fourteenth century a time of transition in thought and of difficulty for the curia at Avignon.

THE FRIARS
I. ORIGINS AND EXPANSION

WHEN Innocent III and other responsible observers throughout Europe were deploring the mounting crisis in the pastoral and spiritual life of the church, the decline of standards and practice in the religious life, the needs of the growing towns and the spread of heresy among the bourgeoisie, they could not foresee the new movement that was to make of the thirteenth century a time of pastoral and apostolic zeal, of keen intellectual life and of a new pattern of the devout life together with an outpouring of mystical graces.

We have marked the appearance of groups of earnest men and women in the towns, practising poverty and the communal life and holding meetings for preaching and prayer. Some of these turned heretics, others were saved for the Church by the breadth of mind of Innocent III, who refused to treat as heretics those who wished to stay within the Church. Poverty and preaching were therefore in the air, but Francis and Dominic did more than develop a movement already in being. Of the two Dominic was the older and received formal approval before Francis, but it was Francis whose personality and message seemed so new and so irresistible to his contemporaries, and it was he who created the image and vocation of the friar. Moreover while Dominic remains a child of his age, though with uncommon sanctity and foresight, Francis is one of the great originals of history who opened windows upon unfamiliar prospects in the world around, in the mind of men, in the gospel message and in the personal religion of multitudes of Christians. Bernard, Francis and Dante, all quintessentially medieval, nevertheless are all three creators from whom the modern world has derived something of its spirit and in whom modern man sees something of himself.

Francis (1181/2-1226) the son of a well-to-do merchant of Assisi, was converted from a youth of prodigality and comfort and from hopes of a career in arms to a hermit's life which became that of a homeless worker and simple preacher when he was joined by others. His primitive brotherhood lived by a few texts of the gospel in total poverty, going out to work for their keep, with no fixed abode, preaching penance (that is, moral conversion) and bound together by brotherly love. His project, after initial rejection, had received verbal approbation from Innocent III in 1210. Francis had at first no intention of founding an organisation of any kind, but his magnetic personality, and his invitation to a way of life for which thousands had been groping, attracted multitudes in central Italy and some kind of formal rule and institution were essential. In 1217 ' provinces ' with ' ministers ' were established and bands were sent on missions beyond Italy and the Alps. Francis resisted further formalisation and himself set out for the East. In his absence the friars left in charge obtained from Honorius III a bull imposing a year's noviciate, formal profession and control of preaching. Francis who had already resigned direct government of the brethren fought against all such legislation, but under pressure composed a Rule (the so-called *Regula Prima*) in 1221 which came as near as words could to the expression of his ideal. It was too strict and too vague for the men of learning and legal training, who were now the spokesmen of the friars. Francis for long held firm, but at last produced another Rule, the so-called *Bullata* of 1223, which was shorter, but contained fresh details of organisation, while it omitted some passages from the gospels which officials of the order had found too severe. Three groups had now appeared in embryo who were to make the history of the Friars Minor for a century: the group of intimate ' first companions ' standing for the integral, literal following of the gospel; the party of the ' ministers ' willing to sacrifice simplicity in the interests of a strong and efficient government, and a third party of learned and zealous men who wished for a strict Rule but with the possibility of sharing in the intellectual and pastoral work of the age. Francis, a prey to illness and to the sufferings that accompanied the Stigmata of 1224, drew apart from his friars, save for a group of early companions, and died at Assisi in 1226 shortly after he had composed a *Testament* in which he reiterated in stark simplicity the prohibitions against possessions and privileges and his distrust of learning.

While the Friars Minor were capturing the enthusiasm of Italy, the Preachers were establishing themselves in Languedoc. The founder, Dominic, a regular canon of Osma, who had left Spain with his bishop to preach to the heathen on the Danish March, had found his vocation in work among the Albigenses, where in 1205-7 he had gathered companions and established a convent of nuns. He visited Rome in 1215 just after the Lateran council had decreed that no new orders should come into being. Innocent approved his design and told him to choose an existing rule, which in fact implied a choice between the rules of Benedict and Augustine. Already an Augustinian canon, he naturally took that of St Augustine, and on its narrow base the Dominican legislation was erected when the founder, after 1218, had widened the scope of his order. It was to be one of clerics, theologically instructed, and their work, after personal sanctification, was to be the preaching of Catholic doctrine wherever need might arise. That simple priests should be trained and dedicated as preachers was a new thing in Europe; the preacher *ex officio* was the bishop; but here again Innocent saw the needs of the time and blessed the Preachers. Their elaborate constitutions were rapidly executed at the chapters of 1216 and 1220. In the first part a quasi-monastic régime was instituted for the friaries; in the second a system of theological training was set up throughout the order with a doctor in each friary, a house of studies in each province, and houses of higher studies at Paris, Oxford, Cologne, Montpelier and Bologna for the whole order. At the same time an intricate system of election and representation was devised for conventual, provincial and general chapters, with a master-general at the head of the order. An original feature was the establishment of temporary superiors at every level save the highest, with a small committee with full powers in the provincial chapter, and a general chapter in which elected members served for two years out of three. It was a departure from the principle of paternal government in favour of one by men chosen by their fellows for qualities of learning and administrative ability. We may almost say that Dominic originated the modern administrative expedient of government by committee.

Francis had no wish to found an order; Dominic had originally no thought of his followers as friars; but within twenty years of the deaths of the two founders the two bodies to a superficial observer differed only in the colour of their tunic. The two saints knew and admired each other and their followers passed each other on the roads and in the market-places of Europe. It has been said that the Minors turned the Preachers into friars and mendicants, while the Preachers turned the Minors into a student order. Both orders reject these statements, and as crude assertions they can be contested; certainly Dominic had chosen corporate poverty before any

direct Franciscan influence can be seen. It is truer to say that both orders
were moulded by the needs and forms of their world. Both orders hastened
to the university towns, the Preachers to learn and the Minors to call souls
to Christ; they were magnets that attracted some of the leading masters
and students, and in a few years the friars' houses contained the leading
theologians of Europe. Each order gave birth to an outstanding mind and
personality that stood for all succeeding generations as a type and example.
Bonaventure with his *Life of St Francis* and the constitutions of Narbonne
(1260) canonised the *via media* of austere compromise between the *Testament* of Francis and laxity. Aquinas, though never taking part in the
government of his order, gave in his works a directory of Christian practice
and conduct with included a view of the religious life and its duties, thus
giving to the Preachers the theoretical spiritual and practical exposition of
their ideals which they had hitherto lacked. Both orders spread rapidly
and with identical aims. The original missionary group made for a principal city in each region and thence to the chief towns, one or more of
which usually contained a university. Thenceforward they spread to all the
greater towns and some of the smaller; it was not usual for one order to
have two houses in a city, however populous. Both orders from an early
date divided themselves into regional provinces administered by a minister-
or prior-provincial; the constitution of the orders had therefore three tiers:
the friary under its guardian (Order of Friars Minor) or prior (Order of
Preachers), forming a member of a province under minister- or prior-
provincial, who in turn were subordinate to a minister- or master-general.
Friary, province and order met in regular chapters. In both the general
chapter, triennial (O.F.M.) or annual (O.P.), was sovereign during its
brief life, but the Franciscan minister-general had wider powers than the
Dominican master. The Dominicans rapidly organised a system of study
throughout the order. Each friary gave elementary teaching in arts, which
came to include philosophy and elementary theology; each province
contained one or more *studia particularia* frequented by the normal run
of theological students; finally there were a few *studia generalia* usually
but not always in university towns such as Paris, Bologna and Oxford, to
which brilliant students could be sent from all provinces. They thus gave
to the western church for the first time the completely articulated and
supra-national religious order in which the individual had no single, permanent home, but might be, and usually was, moved from friary to friary
and even from province to province or to a missionary journey beyond all
provincial boundaries at the command of the general. Moreover, whereas
in the orders of monks and canons the primary concern was the spiritual
advance of the individual within a framework of liturgical and conventual
observance, the superiors of the friars were concerned with the deployment

of their subjects to meet the demands of teaching, preaching and missionary activity. Thus while monks and canons were static, the friars were
dynamic; they could be deployed and exploited like troops for an agreed
object. By an accident of history the two founders were drawn at once
into close reliance upon the papacy; this relationship was confirmed in the
sequel, and in consequence the papacy had at its disposition and service a
new kind of militia which it could use as it could never use monks, canons
or the secular clergy as a body.

The original orders of friars, like the Cistercians a century earlier, had
many imitators. Two bodies in particular were drawn into their magnetic
field. The one consisted of groups of hermits from Mount Carmel driven
from Palestine by the Saracens and establishing themselves in Sicily, Italy
and Spain and above all in England. They gradually adopted the outlook
and work of the friars and a constitution similar to that of the Preachers.
The other was made up of hermit-groups of Italy, united by successive
popes, Innocent IV and Alexander IV, and in 1256 erected into an order
of mendicant friars. These also rapidly assimilated themselves to the others.
In addition a number of splinter-groups appeared, of varied degrees of
respectability, among them the Friars of the Cross or ' Crutched ' Friars.

The tribulations and vagaries of the Minors, which inevitably attract
the attention of historians in the thirteenth century, must not be allowed
to obscure the solid, nay brilliant, achievements of the order. Apart
altogether from the schools, in which they shared with the Preachers the
intellectual leadership of Europe, they were the boldest and most successful of medieval missionaries. They penetrated into China, where for
more than a century they maintained a flourishing church under a partly
native hierarchy, and individual friars were to be found in many regions
at the edge of Christendom. Above all, by their preaching and spiritual
direction, and through the ' third order ' of penance for lay people, they
exercised a widespread and beneficent influence in every country of Europe
in the century after their establishment. It was the friars, and particularly
the Minors, always the most numerous and the closest in sympathy with
the masses, who developed the latent sources of lay piety and brought
religious practices into the homes of the townspeople. The friars are an
integral part of social life in the thirteenth and fourteenth centuries, and
the Minors were more ubiquitous than any others.

The Preachers, numerically second to the Minors, were almost as
ubiquitous, but their more conventual character and their devotion to
theological study gave them something of a monastic tinge. They were from
early days used by popes and kings as emissaries and royal confessors,
filling at the courts of the thirteenth century something of the position
taken by the Jesuits of the Counter-Reformation. Their rigid orthodoxy

and excellent constitution, together with their cult of the rational, preserved them from the aspirations, the anguishes and the feuds of the Minors.

The two remaining orders of Carmelites and Austin Hermits did not achieve the status of a fully organised international religious order till the latter half of the thirteenth century. The period of their greatest influence was in the fourteenth century, as will be seen. Though retaining interesting differences of organisation there is little in the records that remain to show any great difference of spirit or work or ideal between them, or any contrast with the two senior orders. Arriving later they had a smaller, but still notable, share in the great creative age of scholastic theology.

The friars, like the monks before them, attracted women to share their ideals. In the case of St Dominic the sisters of Prouille, near Toulouse, were gathered together to assist the founder and his associates with their prayers and services before the order of Preachers was established. Similarly Clare of Assisi and her first companions took their vows at the hands of St Francis when the brotherhood was still small. Later the Poor Ladies or Poor Clares developed into a contemplative body of great strictness. The contrast between the early followers of Francis, always on the move and without a settled community life, and the enclosed and conventual (one might almost add 'conventional') existence of the Minoresses is very striking. Clearly the thirteenth century would not have tolerated unenclosed religious women, but it is a mark of Francis's breadth of mind and radically unrevolutionary spirit that he should have accepted, in this respect at least, the traditional 'monastic' way of life for his sisters. The Carmelite nuns, for their part, did not appear till the end of the fourteenth century, and the glory of the order dates from its reform in Spain under St Teresa.

The friars, in addition, reawakened the missionary consciousness of Christian Europe, and turned the eyes of the papacy towards the mission field of Islam and the East. St Dominic was on his way to preach to the heathen of northern Europe when he found his life's work in Provence. St Francis had himself voyaged to Egypt to convert the Soldan, and the earliest Minors were encouraged to go forth to preach to Moors and Muslims. Provinces of both orders were soon established in the Holy Land (Minors, 1220; Preachers, 1228) and members of both orders learnt Arabic, in order to preach to the Moors. Under Brother Elias the Minors spread to Georgia, to Damascus and to Baghdad, and the Dominicans followed hard after them to Syria and Persia. Both orders entered Morocco, where each had its martyrs in early years. When the Mongols invaded Europe in 1241 the friars were commissioned by the pope to preach the crusade, and four years later the Franciscan John of Plano Carpini was sent by

Innocent IV to the great Khan at Karakorum in Mongolia south of the modern Irkutsk, and he was followed ten years later by Friar William of Robruck, sent by St Louis as his envoy. Others followed and made converts in China, where an archbishopric was established with ten suffragans. The Avignonese popes, and in particular John XXII, gave constant attention to the Asian field of mission, and churches were established in Persia, with an archbishop, in Turkestan, and in India. For more than a century, until the advent of the great Turk, Tamerlane (1369), there was a tenuous link of traffic and evangelisation across central Asia, and China experienced the second of her recurring glimpses of Christian life. Distance and pagan invasion broke the life-line, and the communities in the east died out, but the stream of friars who made the journey across vast spaces to unknown peoples, and who made converts to the gospel despite all difficulties of language and alien customs, must rank among the most remarkable and daring missionaries of the Christian centuries.

THE FRIARS
II. CONTROVERSIES

THE thirteenth century is rightly regarded as the age of the friars. St Francis and St Dominic, in different but complementary ways, gave to the Church a new form of religious life, which had an immense and permanent appeal, and one which both attracted a new type of recruit and in its turn inspired an apostolate to the laity, to the heretic and to the heathen. Not only did the appearance of the friars rescue the western church from its drift towards heresy and schism, but the new warmth of devotional life, the preaching, the confessing and the daily counsel of the friars gave a new strength to the lower level of Christian society and indirectly acted as a powerful agent of spiritual growth and social union, thus invisibly compensating for the growing power of legalism and political motives at the higher levels of church life. In addition, the friars had a major share in the wonderful flowering of theological genius in the schools. They had thus a twofold influence in the realm of the spirit. They – and among them in particular Francis and his nearest companions – brought back to the Christian consciousness the earthly life of Christ in its love, its poverty and its suffering as an ideal to be followed to the end, while at the same time they presented the theological expression of Christ's message in the lecture-room and pulpit throughout Christendom. The services of the army of friars of all four orders in the age between the

Fourth Lateran Council and the Black Death were indeed innumerable and beneficent beyond reckoning, and should always be present in the mind of anyone considering the fortunes of the church at that period.

Yet at the same time, being men among men, the friars passed through a series of distressing controversies, whether united against bishops and universities, or ranged against each other in rivalry or dispute, or divided each in their own order over matters of theory and practice. The Franciscans in particular were riven with dissension, and their history in the thirteenth century has many of the elements of tragedy along with its many glimpses of heroism and sanctity.

St Francis never desired to found an organised, formalised ' order '; his companions made up a brotherhood, and when, with multitudes of recruits, he yielded to pressure and necessity, it was with sorrow and against his inmost conviction. To the end he preached and commanded absolute poverty (with the prohibition against physical contact with money), entire simplicity, both material and mental, entire submission to pope and bishops, and the literal imitation of the itinerant and crucified Christ. In his *Testament* he reiterated his message: no possessions, no privileges, and the *Rule* observed to the letter. The domestic history of his order for a century or more was conditioned by the bitter struggle between those who wished to judge all activities and works by the *Rule* and *Testament*, and those who wished to adapt the *Rule* and ignore the *Testament* in order to meet the exigencies of the work to be done. In the first phase the influence of the learned clerks who became friars ended by transforming the loose, primarily lay, itinerant preaching body into a tightly organised clerical order, largely student in training and living in convents protected by privileges from episcopal interference. In the gradual erosion of the defences of the *Rule* a large part was played by the great canonist popes. Thus Gregory IX in the bull *Quo elongati* of 1230 declared the *Testament* not binding and that the friars might make use of an agent *(nuntius)* to receive alms and of friends *(amici spirituales)* to hold money in reserve, while in 1231 the bull *Nimis iniqua* gave full exemption. Theological studies soon followed the arrival of the friars at Paris and Oxford (1231) and in 1239, after the *débâcle* of Brother Elias, the autocratic and intransigent minister-general whose spirit and methods had provoked an appeal to the pope, the order was organised from top to bottom as an international body, with diffinitors (a legislating committee) and elected officers similar to those of the Preachers; after *c.* 1242 only clerics were eligible for office, and thereafter the lay element practically disappeared, to be reintroduced later in a more conventional form.

Innocent IV, while safeguarding the letter of the *Rule* by declaring that all the property of the order belonged to the Holy See and was exempt from episcopal control (*Ordinem vestrum* 1245) departed from its letter and spirit by instituting (*Quanto studiosius* 1247) procurators in each province to administer funds. These numerous privileges were consolidated in 1258 by Alexander IV in a bull that became known as ' the Ocean ' *(Mare magnum)*. These relaxations did not go unchallenged; the order repudiated *Ordinem vestrum*, and henceforward there was a considerable minority, of which the hard core consisted of eremitical Italian friars inspired by the group of St Francis's ' first companions ', who became known as extremists or *zelanti* as distinguished from the ' conventuals '. The schism that threatened was averted by St Bonaventure (1221-74) who by his commentary on the *Rule*, his anodyne *Life* of St Francis, and the constitutions passed at the chapter of Narbonne (1260), standardised a *via media* between laxity and rigour and established the ideal of the ' sparing use ' *(usus pauper)* of all things. St Bonaventure has often been considered a second founder of the order, which has ever since held his teaching as a norm, but it would be more historical to regard him as one who, accepting the essential changes already completed, stereotyped them into a way of life that looked to St Francis for inspiration rather than for direct commands. His criterion when interpreting the *Rule* was papal pronouncement and dispensation rather than the *Testament* of Francis. He canonised the ' conventual ' life, monastic rather than eremitical, and showed himself the opponent equally of the rigorous and of the lax, and by preaching the ' sparing use ' in practice and the spiritual and relative rather than the material and absolute observance of poverty, he sowed the seeds of the controversy that was to agitate the order after his death and the whole western church fifty years later. Bonaventure's *via media* needed the saint's presence to give it strength. When he had gone the Laxists and Spirituals (as they were now called) gained ground upon the ' Community '. Poverty, personal and corporate, declined rapidly; friars secured possessions, the order accepted revenues and built great churches. The strict view of poverty was attacked within and without the order, and it was to repel these attacks that Nicholas III composed his bull *Exiit qui seminat* (1279) declaring the renouncement of all ownership to be Christ-like, practicable and meritorious. He also forbade any further discussion on the subject. Martin IV, however, by his bull *Exultantes in Domino* (1283) allowed all Franciscan property to be administered by procurators chosen and controlled by the friars themselves. The procurator became a puppet, and the dominion of the Holy See pure fiction, while the number of friars grew even greater. In reaction the party of Spirituals, heirs of the *zelanti*, emerged; and three leaders appeared of exceptional gifts and outstanding personality, Angelo da Clareno (1247-1337), Ubertino da Casale (1259-1325) and Pierre Olivi (1248-98). Austere of life, they were the confidants of such saintly persons as Conrad d'Offida, Angela of Foligno and Margaret of Cortona. The main points of their programme were: abstention from the study of philosophy (i.e., Aristotle); absolute personal poverty allowing only use of absolutely necessary objects (e.g. food and clothing) as implied by the religious vow of a Franciscan; the *Rule* and *Testament* as obligatory; and that papal dispensations were illicit. As Dante remarked, one party escaped the *Rule*, the other drew it too tight. [1]

The zeal of the Spirituals embittered the community and they were subjected to persecution. In 1294 Celestine V took the fateful step of separating them from the order; Boniface VIII revoked this act and persecution and amnesty succeeded each other, while bitter polemics ensued, in which the Spirituals were handicapped by the Joachimism [2] of some of their supporters, and greatly assisted by the brilliant debating skill of Ubertino da Casale. After many vicissitudes, a commission was set up by Clement V which ultimately pronounced in favour of Ubertino's teaching on all but a few points, and the pope at the Council of Vienne published in the bull *Exivi de paradiso* (1312) a remarkably fair assessment of the controversy, which, by condemning current relaxations while approving of the *usus pauper* rather than the letter of the *Rule* and *Testament*, satisfied the Spirituals in part while denying them in practice the right to secede from the order. Both parties accepted the decision but discord soon reappeared; the Spirituals in Italy were intractable and their adversaries revived their attacks on Ubertino and others. John XXII, at first favourable to the Spirituals, was exasperated by their intransigence and in the bull *Quorumdam exigit* (1317) demanded complete submission on their part to their (conventual) superiors. In the following year the Spirituals who still resisted conformity were condemned. Ubertino left the order; Angelo went into schism and his followers, known as *Fraticelli*, continued to exist in Italy for a century.

None of the other three principal orders of friars had at this time a domestic crisis comparable to that of the Minors, but the friars as a body were in collision with two authorities external to their order, the universities and the episcopate. Arrived at Paris and Oxford to preach and to convert, the friars had become almost in spite of themselves masters and students and struggled to retain their freedom while enjoying the privileges of the university. In particular, they wished to study theology without having qualified in arts, to establish chairs and to attain the master's degree within their own schools, and to be free of obligation to observe the statutes and decrees of the university. The secular masters for their part not only demanded submission of the friars but went on to attack the rights of

1. *Paradiso* XII, 127. ' Ch'uno la fugge, ed altro la coarta. '
2. For this see pp. 406-7.

the friars to be a student and a preaching order. The friars, with St Bona-venture and St Thomas in the lists, had little trouble in defending their ideals, though they were handicapped by one of their number, Gerard of Borgo San Donnino, who adapted the prophecies of Joachim of Flora to serve his presentation of the Friars Minor as the apostles of the coming kingdom of the Holy Spirit. On the whole front they might well have succumbed but for the support of the papacy in the person of Alexander IV who threw all the weight of his authority on their side, condemning their opponents and assuring their status at Paris in the bull *Quasi lignum vitae* (1257). Henceforward their position was secure in essentials, but the action of Alexander IV was as impressive in its hostility to the secular masters as, in the opposite sense, had been the support of Gregory IX in the bull *Parens scientiarum* (1231), the Magna Carta of the university, and some have traced the origins of Gallicanism to the academic resentment at the papal decision in this controversy. The troubles of the friars at Paris were accompanied by a wider and more lasting controversy with the episcopate. St Francis had intended his brethren to preach penance in complete sub-mission to the bishop of the diocese where they might be, and St Dominic had organised his brethren to preach against the heretics in aid of the crusade against the Albigensians. When both orders began to cover Europe and to preach and absolve, with papal privileges and exemption, a new situation arose in which the bishops and parish priests saw their functions and revenues encroached upon. For some decades the papacy continued to heap favours upon the friars, and the attacks on their ideals and rights as mendicants and apostles failed, as we have seen. The practical difficul-ties however remained, and in face of widespread episcopal complaints Innocent IV in his bull *Etsi animarum* (1254) restricted the freedom of access to the friars' churches and forbade them to preach or hear confes-sions in parish churches without the invitation of the parish priest. The pope died a few days later (a circumstance that was exploited by the friars) and his successor Alexander IV suspended the obnoxious bull. Friction nevertheless continued and came to a head at the second Council of Lyons (1274) when a decree was proposed to suppress all new religious bodies. With St Bonaventure, O.F.M., and Pierre of Tarentaise, O.P., among the leading cardinals, and a host of friars among the conciliar fathers, such a proposal was doomed to failure. Nevertheless only Minors and Preachers were unconditionally exempted from the decree; Augustinians and Car-melites enjoyed a temporary reprieve, which in the event was permanent; the Friars of the Sack and other splinter orders were formally suppressed; though some, e.g., the Crutched Friars in England, called themselves canons and remained in existence till the Reformation. The council was followed by further attempts at conciliation, but hopes of agreement were thwarted by Martin IV, who by his bull *Ad fructus uberes* (1281) gave the friars permission to preach and confess everywhere without any permission, while giving the mendicant superiors sole right of examining and appointing preachers and confessors. Privilege could no farther go. *Ad fructus uberes* was the last wash of the spring tide of papal plenary power which under Innocent IV had invaded almost all customary episcopal rights. It was a serious moment. The pope as universal ordinary was bypassing all episcopal and parochial rights. Had the process continued to the end bishops would have become mere ordaining and consecrating papal chaplains, and all benefices would have been filled with provisors, while friars preached, confessed and buried parishioners in their own precincts. The traditional rôle of the monarchical bishop would have been lost for ever. The situation was saved, paradoxically enough, by Boniface VIII, who rearranged matters with the wise decree *Super cathedram* (1300) in which, among other prescriptions, he laid an obligation upon the mendicants to receive the parish priest's permission before preaching and confessing, though the bishop must authorise the ministry of a fixed number from those presented to him. True, *Super cathedram* was revoked by the short-lived Benedict XI, O.P., but it was republished soon after by his successor and remained in force throughout the middle ages. The parish clergy and many bishops were at odds with the mendicants in the years to come, but the friars never again threatened to become a papal militia ministering to the faithful from a privileged position over the heads of bishops and parish priests.

When John XXII silenced the Spirituals he was not yet done with the Minors. Whatever might be their practice or their exegesis of the *Rule*, all Franciscans were committed in principle to the teaching that their poverty was a unique imitation of Christ's poverty, which was absolute. Working downward, they could then be assured that theirs was the only exact imitation of the poverty of Christ; this, they held, had in fact been defined by Nicholas III in his bull *Exiit*. The matter was brought to a head by the refusal by a Franciscan inquisitor to condemn as a heretic a ' spiritual ' who asserted Christ to have renounced all rights to ownership. John XXII was determined to settle the matter once and for all, and after theological consultation issued (March 1322) the bull *Quia nonnumquam*, in which he declared that Christ and the apostles as head and rulers of the Church owned property, though as individuals they had the right of renouncement. The shock was great in all Franciscan circles, and at the general chapter at Perugia in June, under the minister-general Michael of Cesena, they asserted the absolute poverty of Christ to be a doctrine held by all Christians. John XXII replied with the bull *Ad conditorem canonum* (December 1322) revoking papal ownership of the friars' possessions and throwing back at the friars the property of which they disclaimed ownership while enjoying the fruits. Their protests were vehement and the pope modified his action by resuming ownership of real property as opposed to perishable goods, but by his canonisation of St Thomas Aquinas (whose teaching on poverty was sober) and still more by his bull *Cum inter nonnullos* (1323), solemnly condemning the teaching that Jesus Christ had no ownership, he made his position clear enough. The Minors passed through a difficult period; while many accepted the pope's actions and pronouncements, others abounded in their own sense, encouraged by the distant applause of the emperor. Michael of Cesena, the minister-general, remained in opposition; called to Avignon for an explanation he fled (26/7 May 1328), accused the pope of heresy and joined the imperial party. John XXII directed to his address the bull *Quia vir reprobus* (16 November 1329) reaffirming Christ's right of ownership, but for the rest of the pontificate groups of Minors, especially in Germany, remained in schism, while William of Ockham raked the papal position fore and aft with his pamphlets.

30

THE SPIRITUAL LIFE (II)

THE exaltation of material poverty was an important strand in the web of medieval spirituality. It was indeed one of the two strands that were the especial contributions of the Friars Minor. The other was a devotion to the passion and cross of Christ. This again was no novelty in Christendom. It was a sentiment which had inspired liturgical and artistic genius, and had repeatedly sent Europe on the road to Jerusalem in the guise of a pilgrim or a crusader. Nevertheless St Francis gave a new depth and directness to the traditional devotion. Historically speaking he was the first stigmatic, or at least the first to be universally and even officially acknowledged as such, and thus the prototype of a long line. In this identification with the suffering Redeemer he inspired a great army of followers to a new kind of self-dedication and self-sacrifice. Franciscan piety – and it must be remembered that the Franciscans were and are the most numerous of the religious orders, quite apart from their ' third order ' – retained this affective Christo-centric devotion throughout the middle ages. The great Franciscan theologians, in particular St Bonaventure, reflect the message of St Francis in two ways. They stand for the primacy of love, looking to the love of God rather than to the truth and knowledge of God as the key to the universe and the reason for the Incarnation. And they regard theology as primarily the guide to a life which rises by stages to the ecstatic vision of God. All learning is in fact directed towards the love of God; it is, in the form of the title of St Bonaventure's most celebrated book, the *Journey of the mind to God.*

In contrast to the Franciscans the Dominicans had at first no distinctive personal ' message '. They preached Catholic truth in its fulness, and while it would be an undue simplification to say that while the Franciscans aimed at changing the heart the Dominicans were concerned with enlightening the mind, such a statement would not greatly have misrepresented the preaching purpose of the two orders in the early decades of their existence. It was natural therefore that the central body of the Dominican order should see the spiritual life theologically, not to say scholastically, and that Aquinas should in due course become, not only their doctor but also their source of spiritual teaching. St Thomas's presentation of the theological virtues, of the infused moral virtues and of the gifts of the Holy Ghost, as also his teaching on the contemplative life, lie behind the classical ascetical and mystical doctrines of the order and mould the expressions of its saints. Nevertheless the chief influence of the order in the realm of spiritual theology was in a sense ' off centre '. It took place in the Rhineland and owed its character neither to Aristotle nor to Augustine, but to Denis the Areopagite. Aquinas, in common with all the thirteenth-century schoolmen, regarded the opinions of Denis with reverence, however great the difficulty of harmonising them with his Aristotelian outlook. He may have gained some of his knowledge from Albert the Great, who in one of his periods of residence at Cologne devoted himself to Dionysian study. Albert (d. 1280) was the master of Dietrich of Freiberg (d. *c.* 1310) who in his turn inspired Eckhart (d. 1327) who then was chiefly responsible for impregnating medieval mystical theology with Neoplatonism largely derived from Denis. Towards the end of the thirteenth century many convents of Dominican nuns came into being in the Rhineland and these were entrusted to Dominicans for spiritual direction. South Germany proved a remarkably fruitful seeding-ground, and for a century its convents and city parishes received rarefied instruction from a succession of Dominicans of whom the most celebrated were Tauler (d. 1361) and Henry Suso (d. 1366). Eckhart's doctrine was partly condemned after his death, but Tauler his pupil and admirer succeeded in purifying it of dubious material and presenting a system which was an orthodox blend of Thomism and Dionysian Neoplatonism. A feature of his teaching, derived from Denis, is its insistence on both the supernatural character and the darkness of the approach to contemplation, the ' ray of darkness '. Visions, locutions and ecstasy are foreign to his system. From Tauler descended the scheme of ascetical and mystical theology which has since been adopted by Dominican and Carmelite theologians, though often with a lack of emphasis upon the Dionysian elements. Its postulates are that ' contemplation ' is in essence infused knowledge and love bestowed on the soul by the action of the gifts of the Holy Ghost. These, present in every soul in grace, only become perceptible when the theological virtues have reached, so to say, a certain temperature. The mystical life is therefore an intensification, a prolongation, of the sanctifying grace bestowed at baptism and thus an integral part of a theologically ' perfect ' life, though in practice rare in its higher manifestations. It is always the free gift of God and cannot be acquired by labour or even merited. So far the doctrine is wholly traditional, but many mystics and theologians, emphasising principles that are Dionysian rather than evangelical, regarded the mystical life as the only and necessary perfection of the Christian life and therefore the goal of endeavour of all, with the corollary that all who fail to attain it have failed in due endeavour. Tauler, in consequence, urges all his audiences to aim at a life of mystical perfection. There is much evidence to show that in south Germany and later in the Netherlands a flowering of mystical sanctity did in fact take place comparable to that in Spain in the sixteenth century. Historians of mystical theology have seen in this movement two modes of expressing the mystical union and its degrees. The one, ' marriage-mysticism ' (Braut-mystik), emphasises the union of love, basing its expression on the Canticle of Canticles and deriving in part from St Bernard. The other, ' essence-mysticism ' (Wesens-mystik), looks at the relationship of the soul to its exemplar the Word of God and regards the preparation for union as a stripping from the soul of all save its simple being which can be absorbed in the Deity while retaining its distinction as a creature. The two modes of expression are not mutually exclusive, for both are attempts to express the inexplicable, and later mystics, such as St John of the Cross, make use of both.

However we characterise or judge the matter, the mystics of the Rhineland are a remarkable and on the whole a sane and impressive group. Among them the Dominican nuns stand out, and several left written instructions, revelations and lives, of which the best known is by Elizabeth Stagel the biographer of Suso. Hadewijch of the Netherlands may take her place among them.

Closely connected with the Rhineland were the Beghards and Beguines, [1] who existed in great numbers in all the towns of the urban belt between Cologne and Antwerp. The Beguines were a northern and tardy counterpart of the Humiliati and others in north Italy. Their origin is uncertain but from the thirteenth century onwards they were common. Mainly men and women of the middle or lower bourgeoisie, living alone or in small

1. The derivation of the name is uncertain. It may be a corruption of Albeginois; it may be taken from their beige clothing.

groups and giving themselves either to industries such as weaving or to good works such as teaching or nursing, they were devout and often of deep spirituality. Their independence from religious orders and their self-taught piety often gave rise to hostility and criticism and they were on occasion accused of heresy, especially of catharism, and illuminism. Beguine and beguinage became terms of contempt or abuse. Many of the charges, however, were unfounded, and Beguines are found among the notable disciples of the school of Tauler and Suso. They continued to exist; some of them were merged with the communities of the Common Life and still later with some of the independent sects of Protestantism.

The doctrine of Eckhart and Tauler and the practices of the Rhineland mystics gradually filtered into Flanders and a focus of fervent life developed at Groenendael near Brussels, a hermitage chosen by Jean de Ruysbroeck (1343), who remained there as prior of an Augustinian community till his death in 1381. Ruysbroeck is by general consent ranked among the greatest of those who have written of the contemplative union with God in the light of their own experience. He stands indeed, with St John of the Cross and, in the judgment of some, with St Augustine, on the summit of a mountain without other company. Though not a Dominican he is clearly, indeed explicitly, beholden for much of his outlook and theological expression to Eckhart, but he is far more personal in his approach, resembling in this Henry Suso, though with a less emotional and firmer temper of mind. He is in some ways a prolongation of the Rhineland school into another region and language, and a small cluster of mystics looked to him as master.

Ruysbroeck stood also at the source of another and very different current, that of the *Devotio Moderna*. This movement, which had a wide historical influence of a different kind from any school of spirituality, receives fuller mention on another page. Here it is enough to note that it took the form of a reaction against the Rhineland school, both by its exclusive concentration on ascetic spirituality and by an implicit reaction against the autobiographical character and the tremendous claims, whether speculative or actual, of Eckhart, Suso and Ruysbroeck. The last named was visited and admired by Gerard Groot, but was in no sense a founder of the school.

During the greater part of the fourteenth century a series of spiritual writers existed in England who have for long borne the conventional name of ' The English Mystics '. Of the four major members of this group three, Richard Rolle, the unknown author of *The Cloud of Unknowing*, and Walter Hilton, are closely connected with one another either in reaction or in sympathy. The fourth, Dame Julian of Norwich, is of another category and will be mentioned later. Rolle, a university student, turned hermit in

Yorkshire and, writing in both Latin and English, is of interest to philologists as the first known master of the old English literary idiom that had vanished as it were underground shortly after the Norman Conquest. To us he is a writer with a clearly defined and attractive personality who, with many autobiographical details, defends the life of solitude and contemplation and explains his very individual methods and experiences in prayer. In so far as he has masters, they are those who are common to literate Europe, especially Bernard and Richard of St Victor, but it is Rolle's own experience of song and warmth and joy in the Lord that give him the appeal he had throughout the middle ages and that he has regained among readers of today. The unknown writer of *The Cloud* and other short treatises is of another type. Like Rolle a trained scholar, but unlike Rolle a trained theologian, he writes for individuals, in a style of remarkable power, instructions for the first stages of the mystical life. Like Rolle, also, he knows his traditional authorities, Augustine, Bernard and Richard of St Victor, and he appeals directly to Denis, whose *Mystical Theology* he translates. Nevertheless in spirit, in precept and in his firm theological background he resembles Tauler and the Rhinelanders rather than the Victorines, and on a wide view must be regarded as an extension of the Dominican school. Like them, also, he looks forward to the Spanish Carmelites of the sixteenth century. Walter Hilton, a Cambridge master, a hermit, and later an Austin canon, has an almost precisely similar ancestry of mingled Augustinian, Victorine and Dominican provenance. He knows *The Cloud*; whether he drew his firm principles from it or from some other source cannot be said. His scope is wider and embraces a well-developed scheme of spiritual life, both ascetical and mystical. He had no successors, and England in the fifteenth century was remarkably poor in spiritual literature, but Hilton's *Scale of Perfection* remained, until the Reformation and beyond, a manual of the devout life for Englishmen and women, while *The Cloud* retained a similar place among the Carthusians and Bridgettines.

What may be called the academic, traditional stream of spiritual teaching which in its Augustinian form had reached a final formulation in St Bonaventure, and in its Aristotelian branch had come to equilibrium in Aquinas, was to become familiar to multitudes of readers throughout the centuries in the writings of Dante. On this, as on every aspect of his thought, there has been endless discussion, and the old conception of Dante as an orthodox Aristotelian and Thomist has yielded to a far more complex picture. Dante, the poet, even more than St Thomas, absorbed and transcended the opinions of many men and schools, and in the last resort saw reality with the intuition of a poet rather than with the mind of a theologian or a philosopher. A Thomist in his presentation of psychological and moral issues and the powers and destinies of the soul, he regards contemplation, which is the highest pursuit of man and in which the poet himself sees 'things invisible to human sight', as intellectual 'light' rather than as the ineffable superluminous infusion of the mystics, while his doctrine of the active and contemplative lives is in the full tradition of Augustine and the Victorines. Here, as in so many other ways, the poet represents and dominates the traditions of medieval religious thought without himself representing or indeed resembling the opinion of any individual or any school of his age. In his spirituality as in his political thought he is the quintessence of his world, yet stands alone. Aquinas and Dante alike ceased to be guides of the mind in the mid-fourteenth century when the fragmentation of the universe of knowledge began. With the victory of Nominalism in the schools the traditional mystical theology disappears from the universities and the schools of the orders in Italy, France and England, and the famous Parisian masters of the next genera-tion, such as Pierre d'Ailly and Jean Gerson, are in general anti-mystical, and find heresy in Ruysbroeck's teaching.

En revanche the traditional doctrine of the contemplative life, which we have seen becoming domesticated in both the Rhineland and England, finds prophets and preachers among the laity. In England the great and lonely poet William Langland sees the whole world and human life in terms of *Do-well* and *Do-best*, Martha's work and Mary's 'better part', and in Italy Catherine of Siena (1347-80) is giving her mystic's version of traditional theology to the clerics and laypeople of her 'family'. Indeed from 1350 onwards the saints, contemplatives included, and also less repu-table claimants to prophetic gifts, are found more often than not outside the cloister. Catherine herself, Birgitta of Sweden and her daughter, the exquisite Julian of Norwich (1342- after 1413) and the equivocal Margery Kempe, may stand as examples.

Looking back over the nine hundred years surveyed in this book we have seen that for more than half that period the monastic, non-technical, Augustinian expression of spirituality holds undisputed sway, with the bounds of natural and supernatural undefined. In the twelfth century there are the beginnings of a bifurcation. The monastic scheme is on the one hand broken up by scholastic analysis, and the infiltration of Denis the Areopagite with his doctrine of divine darkness and ecstasy is combined with the Augustinian growth in illumination. On the other hand Bernard, with his emphasis on love, with his use of the allegorical bride-mysticism, his direct invitation to the heights, and his autobiographical confirmation of his doctrine, opens a new genre of spiritual writing. In the thirteenth century the academic doctrine splits into the Franciscan, Augustinian, 'affective' school, and the Thomist-Dionysian 'intellective' school. The latter also bifurcates. The main stream becomes thin and confined to academic friars, but a branch in the Rhineland, swollen by great Neoplatonic tributaries, becomes the school of Eckhart, Tauler and Suso, and then passes into the Netherlands to inspire Ruysbroeck. In all academic schools by this time the line between natural and supernatural has been clearly drawn.

Meanwhile the monastic spirituality of Anselm and Bernard continues to nourish the black and white monks who remain for the most part untouched by the mystical outpouring of the fourteenth century and pasture until the end on writers of the twelfth and thirteenth centuries.

31

MEDIEVAL THOUGHT

I. 1200-1277

U NTIL the middle of the twelfth century medieval thinkers depended for their foundations solely upon the logic of Aristotle, available by 1140 in its full extent, and the commentaries composed or translated by Boethius. This circumstance was of the greatest significance for the whole course of medieval thought, for it made of logic the sole discipline and foundation of higher education, thus establishing disputation in set form as the common exercise of students and the method used in every kind of research. This gave to medieval thought the clarity, the accuracy and the subtlety that have been recognised by all historians; it also gave a rigidity which might easily become aridity, in which the technique was prized more than the matter, and verbal dexterity more than original or intuitional thought.

There was something of a pause in the development of systematic thought between the death of Abelard and the first condemnation of Aristotle (i.e., from 1143 to 1210), and it was during this pause in intellectual advance that the universities of France, and above all others, Paris, elaborated their organisation and methods of teaching. It is no part of our task to consider the universities and their development, but it may be remarked that in this period of apparent stagnation in philosophy there came into being for the first time in European civilisation what we still know as the university education: the study by enrolled students at a high level of a fixed syllabus for a fixed time, taught by accredited and highly trained masters, and leading to a serious examination, success in which was rewarded by a ' degree ' of bachelor or master that gave an acknowledged status and qualification throughout western Christendom.

Meanwhile, unseen and sporadically, the philosophical treatises of Aristotle began to filter into France from the sources in Sicily and above all in Spain where the translators had been working since the middle of the century. The intellectual revolution that followed was given a peculiar character by two circumstances. The first was the slow and haphazard process, spread over almost a century, by which translations of Aristotle's treatises reached Paris and Oxford, ever increasing in number and in fidelity to the original Greek. Speaking very generally the scientific treatises were the first to arrive (1170-80), then the great philosophical works on metaphysics, ethics and psychology, and finally the literary and practical treatises, ending with the *Politics* and *Poetics c.* 1250-60. The second circumstance was the ' contamination ' of Aristotle's doctrines partly by apocryphal Neoplatonic works reputed to be his, but more seriously by the commentaries and translations of Arab philosophers who interpreted the Philosopher in their own sense, which in part derived from Neoplatonism and in part was non-religious and determinist in tone.

The works of Aristotle now becoming available were at first of little direct interest for the arts schools, which were concerned with logic only, and they came into notice only when used to support materialistic or pantheistic teaching by individual writers. As a result, a prohibition was issued in 1210 by the archbishop of Sens against their use by teachers in the arts school of Paris. This prohibition did not affect theologians and applied at first only at Paris. By the time that it was reissued by Gregory IX in 1231 as a detail in his great Bull *Parens scientiarum* establishing the constitution and independence of the university of Paris, Aristotle was already entering the curriculum of arts at Oxford and was being used by masters of theology at Paris. Thenceforward the stream became a flood, and theologians and artists alike were compelled to take account of Aristotle's thought. At first they were content to adopt this or that definition or proof that might suit their own opinion, but gradually it became clear that Aristotle's philosophical opinions and naturalistic, perhaps also determinist, outlook accorded ill with the deeply religious outlook of Augustine and the Neoplatonist undertones of his thought. The controversy became open and fierce in the sixth decade of the century, when theologians and philosophers of genius were working at Paris. St Bonaventure, conservative, Franciscan and Augustinian in outlook, used Aristotle little and grew more hostile as the years passed. Albert the Dominican set himself the task of commenting on the whole corpus of Aristotle with a view to making his thought where possible viable for Christian thinkers. Thomas Aquinas, a Dominican pupil of Albert, went still further, by proposing to accept Aristotle's system in general as a basis for Christian thought and theology, to interpret it whenever possible in a Christian sense, and to correct it in a few places. In fact, St Thomas re-expressed much of Aristotle and admitted some elements of Platonic and Neoplatonic thought; his system is in effect an original construction in which the Aristotelian framework is, so to say, turned upside down. Whereas the Greek operates in the universe of experience which is actuated by an impersonal and inflexible First Mover, Thomas works downwards from a personal omnipotent Creator, whose love and care is diffused throughout the universe. In the Paris of the mid-thirteenth century, however, it was impossible for the controversy between the two masters of genius, Bonaventure and Thomas, to work itself out as it were in a sealed vessel, for the currents of thought were disturbed by a third leader. This was Siger of Brabant whose influence originated in the arts school. There also Aristotle had penetrated as a convulsive force. The arts syllabus, previously restricted to logic, had now received the whole of Aristotle, and despite early attempts of authority to contain his teaching and despite also the standing prohibition that kept the artists from debating matters of theology, the metaphysics and psychology of the Philosopher had opened up a whole area of philosophical thought on a purely rational level. Working thus professedly outside the field of theology Siger and his friends had perhaps inevitably interpreted Aristotle (as indeed he wrote) in total separation from Christian belief; they had been led still further away by the Commentary of the great Spanish-Arabian philosopher Averroës, who interpreted Aristotle as holding that all human thought (and thence moral action) was caused by the illumination of a single intellect which enlightened all human minds from outside and from above – a doctrine which carried with it a denial of human individuality, responsibility and immortality. Similarly the doctrine of the existence of the world from all eternity, assumed by Aristotle and asserted by the Arabians, was propounded also by Siger; it was naturally attacked by his opponents as contrary to the Scriptures. The Paris Aristotelians, known by historians till recently as the Latin Averroists, were opposed by both Thomas and Bonaventure and their teaching was condemned by Etienne Tempier, bishop of Paris, in 1272. Siger and his friends defended themselves on the grounds that they taught as philosophers what Aristotle, who personified right reason, had taught; as Christians they accepted the pronouncements of the Church.

Whether they went on to posit, with Averroës, different categories of truth, or the so-called doctrine of the ' double truth ', is not clear. Siger would seem to have been influenced by the condemnation of 1272 and by the arguments of Aquinas, but his school continued to profess integral Aristotelianism, and it is clear that there was in addition a considerable amount of naturalistic, quasi-pagan thought among the masters and students of the arts school. Meanwhile both Aquinas and Bonaventure had died. In the years before the condemnation of 1272 the Franciscans at Paris, led by John Pecham and countenanced by Bonaventure, had attacked certain Aristotelian features adopted by Aquinas, including his interpretation of Aristotle's psychology, in which the soul was presented as the ' form ' of man in the analysis of man's metaphysical constituents (soul = form; body = matter). This teaching, which itself flowed from a primary axiom of Thomism, that being and unity are caused by one and the same principle, appeared to have many inconveniences, philosophical and theological. When therefore Tempier acted again in 1277 and condemned a long series of disparate propositions in which several Aristotelian doctrines were included, some of those in his list were taken from Aquinas.

The Paris condemnations are an important landmark in medieval thought. Though Siger left Paris under a cloud and died shortly after, while Aquinas was vindicated and canonised half-a-century later, the censure of integral Aristotelianism was a victory for the conservative theologians. Aristotle henceforward, save as a logician, was avoided by theologians, and several masters, of whom Duns Scotus is the chief, endeavoured to frame new systems more in harmony with the Christian faith. The tradition of more than a thousand years, that Greek thought was reason expressed in technical terms, was broken, never to be fully repaired, and with it went the conviction, held by all between Augustine and Aquinas, that philosophical and revealed theological knowledge were interlocking parts of a body of known truth accessible to the human mind and reaching from matter to the Divine Trinity, and from the experiences of the senses to the mystical intuition of supernatural knowledge. This conviction rested upon a still more basic assurance, that the human mind was capable of making an adequate contact with reality outside itself, and that the understanding of this reality, in the realm of metaphysics as well as in that of ethics, could be expressed in terms valid for all time. There was therefore an unchanging philosophy *(philosophia perennis)*, which could be formulated with ever greater fullness and precision, and handed on to others as could grammar or mathematics. This assurance, strengthened for a moment by the new knowledge of Aristotle and of the eminent Arabic thinkers who had accepted his words as the expression of the human reason itself, was no longer to be universal in the schools.

The arrival of Aristotle and the work of Aquinas marked an epoch in Christian thought in another respect also. Aristotle, in contrast to Plato and still more in contrast to Plotinus and Augustine, is the philosopher of nature, and of human nature in all its manifestations in social life. While thinkers in the Platonic tradition, reinforced by the Christian emphasis on the transience and imperfection of secular affairs, and on the weakness and insufficiency of human nature, sought reality in a higher sphere of existence, Aristotle restricts his interest strictly to the known universe and to human nature as it is. The thinkers of the thirteenth century were thus for the first time since the collapse of ancient civilisation brought face to face with a view of life which gave to politics and all human relations absolute value. It was upon this basis that Aquinas was able to distinguish clearly between the natural and the supernatural, and to formulate what was perhaps the most seminal of his axioms, that grace and the Christian dispensation did not eliminate but were able to sublimate human nature *(gratia non tollit naturam sed perficit)*. He was thus able to give an absolute value to human activity and human politics and social life, and to vindicate the autonomy, within its own sphere, of human thought. The philosopher, if thinking aright (and this, too, was capable of control and recognition) was in his own sphere unchallengeable. Natural reason, again within its own sphere, was autonomous. Truth could not contradict truth. But this view of the universe was not to be that of the new world of the fourteenth century.

2. ROGER BACON

While almost all the thinkers of the thirteenth century take their place in the orderly development of the schools, there are a few figures who remind us that there is no single and exclusive medieval cast of mind. One such is Friar Roger Bacon (*c.* 1220-*c.* 1292). His external life did not separate him from others. An early teacher of Aristotle as master in the arts school at Paris, a disciple of Grosseteste at Oxford, a late entrant into the Franciscan order, he had many of the aims and prepossessions and mental character-istics of his class. His collisions with authority and the restraints he suffered find a close parallel in those endured by his contemporaries and confrères in another cause, the Spiritual Franciscans. Nor do his criticisms of those in official or intellectual authority differ in anything save their intensity from those of earlier and later embittered or slighted minds. His animus against the theological establishment is largely the outcome of his own frustration. Bacon's significance lies rather in his clearsighted recognition of the basic faults of the scholastic mind: its exaggerated estimate of dialectic as the key to knowledge, its reverence for bookish authority, and its divorce from life and from the facts of the physical universe. He called for a knowledge of Greek and Hebrew, or for exact translations made from accurate texts and, still more urgently, for the use of experiment and the registration of experience in all branches of natural science, and for the recognition of intuition, whether natural or quasi-mystical, in all branches of knowledge.

Original as Bacon certainly was, he remained, as did Wyclif a century later, fully a child of his age and environment, using scholastic methods and subordinating all human knowledge to divine revelation. He had no followers, and natural science at Oxford and at Paris owed none of its discoveries and achievements to him. Yet Bacon, like his younger confrère Scotus, marks a break with the thought of past ages, the eternal philosophy, and it is perhaps not without significance that they and the third revolutionary, William of Ockham, should have been of insular, non-Latin provenance.

3. RAMON LULL

Unlike Roger Bacon in character, in fortune and in method, the great if eccentric Catalan genius Ramon (Raymond) Lull resembles him in his endeavour to reform the whole intellectual and educational system of Europe by a new method and in his sharp criticism of the leading interests of the age such as the strategy of the crusaders and the best way of converting the unbelievers. Born in Majorca c. 1232 Lull, after periods of dissolute and domestic life, experienced a change of heart c. 1262 and devoted himself to the conversion of the infidel, joining the third Order of St Francis. In this period of his life he attacked Averroism, which he regarded as the principal public enemy of the age, in a series of writings, and also elaborated his method of universal knowledge, the *Ars generalis*. This was a system by which the combination in different ways of a number of metaphysical conceptions or Ideas gave insight into the nature and principles of all the subaltern sciences. To make what was a difficult metaphysical process feasible for ordinary intelligences Lull devised a system of significant letters and circles (standing for leading ideas) which would show at a glance, after the necessary shifting and adjustment, the particular intellectual process to be followed. This phase of Lull's life was followed by one of travel and propaganda on behalf of the crusade, and in missionary journeys of preaching, in the course of which in North Africa he was so maltreated by the infidels that he died shortly after in 1315. Lull was an indefatigable and voluminous writer, with many facets to his mind, and his mystical writings are an important part of his work. Thinkers who devise a ready reckoner to solve the riddles of the universe must expect ridicule as well as admiration, and Lull received both from his contemporaries and posterity. He has always had his devotees among thinkers and scholars, but the final estimate of his personality and intellectual stature still awaits the day when scholarship shall have presented all his works for scrutiny.

$$\boxed{32}$$

HERESY

I. EARLY HERESY AND THE CATHARI

THE history of the Church in the Roman empire is in great part a history of the growth and fortunes of heresy, the name given to all deviations from the doctrinal or moral teaching of Catholic Christianity. While these deviations occasionally took the form of moral or disciplinary revolt, the more celebrated and influential were concerned with the deepest mysteries of the faith and gave rise to controversies often conducted on either side by men of great mental power and upright life. From the fifth century to the eleventh heresy was practically non-existent in the West as a public danger or an intellectual debate, and the impact of eastern controversies, such as the monothelite and iconoclastic, was only felt at the high level of papal or imperial diplomacy, while the more domestic issues such as the eucharistic debates of Paschasius Radbert were conducted between a few experts. In the twelfth century, on the other hand, popular and widespread movements appeared, resulting in the formation of veritable anti-churches and the creation of enclaves within Catholic Christendom, and leading to the establishment by church and state of a machinery of repression whose activities are one of the most difficult and painful features of the age. There were in general three different types of unorthodox teaching which blended and divided in various ways. There was the simple revolt against a rich, established, hierarchical and sacramental religion; here the aim was to revive a more spiritual, simple, individual approach to God. There was the invasion of ancient dualistic heterodoxy from the Balkans and beyond. Finally, there was the more systematic or programmatic unorthodoxy of a few trained and gifted minds. A distinguished historian [1] has remarked that all the religious movements of the middle ages left as a deposit behind them either a religious order or an heretical sect. He has also shown that many of the sects owed their origin to economic or social factors. The cult of poverty and the communal life was at once a spiritualisation of existing conditions and a reaction against wealthy and luxurious capitalists. The anti-clerical and anti-sacramental bias was a practical criticism of a sordid clerical proletariate, an aristocratic episcopate and grasping and exclusive monastic and capitular bodies.

The first heretical movements of which any trace remains occurred in the early decades of the eleventh century in several districts of France, such as Champagne, the Orléanais and Aquitaine, and north Italy. They were obscure in origin and apparently resembled one another in rejecting the Incarnation and in consequence the traditional doctrine of the Eucharist, and in denying the need for baptism and the powers of a bishop to ordain. These negative tenets and the call to poverty and a direct communication with God were sometimes combined with more specific opinions such as the rejection of marriage, abstinence from fleshmeat, and the acceptance of a ministery conferred by the laying on of hands by an outstanding leader. These last tenets, which are often referred to an origin in north Italy, strongly suggest some kind of Bogomil or, as it was then usually called, Manichaean influence. Entirely separate from these, and never unorthodox in a technical sense, was the Pataria of the common people in Milan and Lombardy, a movement of revolt against a rich and simoniacal clergy. The frankly heretical sects, antinomian and antimoral in effect, were diffused by popular leaders, some of whom claimed to possess divine powers. They were repressed sooner or later with severity, sometimes by bishops, sometimes by popular violence, and only in Languedoc, long to be a nursery and asylum of heresy, did they become in any sense endemic. Elsewhere they vanish from sight for half a century, possibly losing their attraction to would-be reformers when the Gregorian reform was under way, possibly merely invisible from a lack of documentary evidence of the activities of scattered minorities.

A second wave originated, so far as can be seen, in Italy and southern

1. H. Grundmann.

France in the first half of the twelfth century. This was mainly a movement of reform, in which a return to apostolic poverty on the part of the clergy was demanded. Among the clearly heretical leaders were Peter of Bruis (d.*c.* 1126), who preached poverty and an unsacramental, puritanical religion, Arnold of Brescia (d. 1155) and Ugo Speroni (d. after 1174). Of these Peter was opposed, both in writing and in person, by Peter the Venerable and St Bernard, and was burnt by an excited crowd. Arnold of Brescia, a restless and tireless preacher of poverty for priests and monks, and hostile to the clerical establishment, was regarded, perhaps mistakenly, by St Bernard as an ally of Abelard. He turned to political agitation and shared in the establishment in Rome of a commune in antiquarian clothes; he was ultimately hanged as a revolutionary at the instigation of Hadrian IV and Frederick Barbarossa. Ugo Speroni, a recently discovered lawyer heretic, is an example of a lone teacher constantly in collision with authority. [2]

A third and more formidable wave developed shortly before the middle of the twelfth century. This was an offshoot of the Bogomil heresy of Bulgaria, itself derived ultimately from the dualistic and gnostic teaching of Manichaeism. Striking roots in Constantinople, it acquired the rudiments of a dogmatic and ascetic system which spread to Bulgaria and Bosnia along the routes of the trader and gradually filtered into the populous districts of western and northern Europe by way of the highways of commerce. From about 1140 its adepts multiplied in every direction: in the Rhineland with a centre at Cologne; at Périgord, at Rheims in Lombardy and central Italy, and above all in southern France around Albi, Toulouse and Carcassonne. A feature of the movement was its strict ecclesiastical organisation, which together with its missionary urge gave it dynamic strength and great powers of resistance. In the second half of the twelfth century it was diffused over much of Italy north of Rome owing in particular to the evangelising activity of one Peter of Lombardy. It existed there as a secret and hidden scattering of groups, each centred upon an ordained leader and without organic connection with each other. While the church in Italy was still consolidating itself, apostles crossed the Alps or passed by sea into the Rhône valley. At some moment in this advance the name of Cathari (= ' the pure ') was transferred from the small class of perfect, to which it properly applied, to the whole body. Whereas in Italy the adepts were chiefly merchants and craftsmen, in Languedoc many converts were made among leading feudal families, including Raymond VI, count of Toulouse; monks also and even bishops joined them, and in the relatively polished and luxurious society that gave birth to the troubadours and the

2. For him see Ilarino da Milano, *L'eresia di U. Speroni*, Studi e Testi 35 (Città del Vaticano 1945).

first medieval school of secular music the novel and elaborate teaching and practice spread rapidly.

The doctrines of the sect, though differing at first both in theory and practice from group to group, were in general a residual offshoot of Manichaeism adapted first by Bogomil and then contaminated by Christianity; it became more and more a rival to Catholicism by reason of its imitation of Christian organisation and ritual. The teaching rested on a dualistic theory of good and evil, spirit and matter. The principle of good, the creator of the world of spirit, was opposed by a principle of evil, either a co-eternal but rebellious divine Son or, as held by some, a fallen angel, a demiurge. In either case an evil agent was the creator of the material world. Human souls were fragments of spirit, or according to some, fallen angels, enmeshed in matter, Christ was the highest of the angels (or the best of mankind) adopted by God as Son; his body and death were appearances only, or in any case his death was insignificant, as he redeemed man by his teaching, not by his Passion. The Catholic church was a corrupt descendant of an originally pure body; its doctrines were false, its sacraments unreal. The Catharist church consisted of two classes, one small, the other large. The small class of the ' perfect ' or ' pure ', who gave their name to the body, provided the hierarchy of various degrees who were also the preachers. They were ordained by a sacrament of initiation, preceded by a severe probation, which blotted out sin, gave the Holy Spirit, and conferred powers of ministry. This sacrament, the *consolamentum* as it was called, implied a life of great austerity, with perpetual chastity and abstinence from fleshmeat; fighting and oaths also were forbidden. The others, the ' adherents ', were allowed more freedom and a full use of worldly possessions; when possible they received an abbreviated version of the *consolamentum* on their deathbed. The rejection of the material creation led in theory to a contempt of life, and voluntary suicide by starvation (the *endura*) was not unknown. In theory, which was often put into practice in early days, the ' perfect ' were bound to a life of austere virtue, whereas the others were allowed more laxity. Marriage was regarded as evil and women as a more evil part of creation than men. The strictness of these divisions relaxed with time; the doctrine that all were bound to prepare themselves for ' perfection ' seems to have had a morally good influence, and marriage was in fact recognised. Considerable variety of doctrine existed, especially in Italy; some held that if a ' bishop ' sinned grievously the *consolamentum* received by him was invalid, as were also the *consolamenta* he had conferred. The statements of Catholic polemists that the Cathari, who condemned all sexual relations, made no distinction in consequence between the normal and the perverse, and between lawful and free intercourse, and that therefore the mere ' adherents ' had no morality, may have had some foundation but were not in general correct.

The Cathari had a public liturgy which was a recognisable imitation of the Eucharist. They flourished to an extraordinary degree in Languedoc, Provence and north Italy, where schools were established and industries organised for the believers, who were found among all classes of a society that was notably prosperous and cultivated. The strong appeal of their teaching, which is alien to modern instincts, must be accepted as an historical fact. The Catholic church had lost its hold in many districts and among certain classes; the orthodox clergy in Languedoc were prosperous and lax; Catharism gave to many a sense of corporate life and mutual support which was not to be found in the contemporary Catholic society, and its esoteric character and frigid ritual seem to have been no bar to its appeal.

Of a different family by origin, though sometimes going over into Catharism and often coinciding with it in marginal doctrines and practices were those groups, orthodox in belief, at least in origin, that came into being in many centres and approximated in practices and feeling to the ' nonconformist ' and ' congregational ' sects of later centuries. Such were the Humiliati of the cities of Lombardy who practised a laborious and penurious life in groups, given to preaching, reading the Bible in the vernacular, minimising the priesthood and the sacraments and extolling personal, interior union with God. On the left, so to say, of this group were the Waldenses of the Dauphiné and Piedmont, named after Waldes a rich merchant of Lyons, who gave themselves to piety and good works, Bible-reading and preaching and living upon alms. Waldes himself was wholly orthodox in original intention, and when he left his home for his apostolic vocation he settled his two daughters in the aristocratic abbey of Fontevrault. Nevertheless, some in all these groups became definitely heterodox, regarding the Bible as the supreme authority and denying the real presence in the Eucharist. A few groups adopted the organisation and some of the practices and precepts, though not the theology, of the Cathari. A majority remained professedly orthodox, as the Humiliati and the Poor Catholics; others became and remained Christian ' heretics ', and of these the Waldenses, the ' proto-Protestants ', continued to influence religious history throughout the middle ages and despite persecution remain in existence at the present day.

Heresy was countered by the polemical writings and sermons of eminent men such as Peter the Venerable, St Bernard, Vacarius and Alan of Lille, and later by the collections of nameless friars. Gradually coercion, secular and ecclesiastical, took the place of persuasion. In default of an established procedure punishments differed in severity. The imperial law of Byzantium had decreed death for the Manichees, and in later ages witchcraft was punishable by the fire, but for long bishops and controversialists were averse to the death penalty or severe corporal punishment. At last the Council of Tours, in 1163, at the request of rulers and bishops, established a process of ecclesiastical inquiry. Albigenses convicted of heresy were to be handed over to the secular authorities for imprisonment and the confiscation of their property. This led to armed revolt, against which the third Lateran council summoned a crusade. Five years later Lucius III, after an agreement with Frederick I, promulgated a decretal in which, after a global excommunication of existing heretics, the duty of inquisition by visitation and denunciation in all localities known to harbour heretics was laid directly upon the bishop. Those who were denounced and unable to prove their innocence were handed over to the lay power. No penalty was specified and the lay rulers, who showed themselves active in controlling heretics, maintained at first the traditional imprisonment and confiscation of property. The first appearance of fire for heresy in western Europe has often been seen by historians in a decree of Peter of Aragon in 1197, but several of the early heretics of the eleventh century had been burned. Of all the centres of heresy, by far the most notable was that of the Albigenses in southern France, from Loire to Rhône, with its centre in the county of Toulouse, where a warlike and amoral but luxurious, cultivated and orientalised baronage had made use of Cathari in their private wars against the count of Toulouse, and an aristocratic hierarchy and an uneducated clergy had for different reasons become infected. The real austerity and good works of the ' perfect ' and the ambiguous attitude of Raymond VI contributed to make converts.

Innocent III received notice of heresies from all parts and had personal knowledge of Catharism as existing in Lombardy and Tuscany. Equating heresy with treason he accepted the task of eradicating it and of handing over condemned persons to the secular power, though at first with no thought of capital punishment and with a preference for purely spiritual means. The pope had also directed into the region of Toulouse Cistercian monks, including the abbot of Cîteaux and other legates. They produced little effect, their prosperous and splendid way of life contrasting with the edifying austerity of the ' perfect '. A long-term remedy was found, as we shall see, in the mendicant Dominicans; meanwhile all efforts proved useless. Raymond VI was excommunicated as a supporter and near heretic and the legate Pierre de Castelnau was assassinated by one of the count's officers (January 1208). Innocent III, shocked, assumed the complicity of Raymond and appealed to the king of France, Philip Augustus, to launch a crusade. The king delayed, but barons in large numbers undertook the task, for which the normal crusading rewards were issued. Raymond performed a spectacular penance and offered himself as a crusader but the northerners would not be baulked. The fearful massacre of Bézières followed (21 July 1209) and the crusaders entered in upon their spoils, assisted by the papal legates. The pope, misinformed and overrun by the events, formally acquiesced in the installation in the county of Toulouse of Simon de Montfort, despite the often asserted submission of Raymond VI. Thus ended the first act in the tragic drama of the Albigenses. For the rest Innocent showed himself ready to countenance Waldenses and Humiliati who accepted the common faith and discipline of the Church. At the Lateran Council the matter of the Albigenses was settled by a compromise: Simon de Montfort was allowed to retain his conquests, Toulouse and Montauban, while Provence was to pass to Raymond VII.

2. THE INQUISITION

Nevertheless heresy continued to diffuse itself and the Albigensian territory continued to be the principal centre. In Italy a Catharist church existed in scattered communities, and even penetrated into the Rhineland. To combat this danger the papacy in the thirteenth century organised the inquisition.

This derived directly from the decree of Lucius III reaffirmed by the Lateran council and by Gregory IX, giving to the bishops the duty and right of discovering and punishing heresy, with the ultimate abandonment of the convict to the secular arm for due punishment *(animadversio debita)*. Under Honorius III fighting broke out again between the supporters of the native dynasty of Toulouse and Simon de Montfort and a second crusade with the same characteristics as before was launched (1221) and ultimately adopted by King Louis VIII in person (1226). Meanwhile the sovereigns had adopted the legislation of the fourth Lateran Council. The emperor Frederick II in 1220 and King Louis VIII in 1226 accepted the duty of the bishop to discover and judge heretics and that of the secular power to apply the due penalty. This was defined as the fire by the emperor in 1224; as a practice this was already current in Aragon and Languedoc. Pope Honorius accepted it from imperial Italy in the last years of his reign. Gregory IX, who confirmed the transference of the county of Toulouse to the French crown, took up the imperial legislation into canon law (1231); Louis had meanwhile in 1229 accepted the *animadversio debita*. Gregory IX was further responsible for integrating the inquisitorial procedure into canon law with all its details of penalties. This machinery was immediately set to work. In Rome itself and in Sicily the pope countenanced the translation into secular law of the whole process. The northern cities of Italy followed, and at the same time the pope gave special powers in Germany to Conrad of Marburg who for a year conducted a savage campaign against the Luciferian heretics around Treves. In Italy pope and emperor were in agreement in applying the methods of the inquisition to the Catharist and other groups of heretics. Indeed in the latter years of Gregory IX the inquisition was functioning with ardour in France, Italy, Germany, the Low Countries and north Spain. In Languedoc and the Midi in general papal legates and local inquisitors did their best to extirpate the heretics who were still numerous, active and in some cases edifying. In northern France the Dominican Robert le Bougre, a convert from Catharism, won for himself a name of fear and hatred equal to that of Conrad of Marburg, who was assassinated in 1233. Gradually the inquisition, supported by pope, bishops and the Dominicans, and in general feared and hated by the people, rooted out the catharism of the Midi and the north of France. In Italy the more peaceful influence of St Francis and his friars may have been felt. Henceforward, the institution remained, formalised and with some of its severity mitigated.

The inquisition, which at first supplemented and then supplanted the normal episcopal court, was in origin devised to deal with heresy such as that of the catharists which was deeply ingrained in a district and supported by many of the powerful and wealthy, including highly placed clergy. Proceedings began by exhortation to confession with promise of merciful treatment and a command to the faithful to denounce. The normal procedure of action by the archdeacon or an individual was supplanted by a command that accusations should be made of any person suspected of heresy in a particular district. Those who made such accusations were to remain anonymous, and the persons so accused were examined. The burden of disproof lay upon the accused. If unable to exculpate themselves at once they were subjected to a searching interrogation, the avowed purpose of which was to secure confession of heresy. If this was obtained, a penalty of lesser or greater weight was assigned. The heaviest that the inquisitors could impose was imprisonment of which the extreme form was solitary imprisonment for life; beyond this, and reserved for confessed heretics who refused to recant or who relapsed after recantation, was the punishment of fire, carried out by the secular arm, usually with alacrity but under strict ecclesiastical sanction. Throughout the proceedings the dice were loaded against the accused, and what protection he had in the earliest times – an advocate, the inadmissibility of evidence obtained by violence, protection from torture and from its repetition – were gradually whittled away by legislation and by casuistry and by open and direct equivocation, and the attempts of popes such as Clement V to restore equitable treatment were ignored. We of the present century have some knowledge of the seeming inevitability by which the machinery of the law becomes a snare when used by a sovereign authority for a political end, or indeed by any who hold that a reason of state or ideology or of religion can be invoked against truth and just judgment.

The medieval inquisition was the product of the circumstances of the time and the mental climate of its age. On the one hand a society, integrally Christian in its institutions, beliefs, assumptions and habits, became aware for the first time of a new, large, increasing and for the most part secret body of dissidents in its midst who were actively diffusing doctrines and practices that were an imitation of the most sacred rites and at the same time an explicit repudiation of the Christian faith, besides being in some measure and in many cases a challenge to Christian moral teaching. On the other hand the Church, that is the clerical body under its supreme head, the pope, had as a result of the great movement known as the Gregorian reform, claimed, and in large measure succeeded in attaining, a position of supreme authority and actual power in the body politic of Christendom. The papacy, in particular, was now recognised as having, and was ready to assume, the responsibility and initiative for the protection and discipline of the whole Church, in which the temporal authorities were included as subjects of the pope. Disposing, as he did, of the spiritual arms of the vicar of Christ, the pope claimed and actually had, at least in certain spheres and places, the power of a totalitarian authority.

These circumstances of themselves might not have led either to the endeavour to extirpate heresy by fire or to the novel methods of the inquisition. There was however in addition the conviction of the whole of society that this should be done. The attacks upon the heretics of the eleventh and early twelfth century had been popular and tumultuary; bishops and kings had done no more than acquiesce. The people in northern France and elsewhere had a fear of a heretic that was half superstitious and half akin to xenophobia. In the latter part of the century and throughout the thirteenth the emperor, the king of France, and other rulers took the fiercest action without any incitement and were ready to support the pope and later the inquisition. This action was undoubtedly sharpened by a new familiarity with Roman law, as containing legislation against Manichaeism and other heresy, as sanctioning the extreme penalty, and as regarding heresy as the state crime of treason. To these circumstances must be added a change in sentiment over the greater part of educated Europe, on the one hand in the direction of authoritarian power, and on the other hand to a blunting of the sense of humanity and of natural justice. The twelfth and earlier centuries had been brutal and lawless in many respects, and their customary punishments had been barbarous, but the legalised and deliberate cruelty of the thirteenth century was a new phenomenon. The use of torture, which had been repugnant to an earlier generation, now caused no qualm. The sense of humanity which the old literary and patristic education had fostered had been lost, while the philosophical assertion of natural rights had not been born. A reader of yesterday and today is revolted and indignant as he learns of the procedure of the inquisition. He should not need to be reminded what excesses are caused by fear of the enemy within the gates, by the enmity of warring ideologies, and by the strength of a totalitarian power. In the thirteenth century, safety of society and the responsibility of handing down intact the deposit of faith in Christ's Church seemed to rest with the inquisitors, and the conviction that the unbaptised or heretic had no rights was widespread. Any comparison with the climate of ideas at the present day or indeed at any time since the fifteenth century is fallacious. The medieval heretic was not one who had followed his reason or conscience as best he could among a hundred warring creeds and unbeliefs. He was often one who consciously and sometimes rebelliously set his face against the common belief of his world, and in some cases went on to oppose it and even to blaspheme it, not in order to accept a parallel interpretation of the Christian message. To contemporaries, the Cathari rather than the Waldenses made up the 'image' of the heretic. To say this is not to pronounce the methods and acts of inquisition as just, or as consonant in all respects with the teaching of Christ. In particular the inquisitors in general made no distinction between one who had knowingly abandoned the Christian faith and one who had been brought up from infancy among 'heretics', as had many in the Midi, or between the deliberate rebel and the mentally or psychologically morbid character. And justice and Christian charity were often strangely neglected by men acting in a public capacity when as private individuals they showed themselves both just and humane.

3. JOACHIM OF FIORE

This is perhaps a fitting place to mention a heretic of a very different type. Joachim of Fiore or Flora became a Cistercian in middle life and abbot of Corazzo in Calabria, leaving in 1190 to found a new monastic order at San Giovanni in Fiore, where he died in 1202. In his later years he had written a number of apocalyptic commentaries on Scripture, and an attack on the trinitarian theology of Peter the Lombard, which he considered heretical as implying a fourfold deity of the Three Persons and their divinity. He himself, protesting orthodoxy, in fact denied the real unity of the Three Persons, and was duly anathematised by the Fourth Lateran Council which gave resounding approbation to the Lombard, who was mentioned by name in the definitory decree. [3] Meanwhile, Joachim had

---

3. IV Lateran Council ch. 2. 'Nos autem, sacro approbante Concilio, credimus et confitemur cum Petro Lombardo, quod, etc.' Denzinger-Schönmetzer, 804. 'Nos' is Innocent himself.

died in the odour of sanctity, submitting all his writings to the judgment of the Church.

His three principal works, the *Harmony (Concordia) of the New and Old Testaments*, the *Exposition of the Apocalypse*, and the *Psaltery with three strings*, propounded a wide scheme of world history in three divisions: the age of God the Father and the Law, from the creation to the redemption; that of the gospel and the Son, now nearing its term; and that of the eternal gospel and the Holy Ghost. This last period, for which preparation was to begin about 1200 for its arrival in 1260, was to see a new and spiritual understanding of the gospel message in which a new order of spiritual men, under the guidance of a Christ-like leader, would take the place of bishops. Along with much purely visionary detail there was a considerable depth of religious thought in Joachim's writings, which he revised continually. In particular, also, his conception of the gradual evolution of one epoch from another, and the constant development of clarity in the divine message, implied a recognition of the significance of the historical process as a ' linear ' one, neither static nor cyclic. His prophecies, neglected for years, found fortune when the friars, and in particular the Minors, saw in St Francis and his order the spiritual men and their leader who were to rule the brave new world that was to dawn in 1260, and the programme was expounded by Gerard of Borgo San Donnino in his *Introduction to the Eternal Gospel* of 1254. This was condemned, not without dust and noise, by a papal commission, but henceforth the echoes of Joachim's prophecies never ceased to reverberate in the minds of the Franciscan Spirituals and Fraticelli. John of Parma, Peter Olivi, Ubertino da Casale and a host of lesser men were, or were accused of being, Joachimists and the dose of apocalyptic prophecy in the programme of the reformers had a large part in bringing discredit upon their cause in their struggles with the Conventuals and with the pope. Joachim, indeed, as Dante's line showed, [4] haunted the imagination of men long after the Calabrian abbot, as an historical figure, had faded from the memory of his age.

4. *Paradiso* XII, 140. ' Il calavrese abate Giovacchino/Di spiritu profetico dotato. '

THE JEWS AND USURY

THE men of the later middle ages in Europe assumed as axiomatic both that they composed the universal church (with a tacit neglect of Orthodox Christianity) and that western Christendom was wholly Christian. There was, however, besides the heretical bodies, such as the Albigenses or Waldenses, who from time to time formed hostile groups, one body of convinced non-Christians, who continued to exist throughout the medieval millennium and beyond it, that of the Jews. These, though never attaining demographic importance in western Europe, remained, in their obstinate racial independence and their ability to survive the hardest treatment, a standing challenge to Christianity and a passive measure of the humanity and tolerance of the medieval centuries. By a curious paradox Rome, which in its imperial days had harboured for centuries a large colony, continued throughout to contain a nucleus of Jews, and it has been noted that the Roman Jews were treated in general with tolerance, and that the popes, by deed as well as by word, were the most humane of all the rulers of Europe. Generally speaking the Jews followed population and trade; it was only in the later middle ages and in central Europe that they were found in numbers in small towns and villages and on the land.

Long before our period opens ecclesiastical and civil legislation had discriminated against the Jews and had forbidden intermarriage between

Jews and Christians; they were also debarred from public office, but their financial and mercantile skill made them all but indispensable. Their unchanging traditions and their rich legal, theological and economic lore made them always a busy, sophisticated element in society. Persecution was always officially discouraged and at more than one epoch persuasion and controversy were intellectual interests among educated Christians. The baptism of a Jew was an occasion of triumph, the apostasising of a Christian visited by death.

The sole theatre of persecution in the seventh century was Visigothic Spain. Spain was then the richest and in some ways the most civilised of the Roman provinces, and Jews were numerous and prosperous. This, as commonly happened, provoked envy and hostility, and at several of the councils of Toledo, where royal and secular influence was greater than that of the bishops, measures of proscription were passed with the object of compelling Jews to abjure their faith in baptism or leave the country. It was the first sign of that disastrous policy that was to recur in Spanish history. As later, it had the twofold result of driving the most sincere and gifted Jews into the arms of Spain's enemies, and of transforming the others into false Christians and potential traitors. Jews in fact were among those who encouraged the Muslim invaders, and when these latter were established the Jews found them more tolerable masters than the Christians. Jewish civilisation and genius, indeed, has never in the Christian centuries been seen to better effect than in Spain under the caliphs of Cordova. Poets, scholars and philosophers appeared; among them Solomon ibn Gabirol (Avicebron, 1021-70) and a century later Moses ben Maimum (Maimonides, 1135-1204) both of whom deeply influenced Christian thinkers and theologians of the thirteenth century. Persecution, however, occurred at first sporadically and then universally, with a consequent increase of crypto-Jews.

Meanwhile forced conversion or exile emptied Lombardy and Gaul of Jews in the seventh century, but from the age of Charlemagne onwards the European Jews gradually established a numerical superiority over those in the East. Jewish merchants multiplied along the trade-routes, and were protected and favoured. Lombardy, Provence, the valleys of the Rhône, Rhine, Danube and Elbe admitted many colonies; their entry into England followed upon the Norman Conquest, and the eleventh century marked the summit of their fortunes. Thenceforward catastrophes followed. There were isolated persecutions in France and shocking massacres in the path of the recruits to the first and second crusades, particularly in the Rhineland. All these were the work of crowds and the people; the bishops in many cases, and St Bernard the preacher of the second crusade, did everything possible to protect the Jews, as did the sovereigns in England and elsewhere who needed their services as financiers. Apart from the massacres, the Jews continued to increase and amass wealth. Within the Jewries study of the Scriptures and Talmudic literature flourished, and among learned Christians dialogues between a Christian and a Jew became a favourite literary genre, while medicine as always was cultivated and practised with distinction by Jews. At the same time the twelfth century, which witnessed the successful advance of Catharism and other heresy, especially in Italy and southern France, with the consequent reaction of fear both in the higher and lower levels of church life, saw also a spread of the panic accusation of child-crucifixion and desecration of the Eucharist on the part of Jews, with attendant murders and massacres. Consequently, just as now for the first time in the West severe ecclesiastical sanctions were framed against heresy, so the papal councils opened the series of restrictive legislation against Jews. The Third Lateran Council of 1179 forbade Jews to have Christian servants, and Christians to dwell among Jews. The Fourth Lateran of 1215 ordered Jews to pay tithes and forbade their employment in positions of authority by Christian governments. Above all, the council enacted that Jews must wear a distinguishing badge, which took the form of a piece of yellow or red cloth or (as in Italy) a hat of a particular colour. This twofold legislation, of segregation and distinctive marking, established once and for all in medieval Europe what would now be called a species of *apartheid*, which resulted in the ' Ghetto system ' in the larger towns of Europe, and exposed the Jews as a target for attack or massacre. It is about this time that the monastic artists of Europe, who were exchanging hieratic or ideal figures for those taken from real life in their environment, began to people the scenes of the Passion of Christ with countenances reflecting the characteristics of the Jews they saw about them, thus helping to fasten the guilt of the crucifixion upon their race.

Nevertheless the late twelfth century and the thirteenth were an epoch of relative consolidation and prosperity for the Jewish colonies in Italy, France and England. External and domestic pressures combined to make of the individual companies and the national aggregate a compact, well organised body, a *universitas Judeorum*, more self-contained and regulated than any other class or guild. Wherever peace reigned intellectual life flourished, with particular attention to the Judaic law, but with some interest also in philosophy and literature. In both England and France royal protection and the claim of suzerainty were at first of benefit to the Jews, but in both countries excessive exploitation, confiscation and exaction dried up the golden stream at its source, while at the same time the appearance of the wealthy and technically skilful financiers from Lombardy and Cahors, and later from Florence and Genoa, more than compensated for the disappearance of Jewish capital. Edward I of England, after an attempt to direct the wealthy Jews to merchandise and the lesser to handicrafts, took the decisive step of expulsion in 1290. His policy was imitated with less skill and honesty, and more barbarity, by Philip the Fair in 1306. These two expulsions swelled the Jewries of the German-speaking lands. Here, owing to the decay of imperial, and all central authority, the Jews were neither protected nor expelled in bulk. Instead, as a Jewish historian wrote in 1931, in words so soon to be tragically verified, Germany figures ' as the classical land of Jewish martyrdom, where banishment was employed only . . . to complete the work of massacre '. [1] Accusations of child-murder and host-profanation, or of spreading the Great Pestilence of 1348-9, were used to inflame anti-racial prejudice and the grievances of debtors. The mid-fourteenth-century massacres, indeed, had the same effect as the western expulsions, and the living remnant drifted eastwards. In Austria and Bohemia the same rhythm was followed at an interval of years, and the surviving exiles found comparative peace in Poland, where Casimir the Great (1333-70) gave them a protection which allowed their intellectual heritage to blossom once again. There, large numbers were still in existence at the end of the middle ages. Similarly in Italy colonies remained, particularly in Rome, where expulsion never took place, in Venice, where a peculiar arrangement of a ten-years' lease of life was in force, and in Calabria where the Jews remained the only capitalists of the region.

Spain, by reason of its past history, stood apart from the rest of Europe here as in other matters. The Jews as has been seen had a chequered history under Muslim rule, and when the reconquest came they met with ambivalent treatment, now regarded as the ally of Islam against the Christian, now as the inheritors of a religious and cultural tradition akin to Christianity. In the event, the age of great scholars and poets overlapped into the Christian era with such great names as Abraham ibn Ezra (Rabbi ben Ezra 1092-1167) and Maimonides. Alfonso VI of Castile (1063-1109) was particularly favourable to them, and his was one of the few medieval armies to contain numbers of Jews. It was in this period, and especially at Toledo, that Jews assisted so greatly the researches of northern and Italian scholars among the treasures of Arabic learning in the sciences and in philosophy. The period of toleration and favour ended when Muslim power was finally broken at Las Navas de Tolosa (1212). The Jews now began to be regarded as potential enemies and the decrees of the Lateran Council of 1215 were accepted, though never fully implemented, but for more than a century the Jews enjoyed peace and shared more freely in agricultural and industrial pursuits than in any other European country. A change for the worse came with the Black Death when a series of massacres began, and in 1391 mob-

1. Cecil Roth in *Cambridge Medieval History* VII, 657.

violence over almost the whole peninsula presented the Jewish community
with the alternative of baptism or death. Many yielded, and thus for the
second time Spain contained a large quota of crypto-Jews as well as of
sincere converts who rose to positions of ecclesiastical dignity. This presented a problem unique in Europe. The Jews who had succeeded in
escaping death or who had subsequently entered the country lived side by
side with those – the Maranos – who had ostensibly accepted the Christian
faith by baptism but who continued to think, and in part to practise, as
Jews, and with those of Jewish descent who now belonged heart and soul
to the Catholic church and enjoyed high honours both in church and state.
Isabella the Catholic agreed to the establishment of the inquisition in
Castile and Aragon (1480, 1484), and shortly after the capture of Granada
decreed the expulsion of all Jews from Spain (1492), and Portugal followed
suit in 1496. A few only remained at the risk of their lives, and ultimately,
escaping from Spain, formed the nucleus of the modern communities of
north-western Europe, which, while rarely inter-marrying with Christians,
have identified themselves in large part with the nationalities among whom
they have taken up a permanent abode.

The treatment of Jews by medieval Christians is an inglorious page of
history, though it should in fairness be remembered that the Muslims at
various epochs have shown similar inhumanity, while modern states, both
those nominally Christian and those professedly atheistic, have shown still
worse barbarity. Leaving aside all moral or psychological causes in either
party, there were reasons for friction. The Jewish race is unique in European history both in its persistent survival and diffusion in all epochs and
in its cohesive and strongly marked character. While in certain regions and
epochs, such as Merovingian France and late medieval Europe, Jews have
taken part in the exploitation of the natural resources of the land, their
racial talents and the feudal organisation of Europe, to which were later
added the legal and canonical disabilities, combined to bring about their
concentration in towns and the development of their talent in financial and
later mercantile pursuits. They became and remained, wherever they
enjoyed peaceful existence, capitalists and moneylenders, and this alone,
in a society without an understanding of the function and manipulation of
money as capital, would have inspired distrust and envy. Even in modern
society the forcible recovery of a debt has something odious about it, and
in underdeveloped societies the domination of a lower class by their credi-
tors has always been the classical prelude to a revolt. To this was added
the ideological enmity born of the place taken by Jews in the economy of
Christian origins. While it is true that the Christian Church treated the
Jewish Scriptures as an integral part of its heritage and retained much of
Jewish prayer and ceremony, and that exegetes of the patristic age distin-

guished clearly between the small group of leaders directly responsible for the crucifixion and the race from which Christ himself and his Mother, his apostles and disciples had sprung, it is true also that they, following the lead of Christ himself and the inspired writers, had regarded the Jews as heirs of a national apostasy and as living outside the economy of grace which had passed from the children of circumcision to the children of the baptismal waters. Doubtless their conversion was to be hoped for, prayed for and worked for, but meanwhile they were not only without faith but in a certain sense had broken faith with God: they were the *perfidi* of the liturgy.[2] Human nature is prone to hatred of dissimilarity, both racial and ideological, and the Jews were obstinately dissimilar. On their part too there was hatred and ruthlessness. The step to segregation and the darker step to persecution and massacre were lightly taken.

The treatment of the Jews was rendered more harsh on account of their practice of usury, which was prohibited to Christians of the later middle ages by canon law supported by the strongest sanctions.

Whatever may be thought of the economic or social unwisdom of this prohibition, it cannot be laid at the door of the medieval papacy. Although in the ancient civilisations, both Semitic and Greco-Roman, operations of capital and credit, together with actuarial calculations and the regular use of interest on loans, had been part of the economy, theorists had continued, with Aristotle, to regard money as dead, unproductive metal, a token of account or medium of exchange, not as a commodity equivalent to real estate or natural produce and therefore rightly to be regarded as potentially productive. On the forensic level, no adequate control had been put upon rates of interest, and Roman and Greek history abound in instances of scandalous and intolerable usury. It was therefore perhaps natural that the early Fathers should have endeavoured to go to the root of the matter by forbidding all interest, basing themselves on a passage of the Old Law and the counsel (regarded by them as a command) of Christ to lend freely. Here, as in the later controversies of the Poverty of Christ and the right of Dominion, the attempt to translate into legal language the spiritual teaching of Christ was doomed to lead to a dead end.

Nevertheless, the great authority of SS Basil and Gregory of Nyssa and later of SS John Chrysostom, Ambrose and Augustine carried the day, and usury was forbidden to clerics both by the Council of Nicea and by St Leo I, though imperial law and the code of Justinian recognised its existence in secular affairs. When in the West, at the beginning of our period, the economy contracted and money, now gradually becoming scarce, all but ceased to exist in high denominations save as a token of

2. The word was eliminated in the recent liturgical reform.

account, rates of interest rose and usury became generally extortionate and odious. In a decree of Aachen of 789 Charlemagne, characteristically confusing the secular and religious spheres, applied the canonical prohibitions to secular operations and thenceforward councils continued the tradition, both under Gregory VII and at the Second Lateran Council of 1139. Gratian and Peter the Lombard, reflecting current opinion, accepted the prohibition which was thus stereotyped for the schools. Meanwhile the growth of capital and the extension of commerce reintroduced the complicated monetary economy of the ancient world. It might have been supposed that a reassessment of the whole problem would result, but the force of unanimous tradition was too strong, and the theoretical grasp of economic reality too imperfect, to allow of a revolution. Indeed the existing prohibitions were buttressed by the severe sanctions of suspension and excommunication. This left the field clear for the Jews, and though these were later supplanted in the realm of high finance by the Lombards and Cahorsins and Florentines, with whose operations in governmental and papal finance no interference was attempted, the Jews remained, until their expulsion, the small man's moneylender and the pawnbroker of the medieval world.

But although the prohibitions against usury remained in force, and were defended by a series of distinguished commentators including Giles of Lessines, a disciple of St Thomas and, more than a century later, by the two great friars Bernardino of Siena and archbishop Antoninus of Florence, the necessities of life in a commercial economy reposing on credit and banking demanded and received flexibility of treatment. This was provided partly by casuists, but still more frequently by the civil lawyers, who had as their text the code of Justinian and its commentators who presupposed the reception of interest on money.

From the first allowance was made for contingent damages *(damnum emergens)* and loss of financial opportunities *(lucrum cessans)* consequent upon a loan. Thus failure to repay on a specified date could be penalised by a fine, and compensation could further be obtained for actual and even exceptional opportunities of profit thus lost. Banking and what would now be called joint-stock enterprises were permissible, and in each case the customer or partner could receive interest, for his money was not strictly loaned, but deposited, and he could at any time apply for it to be refunded. Similarly where an element of activity (as in money-changing) or of unusual risk (as in maritime insurance) entered in, the scriptural prohibition, which rested on the claims of neighbourly charity, did not apply.

Annuities or interest-bearing mortgages were more delicate problems, but a wide practical breach was made in the traditional fortress by the forced loans on which the cities of Italy and the northern towns came to depend for their well-being, and which could be repaid only by payments of interest. This encouraged the establishment, originally by the Franciscans, of pools of money available at comparatively low rates of interest to small people in need and easily victimised by unlawful moneylenders. These *monti di pietà*, as they were called, were at first resisted by conservative moralists, but ultimately approved by the Church. [3] How far the ecclesiastical prohibitions, based upon reasoning and exegesis both of which seem invalid to the modern mind, did in fact either hinder the development of lawful commercial enterprise or prevent oppressive dealing cannot be assessed, but it was certainly a topic on which much mental energy was spent and which added to the sum of the *gravamina* brought against medieval theologians by the reformers and humanists of a later age.

3. V Lateran Council 1512-17. Denzinger-Schönmetzer, 1444.

REFORM OR DECLINE?

THE thirteenth century has often been saluted as the golden age of the medieval civilisation, the apogee of its achievement. In many ways indeed it was an age of splendid maturity, and in the realm of literature and art the high light and bright colours of early summer had not yet given way to the sultry calms and mellow tints of early autumn. The cathedral with its sculptures and its glass; the theological supremacy of Bonaventure and Aquinas; the royal saint, vigorous, intelligent, firm, the prince of courtesy, and the lion of justice; the poetry of Dante culminating in *The Divine Comedy*; all in their various ways reached a summit of magnificence in which a culture manifested itself without a sign of decay. Yet in other respects the sun had passed the meridian long before Dante wrote. The springtime purity of Francis departed early and the latter half of the century is filled with controversies; a rigidity and a cruelty appear in action, and a logical intolerance in the realm of thought.

The thirteenth century saw the western church in command of all its resources. Canon law and the Lateran Council had between them established a firm pattern for a pastoral clergy, and the period between 1215 and 1350 was one of general well-being in the diocese and parish. Bishops, many of them *magistri* with a university training elected by their chapters, devoted themselves to the service of their diocese, holding synods and visitations, establishing vicarages, rebuilding or adorning their cathedrals, keeping registers of their doings and ordinations. The friars arrived with a new pastoral zeal, exhorting, instructing, confessing and drawing an army of recruits. The universities were not only deploying the talents of an age unusually rich in speculative genius; they were also giving, to a population more numerous than ever, the basic training of a clerk, a lawyer or a priest. Sanctity as well as genius was present in high places, and it was a century fruitful in canonised saints, ranging from two kings and a queen to unlettered lay-brothers. Not only the new orders, with Francis, Dominic, Albert, Thomas, Bonaventure, Raymond, Antony and many others, but the secular episcopate also, with three canonised bishops in England alone (Edmund of Canterbury, Richard of Chichester and Thomas of Hereford), contained a number of remarkable figures. England indeed was perhaps a palmary instance, rather than a fair sample, of the spirit of reform initiated by Innocent III. For much of the century canonical freedom of election was permitted, and chapters made wise choices often from the ranks of Oxford masters, to which class the three saints and Robert Grosseteste of Lincoln, one of the greatest and most influential of all the bishops of the age, belonged. Not only Canterbury, but York, Lincoln and Salisbury and some lesser sees had a succession of devout and able rulers. Many cathedrals, abbeys and parish churches, among them the new cathedral of Salisbury, gradually developed into the shape they were to maintain to the end of the medieval period. Contact between the bishops and the two universities was frequent and friendly, and the two legatine councils of cardinals Otto (1236) and Ottobono (1268) published reforming constitutions which continued to be the norm until the Reformation, as did the decree on preaching of Archbishop Pecham. In France the Franciscan Eudes Rigaud of Rouen, and the Dominican Pierre de Tarantaise, in Germany St Engelbert of Cologne and in Spain Julian of Cuenca were eminent as able and spiritual prelates. In Italy the first gracious flowers were appearing of that art that was to expand for so many centuries, and in Europe beyond the Alps masterpieces of architecture, sculpture and manuscript illumination were appearing yearly in every region. In Germany, Switzerland and Lorraine urban parish organisation, with its guilds, its hospitals and its festivals was drawing the comfortable bourgeoisie into a social and devotional unity, while the Second and Third Orders of the friars were opening new varieties of religious vocation to classes for whom entry to the aristocratic Benedictine nunneries had been difficult. Women, in particular, were finding a new place and receiving more attention from parish priests and directors than in past centuries.

At the same time the centralisation of the government of the Church had continued to develop. Innocent III, great as a lawyer, administrator and politician, had by his own initiative and intervention tightened the grip of the papacy on the episcopate, on monarchs and on the faithful, and had not hesitated to use the extreme measure of interdict on a country or region as a weapon against the vagaries of its ruler. He had been followed in many of these ways by his successors and by the traditions of the curia. Both Honorius III, for long papal Chamberlain, and Gregory IX, a canon lawyer who put out the five books of Decretals, were reformers, and in their hands the machinery of control and coercion was used on the whole from pastoral motives and for the good of those governed. Under Innocent IV, the great canonist Sinibaldo Fieschi, there is apparent consistently and frequently for the first time in the utterances and actions of a pope the tendency to exalt the papal plenitude of power to the exclusion of any other and to use it for ends that are not strictly religious. In other words Innocent IV seems in some of his utterances and actions to exploit his powers and to use them for worldly and political ends. Whereas earlier popes such as Gregory VII and Innocent III not only declare, but are sincere in declaring that head and members not only exist for each other's mutual benefit, but could not in fact exist without the mutual bond of care, Innocent IV gives the impression that the Church exists for the sake of the papacy. It has often been said, and as often denied, that his reign marks the moment when the papacy ceased to feed and began to fleece. Misleading as a blunt statement, for very many of the actions and interests of Innocent and his successors were truly pastoral, it is in part true and it may be that the element of truth is that which is historically significant.

The tendency can be seen most clearly in the two matters of papal taxation and appointment to benefices. Until the end of the twelfth century there was no taxation for the Church as such. The pope as a regional and feudal sovereign levied imposts and taxes; he had for more than 200 years imposed a very small annual sum on abbeys and churches commended to the Holy See, and he had for centuries received from England (and more recently from Scandinavia) a small goodwill offering of Peter's pence. The feudal surrender made by sovereigns in need of confirmation and support, in Spain, Hungary, Poland and Denmark and lastly and most spectacularly in England, implied a moderate annual payment. Fees or presents were naturally demanded for the expedition of privileges and lawsuits, and once the curia became a general court of appeal and source of employment it was inevitable that accusations of venality should be made. John of Salisbury's frank criticism of Hadrian IV was not the first occasion on which the insatiable Roman thirst for gold was deplored. All these sources of income put together were, however, quite incapable of supporting the administrative and judicial services of a European church centred upon Rome, and when to these were added the demands of the religious and political enterprises of the papacy – missions, crusades of every kind, wars and expeditions – it is clear that neither the revenues of the patrimony nor small presents would meet the needs of the curia. Direct taxation seems to have begun under Innocent III with the crusade tax of a fortieth on benefices and religious houses in 1199. This was repeated and soon two further taxes were instituted, those of first fruits (the assumed annual value of a benefice levied upon a newcomer) and of the tenth of all clerical incomes. These were levied as early as 1225 for the war of Honorius III with Frederick II and they continued throughout the middle ages. Other occasional payments also came in, such as the heavy sums paid at election by the abbots of exempt houses.

Concurrently with taxation went the growing papal control of appointment to benefices. At the level of episcopal elections the reforming papacy had stood consistently for a free canonical election by the clergy of the church and local notabilities, an electorate that was soon reduced in practice to the cathedral chapter. The various concordats that ended the investiture contest sometimes contained a proviso that the election should take place in the presence of the king who would thus in practice control the election. Innocent III and the Lateran Council reiterated the canonical ideal and in England and some other countries considerable freedom prevailed during the thirteenth century. Quite apart, however, from uncanonical action or ancient claims by monarchs, the papacy could in fact gain control of an election in a number of ways. By tradition, old and new, when a bishop was translated to another see, or resigned or was deprived by the pope, or died while visiting or residing in the curia, the pope had the right of appointment. Moreover if an election was carried to Rome on appeal, as often happened, and the pope found legal fault, he could appoint. During the thirteenth century, nevertheless, the régime of the canonical capitular election prevailed save when the pope by canon law or the king by undue force took part in it.

In minor benefices the course of development was different. Here a distinction must be made between the advowson of a church and the appointment to a benefice, such as a canonry or deanery, without cure of souls. In the former the régime of the private church had been broken by the reformers to the extent that all that remained to the lay proprietor was the right to present to the bishop, but this right, even if no simoniacal transaction took place, was a valuable piece of patronage. In the latter, the appointment originally lay either with the bishop or with a royal or lay patron. The intervention of the papacy came during the twelfth century at first in the recommendation of candidates or nominees and then in compulsory appointment. At its origin the process went through four stages; request, admonition, command and peremptory execution, and at any stage the case might be dropped, but gradually all four missives were issued at once, and from the time of Innocent III peremptory ' provisions ' became common. The practice grew naturally and swiftly and in the thirteenth century was used more and more often as a means of subsidising curial officials great and small. Innocent IV and Clement IV in particular extended provisions and the latter, pronouncing the rights of the pope to be universal, reserved to the Roman see all benefices vacated in the curia, by which means numerous benefices could be retained for periods of indefinite length to serve as salary. Papal taxation and provisions produced in western Europe for the first time widespread and organised expressions of resentment even in circles which admitted to the full all the papal claims to universal dominion. Patrons of all kinds resented the loss of patronage and bishops and patriots deplored the intrusion into their parishes of unworthy, uncanonically young and alien provisors, while kings protested against the invasion of traditional rights. The spirited protest of Grosseteste of Lincoln in 1245 and of the French bishops under King Louis IX in 1247 are justly celebrated. On the whole popes refrained from touching the advowsons of private laymen; the bishops were the principal sufferers. The taxation which fell upon a far wider group was equally resented, and the English chronicler Matthew Paris has a number of violent denunciations. Discontent was aggravated both by the methods of the collectors, usually Italian bankers, and by their inefficiency and later by the misappropriation of the funds and also by the employment of spiritual weapons to enforce payment. While it is unquestionable that there was great justice in these complaints their acerbity was due in part at least to the medieval resentment at any kind of taxation. Papal and royal taxation taken together were not crushing by modern standards, but medieval subjects seem never to have realised that the papal administration, of which they made use in many ways, could only be kept going by means of subvention from those who benefited by its services and protection. Nevertheless the appearance of the papacy as primarily concerned with the exploitation of the financial and patronal resources of the universal Church, as using for its instruments brokers and bankers already the object of dislike, who were allowed to make use of spiritual sanctions to achieve their purpose, was a deplorable circumstance, the first but not the least weight of odium that was to be thrown in the balance against Rome when the day of reckoning came.

ART 1150-1300

THE middle decades of the twelfth century, which formed such a watershed in the history of letters and sentiment, of thought and of education, saw also an unparalleled revolution in architectural style. It is difficult to think of another instance in modern Europe of such a complete change of style in the middle of a period when technical advance was steady throughout and both constructional problems and patrons' demands underwent no great or sudden change. The revolution came on the level of the mason's lodge, in the gradual evolution of vaulting from the solid concrete or rubble dome or barrel vault to the groined and ribbed vault in which the pointed replaced the round arch. This in time transformed the sturdy, static fabric with its thick masonry and vertical pressure into a soaring, dynamic cage of thrusts, in which ultimately the masonry was reduced to little more than a stone skeleton, and where glass took the place of stone between the lines of support. On the architect's level grace and height, and the mutual proportions of every element of the building, replaced the earlier achievement of solid power and symmetry. To the beholder, the pointed arch, the innumerable upward lines, the pinnacle, the spire and the geometrical tracery gave an impression of lightness and of exaltation, of intellect inspiring stone, and of stone pointing heavenward.

It is tempting to see this change as another aspect of the change in sentiment from humane letters and platonic thought to logic, mathematics and Aristotle, to establish a relationship between formal logic, dialectic and the disputation on the one hand and the geometrical figures, careful ratios and balanced stresses on the other, between the rigorous legalism of the age and the colder and harder lines of the new architecture. There is perhaps a psychological relationship as well as an aesthetic parallel between the advance from Paris to Amiens, and from Amiens to Beauvais, the stretching of the powers of masonry and calculation up to and beyond the limits of the practicable, and the driving of logical thought over the horizon of reason by the papalists and nominalists of the early fourteenth century, just as there is a recognisable basis of comparison between the architectonics of the *Summa Theologica* and of Salisbury cathedral. Such comparisons, however, must not be pressed. There were other and dissimilar changes at the same moment. In sculpture, if not in architecture, the new humanism appears just when the fabric is attaining its maximum of rigidity.

The first work to be completed in the new pointed style was that of Abbot Suger. He was rebuilding his abbey church of St Denis – the Areopagite, the supreme mystical doctor – the saint whose legendary progress through the ages is as marvellous as his posthumous progress through Paris – and his abbey possessed the translation and commentary by John Erigena. In this, the Plotinian doctrine of the emanation of the One in the form of spirit and intelligence throughout all being had been identified with the sharing by all creation, and above all by angelic and human minds, in the true Light of the world, God the Son. The light of day was linked by analogy to the uncreated Light, and the Christian's mind could rise from light to light in the ascent to God. Hence for Suger the glory of light and colour and the gleam of gold and jewels on the walls and in the windows of his church was an emanation, a faint reflection, of the eternal glory of God. As he wrote on his doors, in verses that indicate both the symbolism and ' anagogic ' power of material beauty:

> The resplendent work is bright, but may this shining work enlighten our minds, so that they may pass through true lights to the true Light where Christ is the true door... the weak mind rises to truth by means of material things. [1]

Suger learnt also from a contemporary, Honorius Augustodunensis, who, in his *Mirror of the Church*, displayed in profusion for the first time a sequence of the symbols or types of the New Testament to be found in

---

1. Suger, *De administratione*, 47, 49: ' Nobile claret opus, sed opus quod nobile claret / Clarificet mentes ut eant per lumina vera / Ad verum lumen ubi Christus janua vera / ...Mens hebes ad verum per materialia surgit '.

the Old. Henceforward symbolism of all kinds, including theological and mystical analogy, became general in all schemes of sculpture and glass, together with groups of personages – prophets and priests, saints and apostles – that typified the old and the new. If, as has been widely held, the Gothic portal, with a new version of the Last Judgment as the sculptural theme of the tympanum, was first seen in his church, and if he is also responsible for the rose window and the tree of Jesse as a subject for a great window, he has every right to stand with those other great men of the twelfth century – Abelard, Gratian, Peter Lombard – who gave a decisive pattern to the age that was to follow.

In the remarkable, indeed unique, memoir which is also a programme and an apologia, the abbot of St Denis shows us also the practical aspect of his work. The Carolingian nucleus of St Denis was too small:

> Often on feast days, when completely filled, it disgorged through all its doors the overflowing crowds only to meet those advancing against them, and the outward pressure of those in front not only prevented those attempting to enter from doing so, but also pushed out those who had already entered. At times... no one among the countless thousands of people could move a foot because they were so closely packed. The pressure was such that no one could do anything but stand as if turned to stone, paralysed and able only, as a last resort, to shout. The agony of the women was unbearable, squeezed as they were as in a winepress by hulking men; their faces went white as corpses, they screamed as if in labour and were often trodden underfoot. Others were lifted up above the crowd by kindly men and walked on people's heads as on a pavement, while yet others were carried out at their last gasp and lay fighting for breath in the cloister garth. As for the brethren who were displaying the Nail and Crown of Thorns, they were unable to turn in the press and often had to escape with the relics through a window. [2]

Suger attended to every detail of the rebuilding himself:

> One night... I began to think in bed after Matins that I should myself go through the forests of those parts and look around everywhere to find beams of the right size ... Rising in haste at early dawn I went quickly with carpenters and the measurements of the beams to the forest called Iveline ... where, summoning the keepers and those who knew other woods I questioned them under oath whether we could find there trees of that size ... they smiled, and if they had dared they would have laughed at me as being ignorant that nothing of that kind was there ... Nevertheless I refused to believe them ... and by midday or before, breaking through dense thickets and tangled briars we had marked twelve timber trees. [3]

2. Suger, *De consecratione ecclesiae S. Dionysii* (ed. and trans. E. Panofsky) 87-9. Suger in two other places (ed. Panofsky, 43, 135) mentions the detail of the women walking on the heads of the men to get to the altar.

3. *Ibid.* 95, 97.

On another occasion he had a share in what he calls ' a notable and amusing miracle ':

> I was gravelled, he writes, for lack of jewels, when ... two Cistercians and a monk of Fontevrault turned up in my little room by the church with an abundance of gems for sale – hyacinths, sapphires, emeralds, topazes... which they had received as alms from the treasures of the late King Henry I of England... We thanked God and gave four hundred pounds for the lot, though they were worth much more. [4]

Did Suger, we wonder, tell the abbot of Clairvaux of this? Be that as it may, the work of Suger marked an epoch. His primary aim, as he has told us, was to give to God, and in particular to the altar on which the Holy Sacrifice was celebrated, all that was most precious and beautiful, but he was also concerned to raise the minds of those who saw his church from material to spiritual things.

It has sometimes been supposed that those who used or who beheld the great medieval churches in their fresh beauty had little appreciation of the fine points of their architectural design. This is not so, and numerous detailed accounts survive that show both aesthetical and technical appreciation. One of the earliest is a long description of the work accomplished at the abbey of St Benignus at Dijon by the great abbot William of Volpiano (abbot 990-1031), which in some respects anticipates that of Suger. The chronicler of the abbey writes:

> It will not be a waste of time to set down in writing for the unlearned the shape and inner significance of the abbot's exceedingly skilful work, for many parts of it have a symbolic meaning which should be attributed to divine inspiration rather than to technical skill.

He proceeds at great length to describe what was a very remarkable and complicated design. He ends with a detailed description of the wooden ark containing the relics,

> which, covered entirely with gold and silver, at one time displayed the Birth and Passion of Christ in reliefs of great beauty. Later, however, this superb work of art was taken to pieces by abbot William during a famine and sold to obtain food for the poor. [5]

A century and a half later Gervase of Canterbury describes in vivid detail the great fire of 1174, the ruined choir of the cathedral, and the council of experts from far and near:

> among whom was a man of Sens, William by name, of great energy and a genius in building with wood and stone. Him the monks chose to act alone in the reconstruction on account of his brilliance of talent and his integrity. [6]

4. Suger, *De administratione*, 59.
5. *Recueil* I, 27, 32. See p. 393 n. 7 for full title.
6. Gervase of Canterbury, ed. W. Stubbs (Rolls Series 73 I, 1879), 3ff. *Recueil* I, 208-9.

The chronicler goes on to recapitulate the architectural history of the church from the Norman Conquest and to describe, stage by stage, the reconstruction, the accident that incapacitated William of Sens, and the continuation of the work by an English William. His account, though more concerned with constructional details than with descriptions of ornaments, must count as second only to that of Suger in bringing before us the picture of a great church lifting its columns and vaulting.

One of the most striking features of what may be called the social religion of the eleventh and twelfth centuries is the share taken by the people of a town or district in the physical labour of building a great church. An early example is at the building of the abbey of St Trond near Liège:

> It was a wonderful thing to see what a multitude of zealous workers brought stones, chalk, sand, wood and other things, by day and by night, in wagons and carts freely provided at their own expense. When the wagons were coming to us from Cologne the population roped them and drew them from town to town without any help from draught animals. [7]

Almost a century later there is the more celebrated case of Chartres:

> In this year [1145] (writes the chronicler Robert of Torigny) men first began to draw with their own hands carts full of stone and wood for the work on the church where the towers were going up, and not only there but almost everywhere in France and Normandy the same thing was happening. [8]

The year 1145 was indeed a year of wonder, if the various notices can be trusted, but it was not unique. When the church of Our Lady at Châlons-sur-Marne was being built (1162-71),

> When the wagons of stone reached the town you would see knights and their ladies, young men and maidens, old and young, hurrying happily barefoot down the streets. Some grasped the ropes, others who had no ropes joined hands and arms to pull... while others with singing and cheering escorted them to the church of the Virgin. [9]

When the cathedral of Chartres was gutted by fire in 1194,

> Since it was now necessary to build a completely new church, wagons were got ready and everyone encouraged his neighbour to help in preparing and completing everything that the craftsmen might bid them do. [10]

---

7. Migne, PL CLXXIII col. 46. *Recueil de textes rélatifs à l'histoire de l'architecture*, etc. vol. I (ed. V. Mortet, Paris 1911), 157-8.
8. *Chronique de Robert de Torigny*, ed. L. Delisle (Soc. de l'Hist. de France) I (1872), 238. *Recueil*, II (ed. P. Deschamps, 1929), 65-6.
9. *Recueil* II, 109-10.
10. *Recueil* II, 169.

Thirty years later at Le Mans, when the relics of St Julian were to be translated,

> After Easter a great multitude of the city, of every age and sex and condition, presented themselves at the church of St Julian. To get the site clear they removed the rubbish, vying with each other in cleansing the church. Housewives and other women, contrary to their normal ways and careless of their fine clothes, carried débris out of the church in cloths of various colours, scarlet and green. Many carried the sweepings of the church in their chemises, and were content to see them soiled. Others filled the aprons of their children with sand, and bore them out. Infants and children of three years old... carried out dust in their little petticoats... the men carried out great beams and heavy stones... and in a short time they achieved what hired labour would have failed to do in a much longer space. [11]

The cathedral or the largest church in a city or town was, during the central centuries of the middle ages, not only the scene of the solemn execution of the liturgy, but the gathering-place for every kind of religious and quasi-religious activity. There was the tomb of a revered saint or a celebrated image, and a show of relics exhibited on holidays. There were the liturgical dramas and the mysteries at Christmas and Eastertide. Thither the people of town and countryside flocked to visit their favourite shrine or simply to walk about the great building, to admire its display of lamps and tapers and to receive a bishop's blessing or indulgence. When the knights entered the dimly lighted cathedral at Canterbury on that December afternoon, with swords drawn seeking the archbishop, they collided with groups of townsfolk walking in the aisle at vesper time. When, four years later, a September gale drove sparks from some burning houses into the roof of the cathedral and destroyed half the building, those same citizens, so the chronicler tells us, beside themselves with grief beat their heads and hands against the walls, cursing God and the patron saints who had not preserved their shrines. At Chartres twenty years later, the clerics and layfolk who had lost all their possessions in the fire made no account of their personal losses but considered that the only catastrophe was ' the loss of the home of the Virgin, the peculiar glory of the city, the cynosure of all the region, the incomparable place of prayer '. [12]

The cathedral of Chartres was indeed, as Emile Mâle wrote, ' the mind of the middle ages made visible '. [13] It has been calculated that six thousand personages appear in its portals and windows – one might say, a complete *dramatis personae* of the Old and New Testaments and of Christian history

11. *Recueil* II, 257-8.
12. *Recueil* II, 168.
13. E. Mâle, *L'Art religieux du XIIIe Siècle en France* (Paris 1910), 453. ' La cathédrale de Chartres est la pensée même du moyen-âge devenu visible... ses six mille personnages peints ou sculptés font un ensemble unique en Europe. '

and legend. Art historians have shown that nothing was accidental or haphazard in the subjects and designs. For three centuries at least the themes and their arrangement were dictated by the best minds of the day, first by monks and then, in the cathedrals, by the leading clergy. As these men had been trained in the schools and had absorbed the lore of scriptural and theological commentators, the display in stone and glass was the visible reflection of the books they read and the doctrines they preached. If the smaller churches were, with their wall-paintings, the ' Bible of the poor ', the cathedrals and larger minsters were, especially in France, not only illustrated Bibles, but ' companions ' in sculpture to the *Golden Legend* of Jacques de Vitry and the *Mirror of History* of Vincent of Beauvais, to the sacramental teaching of Hugh of St Victor and the *Mirror of the Church* of Honorius. Emile Mâle, in a celebrated passage, distinguished one from another the cathedrals of France by their preference for this theme or that: Amiens is the cathedral of the Messiah, whose statue, ' le beau Christ ', is the first to be seen by all who approach; Notre-Dame at Paris is the church of the Virgin, Laon is a lesson in theology, Rheims is the national shrine, Bourges tells of the saints, Rouen is like a richly illuminated Book of Hours [14].

With Chartres (1195-1260) the type-plan of the great cathedrals of central France is all but complete, with the line of double aisles (or aisle and chapel) carried round the apse by ambulatory and chapels and producing a wide oblong space prolonged by an eastern semi-circle, above which the west front, transepts, apses and towers still give the impression of a narrow, cruciform building. Paris, Rheims, Amiens and Bourges show the perfection of its growth, and Toledo and Cologne its forms of exportation. In Normandy, as at Rouen and throughout England, the long and narrow nave and wide transept of the original church were rarely replaced by later changes, and the characteristic Gothic cathedrals, such as Lincoln and Salisbury, are, by contrast with the French, narrow and angular, with pronounced transepts, long presbyteries and square east ends. While no late medieval Gothic cathedrals, when furnished with screens, gave a great assembly a sight of the altar or a sound of the sermon, the English type is perhaps the least accommodating of any in these respects.

We are not concerned with the development of medieval architecture as such, but no attempt to present a view of the monastic life of the middle ages would be complete without a reference to its material setting. Even after the havoc of the Hundred Years' War, the Reformation, the Thirty Years' War, the French Revolution, and the two great wars of our own day, even after the attacks of fire and tempest, and the ceaseless gnawing of wind and water upon the buildings that flout the elements while often

14. *Ibid.* 454.

resting on scanty foundations and watery soil, even after the almost total neglect of the fabric for more than two centuries, the wealth of Gothic architecture that remains in France, England, south Germany, Flanders, Spain and Portugal is immense, and there can be few, even among the natives of each country, who are familiar with all that their land possesses of great buildings. Till yesterday the medieval cathedral dominated every view near or distant of the city or town, and even if today its bulk or height is rivalled by cooling-towers and blocks of flats these serve as a foil rather than as a rival to its beauty. As the cathedral is to the city, and the abbey to the town, so is the parish church to the village or the hamlet; it is still often the only discernible building in a wide landscape. The proportionate size of these great churches to their surroundings must have been even more striking in medieval times than it is now. Ely today, with little more than a village at its feet, allows us to imagine Strasbourg or Burgos in the thirteenth century.

For almost four centuries Gothic art expanded over north-western Europe. At its purest, perhaps, in northern and central France and in England, it took different shapes in other regions. The magnificent, if eccentric churches of the Midi–Albi, St Bertrand de Comminges, Toulouse– the impressive *Backsteingothik* of northern Germany, the cathedrals of south Germany, at once severe and ornate, the rich decorations of Spain, are all parts of a great family. Costly to construct and maintain, unpractical to both ancient and modern ideas of congregational participation, Gothic architecture, more than any other, displays itself as a tribute of human achievement to an unseen God and as a fabric that leads both eye and mind away from the earthly and material to the realm of spirit and light.

As sculpture found a wider scope this art, too, became an influence upon the mind and daily life of western Christendom. To many, the aesthetic appeal of the transitional carving is supreme. The royal portal at Chartres, and some of the figures on the west front of Wells, where the artist discloses rather than portrays human dignity and spiritual power, and emotion is enhanced rather than concealed by the hieratic figure and the conventional drapery, will seem to many, just as does the work of the Greek ' primitive ' artists, more satisfying and more appealing than the maturity of Praxiteles or of the sculptors of the portals at Amiens or Rheims. Nevertheless, the work done in the first half of the thirteenth century must be reckoned as the acme of medieval genius. The statues of St Stephen at Senlis, of St Theodore on the south portal of Chartres, the statuettes on the central portal at Rheims, the gallery of figures on the west front of Amiens, remain unsurpassed as the expression of Christian purity and strength, perfectly human yet with the fragrance of divine grace. The surviving masterpieces at Strasbourg, a few decades later, have the same perfection, while Bamberg and Naumburg translate it into the idiom of Germany.

The subjects as well as the execution show the movement towards the world of living men and women. The barbaric majesty of the Judge and his enormous beasts at Moissac and the terrors of the last day in Gislebertus's tympanum at Autun give place to a victorious redeemer or to the Blessed Virgin as Mother or Queen of Heaven. Art, long the monopoly of the cloister, has now begun to attract and to satisfy the Christian people of the towns. Christ, his Mother, his apostles and his saints become human figures and are surrounded by details of human life and human occupations, or by the foliage and flowers of the hedgerow. The welcome of the church of the twelfth century to the people of the thirteenth is symbolised in the magnificent portals and façades of Notre-Dame de Paris, Amiens, Rheims, Rouen, Strasbourg and twenty more, culminating in the stupendous five-fold entrance of Bourges. In England a distant tradition of the Ottonian westworks preserved the cliff of masonry at the west, treated as a screen for statuary at Wells and Lincoln, but never opening upon the city square as do many of the cathedrals of Italy and Spain.

From the end of the twelfth century art in all its forms is leaving the cloister. The illumination of manuscripts, and still more of service books and books for private use and devotion, is becoming a commercial affair, executed by a lay artist in his house or workroom. The subjects treated and the purpose served in all its departments are still predominantly religious but the life of the world is occupying the artist's mind. Animals, grotesques and nondescripts, already seen in the borders of the secular Bayeux tapestry, now appear in Bibles and psalters, while later still the psalter becomes a picture-book of chivalry and courtly life. Architecture and sculpture become honourable professions, and the experts are called in from afar to accept commissions. In the early thirteenth century architects from the Ile de France are at work in Westminster, in German lands and in south France.

Painting lagged behind sculpture and only attained maturity in the age of Dante. It was never therefore a monastic art; the religious who practised it in later centuries, such as Fra Angelico and Lorenzo Monaco, did so as individuals. Nevertheless, for a century or more painting was predominantly religious in its purpose and subject-matter. Giotto, Simone Martini, Taddeo Gaddi, and Ambrogio Lorenzetti are primarily religious artists; Masaccio and Paolo Uccello are primarily artists who execute religious subjects by request or because the life of Christ or an Assumption is to a young artist what the Lombard's Books of the Sentences were to the young theologians of the age, a formulary of talent and competition. To the end of our period and beyond, wherever the Catholic faith flourished or survived, there was a demand for churches and religious pictures and statues, but Fra Angelico was perhaps the last example of a great artist whose work was an effluence of his spiritual life, and in manner, if not in genius and in technique, he was an echo of an earlier age. We need an art-historian who is also an historian of religious sentiment to set the art of the later middle ages in relation to the thermometer of religious fervour and decline.

If architecture and the pictorial and plastic arts are no longer the expression of spiritual needs and intuitions, religious needs still dominate the world of art even when the works of art themselves are not inspired by religion. Thus the development of church planning, particularly in towns, from 1200 onwards is governed by the needs of the people not by the practices of the clergy. Paradoxically enough, some of the largest medieval churches were either monastic, as Cluny, or cathedrals in ' cities ' little more than villages, and in any case the medieval cathedral, the church of a chapter rather than the centre of a diocese, was not built with the primary consideration of pastoral service. When cities grew and the sermon and procession became popular and universal, the friars led the way in building churches that were preaching halls with an eastern altar – with wide and often aisle-less and pillarless naves, and no architectural presbytery or choir. The style was widely copied when town and village churches, not served by friars, were rebuilt, and at the very end of the medieval period the undifferentiated oblong chapel, of which that of King's College, Cambridge, is the supreme example, was introduced, in which the featureless plan was beautified by every elaboration of carving, moulding, tracery and stained glass.

In Italy the relation of the church to artistic activity of all kinds differed considerably from that·in regions beyond the Alps. In the first place there was material continuity throughout Italy with the church of the Roman empire. Churches of some size were numerous in all the cities of the peninsula and the population was preponderantly Christian. Monasteries existed already in the age of Gregory the Great, particularly in the larger cities, and over the whole period monks exercised a less important function in diffusing culture and the arts than they did in northern lands, though for a century or so Italian monastic leaders formed the spearhead of the Gregorian movement of reform. Moreover Italy retained throughout an urban life, and even the baronage of the diluted feudalism had close links with the towns. Consequently, church building was due to civic or at least lay enterprise in a way to which the transalpine countries could show rare parallels before the thirteenth century. A corollary of this was that architecture and the arts of decoration continued to produce work in the existing tradition, and though Lombardy, as we have seen, exported some of its constructional innovations to France and Germany, the influence of northern Romanesque in the peninsula was slight save in the Norman territories of the south, and above all the neighbouring Sicily.

At Rome and other principal cities building in the traditional style, which made no extraordinary demands upon architect or mason, continued. The ruling plan was the basilica, with or without aisles, and a clerestory supported by marble or stone columns, and usually divided into an unfurnished nave and a presbytery surrounded with marble or metal-work screens and containing ambones and a ciborium. In the eleventh century the mosaic decoration known as Cosmati-work made its appearance. Used on pavements to give rich effects with simple designs, it served also to give the screens, ambones, lecterns and the paschal candlestick a delicate and astringent beauty.

Some of the medium-sized churches that appeal most to modern eyes, such as Santa Maria in Cosmedin, Santa Sabina, San Lorenzo *fuori* and Santa Maria in Trastevere, attained their present form in the eleventh or early twelfth centuries, but show little or no architectural advance upon the churches with which Gregory I was familiar. The contrasting social conditions of northern Europe before *c.* 1200 and Italy are mirrored in the plan of their larger churches. In Italy the church is a congregational one, with wide spaces, a prominent single altar and open vistas; in northern Europe it is liturgical, with long processional nave, spacious choir and presbytery, numerous chapels, an ambulatory for pilgrims, large screens and enclosed choir stalls and sanctuary. The great cathedrals of the north remained, in architecture and furnishing, the churches of monks and canonical bodies; those of Italy were, in form at least, churches of assembly and of the bishop; it is noteworthy that in Italy the normal situation for the choir of monks or canons is beyond the altar, or in a *choretto* alongside the presbytery, whereas in the north, above all in England and Spain, the sanctuary and choir from the thirteenth century onwards form an enclosed and almost invisible chapel within the great fabric.

Secular drama as a serious art-from had never flourished in the Roman Empire and did not exist in the medieval world. It was reborn only when the Greek and Latin classics were studied and imitated in Italy in the fifteenth century. Religious drama on the other hand achieved a stature of some importance. Its beginnings must be sought in liturgical and para-liturgical models. The dramatisation of certain episodes of gospel history took literary and liturgical shape in the Carolingian era. Thus the Palm Sunday procession and the hymn *Gloria, laus* of Theodulf, the Reproaches of Good Friday and the Easter sequence *Victimae paschali* contain the elements of dramatic dialogue, but the first known appearance of religious drama is in the English *Regularis Concordia* (*c.* 970), where a short ' act ' is performed after the third responsory of Easter day nocturns by four monks, one in an alb personifying the angel, three in copes representing the women visiting the sepulchre on Easter morning; the rite was accompanied by solo and choral singing. A fuller description exists in the slightly later Winchester tropers, and it is generally accepted that the practice was introduced from Fleury. There is no record of its continuance, but there is sculptural and other evidence of its existence in France. A century later the procession of the host (i.e., Christ) on Palm Sunday, met by a choir representing the crowds and priests of Jerusalem, appears in Lanfranc's Canterbury statutes. This probably also came from France, perhaps Rouen, but became common in England and served as a model for the later Corpus Christi procession. Other liturgical observances were a procession of prophets, each bearing scrolls of messianic prophecy, at Christmastide, and the procession of the Wise Men at Epiphany. From these sprang a long series of religious dramas, rapidly expanding in subject and treatment, that became known as Mysteries or mystery plays, covering the whole story of the creation, fall and redemption, with particular interest in the infancy and passion of Christ. These drew some of their setting from illuminations and themselves in turn influenced designs on capitals and in windows.

Shortly after the first mysteries there appeared a nearly related type, the miracle play, representing incidents in the life or after-life of a martyr or saint. Here again the earliest explicit reference is in England early in the eleventh century, concerning some scenes of the life of St Catherine played by the children of Dunstable school. The master was a native of Maine, and there can be no doubt that the ' miracle ' as well as the mystery originated in France. The near relationship of the two is seen from the use as stage properties at Dunstable of copes borrowed from the sacrist of St Albans, and both were closely connected till late in the twelfth century, when they went ' out of church ' into the hands of confraternities in France and Germany and guilds in England. They soon became vernacular; in France with the great ' mystery ' *Adam* in the early thirteenth century and in England at Beverley in 1220. While ' mysteries ' remained predominantly religious, though admitting lifelike and even comic incidents and dialogue, ' miracles ' with innumerable legends as their basis became domestic and conversational. It was left for a third type, the ' morality play ', to move half-way from an edifying religious presentation in the direction of a comedy of humours, as the virtues and vices, angels and devils, strove for the conquest of man's soul. In England almost every town in the northern midlands and east Anglia had a cycle of plays, while in Paris the confraternity of the Passion controlled the mysteries and the clerks' society of the Basoche turned the miracles into comedy. From the late fourteenth century the plays were performed on large waggons in the streets, and in England on certain festivals, especially Corpus Christi, the various guilds each presented a ' pageant ' on wheels. Miracles and moralities continued until the early decades of the sixteenth century, and in a few instances, particularly the York plays and the morality of *Everyman*, they have proved capable of holding the attention of modern audiences.

PART FOUR
1304-1500

THE POPES AT AVIGNON

THE residence of the papacy at Avignon and its long duration were due to a number of causes. The transference of the curia began almost by accident, when the archbishop of Bordeaux, elected by a Perugian conclave *in absentia*, delayed his progress to Italy for a series of discussions with Philip the Fair, settling in Avignon in 1309. The delay was prolonged by preparations for the Council of Vienne held 1311-12, and then by the invasion of Italy by Henry VII. Thenceforward three pressures petrified the curia: the disturbed condition of Italy, which led to the revolt of parts of the papal states, and anti-papal risings in Rome itself; the need for French support and security when both empire and Italy were hostile; and finally the gradual establishment of a vast fortified palace in a walled city, housing an elaborate administrative machinery and a large and luxurious court. Strong as these and other pressures were, the prolonged absence from Rome was deplorable. On the political side it deprived the papacy of the security and financial resources of the territory for whose government it was in fact responsible; it began with an improper dependence upon the French which it never wholly shook off; it remained a perpetual scandal that the bishop of Rome should reside in affluence and quasi-permanence beyond the Alps; and it was in a real sense the occasion of the Great Schism that followed, and an aid to its continuance.

Contemporaries, among them the eloquent Petrarch and a series of saintly personages ending with St Catherine of Siena, flayed the Avignon papacy with their criticisms and laments, and these have been echoed by almost all historians down to recent times. Within the last sixty years, largely owing to the long life-work of a single scholar, Mgr G. Mollat, a reaction has set in. It has been shown conclusively that many, indeed most, of the popes at Avignon were men of personally devout life, that some of them seriously attempted reform, both in the curia and in the Church at large, and that as a series they built up an administrative and financial system that surpassed in efficiency those of all the other kingdoms of Europe. Even papal taxation and provisions, which were the object of the fiercest criticism, have found scholars to explain and even to defend their technique. As for dependence upon France, many instances have been discovered of independent actions and policies; the curia itself always contained non-French elements, and the situation of Avignon within the French political sphere may well have helped at times, as did and does the presence of the papal court in Italy in the modern epoch, to foster a spirit of independence. Nevertheless, the spectacle of a rich, luxurious and powerful sovereign and his bureaucracy, living in their palace-fortress completely out of touch with the imperial city of the apostles, which had always been the centre of the faith, was of itself a permanent scandal, and it is certain that during its prolonged stay the papacy and its court compromised with worldly standards and aims in an organic fashion which was more detrimental to the Church than previous excesses of individuals.

Yet despite the luxury, the administrative reforms carried through at Avignon were real and lasting. In the *camera* under the chamberlain and the treasurer diplomatic as well as financial business was conducted: this in its perfect form was the work of John XXII. The chancery in its many branches conducted the correspondence between the curia and the Church throughout the world. The judiciary was particularly the work of Clement V, John XXII and Benedict XII. Hitherto great use had been made in distant regions of judges-delegate, who collected and sifted the evidence and often also gave judgment, but sentence was sometimes, and the right of appeal generally, reserved to the pope. Clement set up standing courts: the consistory of pope and cardinals, acting as a court of appeal for the whole church; and cardinalitial tribunals established for cases referred to them by the pope. The Rota, concerned at its formation in 1331 chiefly with the collation of benefices, later became the final court in matrimonial suits. Finally there was a court dealing with all questions and suits of procedure and the execution of sentences. In addition, the apostolic penitentiary and his assistants dealt with dispensations for marriages and from canonical irregularities and with absolution from reserved cases.

To finance the ever-expanding bureaucracy and the whole life of the papal court, shorn of many of the revenues from its patrimony in Italy, the popes extended very greatly both the weight and extent of taxation and the machinery of collection. Whereas in the thirteenth century much of the revenue, itself modest in size, was collected by bishops and their subordinates, or by Italian bankers to whom sources of revenue had been farmed, now much was done by means of papal collectors armed with extensive powers of coercion in the shape of censure, excommunication and fine. In the curia itself taxes were imposed or increased for every entry into office, visit to the apostolic see, or service given by the papal court. While much of the immense revenue went to the upkeep of the papal court and to alms, largesses and presents, almost two-thirds of the papal income over long periods of years went to finance the papal mercenaries and allies in the long and often disastrous wars in Italy. Knowledge of this, and experience of the ruthless behaviour of the papal collectors, led to fierce and permanent complaints all over Europe. The inquisition, the abuse of provisions, and the harsh and often scandalous rapacity of the tax-collectors combined to bring the papal court into general odium. All three activities, initiated and developed by the papacy, were in their different ways repressive of private liberties or property, and in all three the dice, both procedural and judicial, were heavily loaded in favour of the curia or its emissaries. These elements of harshness and of exploitation, which formed in many cases the only link between the individual and the papacy, sowed the seeds of a great bitterness that was to remain even when some of the most oppressive features of the régime had disappeared.

Clement V, at once heir to the odium of Boniface VIII and a Frenchman unwilling for many good reasons to break with the king of France, was in a peculiarly vulnerable position. He yielded to Philip IV's demand that he should cancel all Boniface's charges against the king, and in 1312 capitulated in the more disgraceful matter of the suppression of the order of the Temple. The Knights Templars had lost their *raison d'étre* with the fall of Acre in 1291, but they had possessions all over western Europe and great wealth, which they used as bankers and financiers to their own profit; neither fervent, nor charitable, they had few friends. They had rejected royal and papal suggestions of amalgamation with the Hospitallers, and Philip IV coveted their wealth and welcomed if he did not inspire accusations against them. Finally in 1307 he anticipated a papal inquiry by ordering Nogaret to arrest and examine the whole order. Trickery, torture and forged confessions yielded matter for a list of charges of heresy, witchcraft, blasphemy and unnatural vice against the Templars in the king's hands. The pope, anxious to safeguard justice, ordered the arrest of the whole order and put the French prisoners under ecclesiastical restraint.

Freed thus from royal control they revoked all that they had already confessed and the pope decided to reopen their case. Thus thwarted, Philip IV
used every means to browbeat the pope and to inflame public opinion in
France. The Templars were tried again, simultaneously, by the papal commissioners and in France, and numbers were condemned to the flames as
lapsed heretics. The pope, for his part, yielded to Philip in 1312 and at
the Council of Vienne, against the wish of the fathers, suppressed the order
uncondemned with the charges unproved. There can be no doubt that the
Templars, if fallen from their early fervour, were guiltless as an order of
the specific crimes imputed to them and that Clement V capitulated to
royal pressure. The brutality, rapacity and inequity of the episode reflected
some of the worst characteristics of the age in high places. As a papal act
of power it was evidence of the degree of centralisation of authority now
attained, as was also the attitude of Clement V towards the Council of
Vienne when the fathers opposed the suppression and the transference to
the Hospital of the possessions of the Templars.

Clement V's successor, elected after a vacancy of more than two years,
was a man of mean appearance and erratic personality but of many talents
and of extraordinary vitality. Crowned pope at the age of seventy-two
John XXII disappointed the prophets and his enemies by living to the age
of ninety through a constant succession of storms and disputes. A financier
of genius, he reformed the papal revenues, greatly increased the taxation
and left his successor a weighty credit balance. Swift and intemperate in
politics he was soon embroiled in a contest unnecessary and vexatious in
itself, and destined to last beyond his pontificate. In 1314, at the beginning
of the papal interregnum, two claimants had emerged from a disputed
imperial election, the Habsburg Frederick, duke of Austria, and the
Wittelsbach Lewis, duke of Bavaria. John XXII when elected long remained neutral from political reasons, but when Lewis overcame his rival
at the battle of Mühldorf, and subsequently threatened the papal interests
in Italy and appointed an imperial vicar, the pope broke silence (1323)
with an angry denunciation of Lewis as having acted as king and emperor
before his election had been examined and accepted by the pope, and
demanded complete submission. Failure to submit would entail excommunication, which duly followed six months later. Lewis, hitherto pacific,
replied in his Appeal of Sachsenhausen (1324) with a vigorous counter-
attack. The pope had no rights whatever in an imperial election, and John
was in fact a heretic, specifically in the matter of the Poverty of Christ.
The long and unedifying feud that followed was in a sense unreal on both
the theoretical and the political level. The high debate of empire and
papacy had gone for ever with the fragmentation of Germany, the decline
of the papacy, and the growth of national consciousness. On the other

hand the quarrel had little effect in the empire, where most laymen and many clerics remained unmoved by papal censures or imperial denunciations and continued to recognise John as pope and Lewis as emperor. Nevertheless, it combined with the other troubles to make the pontificate of John XXII a disturbing and harmful one. After many vicissitudes, Lewis was strong enough in 1327 to invade Italy, and early in 1328 he entered Rome where he allowed himself to be crowned by the civil authorities, following up this performance by the appointment and coronation of an anti-pope. An emperor at odds with the pope attracted a group of unusually notable rebels who were without any other common denominator. Lewis's first manifesto in 1324 owed much to Peter Olivi and in 1327 Ubertino da Casale was in his train. In his entry to Rome he was accompanied by Marsilius of Padua, whom he appointed his vicar-general, and by Jean de Jandun. Finally in 1328 he was joined by William of Ockham and the Franciscan general, Michael of Cesena. With such a galaxy of revolutionary talent in action it is not surprising that a shower of brilliant polemics harassed John XXII, who supplied his enemies with a gratuitous target by his pronouncement on the delayed beatific vision (see p. 411). The pope died with the controversy still alive, and his successor, though more reasonable, refused to acknowledge Lewis without an unconditional submission in return for confirmation of his claims to be king. In 1338, therefore, the emperor hardened his attitude with a solemn delcaration, ratified at a diet in Frankfurt (1338), that a king of the Romans could be elected and enter into all his rights as king and emperor without any papal sanction. For his coronation and assumption of the imperial title, and for this alone, papal sanction was necessary. The pope, now Clement VI, retorted by persuading Charles of Bohemia to make most of the concessions demanded of Lewis, and by then arranging for his election as king. Lewis died almost at once, in 1347, still excommunicate, to be followed as emperor, two years later, by his rival, now acknowledged as Charles IV. The significance of the latter in European history concerns us only in so far as the so-called Golden Bull of 1356 affected both the relations of pope and emperor and the future of the German church. Therein the procedure of election was elaborately defined, the territories of the Electors declared inviolable and indivisible, and the electors themselves formed into a kind of permanent council with the emperor as chairman. The pope is nowhere repudiated, but neither is he mentioned. Ecclesiastically speaking the chief effect of the Golden Bull was to give complete autonomy to the electors who were prelates (the archbishops of Cologne, Treves and Mayence) and thus considerably to enhance the status of other bishops who were lords of territories – a circumstance that has influenced German religious history from that day to this.

John XXII, who could remember the days of Innocent IV and whose life-span overlapped that of Dante at both ends, who was a man of thirty when Aquinas died, and who lived to canonise him half-a-century later, was fated to attract in his old age the attacks of two men who put into currency ideas that were to have a long life in the new world of which they were the harbingers.

Marsilius of Padua, whose *Defensor Pacis* was published in 1324, was a thinker of great power and no spirituality whose mind cut into the fabric of the world around him like an oxy-acetylene flame. An Aristotelian who saw the world denuded of all spirit and grace, he held that the papacy was a human institution that had gradually won its way by force or guile. While admitting so far as words went the authority of Christ and the Scriptures, and the full dignity of the Church, he reduced the spiritual sphere to nothing by a positivist and secularist view of life. Physical material power alone gave real authority among men; this belonged to the people and by them was delegated to the ruler *(princeps, pars principans)* or legislator whose coercion was visibly valid. Spiritual censures were of force only in an invisible, future world. Marsilius thus by a process of argument strikingly similar to that of Ockhamist theologians relegated religion to limbo. While the Ockhamist, by concentrating his attention on the absolute power of God, deprived the normal, known law of God of all real content and significance, so Marsilius, having saluted from afar the sanctions and sacraments of the Church, allowed reality only to the secular ruler and made of the visible church a department of state or a kind of religious guild. Within it the supreme power was a general council, summoned by the community of laymen or their ruler, from whom the pope derived his authority. Christ instituted priests only; bishops and popes were of human institution. Marsilius's vision had a brief and local moment of realisation, when as vicar in spiritual things of the emperor Lewis IV he assisted at the election by the people of Rome of a pope to replace the ' heretic ' John XXII. Marsilius was duly excommunicated and his doctrine condemned by the pope in 1327; it lay in the ground and brought forth fruit in season, the first crop during the Great Schism, the second during the English Reformation.

The name of William of Ockham has often occurred in these pages. His career falls sharply into two parts divided by his long durance at Avignon. When he arrived at the papal court he was a young bachelor of the Sentences, the confident propounder of a new logic with a distinguished career opening before him. When he left the riverside wharf on a night of May, 1328, he was an embittered man pledged to the cause of the schismatic Franciscans and to the consequent assertion of the heresy of John XXII; the associate of Marsilius and Lewis IV. Henceforth for twenty years his pen was rarely idle, but he had said farewell to logic and theology and devoted his great talents to polemics and to political thought. His theses were developed at great length by way of an elaborate *sic et non* exercise. In his first work, the rapidly composed *Opus nonaginta dierum*, he attacked the pronouncements of the pope on the poverty of Christ and other subjects. John XXII assisted him by his dubious opinions on the delayed beatific vision. Having completed this work, Ockham embarked on a long *Dialogue* concerning the errors of the pope. In this, a long conversation between a master and a disciple who favoured the pope, Ockham traversed the whole extent of the papal claims, challenging the divine institution of the papacy and the infallibility of the Church, and setting against them the opinion that the Church consisted of the community of the faithful, not of the clergy. Heresy might ravage the Church from top to bottom, but the faith of Christ would remain intact in a few individuals. Always behind the façade of general propositions lay the mind of the Franciscan embittered by the papal decision on poverty, and of the inceptor in theology who would never become a master. The first part of the *Dialogue* was followed by an open attack on the heresies of John XXII; the pontiff was still alive but his death, when it occurred, did not put a period to Ockham's polemics. In the third part of the *Dialogue* he returned once more to his dissolvent examination of the papacy and of the Church, and to his assertion of the divine right of the German king. He died at Munich unreconciled in 1349. [1]

John XXII, indeed, himself a stormy petrel, was fated to bear the brunt of more than one redoubtable troublemaker. In addition, he caused himself gratuitous tribulation by his theory of the delayed vision of God. This opinion, that the beatific vision of God (though not the presence of the humanity of Christ) was withheld from the souls of the just until the Last Judgment, was unexpectedly propounded by the pope in a series of sermons in the papal court. Supported by interested careerists and attacked alike by conservative theologians and delighted enemies, it was defended by its author with diminishing enthusiasm, and retracted on the pope's deathbed, while the common belief was defined in 1336, by his successor, Benedict XII, in the constitution *Benedictus Deus*. These controversies did not exhaust the activities of the indomitable octogenarian. He continued to perfect the fiscality and to combat the abuses of the curia, to conduct his wars in Italy and to organise the missionary activities of the Franciscan friars. Whatever may be thought of his wisdom and methods in controversy, his energy, his personality and his considerable and varied talents

1. For this see C. K. Brampton, ' Traditions relating to the death of William of Ockham', in *Archivum Franciscanum Historicum* 32 (1960), 442-9. He died 9/10 March 1349 unabsolved.

left their mark upon the medieval Church, and his pontificate is surely the most remarkable of the Avignon period.

John XXII was followed at Avignon by five popes all of whom reigned for a period of eight to ten years. The first of these, Benedict XII, 1334-42, a Cistercian with considerable theological learning, was by disposition a reformer; he directed his attention to the curia and to the distribution of benefices with some success, but he is chiefly remembered for his reforming decrees for the Cistercians, the Benedictines and the Austin canons. It was the last attempt of the medieval papacy to arrest the decline of the old orders; it was a reform with the hope of regularising and stabilising the actual position of the monks rather than an attempt to recall them to their original austerity. Clement VI (1342-52), an aristocrat of genial temper who loved splendour and largesse, made of Avignon the gayest court of Europe and the meeting-place of poets, artists and scientists. At the height of its glory the papal city was struck by the Great Pestilence (1348); the pope rode out the storm in his palace, giving generous aid to the victims whenever possible. His successor Innocent VI (1352-62) was an ageing lawyer of yielding character and no great political ability, who suffered from the extravagance of his predecessors and the wars in Italy. He suffered also from the Free Companies that ravaged Provence after the truce of Bordeaux (1357) and the treaty of Brétigny (1360). Avignon itself was in danger and was hastily fortified. Innocent was something of a reformer, and bore hard upon the Franciscan Spirituals and the Fraticelli, earning for himself some searing criticisms from St Birgitta of Sweden. Urban V (1362-70), the next in succession, was by far the most saintly pope of Avignon. An aristocrat by birth and a Benedictine monk by profession, he preserved throughout his pontificate the spiritual exercises of the cloister, and won the esteem even of Petrarch. Meanwhile the papacy had strengthened its position in Italy largely owing to the energy and the military and political genius of the Spanish cardinal Egidio Albornoz, and Urban V, who gave the recovered papal territory a constitution which endured till modern times, took the courageous step of returning to Rome in 1367. He remained in Italy for three years, but returned to Avignon to die. In the church at large his most notable act was the bull *Horribilis* (1366), limiting plurality of benefices. Gregory XI (1370-8) the nephew of Clement VI was an eminent canon lawyer of blameless life and scholarly interests. Encouraged by St Catherine of Siena, he made the final return to Rome early in 1377, when only a year of life remained to him.

During the seventy years of Avignon western Europe had entered upon a period of distress that was to last for a century. In 1337 the disastrous Hundred Years' War began that was for long to ruin and divide France and later to debase England, and that was to loose upon Europe the lawless savagery of the mercenary Companies. In 1348-49 the Black Death removed about one-third of the total population and accelerated various economic and social changes. How far its effects upon religion were baneful and permanent is a matter of debate, but for several decades the number of religious and clergy, as indeed of the whole population, was greatly reduced. A Europe brutalised and impoverished by war, depopulated and shocked by pestilence, and without a great focus and movement of new life, was about to suffer another unfamiliar and searching trial in the Great Schism.

Portugal firstly Avignon later Roman

Obedience to Rome

Obedience to Avignon

Components of the German Empire
differed in allegiance

SCOTLAND

IRELAND

ENGLAND

SCANDINAVIA

POLAND

GERMAN
EMPIRE

•Paris

•Constance

Basel

HUNGARY

FRANCE

ITALY •Ferrara

•Avignon

•Florence

Pisa•

PORTUGAL

CASTILE

ARAGON

Rome•

Naples•

14. Europe of the Great Schism and the conciliar epoch

THE GREAT SCHISM

WHEN Gregory XI transferred the curia to Rome and put an end to the long Babylonian exile he was only forty-seven years of age. Had time and resolution been granted, he might well have re-established the papacy in its old home and have begun to form a new curial generation. As it was, he had already decided to return to Avignon when death overtook him fourteen months after his arrival in Rome.

Sixteen cardinals were in the city. They were almost without exception wealthy and worldly prelates, aristocrats by birth and disposition. Four were Italians, one Spanish and the rest Frenchmen who were implacably divided into ' Limousins ', the party of three of the last four popes, [1] and the others. They were surrounded and at times mobbed by the people of Rome and the environs, clamouring for a Roman, or at least for an Italian, pope. Before entering the conclave they had canvassed the election and, so it would seem, had pitched upon an eminent curial official, an Italian, long resident in Avignon and now absentee archbishop of Bari, Bartolomeo Prignano, and they rapidly proceeded to elect him, in the midst of alarums and excursions. He was duly enthroned and crowned and entered upon his office as Urban VI. Almost immediately, however, the

---

1. They came from the region of Limoges.

supposedly sedate official showed himself as a coarse, overbearing, sadistic despot, rating the cardinals, demanding their reform, shouting them down, and torturing recalcitrants. As a result, the French cardinals departed in a body, and were ultimately joined by the Italians. After fruitless negotiations, in which St Catherine of Siena played a part, they unanimously elected cardinal Robert of Geneva, a young, able, ruthless, arrogant man, and a cousin of the king of France, who chose the name of Clement VII and betook himself to Avignon. Both parties proceeded to solicit support throughout Europe, creating cardinals and excommunicating their opponents. Within a few years Europe had split into two roughly equal allegiances. The empire in general, Hungary and Bohemia, Flanders, the Low Countries, England, Castile (at first) and parts of Italy held by Urban VI. France, Scotland, Savoy, Austria and later Aragon and Navarre stood for Clement VII. Propaganda was busy on both sides; political motives had their weight and after a few years all parties had given up any hope of agreement as to which of the two popes was the authentic one.

Why, we may ask, did the Schism take place and why did it so fiercely resist healing treatment? And who was the legitimate pope?

As regards the second question, all must turn on the authenticity of the alleged compulsive fear which had brought about the otherwise canonically valid election of Prignano, and despite the reserve shown by a few eminent historians, the existing evidence would seem to show decisively that the undoubted pressure of the Roman populace was not such as to incapacitate a body of reasonably honest and courageous men. Indeed the excuse of compulsion was never more than secondary in the early defence of the cardinals; they stressed rather the impossible, nay insane, temperament of the pope. The insoluble problem, in fact, is not an historical but a psychological one. How could an experienced body of men have been mistaken as to the character and qualities of someone whom they had known for years? Or conversely, how could a character have changed and deteriorated so rapidly?

As for the other question, an immediate reason can be found in the lack of spiritual and moral fibre in a small college of cardinals made up of wealthy and ambitious men resembling each other in background and opinions but divided by personal and national feuds. It was the peculiar vice of the Avignon period that it reduced the Sacred College to a small group of able, narrow-minded careerists, the majority drawn from a single racial group, jealous of their collegiate significance but without any sense of the wider needs of the Church or of their immense spiritual responsibilities. In no account of the crucial conclave is there any evidence of a care for the spiritual welfare of Christendom. If we ask finally why the election of 1378 produced a general and lasting division whereas earlier schisms had been local and either brief or insignificant, the answer must be that the sense of impotence and frustration that fell upon Europe like a fog in the autumn of 1378 was due directly to the fact that the schism was not between two popes elected by two parties or potentates but between two elected by the same very small body of men. Thus all the available guarantors of the first election were also committed to the second, and when in addition the rivals had surrounded themselves (as they did immediately) with a large body of newly created cardinals the vested interests were so extensive as to destroy the possibility of a cool review.

Nevertheless attempts were made to settle the matter by evidence and by force *(per viam facti)*. The cardinals immediately after the second election published a *declaratio* in justification of their action. The curia of Urban VI published in reply a sober memorandum supported by documents, which remains the most important contemporary evidence. The memorandum of the Urbanists is corroborated by the witness of St Catherine of Sweden to a commission set up in 1379. St Catherine of Siena, who was at Rome at the time, was equally convinced that Urban was the rightful pope. On the other side is the account given by St Vincent Ferrer; thus each party had supporters of moral worth. As even modern historians with all the evidence before them have been unable to attain absolute unanimity, it was not to be expected that contemporaries, in default of a full and official enquiry, would do so. Moreover when once Europe had split along national lines any hopes of a reasoned solution were vain. Both parties proceeded at once to anathemas, propaganda, intrigues, and even violence, and it was soon clear that any attempt to establish past facts or create a *de facto* solution was doomed to fail.

When it became clear that two papal obediences, each with an efficient curia functioning on traditional lines, and each pledged to its right to universal jurisdiction, had been clamped upon Europe, attempts to break the deadlock took two forms: the *via cessionis*, that of inducing one or both the claimants to resign; and the *via concilii*, that of superseding the rivals by a general council. The former way proved hopeless; neither of the original pair would move and each line was continued when a death occurred. Promises and offers of resignation were made and dishonoured, but in the event there were still two pontiffs in presence after thirty years.

Meanwhile the canonists and publicists had been active. Modern historians, with long acquaintance with the post-Tridentine and post-1870 Church, and often more familiar with the age of Gregory VII and Innocent III than with that of the Schism, have very generally assumed that between 1076 and 1378 the only alternative to the victorious orthodoxy of papal monarchy was the languishing and ultimately defeated imperialistic position. In fact, however, the social and ecclesiastical background during this period, and canonist reflection, had given birth to a theory parallel to the monarchic, of the Church as a corporation, or rather a hierarchy of corporations, of which the lowest was the body of the faithful and the highest the college of cardinals. According to this view, the pope was the divinely instituted head of all, but the various bodies had certain indefeasible rights. What these were differed in expression from one canonist to another, but the great Hostiensis, so often cited as a papalist, regarded the college of cardinals as forming a corporate body with the pope, with the corollary that in a papal vacancy the cardinals had full authority, while in the case of a total demise of the cardinals authority would fall back to the whole Church in general council. From this position it was easy to proceed, with John of Paris, to consider the pope's power as limited by the needs of the Church; an incompetent pope, as well as an heretical or sinful pope, could be deposed. Here was a line of thought that could be developed in different ways by the cardinals who had made the election of Clement VII and by thinkers faced with the problem of a divided Christendom. It was not the only line of thought available. The more radical and individualistic opinions of Marsilius and Ockham, each in its way exalting the general council, which represented the body of the faithful as opposed to the pope, had penetrated academic circles many years before 1378.

Universities, indeed, and in particular the university of Paris, were to play a leading part in the debates that were beginning. Paris, for some two centuries, had been the intellectual queen of Europe, and the advance of other academies, and in particular that of Oxford, to near parity had not dispossessed her. In the mid-fourteenth century there was a change. The great war between England and France had cut the link between Oxford and Paris, and the Schism thirty years later had deprived Paris of other regions of recruitment. The university became almost wholly a French institution while embracing among its alumni all the leading ecclesiastics and some of the lawyers of the nation. At once narrowed in outlook and stimulated by a sense of having lost prestige, it entered upon a period of mental strife and was represented by a succession of distinguished men. The first of these to enter the lists was (1380) Conrad of Gelnhausen demanding in his *Epistola Concordiae* a general council on the grounds that the Church universal is superior to pope and cardinals and ' what concerns all should be dealt with by or for all '. To the axiom that only a pope can convoke a council Conrad, a follower of Ockham, used the argument that necessity knows no law and that the Schism was a case not contemplated by the framers of canon law. Conrad was followed by Henry of Langenstein who in his *Epistola pacis* (1381) maintained the right of the Church to rid herself of an ill-chosen and harmful pope. These two thinkers headed a great phalanx of publicists. They were to be followed in the next generation by Pierre d'Ailly and Jean Gerson, but for the moment they had little influence.

When Urban VI, the Roman pope, died in 1389 he was at once replaced by Boniface IX without incident, but when in 1394 Clement VII died at Avignon the French king made a determined effort to prevent an election. He failed, and though all the cardinals bound themselves by oath to resign if elected, the Spaniard Pedro de Luna, elected as Benedict XIII, showed no sign of abdicating, and resisted further French attempts to achieve his resignation together with that of his rival. It was at this conjuncture, when a Spanish pope was using all possible means to augment his revenues from France, that the clergy of France in collusion with the university of Paris organised a new move. At an assembly in 1396 it was proposed to withdraw obedience from Benedict XIII in order to force his resignation. The motion was lost, but at another synod of 1398 the university supported by the government had its way. Claiming that liberties of immemorial antiquity had been invaded by the papacy, and that the king alone had the right of taxing the clergy, of enjoying revenues of vacant benefices, and of appointing to all benefices in the church of France, the assembly solemnly withdrew obedience, while maintaining that it still allowed the purely spiritual supremacy of the pope. This, the first appearance of what was later called Gallicanism, represented the fusion of two movements of opinion – the growth of the secularist and nationalist spirit in the kings of France since the days of Philip the Fair, and the jealous attitude of the university towards the papacy which had been growing ever since the papacy had supported the friars in their struggle with the university and with the bishops. With both parties economic motives entered into the reckoning: the king hoped to divert the papal taxes and dues to his own advantage; the university hoped to secure the patronage enjoyed by the popes. For the moment the move seemed successful. The cardinals left Benedict XIII and claimed to rule the Church, and the pope was forced into flight. Nevertheless he held out; all in France were soon dissatisfied by the behaviour and the rapacity of the government and others who replaced the papal agents; a few stalwart bishops had protested from the beginning against the withdrawal, and in 1403 France returned to obedience.

The years that immediately followed saw several movements, sincere or simulated, towards the ' way of resignation ', and a long series of sidling advances, not unlike that of hostile cats, took place, in which the two popes approached each other in the Ligurian Alps without ever making the contact that each professed to desire as a preparation for a joint resignation, and in which the Roman Gregory XII allowed himself to be morally out-manoeuvred. Europe had long been out of patience, and a second withdrawal of obedience by France had been secretly agreed upon in 1407.

At last in the spring of 1408 cardinals of both obediences revolted at the tergiversations of the rival popes and came together to take action. They announced that a general council would meet at Pisa on 25 March 1409 and summoned the two rivals to attend. The two pontiffs responded by convoking councils of their own, Benedict XIII at Perpignan, Gregory XII at Cividale. Nevertheless the council at Pisa, moderate in size but fairly wide in representation, proceeded to depose the two existing popes and to elect Alexander V, a Franciscan, with instructions for reforms which were never implemented. When he died a year later Baldassare Cossa, who lacked all moral and spiritual qualifications, was elected as John XXIII. Among his cardinals were Zabarella and Pierre d'Ailly. Christendom now had three pontiffs of whom the last was certainly personally unworthy and canonically in the eyes of many an intruder, and a complete impasse had been reached. It was broken by the action of King Sigismund. This monarch, who was to be the central figure in the European stage for thirty years, was a younger son of the emperor Charles IV and was successively elector of Brandenburg, king of Hungary (1387), emperor (1411) and king of Bohemia (1419). Able, energetic, ambitious and versatile he grasped the situation and persuaded John XXIII to convoke a council for November 1414 at Constance. Sigismund himself, and the general desire for an end to the Schism, secured a general acceptance and the Council of Constance, which opened quietly, soon had a large attendance and developed a character of its own. The distrust of popes and cardinals, and the contemporary national sentiment, inflamed by the current hostility of England and France, led to two important innovations. The one was that of debating and voting by nations. The other was the admission of non-episcopal theologians in large numbers. This ensured an influential position for the university men who stood for the superiority of council over pope and for the need for recurrent councils. Pierre d'Ailly, now cardinal, was a conciliar extremist; Gerson was more conservative and stood for a limited reform; Zabarella was a qualified conciliarist and Dietrich of Niem an insistent and radical reformer who proclaimed the supremacy of the universal Church. The council, when all its members had arrived, was large and representative and as both curial and imperial business was transacted there, Constance was for three years the metropolis of Europe.

The council began by condemning Hus [2] and by dividing itself into four unequal nations, equal in voting power. John XXIII after much shuffling offered to abdicate if his two rivals would do likewise. Gregory XII was willing but before Benedict XIII had spoken John XXIII levanted in disguise, following a precedent set earlier by his two rivals. The council, left to itself, decided that it had full authority to continue in being, and on

2. See below ch. 41.

6 April, in the celebrated decree *Sacrosancta*, went on to decree that it had authority directly from Christ and claimed the obedience of all, including the pope, in matters of the faith and reform. The fathers then proceeded to try John XXIII on innumerable charges and he was condemned, not unjustly, and deposed. A few days later the resignation of Gregory XII was handed in. Benedict XIII held firm, hoping to survive as the only pope left, and he was not deposed until 1417. Meanwhile the council had run into the doldrums. The absence of Sigismund, war between England and France, and divisions between Burgundians and Armagnacs, national and personal frictions and above all the lack of a single authority paralysed initiative, and the council was entangled in a series of bitter, unnecessary and futile disputes. Nevertheless a committee had been set up to present heads of reform, and each nation sent up its own scheme of priorities; of these the German was the most inclusive and realistic; the English the mildest, and the French the most revolutionary. Sigismund returned to find the council enervated and disunited, and his own prestige decayed. With Benedict XIII eliminated at last (1417) the way was clear for a papal election but the council was equally divided as to whether or no election should precede reform. When this was ultimately decided, controversy broke out afresh as to who should elect; the consolidated college of cardinals, all of whom had doubtful credentials; or the council with questionable canonical authority. A compromise was arrived at, but before the election the Fathers passed another important decree (9 October 1417), *Frequens*, according to which the council must reunite after five years, then after seven, and permanently every ten years thereafter. To this were added decrees limiting to a small extent the financial exactions of the papacy. Shortly before the papal election Cardinal Zabarella died, a sage and moderate conciliarist of blameless life who might well have found favour with the electors. As it was, a short conclave issued on St Martin's day in the choice of a Roman of pure blood, Ottone Colonna, who took the name of Martin V. It was an omen of conservative action, and both France and Sigismund were slighted, but the Schism of thirty-nine years was over.

The extent of ecumenicity in the decrees of the Council of Constance has often been debated. There can be no doubt with regard to the sessions (42 to 45) at which the pope, Martin V, was present, nor of those, such as the eighth, where Wyclif's teaching was condemned, and the fifteenth which condemned that of Hus, for these decisions were taken up by Martin V and republished in his bull *Inter Cunctas* of 22 February 1418. On the other hand Eugenius IV accepted in gross the two Councils of Constance and Basle with the express reservation of any diminution of the rights, dignities, and pre-eminence of the Roman see. The issue is a living one in view of the decree *Sacrosancta* of the fifth session (5 April 1415) which declared that the council derived its authority immediately from Christ and that every-one, even the pope, owed obedience to it in matters of faith and reform. This decree, on strictly theological principles, is not an infallible pro-nouncement for it was never accepted by a pope. Even considered by itself it is questionable whether it could be an authentic declaration of the faith. Quite apart from the fact that important cardinals protested and many withdrew or were absent from the vote, the decree was an unprepared motion to meet an unexpected situation, when the council found itself abandoned by Pope John (who counted himself John XXIII) and without a head, and some recent historians have maintained that in the state of uncertainty that then existed, according to traditional canonical principles, a council had full (temporary) authority, and that therefore John (XXIII) was a lawfully elected pope. In consequence, the Council of Constance was an authentic council not only when the pope was present but also when his flight and condemnation had once more brought about a state of chaos. If this opinion is accepted it was therefore facing extinction, and the decree *Sacrosancta* was framed to meet the particular dilemma by self-preservation. It was not in fact treated afterwards by all in the council as having settled the question of the superiority of a council to a pope. No doubt many of those present wished and intended to settle it thus; probably also, had the Schism lasted, and had the decree *Frequens* come into regular operation, the decree *Sacrosancta* would have been amplified and repeated in a more regular form, but in fact neither of these eventualities occurred and it was not for almost two centuries that *Sacrosancta* became a shib-boleth of the Gallican theologians.

The new pope made it clear at once that any kind of radical reform was unthinkable. His regulations for the curia perpetuated some of the prac-tices included as reprehensible in all the programmes of reform, though in lesser measures of reform and in his efficient restoration of curial machinery he brought about a speedy return to normal working. He devoted the greater part of his energies to restoring order and financial solvency to the papal state in Italy, and here he was remarkably successful. Though from the first he had proclaimed the traditional supremacy of the papacy he observed the decrees of Constance and a council was duly convoked to Pavia in 1423. Poorly attended and transferred to Siena it languished and was soon dissolved (March 1424) by Martin, who must take responsibility for its failure to move towards reform. Growing discontent, and the failure to curb the Hussites in Bohemia, led to a widespread insist-ence on the observance of the date, fixed by *Frequens*, for the next council, and the pope yielded with his bull of convocation to Basle in 1431, appointing as his legate the pure, learned and attractive young cardinal Giuliano Cesarini, already on his way to lead the crusade against the

Hussites. Before the council could meet, Martin V was dead.

The story of the Council of Basle (1431-49) is even more complicated than that of Constance. Though somewhat weaker in numbers and with fewer bishops and more university men and lower clergy, it was a fair cross-section of the church in Europe. Its lack of leaders of the mental calibre of Gerson and d'Ailly was balanced by the guiding influence of the moderate Cesarini; while the great majority of its members were, or became, unsympathetic towards the monarchical supremacy of the pope, there was a great variety of opinion ranging from those who held the papacy to be a divine institution, but without infallibility, to those who considered the body of the clergy or even the body of the faithful to be the ultimate sovereign in matters of faith and government. Almost all members held that a General Council had in the present circumstances authority superior to the pope, though it must be remembered both that all were convinced that the pope was at least the normal executive and head of the Church and that the majority both of bishops and educated laity outside the council, together with a school of conservative and able theologians, remained wedded to the traditional doctrine of the past. Whatever the faults and ultimate failure of the Council of Basle, it is nevertheless a remarkable fact that a large and international assembly should have remained in existence and indeed in energetic life for some eighteen years.

The first phase was the most successful, in which by skilful debate and diplomacy it first composed and then temporarily settled the quarrel between the Hussites and the orthodox Catholics. Its prestige indeed was such as to force the new pope Eugenius IV, a skilful politician and obstinate upholder of the papal supremacy, to withdraw his dissolution of the council and to countenance for a time its proposals. A peak of endeavour was reached with decrees in 1433 abolishing papal reservation of benefices and in 1435 doing away with all fees charged by the curia including those for benefices and appointments, annates and first-fruits. Fortunately for Eugenius IV the current need of the Greek emperor for assistance and consequently for reunion enabled him to regain the initiative. While the council bungled negotiations, the pope met Greek demands by transferring the council to Ferrara (later Florence) with reunion on the agenda. A minority from Basle joined the new assembly and the Council of Florence after considerable debate achieved an artificial union (1438-9). The Council of Basle meanwhile called the pope to account and finally deposed him as a heretic (1439), electing as anti-pope a retired duke of Savoy (Felix V), but the success of Eugenius with the Greeks, and his diplomatic skill in satisfying kings and princes with concordats, deprived the council of support and prestige, though it was ten years in expiring. In 1449 the era of councils and rival popes ended: the age of secular autocracy and theological revolution was already dawning.

The reader or student, who makes his first acquaintance with the conciliar epoch, will probably be amazed that the doctrine of the monarchical supremacy of the papacy, propounded in the thirteenth century by popes, theologians and canonists in harmony, should have apparently crumbled to ruin within a little more than fifty years in favour of opinions almost directly contrary to it, some versions of which were even propounded as Christian teaching by bodies claiming to represent the universal Church. The reply, that a large if silent body of pastors and faithful remained unaffected by this shift of opinion does not wholly meet the difficulty.

In the first place, we must distinguish between basic doctrine and its superstructure. A general belief that the apostolic see had supremacy as the rock of faith and source of authority had been current in the western church from earliest antiquity. The superstructure of the canonists and publicists of the thirteenth century was, in part at least, something individual and temporary, subject, like all movements of sentiment or philosophical opinions, to reactionary change. Next, it would seem historically true that this reaction, seen in the writings of Marsilius and Ockham, was as wide and as deep as had been the movement towards centralisation in the two previous centuries, and it was assisted by the loss of prestige suffered by the papacy at Avignon. Even so, most historians would agree that but for the ' accident ' of the double election of 1378 there would never have been a ' conciliar epoch '. As it was the Schism had lasted for a dozen years or more before the ' conciliarists ' – i.e., not merely those who advocated the calling of a council, but those who attributed some kind of sovereign power to a council – became influential leaders of a large body of opinion, and this body became large not primarily through the intrinsic appeal of the doctrine but through despair of any other means of ending an intolerable situation, and through disgust at the behaviour of almost all the various pretenders to the papal dignity. Even so the ' conciliarists ' were for the most part either academics or politicians. The inarticulate body of the Church probably stood as far away from a Gerson or William of Ockham as their forebears had stood away from Innocent IV or Ptolemy of Lucca. They were neither conciliarists nor papalists, and the confusion of the schism exasperated them. They were orthodox believers without any personal loyalty to the pope, and probably without any practical advertence to the papacy as an influence upon their beliefs or practices, but recognising that the machinery of the Church demanded and possessed a guide and master to ensure its right direction. The ease with which Martin V restored the position of the papacy is an index of the hold it had as an institution in the political consciousness of the epoch, and it is evident that the councils had shown themselves in the long run incapable of dealing with divisions among Christians or with movements of reform. Still more significant, though less in evidence, is the re-emergence of traditional thought as seen in the disputations with the Greeks at Florence, in the apologetics of Thomas Netter and in the writings of the revived Thomist school.

Yet the councils had not been without influence. Without them it is hard to see how the unity of the Church could ever have been restored. On the other hand, both Constance and Basle, the former by its reliance upon Sigismund and the latter by its obstinacy in clinging to its untenable position, gave a great impulse to the strengthening of secular control over religion that was to be such a feature of the two following centuries.

The scandal and disruption of the normal life of the Church during the Schism were undoubtedly very great. Yet it is probable that the administration of church life suffered less than might be thought. Europe was divided regionally, not locally or personally, save for a few exceptions; both obediences, at least until 1409, functioned fairly efficiently, and it is clear that Europe as a whole was still solidly Catholic and therefore undisturbed in belief. At levels below the hierarchy it is probable that clergy and people were affected very little by the schism. As regards England, at least, it is worth remarking that readers of the extensive and far-reaching poems of Chaucer (c. 1340-1400) and Langland (?1330-?1400) and of the reflections of Julian of Norwich (1342-1416) would have no conception that the Church was passing through a crisis of government without precedent or parallel. In two respects, however, the influence of the Schism was felt. The centralised religious orders were perforce split into two, with the general of the order or the head house cut off from half their subjects. As time went on a double organisation came into being in some cases (as the friars) while in others devolution took place. Thus in England the Cluniac, Cistercian and Premonstratensian orders were for the time being centred upon English superiors or an important English house (e.g., Welbeck). When unity returned, the friars had little difficulty in restoring the *status quo ante*, but the older, less firmly centralised, orders tended to petrify in their national groupings. The other widespread consequence was a cheapening of every kind of privilege and exception, owing to the ease with which popes of either party dispensed their favours for cash. Monastic and ecclesiastical discipline suffered, and never wholly regained the ground it had lost.

Above all the schism, by loosening the bonds of spiritual discipline while retaining, and even increasing, the burden of papal taxation, brought a new urgency into the demand for reform in head and members. This demand grew as the years passed and reached its height in the early period of the Council of Basle. If any lesson was learnt by Europe at large from the ' conciliar epoch ' it was that councils could not, and that popes as yet would not, satisfy that demand.

THE FIFTEENTH CENTURY

I. AFTERMATH OF SCHISM

ONE of the most notable and fateful results of the long depression of the papacy and of the political theories rife in the ' conciliar epoch ' was the tighter control of the national churches by the secular power. This took different forms in different countries.

We have seen how in England from the time of the Norman Conquest onwards there had been a long conflict between the kings and their governments, who asserted the ancient custom of the realm as giving control over elections, excommunications, and papal commands, and those ecclesiastics who followed the dictates of canon law. By the end of the twelfth century the Church had won on the level of theory, and, save in a few borderline matters, canon law and the decretals of popes were recognised as binding on English clerks and as sanctioned by the English courts of law. This is not to say that there were no protests or resistance. From the reign of Edward I (1272-1307) onwards there had been repeated protests by king and parliament against papal exactions and provisions, culminating in the statues of Provisors (1351) and Praemunire (1353), which prohibited the acceptance by an Englishman of any benefice from Rome, appeals to Rome in any case pending in England, and the acceptance of any papal bull. Both these statutes were repeated in 1380 and the sending of any money out of the realm to the pope was forbidden. It is true that these measures were in great degree merely enablements, intended by the government to satisfy public discontent, to deter the papacy from further exploitation, and to assist the king to strike a bargain in practice. They represent a counter-response to *Clericis laicos*, leaving the issue between the two powers unresolved, and their immediate practical effect was small. They were certainly in no way directed against the spiritual authority of the pope. Nevertheless, so far as words went they were sufficiently audacious, and they were not without influence across the Channel.

The French church, as has been noted above, had renounced obedience to the Avignon pope in 1398, had restored it, and renounced it again in 1403, and had finally restored it in 1404. This arrangement was not lasting, and at a council in 1406, largely controlled by the university of Paris, with Pierre le Roy, abbot of Mont St Michel, and Jean Petit as spokesmen, drastic decisions were taken, and sanctioned by Charles VI in 1407. In these papal provisions to benefices and papal exaction of annates, procurations, revenues during vacancies, tithes and other taxes were declared inadmissible. Full obedience to the pope in his capacity of spiritual head of the church was reaffirmed save in one important particular; the authority of a general council was set above that of a papal pronouncement. This event has rightly been considered as the birth of historical Gallicanism. It rested in theory on two assumptions: that the king of France had enjoyed from time immemorial certain rights of taxation and revenue and appointment over the French church; and that papal authority was limited by the reputedly ancient canon law which rested principally on conciliar decisions. Of the first assumption the beneficiary was the king, who assumed control over the administration and finances of the church. The resultant ' freedom ' of the Gallican church was based upon the novel assumption that papal decretals and bulls were invalid if they conflicted with, or went beyond, conciliar decrees and pre-Gratian canon law. The later corollary, that a papal pronouncement on doctrine was only irreformable or infallible when accepted by a general council, was an extension of the principle that conciliar decision was the one sufficient and irreversible authority.

Historically, canonically and theologically this position was untenable. That it was taken up and successfully maintained was due partly to the growth of national feeling, exploited by the monarchy, partly to the distress of the papacy during the Great Schism, and partly to the influence of dissolvent thought at all levels, derived from Marsilius of Padua, William of Ockham and his followers.

The arrangements of 1406/7 were not final. Martin V endeavoured to reassert papal rights admitted by the church in general, while in France both king and university were prepared to abate their claims in order to reap immediate advantage. A more lasting settlement was reached at the Congress of Bourges in 1433, and its ordinances were reasserted in the Pragmatic Sanction of 1439. This instrument was not so revolutionary as has been supposed. Broadly speaking, it followed the pronouncements of the Council of Basle and endeavoured to reproduce the state of things that existed before the residence of the papacy at Avignon. Its ordinances may be summarised as follows:

1) The decree *Frequens* (decennial councils) was reaffirmed and the superiority of a council over the pope asserted, with its corollary that the king of France had no superior in political matters.

2) Elections and collations were to be ' free ' and performed by the bodies or persons as of old. The papal reservations of the Decretals and Sext (a constitution of Boniface VIII) were admitted, but not those declared more recently.

3) Annates and papal taxes in general were abolished, but provision was made for the needs of Eugenius IV.

4) Appeals were to be as in the days of Boniface VIII. All cases four days' journey from the curia were to be tried at home, save for grave causes excepted in the canons and for those concerning bishoprics and exempt monasteries.

5) Various reforming decrees reaffirmed celibacy, residence and attend-ance of canons, etc., at choir.

The Pragmatic Sanction of Bourges was regarded as the Great Charter of the church of France. Though constantly attacked by the papacy, it remained until abolished by Louis XI in 1461 and was reaffirmed in the concordat between Francis I and Leo X in 1516.

It is interesting to compare the English and French solutions to the problems raised by the papal claims to universal sovereignty in temporal and spiritual affairs. The English acts of parliament remained valid on the external level of politics; they put a practical weapon in the hands of king and parliament and the result was a compromise that satisfied both parties. The prelates and convocations never explicitly recognised the anti-papal legislation, which was not in fact enforced. The French move, on the other hand, was put on a theoretical basis, and resulted in an alliance of the clergy with the king against the pope and the curia.

In Germany long negotiations issued in the Concordat of Constance (1418) which after many difficulties and discussions was repeated in essentials in the Concordat of Vienna (1448). These concordats were in essence a return to the *status quo* as understood by the papacy, with certain exceptions. Thus papal reservations were restricted to those allowed in the thirteenth century, canonical elections were restored and non-elective benefices were to be filled alternately by the pope and the normal authority; certain benefices were reserved for graduates.

2. THE RENAISSANCE PAPACY

Ever since the coming of age of critical history and of the history of literature early in the nineteenth century there has been debate as to the significance of the terms renaissance and humanism, and as to their relationship to medieval culture on the one hand, and to contemporary fifteenth-century religious belief on the other. Though some kind of division into chronological periods is inevitable if history is to be more than a series of annals, recent historians of every country have deplored hard and fast lines of division or definition. It is clear for example that the seeds and even early blossoms of the renaissance and the Reformation are visible from *c.* 1350 onwards, to say nothing of an earlier ' renaissance ' and ' humanism ' in the eleventh and twelfth centuries. In many ways indeed, the ' modern ' age dawned in the days of Dante, Petrarch, Ockham, Marsilius and Boccaccio, while in other respects much that is characteristically medieval in outlook survived at least until 1650. Similarly the nineteenth-century identification of Italian humanism with religious liberalism or even free thought cannot be maintained. In the field of religious sentiment and theology it is easy to see elements of the Reformation and the Counter-Reformation in the fifteenth and fourteenth centuries. What are sometimes called the spirit and piety of the Counter-Reformation are indeed little more than natural developments from the practices and outlook of late medieval Italy and Spain. And as we have already remarked it was in the fifteenth century that the great national divisions of Europe showed clearly their divergent outlook on every aspect of human life and thought.

Nevertheless in the attitude to human life (restricted, if we wish, almost entirely to Italy) a great change of sentiment is visible. Individualism, and the interest in individuals and of the individual in himself and his achievements and posthumous glory; appreciation of physical, literary, material and artistic beauty regarded as an accomplishment, rather than as a delusion; interest in man and his works, in natural beauty, in the art of living, rather than in a withdrawal from the world as a transitory and deceptive dwelling-place; these were elements in new types of men: the cultured, cool mind of the man of taste; the artist, whether architect, painter or sculptor; the universal man, sane and whole in mind and body; and the successful man, the man of *virtù* who reached distinction by qualities of mind rather than by physical or spiritual strength. But in all this, the difference between Italy and transalpine Europe is great.

As for the relationship, or opposition, between humanism and religion, the debate continues among historians. Whatever may have been the sophisticated paganism of groups of scholars, whatever the refinements of treachery, crime and lust in the high levels of society, the middle and lower ranks of the Italian population remained very much as they had been, some devout, many worldly, very many superstitious with a peculiar extravagance, while some of the most brilliant of the galaxy of talent and genius, and members of the Platonic Academy of Florence such as Marsilio Ficino and Pico de la Mirandola, were instances of that ' devout humanism ' that would perhaps have been characteristic of the century that followed had not Luther and Calvin troubled the waters.

In any case, northern and central Italy in the fifteenth century was a furnace of passion, human and political, a whirlpool of brilliant colours, a teeming field of genius, and an entanglement of cultures and civilisations without parallel in the history of western Europe. The fragmentation of its society into numerous independent centres each of which contained circling groups of elements, and the absence of an institution, a discipline, or a person to dominate the whole or reduce it to a unity, render any summary or description wholly inadequate. It was the misfortune of the church that the clerical order, and above all the papal court, was representative of every aspect of contemporary life, a microcosm with every element of good and evil, and that individuals in high places were themselves children of light and darkness, unable therefore to give the message of the gospel with that exemplary clarity that alone might have averted the revolution that was in fact to come so soon.

The contrast between the humanism of Italy and that of Germany is familiar. Whereas in Italy the original aim of humanism was literary and imitative, to recapture the lost or neglected masterpieces of Latin, and later of Greek, literature, and to reproduce their style and metres in writings that would display the rebirth of fine letters after an intermediate period of semi-barbarism, in Germany and the Low Countries the aim was rather grammatical and philological, embracing Hebrew as well as Latin and Greek, and whereas Cicero was the only model for Valla and Bembo, Erasmus affected the more racy and familiar speech of Plautus and Terence. Similarly, in the later generations Italian scholars edited classical texts and studied Plato, while the northern scholars turned their attention to the Fathers and explored Scripture. Italy sought after visual beauty of all kinds, and pursued the humanist ideal of the many-sided personality and a life of experience and achievement, of *virtù* and posthumous fame. Transalpine scholars in the north lived laborious sedentary lives, with acrid controversies and a longing to return to the simple-seeming Christianity of the early Church. The contrast must not be pressed, but it existed.

While the pure scholars of both regions could meet in mutual sympathy and understanding, and while the northerners could in many ways show a level of accomplishment and originality that equalled anything cisalpine –a Nicholas of Cusa, a Reuchlin and above all an Erasmus–there was, at least in our period, no full ' renaissance ' of life and letters in the north. The great figures, and still more the lesser ones, were direct descendants of their medieval forebears, with the addition of a new scholarship and a stronger hostility towards monks and friars and the court of Rome. Nicholas of Cusa (1401-64), however, stands apart from the later German humanists. His career, which took him into lifelong companion-ship with Italians and with popes, and his intellectual interests, which became more and more turned to Neoplatonism, bridged for him the space between Germany and Italy, just as does his ideal, the harmonisation of philosophy and theology, and (in later life) the restoration of the power of the papacy. Cusanus, alike in his effort to re-establish a metaphysical and rational basis for faith, in his hope of harmonising Aristotle and Plato, and in his reforming zeal, stands apart from his colleagues in the college of cardinals, whom he nevertheless resembles in his struggle for preferment in his assertive litigation and in some of his affluent tastes.

The return of the papacy to Rome at the end of the Great Schism in 1417 would under any circumstances have opened a new chapter in its history. In the event, the restoration of papal government coincided with the development of a great cultural movement and helped to influence the political history of Italy in a decisive manner. An epoch was opened that was only ended by the series of European catastrophes of which the first was heralded by the emergence of Luther exactly one hundred years later.

For the papacy, the essential characteristics of this period were the gradual immersion of the popes in the violent power politics of Italy, and the share taken by Italian ecclesiastics in the movement known as the Italian renaissance. The combined effect of these two activities was to lower the spiritual and moral strength of the Roman curia and, as a consequence, to diminish very notably its prestige.

During the long absence from Rome of direct papal government the political scene in the peninsula had greatly altered. An Italy in which a central papacy was principally concerned with containing or repelling the advances of the German emperor in the north and the Angevin power in the south had given place to a patchwork of states, greater or smaller, almost all controlled by a signore who had become in time a despot, either under the title of a duke or prince, or nominally an influential citizen, or (as at Venice) a small oligarchy. In central Italy lay the void of the papal states, now overrun, now in revolt, now reclaimed by a legate. When Martin V returned to Italy his first task was to gain control of his territory and reorganise its resources and revenues. This he did with success and when he died the papacy was in possession and solvent. He and his successors found themselves as an influential power separating Naples from the three principal northern states of Florence, Milan and Venice, and an active diplomacy was essential to safeguard legitimate interests, but the personal characteristics and dynastic ambitions of a series of pontiffs shortly before 1500 led to adventures and involvements of a political and even of a military nature that put the papacy into a new position – that of a political power with relations of peace and war, diplomacy or discord, with any or all of the new national powers of Europe, quite irrespective of the ecclesiastical or spiritual standing of the power concerned.

At the same time the papacy had to reckon with the great movement of intellectual, artistic and psychological life known as the Italian renaissance.

This movement, as distinct from the gradual development of the arts and civilisation in the twelfth and thirteenth centuries, had shown two new features from about the middle of the fourteenth century onwards. The one was a new interest in, and attitude to, the actions and emotions of the individual human being considered precisely as a living human being and not as a soul meriting or forfeiting eternal life. The other, acting to the first as both cause and effect, was a new interest in the literary and artistic monuments of classical civilisation, regarded as both displaying and aiding the expression of human genius and character in the past and present.

The restoration of the papacy to Rome and the progressive diminution of the conciliar challenge had the result of making Italy the cynosure of Europe at the moment of its emergence as the centre of European civilisation and the mother of a host of men of genius. The cult of ancient literature and the output of painting and other artistic work of the highest quality had begun in the fourteenth century with Petrarch and Boccaccio, with Giotto, Simone Martini and Giovanni Pisano, and the forward movement in art was to be continuous for almost three hundred years. Painting and the representative arts are, indeed, the one important field of achievement of the human mind that bridged the transition in the fifteenth century between the medieval and the modern world.

The appearance of great literature in the vernacular and the emergence of painting, at first in tempera and later on wood and canvas, as an art-form of distinction, might have had no more influence upon society in general than the birth of any other school of writing or painting. Nor did early humanism, with its search for Latin manuscripts and its quest of stylistic purity, threaten to change the doctrinal outlook of its adepts. But when Greek literature and thought were rediscovered, when beauty in every shape or form was sought after, when the classical, pagan, luxurious antiquity was taken as the model in every sphere of life, and when the technique of literary and historical criticism was developed, it became clear that a challenge was being made to the ideals and conventions of the medieval ' ages of faith '.

At first the papal curia accepted the new world without pronouncing upon it. Leading humanists such as Poggio Bracciolini and Aeneas Sylvius Piccolomini became papal secretaries, and whatever their morals might be, religious beliefs were generally orthodox. Eugenius IV, though no aesthete, was celebrated by Benozzo Gozzoli and others. As the renaissance gathered momentum, however, and began to colour society, the attitude of the papacy became a matter of importance. A decisive step was taken by Pope Nicholas V, who as Tommaso Parentucelli had been an enthusiastic humanist and scholar. He decided to capture the spirit of the age for the papacy by making Rome the cultural capital of Italy. Besides surrounding himself with a group of leading scholars including Poggio, Filelfo and Lorenzo Valla, the pope inaugurated two projects of lasting importance. The first was the transformation of the small papal library into a great collection of Latin and Greek manuscripts, the first stage in the amassing of precious, curious and beautiful objects and works within the galleries of the Vatican. The other was the rebuilding of St Peter's, the Vatican, and Rome itself on a scale of unparalleled magnificence. Nicholas called Fra Angelico and Benozzo, among others, to Rome and replanned the Leonine city on lines that have remained to the present day. The successor of Nicholas V, Calixtus III (1455-8), discontinued and even undid some of his work, but the projects remained and bore fruit. Calixtus, elected as an aged nonentity when faction made election difficult, initiated another and more baneful characteristic of the fifteenth-century papacy. A Spaniard and the first of the Borgias, he created two nephews cardinals and a third prefect of the city and vicar of Terracina and Benevento. The death of Calixtus was followed by a conclave in which another *tertius gaudens* was elected. This time it was no ordinary choice. Aeneas Sylvius Piccolomini, Pius II (1458-64), was as much an epitome of his age as Innocent III was of an earlier epoch. A diplomatist and writer of the highest skill and virtuosity, he had lived down his early profligacy while still remaining a worldly rather than a spiritual leader. A conciliarist for long, he lived to publish as pope the bull *Execrabilis* (1460) reaffirming papal supremacy. A diarist and autobiographer of genius, he has attracted more notice and won more affection in the course of the centuries than his work as pope deserved. His diplomacy helped to consolidate the reputation of the curia in this field, but his efforts to raise a crusade against the Turk failed hopelessly. His successor Paul II (1464-71), a nephew of Eugenius IV, was a good-tempered autocrat who alienated the humanists but satisfied the people of Rome with his carnivals and constructions. For the former he cleared the Piazza Venezia, and built and inhabited the Palazzo Venezia which commanded it. He was followed by Francesco della Rovere, Sixtus IV (1471-84), who when elected was Minister-General of the Franciscan order, a man of humble origins who had made his mark as scholar and preacher. After repeated failures in his attempts to mount a crusade against the Turk, he took the fateful step of transforming the papal monarchy into a great Italian power, using his numerous nephews as lieutenants. Two were cardinals, both of loose morality and wholly unspiritual, three were laymen; between them they executed the papal diplomacy with a dexterity which kept Italy in perpetual ferment. Sixtus IV was a munificent patron of the arts. He built the world-famous chapel named after him, and marshalled a galaxy of genius to decorate it: Ghirlandaio, Botticelli, Perugino, Pinturicchio and Melozzo da Forli among them. He also built or began to build several churches, including Santa Maria della Pace, and his features and those of his librarian, Platina, are familiar from the fresco of Melozzo. When Sixtus died another stalemate and bartered election produced Battista Cybo, Innocent VIII (1484-92). With his pontificate the reputation of the papacy fell steeply. The pope acknowledged an illegitimate son and daughter of his pre-clerical days, and celebrated the marriage of his grand-daughter with a banquet at which ladies were present at a papal reception for the first time. Bribery and the purchase of office were common form in the curia and forged bulls and privileges abounded. Sixtus IV and Innocent VIII both created numerous cardinals from their families and supporters and the large college, made up of wealthy and ambitious men, was split into factions which carried on party strife and intrigues in the City and its neighbourhood. Innocent died shortly after the Catholic kings had conquered Granada, and shortly before Columbus discovered America, in the year which has often been taken as the notional beginning of the modern world. The popes since the Schism had now contributed every element that made up the papacy of the next forty years – political intrigue, worldly aims, corruption, lax morals, dynastic hopes – in a city which had attracted and continued to attract the greatest artists of the supreme century of European art. When the fifteenth century ended Alexander VI (1492-1503) occupied the papal throne.

MONASTIC AND REGULAR LIFE IN THE LATER MIDDLE AGES 1216-1500

O N an earlier page we followed the story of the monastic and regular life down to the end of the twelfth century. The Fourth Lateran Council is often taken as the beginning of a new period. It neither attempted nor effected a spiritual revival among the monks and canons, but it set up canonical measures and sanctions which endured. In the first place it applied to all religious the successful disciplinary innovations of the Cistercians. The two oldest families of regulars, the black monks and the black canons, were to form provincial groups for the purpose of legislation and visitation, to be regulated in quadrennial chapters conducted on the lines of the assemblies at Cîteaux and Prémontré. Another canon declared the right and duty of the ordinary of the diocese to visit all non-exempt religious houses, while a later decree imposed upon all superiors the obligation of presenting the accounts of the house in chapter annually and of obtaining the consent of the chapter for all notable expenditures. These were necessary and useful reforming decrees, but they affected the administrative rather than the spiritual life, nor were they punctually and universally executed; England, indeed, seems to have a better record in this respect than any other country.

Quite apart from questions of internal discipline the orders of both monks and canons entered upon a new era in the thirteenth century. In the first place, the monastic and regular canonical way of life which for so many centuries had been the only recognised way of following the evangelical counsels in a life solemnly dedicated to God, had now been challenged by a new way, that of the friars. Just as the Cistercians and Premonstratensians had captured many of the sources of recruitment which had hitherto profited the black monks and black canons, so now the friars could outbid the monks and canons of every habit. Secondly, the rise of the universities had drawn off another type of recruit, the able young man attracted by learning. Such talented boys now went into an arts school at thirteen or so and later followed an administrative or academic career before the coming of the friars; thereafter they might take the friars' habit themselves. In any case, the development of higher education throughout Europe, with logic followed by law or theology as the ruling discipline, sounded the death-knell of the old literary humanist education of the cloister. The age of monastic culture had passed, and between the Lateran Council and the appearance of the humanistic culture of the fifteenth century the universities, and the friars' schools within the universities, were the centres of intellectual life. This became so apparent, and the charge of ignorance pressed the monks so hard, that they also betook themselves to the universities towards the end of the thirteenth century. The move was probably beneficial and certainly inevitable, but neither as a career nor as an intellectual occupation could medieval academic life be satisfactory for the majority of monks and regular canons, and no monk is recorded among the great names of scholastic thought.

Speaking generally the old orders continued to flourish during the thirteenth century. Great abbots and notable spiritual writers appeared, and in north-western Europe the monks as landlords profited by an expanding economy and commonly themselves exploited their estates. The general regression of demesne farming as practised in the fourteenth century, which was accentuated by the Black Death and its consequent social and economic readjustments, helped to bring about a slow change. The older orders, even the Cistercians, who had by now found lay brothers both scarce and economically undesirable, went gradually over to an economy of leases and rents, and in the fifteenth century almost all the orders were *rentiers* living on the rents and spiritual revenues of their estates.

Meanwhile there had been a slow change also within the cloister. The monastic life of the eleventh century had been largely liturgical. Benedictine and Cistercian monachism continued to cherish this element but both administrators and students found the working day short, and some of the additional psalmody was reduced. In the matter of diet the absolute prohibition of fleshmeat, though in some houses held not to exclude bipeds, had always been difficult to maintain. A rota system of sharing the abbot's table, or visiting the infirmary after regular blood-letting, had been widely adopted. In the fourteenth century the establishment of a ' meat-refectory ' was common, attended by brethren in rotation while the regular fare was served in the main dining hall. These and other innovations were codified and imposed on the monastic world of Europe in a series of constitutions by the Cistercian pope Benedict XII. The ' Benedictine Constitutions ' promulgated for the black monks (1336), and similar decrees for the white monks and the black canons (in 1335 and 1339), were essentially a ' holding operation ' legalising certain relaxations such as meat-eating and enforcing the frequenting of universities, while forbidding the more flagrant violations of personal poverty and religious obedience. They represent the last reforming action taken for the whole Church by the papacy in the middle ages, and they had no enduring success. Relaxations became more common. During the fifty years of the Great Schism the rival popes, short of funds, sold dispensations of every kind to individual religious, while the spirit of the times everywhere tended to make every office into a benefice. Superiors had long enjoyed the use of revenues and quarters separate from the community. Gradually the other officers (or obedientiaries) of the community acquired by custom or formal distribution the administration of certain sources of income and the use of special chambers and servants, while the daily needs of the brethren, hitherto found from the common store of food, clothing, medicine, etc., came to be met by an annual sum of money known as ' wages ', from which the individual could also acquire spices (the equivalent of modern confectionery or tobacco) and books. Thus even a house of respectable observance was coming to resemble a collegiate establishment.

This gradual slackening of the rhythm of monastic life was accentuated by public disasters and abuses. Among the former may be counted the great pestilences, with their toll of lives varying in incidence from a tenth to a half of a large community and the total obliteration of a small one; the wars of the age, in particular the outrages and wanton destructions of the Hundred Years' War and the Free Companies in France; and the loss of estates owing to inflation and labour shortage in Italy. Among the latter pride of place must be taken by the plague of *commendam*. This, the bestowal of a title and emoluments of a monastic prelacy upon a secular or lay holder by pope or king, was an old institution which had been misused in an earlier age. Practically non-existent in the age following the Gregorian reform it returned as a means of providing employment and a livelihood for prelates driven from their sees in the Levant. In the period of the Avignon papacy it was revived on a large scale to compensate cardinals and others for the loss of Italian revenues and in general to support the bureaucracy, while during the Schism rival popes used it to reward or retain supporters. It was adopted by kings of France and lesser rulers in Italy and elsewhere, and in the concordats of the conciliar epoch was sometimes renounced by Rome and inherited by the monarch. Almost universal in France, Italy and Spain, it was rare in German countries and nonexistent in our period in England. It took the usual form of substituting for the abbot a titular and absentee head who might be a bishop or other prelate but was later often a layman, who held office for life. He drew at least the annual revenue previously allotted to the head of the house, and an unscrupulous holder could draw considerably more, and do much to ruin the finances of the house. Meanwhile the house was governed by a prior, often the nominee of the commendatory abbot, who lacked both the prestige attaching to the consecrated abbot of the Rule, and also the authority to undertake great works whether spiritual or material. In exceptional cases the titular head could be an incubus, starving or maltreating the monks or, as in Scotland in the late fifteenth century, residing as laird in a house inside the precinct. As a consequence of all these misfortunes, together with the gradual decline and secularisation of many kinds of religious life in the fourteenth and fifteenth centuries, there was a general loss of fervour and a general, though not a universal, decline of observance, and many houses in rural surroundings sank deep into the soil so as to resemble a large farm or small manor-house, while some became and remained frankly scandalous, resisting all forms of regular discipline. In default of statistics no attempt to assign proportions to the good and the bad is possible, but on the whole the largest and most celebrated houses were the most respectable. France was probably the hardest hit economically, while Germany and parts of Italy showed the more deplorable scandals. England, saved from the *commendam* of France and the aristocratic ' closed shop ' of Germany, was probably in better fettle than either of these countries, though by no means exemplary.

Another abuse, most common in the German empire, was the restriction of recruitment to those belonging to the nobility or to recruits able to show title of heraldry. This exclusiveness was seen at its worst in convents of women, where it intensified the secular atmosphere often already present for reasons of recruitment mentioned below. Records of visitations in houses of this kind sometimes reveal a community in which aristocratic pride, unhappiness and hysteria combined to produce a deplorable disorder.

When the strict monastic life no longer attracted large numbers, when the religious houses, as was the case throughout Europe, were more numerous than the numbers of recruits justified, it was inevitable that the dedicated claustral life, from being a strong vocation, should become simply a career for those attracted to a regular, peaceful and studious existence, flavoured with religious devotion. Throughout the middle ages there was a slow, but by no means universal, shift in the class of recruit. Whereas in 1100 the great abbey would draw many of its recruits from the feudal, land-owning class, many of whom would come from afar, by the fifteenth century the main intake would be from the class of small farmers or burghers in the neighbourhood or on the lands of the abbey. In the case of women the strong vocation was still rarer. The nuns of medieval Europe, somewhat surprisingly to our minds, were very much less numerous than the monks, and almost all drawn from what we should call the upper and upper middle class of society. In those classes the unmarried daughter was a liability, and there was everything to be said for finding her a comfortable place in a nunnery.

When spiritual and economic saturation point had been reached by the end of the twelfth century in all the main countries of Europe, and when the orders of friars were calling powerfully to the classes unaffected by the monasteries, new monastic institutes were not to be expected. Such new orders as arose were strict groups within the Benedictine framework. Thus the Silvestrines or blue Benedictines began at Monte Fano in 1231 and were named after their founder Sylvestro Gozzolini; the Celestines, an eremitical family (1264), took their name from that briefly held by their founder, the unfortunate Peter of Morrone, Pope Celestine V; the Olivetans, established on Monte Oliveto, had for founder Bernard Ptolemei (1344). All these had a limited success, and the first and last still exist.

Alone of the monastic orders the Carthusians continued both to grow, slowly but steadily, and to maintain their observance and fervour throughout the middle ages. Originally settling on wild and uninhabited sites, they began in the mid-fourteenth century to found in the centre of cities, as at Paris and Cologne and the celebrated Charterhouse of the Salutation in London (1370). At the same time, the tempo of their increase became notably more rapid. It was the ' century of the mystics '. It was also the century of great catastrophes. In any case the Carthusian order in the mid-fourteenth century was both more numerous (with 107 houses) and more familiar to its world than ever before, and produced in Denis the Carthusian one of the most notable mystical writers of the middle ages. With the exception of the Carthusians few orders saw any new foundations after 1300, though a distinguished exception to the rule may be seen in the large and wealthy abbey of Syon near London, founded in 1415 by Henry V to house a large community of Bridgettines, in origin a Swedish order, and their attendant confessors and chaplains. The latter class, like the communities of city charterhouses, contained a considerable proportion of ' late vocations ' of priests of high or academic standing.

We have already considered the friars during their first century of expansion. The Dominicans, unlike the Franciscans, remained a single order throughout, but they too suffered from a decline of fervour, and the disasters of the mid-fourteenth century. Recruitment slackened, scandals were common, and the observance of poverty was lax. The number of Dominican canonised saints and *beati* was small. When the Great Schism came it divided the order, but gave to it two saints. Vincent Ferrer, a Spaniard, supported the pope of Avignon, and was involved in diplomacy with the court of Aragon. Catherine of Siena, a Dominican tertiary, was even more deeply interested in the defence of the Roman pope. Saint Catherine is perhaps the most attractive saint and woman of her age. Virile in spirit, an ecstatic with a fund of common-sense and mental power whose letters are one of the earliest jewels of Italian prose, she was a radiant character with a maternal affection for her ' family ' of counsellors and disciples. She played her part in the history of the age not, as was once thought, by direct action upon Urban V so much as by the formation of a group of followers who carried far and wide her spirit of reforming ardour. Among them were Raymund of Capua, later (1380) master-general of his order, and Blessed John (later cardinal) Dominici, who, together with Conrad of Prussia, was the originator of the Observance, a family of friaries practising strict observance of the Rule. From these, in the next generation, came Fra Angelico of San Marco, Florence, and St Antoninus, both disciples of Dominici, and the movement spread to Germany and Spain, without ever becoming ubiquitous.

The Franciscans, also, by far the most numerous of the friars, had suffered from the ills of the times. The condemnation of the unwise and unfortunate Spirituals by John XXII had for a time left the orthodox main body alone in the field, though ' Spiritual ' currents still flowed in Italy and Provence. Before the end of the century, however, the differences within the order reasserted themselves. A reform, with convents of ' observant ' friars, appeared in 1368 and after slow beginnings grew into a strong body, at first in convents within the bounds of the order but later as a separate order under their common patron. With three notables saints of the fifteenth century in Bernardino of Siena, John Capistran and James of the March, the Observants developed into an order distinguished as much by their frank and outspoken criticism of men and policies as by their rigid observance.

It is difficult to make a general judgment on the state of the religious orders during the two last centuries of the middle ages; it is equally hard to assess their popularity or prestige. Monks had been targets for satire in every age when literary activity was common. Their luxury, worldliness, rich clothes and rich food, before and after Gerald of Wales, had inspired countless writers and continued to do so, and when criticism sounded a harsher and more threatening note in Wyclif and his imitators it is difficult to separate charges against existing bodies from attacks on the very principles of the monastic life. One charge, indeed, made by almost all those who survey the social scene, is that the friars were numberless and ubiquitous, in Chaucer's phrase they were ' as thikke as motes in a sonne beame '. No doubt their presence at every street corner or in every churchyard irked many observers, but it is a witness that the life, if not the vocation, of a friar still had its appeal, and that he had a share in the affairs, as he had a place in the wills, of the little people of the marketplace and the faubourg.

The fifteenth century, in general so ineffective in its velleities for reform, gave birth to more than one new focus of observance and created a new form of monastic constitution which crossed the great divide of the Reform and inspired important institutions of the modern world. This was the new model of Santa Giustina of Padua. This ancient Cluniac monastery was in a state of advanced decay when in 1418 the Venetian canon Louis Barbo (d. 1443) was commissioned by Gregory XII to restore the abbey. The house prospered and reformed several houses and Barbo, anxious to avoid the scourge of *commendam*, created a congregation finally stabilised by Eugenius IV in 1431. In this no life-abbot existed and the houses had no autonomy. The sovereign power was the general chapter and the diffinitory of nine members who had full legislative and executive power; in addition they elected the triennial abbots and all officers of the monasteries. Between chapters visitors elected by the diffinitors applied their decisions. The monks belonged to the congregation, not to the monastery, and the abbots if successful were transferred from house to house at set intervals. This was a radical change, many would say a deformation, of the system of St Benedict. The monarchical abbot, father for life of all his monks, was replaced by a temporary nominee of a general chapter whose activities were restricted and controlled by a board and visitors responsible to chapter. Devised to avoid *commendam*, and perhaps influenced by the prevailing conciliar thought, this revolutionary constitution was akin in spirit to the system of the Dominicans. It was to have a future so long as *commendam* endured. Its observance was adopted by all the Benedictine monasteries of Italy and its system by the fervent Valladolid congregation of Spain (1492). When Monte Cassino joined in 1504 it became known as the Cassinese congregation and a number of the new congregations of the Counter-Reformation adopted its principles.

Two other reforms sprang from conciliar zeal. The first was a result of action at Constance. The ancient abbey of Melk on the Danube was chosen by Duke Albert V of Austria as the focus of a strict observance based upon that of Subiaco (1418). The movement spread all over Austria, Bavaria and Swabia and endured for a century, but it never acquired the firm bonds of a constitution and it disappeared in great part with the onset of the Reformation. The more celebrated reform of Bursfeld owed its origin to the abbots gathered at Basle and its execution to John Dederoth and John de Rode, the latter a Carthusian turned Benedictine (1434). A congregation was formed with Bursfeld as head-house and its abbot as perpetual president. A general chapter had legislative power when sitting, but the normal executive control lay with the abbot of Bursfeld as visitor-general. The monasteries were autonomous under their own abbots, and monks made profession to their own houses. Bursfeld was thus a reform on traditional lines, and though fervour diminished with the passage of time, the congregation endured till the Napoleonic era.

The fifteenth century, therefore, though in so many respects a time of decline and laxity, gave birth to a series of movements of reform which not only carried many of the monasteries through the storms of the Reformation but evolved a machinery which, though contrary in some important respects to the precepts of St Benedict, served to give to the post-Reformation world a pattern which proved able to withstand many of the dangers of the times.

Women religious, as we have noted, were less numerous and had far less scope than men. From the beginning there were a fair number of abbeys, recruited from the seignorial and later also from the bourgeois class, all living a liturgical, contemplative life usually under the rule of St Benedict. In the twelfth century houses of Austin canonesses appeared, scarcely distinguishable from the Benedictines, and some new institutes were formed for women. Thus the celebrated preacher Robert of Arbrissel founded the large establishment of Fontevrault consisting of three austere nunneries and a monastery all following the Rule of St Benedict under the control of an abbess (1106). In this establishment the chief function of the men was to act as chaplains and confessors to the women. A few decades later an English priest Gilbert founded in the Lincolnshire hamlet of Sempringham an order intended principally for women, but embracing also small groups of canons, to act as chaplains, and numerous lay brethren and lay sisters. This order for a century or more was distinguished by the numbers and the spiritual gifts of its members. When Cistercians and Premonstratensians multiplied there was a demand, which the founders resisted for a time, but vainly, for female branches of the orders. In the event, both orders came to have nunneries, though never so numerous as the monasteries. Henceforth it was the general practice that each order had its female counterpart, but in a society which could not tolerate religious women at work outside the cloister in school or hospital, all the orders tended to be of the same liturgical and contemplative type. Even the Poor Ladies of St Francis differed from the others only in the matter of austerity, and neither they nor the Dominicanesses could resemble their friars in number or in ubiquity. In England, for example, where there were some 3,400 Friars Minor and Preachers (c. 1330), there were only three small houses of the Poor Clares and one moderately-sized house of Dominicanesses. At the peak of the national population c. 1320 there were some twelve thousand men and two thousand women religious in England, the only European country where numbers are known with any accuracy. On the continent indeed, and especially in the towns of Flanders and the Rhineland, numerous beguinages gave scope for those who wished for a more active life of devotion, and throughout the earlier medieval centuries there were groups of devoted women not belonging to any order but attached to hospices or hospitals.

In the very last century of the middle ages two new orders of women came into being. The one was the female branch of the Carmelites, which started in Italy and spread to Spain where, more than a century later, it was to prove in its reformed branch a cradle of sanctity and a powerful weapon of the Counter-Reform. The other was the order known later as the Bridgettine from its Swedish founder St Birgitta. Like the earlier Fontevrault it was intended primarily for women, assisted by a group of ' confessors ' and lay brethren and sisters. The mother house, Vadstena, was one of the glories of Sweden in the age before the Reformation, and its foundress a national patron, but there were only a few foundations in Scandinavia, and apart from Vadstena the only great abbey was that of Syon in Middlesex.

The two last centuries of the middle ages saw also the multiplication of secular colleges and chantries, which were in some sense the last vestigial descendant of the monastic institute. These colleges were communities of secular priests living together and bound to certain religious observances, but not forming an order. They were of three kinds: a group of priests serving and ' owning ' a large church and parish and bound to the full liturgical service; a group attached to one or more chapels of a large church, without a cure of souls, but bound to offer Masses and liturgical prayers for the founder and others; and finally the scholastic or academic college, a group of priests or clerics with an obligation of learning or teaching. The two latter kinds were in origin ' chantries ' rather than colleges, and the numerous chantries served by one or two priests were a sub-species; but the academic colleges, prominent at Paris, Oxford and Cambridge, survived subsequent upheavals and remain the only type of medieval college familiar to the modern world.

MEDIEVAL THOUGHT 1277-1500

As we have seen, the deaths of St Bonaventure and St Thomas, and the twofold condemnation of the Paris Aristotelians, all of which took place within the space of seven years, marked the end of an epoch, that in which masters of all schools were endeavouring to make a wide synthesis of traditional theology and Greek philosophy. The full significance of the change was masked for a time by the apparent survival of the school of Bonaventure in the teaching of John Pecham, who had moulded doctrines of Augustine, the Neoplatonists and the Arabians into something of a system, known to historians as Augustinianism, which he endeavoured to impose on Oxford when archbishop of Canterbury. The resistance he met with from young Dominican enthusiasts, who defended Thomism with great energy, seemed likewise to show that their school also remained alive. In the event, however, both Augustinianism and Thomism went rapidly into eclipse, the former by reason of its philosophical vulnerability, the latter through lack of able defenders against the attacks on Aristotle. In their place three new currents of teaching appeared. At Paris, and in France generally, the *Summa* gave place to the study of individual topics; at Oxford there was a movement to rethink the whole body of philosophical doctrine; in the Rhineland arose a new form of Neoplatonism which influenced both dogmatic and mystical theology.

During the last quarter of the thirteenth century Oxford drew level with Paris as the home of original thought, and remained on an equality until 1350. Hitherto many of the greatest English masters, such as Stephen Langton, Alexander of Hales, Robert Kilwardby and John Pecham, had received their early training and won their first laurels at Paris. Now, the acutest minds of Britain such as Duns Scotus, William of Ockham, Thomas Bradwardine and Robert Holcot received their formation at Oxford and often remained in England for most of their teaching life. Oxford had long been the home of logic and mathematics. From William of Shireswood (d. 1249) to William of Heytesbury (d. 1380) and Ralph Strode (d. *c.* 1400) Oxford logicians had been the masters of Europe, and in mathematics and science there had been a succession of great names from Grosseteste and Roger Bacon to the long line of Mertonians, fellows of the Oxford college of that name. The achievement of Scotus was to criticise the various systems of thought and to frame a new metaphysical doctrine of his own, with new concepts and terms, thus becoming a harbinger of modern philosophy, while still retaining the methods, and many of the traditional ways of thought and expressions, of medieval thought. Scotus died young, leaving his system unfinished, but a succession of followers in his order continued his thought and wove it into the theological doctrine of Bonaventure, making of it a rival to the Thomist body of thought. Scotus was unsparing in his criticism of predecessors and contemporaries, friends and foes, and did not hesitate to jettison the divine illumination of the intellect, hitherto a shibboleth of the Augustinian traditionalists, in favour of the epistemology of Aristotle. Perhaps his chief significance is his insistence on the infinity and absolute freedom of God, which led him to erect a barrier between the objects of philosophical (rational) and theological (revealed) knowledge, and to defend in man the ' primacy of the will ' as against the Thomist ' primacy of the intellect '. God's freedom and love, rather than his law and truth, are the keys to an understanding of the universe, and the sphere of demonstrable knowledge is restricted. Natural theology is of little importance and an uncrossable gulf separates it from the supernatural, revealed knowledge of the theologian.

Though in fact a revolutionary thinker, Duns Scotus was an orthodox and great theologian. William of Ockham, known as the ' venerable inceptor ' because he never proceeded to the master's degree, was primarily a logician, but his powerful mind and audacious temper allowed his logic to determine his theory of knowledge and metaphysics. The tendency of his thought was to reduce knowledge to an intuition of individual experience, thereby depriving such terms as ' essence ' or ' nature ', and indeed all ' universals ' such as man, rose, etc., of any real meaning; they were mere names or signs attached to mental experiences, and any use made of them by the mind was purely notional or subjective. Similarly the concept of causality was unnecessary and undemonstrable. All one could say was that A happened and then B. The mythical razor of Ockham does in fact describe his aim, which was to throw away the intellectual framework of philosophy and theology, while retaining a novel and extremely elaborate logic. Between our indefinable experience of individual things and the God-given knowledge of revelation there was no mental bridge. Just as no general statement about the external universe could be called true, so no type of action could be called good. The true was what God had revealed, the good what he had commanded, and Ockham's followers, if not Ockham himself, made great play with the distinction between the absolute and the conditional power of God. The former, implying absolute freedom, was alone certain; the other, God's declared way of acting at present in the universe, was of no speculative significance, either theological or philosophical.

Ockham was delated to the curia at Avignon in 1324, when still only twenty-five, and his teaching ultimately received a mild censure. Meanwhile he had been won by Michael of Cesena to join him in opposition to John XXII and the two escaped together from Avignon in 1328. For the rest of his life (he died in 1348/9) Ockham was engaged in polemics on behalf of the emperor Lewis and showed himself as ruthlessly destructive in political theory as he had been in pure thought. His followers, while remaining orthodox in practice and profession, effectually disrupted the medieval synthesis of reason and revelation, natural and supernatural, and both philosophy and speculative theology became a subtle mental exercise in a field strictly enclosed and delimited. The comparison that has often been made between the Ockhamist logicians and Anglo-Saxon philosophical thought since Russell and Whitehead will not bear emphasis, but the crisis behind the two movements is similar. The attempt made in recent years, mainly by American and German scholars, to rehabilitate Ockham and his immediate followers as good Aristotelians and orthodox theologians is welcome as deepening our understanding of the thought of the age and as presenting us with serious and often devout thinkers whose opinions deserve consideration, but it cannot be fully accepted as a reversal of all past criticism.

After a period in which Ockhamist logic was used at Paris to demonstrate the relativity of all truth, a kind of equilibrium was established among Nominalist theologians between destructive or at least arid speculation and a devotional exposition of dogma that was often orthodox to the point of extravagance. In reaction, the rare masters of a realist outlook, such as Thomas Bradwardine and later John Wyclif in England, went to extremes in the opposite direction, the former verging upon determinism in his opposition to what seemed to him the ' Pelagianism ' of Ockham, the latter allowing his realism to affect his attitude towards Catholic doctrine in the Eucharist. Though at first opposed at Paris, the ' new way ' had a fair hold in the university in the second half of the century and Paris remained Nominalist with short intervals of reaction until the end of the medieval period. Indeed almost all the universities of north-western Europe were wholly or partly Nominalist by 1400, the only citadels of realism being in Bohemia and some of the Spanish academies. Much has been written in recent years of the influence of Nominalism on the outlook of the great Reformers. In the decades before Luther, the age of Erasmus, its influence was chiefly negative, in paralysing apostolic or apologetic presentations of the faith. By denying the axioms of traditional meta-physics, whether Platonic or Aristotelian, it tended to take speculative theologians away from their real task of penetrating Christian life and dogma, and to set them discussing hypothetical problems in a Nominalist universe of thought. Whatever may be said of the orthodoxy, intended or actual, of Nominalist theologians, there were two influential and religiously ambivalent currents of thought in the mental climate of a Nominalist world: the abandonment of metaphysics and natural religion as a rational base for theological and moral argument, thereby encouraging either a humanistic or a mystical approach to the Christian life; and the abandon-ment in every sphere of life of a reliance upon the reason to attain abstract truth, thereby opening the way to an authoritarian attitude towards all issues in theology and politics.

We are not concerned here with the notable advances in scientific and mathematical thought, due partly to the abandonment of metaphysics; recent research has shown that the fourteenth century was in many ways the first dawn of the modern world. Nor are we concerned to delate Nominalism at the bar of an historical Holy Office. Those, however, who profess to find little or nothing of credal deviation in Nominalist theolo-gians forget perhaps that Christian theology and spirituality extend far beyond the field of defined propositions, and that Nominalist thinkers did not confine themselves to logic. By their principle of economy and their elimination of venerable theological expressions, they did in effect expel from the Christian consciousness many real and deep relationships in the life of grace and the dealings of God with man which may never have been defined as essential articles of faith, but which nevertheless had hitherto been taken for granted by all theologians and spiritual writers.

In theology as in philosophy, the fourteenth century followed a new path. Whereas hitherto the great teachers of the thirteenth century had been concerned with elucidating and systematising the deposit of faith, and discussing the various articles of belief handed down in the Scriptures and writings of the Fathers, the theologians of the next generation began to isolate ideas and theological propositions and subject them to philosophical rather than theological criticism. The manner in which this was accomplished was profoundly modified from the third decade of the century onwards by the influence of William of Ockham and his many followers, and to a very large extent the writings of theologians in the century following Ockham's death (1349) represent a dialogue between traditional doctrine and Ockhamist axioms, in which both natural theology and theodicy and the patristic and scholastic framework of the supernatural life of grace, virtues and gifts of the Holy Ghost were shorn away, leaving a chasm between the experimental, positivist, mental content of the Nominalist and the revealed truths and commands of a loving but absolutely free and inapprehensible God. Concurrently, the new preoccupation of thinkers and poets with the individual man rather than with human nature as such directed attention to the problems of free will, merit, justification and salvation. The Ockhamist theologians stressed human free will on the one hand, and divine liberty on the other; the one impulse leading them to the edge of Pelagianism, the heresy that denied the need of supernatural assistance for meritorious action or at least for the first turning of the soul to God, the other tendency leading to a separation of God's justifying choice from any disposition on the part of the subject, and ultimately to equating justification with a mere relationship of man to a benevolent God, and even to an imputational view of righteousness. Similarly, debate began on the deep problems of predestination and God's knowledge of free future actions between the extreme Ockhamists and the traditional followers of Augustine. Among the latter the most eminent was the great Oxford master Thomas Bradwardine, later (1349) for a few weeks archbishop of Canterbury before he was carried off by the Black Death at almost the same moment as the venerable inceptor whose teaching he attacked with such burning force. Bradwardine, indeed, in his construction of a universe wholly controlled by the foreknowledge of God, and of a human race predestined to glory or foreseen in damnation, whose every meritorious action was determined by God's decree, departed as far from the golden mean of tradition as did Ockham. Far less influential on his generation, he could yet have counted Wyclif among his disciples.

At the same time Ockhamist opinions on justification were being used to support the view that ' good ' pagans might be saved, and that unbaptised infants might attain to heaven. It is an index of the theological confusion of the age that William of Ockham himself escaped with a very mild theological censure and that Bradwardine's orthodoxy was never questioned. Trials and anathemas were reserved for the less abstruse and more shocking aberrations of Wyclif, the Lollards and the Hussites, and these troubles and the prolonged and violent conciliarist debates overshadowed the last decades of the fourteenth century. Here as in so many other spheres, problems were broached and seeds were sown that waited for solution or growth till the epoch of the Reformation, when both Ockham and Bradwardine could if still alive have shared in the debates with a familiarity of mind.

Apart from the Ockhamist, the conciliar and the Wyclif-Hus issues, few new points of theology were raised in the fourteenth and fifteenth centuries. Benedict XII quashed the private opinion of his predecessor John XXII by defining the doctrine that pure or purified souls passed to the beatific vision as soon after death as their freedom from guilt of sin allowed. A century later in the statements of doctrine prepared at Rome for acceptance by the Greeks, Armenians and others, the traditional teaching on purgatory and the sevenfold number of sacraments was included as if common form though it appeared for the first time in an authentic and solemn statement of the faith. On the same occasion (1439) Eugenius IV defined the supremacy of the Roman pontiff.

Historians of doctrine have sometimes paid insufficient attention to the revival of Thomism in the fifteenth century. After a period in which Nominalism had found favour even among Dominicans, a reaction set in with Capreolus (1380-1444), the ' first Thomist ' *(princeps Thomistarum)* as he has been called. In his great commentary on the *Summa* he went far towards creating Thomism, that is a complete theological system resting on a particular interpretation of the mind of St Thomas, to be perfected by Cajetan in the early years of the sixteenth century and finally prolonged by Bañez eighty years later. A few decades after Capreolus, Turrecremata (Torquemada), another orthodox follower of St Thomas, used the *Summa* in defending the papalist doctrine of the constitution of the Church, while Henry of Gorkum applied the principles of Thomism to moral theology and gave the young university of Cologne its bias towards traditional philosophy. The first great epoch of Thomism, indeed, which is often said to begin with Cajetan and Vittoria, began in fact almost a century earlier, and is another instance of a revival begun before the Reformation and spanning the century of division.

HERESY AND REVOLUTION

THE last decades of the fourteenth century saw the reappearance of heresy on a large scale in Europe, at first in England and later in Bohemia. As we have seen, the heretics of the twelfth and thirteenth centuries had been of two kinds – those such as the Cathari with dualistic tenets and anti-Christian practices and ethics, and those such as the Waldenses who strove to recreate a supposedly pure and primitive Christianity.

The fourteenth century heresy was of the latter type, and its first leader was the Oxford scholar John Wyclif. There was little intellectual originality in Wyclif. Whatever its immediate ancestry, his religious teaching greatly resembled that of the Waldenses, while in the realm of church polity he adopted some of the positions and arguments of Marsilius and of Ockham and his school. He differed from his predecessors only in the apparatus of learning that he used and the ruthless logic and wide scope of his criticism. Wyclif in early manhood was a distinguished Oxford master of arts. Influenced by Bradwardine, the great opponent of Ockhamism in the previous generation, he was an extreme realist in philosophy and an Augustinian in theology, but in this phase he was neither unorthodox nor anti-papal. His career was interrupted by his assertions on the topic of dominion and grace, a long-standing controversy in which he was influenced by Richard

FitzRalph, an opponent of the friars. Wyclif's view was a conflation of two opinions: that only those in a state of grace had a true moral right of ownership; and that Christians, and above all clerics, should follow the evangelical law of poverty. He expressed his opinions in terms of Augustinian theology, asserting that the true Church was invisible and was composed of those predestined to salvation; the hierarchy of the visible Church, all too clearly tainted with sin, was doubly disqualified from possessing wealth, and the secular power was justified in confiscating this wealth when necessary. In this attitude the strands of idealism and political opportunism at a moment of national disaster were inextricably entangled. Wyclif was delated to Gregory XI in 1377, but the proceedings taken against him in response to papal commands were not carried through to a decision, owing partly to political protection. Some years later, however, Wyclif published works in which the orthodox teaching on the Eucharist was controverted, and transubstantiation and the real presence were in effect denied. Wyclif passed from the philosophical conviction that the substance of the elements was unchanged by consecration to the assertion of a purely spiritual presence, non-existent in the case of unworthy recipients. In origin Wyclif's eucharistic opinions derived from his extreme realism and his unwillingness to accept the scholastic explanation of ' substantial ' change, but he soon passed to the controversial level of an attack on eucharistic reverence and devotion. This alienated many of his supporters and brought upon him the concentrated assault of the friars who were the leading academic theologians, and in 1382 a number of propositions extracted from his teaching were condemned by Archbishop Courtenay in a council at London. His school of thought was stamped out at Oxford and he himself retired to his country living at Lutterworth, where he died in 1384. During the last years of his life he developed an intense literary activity in which he attacked the papacy, the priesthood, and all religious orders – the friars above all – as well as eucharistic piety and devotion to the saints, and preached a simple scriptural ' primitive ' Christianity without sacramental or sacerdotal trappings. The violence of language in some of these writings has rarely been surpassed even in the realm of religious polemic.

Wyclif's teaching both in its theological aspects and in its secularist attack on church endowments was effectively sterilised by the firm action of Archbishop Courtenay, by the able theological counter-offensive of the friars, and by the ruling orthodoxy of established authority. The Lollards, an ill-defined, unorganised but influential body of sentiment rather than a sect, who preached and held a simple ' evangelical ' faith buttressed with passionate denunciations of the established church similar to and probably derived from the later works of Wyclif, were driven underground by episcopal repression and disappeared in all save a few woodland regions of the country. Nevertheless Wyclif is a figure of great significance. In his writings are to be found, collected together for the first time and pungently expressed, almost all the popular charges against the Catholic church of the later middle ages, and almost all the features of early Protestant opinion on such matters as the sole authority of Scripture, sacramental absolution, indulgences and church order. As will be seen, his writings, transplanted to central Europe, exercised a decisive influence in Bohemia and later, perhaps, in Germany. In England in particular John Wyclif, alike in the simple piety of his earlier treatises and the individualistic, anti-sacramental and anti-sacerdotal enthusiasm of his polemic works, is the first recognisable appearance of the ' nonconformist ' presentation of Christianity that was to be such a characteristic feature of Anglo-Saxon society in the next age.

Meanwhile a movement with some resemblance to Lollardy was taking place at the eastern extremity of Roman Christendom in Bohemia. This country of Slavonic population had been nominally Christian since 1000 and had gradually become assimilated to the ecclesiastical pattern of the west without losing its natural and racial characteristics. During the greater part of the fourteenth century it was ruled by two monarchs of the house of Luxembourg. King Johan (1310-46), largely an absentee, a brilliant knight errant, left the government of the country to the nobles but added considerably to its territories. Blind in his last years, shortly before his death on the field of Creçy he had arranged for his son Charles to be elected King of the Romans. Charles IV, king of Bohemia and emperor (1346-78), was the founder of Bohemian national greatness. He introduced arts and crafts of every kind from the western countries, erected Prague into an independent archbishopric, and founded the university (later split into two) in that city which, as the only considerable centre of population in the country, came to be the barometer of national life. His son Wenceslas (1378-1419), an unbalanced character, had to deal with the problems following his father's reign. Bohemia at this time was a country with no bourgeoisie; it was a peasant land dominated economically and politically by the class of nobles. The Church was rich, and had the usual medieval surplus of priests and clerks, many of whom were ignorant and vicious of life. A small but influential immigration of Germans introduced racial and religious differences; the Germans resembled their western cousins in a more ordered and sober way of life. Owing perhaps to the changes of wind that were blowing through the country, there was a stirring in popular religion. Bohemia had in the past been infected both with the Bogomil or Catharist heresy and with the sect of Waldensians, and it is possible, perhaps probable, that the influence of the latter may have continued to work unseen, but the perpetual orthodoxy of Bohemia was a rallying-cry at the end of the fourteenth century. Nevertheless, before that date a succession of preachers of enthusiastic and unorthodox type made reform a living issue. The Moravian John Milič announced in Prague that the reign of Antichrist was near and indicated Charles IV as filling the rôle. He, John, had been sent by the Spirit to reform the church in Bohemia, and he advocated frequent or daily communion as a principal means. Mathias of Janov, an alumnus of Paris and a disciple of Milič, saw in the papal schism the end of the world. Like his master he advocated frequent reception of the Eucharist; he condemned excessive devotion to the saints, and preached against monks, ceremonies and Greek philosophy. He wished to return to the piety of the early Church and, though not explicitly attacking the existing hierarchy, proclaimed that the Holy Spirit and the Bible were the guides of faith for the individual Christian.

These and similar opinions, together with a real religious revival, were the background of the life of John Hus. The son of poor parents and an alumnus of Prague, Hus began his preaching career early and with great success. Like Luther, he had the fire of passionate sincerity and a vernacular eloquence, rather than intellectual or theological brilliance. His outlook was influenced by the writings of Wyclif and this transference of teaching across Europe into an entirely different environment is one of the most curious and decisive examples of the journeying of ideas. There had been contact for some time between Prague and Oxford, the two universities of the Roman obedience in the Schism, and the link between England and Bohemia had been further strengthened by the marriage (in 1382) between King Richard II and Anne daughter of Charles IV. Wyclif's works, and students imbued with his teaching, circulated widely in Prague and elsewhere, and from his university days onwards Hus took Wyclif as an authority for his own expositions. The older and conservative academics and clerics, however, thought differently, and in 1403 the university of Prague condemned forty-five propositions taken from Wyclif's writings by a majority vote.

This was the beginning of a long struggle in which the future of Bohemia as well as that of Hus was at stake. The Prague condemnation was followed by the prohibition of Wyclif's doctrines by Pope Gregory XII in 1408 and 1412. Ironically, Gregory was the pope held as authentic by Bohemia and by Hus, but when in 1409 King Wenceslas wished to support the proposal for convoking the Council of Pisa, against a majority of three to one among the ' nations ' of the universities at Prague, Hus stood by him in an act of power by which the king decreed threefold value to the vote of the Czech nation which had supported him. As a direct result the German ' nation ' left the university in large numbers and transferred themselves to the newly founded Leipzig, and their loud accusations of heresy against Bohemia had their effect in prejudicing the council against Hus. A period of confused intrigue followed in which Hus, maintained by the king, was excommunicated by the archbishop as a supporter of heretics. Hus, encouraged by royal and popular support, became more and more violent, writing, and staging a disputation, against indulgences. Much of his tract *adversus indulgentias* is taken from Wyclif. He now denied the worth of priestly absolution, thus returning to an early medieval opinion long discountenanced, and proposed Scriptural authority as the test of belief. In 1413 John XXIII condemned Wyclif's doctrines anew, and Hus in answer wrote his *De ecclesia* based on Wyclif's work. The predestined only, and not sinners, make up the body of believers, but Hus, unlike Wyclif, always accepted an hierarchical church. He now saw himself excommunicated by his archbishop and accused of heresy by the theologians, but supported by king and people.

It was at this juncture, in the summer of 1414, that the emperor Sigismund turned his attention to Hus. Sigismund was heir to Bohemia and had no mind to have a country at odds with itself. To arrive at peace he proposed to Hus that he should present his case to the council at Constance. All parties at Prague encouraged him, and Pope John XXIII (later regarded as anti-pope) suspended his excommunication. Hus, though not without forebodings, went to Constance in high hopes. Bred in a country far from the centres of European thought, and educated in a university that stood apart from all others theologically and philosophically, saturated with the thought of Wyclif and accustomed to sway the emotions and lead the reforming zeal of his own people, Hus had no conception of the weight of traditional theology and canonical discipline that was still taken for granted by the prelates assembled at Constance. He had hoped to argue and to convince, but it was clear that the fathers were prepared only to judge, and they could only judge one way.

Hus rightly denied that he followed Wyclif in all things (he never held Wyclif's views on the Eucharist) but his conception of the Church and of the sacerdotal office would alone have secured his condemnation. He refused to condemn all of the articles from Wyclif's teaching that the council had anathematised and he refused to recant the propositions imputed to himself, on the ground that the charges were false. He refused to withdraw and insisted on taking Scripture alone as the test of doctrine. After condemnation he was handed over to the emperor. The circumstances of his burning, which he suffered with courage and piety, were unusually revolting. He was followed to the stake almost a year later by his disciple Jerome of Prague who recanted in prison but withdrew his recantation and publicly proclaimed his adherence to Wyclif and Hus. He died courageously in May 1416.

The sincere and forthright, if tactically unwise, conduct of Hus and his betrayal by Sigismund, have rightly won sympathy for his fate. His life in the ardent and fermenting society of an isolated province of Europe, his great reputation among his own people and his conviction that he had found a new and purer interpretation of the Christian message blinded him to the realities of contemporary religious life and to the folly of expecting that a council of the Catholic West would be convinced or attracted by what he had to say. The council of theologians claiming supreme power and convoked to restore unity was in its element when faced by an assertive heretic holding fast, as they supposed, to propositions condemned again and again by authority and palpably subversive. Sigismund's breach of faith was deplorable; but he had made a grave error in promising what he dared not and perhaps could not as the patron of orthodoxy perform. At the present moment a current of sympathy with Hus is running strongly, and serious attempts have been made to show that he was heretical only on the matter of papal supremacy, where the council that condemned him could in truth throw no stones. Others will feel less convinced of his radical orthodoxy.

The council still had the large following of Hus on their hands. A representative gathering of the Bohemian nobility in the autumn of 1415 pledged themselves to honour his memory. Like Hus they declared their perfect orthodoxy and their submission to the pope, bishops and priests, in so far as their teaching was consonant with the will of God and Scripture. The arbiter was to be the university of Prague. The council replied by suspending the university and scattering condemnations. The shibboleth of the reformers was the use of the chalice by the laity. This was not an original demand of Hus, though he was prepared to countenance it. It seems to have originated among those who advocated frequent communion for the laity, and it was based partly on the use of the primitive Church, but mainly on an interpretation of the words of Christ cited by St Paul (1 Cor. 11: 23-25). It was specifically prohibited by Constance, but the Hussites were now travelling further away from orthodoxy by a denial of sacerdotal, and therefore episcopal and papal, powers of any kind. The death of Hus had resulted immediately in a league of five hundred nobles against the established Church, and this was followed by a long period of warfare, partly of the Bohemian nation against invaders in the guise of crusaders, partly of the factions of the reformers among themselves. While the Calixtines, taking their name from the chalice which was the centre of their devotion, remained faithful to the mind and moderation of Hus, the Taborites, the first sect to look back to the wars of the Israelites, were extremists whose actions foreshadowed alike the virtues and the excesses of the Puritans and the later wars of religion, and who combined intense nationalism with economic and social revolution.

The death of King Wenceslas in 1419 and the unsuccessful attempts of Sigismund to conquer the Czechs with a succession of ' crusades ' are part of the political history of Europe. The celebrated Four Articles of Prague (1420) represented an early attempt at uniting various groups. They established 1) freedom from control of preaching; 2) communion under both kinds; 3) that priests should not be owners of worldly possessions, but simple apostolic pastors; 4) public sanctions against mortal sins, especially simony. In the years that followed every kind of medieval heresy – Wyclifite, Waldensian, Catharist and Millenary – had its preachers in Bohemia. When at last the tide of war ran against the Czechs and Sigismund was recognised as king a determined effort was made to regularise matters and in 1433 envoys of the Hussites were received courteously by Cesarini and the Council of Basle and the so-called Compacts were agreed upon between delegates of the council, Sigismund and the Czechs. These were a modified version of the Four Articles, in which the use of the cup was greatly restricted. Even so, and in spite of their formal ratification in 1436, followed by a reconciliation of Bohemia with the church, there was no hope of complete or final reunion when Sigismund died. Bohemia, in the latter half of the fifteenth century, was in fact separated in practice and belief from the rest of western Christendom.

This fact was to some extent concealed by repeated attempts at reunion and by fluctuations in the strength of the Catholic party. It was nevertheless a portent, and it is this that gave a permanent significance to John Hus, and, behind him, to Wyclif. Between them, in word and in work, they had challenged the doctrine and the constitutional framework of the Catholic church all along the line, and for the first time a province of western Christendom, which was also a nation, had de facto separated itself from obedience while claiming to represent the true shape of Christianity. For the apostolic hierarchy under the successor of Peter had been substituted the judgment of the individual based on the word of Scripture. Time was to show whether this was an isolated splinter or the first rock in a great avalanche.

THE RELIGIOUS CLIMATE
OF THE FIFTEENTH CENTURY

THE election of Pope Martin V in 1417 marked the beginning of the end of the conciliar epoch, and its significance was recognised almost immediately by contemporaries. Exactly a century later Martin Luther nailed up his propositions (if indeed he did so) on the door of the castle church at Wittenberg. The events and circumstances that led up to the religious revolution of the sixteenth century fall within the province of the succeeding volume of this history, but it may not be out of place to consider the quality of the religious life in the earlier and central years of the fifteenth century.

Just as the fourteenth century saw many of the countries of modern Europe growing into what may be called nationhood, and the old conception of a single cultural unit, *Latinitas*, dissolving, so in religious matters central and western Europe in the early fifteenth century showed a pattern more diverse than at any time during the previous four hundred years. Scarcely any broad statement as to religious practice and sentiment is true of all the countries of Christendom. At one end of the scale is Bohemia, the first regional or racial group of modern Europe to secede with violence from the unity of the western church, a notable harbinger of things to come. Strong as were the political and patriotic issues in Bohemia, there was also the radical doctrinal and ritual element received in large part from

15. European ecclesiastical divisions in the later middle ages

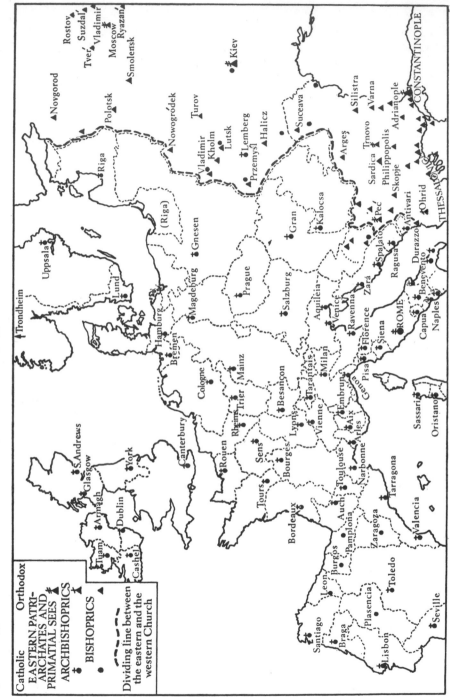

Catholic   Orthodox
EASTERN PATRI-
ARCHATES AND
PRIMATIAL SEES ♱ ▲
ARCHBISHOPRICS
♱   ▲
BISHOPRICS
♱   ●
Dividing line between
the eastern and the
western Church

Trondheim
Uppsala
Lund
(Riga)
Riga
Polotsk
Novgorod
Rostov
Tver' Suzdal'
Vladimir
Moscow Ryazan'
Smolensk
Kiev
Nowogródek
Turov
Vladimir
Kholm
Lutsk
Lemberg
Przemysł
Halicz
Suceava
Silistra
Varna
Adrianople
CONSTANTINOPLE
Arges
Trnovo
Sardica Philippopolis
Skopje
Pec
Antivari Ohrid
THESSALONICA
Durazzo
Ragusa
Benevento
Capua Naples
ROME
Spalato
Zara
Ravenna
Venice
Aquileia
Florence Siena
Pisa
Genoa
Milan
Salzburg
Prague
Gran
Kalocsa
Gnesen
Magdeburg
Hamburg
Bremen
Cologne
Mainz
Trier
Besançon
Rheims
Tarantaise
Embrun
Aix
Arles
Vienne
Lyons
Bourges
Sens
Tours
Rouen
Toulouse
Auch
Narbonne
Bordeaux
Pamplona
Zaragoza
Tarragona
Valencia
Burgos
León
Plasencia
Toledo
Braga
Lisbon
Seville
Santiago
Sassari
Oristano
Canterbury
York
Glasgow
S.Andrews
Dublin
Armagh
Tuam
Cashel

Wyclif, and Wyclif's teaching itself focused and sharpened the points of criticism that had been familiar to the heretical sects of Lombardy and Savoy since the twelfth century. With the Bohemian revolt a point of no return had been reached, though this was not fully grasped at once either by the patriots or by their enemies. At the other end of Europe lay the Iberian peninsula, a late-comer to the season of flower in medieval culture, and now about to enter upon its golden age of achievement and to form in the crisis of the sixteenth century a land of saints and thinkers and leaders, the citadel and the spearhead of the Counter-Reformation. Between these two extremes lay the other principal regions of Europe. Italy, by far the richest in genius and in intellectual and artistic power, with its humanism turning to paganism and its harvest of political vice and crime existing side by side with instances of sanctity and ascetic virtue, was in some ways the least Christian of countries, with the highest proportion of non-resident bishops, yet it was also the most tenaciously Catholic, both on the lowest level of the Neapolitan or Calabrian proletariate and the highest of the Roman curia.

The Low Countries, which we shall see as the home of *devotio moderna*, were, with their galaxy of towns and affluent *bourgeoisie*, a focus for all the popular manifestations of religion and secularity of the day. The numerous beguinages of men and women of every degree of sentiment from strict orthodoxy to sheer heresy, the recurring processions, some reflecting social rather than religious interests, others, such as those of the penitents or the flagellants, devotional even to extravagance, together with the civic and guild observances have recently received attention from historians and sociologists alike. The morbid and febrile qualities that appear, not only in the Low Countries, have won for the age the misleading name of ' the waning of the middle ages ', and stress has been laid on the widespread absence of earnest, simple, faithful Christianity that some researches have revealed. In England a little earlier the devout, much travelled and unbalanced Margery Kempe (*c.* 1373-*c.* 1440) of King's Lynn has some of the same characteristics, but her autobiography reveals also the presence of traditional piety, of the cult of the sermon and the presence of enlightened spiritual direction, and among Margery's older contemporaries was the homely and exquisite Julian of Norwich (1342-*c.* 1413). In the pilgrimages, in the popular devotions to the Holy Name, to the Precious Blood and to the details of the Passion, and in the sermons of the eminent nominalist Gabriel Biel (1410-95) we can see the divorce between speculative theology and the devotional life, the one finespun and arid, the other pietistic and emotional, that prepared the way for the Lutheran Reformation.

Germany, the greatest sufferer from the abuses old and new of feudal society and papal autocracy, was still in many districts and towns profoundly devout. Recent historical and sociological research can find little change in the religious climate during the fifteenth century. Here, as elsewhere, the new industry of printing was directed primarily to the production of religious books, whether service books or spiritual reading for a public of layfolk whose piety was on the whole more remarkable than that of the priests, religious and bishops.

France, ravaged and ruined by the Hundred Years' War, and with its church fettered more closely than any other by the evils of *commendam*, provision and royal control, nevertheless witnessed a national resurgence in which a real revival of religion had a share. England, isolated for decades from France by the Schism and by war, and with her political life little more than a series of struggles for power between a few magnates around the king, passed through a particularly arid century of church life, without any spiritual or intellectual leadership after the death of Henry V. Yet here also the devout life of the middle ages continued, with a stream of devotional books from the press and the accumulation, by foundations and legacies, of chantries, Masses and prayers for the dead. Scotland, a small country whose religious energy was sapped by almost all the abuses and misfortunes of the age, had nevertheless a reserve of strength to meet her destiny and to play more than a small part in the religious changes that were to come.

What was the legacy of the fourteenth century to this age? All would agree that there had been a catastrophic decline in the power and prestige of the papacy. The recalcitrant behaviour of the pontiffs of each party allowed a conciliar doctrine to emerge into the realm of practical politics from the pages of academic discussion. That the papacy should have survived forty years of such anarchy is indeed remarkable and it emerged with its powers not only intact, but with an ability to fight off a rearguard action of the conciliarists. It thus entered upon a century in which, deeply involved in Italian power politics, it attained considerable success in devious statecraft and lavish patronage of the arts and luxurious living, while ceasing to give effective spiritual leadership and guidance to the Church and sinking very low indeed in moral esteem. This must be borne in mind as a background to the religious life of the century: a worldly papacy, principally interested in Italian politics, and the centre of a rich, brilliant, worldly and often vicious court.

Meanwhile in the realm of ideas the fifteenth century was still under the influence of what had long been known as the *via moderna*, the new outlook, that is, the cast of thought inspired by Ockhamism or Nominalism. Victorious at Paris and Oxford in the fifty years before 1350, it had spread during the latter part of the fourteenth century into most of the universities of Europe as the ruling way of theological expression. Only at the extreme borders of east and west, in Bohemia swayed by Wyclif, and in Spain still retaining Thomism and Scotism in a fairly pure state, was Nominalism unfamiliar. Paris, where Ockham had found early entry, swung backwards and forwards between Nominalism and realism for a century and a half, but the periods of Scotist realism were brief, and the Nominalists were leading at the end of the fifteenth century. Oxford throughout the same period was preponderantly Nominalist, though some of the friars were realist. In central Europe Vienna and Erfurt were Nominalist, and at all the other German and Austrian universities Nominalism was either in control or at least strongly represented; almost the only exception was the newly founded Cologne. Prague indeed, influenced by Wyclif, was realist, but with a realism of an unexportable brand. Even in Spain, soon after 1500, Salamanca had three chairs – Thomist, Scotist and Nominalist.

While Nominalism was no longer – if indeed it ever had been – an instrument of intellectual agnosticism, it still continued to make of theology an exercise in dialectical ingenuity with little reference to tradition, and many of the eminent doctors of the day, such as Gabriel Biel, show two distinct faces, the exigent theologian thinking in the categories of later Ockhamism and the devout preacher presenting the familiar pieties of the age, sometimes in an extremely advanced form. Thomists and Scotists were often nominalists in outlook, and this tended to confine them to arid technical disputations which did not touch upon the Christian life. Nominalism, wherever present, discouraged any attempt to attain to a certain and true intellectual recognition of God, and eliminated as an unnecessary assumption any God-given habit or capacity, the ' sanctifying grace ' of the theologians, in the soul of man. Moreover, its distinctions led almost always to an elimination of grace as a supernatural help or habit; Bradwardine was not mistaken when he caught the scent of Pelagius in the wind of Ockhamism. The only systematic rival to nominalism was the Averroism of some northern Italian universities, particularly Padua. This was a materialistic, determinist version of Arabian philosophy, particularly strong in the schools of medicine.

Meanwhile a new mental interest was steadily growing, chiefly in lay circles and in cities rather than in universities. This was humanism in the widest sense of the term. Admiration for literary perfection of style, interest in the individual, devotion to classical literature and learning, all these were inimical to the arid contemporary theology. Humanism had fashioned for itself for a brief space a philosophy in Italy, but it was of a very different type from Nominalism. The latter, professing to be a true presentation of Aristotle, had in effect killed traditional Aristotelian philosophy, which proceeded by way of abstraction from sense perception to the most subtle analysis and deduction. A century earlier, the victorious Aristotle had vanquished in the field of metaphysics the relics of Neoplatonism that had come down the centuries from St Augustine and the Arabian and Jewish philosophers. Now, with a knowledge of Greek spreading throughout Italy, and with Greek texts of Plato and Plotinus available for the first time, there were attempts to present Christianity in terms either of traditional Neoplatonism as seen in the pseudo-Denis and Eckhart, or of the redis-covered historical Plato. Of the first stream Nicholas of Cues or Cusa, Prince-Bishop of Brixen, is a leading example, a figure who could have ap-peared in no age but this. An efficient reformer, a good administrator, a scientist and a humanist, an archbishop and a cardinal, a pluralist and a litigant of parts, he was also a bold Neoplatonist with little sympathy for authoritarian pronouncements or for the traditional emphasis on sacra-mental grace, and with a tendency to translate Christian dogma into Neoplatonic terms.

Of the second stream of pure Platonism, consequent upon the appe-arance in Italy of the great Platonic dialogues unknown throughout the middle ages, there were two eminent practitioners, the Tuscan Marsilio Ficino (1433-91) and Giovanni Pico della Mirandola (1463-94). Ficino, while remaining a cleric and professedly a Christian, constructed a system, partly from Plato, partly from Plotinus, which was in effect a simplified version of Christianity expressed in philosophical rather than in religious terms. Pico, a young aristocrat and disciple of Ficino, was less cautious than his master. He supplemented Plato with doctrines from the Jewish and Arabian mystics and teachers and was frankly unorthodox, half pagan, half Wyclifite in his views, denying transubstantiation and eternal punish-ment. He escaped papal condemnation by flight, and in his last years he lived the life of a penitent, though never recanting his opinions. A small circle in Florence continued this Neoplatonic school, but it never had a wide influence.

The Italy of Pico and Ficino was also the Italy of the Borgias and of Savonarola, the Italy of the Quattrocento in which the peninsula harboured great men and bad men without number. Yet we have only to look at the array of Italian saints in the century to realise that we must think twice before bringing a charge of universal irreligion against the country. There were, for example, the two eminent patrician archbishops, St Antoninus of Florence, the Dominican (d. 1459), and St Lorenzo Giustiniani of Venice (d. 1455). There were the two sainted mystics, the noble Catherine of Bologna (d. 1463), an artist in illumination, one of whose works is pre-served at Oxford, and the extraordinary and in some respects modern and forward-looking Catherine of Genoa (d. 1510), daughter of the viceroy of Naples. There were the three great Franciscan Observants, Bernardine of Siena (d. 1449), James of the March (d. 1476) and John Capistran (d. 1456), the last of whom saved Hungary from the Turks by leading the host that raised the siege of Belgrade. There were Frances (d. 1440), the married woman who had the distinction of taking her title as saint from Rome itself, and the fiercely ascetic Francis of Paola (d. 1506), who was summoned to France by the express command of Louis XI. In the fifteenth century also lived two French saints who fall less easily into comfortable categories: St Joan of Arc canonised in 1920 and Jeanne, daughter of Louis XI, who attained canonisation as recently as 1950. Moreover, Italy in the fifteenth century gave birth to three new and austere orders, the Franciscan Observants, the Minims, order of St Francis of Paola, and the Carmelite nuns who were to have such a distinguished history a century later. Italy indeed could show the extremes of luxury and worldliness, of austerity and sanctity, but in the midst of her dazzling company of artists, poets and humanists Savonarola was the only harbinger of reform, and his reform was of the traditional type of the middle ages, just as Ficino and Pico, appealing to ancient and oriental wisdom, were in the traditional line of medieval heterodoxy seen earlier in John Erigena and Siger of Brabant.

Meanwhile in north-western Europe a religious movement of a very different character was developing in the first half of the century. This derived from the Brothers of the Common Life founded at Deventer, in what is now central Holland, in the last years of the fourteenth century, and from their offshoot, the congregation of Austin canons of Windesheim. Both these institutes derived much of their spirit from the Flemish mystic Ruysbroeck and the Flemish Carthusians, but they were ' active ' rather than ' contemplative ' in character and multiplied widely with schools and hospitals. Their principal characteristic was what might be called an ascetic Ockhamism, a reduction of the Christian life to its bare essentials. Dropping the penances, the long rites and prayers and the complications of ritual and chant usual in the traditional religious orders, avoiding also all technical expertise in theology, and all prelacy and privilege, they aimed at living in common a simple life of useful work and prayer, and the spirtuality surrounding this life became known as the *devotio moderna* and diffused itself far and wide over north-western Europe. With the *devotio moderna* we touch a new creation, not perhaps so much a harbinger of the Reformation as a symptom of the needs of the new age. A community of the Common Life stands half-way between a medieval friary and a devout Puritan or Quaker household of the sixteenth or seventeenth century. Theologically and morally entirely orthodox, it stands nevertheless at the very opposite end of the spectrum to, let us say, Cluniac monasticism or the metaphysics of Scotism. It is Catholicism reduced to its lowest terms, and it is significant that its noblest literary legacy to the world, the *Imitation of Christ*, has always, even in the seventeenth and eighteenth centuries, maintained its position as a spiritual classic of the first water among Catholics and Protestants alike, a truly ecumenical achievement. The note of the Brethren was simple, affective piety, directed towards the God made man with an emphasis on his passion and cross. They were great educators, taking from Italian humanism its methods of teaching and its manuals of grammar, but not its aesthetic and emotional overtones. Erasmus was the greatest of the many scholars produced by the Brethren, and his Christian philosophy is a recognisable descendant of the *devotio moderna*, though he injected into his outlook a passionate love of letters and a more emphatic flight from theology and from the traditional conception of sanctifying grace.

Allied to the *devotio moderna* was the spirit of the Carthusian revival. This produced a number of spiritual writers of whom Ludolph of Saxony, the author of an immensely popular meditative *Life of Christ* in the late fourteenth century, and Denis the Carthusian, a prolific mystical writer, were the most celebrated. Unintellectual, meditative and pietistic, they came very near to the spirit of Windesheim with their silence, their simplicity and their lack of ritualistic display, though they maintained intact their rigour and their penances.

In contrast to the *devotio moderna* stand the currents of religious sentiment that are revolutionary, or at least pre-revolutionary. When historians search for the causes of the Reformation they often catalogue what may be called the dispositive or irritant causes and neglect those that are inner and spiritual. Perhaps we touch here the one great topic in modern European history where complete understanding will never be reached. A Roman Catholic will rarely be able to comprehend that anything more could be desired than a purified church; a non-Catholic Christian will never cease to feel thankful for the liberating spirit of the Reformation. Most would agree that one great religious need felt by many, and particularly by the educated lay population of the towns of Europe, was that for personal action and personal self-realisation in the sphere of religion; it was a need satisfied alike by the individual and the congregational activities of the Reformers and by the spirit of the *Exercises* of St Ignatius and the new education of the Jesuit colleges. Alongside this, and certainly one of the earliest and deepest motives and desires among the leaders of the pre-Reformation, was the desire to discover and to reproduce the supposed purity of the early Church. This desire had lain behind some of the earliest western movements of discontent such as that of the Waldenses, and had flared up for all to see with Wyclif and his followers, but before the fifteenth century the reformers had nothing to work upon but a few texts and an imaginary picture of a golden age. Now the discovery of some of the early Christian literature, together with a knowledge of the Greek New

Testament and the critical methods of Valla adopted and extended by Erasmus, made possible a new appeal to the New Testament as giving a clear view of the human life of Christ and also of the manner of life (so it was thought) of the early Christians, seen now directly in the letters of St Paul and not through the refracting medium of the liturgy and speculative theology. This gave a new vividness to the prevailing devotion, seen in such writers as Ludolph of Saxony, to the events of the life of Christ, and it was the beginning of what may be called the Pauline movement, the focusing of interest upon the moral and devotional, rather than upon the strictly theological, teaching of St Paul. It was a further aspect of the return to the Bible. If the gospels, and in particular the synoptic gospels, show us Christ as a man in his earthly life, the letters of St Paul show us the earliest and greatest of all the interpreters of the gospel message working among the first generations of Christians. In France Lefèvre d'Etaples (1461-1536) was the prophet of this outlook; in England there was Dean Colet (1467-1519) with his lectures at Oxford and his sermons at St Paul's. Erasmus, who was perhaps thirty-five years of age in 1500, shows us all these northern tendencies meeting. He, beyond all others, was equipped with the learning and linguistic and critical skill that he had acquired from schools of the Brethren of Common Life on the one hand, and from the writings of Lorenzo Valla on the other. He had also the current aversion from metaphysics and speculative theology, which again derived partly from his humanism and partly from the *devotio moderna*. From all these sources came his persuasive, reasonable, picture of the Christian man with the familiar human virtues, and his attractive version of the gospel story in which the characters are living, and no more than life-size.

In contrast to the splendour and fever of Italy, the fifteenth century in England is peculiarly barren of great men and genial ideas. For whatever reason, the promise of the fourteenth century was not realised. Neither the great poets, nor the English mystics, nor the radical views of Wyclif had any succession. Yet even in England we can see currents of thought that were carried across the divide of the Reformation. One such current was the apologetic of Thomas Netter (d. 1430), the English Carmelite commissioned to defend the orthodox faith against the Lollards. His first treatise was so effective that Pope Martin V called upon the author to write a continuation, and then to add a third part. Netter abandoned the dialectic framework of the disputation *(quaestio)* for the more direct method of answer and proof, and his book was reprinted again and again in the sixteenth and seventeenth centuries as a piece in the armoury of the Counter-Reformation. At almost the same time in Italy the Dominican cardinal Turrecremata, in his treatise on the power of the pope *(De Potestate Papae)* was composing a defence of the traditional papal position in moderate terms which contained a remarkable anticipation of the doctrine of indirect power later rendered familiar by Bellarmine – the doctrine, that is, that the pope has no direct power to control or intervene in temporal affairs, but the indirect power of pronouncing on the morality of a particular act of policy of the secular ruler.

This, then, is the religious climate of the fifteenth century: a church sick, indeed, in head and members, and crying for reform, but with no fear of a catastrophe such as was so soon to occur. It was a church in which the traditional theological education had become petrified, largely owing to the new logic of Ockham and its derivatives which had disrupted the traditional intellectual progress from reason to faith and from ' natural theology ' to revelation. With traditional philosophy in eclipse, and with no positive system to replace it, the door was left open to the creators of new philosophies based on Platonism or Neoplatonism, and, at the other end of the scale, to those who fled from all technical theology to humanism or to a supposedly primitive and simple Christianity. The way was open, though contemporaries did not perceive it, for a revolutionary who should break sharply with the hierarchical church and appeal to the inner light of the individual and to the words of Scripture that had now become familiar to the layman. The essential note of the new age, the inner conviction which made a strong appeal to religious men all over northern Europe, was a direct faith in the living Christ of the gospels, accepted as Redeemer by a personal, experiential faith. To such men the historical development of Christianity, the mediating priesthood, the graces of the sacramental life, the word of authority, the visible Church, all meant nothing. Faith was not a set of articles handed down, but a realisation, and acceptance, of the redemption and of the living Christ.

EPILOGUE

The stream of human actions that are the stuff of history never ceases to flow, and in this history of the Church another pen has taken up the story of the next phase of Christian life. But the long age we have reviewed has a broad unity of landscape, with a rhythm within it of growth, maturity and change in European society and religion, and it may not be out of place to end this volume with a backward glance.

Since the days of Gregory the Great Christendom had seen great progress and endured great losses. An eminent historian of Christian missionary endeavour has pointed out to us the somewhat surprising fact that in ecumenical terms the church was no more widely or numerically extended in 1500 than it had been in 600; the losses had cancelled out the gains. [1] The flourishing churches around the eastern and southern Mediterranean from Salonika to Spain, together with those in the lands of the Near East, had been overrun by Islam, and by Mongol and Turk, till at the end of the period and the fall of Constantinople no politically free Christian state existed east and south of Italy. To balance these losses could be set the reconquest of Spain, never wholly lost to the faith, and the

---

1. K. S. Latourette, *A History of the Expansion of Christianity,* II (London, 1939), 2. ' Probably in A. D. 1500 it [*sc.* the area in which Christians were to be found] was more restricted than it had been in A. D. 500. '

evangelisation of a wide arc of territory from Gaul and the British Isles through Scandinavia with its outposts in the Arctic and through central Europe down to the Russian state and Bulgaria, though some of the northern and eastern parts of this arc had been submerged again by pagan invasion more than once, and some were still under heavy pressure in the fifteenth century.

Moreover, Christendom itself had suffered irretrievable harm by the permanent separation of East and West. The Muslim invasions, by constricting and in some cases obliterating the eastern churches which had given so much of early glory and later lustre to Christian life and thought, and had given to the world so many great saints and doctors, had swept away for ever the dynamic forces of Syria, of Alexandria and of Africa, leaving only a single great church still flourishing, that of Constantinople. The writings and traditions of so much of the East were thus lost, for all practical purposes, to the medieval West, with a consequent impoverishment of its life-blood which cannot be measured but which was assuredly very great. The loss to the eastern church was almost as great, and the disappearance of these churches as living forces was undoubtedly a major cause of the rift between the surviving Orthodox church and the church of Rome. The isolation of the church of Constantinople, and its position both of prestige and of dependence as the church of the emperor and the capital, made rivalry with Rome all but inevitable. In the event, each part suffered grievous loss, and has ever since lacked the peculiar strength in combination which union might have brought. The historian must always warn himself and his readers that the predominantly Latin and Franco-German character of the Roman Catholic church in the middle ages was not the only outward habit that Roman Catholic Christianity could have worn.

Within the ambit of the western church the most significant development was the gradual emergence of the papacy to supreme monarchical rule. From a position of ecumenical presidency and honour as the depository of apostolic faith, and from a wide patriarchal authority in the West, the popes of the early medieval centuries lost all hold over the eastern church, while their practical authority in the West was greatly reduced at different times by their own lack of energy and moral fibre, by the claims and usurpations of kings and emperors, and by the creeping paralysis of lay control. Their prestige was restored and their unique and paramount authority to teach, to judge and to govern the Church was vindicated by a series of energetic pontiffs from Leo IX to Innocent III. While Gregory VII had exalted the papacy above the imperial power, Innocent III extended his surveillance to the political sphere and at the same time to the well-being of the laity, and for almost a century the papacy extended ts claims over the clergy and over the rulers of Catholic peoples.

Along with the expansion of papal power went an unparalleled growth in every institution and activity. Theology was shaped into a system, based upon, though not dependent upon, Aristotelian philosophy and some elements of Platonic thought, canon law was erected into a discipline and a profession, the administration of the curia, of the diocese, and of the parish was perfected, new religious orders arose and the fully centralised and international order was organised. A succession of saints, many of whom have remained present in the Catholic consciousness as embodying for all time a reflection of the life of Christ – an Anselm, a Bernard, a Francis, an Aquinas, a Catherine – and an equally majestic series of theologians made of the twelfth and thirteenth centuries a summit of achievement. Concurrently, architectural and artistic genius, and a technique of construction superior to all that had been known since the decline of Rome, gave expression to religious sentiment and belief in a way more adequate, perhaps, than anything that has been seen since that day.

The age changed in the decades around the year 1300. Aristotelian philosophy was challenged, and the age of individual systems with a flight from metaphysics began. The marriage of philosophy and theology was broken. At the same time, national sentiment and a ' lay outlook ' developed rapidly in a society that was steadily becoming more complex and more deeply involved in the exploitation of material resources and in manipulating the financial controls of a commercial and incipiently capitalist society. Meanwhile the papacy lurched from one catastrophe to another, and, unwilling to reform itself, was in consequence unable to reform the Church.

For the first centuries of its life the Christian Church had remained disengaged from ' the world ' as a self-contained body with its own life within an alien society whose secular authority it respected without sharing in its administration. Then, in the West, during some seven centuries the church, and in particular the clergy, had come gradually to dominate and penetrate every activity and class, and to vindicate its claim to lead and control a society that was at least nominally Christian in all its ways. Now, in fourteenth-century Europe, purely secular and material motives and forces were once more beginning to assert their claims, and the pattern of the early modern period of history was beginning to emerge, as one of rivalry between church and state, cleric and layman, unaided reason and revealed truth, authority and personal freedom, and one in which the majority of educated men had a dual allegiance. It was the misfortune of the medieval Church that the new winds blew at a moment, or rather in an age, when the old garments were threadbare, when the weaknesses and abuses of papal government, and the decline of old institutions and ideals, rendered an energetic recovery all but impossible.

The weaknesses and abuses of the late medieval Church have often been exposed: namely, the extravagant claims of the curia, papal taxation and provision, the plagues of *commendam*, plurality and absenteeism, the inability of bishops to enforce regularity when faced with the manifold exemptions and immunities of privileged bodies. Concurrently, on a deeper level, there was an impoverishment of the gospel message in those nurtured on later scholastic theology, and a mechanisation and lack of spiritual content in much of popular sentiment and devotion. Looking back upon the centuries from Gregory I to Boniface VIII or Martin V, we can see three principal sources of weakness, always present as dangers to the Christian Church in this world and progressively harmful in the middle ages. The first is wealth. The excessive endowment of the Church, at first by piety in the eleventh and twelfth centuries, and then by careful administration and deliberate aggrandisement, stifled the spirit of Christian renunciation and simplicity, and created in the clergy and religious an aristocracy of wealth and landed property, a vast vested interest in mammon. Secondly, there was the involvement in secular affairs. Thrust upon the Church at first in times of need, and demanded from her in a later age by a secular power which lacked the resources of an educated and professional class of laymen, the co-operation of the clergy in the business of government changed gradually from a control which allowed the application of Christian principles, to a bond of economic and political dependence which made the bishops in many countries king's men. Beyond this, the spectacle of the pope as a temporal monarch negotiating with other powers, and even directing armed conflict against Christian kings, was not calculated to assist bishops or abbots in taking a firm stand against implication in secular affairs. Moreover, the economy, which was for long predominantly agrarian, and the feudal link between landholders and an overlord who was also a monarch, made feudal lords of abbots and bishops, and imposed on them duties corresponding to their privileges. The wealthy bishop, often a confirmed absentee from his diocese in his king's service, or looking for a career in the papal court, was one of the major sources of weakness in the late medieval Church.

Thirdly, there was the lack of a trained clergy, combined with a superfluity of priests. Contemporaries perceived this, but between the age of Innocent III and the Council of Trent no serious attempt was made to find a remedy. The universities, perhaps the greatest institutional creation of the middle ages, multiplied clerks while they hindered rather than helped the education of the clergy as such. The cathedral school, controlled by the bishop, disappeared before the victorious advance of the university; theological training, prolonged and expensive, became the attainment of the few; and the control of young clerks passed from the bishop to the chancellor of the university. The arts school had no theological relevance, and the ordinary candidates for ordination had no training in discipline, in the spiritual life, in pastoral method or even in theology.

Nevertheless, the legacy of the medieval Church was great and splendid. The unity of all under the Roman pontiff was to be broken in part, but remained and was strengthened in the sequel. The schools had achieved a presentation of the totality of Christian doctrine and practice which has continued ever since to form the basis of speculative theology. The orders of monks and friars continue their work of liturgical prayer and pastoral service. The architecture and the art remain after the lapse of centuries as memorials of an age of faith, and of a Christian Europe. Above all, and throughout the whole period, the life of the spirit continued, hidden, as always, for the greater part, but appearing again and again on the surface of history in individuals or communities. No century was without its saints, among both pastors and people, or without the hidden servants of God, whose prayers and self-sacrifice fill up what is wanting to the sufferings of Christ, and who are in every age the unseen pillars of the building.

BIBLIOGRAPHY

Chapter I
INTRODUCTORY

The whole period, save for a single century (1274-1378), is now (1968) covered by the *Histoire de l'Église*, founded by A. FLICHE and V. MARTIN and now directed by J. B. DUROSELLE and E. JARRY. The later medieval volumes reflect a gradual change of approach, which may be due to change of editing, or, more probably, to a development of historical resources and fields. From Gregory the Great to Innocent III the approach was primarily the traditional political and chronological narrative; since the second World War the volumes have tended to treat a long period from a doctrinal, sociological and institutional viewpoint. Bibliographical material has become lavish, and has included a wider selection of works from England, Germany and Italy than before. With all its excellences, the time-lag in production and the vastness of the undertaking have always made of it a student's, rather than a reader's history. Nevertheless, certain volumes, such as those of E. AMANN on the Carolingian age (vol. VI and parts of vol. VII) and of A. FLICHE on the Gregorian Reform (vol. VIII) rest upon the original work of eminent scholars and remain in many respects the best accounts yet published of the periods concerned. The work will be referred to as FLICHE & MARTIN, V, etc. Of the older general histories A. HAUCK'S *Kirchengeschichte Deutschlands* (5 vols subdivided, Leipzig, 1887-1920, often revised and reprinted), remains indispensable up to *c.* 1350. Until *c.* 1100 it includes virtually all continental Europe west of Russia and north of Spain and Bulgaria, and the range of information and command of the contemporary authorities are throughout admirable. H. K. Mann's *Lives of the Popes in the Early Middle Ages*, 18 vols., London 1902-32, give a continuous account of papal activity, not always critical and never attempting synthesis or analysis. Over the whole period the fullest and most reliable source of information is often to be found in one or more of the five great French dictionaries; *Dictionnaire de théologie catholique* (1905-50 complete), *Dictionnaire d'histoire et de géographie ecclésiastiques* (1912-to letter Fa), *Dictionnaire d'archéologie chrétienne et de liturgie* (1907-53 complete), *Dictionnaire de Spiritualité* (1932 to Fu), and *Dictionnaire de Droit canonique* (1935 to Reg), though the earlier volumes of the three first have become

antiquated in the half-century since their appearance.   For all doctrinal
pronouncements, K. J. Hefele and H. Leclercq, *Histoire des Conciles*, 8 vols.
in 16, 1907-21 with supplements, and for all purposes *Lexicon für Theologie
und Kirche*, 2nd ed., Freiburg-i-B., 1957f.   Of other works of reference
A. HAUCK's *Realencyclopädie für protestantische Theologie und Kirche*
(23 vols., Leipzig, 1913) is often useful especially on economic and legal
topics.   The following books also are of use for the whole or a great part
of the period:

C. MIRBT, *Quellen zur Geschichte des Papsttums und der römischen Katholizismus*,
    Tübingen, 1924.
H. VON SCHUBERT, *Geschichte der christlichen Kirche im Frühmittelalter*, 2nd ed.,
    Tübingen, 1962.
K. BIHLMEYER and H. TÜCHLE, *Kirchengeschichte*, vol. II, 17th ed., Paderborn, 1962.
F. GREGOROVIUS, *Geschichte der Stadt Rom im Mittelalter*, 8 vols. Stuttgart, 1859-72.
    Engl. trans., A. Hamilton, 8 vols. in 13, London 1894-1902.   Outdated in
    parts, but the only survey.
A. DENZINGER and A. SCHÖNMETZER, *Enchiridion Symbolorum*. ed. 32 (K. Rahner)
    Freiburg-i-B., Rome, New York, 1963.

Tables générales of indices and up-to-date bibliographies are in course of publication
    in *fascicules*.

Within the past twenty years a new kind of historical source of great importance
    has appeared, especially in Italy, in the form of a conference or *Centro di
    Studi* where a number of experts deliver essays on various aspects of a broad
    topic, and subsequently take part in a general discussion with their colleagues;
    the published result gives both a detailed and a scholarly account of the topic,
    together with the reasons for and against all controversial opinions.   In
    medieval studies, three bodies are pre-eminent:

SPOLETO: Centro italiano di studi sull'alto medioevo, holding an annual *settimana
    di studi* of which the results are published.   The following are of interest
    for ecclesiastical history:
I (1954) *I problemi della civiltà carolingia.*
III (1956) *L'Italia meridionale nell'alto medioevo e i rapporti con il mondo bizantino.*
IV (1957) *Il monachesimo nell'alto medioevo e la formazione della civiltà occidentale.*
V (1958) *Caratteri del secolo vii in occidente.*
VII (1960)*Le chiese nei regni dell'Europa occidentale e i loro rapporti con Roma fino all'800.*
IX (1962) *Il passagio dall'antichità al medioevo in occidente.*

TODI: Centro di studi sulla spiritualità medievale.
II (1960) *Spiritualità cluniacense.*

MILAN (Università del Sagro Cuore): Centro di studi medioevali, Mendola.
I (1959) *La via commune del clero nei secoli XI e XII.*
II (1962) *L'eremitismo in occidente nei secoli XI e XII.*
III (1965) *I laici nella ' societas christiana ' dei secoli XI e XII.*

Chapter 2

THE EVANGELISATION OF EUROPE

K. S. LATOURETTE, *A History of the Expansion of Christianity*, vol. II, London, 1938-45.

F. Lot, *La fin du monde antique*, 2nd ed., Paris, 1952.

L. Duchesne, *L'Eglise au VIe siècle*, Paris, 1925.

Sankt Bonifatius (a volume for the twelfth centenary) Fulda, 1954. Essential.

M. Tangl, *Die Briefe des heiligen Bonifatius und Lullus*, in *MGH Epistolae selectae*, Berlin, 1916.

E. Emerton, *The Letters of St Boniface*, trans. with introduction, New York, 1946.

S. J. Crawford, *Anglo-Saxon influence on Western Christianity*, 600-800, Oxford, 1933.

W. H. Levison, *England and the Continent in the Eighth Century*, Oxford, 1946.

L. Gougaud, *Christianity in Celtic Lands*, London, 1932. An improved version of the French *Les chrétientés celtiques*, Paris, 1911.

F. Dvornik, *The Making of Central and Eastern Europe*, London, 1949.

The Anglo-Saxon Missionaries in Germany, trans. C. H. Talbot, London, 1954.

L. Bieler, *Ireland, harbinger of the middle ages*, London, 1963.

Ebo and Herbordus, *The life of Otto, Apostle of Pomerania*, trans. C. H. Robinson, London, 1920.

Adam of Bremen, *History of the archbishops of Hamburg-Bremen*, trans. F. J. Tschan, New York, 1959.

Helmold, *Chronicle of the Slavs*, trans. F. J. Tschan, New York.

F. Dvornik, *The Slavs. Their early History and Civilization*, Boston, 1956.

Chapter 3

THE ORTHODOX CHURCHES OF EASTERN EUROPE

On **Cyril** and **Methodius** the following are of special importance:

F. Dvornik, *Les Slaves, Byzance et Rome au IXe siècle*, Paris, 1926.

F. Dvornik, *Les Légendes de Constantin et de Méthode vues de Byzance*, Prague, 1933.

F. Grivec, *Konstantin und Method, Lehrer der Slaven*, Wiesbaden, 1960.

F. Grivec and F. Tomsic, *Constantinus et Methodius Thessalonicenses. Fontes*, Zagreb, 1960 (Radovi Staroslavenskog Instituta 4).

C. J. Potocek, *Saints Cyril and Methodius*, New York, 1941

Chapter 4

THE CHURCHES OF WESTERN EUROPE

(a) The Merovingian and Frankish Churches

J. M. Wallace-Hadrill, *The Long-haired Kings*, London, 1962.

E. Delaruelle, *L'Église Romaine et ses relations avec l'église franque jusqu'en 800*, in *SSS* 7 (1959), Spoleto, 1960, 143-184.

C. De Clercq, ' La législation religieuse franque de Clovis à Charlemagne ', Paris, 1936, with supplementation in *Revue de droit canonique*, 1954-5 and 1956-8.

F. L. Ganshof, *L'Église sous Pépin III et Charlemagne*, ibid., 95-141.

P. Imbart de la Tour, *Les paroisses rurales du IVe au XIe siècle*, Paris, 1900.

Les élections épiscopales en France, Paris, 1891.

E. Mâle, *La fin du paganisme en Gaul*, Paris, 1950.

E. de Moreau, *Histoire de l'Église en Belgique*, I, 2nd ed., Brussels, 1945.

F. L. Ganshof, *La Belgique carolingienne*, Brussels, 1958.

SSS V 1958. *Caratteri del secolo VII in occidente.*

SSS IX 1962. *Il passagio dell'antichità al medioevo in occidente.*

P. RICHE, *Éducation et culture dans l'Occident barbare*, VIᵉ-VIIIᵉ siècles, Paris, 1962.

E. S. DUCKETT, *Alcuin, friend of Charlemagne. His world and his work*, New York, 1951.
  Carolingian portraits. A study in the ninth century, Ann Arbor, 1962.

(b) The Anglo-Saxon Church

D. WHITELOCK, ed., *English Historical Documents*, ed. D. C. Douglas, I, London, 1955.

M. DEANESLY, *The pre-Conquest Church in England*, London, 1961.

P. HUNTER BLAIR, *An Introduction to Anglo-Saxon England*, Cambridge, 1956.

W. H. LEVISON and S. J. CRAWFORD, as above ch. 1.

Bede: his Life, Times and Writings, ed. A. H. Thompson, Oxford, 1935.

S. Beda Venerabilis, B. Capelle and others, Studia Anselmiana 6, Rome, 1936.

BEDE, *Historia Ecclesiastica, Historia Abbatum* and *Letter to Egbert.* The best edition
  is still that of C. Plummer, *Venerabilis Baedae Opera Historica*, 2 vols.,
  Oxford, 1896. There are many adequate translations.

J. E. LLOYD, *History of Wales to the Edwardian Conquest*, 3rd ed. London, 1939.

E. S. DUCKETT, *Anglo-Saxon saints and scholars*, New York, 1947.
  Saint Dunstan of Canterbury, New York, 1955.

(c) The German Church

A. HAUCK, as above.

THEOD. SCHIEFFER, *Angelsachsen und Friesen*, Mainz, 1950.

T. SCHAEFFER, *La chiesa nazionale di osservanze Romana. L'Opera di Willibrord et
  di Bonifacio*, in *SSS* 1959. Spoleto, 1960.

G. BARRACLOUGH, *The Origins of Modern Germany*, 2nd ed. Oxford, 1948.

(d) The Spanish Church

G. VILLADA, *Historia ecclesiástica de España*, I, Madrid, 1929.

R. MENENDEZ PINAL, *Historia de España*, vol. IV, *España cristiana*, 711-1038, by
  J. Pérez de Urbel and R. del Arco y Garay, Madrid, 1956.

RAIMOND BIDAGOR, *La iglesia propria en España*, Rome, 1933.

(e) The Church in Lay Hands

E. LESNE, *Histoire de la propriété ecclésiastique en France*, Lille, 6 vols, 1922-36.

U. STUTZ, *Die Eigenkirche als Element des mittelalterlich-germanischen Kirchenrechtes*,
  Berlin, 1895.

U. STUTZ, *Geschichte des kirchlichen Benefizialwesens von seinen Anfangen bis auf die
  Zeit Alexanders III*, Berlin, 1895. Engl. trans. G. Barraclough, *The
  proprietary church as an element of medieval ecclesiastical law*, vol. 2 of
  Medieval Germany*, 911-1250, Oxford, 1938.

P. THOMAS, *Le droit de propriété des laïques*, Paris, 1906.

Chapter 5

THE FORTUNES OF THE PAPACY 604-1049

H. VON SCHUBERT and C. DE CLERCQ, as above, General and ch. 4.

A. HAUCK, as above.

L. DUCHESNE, *Les premiers temps de l'État pontifical*, 3rd ed. Paris, 1911; Engl. trans.

by A. H. Mathew, *The Beginnings of the Temporal Sovereignty of the Popes*, London, 1907. Old, but not yet replaced.

Le ' *Liber Pontificalis* ', 2nd ed. with additions and corrections by C. Vogel, Paris, 1955, 1957. This is still the best ed., and is essential.

E. Caspar, *Geschichte des Papsttums*, 2 vols., Tübingen, 1930-3.

' Das Papsttum unter frankischer Herrschaft ' in *Zeitschrift für Kirchengeschichte*, 3 ser. 5 (1935), 132-255. Important.

H. Fichtenau, *Das karolingische Imperium*, Zurich. Engl. trans. P. Munz, *The Carolingian Empire*, Oxford, 1957.

R. Folz, *Le couronnement impérial de Charlemagne*, Paris, 1964.

P. Munz, *The Origin of the Carolingian Empire*, Leicester, 1960.

H. Beumann and others, *Karl der Grosse, Lebenswerk und Nachleben*, 4 vols., Düsseldorf, 1965.

P. E. Schramm, *Kaiser, Rom und Renovatio*, Darmstadt, ed. 1961.

Chapter 6

THE SOURCE OF AUTHORITY

J. Haller, *Das Papsttum, Idee und Wirklichkeit*, 2nd ed. Stuttgart, 1950.

H. X. Arquillière, *L'Augustinisme politique*, 2nd ed. Paris, 1955.

R. W. and A. J. Carlyle, *The History of Political Thought in the West*, vols. I-V, Edinburgh, 2nd/3rd ed., 1930-8.

W. Ullmann, *Medieval Papalism*, London, 1949.

The Growth of Papal Government in the Middle Ages, 3rd ed., London, 1965. *Principles of Government and Politics in the Middle Ages*, London, 2nd ed. 1966.

For a critique of Ullmann's thesis see F. Kempf, ' Die päpstliche Gewalt in der mittelalterlichen Welt ', in *Miscellanea Historiae Pontificiae*, XXI, Rome, 1959, 117-169.

O. Gierke and F. W. Maitland, *Political Theories of the Middle Ages*, Cambridge, 1900 (Beacon paperback 1958).

Chapter 7

THE BYZANTINE CHURCH

General works on the history and civilisation of Byzantium contain much information on the Church. The following books may be noted:

G. Ostrogorsky, *Geschichte des byzantinischen Staates*, 3rd ed., Munich, 1963. Engl. trans. J. Hussey, *History of the Byzantine State*, Oxford, 1956.

The Cambridge Medieval History, IV, 2nd ed., ed. J. Hussey, Cambridge, 1966-7.

General works on the Byzantine Church:

J. M. Hussey, *Church and Learning in the Byzantine Empire* 867-1185, Oxford, 1937.

G. Every, *The Byzantine Patriarchate* 451-1204, 2nd ed., London, 1962.

An important work of reference:

H.-G. Beck, *Kirche und Theologische Literatur im byzantinischen Reich*, Munich, 1959.

On **Maximus the Confessor:**

W. Volker, *Maximus Confessor als Meister des geistlichen Lebens*, Wiesbaden, 1965.

L. Thunberg, *Microcosm and Mediator. The Theological Anthropology of Maximus the Confessor*, Lund, 1965.

On the **Iconoclast Crisis:**

K. Schwarzlose, *Der Bilderstreit, ein Kampf der griechischen Kirche um ihre Eigenart und um ihre Freiheit*, Gotha, 1890.

L. Brehier, *La quérelle des images*, Paris, 1904.

G. Ostrogorsky, *Studien zur Geschichte des byzantinischen Bilderstreites*, Breslau, 1929.

E. J. Martin, *A History of the Iconoclastic Controversy*, London n.d. (1930).

H. Menges, *Die Bilderlehre des hl. Johannes von Damaskus*, Münster, 1938.

P. J. Alexander, *The Patriarch Nicephorus of Constantinople. Ecclesiastical Policy and Image Worship in the Byzantine Empire*, Oxford, 1958.

On **Byzantine Art** of the post-Iconoclast period:

G. Mathew, *Byzantine Aesthetics*, London, 1963.

O. M. Dalton, *East Christian Art*, Oxford, 1925.

D. Talbot Rice, *The Art of Byzantium*, London, 1959.

O. Demus, *Byzantine Mosaic Decoration. Aspects of monumental art in Byzantium*, London, 1947.

On **Hymnography:**

E. Wellesz, *A History of Byzantine Music and Hymnography*, 2nd ed., Oxford, 1961.

On the **Liturgy:**

E. Mercenier, F. Paris and G. Bainbridge, *La prière des églises de rite byzantin*, 2nd ed., I, II, Chevetogne n.d.

J. M. Sauget, *Bibliographie des liturgies orientales* (1900-1960), Rome, 1962.

On **Monasticism:**

A. Gardner, *Theodore of Studium, his life and times*, London, 1905.

P. Sherrard, *Athos, der Berg des Schweigens*, Olten, 1959. Engl. trans. *Athos, the Mountain of Silence*, London, 1960.

Le millénaire du Mont Athos 963-1963. *Etudes et mélanges*, I, II, Chevetogne, 1963-64 (with exhaustive bibliography).

On **The Church and The Imperial Power:**

A. Grabar, *L'empereur dans l'art byzantin. Recherches sur l'art officiel de l'empire d'Orient*, Paris, 1936.

A. Michel, *Die Kaisermacht in der Ostkirche* (843-1204), Darmstadt, 1959.

H. Rahner, *Kirche und Staat im frühen Christentum. Dokumente aus acht Jahrhunderten und ihre Deutung*, Munich, 1961.

On the **Photian Dispute:**

F. Dvornik, *The Photian Schism, history and legend*, Cambridge, 1948.

On the **Byzantine Attitude to the Roman Primacy:**

F. DÖLGER, *Byzanz und die europäische Staatenwelt*, Ettal, 1953.

F. DVORNIK, *The idea of Apostolicity in Byzantium and the legend of the Apostle Andrew*, Cambridge (Mass.), 1958.

J. MEYENDORFF, A. SCHMEMANN, N. AFANASSIEFF and N. KOULOMZINE, *La primauté de Pierre dans l'Église Orthodoxe*, Neuchâtel, 1960. Trans. *The Primacy of Peter in the Orthodox Church*, London, 1963.

F. DVORNIK, *Byzance et la Primauté Romaine*, Paris, 1964.

For the **Filioque** viewed by a theologian of the Orthodox Church:

V. LOSSKY, *Essai sur la théologie mystique de l'Église d'Orient*, Paris, 1944. Engl. trans. *The Mystical Theology of the Eastern Church*, London, 1957.

On the **Breach** of 1054:

A. MICHEL, *Humbert und Kerullarios. Quellen und Studien zum Schisma des XI Jahrhunderts*, I, II, Paderborn, 1925-30.

1054-1954. *L'Église et les églises. Neuf siècles de douloureuse séparation entre l'Orient et l'Occident*, I, II, Chevetogne, 1954-5.

S. RUNCIMAN, *The Eastern Schism. A study of the Papacy and the Eastern Churches during the XIth and XIIth centuries*, Oxford, 1955.

Chapter 8
ROME AND CONSTANTINOPLE (I)

See bibliographies for ch. 5 and 7.

Chapter 9
THE MONASTIC CENTURIES (I)

P. SCHMITZ, *Histoire de l'Ordre de S. Benoît*, 7 vols., Maredsous, 1942-56. Engl. trans. of early vols. The only historical survey, but necessarily somewhat superficial.

P. COUSIN, *Précis d'histoire monastique*, Paris, 1956. Rich in information and bibliographical detail, but with very many small inaccuracies.

Il monachesimo nell'alto medioevo e la formazione della civiltà occidentale (= *SSS* IV, 1957), Spoleto, 1959.

La vita commune del clero nei secoli XI e XII (= *SSM* I, 1959), Milan, 1961.

L'eremitismo in occidente nei secoli XI e XII (= *SSM* II, 1962), Milan, 1964.

J. RYAN, *Irish Monasticism*, Dublin, 1931. Still the best work.

C. BUTLER, *Benedictine Monachism*, London, 1919, 2nd ed., reprinted Cambridge, 1961.

G. PENCO, *Storia del Monachesimo in Italia*, Rome, 1961.

E. SACKUR, *Die Cluniacenser*, 2 vols., Halle, 1892-4.

Neue Forschungen über Cluny und die Cluniacenser, ed. G. Tellenbach, Freiling, 1959.

G. FERRARI, *Early Roman Monasteries*, (Studi di antichità cristiana, XXIII), Vatican City, 1957.

B. HAMILTON, ' The monastic revival in tenth century Rome ' in *Studia Monastica*, 4 (1962), 35-68.

G. DE VALOUS, *Le monachisme clunisien des origines au XVe siècle*, 2 vols, Paris, 1935. Much information, but without critical or analytical force.

K. Hallinger, *Gorze-Kluny* (Studia Anselmiana 42), 2 vols, Rome, 1950-1. Learned and essential, but exaggerates the differences within a single monastic framework.

H. Dauphin, *Le bienheureux Richard, abbé de Saint-Vanne de Verdun*, Louvain, 1946.

M. D. Knowles, *The Monastic Order in England*, 2nd ed., Cambridge, 1963.

Gérard de Brogne et son œuvre réformatrice, Maredsous, 1960.

Chapter 10

THEOLOGY 604-1050

In general the relevant articles in the *DTC*, and the chapters by E. Amann in Fliche & Martin, vols. VI and VII, are indispensable and have not been superseded, though all are now in various degrees in need of *aggiornamento*. The articles in *Lexikon für Theologie und Kirche*, where available, signalise recent literature. For the insular penitentials, see also histories of the Anglo-Saxon church, above. For John the Scot Erigena, M. Cappuyns, *Jean Scot Erigène*, Paris, 1933, is still authoritative.

A. Teetaert, *La confession aux laïques dans l'église latine depuis le 8e jusqu'au 14e siècle*, Louvain, 1949.

O. D. Watkins, *A History of Penance*, London and New York, 1920.

B. Poschmann, *Penance and the anointing of the sick*, trans. from German and revised by F. Courtney, London, 1964.

J. Macneill and H. Gamer, *Medieval Handbooks of Penance*, New York, 1938.

B. Anciaux, *La théologie du sacrement de pénitence au XIIe siècle*, Louvain, 1949.

N. Paulus, *Geschichte des Ablasses im Mittelalter von Ursprung bis zur Mitte des 14 Jahrhunderts*, 3 vols., Paderborn, 1923.

Chapter 11

CANON LAW FROM DIONYSIUS EXIGUUS TO IVO OF CHARTRES

A. van Hove, *Prolegomena ad Codicem Iuris Canonici*, 2nd ed., Mechlin-Rome, 1945.

G. Le Bras, *Histoire du droit et des institutions de l'église en occident* : vol. 7, *L'âge classique*, Paris, 1965.

H. Feine, *Kirchlicherechtsgeschichte*, 4th ed., Weimar, 1964.

P. Fournier and G. Le Bras, *Histoire des collections canoniques en Occident*, 2 vols., Paris, 1931-2.

P. Hinschius, *System des katholisches Kirchenrechts*, vols. 1-6, Berlin, 1869-97.

J. J. Ryan, *St Peter Damian and his Canonical Sources*, (Studies and Texts 2, Pontificial Institute), Toronto, 1956.

Articles in *Dictionnaire du droit canonique*. This is a rapidly expanding field of study.

C. Vogel, *La discipline pénitentielle en Gaule des origines à la fin du VIIe siècle*, Paris, 1952.

J. Laporte, *Le Pénitentiel de S. Columban*, Tournai, 1958.

Chapter 12
PUBLIC WORSHIP AND THE DEVOTIONAL LIFE

J. A. JUNGMANN, *Missarum Sollemnia*, Freiburg, ed. 1952. Engl. trans. F. A. Brunner, *The Mass of the Roman Rite*, 2 vols., New York, 1951-5.
Die lateinischen Bussriten in ihrer geschichtlichen Entwicklung, Innsbruck, 1932.

J. BRAUN, *Die liturgische Gewandung im Occident und Orient*, Freiburg i. B., ed. 1964.

A. BAUMSTARK, *Comparative Liturgy*, revised by Dom Botte and trans. F. L. Cross, London, 1958.

C. A. VOGEL, *Les échanges liturgiques entre Rome et les pays francs jusqu'à l'époque de Charlemagne*, in *SSS* VII, 1959, publ. 1960.

E. BISHOP, *Liturgica Historica*, Oxford, 1916.

P. BATIFFOL, *Histoire du bréviaire romain*, Paris, 1893. Engl. trans. Baylay, *History of the Roman Breviary*, London, 1912.

E. WELLESZ, *A History of Byzantine Music and Hymnography*, 2nd ed., Oxford, 1961.

F. J. E. RABY, *A History of Christian Latin Poetry*, 2nd ed., Oxford, 1953.

See also articles in *Dictionnaire d'Archéologie Chrétienne et de Liturgie.*

Chapter 13
CHRISTIAN CULTURE IN THE WEST

G. SCHNURER, *Kirche und Kultur im Mittelalter*, 3 vols., Paderborn, 1936. Engl. trans. C. J. Undreimer, *Church and Culture in the Middle Ages*, Paterson (U.S.A.), 1956.

J. DE GHELLINCK, *Littérature latine au moyen âge*, 2 vols., Paris, 1939.

I problemi della civiltà carolingia, (*SSS* I), Spoleto, 1954.

M. LAISTNER, *Thought and Letters in Western Europe, A.D. 500-900*, London, 1931.

Chapter 14
THE GREGORIAN REFORM

Studi Gregoriani, ed. G. BORINO, I-VIII, Rome, 1947-1960. Indispensable to study.

Registrum Gregorii VII, ed. E. CASPAR in *MGH Epistolae selectae*, Berlin, 1923, see also Caspar's *Studien zum Register Gregors VII* in *Neues Archiv* XXXVIII (1913), 143-226.

A. FLICHE, *La Réforme grégorienne*, 2 vols, Louvain, 1924 and in Fliche and Martin, VIII. Still valuable though partly outdated.

H. X. ARQUILLIÈRE, *Saint Grégoire VII et sa conception du pouvoir pontifical*, Paris, 1934.

E. VOOSEN, *Papauté et pouvoir civil à l'époque de Grégoire VII*, Gembloux, 1927.

W. VON DEN STEINEN, *Canossa, Heinrich IV und die Kirche*, (Janus-Bücher 5), Munich, 1957.

F. KERN, *Gottesgnadentum und Widerstandsrecht*, ed. R. Buchner, 3rd ed., Leipzig, 1963.

G. H. WILLIAMS, *The Norman Anonymous of 1100*, Cambridge, Mass., 1951.

G. BARRACLOUGH, *Medieval Germany, 911-1250*, 3rd reprint, 1961.

G. Tellenbach, *Church, State and Christian Society at the time of the Investiture Contest*, Oxford, 1945.

Z. N. Brooke, ch. 2 and 3 in *Cambridge Medieval History*, vol. V (1926) with bibliographies.

F. Kern, *Kingship and Law in the Middle Ages*, Oxford, 1939.

J. P. Whitney, *Hildebrandine Essays*, Cambridge, 1932.

Imperial lives and letters of the eleventh century, trans. T. E. Mommsen and K. F. Morrison, New York, 1962.

M. Maccarone, *Vicarius Christi*, Rome, 1952.

Chapter 15

THE MONASTIC CENTURIES (II)

M. Heimbucher, *Die Orden und Kongregationen der katholischen Kirche*, 2 vols., 2nd ed., Paderborn, 1933-4. Valuable, but occasionally uncritical.

Ph. Schmitz, cf. ch. 9 above.

F. Dressler, *Petrus Damiani: Leben und Werk* (Studia Anselmiana 34), Rome, 1954.

J. Ryan, *Peter Damian*, Toronto, 1956.

Ch. Dereine, ' Vie commune, règle de S. Augustin et chanoines réguliers au XIe siècle ' in *RHE* 1946, XLI, 365-406.
article ' Chanoines ' in *DHG*.

H. M. Colvin, *The White Canons in England*, Oxford, 1951.

M. D. Knowles, *The Monastic Order in England*, (940-1216), 2nd ed., Cambridge, 1963.

J. C. Dickinson, *The Origins of the Austin Canons*, London, 1950.

J. Lekai, *Les Moines blancs*, Paris, 1957, an expanded and improved version of *The White Monks*, Okauchee (Wisconsin), 1953.

J. B. Mahn, *L'Ordre cistercien*, 2nd ed., Paris, 1951. Some early pages now outdated, but still valuable.

E. Vacandard, *Vie de S. Bernard*, 2 vols., Paris, 1895-7, frequently revised and still unreplaced and fundamental.

Walter Daniel, *Vita Ailredi*, ed. F. M. Powicke, Edinburgh, 1950.

M. Thompson, *The Carthusian Order in England*, London, 1930. Valuable chapters on the origin and legislation of the Carthusians.

Petrus Venerabilis, ed. G. Constable and J. Kritzeck (Studia Anselmiana 40) Rome, 1956.

Spiritualità Cluniacense, Todi, 1960. See ch. 1 above.

R. W. Southern, *St Anselm and his Biographer*, Cambridge, 1963.

R. W. Southern, ed., *The Life of St Anselm by Eadmer*, Edinburgh, 1962.

Chapter 16

THE CHURCH IN THE TWELFTH CENTURY

D. C. Douglas and G. W. Greenaway, *English Historical Documents*, II, London, 1955.

H. Boehmer, *Kirche und Staat in England und in der Normandie in XI und XII Jahrhundert*, Leipzig, 1899. Antiquated as to Normandy, but still indispensable for England.

G. Villada, *História ecclesiástica de España*, I and II, Madrid, 1929-32.

A. Morey and C. N. L. Brooke, *Gilbert Foliot*, Cambridge, 1965.

M. Maccarone, *Papato e impero dalla elezione di Federico I alla morte di Adriano IV*, Rome, 1959.

M. Pacaut, *Alexandre III*, Paris, 1956.

Sacerdozio e regno da Gregorio VII a Bonifacio VIII, (Miscell. Historiae Pontificalis 18) Rome, 1954.

E. W. Kemp, *Canonization and authority in the Roman Church*, Oxford, 1948.

G. Barraclough, *The Origins of Modern Germany*, 2nd ed., Oxford, 1948.

Menéndez Pidal, *Historia de España*, III, Madrid, 1940.

See also articles and reviews in *Studia Monastica*, Montserrat.

S. Runciman, *History of the Crusades*, 3 vols., Cambridge, 1951-4.

P. Throop, *Criticism of the Crusades: a Study of Public Opinion and Crusade Propaganda*, Amsterdam, 1940.

A. Frolow, *Recherches sur la déviation de la IVᵉ croisade*, Paris, 1955.

See also lives of St Bernard, above.

A. Luchaire, *Innocent III*, 6 vols., Paris, 1904-8.

H. Jedin, *Ecumenical Councils of the Catholic Church.* Engl. trans. E. Graf, Edinburgh-London, 1960.

Kleine Konziliengeschichte, Freiburg, 1959.

S. Küttner and A. Garcia y Garcia, 'A new eyewitness account of the Fourth Lateran Council', in *Traditio*, 20 (1964), 115-178.

Chapter 17

THE SHAPE OF THE MEDIEVAL CHURCH

G. Le Bras, *Les Institutions de la Chrétienté médiévale*, Fliche and Martin, 12, Paris, 1959.

F. Lot and R. Fawtier, edd., *Histoire des Institutions françaises au moyen âge*, III, *Institutions ecclésiastiques*, by J. F. Lamarignier, J. Gaudemet, and G. Mollat, Paris, 1962.

J. Guiraud, *Histoire de l'inquisition au moyen* age, 2 vols., Paris, 1935-8.

H. Maisonneuve, *Études sur les origines de l'inquisition*, 2nd ed., Paris, 1960.

H. C. Lea, *The Inquisition of the Middle Ages*, (i.e. ch. 7-14 of vol. I of the 3 vol. *History*) ed. with introd. by W. Ullmann, London, 1963.

J. Forchielli and A. Stickler, edd., *Studia Gratiana*, in progress, Bologna, 1953.

S. Küttner, *Repertorium der Kanonistik (1140-1234)*.

Chapter 18

THEOLOGY 1050-1216

M. D. Chenu, *La théologie au XIIᵉ siècle*, Paris, 1957.

J. de Ghellinck, *Le mouvement théologique du XIIᵉ siècle*, 2nd ed., Bruges-Brussels, 1948.

B. Smalley, *The Study of the Bible in the Middle Ages*, 2nd ed., Oxford, 1952.

D. A. M. van den Eynde, *Les définitions des sacrements... 1050-1240*, Louvain, 1950.

M. Grabmann, *Geschichte der katholische Theologie*, Freiburg i. B., 1933.

Mittelalterliches Geistesleben, 3 vols, Munich, 1926, 1936, 1956.

Chapter 19

MEDIEVAL THOUGHT 1000-1200

M. GRABMANN, *Geschichte der scholastischen Methode*, 2 vols., Freiburg i. B., 1909, 1911.

B. GEYER, *Die patristische und scholastische Philosophie* in F. Ueberweg, *Grundriss der Geschichte der Philosophie*, vol. II, Berlin, 1928, anastatic reprint, Basle, 1951. Still the basic authority.

E. GILSON, *Histoire de la philosophie médiévale*, 2nd ed., Paris, 1943. A translation of this in English exists, but is out of print; it is superseded by a similar but not identical work by Gilson himself, *History of Christian Philosophy in the Middle Ages*, London, 1955 (with full bibliography to 1953).

F. COPLESTON, *History of Philosophy*, II, III, London, 1952-3.

G. PARÉ, A. BRUNET and P. TREMBLAY, *La renaissance du XIIe siècle*, Paris, 1933.

H. RASHDALL, *The Universities of Europe in the Middle Ages*, ed. F. M. Powicke and A. B. Emden, 3 vols, Oxford, 1936.

C. C. J. WEBB, *John of Salisbury*, London, 1932.

C. N. L. BROOKE and others, *The Letters of John of Salisbury*, I, Edinburgh, 1955.

J. RIVIÈRE, ' Les " capitula " d'Abélard, condamnés au concile de Sens ', in *Recherches de théologie ancienne et médiévale*, V (1930), 5-22.

J. LECLERCQ, F. VANDENBROUCKE and L. BOUYER, *La Spiritualité du moyen âge* (vol. II of *Histoire de la Spiritualité chrétienne*), Paris, 1961.

P. POURRAT, *La Spiritualité chrétienne*, II, Paris, 1925. Superseded in interpretation by the above, but still useful for names and facts.

E. GILSON, *La théologie mystique de S. Bernard*, Paris, 1934. Engl. trans. *The Mystical Theology of St Bernard*, London, 1940.

Chapter 20

THE SPIRITUAL LIFE (I)

J. LECLERCQ, *L'Amour de lettres et le désir de Dieu*, Paris, 1957. Engl. trans. *The Love of Learning and the Desire of God*, Fordham (U.S.A.), 1960. This is only one, though perhaps the most notable, of Dom Leclercq's excellent works.

D. KNOWLES, *The English Mystical Tradition*, London, 1961.

L. GOUGAUD, *Dévotions et pratiques ascétiques du moyen âge*, Paris, 1921.

Chapter 21

THE RELIGION OF THE LAITY

H. GRUNDMANN, *Religiöse Bewegungen im Mittelalter*, 3rd ed., Darmstadt, 1961, supplemented by ' Neue Beiträge zur Geschichte der Rel. Bew. im Mittelalter ', in *Archiv für Kulturgeschichte*, 37 (1955), 129-82.

I laici nella ' societas christiana ' dei secoli XI e XII (= SSM III, 1965) Milan, 1967.

Chapter 22

LITERATURE IN THE ELEVENTH AND TWELFTH CENTURIES

J. DE GHELLINCK, *L'Essor de la littérature latine au XIIe siècle*, 2 vols., Brussels-Paris, 1946.

See also RABY, *Christian Poetry*, WEBB, *John of Salisbury*, and articles in *Histoire littéraire de la France*, vol. IX onwards.

Chapter 23

ART AND MUSIC 600-1150

From the limitless literature may be mentioned:

H. FOCILLON, *Art d'Occident*, Paris, 2nd ed., 1942. Trans. as *The Art of the West in the Middle Ages*, 2 vols, London, 1963.

C. R. MOREY, *Medieval Art*, New York, 1942.

M. AUBERT, *L'art français à l'époque romane*, 3 vols., Paris, 1930-3.

H. JANTZEN, *Ottonische Kunst*, 2nd ed., Hamburg, 1959.

G. DEHIO, *Geschichte d. kirchliche Baukunst d. Abendlandes*, edition with revisions and supplement, 6 vols., Berlin and Leipzig, 1919-34.

   Handbuch d. deutschen Kunstdenkmäler, latest edition, many vols., Munich and Berlin, 1935-64.

E. PANOFSKY, *Abbot Suger on the Abbey Church of St Denis*, Princeton, 1946.

   Renaissance and Renascences in western art, Stockholm, 1960.

THEOPHILUS, *De diversis artibus*, ed. C. R. Dodwell, Edinburgh, 1961.

J. BECKWITH, *Early medieval art: Carolingian, Ottonian, Romanesque*, London, 1964.

Larousse Encyclopedia of Byzantine and Medieval Art, ed. R. HUYGHE, London, 1963.

E. MÂLE, *L'art religieux du XIIe siècle en France*, 3rd ed., Paris, 1928.

   L'art religieux du XIIIe siècle en France, 2nd ed., Paris, 1923. Engl. trans. D. Nussey, London, 1913.

   L'art religieux de la fin du moyen âge en France, Paris, 1921.

This trilogy marked an epoch in dating and grouping French sculpture and in showing its religious and social significance.

O. E. SAUNDERS, *A History of English Art in the Middle Ages*, Oxford, 1932.

See also the volumes of the Pelican History of Art, especially that on *Carolingian and Romanesque Architecture*, by K. J. CONANT, London, 1959.

L. GRODECKI, *Au seuil de l'art roman: L'Architecture Ottonienne*, Paris, 1958.

K. J. CONANT, 'Medieval Academy excavations at Cluny', in *Speculum* XXIX (1954) 1-45, with list of previous articles on the subject.

F. L. HARRISON, *Music in Medieval Britain*, London, 1958.

The New Oxford History of Music, II, ed. A. HUGHES, Oxford, 1954.

E. WELLESZ, see ch. 7, Hymnography.

Chapter 24

THE THIRTEENTH CENTURY

A. LUCHAIRE, A. FLICHE (Fliche and Martin) as above.

F. X. Seppelt, *Geschichte der Päpste*, 5 vols, Munich, 1954-9. Cf. Vol. III here.
H. Tillman, *Papst Innocenz III*, Bonn, 1954.
F. Kempf, *Papsttum and Kaisertum bei Innocenz III*, Rome, 1954 (Miscellanea historiae pontificiae 192).
M. Maccarone, *Chiesa e stato nella dottrina di papa Innocenzo III*, (Collect. Lateranum, new series VI, 3, 4), Rome, 1940.
G. Digard, *Philippe le Bel et le saint siège*, 2 vols, Paris, 1936-7.
A. Hauck, ' Die Rezeption und Umbildung der allgemeinen Synode im Mittelalter ', in *Historische Vierteljahrschrift*, 10 (1907), 465-82.

Chapter 25

PAPAL SUPREMACY — THE SPREAD OF THE FAITH

As previous chapter, and:

W. E. Lunt, *Papal Revenues in the Middle Ages*, 3 vols, New York, 1934-62.
G. Barraclough, *Papal Provisions*, Oxford, 1935. Learned but perhaps tendentious.
F. Dvornik, *The Slavs. Their early history and civilization*, Boston, 1956.

On the **Bulgarian Church:**

S. Runciman, *A History of the First Bulgarian Empire*, London, 1930.
M. Spinka, *A History of Christianity in the Balkans*, Chicago, 1933.
D. Obolensky, *The Bogomils. A study in Balkan Neo-Manichaeism*, Cambridge, 1948.

On the **Serbian Church:**

K. Jireček, *Geschichte der Serben*, I, II, Gotha, 1911-18.
A. Hudal, *Die serbisch-orthodoxe Nationalkirche*, Graz, 1922.
Yugoslavia: Mediaeval Frescoes, Paris, 1955 (UNESCO World Art Series).

On the **Russian Church:**

A. M. Ammann, *Abriss der ostslawischen Kirchengeschichte*, Vienna, 1950.
I. Smolitsch, *Russisches Mönchtum: Entstehung, Entwicklung und Wesen 988-1917*, Würzburg, 1953.
G. Fedotov, *The Russian Religious Mind: I. Kievan Christianity: the tenth to the thirteenth centuries. II. The Middle Ages: the thirteenth to the fifteenth centuries*, Cambridge, Mass., 1966.
A Treasury of Russian Spirituality, New York, 1961.

Chapter 26

ROME AND CONSTANTINOPLE (II)

J. Gill, *The Council of Florence*, Cambridge, 1959.

On the **Relations between Rome and Constantinople** between the XI and the XV centuries:

W. Norden, *Das Papsttum und Byzanz. Die Trennung der beiden Mächte und das Problem ihrer Wiedervereinigung bis zum Untergange des byzantinischen Reichs*, Berlin, 1903. Reprinted in New York, 1958.

R. L. WOLFF, 'Politics in the Latin Patriarchate of Constantinople, 1203-1261 ', in *Dumbarton Oaks Papers*, VIII (1954), 225-303.

On Byzantine Spirituality:

B. TATAKIS, *La philosophie byzantine*, Paris, 1949.

B. KRIVOSHEINE, *The Ascetic and Theological Teaching of Gregory Palamas*, London, 1954. Reprinted from *The Eastern Churches Quarterly*. III (1938), nos. 1-4.

J. MEYENDORFF, *Introduction à l'étude de Grégoire Palamas*, Paris, 1959. Engl. trans. *A Study of Gregory Palamas*, London, 1964.
   S. Grégoire Palamas et la mystique orthodoxe, Paris, 1959.

L. BOUYER, *La spiritualité byzantine*, in L. BOUYER, J. LECLERCQ, F. VANDENBROUCKE and L. COGNET, *Histoire de la spiritualité chrétienne*, II: *La spiritualité du moyen âge*, Paris, 1961, 645-696.

Chapter 27

THESIS AND ANTITHESIS IN CHURCH AND KINGDOM

R. W. and A. J. CARLYLE, as above ch. 6.

T. R. S. BOASE, *Boniface VIII*, London, 1933.

M. J. WILKS, *The Problem of Sovereignty*, Cambridge, 1962.

J. LECLERCQ, *Jean de Paris et l'ecclésiologie du XIIIᵉ siècle*, Paris, 1942.

G. DIGARD, *Philippe le Bel et le Saint-Siège de 1285 à 1304*, 2 vols, Paris, 1936-7.

V. MARTIN, *Les origines du Gallicisme*, 2 vols., Paris, 1939.

J. RIVIÈRE, *Le problème de l'Église et de l'État au temps de Philippe le Bel*, Louvain, 1926.

G. LIZERAND, *Clément V et Philippe le Bel*, Paris, 1911. Important for Templars.

Chapters 28-9

THE FRIARS

Several of the basic studies on the early history and constitutional development of the orders of friars, and on the schism of the Franciscan Spirituals, are by H. Denifle and F. Ehrle in their joint publication *Archiv für Litteratur- und Kirchengeschichte des Mittelalters* (6 vols., Berlin and Freiburg i. B., 1885-92). For a list of these, see D. Knowles, *Religious Orders*, I, 332-3.

There is no adequate life of St Francis embodying all the critical findings of the past seventy years. The epoch-making *Vie de S. François* of P. Sabatier (Paris, 1894, and repeatedly revised and reprinted) is a literary classic, but is historically outdated and reflects its author's questionable viewpoint. That of Fr Cuthbert, *St Francis of Assisi* (2nd ed., London, 1912), is almost equally outdated, but remains useful for the general reader. All other *Lives* are either tendentious or superficial.

H. BOEHMER, *Analekten zur Geschichte des Franciscus von Assisi*, 2nd ed., Tübingen, 1930.

P. GRATIEN, *Histoire de la Fondation et de l'Évolution de l'Ordre des Frères Mineurs, au XIIIᵉ siècle*, Paris, 1928. Over-discreet at times, but still essential.

M.-H. VICAIRE, *Histoire de S. Dominique*, Paris, 1957. Magisterial. Engl. trans. Kathleen Pond, *St Dominic and his Times*, London, 1964.

W. A. HINNEBUSCH, *History of the Order of Preachers*, I, New York, 1966.

D. L. DOUIE, *The Nature and Effects of the heresy of the Fraticelli*, Manchester, 1932.

R. B. BROOKE, *Early Franciscan Government*, Cambridge, 1959.

G. R. GALBRAITH, *The Constitution of the Dominican Order*, Manchester, 1925.

The coming of the Friars Minor to England and Germany (= ' Chronicles of Thomas of Eccleston and Jordan of Giano ', trans. E. G. Salter). London 1926.

A. WALZ, *Compendium historiae ordinis Praedicatorum*, 2nd ed., Rome, 1948.

Chapter 30

THE SPIRITUAL LIFE (II)

See ch. 20.

Chapter 31

MEDIEVAL THOUGHT 1200-1277

Copleston, Geyer, Gilson, Rashdall as above. Also, ch. 19. Denifle and Ehrle, ch. 28 and Smalley, ch. 18.

F. VAN STEENBERGHEN, *Aristote en Occident*, Louvain, 1946. Engl. trans. *Aristotle in the West*, Louvain, 1955.

A. FOREST, F. VAN STEENBERGHEN and M. DE GANDILLAC, *Le mouvement doctrinal du IXe au XIVe siècle* (= Fliche and Martin, XIII), Paris, 1950.

D. CALLUS, ed., *Robert Grosseteste*, Oxford, 1955.

G. DE LAGARDE, *La naissance de l'esprit laïque au déclin du moyen-âge*, vol. II, 3rd ed., Paris,1957.

Chapter 32

HERESY

E. D. THESEIDER, *Introduzione alle eresie medioevali*, Bologna, 1954.

A. DONDAINE, ' La hiérarchie cathare en Italie ', in *Archivum FF. Praedicatorum* 19-20 (1949-50), 280-312; 234-324.

A. BORST, *Die Katharer*, (Schriften der *MGH* 12), Stuttgart, 1953.

E. W. MCDONNELL, *The Beguines and Beghards in Medieval Culture*, New Brunswick, 1954. Full of information but lacking in analysis.

ILARINO DA MILANO, *L'eresia di U. Speroni*, Studi e Testi 35, Vatican City, 1945.

G. LEFF, *Heresy in the later Middle Ages*, 2 vols, Manchester, 1967. Very thorough but begins *c*.1250.

' JohnWyclif: the path to Dissent ', in *Proceedings of the British Academy*, LII (1966), 143-180.

For the Inquisition, see above ch. 17.

J. TRIER and H. GRUNDMANN, *Neue Forschungen über Joachim von Fiore*, (Münsterche Forschungen), Marburg, 1950.

M. W. BLOOMFIELD, ' Joachim of Flora ' in *Traditio*, 13 (1957), 249-312.

Chapter 33
THE JEWS AND USURY

CECIL ROTH, ch. 22 in *Cambridge Medieval History*, VII (1932), with excellent bibliography to date.
    History of the Jews in England, 2nd ed., Oxford, 1949.
H. GRAETZ, *Geschichte der Juden*, Leipzig, 13 vols., 1890-1911. Engl. trans. from earlier ed., Philadelphia, 1891-8.
Jewish Encyclopedia, 12 vols., New York, 1901-6.
Usury, see article in *DTC*.
J. T. NOONAN, *The Scholastic Analysis of Usury*, Cambridge, Mass., 1957.
J. W. BALDWIN, 'The medieval theories of the just price: Romanists, Canonists and Theologians in the 12th and 13th centuries', in *Transactions of the American Philosophical Society*, new series, XLIX part 4, Philadelphia, 1959.

Chapter 35
ART 1150-1300

See above ch. 23.
H. JANTZEN, *Die Kunst der Gotik*, Hamburg, 1947.
J. HARVEY, *The Gothic World, 1100-1600*, London, 1950.
J. HUIZINGA, *The Waning of the Middle Ages*, London, 1955.

Chapter 36
THE POPES AT AVIGNON

G. MOLLAT, *Les Papes d'Avignon, 1305-78*, 9th ed. revised, Paris, 1950. Engl. trans.,
    A classic but needs to be supplemented by recent work such as the following.
B. GUILLEMAIN, *La Cour pontificale d'Avignon*, (1309-76) in *Bibliothèque des Écoles Françaises d'Athènes et de Rome*, fasc. 201, 1962.
Y. RENOUARD, *La Papauté à Avignon*, Paris, 1954.
G. DE LAGARDE, *La naissance de l'esprit laïque au déclin du moyen âge*, 6 vols., Saint-Paul-Trois-Fontaines, Paris, 1934-46; new ed. 1956-63.
G. LEFF, *Bradwardine and the Pelagians*, Cambridge, 1957.
L. BAUDRY, *Guillaume d'Ockham*, Paris, 1950.
P. VIGNAUX, *Justification et prédestination au XIVe siècle*, Paris, 1934.
Article 'Nominalisme' in *DTC*, XI (1931), 717-84.
Histoire littéraire de la France. Many excellent articles by N. Valois and others.
Y. RENOUARD, *Les rélations des papes d'Avignon et des compagnies commerciales et bancaires de 1316 à 1378*, Paris, 1941.

Chapter 37
THE GREAT SCHISM

BRIAN TIERNEY, *Foundations of the Conciliar Theory*, Cambridge, 1955.
W. ULLMANN, *The Origins of the Great Schism*, London, 1948, reprinted 1967.

N. VALOIS, *La France et le Grand Schisme d'Occident*, 4 vols., Paris, 1896-1902.
V. MARTIN, *Les Origines du Gallicisme*, 2 vols, Paris, 1939.
N. VALOIS, *Le pape et le concile*, 2 vols., Paris, 1909.
Articles in *Histoire littéraire de la France* and *DTC*.
E. F. JACOB, *Essays in the conciliar epoch*, Manchester, 2nd ed., 1963.
The Council of Constance, documents trans. L. R. LOOMIS, New York, 1961.
A. FRANZEN, W. MÜLLER, *Das Konzil v. Konstanz, Beiträge zu einer Geschichte v. Theologie*, Freiburg i. B., 1964.

Chapter 38

THE FIFTEENTH CENTURY

Every aspect of the times up to 1450 is touched upon, with lavish bibliographical information, by E. Delaruelle, E. R. Labande and P. Ourliac in vol. XIV (two large parts) of Fliche and Martin.
V. MARTIN, see above ch. 37.
F. GRAGG and L. GABEL, *The Commentaries of Pius II:* Books X-XIII, Northampton, Mass., 1957.
P. PARTNER, *The Papal state under Martin V*, London, 1958.
D. AENEAS SYLVIUS PICCOLOMINI (Pius II), *Commentaries*, ed. and trans. D. Hay and W. K. Smith, Oxford, 1967.
A. S. ATYA, *The Crusade in the Later Middle Ages*, London, 1938.
A. LUTTRELL, 'The Crusade in the Fourteenth Century', in *Europe in the Late Middle Ages*, ed. J. Hale and others, London, 1965.

Chaper 39

MONASTIC AND REGULAR LIFE IN THE LATER MIDDLE AGES

An excellent conspectus of monastic and regular life in the XIV-XV centuries is given in Fliche and Martin, XIV, part 21 (Paris, 1964), with exhaustive bibliographies. This replaces all previous work on the European scene.
W. A. PANTIN, *The English Church in the Fourteenth Century*, Cambridge, 1955.
D. KNOWLES, *The Religious Orders in England*, II, III, Cambridge, 1955-9.
H. DENIFLE, *La désolation des églises, monastères et hôpitaux de France pendant la guerre de Cent Ans*, 2 vols., Mâcon, 1897. This work, principally a collection of documents, must still form the 'composition of place' for any consideration of French religious history in this period.
G. M. COLOMBÀS, M. M. GOST, 'Estudios sobre el primero siglo de S. Benito de Valladolid', in *Scripta et Documenta* III, Montserrat (Barcelona), 1954.

Chapter 40

MEDIEVAL THOUGHT 1277-1500

General works as above ch. 31.
L. BAUDRY, *Guillaume d'Ockham: sa vie, ses œuvres, ses idées sociales et politiques*, I, Paris, 1950.

P. BOEHMER, *Collected articles on Ockham*, ed. E. M. Buytaert, St Bonaventure, New York, 1958. Important, but to be used with discretion.

A. MAIER, *Ausgehendes Mittelalter: Gesammelte Aufsätze zur Geistesgeschichte des 13 Jahrhunderts*, Rome, 1965. Essential.

A. COMBES, *La théologie mystique de Gerson: profil de son évolution*, 2 vols, Rome-Paris, 1963-5.

G. DE LAGARDE, as above, ch. 31, vols IV-VI.

P. E. SIGMUND, *Nicholas of Cusa and Medieval Political Thought*, Harvard, Cambridge, Mass., 1963.

E. COLOMER, *Nikolaus von Kues und Raimund Lull*, Berlin, 1961.

E. GILSON, *Jean Duns Scot*, Paris, 1952.

H. A. OBERMAN, *The Harvest of Medieval Theology*, Cambridge, Mass., 1963. Excellent bibliography.

Chapter 41

HERESY AND REVOLUTION

H. B. WORKMAN, *John Wyclif*, 2 vols., Oxford, 1926.

K. B. MCFARLANE, *John Wycliffe*, London, 1952.

M. VISCHER, *Jan Hus, sein Leben und seine Zeit*, 2 vols., 2nd ed., Frankfurt a. M., 1955.

P. DE VOOGHT, *L'hérésie de Jean Huss*, Louvain, 1960.

Hussiana, 2 vols., Louvain, 1960.

R. R. BETTS, 'English and Czech influences on the Hussite Movement', in *Trans. of the Royal Historical Society*, 4 ser. XXI (1939), 71-102.

S. HARRISON THOMSON, *Magistri Joannis Hus Tractatus de Ecclesia*, Boulder, U.S.A., 1956. In this Professor Thomson shows that Wyclif has less influence on Hus than had been thought.

Chapter 42

THE RELIGIOUS CLIMATE OF THE FIFTEENTH CENTURY

J. L. CONNOLLY, *John Gerson: Reformer and Mystic*, Louvain, 1928.

F. COMBES, *Jean Gerson, commentateur dionysien*, Paris, 1940.

A. HYMA, *The Brethren of the Common Life*, Grand Rapids, 1950.

H. A. OBERMAN, see above ch. 39.

W. J. ALBERTS, *Zur Historiographie der Devotio Moderna und ihrer Erforschung*, Westfälische Forschungen, 11 (1958).

J. GUIRAUD, *L'Église romaine et les origines de la Renaissance*, 5th ed., Paris, 1921.

H. BARON, *The Crisis of the Early Italian Renaissance*, 2 vols., Princeton, 1955.

R. MARCEL, *Marcile Ficine*, Paris, 1958.

J. HUIZINGA as above, ch. 35.

J. TOUSSAERT, *Le sentiment religieux en Flandre à la fin du moyen âge*, Paris, 1963.

L. PASTOR, *Geschichte der Päpste*, I, Freiburg i. B., 1886. Engl. trans. L. Antrobus, London, 1891.

INDEX OF PERSONS AND PLACES

abp = archbishop   bp = bishop   card. = cardinal   ct = count   d. = duke
emp. = emperor   metr. = metropolitan   patr. = patriarch

INDEX OF SUBJECTS